M000221057

FIELD MARSHAL VON MANSTEIN, A PORTRAIT

The Janus Head

Marcel Stein

Translated by Marcel Stein
English edition edited by Gwyneth Fairbank

Helion & Company Ltd

Helion & Company Limited
26 Willow Road
Solihull
West Midlands
B91 1UE
England
Tel. 0121 705 3393
Fax 0121 711 4075
Email: publishing@helion.co.uk
Website: www.helion.co.uk

Published by Helion & Company 2007

Designed and typeset by Helion & Company Limited, Solihull, West Midlands
Cover designed by Bookcraft Limited, Stroud, Gloucestershire
Printed by the Cromwell Press Ltd, Trowbridge, Wiltshire

This English edition © Marcel Stein 2006. Translated by Marcel Stein, English edition
edited by Gwyneth Fairbank.
Originally published as: *Der Januskopf – Feldmarschall von Manstein. Eine Neubewertung.*
German edition © Biblio Verlag, Bissendorf 2004. All rights reserved.
Maps © Helion & Company Limited. The publishers would like readers to note that the
maps of Stalingrad and Kursk (pages 122 and 174) are substantially based on those
appearing on pages 37 and 107 of John Erickson's *The Road to Berlin: Stalin's War with
Germany Volume 2* (London: Weidenfeld & Nicolson, 1983). Due acknowledgement is
hereby given to the copyright holders.
Photographs © Ullstein Bild, Biblio Verlag. Front cover photograph © Ullstein Bild.

ISBN 978–1–906033–02–6

British Library Cataloguing-in-Publication Data.
A catalogue record for this book is available from the British Library.

For details of other military history titles published by Helion & Company Limited contact
the above address, or visit our website: http://www.helion.co.uk.

We always welcome receiving book proposals from prospective authors.

Contents

Acknowledgements

L ike all authors, I owe a debt of gratitude to the many who assisted me in my work. I shall never forget the late Professsor Dr Oswald Hahn. Back in 1999, he was the first to encourage me to put the knowledge accumulated over the years, on Manstein, into a book. My research in the German archives was facilitated by the daily assistance of Dr Georg Meyer, at that time head of the Freiburg office of the MGFA and Dr Manfred Kehrig, until his recent retirement, head of the German military archives. I have received valuable advice from Professor Martin van Creveld, Professor Manfred Messerschmidt, Dr Gerd Ueberschär and Professor Yehuda Wallach.

For this new expanded version of my first study of Manstein, published in 2000, I am indebted to advice received by *Generalleutnant (Bundeswehr)* Bernd, Baron Freytag von Loringhoven, *Generalleutnant (Bundeswehr)* Dr Franz Uhle-Wettler, Colonel Karl-Heinz Frieser, *Oberst* iG aD Günther Reichhelm, my schoolmate of the 1930s, Major iG aD Winrich Behr, Major Clemens, *Graf* von Kageneck, decorated with the Oak Leaves, Mr Horst Krönke and Mr Roman Töppel. My special thanks go to my publisher, Mr Wolfram Zeller, owner of Biblio Verlag, and his unwavering support of my work. A special mention must be made of Karl-Günther von Hase. He was former Secretary of State, former Ambassador to London, and former head of the state-owned ZDF television station. He provided me with the recently uncovered text of the shameful speech by Manstein on Hitler's 50th anniversary, 20 April 1939. My special thanks go to my wife Alla for her patience and her assistance with all technical problems at this end.

I would like to extend my thanks to Duncan Rogers and Claire Hill at Helion & Company for their professionalism in seeing this book through to publication. Gwyneth Fairbank, who undertook the editing of the translated text also performed a very thorough job.

This book is not a *verbatim* translation of the German original. Although it stays close to it, certain sections, which have no interest for a foreign reader, have been removed. Other sections have been added, in order to help the foreign reader's understanding of details that are clear to a German reader, but which require further elaboration in a foreign version.

I dedicate this book to the memory of my 33,000 fellow Jews who were murdered in the Southern Ukraine and the Crimea when Manstein was commander of 11th Army and held supreme territorial authority.

Introduction

This book is not a traditional biography, but rather a portrait. In his book on Trotsky, the Russian historian, General Dimitri Volkogonov, explains the distinction:

> I see a serious difference between a biography and a portrait. If the author of a portrait adheres strictly to historic truth, he is entitled to give events and individual actions his personal interpretation that may well extend beyond purely scientific research. The difference between a political portrait and a political biography is the same as the difference between a painting and a photograph.[1]

A complete biography of Manstein would have to dwell in detail on the military operations that took place under his command. Such accounts can be found in great detail in every work of military history dealing with the Russo-German war and with the general history of World War II. This book will not add new elements. It will only mention operations in order to describe Manstein's personal part in them and to arrive at a critical evaluation.

Volkogonov sees Trotsky as the Janus Head of the Revolution. Trotsky will remain history's pantheon as the uncompromising prophet of the communist idea, and as its perpetual prisoner. One could describe Manstein as the Janus Head of the *Wehrmacht* who saw himself as the uncompromising prophet of centuries of tradition, and yet its perpetual prisoner. The Roman God Janus had one head with two opposing faces. To paint a portrait of Manstein on canvas would require the art of Picasso, from the period in which he painted heads with more than one face. Manstein was a split personality with more than two different heads. Almost all of his personalities harbour sharp contradictions, many of them negative.

For example, he was:

- a man whose military leadership was admired by fellow Generals, to a point where *Feldmarschalls* senior to him in date of promotion, declared themselves willing to subordinate themselves to him, if Hitler were to be removed by a *coup*. At the same time, many disliked him and not a few, among them his first sponsor, *Generaloberst* Beck, held him in open contempt.
- a scion of a military dynasty, on his father's, his adoptive father's and his mother's side, all of whom had served Prussia and Germany for centuries. He had been brought up in the best traditions of the German Officer Corps. As supreme territorial commander in the Crimea he would not hesitate to actively participate in the most heinous crimes committed in Russia. He lowered himself to Hannah Arendt's 'banality of evil,' with the request for a few watches taken from the bodies of 14,500 Jews in Simferopol who had been murdered on his order.

---

1   D. Volkonow, *Totzki, Das Janusgesicht der Revolution*, Düsseldorf 1992, p. 19 f

- an unusually well-read man, with a broad knowledge of philosophy and the literature of many countries. He was a connoisseur of classical music way beyond average, but his knowledge and understanding of history showed surprising ignorance.
- a man who extolled the sanctity of the oath, and yet would repeatedly perjure himself at Nuremberg, and at his own trial.
- a man who, in the first volume of his memoirs, describes his total devotion to the sponsor of his career, *Generaloberst* Beck, and professes the greatest respect for his former commander, *Feldmarschall* von Witzleben. In the second volume of his memoirs, he would not even mention their ultimately tragic fate, after the failure of the 20 July 1944 plot, let alone write one word of commiseration.
- a man so convinced of his own infallibility that he would blame his own every error or shortcoming on his subordinates.

Many more such contradictions will appear in this book.

Manstein in Military Literature

One would have to search through many books dealing with the overall history of World War II, or concentrating on the war in Europe, in order to find a work that does not contain numerous mentions of Manstein. Surprisingly, there is no biography. Other German commanders, among them Rundstedt, Guderian, Rommel and Wenck have had biographies written in Germany and abroad. *Feldmarschall* Walter Model has been the subject of three biographies by K. Leppa, Walter Görlitz and this author, M. Stein.[2] Even the almost forgotten *Generaloberst* Blaskowitz has found a biographer.[3]

Books in German, and in foreign literature, that treat Manstein some detail, can be divided into three main groups as to their subject. Firstly, every work describing the battle for France mentions him. He was the creator of the master plan *Sichelschnitt*, that was finally adopted and eventually led to the rapid collapse of the French Army. These books tend to concentrate on military aspects and do not dwell on Manstein's personality.

Secondly, many works have been written about Stalingrad, both by historians and by survivors. With few exceptions, they are highly critical and charge Manstein with not having lived up to his highest duty. Every book dealing with the 'resistance' movement and the events of 20 July 1944 contains chapters dealing with Manstein. Almost all authors are critical of his refusal to join the plot. They tend to focus on Manstein because he was the prominent figure among the top German commanders. In as much as such attacks concentrate on him, they are exaggerated, since almost all Generals acted similarly.

---

2 K. Leppa, *Generalfeldmarschall Walter Model von Genthin bis zu Moskaus Toren*, Nürnberg 1982, W. Görlitz, *Der Feldmarschall und sein Edkampf an der Ruhr*, Berlin 1975 and M. Stein, *Generalfeldmarschall Walter Model – Legende und Wirklichkeit*, Bissendorf 2001

3 R. Giziowski, *The Enigma of General Blaskowitz*, London 1967

Thirdly, Holocaust literature mentions him extensively, as he was one of the German commanders who participated most actively in the extermination of Jews in Russia, by the *Einsatzgruppen*, the death squads. So too does the literature covering the war-crimes for which Manstein was indicted and also the minutes of Manstein's trial, numbering more than 2,000 pages.

Manstein in German Military Literature

A small number of German books deal with Manstein's personality, but they only cover separate short periods. An important work, *Die verdammte Pflicht*, ('Bounden duty' in the English version)[4] has been written by Alexander Stahlberg, Manstein's ADC between 1942 and 1945. Stahlberg was the son of a wealthy industrialist. He had remote Jewish ancestry and volunteered for reserve officers' training, in 1935, as the Army continued to provide a 'small umbrella' with its own justice system. Stahlberg was a cousin of Henning von Tresckow who would become the head of the military 'resistance' movement. Tresckow arranged for Stahlberg to become Manstein's adc in 1942, hoping that Stahlberg could become a vehicle in the attempts to bring Manstein closer to the 'resistance' movement. Stahlberg stayed with Manstein after the *Feldmarschall's* dismissal in 1944 and negotiated the terms of his personal surrender with Montgomery. His book is well written and shows a good intellectual level.

Stahlberg gives no detailed account of military operations, but concentrates instead on Manstein's personality. There was something of a father-son relationship between the two. When Stahlberg took up his duties, Manstein's eldest son, Gero, had just been killed in action. Manstein looked on Stahlberg as something close to a surrogate son and took him into his confidence. Stahlberg's description of Manstein is a mixed picture. On one side, he shows sympathy for the man and high respect for the commander, but he also discloses Manstein's attitude to the Holocaust. He mentioned what eyewitnesses of slaughters had told him and that he had communicated those reports to Manstein who refused to take notice. When he joined Manstein's staff, Stahlberg was not aware of Manstein's 11th Army's participation in the genocide in the Southern Ukraine and the Crimea. The *Feldmarschall* had already taken command of Army Group Don and had attempted the relief of Stalingrad.

Stahlberg has been attacked by some of Manstein's defenders for having written his book fourteen years after the *Feldmarschall's* death. This is hardly a valid argument. The time at which a book appears is unimportant, only the content is relevant. His book is not exempt from criticism. After the war, Stahlberg opened a restaurant in Berlin. When the first edition of his book came out, he was in the middle of an expensive third divorce and needed money. His book became a best-seller and yielded high returns. At times Stahlberg 'strays away' from the truth or simply copies from other works, without mention of their authors. He grossly exaggerated his own role in the 'resistance' movement. Notwithstanding this, his work today is accepted by most historians as a prime source on Manstein's character.

---

4 A. Stahlberg, *Die verdammte Pflicht, Erinnerungen 1932–1945*, Berlin 1987 (henceforth: Stahlberg)

Manstein himself held a high opinion of Stahlberg. In the more important of his two-volume memoirs, *Verlorene Siege* (Lost victories) he mentions him:

> ... Our thoughts were constantly with our comrades surrounded at Stalingrad. My ADC, Lieutenant Stahlberg, was a gifted violinist. He was able to provide some distraction by playing records of classical music, and discussing a variety of other topics. My former close associate Tresckow had brought him to me. He remained constantly at my side until the end of the war. During all the years until the surrender he remained my faithful *aide* in all personal matters.[5]

Oberst Hans Breithaupt, a friend of the Manstein family, published a short book *Zwischen Front und Widerstand – Ein Beitrag zur Diskussion um den Feldmarschall Erich von Manstein* (Between Front and Resistance, a contribution to the discussion about *Feldmarschall* Erich von Manstein).[6] His book is apologetic and inspired by a wish to respond to the growing criticism of Manstein Germany. However, the sources quoted by him are very limited in number and contain mainly statements that tend to support his purpose. Breithaupt, whose book did not elicit much interest from the public, is strongly critical of Stahlberg. While he can point to some inconsistencies of detail in Stahlberg's book, some of which will be mentioned in this volume, his main objection is that Stahlberg wrote down conversations with Manstein verbatim, something he feels could not be possible after forty years had elapsed. One should, however, not discount the possibility that an educated man, such as Stahlberg, may well remember conversations that appeared fateful to him, and that he also made notes on a daily basis.

Chapters about Manstein appear in many books of German military history, and in the works on the Second World War published by official German institutions. Their tendency always is to be influenced by the personal views of the authors.

Die Geburt der Tragödie aus dem Geist des Gehorsams, Deutschlands Generäle und Hitler, Erfahrungen und Reflexionen eines Frontoffiziers. (The birth of a tragedy resulting from the spirit of obedience: Germany's Generals and Hitler. The experience and reflections of a frontline officer.) This book is by the German historian Professor Erich Kosthorst. In it there is a chapter devoted to Manstein, under the heading: *Generalfeldmarschall Erich von Manstein – Exponent eines verabsolutierten Soldatentums* (a representative of militarism turned into an absolute).[7]

Professor Guido Knopp's TV series for the public German station ZDF, and the accompanying books are an important source. In the book accompanying his video *Hitlers Krieger,* (Hitler's warriors) a chapter is devoted to Manstein.[8] Knopp is a very influential reporter, who has specialised in producing lengthy TV series

---

5 E. von Manstein, *Verlorene Siege*, Bonn 1955, p. 339 f (henceforth: *Verlorene Siege*)

6 H. Breithaupt, *Zwischen Front und Widerstand – Ein Beitrag zur Diskussion um den Felmarschall von Manstein*, Bonn 1994 (henceforth: Breithaupt)

7 E. Kosthorst, *Die Geburt der Tragödie aus dem Geist des Gehorsams, Deutschlands Generale und Hitler – Erfahrungen und Reflexionen eines Frontoffiziers*, Bonn 1998 (henceforth: Kosthorst).

8 G. Knopp, *Hitlers Krieger*, Bonn 1998 (henceforth: Knopp).

about the Third *Reich* and World War II. These are shown on public German television and are always accompanied by a book. His technique consists of combining newsreels with statements by survivors. His influence is such that few feel able to abstain from appearing. Knopp's productions have a tinge of journalism. However, he has been instrumental in bringing the personalities of a number of high *Wehrmacht* commanders, and their darker sides, to the awareness of a wide public. His book is an important source, both for the views of former fellow officers, and of the members of Manstein's family, that had not been previously put on record.

The almost daily correspondence during the war, between General Heusinger and his wife, has been revealed in Georg Meyer's recent biography of General Heusinger. Throughout the war, General Heusinger was chief of operations at *OKH*. After the war he became the first inspector general of the *Bundeswehr*.

During recent years, since this book had already appeared in Germany, there has been an upsurge of books dealing with Manstein's occupation of the Crimea. In 2003, Martin Oldenburg published his doctoral thesis, *Ideologie und Militärisches Kalkül. Die Besatzungspolitik der Wehrmacht in der Sowjetunion 1942* (Ideology and Military Calculation. Occupation policies in the Soviet Union 1942).[9] Most of Oldenburg's book deals with Manstein's policies in the Crimea. Apart from the his participation in the genocide, Oldenburg deals with other cruel aspects of Manstein's policies, in particular the systematic famine which he enforced upon the civilian population. In 2005, Norbert Kunz published his thesis, *Die Krim unter deutscher Herrschaft 1941–1944. Germanisierungsutopie und Besatzungsrealität* (The Crimea under German domination 1941–1944. Germanic utopia and the reality of occupation).[10] In 2006, Dr. Oliver von Wrochem's thesis *Erich von Manstein. Vernichtungskrieg und Geschichtspolitik* (Erich von Manstein. War of annihilation and historical politics) was published. This book deals mainly with Manstein's trial and the years after 1945.[11]

Manstein in British Military Literature

Many British books about the *Wehrmacht* tend for obvious reasons to emphasise Rommel, whose operations were mainly conducted against the British Army. He was depicted in a heroic image, way beyond his real capacity, by both Churchill and General Auchinleck. Churchill mentioned him favourably in a speech in the House of Commons, and Auchinleck admonished his soldiers not to be blinded by the 'Rommel myth'. The Rommel hero epic in British literature overlooks the fact that Rommel was, for a lengthy period of time, and not without reason, Hitler's favourite General. However, his superiors considered his operations in Africa to be 'total lunacy'.

A number of British works, detailing with 19th century wars and events in Europe, convey the impression of a nostalgia for times long gone by. Commanders who fought each other were not considered to be enemies, but honourable opponents, bound together by a professional camaraderie, and living in times when foreign

---

9   henceforth Oldenburg
10 henceforth Kunz
11 henceforth Wrochem

employment was taken for a variety of reasons. Lack of promotion at home could be a reason for moving on, in hopes of higher rewards looming elsewhere. Quarrels with the local sovereign, simple financial rewards, or a nascent nationalism, could be reasons for taking up service in a foreign Army.

Scharnhorst, who became the prime reformer of the Prussian Army in the 19th century, was an officer in the Army of the Count of Schaumburg Lippe. For personal reasons he chose to serve the Prince Elector of Hanover who was also King of England. Since Scharnhorst was not an aristocrat, he was denied promotion to Colonel. The King of Prussia then offered him an aristocratic title and a regiment. Clausewitz, the father of German strategic thinking, served as a Colonel in the Russian Army, after Prussia had been reduced to a Napoleonic satellite state. One of Manstein's remote ancestors was a Russian General.

A scion of the famous German military dynasty, von der Schulenburg served in the Venetian Army against the Turks. The Prussian General Yorck became a German corps commander in Napoleon's Army, after Napoleon had ordered the King of Prussia to join his war against Russia. The British General Macdonald, a follower of the House of Stuart, became a Marshal of Napoleon's army. When Napoleon annexed the province of Hanover, many officers escaped to England and joined the 'King's German Legion.' After Bismarck incorporated Hanover into Prussia, others also joined. In the British Army's seniority list of 1914, 100 names were preceded by a 'von' title.

A somewhat curious work is Richard Brett-Smith's *Hitler's Generals*. In his conclusion, Brett-Smith is highly critical of the *Wehrmacht*, but he turns two of his heroes, Manstein and Kesselring into cult figures. Brett-Smith ends his chapter on Manstein with the sentence: "If it be by his peers that a man's qualities should best be judged, then *Feld-Marschall* von Manstein's reputation is safe for all time."[12] The book appeared in 1976. At that time, a number of Manstein's former fellow Generals had gone public in their criticisms of him.

Albert Seaton, who wrote comprehensive books in English about the Russo-German war and the German Army, expressed unfavourable opinions of Manstein:

> Among Manstein's successes were his contributions to the French campaign in 1941, the overrunning of the Crimea, and the containing of part of the spring 1943 Soviet offensive in the Ukraine. He achieved little else. Yet, by the late summer of 1944, his opinion of his own and the German Army's capability had become bizarre. He even thought that, with himself as C-in-C, he could outfight both East and West and force his enemies to the conference table. The Allied and Russian leadership, according to Manstein, was 'wretched' (*miserabel*). He said this at a time when German Armies, even Army Groups, were being completely destroyed, both in the East and in the West.[13]

---

12   R. Brett-Smith, *Hitler's Generals,* London 1966, p. 235 (henceforth Brett-Smith)
13   A. Seaton, *The German Army 1933–1945*, New York 1982, p. 216 (henceforth Seaton, Army)

Seaton's criticism of Manstein's 'draw theory' is well founded, but the remainder of his statement is somewhat exaggerated. It will be referred to in more detail later on. Seaton added:

> Manstein was indeed very ambitious, a man of operative genius whose great abilities were clouded by a pose of arrogance and conceit. He wanted the powers of a Hindenburg and the fame of the elder Moltke, plus a unified *Oberkommando* with himself at its head. Yet, in truth, he was uncertain of himself. He had little understanding of human nature and his attitude towards his subordinates could be very unpleasant ... How close Manstein was to his troops must remain a matter of doubt, for he had become stale. He was a man of habit and routine, absorbed by the evening ritual of bridge that was forced on his immediate circle.[14]

This criticism is also partially exaggerated. Manstein did indeed seek the authorities mentioned by Seaton, but not because he was unsure of himself. His requests, which will be referred to at length, were logical. In fact he was the only German commander capable of filling the positions he aspired to. It is obvious that his ambitions were doomed to failure under a man like Hitler, but he cannot be blamed for that.

The term 'bridge ritual' was appropriate. Manstein had a passion for that card-game and it had developed into fanaticism. An officer who had served on Manstein's staff remembers that when a candidate was proposed to Manstein for a position on his staff, the first question to him by the *Feldmarschall* was: "Do you play bridge?" If the answer was negative, the officer was ordered to learn to play bridge within three weeks, if he wanted to remain on Manstein's staff. It is somewhat doubtful if Manstein can be criticized for his love of bridge. Every man needs some element of distraction after hours of intensive work, with Manstein it was bridge. The 'bridge ritual' was hardly the burden that Seaton implies. Manstein's staff was totally devoted to him and not one of his staff officers ever requested his transfer on the ground of the daily bridge constraints.

Manstein had indeed inherited what could be called 'unbridled arrogance.' General Heusinger wrote about a General von Manstein who had taken part in the victorious war against the Austrians at Königgrätz in 1866. During the battle, that General Manstein had received an order from his commander in chief, Moltke the elder, and his response was: "Who is this General von Moltke?"[15]

Manstein's British defence attorney, Reginald Paget, wrote a book that should have remained unwritten.[16] Paget not only performs a disservice for his client but, at times, he simply subjects him to ridicule. Paget had already incurred the wrath of the British military tribunal for statements at Manstein's trial that were gross National-Socialist propaganda, and for his endeavours to play up to anti-Semitic feelings in the German public. "The number of Jews now living in Germany is

---

14 Ibid.
15 A. Heusinger, *Der unbequeme operative Kopf,* Aufsatz in einer Festschrift der Bundeswehr anläßlich des 80. Geburtstags Mansteins 1987. (henceforth Heusinger, Kopf)
16 R. Paget, Earl of Northampton, *Manstein – seine Feldzüge und sein Prozeß,* 1952 (henceforth Paget)

such that I ask myself where they have come from." As a 'denier' of the Holocaust, Paget puts himself on the same level as David Irving. His book shows a total lack of understanding of the conditions under which Manstein exercised his Commands. He gives calculations bordering on absurdity about the number of Jews murdered in the Crimea with the participation of Manstein's 11th Army. Paget's descriptions of Manstein's character and his opinions are simply childish. His book has no historic value. However, excerpts from it have been repeatedly quoted, because Manstein is its central figure. Parts of it refer to war crimes in which Manstein certainly did participate.

Manstein in French Military Literature

French writings on the Second World War are concerned mainly with the battle for France, and Manstein's '*Sichelschnitt*' plan, which was the decisive element in the German victory. Manstein's personality is treated only incidentally.

Manstein in Russian Military Literature

The official Russian Military History *Otetchesvennoi Voiny Sovietskogo Soyuza* (IVOVS), and the memoirs of Russian Commanders were written after Stalin's death, but decades before the collapse of the Soviet Union. All reflect the 'official doctrine' at the time of their appearance. Also they were submitted to censorship. The first five volumes were written during Krushchev's period. While Stalin as war-lord could not be ignored, Krushchev's achievements are extolled beyond reality. The last volume, which is a summary, came out after Krushchev's dismissal. Suddenly, Breshnev's insignificant achievements as political commissar of an Army became an 'exceptional performance'. *IVOVS* mentions every important German commander and his memoirs. The main purpose was to reject their conclusions, and to emphasise that their objectives were thwarted by the Red Army. The recollections of Marshal Zhukov are believed to have been written with the assistance of ghost-writers. A typical mention of Manstein by Zhukov reads: "In the eyes of the Hitlerian leadership, Manstein was the most outstanding German commander."[17]

In their memoirs, Soviet Generals are often critical of their fellow commanders, particularly in the books written by the 'Southern Generals'. Their operations took place in the southern operational theatre where Krushchev was the head of the political directorate. Relations between Stalin and Krushchev had deteriorated during the war, so that Generals who served under Krushchev's political authority were overlooked for the highest promotion until after Stalin's death. Yeremenko was still an Army General at the end of the war. Chuikov never commanded more than an Army. During Krushchev's reign, both became Marshals of the Soviet Union.

Some care must be exercised when reading German recollections about the number and strength of the Red Army units opposed to them. This can lead to

---

17 G. Zhukov, *Vospominana i Razmychlenia*, Moscow 1969, p. 451 (henceforth Zhukov)

erroneous conclusions. Red Army units were smaller than their German equivalents. A Russian Army was at best the size of a German Corps. A Soviet 'Front', which grouped a number of armies, is often defined as the equivalent of an Army Group. However, its size was at best comparable to a German Army. Often several 'fronts' were temporarily placed under the authority of one commander and his unit was named 'direction' in Russian. English literature used the term 'theatre'. Theatres would be disbanded after completion of the operation for which they were established. Before the war, the prescribed strength of a Russian division was more or less 8,000 men. During the winter of 1941 many divisions were reduced to 2,000 – 3,000 men. However, Red Army divisions were assisted by separate special units that carried their supplies. Russian divisions were commanded mostly by Colonels, and in certain instances by Lieutenant-Colonels.

Autobiographies: Manstein's and Other's

In the absence of a biography, a complete account of Manstein's life can only be gathered from his memoirs. The first volume, *Verlorene Siege*, was published in 1955. It was one of the first memoirs to appear that was written by a senior German commander, and was widely sold, both in Germany and abroad. The book is an account beginning with the outbreak of the war, and ending with Manstein's dismissal in March 1944. In 1958, Manstein published a second shorter volume, *Aus einem Soldatenleben* (From a soldier's life) which covers the years up to 1939.[18] Finally, Manstein's son, Rüdiger von Manstein, and Theodor Fuchs, published *Soldat im 20 Jahrhundert* (A Soldier in the Twentieth Century) after Manstein's death. The first part is simply a condensing of Manstein's two memoirs and is mostly written in the first person singular. The second part is an account of his life after the war and of his trial.[19] The book is, at best, second-rate.

Verlorene Siege conveys a negative impression. There are well-founded suspicions that part of the book was not written by Manstein, but by his close aide, General Busse. The description of military operations reflects the knowledge which could be expected from Manstein's talent as a *Generalstab* officer. They are not conclusive. Other authors, both in Germany and abroad, have been able to avail themselves of new sources which put in doubt many statements in Manstein's books. The main interest in Manstein's book is how he himself viewed his operations, and how he planned them.

Manstein's books show the weakness that Clausewitz criticized in all military memoirs:

> Only from time to time do memoirs of military commanders and their *confidants* show the many 'threads' which create a 'cloth.' Many reflections and internal struggles of authors are purposely hidden, because they concern political events. Sometimes they are omitted because the authors view them simply as rumours, which can be disregarded.

---

18   E. von Manstein, *Aus einem Soldatenleben*, Bonn 1958 (henceforth *Soldatenleben*)
19   R.von Manstein/T. Fuchs, *Soldat im 20. Jahrhundert*, Munich 1091 (henceforth Manstein/Fuchs)

The title chosen by Manstein caused many raised eyebrows. There were no 'lost' German victories in the Second World War, with the possible exception of the victory over France, which turned into a 'victory in the void'. This expression was coined by *Generalleutnant* (ret) *Bundeswehr*, Dr Franz Uhle-Wettler. It will be referred to in the chapter describing the campaign in the West. Manstein's book conveys the impression, as do other German Generals' memoirs, that their war was primarily waged against Hitler and only in a secondary manner against Germany's enemies. The historian Colonel Dr Hans Meier-Welcker comments:

> Many high ranking German commanders attempted, during the war or after its end, to win battles in a spirit of retrospective apology. This is convincingly shown in their memoirs and in their biographies. Titles were such as *Verlorene Siege* (Lost Victories) by Manstein: *Verratene Schlachten* (Betrayed battles) by Friessner: *Soldat bis zum letzten Tag* (Soldier until the final day) by Kesselring: *Ordnung im Chaos* (Order within the chaos) by Balck ....The exceptional conditions that prevailed during the war in Germany should not permit an attempt to exit from history after its end. The attempt is a self justification, and a desire to confer sense on the 'senseless belief' in the final victory of National-Socialist Germany.

Verlorene Siege includes many attempts by its author to hide unpleasant incidents that could be damaging to him. Others are recounted in a manner that is divorced from the truth. The book ends abruptly with Manstein's dismissal. This is not a coincidence. Perhaps it provides the key to Manstein's personality. Manstein was far too intelligent not to realise that his personal account of the decisive events of the war, that occurred in the months following his retirement, would be a contribution to history. One will not find a memoir writer, active or not, who would not write about the attempt on Hitler's life on 20 July 1944, the invasion in 1944, and the final collapse.

But Manstein's world was different. Manstein perceived the Army as an entity, separate from society, and subject to its own moral precepts. He believed it had to be judged solely by those criteria, but without considering the overriding principles. Manstein himself was the personification of the Army. As long as he held an active command, his vision of the Army was unimpaired. He believed that destiny had selected him to be its standard-bearer. The moment he was no longer active, the Army, as he wanted to view it, had come to an end and he became an apparently indifferent observer.

He mentioned his trial in a few short paragraphs, but only to show his regret that he was unable to convince the tribunal of the absurdity of the charges brought against him. His own confused defence at his trial was likewise no coincidence. Manstein always expressed himself with total clarity. But the tribunal was a forum to which his vision of the world was alien. He was unable to find arguments that would convince his judges of a logic which was not their own. The reader of *Verlorene Siege* could get the impression that, with Manstein's removal, a chapter of world history had come to an end.

Soldatenleben is a well-written book, with interesting descriptions of Manstein's youth and his service in the First World War. He writes of the establishment and the functioning of the *Reichswehr* after 1918, and of the *Wehrmacht* up to 1939. The book shows Manstein's ambivalence towards the Weimar Republic, but he refrains from one-sided judgements. In particular his account of the Kapp-*Putsch* is well balanced. Outside Germany, *Soldatenleben* was not met with the same interest as *Verlorene Siege*. When the book was published in 1959, the influential German weekly *Der Spiegel*, on 14 January 1959, wrote a scathing article *In Treue Keß* (Pert in Loyalty). The title chosen by the magazine was a parody of Manstein's personal motto: *In Treue fest* (Firm in loyalty). The article said:

> The most self-satisfied autobiographer among the German military, *Generalfeldmarschall* Erich, born von Lewinski, and by adoption von Manstein, has produced an 'effect' with his memoirs. Other military memoir writers in Germany are eager to avoid such 'effects' by engaging in only gentle criticism of themselves and their fellow Generals. In the first volume of his memoirs, *Verlorene Siege*, the author presented himself with aplomb as an infallible commander. Manstein had already incurred the wrath of his *Wehrmacht* fellow Generals, who then engaged in an unsparing whispering campaign that was not made public. Manstein had extolled his own performance beyond a tolerable level. It was at the expense of other Generals, those who in battle had operated on his left and his right. He wrote of them in the same manner in which he had given them no consideration in his command decisions during the war. *Verlorene Siege* caused malicious glee among the public, because not a single commander in chief, corps commander or chief-of-staff, with whom the author was in contact during the war, was left blameless. In particular, the former Chief of the *Generalstab* Halder is treated in an unfriendly manner. The impression arises that everybody made mistakes, only Manstein committed none.

Structure of this Book

Chapter One is devoted to a summary of Manstein's career. It deals with the main aspects of his life, and also with the campaigns which are not the subject of separate chapters, such as the battle in the West 1940, Stalingrad 1942, and the battles for Kursk 1943, which were the turning point of the war in the East. In a conclusion to this chapter, I will attempt to answer the following questions:

* Was Manstein <u>the</u> *primus inter pares* of the highest German commanders or was he one of the few *primi inter pares*?
* Can Manstein be called a strategist, or was he the war's outstanding leader of operations by using large mobile units?
* Was Manstein a National-Socialist?
* Was Manstein an anti-Semite in the sense of the German racial laws?
* What were Manstein's personal relations with Hitler?

Chapter Two deals with the battle of France in 1940, with emphasis on Manstein's master plan. A long *excursus* deals with the weakness of the French Third Republic and the degradation of the French Army after 1918, which rendered its rout unavoidable, regardless of the plan adopted by the Germans. A second *excursus* shows a comparison between the plans of the battle for France in 1940, and those of the Battle of the Bulge in 1944.

Chapter Three examines if Manstein failed in his duties during the battle for Stalingrad.

Chapter Four describes the battles for Kursk, and operation 'Citadel' in the light of recent discoveries.

Chapter Five deals with the attempts to gain Manstein's adherence to the 'resistance' movement.

Chapter Six is concerned with the 'Commissar Order', with particular emphasis on Manstein's attitude towards it. An *excursus* describes the evolution of the Commissar Institution in the Red Army.

Chapter Seven deals with the murder of Jews in the Southern Ukraine and the Crimea, both areas controlled by Army Group South and Manstein's 11th Army. It contains reports of the slaughter in every city under Manstein's territorial authority. It gives the most complete list, published to date, of relevant reports that reached Manstein, and of the orders issued by Manstein's 11th Army. The attitude of other German High Commanders towards the genocide is shown in some detail. The chapter likewise deals with the first excesses against the Jews in Poland immediately after the end of the Polish campaign.

Chapter Eight attempts to assess Manstein's human values and deficiencies. New and negative material about Manstein, that has recently come to light, has caused some differences in the content of the German original and of the English translation.

The reader will notice that I have widened the subject well beyond the personality of its central figure. The reason for this is obvious. The purpose of this book is not to limit itself to Manstein. It intends to show, with the most capable German commander as its central figure, how the *Nazi* system, step by step, succeeded in perverting the centuries old traditions of the Prussian and German Officer Corps. Therefore additional German high commanders have to be described, to show how the moral decrepitude, of more than one high commander, set in.

German Generals' ranks, all ranks of the *Waffen-SS*, and German military terminology will be given in the vernacular. In this I follow the example of a number of contemporary historians. A few ranks, and other elements of military terminology, lend themselves to exact translation. There is little sense, for instance, in translating the German *Generaloberst* into Colonel-General, since no such rank exists in the British or US Armies. A *German Generalleutnant* is one rank below a British or US Lieutenant General, since the German Army had no Brigadiers. A further confusion may arise with the Red Army, which contains a number of ranks and other terminology adapted from the German. The Red Army has likewise a Colonel-General (General *polkovnik*) whose rank is lower than a German *Generaloberst*. A Russian Marshal of Artillery, Tanks etc. ranks not only below a Marshal of the Soviet Union but also below an Army General.

In German military terminology, the rank of *Feldmarschall* comes close to a myth. In the British Army, Field Marshal is simply an additional rank. One could write that, at Stalingrad, Manstein did not act like a *Feldmarschall*. However, one could not make a similar statement about a British Field Marshal.

To give another, from many examples, the German *Generalstab* was a unique institution with no equivalent in any other Army. To translate it by 'General staff' makes no sense. Until the end of the First World War, the *Generalstab* was the highest military authority in the Imperial Army and its chief outranked the Commander in Chief of the Army. After 1933, this was no longer the case. However, an officer who had succeeded in joining the *Generalstab* after years of training, continued to enjoy a particular status. Until they reached General's rank, officers of the *Generalstab*, whether they served in staff duties or performed troop service, always added the letters 'iG' ie member of the *Generalstab*, after their rank. They wore special uniforms with carmine striped trousers and special shoulder straps and collar tabs.

Functions of the officers of the *Generalstab:*

- The Ia was the first *Generalstab* officer and head of all other officers of the *Generalstab*. Since German divisions had no staff, the Ia was de facto the chief-of-staff of the division:
- Ib was the second officer and responsible for supply.
- Ic was the third officer and responsible for general intelligence.
- Ic/AO was his subordinate and responsible for enemy intelligence.
- Id was a direct assistant to the Ia.
- IIa was responsible for the assignment of officers of his units.
- IIb was responsible for the nco and officers of his unit.
- O1 was the first aid to the Ia.
- O2 was the first aid to the Ic.
- O4 was a 'dogsbody', to be given any available task.

Designation of German military archive documents: The first comprehensive collection of German military archive documents was put together by the Americans during the immediate post-war years. They remain deposited with the city of Nuremberg and are designated by *NOKW*, followed by generally four numbers, eg *NOKW* 2458.

The archives of the German military archives (BA-MA) are given in a key which enables an archivist to immediately locate them:

Example:

> BA-MA, RH 20 – 11/488
> BA-MA = *Bundesarchiv-Militärarchiv*
> RH = *Reichsheer* – Ground forces of the *Reich*
> 20 = Second World War
> 11 = 11th Army
> 488 = File 488 of the 11th Army documents.

For a general reader this is unimportant as the contents of the relevant documents are in the text and the reference to the BA-MA is given in the endnote.

Gradually, German military terminology developed into a separate language of its own. Books that have used only translated words tend to be meaningless, and as a result are mocked by serious critics. The literary translation of *Kessel* would be cauldron. In German military terminology it means a group of forces encircled by the enemy. A *Kesselschlacht* is an encounter that results in a *Kessel*.

I have chosen the following method. At the first mention of a German term, a short explanation in English is added in brackets.

Chapter 1

The Career

Section I. The Ascent

Apart from his removal as *Oberquartiermeister* I (Deputy Chief of the *Generalstab*) during the 1938 *Revirement* of the Army top, Manstein's life resembled a curve with a sudden break at its height. It continued uninterruptedly until 1941. But thereafter, the course of the Second World War produced a downward curve in his career, interrupted only by temporary local successes. As the war progressed, a moral decay set in. At the end, he was tried and sentenced for war crimes.

1887 to 1918 and the end of World War I

Erich von Manstein was born in Berlin on 24 November 1887. He was the tenth child of Major Eduard von Lewinski and his wife Helene von Sperling. Helene von Sperling's sister, Hedwig, was married to Major Georg von Manstein. The Manstein marriage was childless and the two families had agreed, some years before the birth of the future *Feldmarschall* that, if a tenth child were to be a boy, the Mansteins would be his guardian. Later, Erich von Manstein was formally adopted by his foster family. Both families were wealthy.

In *Soldatenleben*, Manstein gives a picturesque description of the circumstances of his birth:

> The clerk at the post office in the small Thuringian town Rudolfstadt, must have cast a nonplussed look at a cable received from Berlin on 27 November 1887. It was addressed to Major Georg von Manstein, commander of the battalion stationed there, and his wife Hedwig, née Sperling. The telegram had the following text: 'Today a healthy son was born to you. Mother and child are well. Heartiest congratulations!' Helene and Lewinski.[1]

In accordance with prevailing regulations, Manstein's official name eventually became Erich von Lewinski, gen. von Manstein (v. Lewinski, named v. Manstein). In most official documents and Army lists, he was mentioned under this double name. However, in the last seniority lists of the *Wehrmacht*, the prefix v. Lewinski gen. was dropped. Apart from official documents he was always written about and addressed as von Manstein.

When discussions about Manstein gained increasing ground in recent years, some authors advanced the opinion that the adoption caused Manstein to choose a military career, since he was looking at the Army as a substitute for a family. Adoption will indeed often cause problems to the adopted child. Sometimes the child does not know who its real parents are or he has no relationship with them. This was not the case with Manstein. His adoption was never kept secret from him and

---

1 *Soldatenleben,* p.11

the relationship between his real and his adopted parents remained harmonious. Manstein emphasises repeatedly that the close ties between the two families prevented any conflict. The reasons for Manstein's choice of a soldier's career are obvious. Majors von Lewinski and Manstein would both become Generals. The families Lewinski, Manstein and Sperling had served as officers over centuries.

The original name of the Lewinski family was Royk. Later they added the name Lewinski as a designation of their large estate Lewyn (today the Polish Lewino). General von Lewinski's grandfather was an officer in the Army of Frederick the Great. The father of the Sperling sisters was successively chief-of-staff of the armies commanded by Generals Goeben and Steinmetz during the Franco–Prussian war of 1870–1871. Male members of the Manstein family had served as officers in the Armies of the *Große Kurfürst*, the 'great' Prince Elector of Prussia, whose son would become the first Prussian King. Another General von Manstein, possibly a distant relative, had served as a Russian General in the Crimea. The *Feldmarschall* was to discover his past when his 11th Army occupied the Crimea in 1941–1942. Through interactions of marriage, Manstein had become a nephew of *Feldmarschall* von Hindenburg. Manstein could write in good conscience that he was born with a military inheritance. No additional psychological search is required.

An interesting example of how an adoption can affect a man's character and determine a famous career is provided by the French general Weygand. Until his death at the age of 97, Weygand did not know who was his father. Rumour had it that he was the illegitimate son of either King Leopold II of Belgium, or the Habsburg Emperor Maximilian I of Mexico. In fact neither rumour was ever established. However, Weygand always had considerable funds at his disposal during his childhood and his upbringing. Maxime Weygand was born in Brussels in 1867. Two men notified his birth to the capital's registry, declaring him to be the child of unknown parents. They did not sign the register, stating that they could neither read nor write. Weygand was first raised by the midwife who delivered him, Mrs. Saget, and bore her name.

At the age of 6, he was taken to France under circumstances that have always remained unclear, and was raised in Paris by a Jewish leather article merchant, David Cohen. Cohen's wife was born Denimal, a name which the young Maxime turned into the aristocratic de Nimal under which he entered the St. Cyr officers' academy as a foreign national. At the age of 18, Weygand applied for French citizenship and was formally adopted by Cohen's bookkeeper, François Joseph Weygand, with whom he never had personal contact.

A few years prior to his death, Weygand told his biographer Guy Raissac that he had never been able to overcome the mystery of his birth. Those circumstances may well have been the root of his later extreme nationalism, which came close to xenophobia, his anti-Semitism, and his idealisation of the French Army which became his ultimate home. Fate would have it that Manstein's and Weygand's paths crossed in 1940. Manstein was the author of the German plan that destroyed the French Army. Weygand became the unsuccessful French *Generalissimo* on 19 May 1940.

In accordance with family tradition, Manstein was educated at the cadet schools at Plön and Berlin-Lichterfelde. At the end of his schooling, Manstein was not content with the *Selecta* that allowed cadets, after seven years of high school, to enter directly into final officers' training. But after two additional school years he went on to pass the *Abitur* of a *Realgymnasium*. In his last school year, after he had passed the *Selecta* as first in his class, he was assigned, as personal page, to the Russian Grand duchess Vladimir at the wedding of the German Crown Prince. The bride was the daughter of the Duchess. The *Abitur* does not confer outstanding erudition. However, Manstein read extensively and developed a wide knowledge of classics, literature and classical music. But history remained close to a blank. While he cannot be placed in the small group of intellectual officers, his general knowledge and erudition were far above average.

After passing his *Abitur* examination in 1906, Manstein entered the aristocratic 3rd Guard Infantry Regiment as a *Fähnrich*, an officer cadet, and remained there until the outbreak of World War I. During the years 1913–14 he entered the War Academy. His studies were interrupted by the outbreak of World War I. During the war he attended the short 'Sedan' *Generalstab* course of four weeks. Curiously, the man who would later become the undisputed brain of the *Generalstab* had never completed the prescribed full *Generalstab* training.

When World War I began, Manstein was a Lieutenant and took part in the battles around Namur, in East Prussia, and in Poland. He finished the war as Captain. During World War I, promotions were slow. In November 1914 Manstein was severely wounded. After his release from hospital, he served only in staff positions until the end of the war, first in the Army of General von Gallwitz, and then under General Fritz von Below. There the latter's chief-of-staff, General von Lossberg, became his first tutor in higher staff assignments. His progress was fast. By 1917 he was already First Staff Officer and Head of Operations of a Division. Uninterrupted staff service during the whole war was exceptional, evidently his unusual talent for staff work had already been recognised. In 1917 Manstein was appointed first general staff officer, *Ia*, with the 4th Cavalry Division in Kurland, and in 1918 he became *Ia* with the 213th Infantry Division on the Western front. German divisions had no chief-of-staff, the *Ia* was thus the foremost staff officer of the unit. Usually this assignment was given to a major or an older captain, with longer experience than the 27 year old Manstein. Obviously his unusual talents had already been recognised. After the signature of the Treaty of Versailles, Manstein was accepted into the small *Reichswehr* of 100,000 men, which was the size of Army permitted in Germany by the Treaty. His acceptance into the *Reichswehr* was never in doubt and no special recommendations were required. The new Army knew that it could not spare a man with his proven talents.

During the Weimar Republic

The end of the Empire was a trauma for German officers. Contrary to their Austrian fellow officers who were attached to the person of the Sovereign, the German officers, in particular the Prussians, served an institution. Wilhelm II enjoyed little personal respect. Manstein later wrote that the Emperor had simply abandoned his authority to his advisers, since before the war, and during the conflict it would devolve on Ludendorff. Manstein added that he had experienced a personal blow when his commanding officer, general von Below, simply paid no attention to a nonsensical order by Wilhelm II, since he had been raised in the belief of an unimpeachable Imperial Royal authority.[2] He wrote:

> The fact that an order, a wish, regardless how the Emperor's words could be interpreted, could simply fall into the waste paper basket, showed me like a flash of lightning the extent to which the Emperor had given up influence on the conduct of the war.[3]

The Prussian Army had always defined itself as a 'Royal Army.' It did not serve the state, or an individual ruler, but spoke of 'Royal Service.' Already Bismarck had written that German patriotism could only flourish if it was bound by devotion to a dynasty. When the Weimar Republic was established, and became a stable institution, the Officer Corps served it loyally without ever adopting a sentimental attachment to it. Manstein wrote in *Soldatenleben*:

> The officers were duty bound to serve a state, whether they approved of its new form or not. The new attachment of the German soldier, who had lost his attachment to a dynasty, was to a new mythical or idealistic form of a state. It may be incomprehensible to foreigners, but was regrettable to many Germans. However, it was 'typically' German.[4]

"Incomprehensible to foreigners?" "Typically German?" Is patriotism suddenly a German monopoly? Manstein's words are a 'typical' example of his ignorance of history, and his lack of knowledge as to how 'foreigners' thought and acted. The 'legitimacy conflict' mentioned by Manstein, had already arisen a century earlier in France and in the French Army, and persisted at that time.

After the French Revolution, the forms of the French state were subject to constant changes. The first Republic was followed by the Directoire, Bonaparte's Consulate, the Empire of Napoleon, the restoration of the Bourbons, the bourgeois Monarchy of Louis Philippe, then the second Republic of Louis-Napoleon. After a few years, the Second Republic became the Second Empire, followed by the Third Republic, the Vichy government, and finally the Fourth and Fifth Republics. The French Army was no less tradition bound than the German, but it subordinated itself to every new form of state. Few soldiers look beyond their limited duties. Personalities such as de Gaulle are exceptions.

Until 1921, Manstein served in the *Grenzschutz Ost* under his former superior, General von Lossberg. The two *Grenzschutz* were regular Army units consisting of regiments stationed in Germany's eastern provinces. The regiments were manned by volunteers, the commanders were active officers. The new borders between Germany and Poland had not yet been finally determined, and Polish troops made frequent incursions into German territory. Since the *Reichswehr* had not yet been established, the *Grenzschutz* units became the German body of defence in the East. Both were disbanded under the provisions of the Treaty of Versailles that provided for the creation of the *Reichswehr*. Manstein did not join a *Freikorps*, or other paramilitary unit, nor did he take part in the Kapp-*Putsch*. It was the short-lived and failed attempt to overthrow the government of the Republic, which he opposed.

---

2 *Soldatenleben*, p. 45
3 Ibid, p. 55
4 Ibid

His description of the Kapp-*Putsch* in *Soldatenleben* is balanced, and shows an understanding of political conditions in Germany at that time. Manstein never hid behind the facade of the 'non-political' officer, which *Generaloberst* von Seeckt, the first commander in chief of the *Reichswehr* had turned into law. Seeckt's law prohibited officers from engaging in any political activity and deprived them of the right to vote.

After the Second World War, many officers referred to the Seeckt doctrine in order to justify their failures. That does not stand up. The law enacted, after pressure by Seeckt, forbade officers from engaging in active politics, but it could not forbid them from thinking. However, Manstein was never able to extend his political understanding beyond the German borders. He showed sympathy for the patriotic feelings that guided the perpetrators of the *coup* attempt, *Generallandschaftsdirektor* Kapp and General von Lüttwitz. He also recalled a private conversation with Lüttwitz's son-in-law, General von Hammerstein-Equord, later Commander in Chief of Germany's armed forces. He told him that his father-in-law acted in a state of inner compulsion, to save the fatherland while there was still time.

At the same time, he strongly castigated the fact that it was the first time in the history of the German Army that some of its generals and officers had openly risen against the legitimate government. He recognised the measured attitude of the government under the authority of *Reichspräsident* Friedrich Ebert that had prevented a cleavage of the officer corps.[5] In the eyes of General von Fritsch, later Commander in Chief of the Army, Ebert was simply a 'swine', a *Schweinehund*. At that time, Manstein understood German political realities better than most of his fellow officers.

In 1920, Manstein married Jutta Sibylle von Loesch. The von Loesch family belonged to Silesian aristocracy and owned a large estate. The marriage was happy and lasted until the death of Ms von Manstein 1966. She had joined the NSDAP and become an active Party member. Stahlberg wrote that Tresckow had warned him to beware of Manstein's wife since she was a '150% *Nazi*.' Stahlberg suggested that Manstein had come under his wife's political influence. However, such a statement can be dismissed as one of his fantasies. Manstein was of a highly independent mind and his opinions were certainly not subject to his wife's influence. To bring Ms von Manstein into the discussions about her husband simply shows poor judgement.

In 1921, Manstein became company commander in the 5th Infantry Regiment at Angermünde. Only two years later he had rejoined the *Generalstab*. The *Generalstab* had been forbidden by the Treaty of Versailles. However, it continued to function through 'semantic artefacts', or the 'playing with words'. It was named *Truppenamt* and its officers *Führergehilfen*. Manstein joined the *Truppenamt* as a *Führerstabsoffizier*, the official term for officers of the *Generalstab*. He served in that capacity at the *Wehrkreiskommando* II, in Stettin, and IV in Dresden. The *Wehrkreise* were the territorial units of the Army, by 1939 they numbered 21. They were headed by a corps commander. Manstein became a teacher at the *Führergehilfenausbildung*, the central three years' course for officers expected to become members of the *Generalstab*. His pupils held him in high esteem. In an

5   Ibid, p. 76

interview in 1982, Heusinger recalled that, as a teacher, Manstein was very demanding, while always remaining courteous:

> Undoubtedly Manstein was anointed with a 'drop of Samuel's oil'. At first he made life difficult for me. He presented me with problems that were entirely new, within a large operational framework of which I had no previous experience. Furthermore, I came under the orders of a superior mind, a man who worked very quickly. He always put his finger on the right solution, while demanding the same quick understanding and response from his pupils. It was certainly not easy. But after a few months I had grown into my assignment and thereafter I had enthusiastic years under such a superior officer. Even then, Manstein was considered to be the coming man.[6]

Between 1927 and 1929, Manstein served on the staff of the Infantry Command IV at Magdeburg. Two years later he was returned to the *Reichswehr* Ministry as head of group I within the T–1 department, ie the equivalent of the operational department of the *Generalstab*. He took part in the plans for a new mobilization of the Army that had been forbidden by the Treaty of Versailles. Several suggestions were put forward. Lieutenant Colonel Wilhelm Keitel, later a *Feldmarschall* and head of OKW, presented a plan to establish Divisions to which troops, but no arms and no equipment would be allotted. Manstein dismissed that concept as nonsensical, since Divisions created without armament would not have combat efficiency if activated. He submitted his own plan, which foresaw a three-fold increase in the total number of Divisions, through internal regroupings, and shifting of units from one Division to another.

His plan was adopted. Keitel had to start again, and adapt his paper to Manstein's conclusions. The incident was evidence of the early recognition of Manstein's talent. In spite of being a newcomer to the ministry, he could success-fully promote his views and overcome traditional bureaucratic resistance. In *Soldatenleben* Manstein wrote that, "from this moment, my views began to gain increasing weight in the operational department."[7]

In 1931 and 1932, Manstein paid two visits to the Soviet Union. Like every foreign visitor to Russia, Manstein was carefully prevented from having any contacts with the population and only met with the officers to whom he was assigned. Manstein's account of his visit makes interesting reading, while showing that he, like his fellow officers, returned with an unchanged ignorance of the USSR. Manstein described his visit as "revealing in military knowledge".[8] In 1941 there was little trace of such 'insight' and Germany paid the price of having under-estimated Russian strength.

After his return from his second visit, Manstein assumed Command of a Battalion of an Infantry Regiment in Kolberg. He was still in Kolberg when Hitler became *Reichskanzler* in 1933.

---

6 Heusinger, Kopf, p. 36
7 *Soldatenleben*, p. 131 ff
8 Ibid, p. 132

In the *Wehrmacht* until the outbreak of World War II

In 1933 Manstein was witness to excesses against Jews in Kolberg. He writes that he expressed outrage:

> In Kolberg attempts were made to dismiss the outstanding head physician of the Siloah children home, because he was half 'non-aryan'. Since he had fought in the First World War, and been decorated with the Iron Cross first class, my regimental commander, the future *Generaloberst* Strauss and I intervened successfully in his favour and prevented his replacement by other willing candidates. We continued to invite him to take his meals in the officers' mess, much to the anger of the party, which left us unperturbed.[9]

On 1 February 1934, Manstein reverted to the *Generalstab* and became chief-of-staff of the *Wehrkreis* III in Berlin. The *Wehrkreis* commander was the future *Feldmarschall* von Witzleben. In *Soldatenleben*, Manstein showered his commander with praise:

> Witzleben had begun his service in the Royal Grenadier Regiment. He was a Prussian nobleman of the very best kind, a most talented soldier, whom everybody liked and admired for his warm heart and his charming behaviour. He never hid his opinions. Generous, and able to immediately grasp the essentials of a problem, he had the gift of not attempting to do everything himself. For a Chief-of-Staff like myself, who placed value on his independence, this was more than convenient. I enjoyed his full trust. Our co-operation was never troubled by the slightest shadow, nor did we have different political opinions. He would never hide his contempt for the NSDAP, and its shady officials, with whom we were in contact. He was generous, and honoured me with total confidence. He would never hide his contempt for the Party.[10]

In *Verlorene Siege*, Manstein would not find a word of regret for the tragic end of the 'Prussian nobleman', who was hanged after 20 July 1944.

In his description of the night of the long knives of 30 June 1934, Manstein engaged in a 'semantic artefact,' a euphemism. Generals von Schleicher and von Bredow were 'murdered', the other victims were 'shot'.

On 21 April 1934, Manstein lodged a formal protest against the retro-active introduction of the racial laws into the *Reichswehr*. He was the only German officer who dared to take such a step. Manstein sent his letter to General Beck, at that time head of the *Truppenamt*. A lieutenant, Klaus von Schmeling-Diringshoven, was a victim of the law. He had served under Manstein at Kolberg. Manstein undoubt-edly showed courage in coming out into the open against one of the cornerstones of the National-Socialist regime. Beck transmitted Manstein's memorandum to the *Reichswehrminister, Generaloberst* von Blomberg, through the intermediary of the head of the ministerial office, General von Reichenau. Blomberg expressed outrage and declared that he would take disciplinary steps against Manstein. The Army

---

9   Ibid, p. 177 f
10   Ibid., p. 181

commander in chief, *Generaloberst* von Fritsch refused. He stated that the matter was within his competence and then simply put it aside. Thanks to Fritsch's attitude, Manstein was spared the negative consequences of his step.

Remarkably, Manstein succeeded in his endeavours for his *protégé*. He managed at first to have him sent to the German military mission in China and, when the latter was disbanded, to maintain him on the active list. The officer was killed in action during the Polish campaign. Significantly, no other officer would emulate him. The future *Generaladmiral* von Friedeburg, himself not a pure Aryan, was confronted with a similar request by one of his subordinates. He refused to intervene, gave his officer a lengthy explanation about the political dimensions of the racial laws, and advised him to quietly await his future destiny.

Manstein's accompanying memorandum reveals singular aspects of his motivation. It can be considered as evidence of his perception of the Army as an institution, exempt from any rules that it had not imposed on itself. Manstein wrote of his general approval of the racial laws and parts of his accompanying memorandum contain strong anti-Semitic words. It is unimaginable that a highly intelligent and educated man, like Manstein, believed in the nonsense of the 'aryan race'. Undoubtedly Manstein had to write a memorandum of general approval of racial legislation if he were to have any success in the instance that prompted him. Some sentences are however, mildly speaking, strange – indeed, they verge on absurdity.

> There can be no doubt that we all stand without reservation behind National-Socialism and racial doctrine. But at the same time, we may not forget our soldiers' honour that has always inextricably bound us together … There is a lack of justice if we expel officers who have a clean conscience, and who cannot be blamed if their grandparents lacked racial consciousness. Meanwhile, we allow officers to remain who have shown lack of racial consciousness by marrying non-aryans …

Manstein then proposed a general review of all active officers, in order to determine who had married a wife with some Jewish blood. (!) Manstein's memorandum evidences that he is primarily concerned with the interference of 'outside elements' in Army matters.

> The soldier has to be judged in a manner different from others. He has not only devoted his work to the country, by joining the Army, he has shown his willingness to fight, even to die for Germany … The honour of these young officers is the honour of all of us. They have shown their patriotism in volunteering for service in the *Reichswehr* at a time when a military career is certainly not a bed of roses.

One paragraph in his memorandum is prophetic and shows that Manstein was clearly aware of the future dangers of National-Socialist doctrine:

> If we agree to sacrifice our young soldiers, the smears will not cease. Then it will be said that further up the hierarchy, you continue to have non-aryans. If we dislodge them, the 'reactionaries' will become the next victims. And this will continue, until the day when those who today attack the Army see a convenient target. If we sacrifice a small number of our comrades, they will immediately demand more heads.

On 1 June 1935, compulsory military service was reintroduced in Germany and Manstein was appointed head of the operational division of the reborn *Generalstab*. On 1 October of the same year, he was promoted to *Oberquartiermeister* I and Deputy Chief of the *Generalstab*. Manstein's rapid rise can be described as meteoric, and is solely due to his extraordinary talent. He had risen to that top position without having served in a troop command, for any lengthy period of time, since entering the Army. Even then it was unusual, since troop commands, at regular intervals, were the rule for those officers intended for higher *Generalstab* assignments. In terms of seniority, Manstein was unknown. He had become a *Generalmajor* only on the day of his appointment.

In the complete seniority list of the Army of 1938, his successor Halder was ranked 17. Manstein was 49 among the *Generalleutnants*. When Halder was appointed *Oberquartiermeister* II, he was already a *General der Artillerie*, with seniority dated 1 February 1936. Manstein was convinced that he had been intended to succeed Beck as Chief of the *Generalstab*. However, there were some doubts. At that time, the personnel department of the Army made promotions strictly in accordance with seniority. No previous *Oberquartiermeister* I had risen directly to Chief of the *Generalstab*. Halder was the only exception. However, his promotion had already been decided on, when he succeeded Manstein as *Oberquartiermeister* I. Undoubtedly, Manstein was looked on as a potential Chief of *Generalstab* at some future date.

During his tenure as head of operations and *Oberquartiermeister* I, Manstein was a strong advocate of modern methods and equipment. In that respect he was far ahead of Beck. He supported Guderian's urge for the creation of *Panzer* divisions, while at the same time recognising that Guderian advocated a one-sided view that only took the new *Panzer* formations into consideration. In fact the bulk of the Army would still consist of infantry divisions, which Guderian looked on as simple *Wollröcke* ie wearers of woollen uniforms. Manstein told Guderian: "Just leave the church in the centre of the village, you can't do it all on your own."

Manstein understood that the mass of the Army would continue to consist of infantry divisions that had to be trained for purposes of attack. Manstein was the prime mover in developing a new artillery weapon, the *Sturmartillerie*, literally assault artillery. It had the chassis of a tank, with a 7.5cm gun replacing the turret. He knew that he would walk straight into a hornet's nest. Until 1933, the artillery had been a stepchild of the German Army. With few exceptions, such as Generals von Gallwitz, von Kirchbach, Scholz and Schubert, artillery officers did not rise above the position of inspectors of their arm. When *Generaloberst* von Fritsch became Commander in Chief of the Army and General Beck Chief of the *Generalstab*, something akin to an artillery lobby emerged at the head of Army command. Fritsch and Beck were artillery officers, as were their respective successors, von Brauchitsch and Halder.

Manstein was convinced that a future war would be one of movement, with rapid advances of infantry and tanks needing the support of artillery. Heavy motorized artillery was never available in sufficient quantities to German infantry divisions. Instead, it was concentrated under the direct control of *OKH*. *OKH* would dispatch units to infantry divisions whenever operations required them, and thereafter returned them to *OKH*. Manstein developed a hybrid solution. The assault gun was to remain part of artillery weaponry but it was to be assigned to infantry units and not be returned to *OKH*. When he showed his idea to his sponsor Beck, he received the reply: "My dear Manstein, this time you have hit wide of the mark."[11] Manstein persisted. Finally his concept was adopted, although Brauchitsch later strongly reduced it in scope.

During 1937 Manstein wrote a series of memoranda about the high command structure. He demanded that in the event of war, the Army Commander in Chief should be invested with supreme authority over all branches of the forces, including Navy and Air Force. He kept in line with the traditional concept of the Prusso-German Army, but this already belonged in the past. In modern war, large as the army might be, superior economic potential, and control of the oceans, would be the dominating factors. Germany possessed neither. Beck had already recognised this in 1937 and had begun to issue warnings that a 'new' World War would inevitably lead to a German defeat. General Blumentritt commented:

> Given Germany's geography, any lengthy war would be deadly for us. Naval powers can permit themselves extended operations, since they cannot be attacked in their core and remain immune to economic warfare.[12]

The absurd future structure of the German High Command with two rival headquarters, *OKW* and *OKH* competing with each other, could obviously not have been foreseen. What was required was a *Generalstab* with authority over Army, Navy and Air Force, like the US joint chiefs-of-staff.

Manstein's dismissal as *Oberquartiermeister* I

In the immediate aftermath of the Blomberg-Fritsch scandal there was a major reshuffling. The *Revirement* took place within the *Wehrmacht*, and the senior civil service, primarily in the Foreign Service. Sixty high ranking officers were placed on the retirement list. However, a number were reactivated, first during the Czecho-slovakian crisis, and then when the war broke out a year later. Ritter von Leeb and von Kleist would rise to *Feldmarschalls*. Hoth became a *Generaloberst* and one of the outstanding *Panzer* commanders.

In his comments on the dismissal of Fritsch, Manstein wrote in *Soldatenleben*, that the background of this shameless intrigue was by then widely known. That was not the case at the time. Only the book by K.H.Janssen and F.Tobias, *Der Sturz der Generäle*, published in 1994, has shed probably the final light on the Blomberg/Fritsch scandal.[13] Manstein's analysis was not realistic. However, he could hardly be faulted for ignoring at the time what future research would bring to light, half a century later.

---

11 *Soldatenleben*, p. 247
12 G. Blumentritt, *Moscow*, in W.Richardson and S.Frei (ed). *The fatal decisions*, London 1956, p. 49
13 K.-H. Janssen/F. Tobias, *Der Sturz der Generäle. Hitler und die Blomberg-Fritsch-Krise –1938*, Munich 1994 (henceforth Janssen/Tobias)

In his reference to Fritsch's dismissal, Manstein wrote that "he had intended to throw his sword at Hitler's feet and that he always regretted not having done so."[14] This was a typical attempt by a memoir writer to gloss over the facts. No general retired from his command in protest against Fritsch's dismissal. When Ritter von Leeb saw the happy faces of his comrades during his farewell ceremony, he commented with disdain: "Just a bunch of job-seekers."[15] Only Fritsch's successor, von Brauchitsch, upon whom his fellow officers would shower blame after the war, was untiring in his efforts to obtain a complete a rehabilitation of Fritsch.

In his comments on the Blomberg-scandal, Manstein wrote: "What a humiliation that the politician Hitler can now appear as the guardian of the Army's honour." However, at that time, Hitler was no longer the 'politician Hitler', he was Head of State and Supreme Commander of the Armed Forces. As Blomberg's witness at the marriage ceremony, he was certainly entitled to feel that he had been debased.

The Blomberg/Fritsch scandal had a fatal consequence for the officers' corps. Blomberg's marriage to a registered prostitute, and Fritsch's clumsy defence when Hitler showed him a police file that accused him of homosexuality, led Hitler to lose his previous respect for his generals. In a speech on 3 January 1935 to party officials, he had said:

> Perhaps someone from the party will come to me and say: "Everything nice and fine, my *Führer*, but General so and so speaks and works against you!" And when another says: "My *Führer*, I have written evidence." Then I tear up this "bumph," because my faith in the *Wehrmacht* is unshakeable." This was now dead and buried.

In the course of the *Revirement*, a number of junior officers were given new commands and Manstein was dismissed as *Oberquartiermeister* I. This was a setback in Manstein's career which he was never able to overcome. In *Soldatenleben* he wrote: "The dream belongs to the past. The greatest honour for an officer, to find himself in the place that a Moltke, a Schlieffen and a Beck had occupied, was now in the grave as far as I was concerned."[16]

It was certainly the way Manstein felt. However, Moltke and Schlieffen on the one hand, and Beck on the other, cannot be compared. In the Imperial Army, the position as head of the *Generalstab* was the Mount Olympus for an officer. He had direct access to the Emperor and was his main adviser in all military matters. In the new *Generalstab*, its chief was one of the *primus inter pares* among the other department heads of the Army high command. He was an adviser without responsibility, something akin to a quartermaster. During World War II, the split between *OKW* and *OKH* relegated the *Generalstab* solely to the Eastern front. Beck had thus occupied the same 'place' as Moltke and Schlieffen, but he never had their authority.

The embittered Manstein sold his house in Berlin, and declared to his family that he would never return to the capital.[17] For years he searched for the reasons of his abrupt dismissal. He felt that Hitler was not responsible, since Hitler had barely

---

14 *Soldatenleben,* p. 396
15 Janssen/Tobias, p. 151 with reference to Leeb's Diaries, p. 41 f
16 *Soldatenleben,* p.319
17 Told by Manstein's daughter, Gisela von Lingenthal to Knopp, Knopp, p. 127

known about him. That was certainly not the case. Although Hitler had never met Manstein person, he obviously knew who the *Oberquartiermeister* I was, and what opinions he held. Manstein believed that his dismissal occurred through an intrigue by Blomberg or Keitel. In *Soldatenleben* he wrote that Beck had ordered Keitel to appear at his office. Outraged, he had asked him how anyone could have dared to remove his closest associate without asking for his prior consent.[18] To imagine that Blomberg stood behind this intrigue was obviously absurd since Blomberg had already been cashiered and stricken from the Army list. Keitel, who was hanged at Nuremberg, was always a convenient scapegoat.

After the war, to his surprise, Manstein heard from Hitler's Air Force adjutant, Colonel von Below, that none other than his first sponsor, Beck, had requested his removal and his replacement by Halder. Beck felt that Halder was more reliable. In his recollections, Below wrote:

> Many years after the end of the war, I had the occasion to tell *Feldmarschall* von Manstein about a conversation that I had with Hitler at the time of Beck's resignation. Brauchitsch had told Hitler that he had chosen Halder to succeed Beck as chief of the *Generalstab*. I asked him if he felt that Halder would bring a new spirit into the *Generalstab*. Hitler replied: 'In fact, I wanted to appoint Manstein but I was told by Brauchitsch that he was too young.' I then asked him why he did not pursue his idea and he answered that he did not wish to encroach on Brauchitsch's authority. Manstein professed complete surprise and initial disbelief and still felt that Hitler had been instrumental in his dismissal. He only dropped his doubts when I reminded him that Halder had been instrumental in having him dismissed as Rundstedt's Chief-of-Staff in February 1940.[19]

At the time of Manstein's dismissal, Beck had already begun to distance himself from him. The estrangement was one sided. Beck would increasingly speak to close friends with contempt for Manstein, but never to Manstein personally. Manstein was thus not aware of the change in Beck's attitude. Manstein's respect for Beck remained unchanged to the very end. When he heard of Beck's intention to resign, he wrote him an imploring ten page letter, urging him to reconsider his decision: "No successor to the *Herr* General will have the same position, the same respect and the same moral authority as the *Herr* General. No other officer in the Army has the knowledge and the strength of character as the *Herr* General."[20]

A copy of this letter is in the Beck Estate at the German military archives, with some handwritten ironic comments. Beck wrote a short and dry reply:

> Dear Manstein, Thank you for your letter and for your opinions. I take them as you intended them to be and in their main points they are certainly correct. Time has however progressed faster than you think and the conditions advanced by you, if they ever existed, are no longer valid.

18 *Soldatenleben*, p. 318
19 N. von Below, *Als Hitlers Adjutant 1937 – 1945*, Mainz, 1980, p. 114, henceforth: Below
20 BA – MA, RH 08 – 28/4, Beck Estate

From my point of view, I can say, not only today but for some time now, 'Too late.' I would prefer to give you further comments verbally, perhaps you will come to Berlin the near future.[21]

Manstein was then appointed Commander of 18th Infantry Division at Liegnitz. Beck asked him to remain a few more weeks at the *Generalstab*. Halder was to be given some time to familiarise himself with his new assignment and, more important, the Austrian Anschluss was impending. Hitler had given the order to march into Austria at 24 hours notice and Beck had not prepared a detailed plan for this contingency. Manstein was to produce another masterpiece of staff work. The *Wehrmacht* had no armies in peace time, yet an Army was required for the operation. In one day, Manstein succeeded in amalgamating two Corps into an Army, with a complete Army staff. Every military expert knows the enormous amount of detailed work required to create an Army and to bring it into 'mobile' shape. Probably Manstein was the only officer on the *Generalstab* who was capable of accomplishing such a feat.

Manstein's handing over of his duties to Halder was hardly a display of good manners. As Halder recalls, Manstein simply handed him the keys to his safe with the words: "There! You can read what is in there. Goodbye!" and walked out.[22]

Relations between Halder and Manstein had always been tense, and Halder was a very resentful man. But, at their last meeting after the war, in 1957, at the funeral of General von Tippelskirch, Halder hardly showed better manners. Manstein went to meet him and extended his hand, Halder demonstratively refused the handshake. *Generalmajor* Alfred Philippi, who was present, told Halder: "*Herr Generaloberst*, this time you have certainly gone too far." Until Halder's dismissal in 1942, Manstein was to feel his heavy hand repeatedly, often in a petty manner.

Against the background of Manstein's later career, his dismissal as *Oberquartiermeister* I can be looked on as his destiny's good fortune. Manstein would not have fared better at Hitler's hand than Halder or Zeitzler, who succeeded Halder after the latter was dismissed. Like them he would have been dismissed after months of fruitless discussions and the coveted *Feldmarschall's* baton would have eluded him.

Manstein was promoted to *Generalleutnant* on 1 April 1938. During the Sudeten crisis, he became Chief-of-Staff of a newly formed Army under *Generaloberst* Ritter von Leeb who had been recalled from retirement. Thereafter he returned to his division at Liegnitz until the beginning of the war. In 1938 his division was by no means combat-ready, some of its units had been diverted to another corps during the march into Austria. Manstein had thus to overcome a number of problems. However, when the war broke out, his division was in excellent shape.

---

21   Ibid. The copy of the letter has the handwritten comment: Letter not sent, contents communicated verbally to *Generalleutnant* von Manstein when he visited me on August 9.

22   Knopp, p. 211

Manstein's Commands in World War II

Three important battles will be treated in detailed separate chapters and only summarised here. The battle for France, where Manstein's plan was the architect of the German *Blitzkrieg* victory, Stalingrad, and thereafter the planning of operation 'Citadel,' the most disastrous offensive launched by the *Wehrmacht* in the East. Excesses against the civilian population in Poland will be described in detail in an *excursus* in the chapter on the Holocaust.

Poland

Manstein was Chief-of-Staff of Army Group South, commanded by *Generaloberst* von Rundstedt. Even in such a short campaign, Manstein received reports about excesses committed by police, *SS*-units and some *Wehrmacht* units against the civilian population and, in particular, against Jews. At that time some German generals, including Manstein, protested. However, Manstein's knowledge of the occurrence, and his protests, show that he perjured himself at Nuremberg, when he stated under oath that he had never heard of the murder of Jews, either in Poland or later in Russia. Since Rundstedt remained in Poland until 24 October 1939, as Military Commander Poland, Manstein likewise had knowledge of the sharp memoranda sent by Generals Blaskowitz and Ulex.

France

On 14 October 1939, Rundstedt's Army Group was renamed Army Group A and sent to the West, with headquarters at Koblenz. Originally Rundstedt's Army Group, which was located between B in the North and C in the South, was relatively weak. It consisted of two armies, 12th Army, again under *Generaloberst* List and 16th Army under General Busch. The original operational plan called for Bock's Army Group to deliver the main thrust. In the West, Manstein came into close contact with Henning von Tresckow, who was the Army Group's Ia and who had been one of Manstein's pupils at the *Generalstab*. Tresckow was initially one of Manstein's admirers, but later gradually distanced himself. During the war, Tresckow was to become the 'soul' of the military 'resistance' movement. He was a close friend and regimental comrade of General Schmundt. As Hitler's personal *Wehrmacht* adc and head of the Army's personnel department, Schmundt wielded considerable influence.

Manstein considered the first German plan – first version of plan 'yellow' – as insufficient, and developed his own plan *Sichelschnitt* in a series of memoranda. After strong resistance by the High Command, Manstein's plan was finally adopted. It established his fame as the main architect of the victory over France.

Manstein's memoranda, which Rundstedt transmitted to *OKH*, led to increasing irritation there, particularly with Halder, who succeeded in having Manstein removed from his position with Rundstedt and entrusting him with the command of XXXVIII Corps only. Manstein was replaced by General von Sodenstern as Chief-of-Staff at Army Group A. His replacement could have been Halder's first payback for the incident in 1938, obviously there were also other reasons. *OKH* became increasingly insecure and began to fear Manstein's superior brain. Therefore he had to be sent away, regardless of where. Halder added a few 'drops of poison' because the corps did not yet exist and had to be formed and mobilized at Stettin. *Generalmajor* von Mellenthin, at that time a Major and Ia in 197th Infantry Division, which was part of Manstein's new corps, recalls a chance encounter with Manstein:

> A tragi-comic incident deserves to be mentioned. During my journey by train to the East, I happened to encounter *Generalleutnant* von Manstein, chief-of-staff of Army Group A in the West, at a Berlin railway station. In his usual straightforward manner, he asked me: 'Mellenthin, what on earth are you doing in the Warthegau, when matters will start in the West within the next coming weeks?' ... To my surprise, the Corps Commander, who inspected our division a few weeks later, turned out to be General von Manstein. After the inspection, which proceeded in an excellent manner, I could not resist the temptation of saying to him: '*Herr General*, things often turn out to be different than expected.'[23]

Manstein was understandably irritated at his removal. However his appointment to Corps Commander was a promotion in accordance with German military practice. Other Generals of the same rank, Hansen, Vietinghoff, Stumme, Rudolf Schmidt, Reinhardt, Brockdorf-Ahlefeld, were likewise given corps at the same date. Manstein was also irritated that he was not entrusted with an armoured corps. However, at that time he had as yet no experience of command of armoured units, whereas other new commanders, among them Wietersheim, Hoth, Hoepner, Guderian and Rudolf Schmidt had already distinguished themselves in this field. Manstein had the reputation of a superior mind in staff work, but who lacked experience in troop command.

In 1941 however, Manstein would show that he was at least the equal of the best commanders of armoured units. Rundstedt had already informed him of his impending replacement, since General Reinhardt, junior to Manstein, would be given a corps and therefore Manstein's promotion could not be delayed. In *Verlorene Siege*, Manstein wrote that the problem could have been solved in 'a different manner', without doubt there were corps, which were already combat ready and which could have been entrusted to him.

During a war game at 12th Army (*Generaloberst* List) on 14 February 1940, which was attended by Halder, differences arose over the crossing of the Meuse River. Guderian wrote that "matters became even more muddled, when it turned out that *Generaloberst* von Rundstedt had no clear idea of the capacity of tanks and advocated a careful solution. Now Manstein was missed."[24] Conceivably Manstein was missed during the attack, since Rundstedt showed himself incapable of understanding and promoting Manstein's ideas. This would show itself at Dunkirk.

Until the mobilization of his corps was completed, Manstein was reduced to boredom. He assembled a staff, waited for the arrival of an intelligence unit, and

---

23   F.von Mellenthin, *Schach dem Schicksal*, Osnabrück 1989, p. 79 f. The excerpt is also quoted in K.-H. Frieser, *Blitzkriegs-Legende, Der Frankreichfeldzug 1940*, Munich 1994, p. 80 (henceforth: Frieser)

24   H. Guderian, *Erinnerungen eines Soldaten*, Stuttgart 1998 (new edition), p. 81 (henceforth Guderian)

inspected his units in Pomerania, and in the Warthegau, the western province of Poland with Lodz as its main city, which had been incorporated into Germany.

On 10 May 1940, when the German attack began, Manstein wrote in his diary: "It has started, and I am sitting at home." In *Verlorene Siege*: "One can certainly understand that I harboured no tender feelings for the body which had removed me far back home, and away from the execution of an operational plan for which I had fought with unbending energy."[25]

Manstein's Corps was ready for combat on 10 May 1940, but he had to wait until 27 May for it to go into action. He spent the first two weeks of the battle in Düsseldorf, in his own words like a *Schlachtenbummler*, a fan watching a sports game. He was confined to touring the localities that the Germans had taken by storm, and obtaining daily information from *OKH* about the *Wehrmacht* progress. On 16 May, his Corps became part of List's 12th Army. His, in his own words, 'boring' assignment was to supervise the dispatch of reserve divisions to the newly activated 2nd Army under General von Weichs. Finally, on 27 May, he was ordered to relieve General von Wietersheim's XIV Corps. He now came under the orders of the future *Feldmarschall* von Kleist whom he heartily disliked and who reciprocated his feelings. Both *Feldmarschalls* would finally be dismissed on the same day. Hitler had sent a plane to pick both of them up at their headquarters. Their Army Groups were neighbours.

Stahlberg, who had accompanied Manstein, recalls that the two *Feldmarschalls* had seated themselves on opposite sides of the plane and did not exchange a word during the long flight to Hitler's residence. Manstein brooded silently on his fate that was no surprise to him, since Zeitzler had told him, a few days before, that he would be informed face to face by Hitler of his dismissal. Kleist was unperturbed and spent most of his time explaining to Stahlberg the best way to prepare a cigar before lighting it.[26]

Manstein's Corps came into action on the Somme, on 27 May 1940. In *Verlorene Siege*, he wrote: "My part in the actual battle was so insignificant that it is hardly worthwhile a mention."[27] This unusual modesty not withstanding, his corps operated successfully throughout, and on 6 June he was rewarded with promotion to *General der Infanterie*. His 'nemesis,' Halder, would see to it that he had to wait for two more years before being promoted to *Generaloberst*. Other corps commanders, who were far inferior to him, became *Generaloberst* on the day of their promotion to army command.

The plans for *Seelöwe* – the intended landing on the British Isles after the defeat of France

Rundstedt's Army Group A, with two armies, 16th Army under Busch, and 9th Army under Strauss, was to be the spearhead of the planned landing. Manstein had received command of XXXVI Corps which was part of Strauss' Army.

---

25   *Verlorene Siege*, p. 126
26   Stahlberg, p. 339
27   Ibid., p. 125

Since the quixotic *Seelöwe* idea never went beyond the planning stage, there is no need to dwell in detail on Manstein's views. They must be mentioned briefly because they show how little Manstein understood the world of politics. Manstein expressed initial optimism, since the British Expeditionary Force had been decimated in France. The units that had been repatriated at Dunkirk could certainly not fight a successful battle against a German Army that had successfully landed. However, Manstein's optimism was guarded. In *Verlorene Siege* he qualified it repeatedly. Manstein admitted that he had not paid sufficient attention to the problems of the Navy and the Air Force. He then indulged in political speculations that were far removed from reality. He conceded that Churchill would not have surrendered in the event of a German invasion, but that he would have continued the war from Canada. However, Manstein expressed doubts that the Dominions would have followed suit, and whether America would have been prepared to take the major burden of the war upon itself. Stalin might, after securing Hitler's agreement, have turned his forces towards the Far East.[28]

The war against the Soviet Union

As Corps Commander, Manstein was not asked to participate in the planning of the war against Russia. However, he was present at Hitler's address of 30 March 1941 to all the Generals who had been intended for Commands on the Eastern Front. He was thus made aware of the methods under which this campaign was to be conducted. The words 'Jewish *Bolshevist* subhuman' were introduced into the vocabulary.

Manstein's ambition to command an armoured corps was finally fulfilled. He was given command of LVI Motorized Corps. In 1942, the 'motorized corps' was renamed '*Panzer* corps.' Army Group North, commanded by *Feldmarschall* Ritter von Leeb consisted of two armies, 18th Army under Küchler and 16th Army under Busch. Hoepner's *Panzergruppe* 4 included two Corps under Manstein and Reinhardt. Some weeks later, Manstein's Corps was transferred to Busch's 16th Army. Manstein immediately showed himself the equal of Germany's best *Panzer* Commanders.

During his operations he developed his mastery in conducting mobile operations of large units. He would be unsurpassed in this by any German commander during the war. His Corps was given the most far-reaching assignment within Army Group North, that of capturing Dünaburg and pushing all opposing forces into a narrow stretch along the Baltic coast. Once again, Halder loomed in the shadow. Manstein did not receive the best, armoured units that he required. They were given to Reinhardt's corps that had been assigned a more limited advance. Manstein had complained to Heusinger who had become head of operations at *OKH*. Heusinger transmitted his request to Halder who replied: "The commander in chief of the Army Group, Ritter von Leeb, has decided and *OKH* will not intervene."[29]

Manstein had thus to make do with the units left to him, but still he conducted his operation in true *Blitzkrieg* fashion. As always in his commands, he had a very capable staff. His chief-of-staff was Major von Elverfeldt, to whom he

---

28 *Verlorene Siege*, p.152-171
29 Heusinger, awkward, p. 42

paid the highest compliments. As chief-of-staff of 9th Army, von Elverfeldt would later have to suffer General Model's outbursts of temper, something that never occurred in Manstein's staff. In his relation with his staff officers, Manstein was always what the Germans called *Ein Herr*. On the first day, Manstein's Corps advanced 60 kilometres. The capture of Dünaburg was planned after an offensive of two weeks. Manstein took the city after four days. At times his Corps was isolated up to 60 kilometres from the *Panzer* group and he was personally at risk of being captured.

As Corps Commander, Manstein commanded in the front line. In *Verlorene Siege* he extolled the virtues of this method:

> The Second World War required new Command Methods, especially with the fast units. Their situation is subject to rapid change. The possibilities of taking advantage of a successful situation are so brief that the commander is unable to judge them from a remote headquarters ... More importantly, the soldier must never have the feeling that orders are given in the rear without knowledge of how things really are in front. He also gets satisfaction when he sees that his commander can get involved in a 'real mess' and that he can also partake in the soldiers' joy at success. Only through daily presence in the front line can the commander know about the many worries of his troops and provide remedies. The commander cannot limit himself to issuing orders. He must be a comrade to his soldiers. His presence at the front line is his main source of renewed inspiration.[30]

Many German corps and division commanders led in this manner. It was one of the main reasons of their superiority over their opponents. Some Army and Army Group commanders led in a similar way. However, when Manstein became commander of an Army and later of an Army Group, he commanded 'from behind' at his headquarters. He understood correctly that command of the largest units required an overall knowledge of the situation and that it required a highly competent staff to be always available to him. The commander of the largest units, who lead from the front line, had only a limited view of the position where they happened to be at any given moment.

Every medal has an obverse. The ease with which Manstein obtained his first successes in the East, would lead him to view the Russian leadership with contempt. He did not realise that the Russians had recovered from their first setbacks and that they now had brilliant high commanders. Manstein's ill-informed views of the Russian leadership will be referred to in a number of specific instances, his general opinion can already be summarised here:

> Deficient ability at the highest levels of command, lack of responsibility resulting from a totalitarian system, [a somewhat strange statement, given the nature of the Third Reich], inadequate staff performance at units, lack of independence of the junior officers and the soldiers, all contributed to the defeat of the Russians in the first months. Undoubtedly the Red Army Generals learned something as the war progressed. But their successes

---

30 *Verlorene Siege*, p. 189

were only due to the mistakes of the German supreme leadership and to their own increasing superiority in men and equipment. When the ratio grows to 5:1, even 7:1, art is no longer required. Blood and iron was available to the Russians in sufficient quantity to enable them to dispense with leadership art. Had the Soviet command possessed the ability to lead, we would not have been able to survive 1943.[31]

Manstein's advance was halted when Busch's 16th Army was in danger of being encircled and Manstein had to go to his rescue. Once again, Busch had shown himself incapable of commanding a large size unit. While commanding his Corps, Manstein was for the first time confronted with the Commissar Order.

Commander in Chief of 11th Army

On 12 September 1941, *Generaloberst* von Schobert, commander in chief of 11th Army was killed in an air crash and Manstein was appointed his successor. General Heusinger commented in a letter to his wife, "He has an Army and appears finally to be satisfied."[32] Manstein had to wait until March 1942 for his promotion to *Generaloberst*, as probably Halder once again put on the brakes. *Wehrmacht* rules, which were still valid in 1941, called for a commander to hold the rank provided for the unit that was under his orders. When he gained command of a larger formation, he was promoted to a higher rank, either immediately or after a short period, during which he had to show his aptitude. The normal rank for an Army commander was *Generaloberst*. There were only few exceptions, such as *General der Infanterie* Carl-Heinrich von Stülpnagel, who was made Commander in Chief of 17th Army at the beginning of the war against Russia, and never promoted thereafter. Another exception was Manstein. Given his previous performances, his promotion should have occurred immediately.

Without doubt, Manstein was due for an army command, however 11th Army was 'a Trojan horse'. Until the beginning of the war against Russia, Halder was the epitome of caution. But after the first *Kessel* ie encirclement victories, he became the victim of an increasing *hubris*. On day twelve of the Russian campaign, he wrote in his diary that the war had already been won and that only mopping up remained. For a number of weeks he kept to that opinion, although the Russian defence at Smolensk, which halted the *Wehrmacht* advance in that sector for nearly a month in July, should have been an eye-opener. In other armies, a Chief of the General Staff who had been faulty to such an extent in his judgement would have been immediately relieved. Hitler, in spite of his threats, would continue to show a surprising leniency with generals, and retained Halder at the head of the *Generalstab* until 29 September 1942.

As the Russian campaign, *Barbarossa*, did not develop in the manner foreseen by *OKH*, Brauchitsch and Halder became increasingly insecure. Once again they could feel Manstein breathing down their necks. Therefore, as before in the West,

---

31 *Soldatenleben*, p.158

32 G.Meyer, *Adolf Heusinger, Dienst eines deutschen Soldaen 1915–1964*, Hamburg 2001, p. 107 (henceforth Meyer, Heusinger

the 'uncomfortable operating head' had to be quickly sent far away. General Heusinger wrote:

> What was Manstein's assignment? The conquest of the Crimea, a theatre of limited size which did not allow for large scale operations. The main purpose was to take Sevastopol, a fortress. Was Manstein now looked upon as a fortress expert? I have never been able to ascertain why he received that command. It was simply said that it was his turn to receive an Army.[33]

11th Army contained a sinister element which, at that time, could not be foreseen. Manstein got stuck in the Crimea for nine months. Meanwhile, Ohlendorf's *Einsatzgruppe* D engaged in the mass murder of the Crimean Jews, along with the active participation of units from Manstein's Army. Manstein became one of the major Holocaust perpetrators among the German generals.

Manstein had likewise become victim of a sudden *hubris*. His *Blitzkrieg* successes in the North apparently made him believe that it would be likewise in the Crimea and he let it be known that he would take Sevastopol before Christmas. No general has universal knowledge, every commander has weaknesses. Manstein was the foremost specialist in mobile warfare. The battle for the Crimea would turn into a prolonged position campaign in a small theatre, with hand-to-hand fighting reminiscent of World War I, accompanied by exceptionally heavy losses. Survivors of the battle, who appear on Knopp's video, still find it difficult to talk about their experiences without deep emotion. The campaign in the Crimea ended with the capture of Sevastopol and brought Manstein the *Feldmarschall* baton. However, it must be viewed as his weakest performance in the whole war.

At first all seemed to go in the direction of Manstein's view. By November, every major city of the Crimea was in German hands, only Sevastopol remained to be taken. Manstein's prophecy to take the fortress before Christmas appeared close to fulfilment. But in December 1941, the tide of the war in the East had turned on the entire Front. *Blitzkrieg* operations belonged to the past. In the Crimea, sizeable Red Army forces had landed at Kerch, Feodosia, and Eupatoria. Basically Manstein was back to square one. When confronted with that unexpected situation, he would, for the first time, display the ruthlessness, shown to a subordinate commander, whose actions could cast a shadow on his own unblemished reputation. Such was his brutal relief of General Count von Sponeck, which would have a tragic conclusion for a most distinguished officer.[34]

General von Sponeck had been Manstein's subordinate as Ia of the Berlin *Wehrkreis* during the period when Manstein was its chief-of-staff. He was a highly decorated officer who had shown himself an opponent of National-Socialism since before the war. During the trial of *Generaloberst* von Fritsch he volunteered to appear as a character witness for his Commander in Chief. His address to the court was interrupted by Göring, who ordered him to "stop making irresponsible political statements."

At the beginning of the war, Sponeck commanded the 22nd Infantry Division. When the war against Russia began, he was on sick leave. He returned to

---

33 Heusinger, Kopf, page 39
34 Details in E.Einbeck, *Das Exempel Sponeck*, Bremen 1970

active service in December 1941 and received command of XLII Corps, stationed on the Crimean Kerch peninsula. After Kerch was taken, he was ordered to prepare operation 'Wintersport,' a landing at Taman. He had had to give up two of his divisions. One was needed when the Russians broke through on the Mius River in the Ukraine, the other was required by Manstein to strengthen the attack on Sevastopol. He thus remained with only one complete division, the 46th Infantry Division, commanded by *Generalleutnant* Himer. The Division had no artillery or *Panzer* units and was thus limited in its actions. Communications with 11th Army headquarters were technically deficient.

On 26 December 1941, massive Red Army contingents landed at Kerch. Sponeck had repeatedly requested reinforcements from 11th Army, which were denied. He felt that his corps was not in a position to hold the peninsula and requested Manstein's permission to evacuate it. Manstein forbade the retreat. On 29 December 1941, a new Russian landing occurred at Feodosia. Sponeck considered his situation to be hopeless and decided to abandon the Kerch peninsula on his own responsibility. Manstein issued a contrary order at 10.09 am which, because of faulty communications, did not reach Himer's division before 1 pm. The evacuation had already begun and Himer was unable to halt it.

There is no doubt that Sponeck acted in accordance with his conscience and his appreciation of the situation of his corps. Manstein was furious. He immediately relieved Sponeck, not on grounds of his independent action, but because he felt that Sponeck was not able to face a critical situation of the kind that had arisen at Kerch.[35] Manstein reported his decision to the Commander in Chief of Army Group South, *Feldmarschall* von Reichenau. Manstein knew Reichenau's ruthlessness well enough to be aware that this reporting would put Sponeck's head on the block. As could be expected, Reichenau reported immediately to *OKH*. Sponeck requested a court-martial in order to vindicate himself. Hitler pre-empted the request, and himself ordered Sponeck's immediate court-martial.

A few weeks earlier, when the Russians launched their massive counter offensive at Moscow, Hitler had issued a 'stay put' order which forbade any voluntary retreat. The 'stay put' order remains a subject of contest to this day. However, Hitler viewed himself as the saviour of the Eastern front with the 'stay put' order. Sponeck was the first victim of a disobedience to the order. He was to be followed by Guderian and Hoepner. When Hitler heard that Hoepner had given an order for a local retreat, he became enraged and yelled at Halder:

> Has the man gone crazy? This is total madness. First General Sponeck evacuates the Kerch peninsula because a few Russians have landed in his rear, and now Hoepner does the same in front of Moscow. I am the one who commands and everyone has to obey me without condition. Where would we be if every general starts to ask himself whether an order was justified or not? This is simply cowardice before the enemy. I am the only

---

person responsible. I alone and no one else. I will ruthlessly eradicate any other opinion.[36]

A commission of inquiry against Sponeck was formed under the presidency of *Generaloberst* Haase, who accepted his appointment on the condition that an eventual death sentence would be commuted to fortress detention. Hitler communicated his agreement through Göring, who would preside over the court-martial. The two assistant judges were General Eugen Müller, and General von Seydlitz-Kurzbach who had vainly tried to be excused. Sponeck had previously been his commander. At his trial Sponeck stated that he would not hesitate to act in the same manner again if faced with a similar situation. A few days later, Hitler met with the Romanian dictator, Marshal Antonescu and vented his fury at Sponeck. Antonescu replied that he would have acted just as Sponeck. On that same day, at his regular evening meeting, Hitler said that Antonescu understood no more about warfare than Franco.

Sponeck was sentenced to death and Hitler immediately commuted his sentence to six years' fortress detention. Sponeck was cashiered from the Army but continued to receive full pay. Hitler was always generous in financial matters. Manstein repeatedly attempted to have the sentence quashed, but was told that 'Sponeck's bad political behaviour' during his imprisonment would not permit his release, let alone his reinstatement. On 22 July 1944 Himmler gave a personal order to have Sponeck shot. His widow was sent to a concentration camp and her property was confiscated, leaving her with 40 marks.

Manstein was certainly acting within his authority in relieving Sponeck, but the manner in which he reported it to a higher level is questionable. Manstein had repeatedly turned down Sponeck's requests for reinforcements and thus had his share of responsibility. Compared with other commanders-in-chief, Manstein does not appear in a favourable light. *Feldmarschall* Model probably held the record for the number of corps commanders relieved. He always moved them towards higher *echelons* and none suffered any future damage. Even Manstein's admirer Brett-Smith would write that the relief of a distinguished officer may have been justified on the grounds of discipline, but that it was unnecessarily harsh.[37] Reichenau did not content himself with reporting Sponeck to the highest level. He issued an order stating that 46th Division had forfeited its honour and forbade any decoration awards to its troops. Reichenau died of a stroke in January 1942. His successor, *Feldmarschall* von Bock, rescinded his order.

In the light of Manstein's later failure at Stalingrad, his conclusions about the conduct of Sponeck must be viewed with scepticism:

> The case of General Sponeck shows the tragedy of a commander, who is torn between his duty to obey orders, and his own understanding about required operative steps. He knows that he risks his head if he disobeys,

---

36   A. Heusinger, *Befehl im Widerstreit, Schicksalsstunden der deutschen Armee 1923–1945*, Tübingen 1950, p. 162 f (henceforth Heusinger Befehl)
37   Brett-Smith, p. 224

but he can still find himself compelled to act contrary to orders. Only a soldier can be confronted with such a conflict.[38]

A year later at Stalingrad, Manstein would face a similar conflict, but he was not prepared to risk his head. Sponeck had given up a piece of territory to save a division from annihilation. Manstein recoiled from his responsibilities and blamed his subordinates.

The fighting in the Crimea continued until 1 July 1942. The capture of Sevastopol was very difficult. Two giant artillery guns, 'Dora', which had been built for the destruction of the strongest forts of the Maginot line, had to be brought from France.

After the fall of Sevastopol Manstein was promoted to *Feldmarschall*. His promotion to Generloberst had taken place on 7 March 1942.

Section II: The Descent

The absurd commands. The Leningrad *intermezzo* and the guest performance at Army Group Centre

After the fall of Sevastopol, 11th Army had to be refreshed with replacement units. Manstein took a leave of a few weeks in Romania. On his return, he was surprised to learn that his Army was to be sent to Army Group North, in a new attempt to take Leningrad. General Heusinger commented:

> After Manstein had taken the Crimea with a few elegant moves, he was now asked to put his experience to use, in order to take Leningrad. For the second time he was ordered to take a fortress, a task which required more technical knowledge than operative talent.[39]

Manstein looked upon his new assignment as an absurdity. As a Corps Commander he had been part of Army Group North which had been ordered to take Leningrad. He knew that if an Army Group, consisting of 2 Armies and a *Panzer* Group, was unable to take the city, parts only of 11th Army would not be able to take 'the remaining ten kilometres'. In fact only two Corps and four additional Divisions had been sent north. In 1941, Hitler had boasted in a speech that "he, who had marched all the way up to Leningrad, would have no difficulty in overcoming the remaining 10 kilometres." Manstein was also aware that the *Wehrmacht* was no longer capable of simultaneous actions on the whole Eastern front. He knew that 1942 would find the South the centre of gravity of major actions. Offensive 'Blue' had already been launched.

On his way to the northern 'theatre', Manstein stopped at Vinniza where Hitler had established a temporary headquarters, and spoke with Halder. In *Verlorene Siege* he wrote that Halder stated clearly "that he was opposed to Hitler's idea to launch a new attack on Leningrad simultaneously with 'Blue'. However, Hitler had stuck to his decision and would not depart from it. When I asked

---

38   Ibid.
39   Heusinger, Kopf, p. 39

Halder if he really felt that my Army could be spared from the South, he replied in the affirmative. I remained sceptical, but at that stage I felt unable to contradict."[40] A few weeks later Halder was dismissed.

Still Manstein had to develop an operational plan, *Nordlicht*. He did this only half-heartedly. "We were obviously aware that success would at best be problematic. That the whole operation could turn out to be superfluous did not make it more attractive."[41] However Manstein carefully omits mentioning the central sentence of his order: "The main purpose of the operation is to strengthen the encirclement, in order to totally cut off the minimal supplies reaching the city over Lake Ladoga." [42]This was no novelty, it was a continuation of the famine policy which *Heeresgruppe Nord* had initiated and which Manstein had practiced in the Crimea. More than a million civilians died during the siege of Leningrad, mostly of famine, twice the number of the Germans who were killed during the air raids on German cities.

No important operations took place in the North, and they are reported in only a cursory manner in the literature of the Second World War. Along the shores of Lake Ladoga, the units of 11th Army encountered the Red Army's Novgorod 'front' under General Vatutin, and suffered a setback. Manstein does not mention this in his memoirs and writes only about the annihilation of the Russian Army. Conceivably both events occurred.

At Vinniza, Manstein was horrified when he heard of the decision to create twenty-two *Luftwaffenfeld* divisions, ie air force field divisions. The divisions were inefficient and were the subject of jokes in the *Wehrmacht*, with expressions such as *Luftwaffenfluchtdivisionen*, ie air force 'run-a-way' divisions. They were created by a direct order of the vain Göring, who, until he fell from grace, was always eager to emphasise his position as 'the second man' in the state. The soldiers had been superbly trained in the air force, but had insufficient time to adjust themselves to infantry warfare and suffered losses out of all proportion.

After the end of its operations in the North, 11th Army was transferred to Army Group Centre. Hitler had told Manstein at Vinniza that he expected a major Russian offensive in the central area. At Vinniza, Manstein again became a *Schlachtenbummler*. There was no offensive in the centre. Hitler had become the victim of a clever deceit by the Russians. They created the appearance of a strong offensive against Army Group Centre, in order to conceal their preparations for their successful counter-offensive at Stalingrad. The Russian attack began on 19 November 1942. A few days later, 6th Army was encircled. A new Army Group Don was hastily formed on 20 November, with the task of bringing relief to 6th Army, and Manstein was given its command.

Stalingrad

The battle of Stalingrad was the biggest defeat ever suffered by the German Army. One has to look back at the annihilation of the Prussian armies by Napoleon at

---

40   *Verlorene Siege,* p. 291 f
41   Ibid.
42   J. Ganzenmüller, "Das belagerte Leningrad 1941–1944. Die Stadt in den Strategien von Angreifern und Verteidigern", Paderborn 2005, p. 81

Jena and Auerstädt to find a similar occurrence. Never before had a whole German Army, in this case the largest Army on the Eastern Front, been encircled and annihilated. Both German commanders in chief involved, Manstein as head of Army Group Don, and Paulus as commander of 6th Army, showed themselves not up to the demands of their duties. Certainly Manstein, whose Army Group included 6th Army, bore a heavier responsibility than Paulus, who simply was not up to the requirements of an Army command. At first, Manstein viewed the situation with some optimism, but reality soon set in. The almost daily conversations between Manstein and Hitler, Zeitzler and Schmundt, are recorded in the war diary of Army Group Don. They show that Manstein had a clear grasp of the crisis and did his utmost in his talks with Hitler and *OKH* to convince them of the necessity to extricate 6th Army from its predicament. But he could not bring himself to issue orders on his own authority, although in his memoirs he pretends to have done so.

One may well ask what kind of risk he ran, if he had issued a clear order to break out in a *Donnerschlag*, and thus acted against Hitler's order to have 6th Army remain the *Kessel*. It would not have cost Manstein his head. Hitler never had generals executed for disobedience. But suppose Manstein had been sentenced to death. A *Feldmarschall* puts the lives of hundreds of thousands of his soldiers at daily risk, therefore he has to be prepared to put his own head on the block, as his conscience dictates. Without doubt Manstein would have been dismissed, probably also cashiered, and his dream of being the final saviour of the Fatherland as chief of a new *Generalstab* or Supreme Commander would have come to an end.

Manstein was not the only *Feldmarschall* to put more value on his own life than on the fate of his soldiers. In 1946, at the British POW camp at Bridgehead, *Feldmarschall* von Rundstedt was questioned by a Professor Gerhard Leibholz. He was an expert in constitutional law who had emigrated to Britain 1939. Leibholz asked him about the Ardennes offensive, the 'Battle of the Bulge'. He wondered if Rundstedt had not been aware that it was doomed to failure. Rundstedt replied that he had looked on the planning of this battle as nonsensical. Leibholz than asked him why he did not rescue himself from that command. He received the reply: "Had I opposed, I may have been shot."[43] In *Verlorene Siege,* Manstein's description of his former commander, Rundstedt, came close to panegyrics, a eulogy. In a conversation with Stahlberg, during his journey to his new Army Group command, he was more realistic. Questioned about his opinion of Rundstedt he replied drily, "He is the most senior on the list."[44]

Manstein's counteroffensive after Stalingrad and *SS-Obergruppenführer* Hausser's open disobedience to Hitler

After the defeat at Stalingrad, Manstein launched a brilliant operation which recaptured Charkov and Belgorod, and re-established parts of the 1942 front line in the southern Ukraine. Manstein would again show his unchallenged mastery in the conduct of large-scale mobile operations. Manstein's counter-offensive was unquestionably an operational masterpiece. However, his own comments, and

---

43   quoted in Kosthorst, p.134 f
44   Stahlberg, p. 234

statements by his admirers, would cast a cloud over it. In *Verlorene Siege* Manstein wrote that the winter of 1942 had again ended in 'victory'.[45] To talk about 'victory' after the disasters at Stalingrad and in the Caucasus, and the recapture of territory which would soon be overrun again by the Red Army, sounds somewhat divorced from reality. The word 'success' would have been more appropriate.

In Knopp's video, the *Bundeswehr* four-star General von Kielmansegg labels Manstein's operation as "the greatest stroke of genius during the whole war." However, compared with Manstein's operational plan for the battle of France, the Allied landing in France 1944 'Overlord,' and the great Russian counter-offensive at Stalingrad, *Uranus,* such a superlative may give rise to some doubt. Breithaupt goes one step further in his statement that Manstein's attack had "a world historical importance" since it prevented Stalin from reaching dominance over all of Europe.[46]

However, Manstein's efforts may well have come to naught, if *SS-Obergruppenführer* Hausser had not done what Manstein would never dare do. Hausser commanded the *Waffen-SS Panzer* Corps within Manstein's Army Group. At that time it was the only corps unit of the *Waffen-SS.* It was part of an *Armeegruppe* [47] commanded by General Lanz. Like all *Waffen-SS* units, the corps was provided with the best equipment available. All *Waffen-SS* senior commanders were volunteers and the relation between officers of all ranks were less formal than in the *Wehrmacht.* Hausser's Corps held Charkov, which was besieged by over-whelming Red Army units. Hitler had issued a direct order to Hausser to hold Charkov at all costs. Hausser knew that his corps would be doomed if he obeyed.

On 15 February 1943, at 1 pm, Hausser assembled his staff and told his offi-cers: "Although I have received a formal order from the *Führer* and my commander to hold the city, I have decided to evacuate it under my sole responsibility and without any cover from above."[48] Hausser was faced with the conflict of loyalty that Manstein explained, at length, after his dismissal of General von Sponeck. Manstein would never solve it. Hausser placed his responsibility toward his troops and conscience ahead of military obedience. Hausser received an additional order, to hold the city, from General Lanz. He paid no attention to it and withdrew his corps with all its equipment. The clash between Lanz and Hausser would drive yet another thorn into the legend of the 'totally clean and non-*Nazi Wehrmacht,*' and the 'totally criminal *Waffen-SS.*'

Lanz was in opposition to the regime. On one occasion he had exhorted his Army commander to arrest Hitler when he visited his Army headquarters. Yet he felt bound to follow an order by Hitler which he knew to be insane. After the war, he would be sentenced to fifteen years by the IMT for massacres committed by his troops on the Greek Island Kephalonia. Hausser, a high *Waffen-SS* commander,

---

45   Ibid., p. 475

46   Breithaupt, p. 112

47   The term 'Armeegruppe' may lead to confusion. It was not an Army Group, Heeresgruppe in German terminology, but a temporary ad hoc formation of two armies, placed under the command of one of their commanders in chief.

48   E.Syring, *Paul Hausser Türöffner und Kommandeur seiner Waffen-SS* in *Die SS-Elite unter dem Totenkopf, 30 Lebensläufe,* ed. R.Smelser/E.Syring, Paderborn 2000, p.190

would be looked on as a totally committed *Nazi*, something he never was. He chose to disobey and he was never indicted for war crimes.

Hausser was born in 1880, a scion of a family of Prussian officers over generations. At cadet school, he was a contemporary of the future *Feldmarschalls* von Bock and von Kluge. He became a member of the Imperial *Generalstab* and held troop commands and staff assignments during World War I. He was accepted into the *Reichswehr* and rose to *Generalmajor*. In 1932 he had reached the age limit for a *Generalmajor* and was retired with the rank of *Generalleutnant*. When the *Waffen-SS* was established, Himmler was eager to recruit Army officers in retirement and Hausser was an obvious candidate. He never hid that he would have preferred to return to the *Wehrmacht* but he saw no prospect for further advancement there.

Hausser became one of the 'rebellious' *Waffen-SS* commanders. He frequently made fun of Himmler, who would label him as the "typical *Generalstab* officer in black uniform." He never issued 'orders of the day' in which he eulogised Hitler's military genius, and never engaged in open *Nazi* propaganda. In 1945, he was one of the few commanders who would openly refuse to obey Hitler's *Nero* order for the total destruction of the German infrastructure. In 1944 he became commander of 7th Army, after *Generaloberst* Dollmann committed suicide. *Generalmajor* von Gersdorff became his chief-of-staff. A few weeks before 20 July 1944, Gersdorff felt confident enough to inform Hausser of his opposition to Hitler. Hausser did not report this conversation to higher levels and replied, "I can fully understand your motives, but please accept that I still feel bound by my oath of loyalty."[49]

Without the help of Hausser's intact corps, Manstein would have been unable to retake Charkov. Since Hausser's corps played the decisive part in Manstein's operation, its mention could not be omitted in *Verlorene Siege*. Manstein did not mention Hausser by name and limited himself to the somewhat contemptuous comment that 'a *Waffen-SS* commander could of course get away with anything', while a *Wehrmacht* General would have been court-martialed.[50]

The conclusion was typical for the Third *Reich*. Lanz, who had insisted on obedience to an order by Hitler, was dismissed and never promoted. Hausser, who had chosen to disobey, heard a few grumbling words from Hitler's distant headquarters about the undisciplined and independent *SS*-generals and had to wait for five months for the award of the Oak Leaves to his Iron Cross. He was later promoted to *SS-Oberstgruppenführer*, a rank corresponding to *Generaloberst*.

When Hausser read *Verlorene Siege*, he told one of his comrades that he longed to meet Manstein person, to ask him how he would have fared at Charkov without the assistance of his corps.

Operation 'Citadel'

The battles for Kursk and the 'Citadel' phase have their own chapter in this book. Kursk was the turning point of the war in the East. After that defeat, the Germans could launch no further initiatives. Manstein's Army Group, renamed 'South' after Stalingrad, was one of the two Army Groups engaged in the failed offensive.

---

49   R. von Gersdorff, *Soldat im Untergang*, Berlin 1977, p. 153
50   *Verlorene Siege*, p. 453

Manstein's dismissal

After the failure of 'Citadel,' Manstein's Army Group conducted a series of defence operations. He would still be able to show his operational skill and obtain temporary local successes. Manstein's relations with Hitler deteriorated rapidly. On 30 March 1944, he was relieved of his Command, never to be employed again. The dismissal occurred under unusually polite circumstances. While Hitler resented Manstein, the *Feldmarschall's* impressive bearing reminded him of the Generals he had once admired, and he could not fault his performance. Hitler began the meeting by handing Manstein the Swords to his Knight's Cross. He then told him that he was very satisfied with his performance, but that Manstein obviously needed a rest and to take care of his eyes. Later, he said he would certainly employ him again, and hinted vaguely that he might make him Supreme Commander West. Manstein, who should have known what to make of Hitler's words, was naive enough to believe him.

Hitler then annoyed Manstein by saying that the time for 'operating' was past, and now he needed a 'stayer' like Model, who would rush from one point of danger to the next and re-establish a situation. Manstein replied testily that his Army Group had completed what could be done and that Model could be sufficient for what remained. Manstein took leave of Hitler with the words: "I hope that you will never have to regret the decision you took today."

After his dismissal, Manstein became a spectator until the end of the war. He did not take part in the 'resistance' movement, although he was courted. Until the very end, he remained convinced that Hitler would recall him if the situation became desperate and would entrust him with supreme command. Manstein had moved from Liegnitz to Berlin. A statement by Knopp, that Manstein had visited *OKH* headquarters at Zossen during the last months of the war, and asked for command of a battalion, can be dismissed as 'journalistic fantasy.'[51]

On 29 January 1945, he suddenly decided to call on Hitler at the chancellery of the *Reich*, where Hitler had transferred his headquarters. He had ordered Stahlberg to accompany him but did not mention what he intended to say to Hitler. Hitler refused to receive him. One can have some understanding that Hitler was in no mood at that time to be subjected once more to a lecture by Manstein. He knew quite well what Manstein would say to him. However, Hitler's refusal to permit Manstein to meet one of his adc was an unnecessary snub.

During the last days of the war, Manstein left Berlin and found refuge at Weissenhaus, near Hamburg. After the partial German surrender to Montgomery's Army Group, Manstein asked Stahlberg to go to Montgomery's headquarters, tell him where he was and ask him what Montgomery expected him to do. He received the reply that he should stay at his home and await developments. The British troops were informed and no personal harm would accrue to him. A few days later the British placed him under arrest.

---

51 Knopp, p.221

The Trials

The Trial of the *OKW* and the *Generalstab*

In 1946 Manstein was sent to the prison at Nuremberg in order to participate as expert in the defence at the trial of the *OKW* and the *Generalstab*, both of which had been indicted as 'groups'. If found guilty, all their members would become automatically subject to indictment. A team of five Generals was designated to prepare the defence, *Feldmarschalls* von Brauchitsch and von Manstein, *Generaloberst* Halder, and Generals Warlimont and Westphal. For once, Manstein and Halder would find themselves on the same side. Manstein became the spokesman of this team. His selection was logical. His reputation was still sky high, Brauchitsch had been forgotten since his dismissal in 1941 and he was already critically ill. Manstein would not have accepted Halder as spokesman, and Westphal and Warlimont were junior to him in rank. Moreover Manstein was known to express himself with great clarity.

Manstein wrote to his wife: "There were the three of us, the other two were Brauchitsch and Rundstedt, who were called as witnesses." Given Manstein's reputation, the other generals of the panel agreed to let him present the arguments. "I became the centre of their attacks, since they knew that I had been the main instrument in preparing the defence."

Manstein and the head of the team of German attorneys, Dr Hans Laternser, had at first agreed upon a strategy that was doomed from the start, ie to blame everything on the *SS*. After careful study of the files, Dr Laternser came to the conclusion that it could not succeed. He advised Manstein to insist that the Generals had fought Hitler and Himmler's criminal orders with their utmost energy. Such a statement by Manstein was somewhat strange, since he would affirm at his own trial that he had no knowledge of such crimes. The historian Hans-Heinrich Wilhelm commented on the paper submitted by the panel:

> A *cliché* which has remained for years with the public, and also in part of the historical literature, purports that, apart from the *SS*, no one had participated in the *Nazi* crimes and, above all, not in the genocide of the Jews. All witnesses of the ministry for the East and the civilian administration stated solemnly, in many words, that they knew nothing and that they were powerless. Even *Reichsmarschall* Göring pretended that he had no insight into the organisation and the actions of the *SS!* Even among the members of the *SS* only a few would acknowledge what they had done and what they had known, and put the blame on comrades who had either been killed in action or already sentenced at other proceedings. Only a few, among them *SS-Obergruppenführer* von dem Bach-Zelewski, who appeared as a prosecution witness, broke the taboo at times, in their

disgust on hearing denials of actions which only the day before were considered to be sacred.[52]

Dr Laternser stated:

They [the officers] are here because their fate had it that they had been brought into a situation by the leadership of the state from which even the prosecution is unable to show an escape. My Lord Justices! Never before have military leaders in any country had to face a comparable situation.

The Italian Generals had certainly faced a similar situation. They had also served a dictatorship. However, they found an escape. Despite formal orders by Mussolini, they refused to proceed with the deportation of Jews from territories occupied by them. They protected all Jews, not only Italians, from any discriminating measures such as the wearing of the yellow star.

Contrary to Dr Laternser's arguments, the prosecution did find a way. The *Generalstab* and the *OKW* were acquitted because the war crimes tribunal decided that neither responded to the criteria which had been established for the definition of a 'group.' However, a number of generals and *Generalstab* officers were individually indicted and were hardly impressive in their defences.

The acquittal gave birth to the untenable legend of the 'clean *Wehrmacht*' which remained for years.

After the acquittal, Manstein wrote to his wife on 2 October 1946 that he experienced the utmost satisfaction of having rendered the Army a last service and that the 'unpleasant' accompanying comments by the tribunal could have been expected. However, they contained much more than 'unpleasantness.' Already the prosecution had argued:

We are still searching, in vain, for a German General who chose to resign rather than obey an order that led to criminal war, or which caused murder and ill-treatment of tens of thousands of helpless civilians and prisoners of war.

It would be difficult to find a more scathing condemnation than the concluding 'unpleasant' statements by the presiding judge, Lord Justice Geoffrey Lawrence:

They have been responsible in large measure for the miseries and sufferings that have fallen on millions of men, women and children. They have been a disgrace to the honourable profession of arms. Without their military guidance the aggressive actions of Hitler and his fellow *Nazis* would have been academic and sterile. Many of these men have made a mockery of the soldier's oath of obedience to military orders. When it suits their defence they say that they had to obey. When confronted with Hitler's brutal crimes, which are shown to have been within their general knowl-

---

52 H.Krausnick/H. Wilhelm, *Die Truppe des Weltanschauungkrieges. Die Einsatzgruppen der Sicherheitspolizei und des SD 1938–1942*, Stuttgart 1981, p. 598 (henceforth Krausnick)

edge, they say that they disobeyed. The truth is that they actively participated in all these crimes, or sat silent and acquiescent.[53]

Like all cross-the-board judgements, this is not entirely fair. A number of high ranking officers had participated in the attempt of 20 July 1944 and paid with their lives. Others, like *Generalleutnant* Groppe had taken positive action. General Groppe commanded a division in the West. In September 1939, local party officials in the Saar planned a *pogrom* against the Jews who had remained. General Groppe ordered his troops to disband them, if necessary by force of arms. After publicly attacking a speech by Himmler, Groppe was cashiered, and thereafter sent to a concentration camp.

Manstein's trial

Manstein was put on trial before a British military tribunal in 1949. It was to be the last trial for war crimes against a German General, and none caused more emotion. At that time, paper was still short in Germany and the press reported only summarily. Manstein's trial continues to be written about even now. On the fiftieth anniversary of Manstein's sentencing, the most influential German daily, *Frankfurter Allgemeine Zeitung*, published on 20 December 1999, a full page article by Bert-Oliver Manning with the title: "What one does not admit, one does not know."

The initial intention was to try four commanders, *Feldmarschalls* von Brauchitsch, von Rundstedt, von Manstein and *Generaloberst* Strauss. Brauchitsch died of angina pectoris before the proceedings began. Rundstedt and Strauss were deemed to be physically and mentally unfit to submit to proceedings. Thus Manstein alone remained.

The British government showed considerable reluctance to opening the proceedings. Churchill's 'Grand Alliance' no longer existed. Russia had turned from ally to potential enemy, and Germany was a factor in the European Defence Strategy. The establishment of NATO had been decided. German participation with a new Army was under tacit consideration, although it was not yet a subject of public discussion.

The questionable McCloy amnesty had taken these considerations into account. The Generals who had been sentenced by the IMT were set free after a few years. They wrote memoirs and appeared as unblemished heroes at meetings of soldiers' associations. Particularly outrageous were the amnesties after the trial of the *Einsatzgruppen.* (IMT, case 9). Seventeen accused were sentenced to death. Only four, Ohlendorf, Dr Braune, Naumann and Blobel were hanged. The others were soon freed and engaged in lucrative business activities.

The British military government in occupied Germany was in favour of a mild attitude towards the German generals, both in a spirit of comradeship and in their desire to avoid a burden in the new relationship between Britain and Germany. There was also fear of the risk that a rigid attitude towards former *Wehrmacht* generals could put German rearmament in jeopardy. Pressure for a trial of Manstein came from the US. The head of the American prosecution team at

---

53 Brett-Smith, p.280

Nuremberg, Telford Taylor, had found voluminous evidence against him, and communicated the documentation to the British Attorney General, Sir Hartley Shawcross. His documentation convinced Shawcross' parliamentary under-secretary Elwyn Jones, that a trial against Manstein was called for. Elwyn Jones, who later belonged to the prosecution team at the Manstein trial, in turn persuaded the Foreign Secretary, Ernest Bevin and the Defence Secretary, Emanuel Shinwell that proceedings against Manstein were necessary.

The openings were delayed by the British High Command in occupied Germany. Their head, General Sir Sholto Douglas, wrote to the British Foreign Office: "We know that the Americans will make use of a lot of evidence of a very dubious nature."[54] In an effort to put an end to disputes between different British authorities, the British government asked the American military command in Germany to consider trying the Generals before an American tribunal. General Clay turned down the request. In March 1948, the Soviet Union requested the British government to hand over Rundstedt and Manstein for a Soviet war crimes trial. The British government was opposed but did not want a major incident with the Soviet Union. The reply was that the Generals would be tried before a British court. The official decision was reached on 5 July 1948.

Loud protests arose in Germany and Britain. Manstein was viewed as the least suitable man for a war crimes trial. His fame as a commander had remained unaltered. He was considered to be the ideal representative of the traditional German Army. His military reputation had remained unaltered. He was known to have kept a clear distance from the Party. He had been courted by the 'resistance' movement. In 1944, he was dismissed by Hitler. That occurred only a few weeks after he had come close to glorification in a cover story in TIME magazine. Opposition in British Conservative circles ran high. Churchill said that the trial was simply 'political idiocy.'

A defence fund was created to which Churchill, Montgomery and Liddell Hart made contributions. The sums raised in Germany and Britain reached 50,000 DM, an immense amount at that time, since the German currency reform had just taken place. During the trial, Countess Marion Dönhoff wrote in the influential weekly *Die Zeit*:

> The shadows of total war have penetrated fully into the so-called peace. During the war, the state demands the utmost from its citizens, now the desire to re-educate him is also total. Even justice becomes subservient and loses its majesty.

At first the trial was considered to be a simple formality which would end in certain acquittal. Manstein's defence team was headed by Dr Laternser and Dr Leverkuehn. Both felt that a British lawyer was required for a trial before a British court. Whether this was really so is questionable. Dr. Laternser and Dr. Leverkuehn were exceptionally capable attorneys. Dr Laternser had been defence counsel at the trial of the *OKW* and the *Generalstab* and he had defended *Feldmarschalls* v. Leeb and List at their respective trials. Dr Leverkuehn had practised in the USA and Britain before the war, and was thus well acquainted with

---

54   Public Record Office (PRO), FO 371/64475, Douglas to Foreign Office, October 23, 1947

both countries' procedures. He spoke perfect English. Also British and American procedures were much more favourable to the defendants than the German code. Other German lawyers had appeared at the IMT trials and foreign procedures had not proved to be an obstacle.

Given the reactions in parts of British Conservative opinion, the Labour government felt that it had to yield to the request and to provide a defence counsel from its own ranks. Since the Conservative Party in Britain spearheaded the protest against a trial of Manstein, the Labour party, which was in power, felt that it had to provide a defence attorney from its own ranks. The Labour MP Reginald Paget was chosen as the main attorney and was assisted by his Jewish junior partner, Sam Silkin. Manstein had tried to refuse Silkin because he was a Jew.[55] Manstein's imbued anti-Semitism had the better of his intelligence, since a Jewish lawyer on his defence team was a major asset. The German public was elated with this tandem, 'the pacifist and the Jew' became a common slogan.

The choice of Paget turned out to be unfortunate. Paget was not a star lawyer. His defence performance was mediocre and consisted mainly of 'hymns' about Manstein and interventions which breathed National-Socialist 'propaganda'.

Manstein had no influence over this choice and since he was in jail, he had to rely on outside assistance in the preparation of his defence strategy. His last chief-of-staff, General Theodor Busse, advised him to simply stick to the arguments used at the trial of the *OKW* and the *Generalstab*, with the *Wehrmacht* having only been a combat force, with no knowledge of the ideological war waged by the *SS* behind its lines. Knowledge of genocide had to be denied at all costs.

The trial opened on 23 August 1949, at the Curio house in Hamburg and large crowds had assembled in the street to demonstrate open support. Manstein appeared in a dark suit, and his appearance remained impressive. At first, matters went as Manstein and his supporters had expected. However, 8 September 1949 was the 'black day' for the defence. The prosecution produced a series of documents:

Manstein's infamous order of the day of 20 November 1941, which followed a previous order by Reichenau, in which Manstein demanded that his soldiers showed understanding for the harsh punishment meted out on Jews. There was evidence that showed that Manstein's 11th Army had requested that the 15,000 Jews of Simferopol were to be shot before Christmas 1941.

The correspondence between the staff of 11th Army and the commander of *Einsatzgruppe* D, Ohlendorf, with the request to hand over 120 watches which had been retrieved from the victims of the massacre.

A page in the war diary of 11th Army, signed by Manstein, that it was unworthy for a German officer to watch the execution of Jews. Only the last document was a novelty.

Manstein's order of the day, of 20 November 1941, the massacre at Simferopol, and the 'watch action' had already been part of the charges against Manstein's chief-of-staff, General Otto Wöhler, at his previous trial before the

---

IMT. However, the Holocaust was not a central point at the preceding trials. At Nuremberg, Raul Hilberg had asked Robert Kempner, a former German senior justice official, who had emigrated to the US during the 1930s, and was a member of the prosecution team, why so little attention was paid to the Holocaust. Kempner replied that the notion 'final solution' simply did not exist at that time.

Suddenly Manstein was proved a liar. As a witness at Nuremberg he had stated under oath that he had never heard of executions of Jews. Moreover, it appeared unbelievable that a man like Manstein would lower himself to the banality of an official request for 120 watches. Until that day, Manstein had remained impressive. Suddenly he became totally confused. Paget could no longer continue with his laudatory exposition and began to appeal to anti-Semitic feelings in the court. One might be surprised that Sam Silkin did not withdraw from Paget's defence team. When shown the Reichenau order, which had served as a pattern for Manstein's order of the day, he simply commented that he saw no difference between that order and an Allied document which requested the elimination of German militarism. "To label the Reichenau order as criminal is only evidence of a short memory."

The German press made an immediate turn-a-round. It became suddenly struck with silence. Until that day, it had daily reported the proceedings. After the disclosures, only the Hamburg daily *Die Welt*, the main paper in northern Germany, which was still under British supervision, continued its daily reporting. The other media ignored the trial and began to write about "false witnesses at the Malmedy trials" and other war crime proceedings which they considered to have been unfair. The weekly *Sonntagzeitung* demanded that German courts be permitted to try Allied commanders who had been guilty of crimes against Germany. In his final plea, Paget again resorted to pathos:

> I refuse to believe that the victor has the right to sit in judgement upon the vanquished. Manstein, the Hector of his nation, will never be considered by Germans as a war criminal. He is a hero of his nation and will remain so. Here, at this tribunal, he has fought his last and fearless battle for the reputation of the men whom he led in combat and who laid down their lives.

The judges were not impressed and Manstein was found guilty on the following charges:

- He had neglected his duty as military commander to see to the humanitarian treatment of prisoners-of-war. As a consequence thereof 7,993 prisoners within the area of 11th Army had either died, been shot, or delivered to the *SD*. The tribunal emphasised however that Manstein had not acted deliberately and recklessly.
- He had executed an order from *OKH* that escaped Russian prisoners-of-war, who had been seized behind the German lines, in uniform or in civilian clothes, would be treated as guerillas.
- He had ordered prisoners-of-war to be engaged in work which endangered their lives and which was prohibited by the Geneva convention.
- He had permitted the execution of the 'Commissar'order.

- He had tolerated the execution of Jews by *Einsatzgruppe* D. However, the tribunal could not find sufficient evidence that he had acted deliberately or recklessly.
- He had ordered the deportation of Russian civilians to hard labour in Germany.
- He had implemented 'scorched-earth' measures during the retreat of his troops in Russia.

Manstein was sentenced to 18 years. Upon hearing the judgement, he removed his headset and threw it on his desk. In a letter to his wife, he wrote that this was not a gesture of uncontrolled rage, he wanted to show his contempt for British justice. Many German papers did not report the sentence. It was reduced in routine manner to 12 years. In 1952, he was given leave, against the pledge of his word of honour, to submit to an urgent eye operation. An increasing number of generals were being released and it was apparent that Manstein would not have to serve his sentence out. German pressure on the British increased. The British took time. Manstein became increasingly annoyed and wrote to Busse that the British acted like Jewish horse-traders.[56] Busse saw the Manstein trial as 'Jewry's vengeance'.[57]

Manstein was finally released in May 1953 but was not spared an ultimate humiliation. His release did not occur within the framework of an amnesty, but because he had served sufficient of his time for release on grounds of 'good conduct in prison.' For Adenauer, who was in the middle of an election campaign at that time, a meeting with Manstein was a welcome opportunity to shake his hand in public.

The final years

Manstein's attempts to play an active part in the setting up of the *Bundeswehr* have to be mentioned, although they remained without result. They were not requested, Manstein took the initiative. Georg Meyer, in his recent 1,000-page biography of General Heusinger, who had become the first inspector general of the *Bundeswehr*, heads this section with the title: 'Manstein meddles.'[58] He described the background to Manstein's intervention:

> General Heusinger had wished to have former high commanders, who had retained influence in military circles, express their verbal encouragement to the new conditions under which a German Army had to be built up, while at the same time hoping that they would remain benevolent silence. In the spring of 1955, after informing the Chancellor, he had sent out invitations to a meeting at Östrich and addressed them to Manstein, the *Generaloberst*s Stumpff and Reinhardt, and Generals Crüwell, Eberbach, Kuntzen and Busse. Manstein's old opponent Halder was not among the guests. Heusinger had hoped in vain that this reunion, which

---

56   Wrochem, p.213
57   Wrochem, p. 127
58   Meyer, Heusinger, p. 545

he saw as a 'farewell party', would lead them to abstain from future meddling and unsolicited advice. He was to be disappointed.[59]

On 28 December 1955 Manstein took the initiative of a controversy with Heusinger which was politely worded but sharp in content. One of his letters contained a typical Manstein sentence: "As a soldier of some [sic] experience, I cannot give up my responsibility to see to it, that our country receives an Army which I consider to be more appropriate than the plans presented here." Manstein had more than just 'some' experience. However, in 1955, it was already worthless. The French generals of the Second World War were also experienced soldiers. However, they led with the methods of the previous war and were thus condemned to failure. Technical progress between the two World Wars was somewhat limited and the armies of the second were to some extent provided with equipment of the first. After the end of the Second World War, nuclear arms and rapidly developing electronics created entirely new types of armament, which required new methods. No war can be fought with the methods of the previous one. A responsibility can be given up only by someone who has been entrusted with it. That was not the case with Manstein.

Manstein, in another document, added that "loyalty to the new international agreements, national sovereignty, and equal rights within the new alliance, would require the new Army units to be structured as we deem it necessary".[60] What is meant by 'we'? Does Manstein even now personify the new Army? Manstein then turned to Franz-Joseph Strauss. Georg Meyer wrote that Manstein was unaware of the damage caused by him. The views of Strauss were in strong opposition to those of the Blank office, the body preceding the new German ministry of defence.

The reasons for Manstein's insistence have been the subject of speculations. Kunrat von Hammerstein, the son of the *Generaloberst*, voiced the opinion that Manstein viewed himself as a second Hindenburg, with the ambition to succeed Theodor Heuss as President of the *Bundesrepublik*. Manstein's view remained without effect on the final plans of the government. There was some criticism abroad and an intervention in the House of Commons.

Manstein spent his remaining years surrounded by his family and a group of close friends. He completed his memoirs and wrote articles in military journals. On his 80th birthday the *Bundeswehr* celebrated him with a *Grosser Zapfenstreich*, a torch-light ceremony to honour high dignitaries. He died of a stroke in 1973 and was buried with military honours. He would never acknowledge his responsibility in the criminal policies of the Second World War.

---

59   Ibid
60   Ibid, p. 546 f

Concluding appreciations

Was Manstein the *primus inter pares* of the German commanders?

In terms of military knowledge and performance, the answer is 'Yes'. No other German general would come close to him. Historians worldwide share this view. He cannot be called a great commander since he lacked the moral greatness that Clausewitz had long considered to be the indispensable attribute of greatness. A man who failed in his overriding moral duty at Stalingrad, who issued the order of the day of 20 November 1941, who perjured himself in court, and who became a major perpetrator of genocide cannot be called great.

Was Manstein a strategist?

While Manstein had strategic knowledge, he was no strategist, although many historians and military experts continue to view him as such.

Sun Tzu is considered to be strategy's father. Over the centuries new concepts have been put forward. In modern times, notions like Liddell Hart's 'Grand Strategy' have gained ground. At the highest level, strategy is the guiding element of warfare which combines the political, economical and military leaderships of a state in order to arrive at a final political result. In modern war, the strategists are no longer the military commanders, but the statesmen to whom the commanders are subordinate.

Against this backgound, one certainly cannot deny Hitler's strategic capability. The Israeli military historian, Professor Martin van Creveld, who wrote his classic study of the *Wehrmacht*'s fighting power, wrote:

> Hitler was not an educated expert, but he had a better understanding of all problems of warfare at the highest level than did his generals. In autumn 1941, a dispute arose between Hitler and his Generals about the continued direction of the advance in Russia. The commanders wanted to proceed to Moscow. Hitler gave the order to turn southwards and secure the raw materials of the Ukraine. Guderian went to Hitler and made a plea, lasting some hours, for the attack on Moscow. Hitler listened patiently to him and when Guderian finished, he cut him off with one sentence: "My generals understand nothing about war economics." Van Creveld added: "That was true and both knew it."[61]

Manstein disqualifies himself with the first paragraph of the introduction to *Verlorene Siege:* "This book is the recollections of a soldier. I have intentionally refrained from giving attention to problems of politics, or other matters which had no immediate relation to military events." Manstein's thoughts were limited to land Army considerations and had no comprehension of the importance of the

---

61   M. van Creveld, *Die deutsche Wehrmacht: eine militärische Beurteilung* in *Die Wehrmacht, Mythos und Realität*, anthology published by the MGFA, Oldenburg, 1999, p. 330 ff, henceforth: van Creveld

economic potential of Germany's adversaries, or the decisive control of the seas. He would increasingly subordinate his views to his abstruse 'draw theory' which remained a credo until the very end.

Stahlberg reports a significant conversation in 1943 between the two:

> Assuming that I have understood his memorandum, he had the opinion that Hitler could force Stalin, Roosevelt and Churchill to a conference table and to agree upon a compromise. Manstein agreed, that was indeed a summary of his views. I told him that this was an illusion. He had to remember that Hitler had called Churchill a 'whisky drunkard', and Roosevelt a 'paralytic', in a number of public speeches. Such utterances were sufficient to preclude any conversation between them. Furthermore, Hitler had broken every agreement soon after having signed it. Thus he could not be looked upon as a serious partner for negotiations, let alone for agreements. Finally, Germany had committed many crimes in occupied territories which had violated every international law.
>
> Manstein replied that he could not dispute my arguments, but still I was mistaken. Such considerations carried little weight in politics and a soldier was not entitled to judge political morality. Germany still had many trump cards which had not yet been shown. No Allied soldier had yet landed on European soil. He assumed that the Americans and the British would land in the not distant future in Italy, the Balkans and on the Atlantic shores. Germany could then retreat to the Alpine mountains which could be defended with greatly reduced forces. Hitler would be well advised if he would give him, Manstein, supreme authority over planning and command. If military leadership would remain as wretched as in recent times, the situation could indeed become critical. But this was still far away.[62]

There is no reason to doubt Stahlberg's *verbatim* account, since Manstein would express himself in similar vein several chapters of *Verlorene Siege*. After the fiasco of operation 'Citadel' in July 1943, he wrote:

> Today, long after the war, people may think that the thought of a possible compromise in the East was just 'pie in the sky'. We soldiers could not fully judge if a political agreement could still be achieved with the Soviet Union. But it certainly could not be entirely excluded, provided Hitler would agree to it. At Army Group Don, later renamed Army Group South, all of us were convinced that with correct operational leadership, a 'draw' [that always recurring phrase], could still be reached in the East. The road from Stalingrad to the Donez basin had caused the enemy to suffer heavy casualties. At the end, he had suffered two defeats. [Manstein's recapture of Charkov and Belgorod]. He had not succeeded in encircling our entire southern wing. We had regained the initiative. During the winter combats the superior value of German troops and commanders had again asserted itself. Admittedly, we had sustained heavy losses at Stalingrad, but according to *OKH* estimations, the Red Army had

suffered more than 11 million casualties since the beginning of the war. Thus the offensive power of the enemy would have to come to an end. This was our understanding, particularly since we had been able to turn a situation that appeared hopeless into ultimate victory. Once again we were on a sound footing. It would certainly not have served our purpose to follow the opinion of today's critics and consider the war as having been irretrievably lost.[63]

The simple fact is that the *Wehrmacht* had no strategists among its commanders. Professor van Creveld wrote:

It is hardly a coincidence that all German commanders, with the possible exception of Rundstedt and Kesselring, only acted on an operational level and commanded Armies and Army Groups at the utmost. This was the case of Generals like Manstein, Guderian, Rommel and Manteuffel, to name a few examples. It is as if the US Army had only consisted of Pattons. The *Wehrmacht* could never produce a commander who would have authority over an entire theatre like Eisenhower, MacArthur and to some extent also Zhukov. The German staff doctrine was simply inadequate for training top command positions.[64]

The historian Karl-Heinz Frieser emphasised that the German generals of the Second World War led with the most modern methods in the field. Their strategic views were anachronistic. Already the American Civil War had shown that the military in the more efficient South could not prevail against the economic strength of the North.[65]

In the art of leading mobile operations of large units, Manstein was the undisputed master of World War II. No other General, German, Allied or Red Army, could come close to his performance. Manstein operated like a chess grandmaster who, willingly, weakens one part of his position, lures his opponent into attacking it and then pounds him with his pieces from the other part of the board. Manstein was an enthusiastic and capable chess player, hence his repeated use of chess game expressions like *Remis* (draw) and *Rochade* (castling). His mobile operations could be likened to 'castling'. He had developed a concept devised by him, and brought it close to perfection. He would withdraw divisions from one sector of the front, and let the Red Army pour into it. Then he used the units he had withdrawn, moving to a neighbouring sector, counterattacking and often destroying the enemy who had infiltrated. Frieser wrote that Manstein's system, at highest operational level, consisted of deviating from systematic thinking. In his view, the right solution for the commander was not to act within logic since that was to be expected by the opponent. Better to proceed illogically and thus surprise the enemy."[66]

After his dismissal of Manstein, Hitler said to *Generaloberst* Jodl, head of operations at *OKW*:

---

63 *Verlorene Siege*, p. 472 f
64 van Creveld, p. 335
65 Frieser, p. 448
66 Ibid, p. 85

In my eyes Manstein has a tremendous talent for operations. There is no doubt about that. And if I had an Army of twenty divisions, at full strength and in peacetime conditions, I could not think of a better commander than Manstein. He knows how to handle them and will do it. He would move like lightning, but always under the condition that he had first-class material, petrol and plenty of ammunition. If something breaks down, he does not get things done. If I got hold of another Army today, I am not at all sure that I would employ Manstein, although he is certainly one of our most competent officers. He can operate with divisions as long as they are in good shape. If, in battle the divisions are roughly treated, I have to take them away from him in a hurry, because he cannot handle such a situation.[67]

That was obviously unfair to Manstein. Hitler knew well that Manstein had to lead during the later years of the war with under-strength formations and his leadership remained brilliant. Perhaps Hitler's words reflected his weariness of Manstein's repeated requests for freedom of action. They may also contain a shade of bad conscience at having relieved Manstein, without being able to fault him with any military failure.

Was Manstein a National-Socialist?

As an active officer, Manstein was forbidden by the *Reichswehr* law of 1921 to engage in any political activity. Like most of his fellow officers, Manstein welcomed the emergence of the Third *Reich* as an authoritarian state. When Hitler assumed power, Manstein was a lieutenant-colonel and could not detect opposition among his superiors. His sponsor, General Beck, had written to Ms Gossler, the daughter of his commander in the First World War, that 30 January 1933 was his first beam of light since the defeat 1918. After his last meeting with Hindenburg, *Generaloberst* von Hammerstein-Equord resigned quickly. He said that Hitler had simply become Germany's fate and that the country would have to bear with him in the coming ten years.

Manstein himself can be described as a monarchist. He was an adherent of the theories of leading German constitutional scholars who viewed the state as a body to be guided by its elites. Manstein's son Rüdiger said, on Knopp's video, that his father certainly was no democrat. At his trial Manstein said:

The democracy of the *Weimar* Republic could not impress me. I was at first impressed by the accomplishments of the party. Like most Germans I had hoped that the party would succeed in removing the gap between the working man and the middle class.[68]

---

67   quoted in Brett-Smith, p.234 f
68   Minutes of the Manstein trial, English version at the Yad Vashem Holocaust Memorial, Jerusalem. A number of pages lack numbers (henceforth Trial). Also quoted in P. Leverkuehn, *Verteidigung Mansteins*, Hamburg 1950, p.3 (henceforth Leverkuehn)

Until very recently, historians were unequivocal in their statements that Manstein was not a National-Socialist and that he always kept his distance from the party. He held most party officials in contempt and looked on them as plebeians. Since Manstein was particularly vilified in Goebbel's diaries, the contention that he was never a National-Socialist was further strengthened. Some of Goebbel's statements are given below:

> 2 March 1943: "In the eyes of the *Führer*, the only trustworthy general is Schmundt. All the others avail themselves of the difficult war situation and create difficulties for him. Göring has told me that Manstein has had the impudence to suggest that the *Führer* abandons Supreme Command. This led to nothing, since he was seriously called to order, but the *Führer* has not forgotten it and let Manstein feel the consequences. The *Führer* had intended to dismiss Manstein, during his recent visit to the southern front, but he did not follow it through."

> 12 March 1943: "During the evening I heard that the *Führer* has again visited the front. He paid a new visit to Manstein and complimented him on his recent performance in the East. I am not happy. The *Führer* does not appear to know how meanly Manstein behaved towards him. If he knows, he shows again that he is much too lenient with the military".

> 9 November 1944: "Himmler is sharply critical of Manstein whom he considers to be defeatist. The crisis in the South would never have reached its present proportion if a man with stature had commanded there instead of Manstein. I have heard in Berlin that the *Führer* has received Manstein at his headquarters. Contrary to expectation, their conversation appears to have been positive and it is assumed that Manstein will remain his command. I would consider this as a fateful mistake. But I need to obtain full knowledge of their conversation."[69]

Even after Manstein's dismissal Goebbels feared that Hitler could employ him again. On 18 April 1944 he wrote:

> The *Führer* is not as ill-disposed towards Manstein as I have assumed. He does not view him as a rousing commander who can create enthusiasm in his troops, but considers him to be an able tactician whom he could put to use when we can regain the offensive. But this will take time and should this occur, we will know how to dissuade him.

November 1944. In a conversation with Goebbels, Himmler had called Manstein 'Marshal backwards', i.e *Marschall Rückwärts*.

In 2005, the German historian Roland Kopp 'caused a bomb to explode', by unveiling an address by Manstein to his Division in Liegnitz on 20 April 1939, Hitler's 50th birthday. It is historians' luck that even after more than fifty years, hitherto unpublished documents suddenly appear, which permit revised judgments of former statements. These are the words of Manstein's speech to his division:

---

69 *Goebbels Tagebücher aus den Jahen 1942–1943 mit anderen Dokumenten*, ed. L.Lochner, Zürich 1941, p.241,267,470 (henceforth Goebbels)

Soldiers, Comrades! To-day, on the 50th birthday of our *Führer*, the *Wehrmacht* joins the whole German people in admiration, gratitude, in love and faith to our Supreme Commander. On this day, we thank the Lord that he has given the German people the gift of this great German son. The Lord kept his protective hand over him, in his days as a brave front soldier. The Lord held his protective hand over him during the years of the struggle for power, and then blessed his activities as the *Führer* of the *Reich*. We all remember the path on which our *Führer* has led us during the past six years. He took us from our inner conflict, to the unity of the German people, when, after years of misery he gave work and bread. From a defenceless position, he restored our military might and led us from weakness to greatness. We will always remember the accomplishments of the *Führer* which are the milestones on the path of the Greater German *Reich*. The Rhineland, German-Austria, the Sudeten provinces, Bohemia/Moravia [so even the robbery of the remaining Czechoslovakia is included in the great deeds] and the Memelland.

If the German people are now in a position to the *Führer* that he had been able to accomplish these great deeds without war, we will never forget that Adolf Hitler has walked this way as a soldier and a fighter. We swear that we will emulate his soldierly virtues, we will follow his endless love for his people, his unshakeable belief in Germany's destiny, his boundless courage and his total personal devotion to the fate and future of our country. And if it seems that a hostile world will surround Germany with walls to keep her from finding her deserved future, we soldiers swear to our *Führer* that we will remove every obstacle in his way. We will see that his will is obeyed, to give him all our assistance in his future struggle, regardless of where he will lead us. May our today's pledge resound through the whole world: Adolf Hitler, our great *Führer*, *Sieg Heil!*

The speech was recorded in the Liegnitz daily but did not find its way into the national press. It thus remained unknown, since hardly anyone, except the people of Liegnitz, took any notice of the local press. (A Baedeker guide of Germany from the 1930s contains only one mention about Liegnitz: 'Not worth a visit.')

Other commanders made addresses in honour of the *Führer*, but only a few engaged in superlatives like Manstein, even glorifying the march into Prague a few weeks earlier. Some commanders, among them General von Sponeck, later to become a victim of Manstein's vindictiveness in the Crimea, refrained from making any speeches and simply reviewed their troops.

The time-frame, 1939, in which Manstein made this speech, has to be recalled. A year before, Manstein had been dismissed from his post of *Oberquartiermeister I* during the *revirement* and sent as divisional commander to Liegnitz. In one of his typical exaggerations, the memoir-writer Manstein wrote that he was tempted to throw his sword at Hitler's feet and regretted not having done so. Then follows: "What a humiliation that the politician Hitler watches upon the honour of the Army." A few weeks later the 'politician Hitler' becomes 'God's gift' to the nation, the *Wehrmacht* and to Manstein himself.

The hostile comments to Manstein by Goebbels have to be seen against the years in which they occurred. They were entered in Goebbel's diary in 1943. By that time, the successful period of Manstein's service had practically come to an end and Manstein had begun his increasing attempts to be appointed Commander in Chief East or head of the new *Generalstab*. During all of the years of the Third *Reich*, Hitler's close associates were engaged in internal struggle for influence, and when a new candidate for a position of power like Manstein appeared, he immediately became the target of their attack.

One can describe Manstein as the kind of careerist found among many high-ranking *Wehrmacht* commanders. He was certainly never a convinced National-Socialist, neither were his comrades of the highest ranks. Like them, he was a typical fellow-traveller who believed in Hitler's 'luck'.

While talking to their aristocratic friends, it was 'good form' to make disparaging comments about party leaders. However, on the other side, when Manstein visited the *Führerhauptquartier*, he often made a point of sitting close to Schmundt, to be sure that his words of devotion would be repeated to Hitler. In several letters to his wife, General Heusinger noted this with disgust. Like Albert Speer, Manstein succeeded in the course of half a century in fooling a generation of historians about his real nature. His unrivalled stature as a commander, and the esteem in which he was held by many Allied historians, among them Liddell Hart, contributed to a fictitious picture of the man's real nature.

Was Manstein an anti-Semite in the National-Socialist sense?

Against the background of his order of the day of 20 November 1941 and his subsequent actions in the Crimea, the logical answer would be an unequivocal 'yes.' However, this requires some qualifications. Manstein was not an anti-Semite because he was a National-Socialist. His anti-Semitism was an inheritance of the traditionally anti-Semitic Prussian army. Although Jews theoretically enjoyed all political rights in Imperial Germany, certain self-styled elitist groups, like the Army and the senior civil service would not accept them in their ranks. In the Prussian army, Jews could not even become reserve officers. The Bavarian army was more liberal – Jews could become reserve officers, in certain instances even active officers. This anti-Semitism was not racist, if a Jew converted to Christianity the obstacles were removed. This is a typical example of narrow Prussian provincialism. In no other major Western European army were there similar restrictions. In 1916, during the war, it reached its climax with the infamous *Judenzählung*, a census of all Jews serving in the German armed forces, under the pretext that there were complaints about many Jews being shirkers. The census showed that there was no substance in its premises. But no apology was forthcoming. The census cost Germany much of the sympathy which it had enjoyed among American Jews, who had previously been strongly opposed to the US entering the war on the side of the *Entente*. The attitude of German active officers towards Jews in general was one of indifference coupled with a feeling of inborn superiority and disdain. Social contacts did not exist.

Manstein's attitude has to be described as having been ambivalent. In 1933, He had gone on record in interceding for a non-aryan physician in Kolberg. With his protest against the introduction of racial legislation in the Army, Manstein may have endangered his career. At that time he was not a violent anti-Semite.

Paget's comments about Manstein's racial views are however grotesque:

> Manstein knew little about racial persecution. He was aware that Jewish emigration was encouraged and that Jews were encountering some difficulties in their professional activities. He also knew that the *Nazis* would sometimes treat Jews less than gently. However, he was totally unaware of concentration camps and their brutality. These camps were totally isolated and guarded by carefully selected *SS* henchmen. Inmates who were released would be afraid to mention a word about their experience.[70]

This calls for some comment. Manstein was neither blind nor deaf. He had heard Hitler's speeches with their increasing appeal for violence against Jews. He read the press that would publish the successive measures of racial legislation taken by the government. He had witnessed the one-day boycott against all Jewish stores in Germany on 1 April 1933. He could not have failed to see the showcases on many streets in which the nearly pornographic anti-Semitic weekly *Der Stürmer* was displayed. The paper was so revolting that the showcases were removed during the 1936 Berlin Olympics, for fear of reaction by the many foreign spectators of the games. Manstein had witnessed the horrible 'Crystal-Night' of November 1938, during which the German synagogues and remaining Jewish stores were set ablaze. Paget confuses the first concentration camps with the future extermination camps. Most inmates of the first camps were not Jews, but political opponents and former union heads. They were guarded by the *SA* and not by the *SS*. They were widely reported in the press and in newsreels as a 'useful instrument of re-education' and names like Dachau and Sachsenhausen were household names in the German public.

To sum up: Manstein was certainly a traditional German anti-Semite. Such an attitude could easily lead to indifference to the later extermination, and in the case of Manstein, even to active participation.

---

70 P.t, p. 27

Manstein's relations with Hitler

Hitler's opinion of his Generals

The Blomberg scandal shattered part of Hitler's world. Below wrote that, "up to this day," his respect for the aristocracy and the generals had remained unaltered. His private secretary Wiedemann recalled that he walked back and forth around his room for hours like a broken man and repeated incessantly: "If a Prussian *Feldmarschall* marries a whore, the world simply crumbles." One of his domestic servants wrote that Hitler had taken no less than seven hot baths on that day, to remove every trace of the hand of Blomberg's wife which he had kissed at the ceremony. Rundstedt confirmed that "Hitler was in a state of shattered nerves, the like of which he had never seen before. Something inside him was broken and he had lost all trust in humanity. It was certainly no show."[71] After the first reverses of the war, Hitler would show an increasing aversion, which would turn into contempt. He then progressed towards visceral hatred.

His frequent outbursts are recorded in Goebbels' diaries of the years 1942–43:

The *Führer* has only negative opinions of his generals. Whenever possible they simply lie to him. Furthermore they have no general education and they don't even understand their military task, something which one should be able to expect from them. That they have no high educational level is not surprising, since this was not part of their upbringing. However, the ultimate condemnation of them is that they have no inkling about warfare. Their education had been wrong over generations and our present Senior Officer Corps is the result …

The *Führer*'s judgement of the generals' moral qualities is simply devastating. '*A priori*,' he no longer believes a single word of a general. All lie to him, pretend that the weather is always fine and advance figures which a child can disprove. This imposition on the *Führer*'s intelligence comes close to insult … The *Führer* talks again at length about the generals whom he holds in total contempt. One should only imagine how they would look in civilian clothes, this would be sufficient to lose any respect for them. When Keitel's name is mentioned, the *Führer* can only smile and say that he has the brains of the doorman of a movie theatre …

After the war, the *Führer* will be happy to don his brown jacket again and he will have no more contact with any general … Most generals hate the *Führer* and look at him as an upstart. They have not sufficient intuition to understand his genius. The *Führer* will spare no effort to bring fresh blood into the Officer Corps. The selection of high commanders will slowly but surely become different …

The *Führer* is most annoyed with the generals' lack of knowledge and understanding of technical matters. They always pretend to know better, in reality they know nothing. These so-called intellectual heroes are insig-

71   Janssen/Tobias, p. 52

nificant, it is sufficient to remember Seeckt. But the *Führer* is no longer fooled by appearances. As soon as he sees shortcomings, he takes strong measures and nothing deflects him. I have the impression that he vents his anger at present more in words than in deeds. But with him, words are always a prelude to action.[72]

The actions predicted by Goebbels did not occur. Hitler would show astonishing leniency to officers whose judgement had faulted him and many would retain their commands. Hitler would gradually dismiss an increasing number of generals, but the core of the *Wehrmacht* Officer Corps would remain unaltered until the end of the war. The generals would only increasingly experience Hitler's outbursts. Guderian attempted once to show Hitler some faulty aspects of his operational judgement. Hitler cut him off rudely:

You cannot lecture me. I have commanded the Army throughout five years of war and in that time I have accumulated more experience than the gentlemen of the *Generalstab* will ever have. I have read the works of Clausewitz and Moltke, and every plan of Schlieffen. I have a much better view than you.[73]

Manstein was never the victim of such outbursts, besides him, only Rundstedt was spared. Hitler was under no illusion about Rundstedt's performance during the Second World War. Age had rapidly caught up with the general, who had become something akin to a marionette: "My *Führer*, whatever you may order, I will obey until my last breath." However, Rundstedt's personal appearance reminded Hitler of past times. When Hitler became Chancellor, Rundstedt was already a *General der Infanterie* and second only to the commander in chief of the Army on the ranking list. During the Blomberg/Fritsch crisis Rundstedt had acted as spokesman of the generals. He had prevented the appointment of Hitler's favourite, Reichenau, as Army commander in chief, forcing him to accept Brauchitsch instead. At the end, Rundstedt sank to so low a level that he accepted the presidency of the court of honour, the *Ehrenhof.* After 20 July 1944, that court expelled from the Army officers who had participated in the failed assassination attempt. They were remanded to the gallows.

Hitler's relations with Manstein

The relationship can be summarised as a growing mutual dislike in an atmosphere of icy reciprocal politeness. When he received command of an Army Group, Manstein became Hitler's direct subordinate. He was the most important commander in the East and met more frequently with Hitler than other generals of similar rank and command. A close relationship could not arise, both personalities were entirely opposite. Manstein was an aristocrat down to his fingertips. As an officer he had been brought up in the spirit and the traditions of his profession. Manstein recognised Hitler as the legitimate Head of State and Supreme Commander of the armed forces, while at the same time feeling that Hitler should

---

72 Goebbels p. 244 ff
73 Guderian, p. 343

pay attention to his logical criticism, so much the more since he never attempted to encroach upon his authority. While Hitler never insulted him to his face, he witnessed many occasions when Hitler behaved in a coarse manner towards other high ranking officers. Hitler vented his anger with Manstein only to third parties.

Manstein would never lower himself to speak contemptuously of Hitler, as the 'corporal of World War I.' However, two of his comments deserve to be quoted here:

> He possessed a number of qualities which are the prerequisite of a great commander, strong will-power, stable nerves even in moments of crisis [Here Manstein errs, Hitler was often panicky], an unquestionably sharp mind, and some talent for operative leadership.[74]

And further:

> Hitler had an astonishing knowledge and memory, and displayed creative imagination in all technical matters and in all problems of weaponry. He would always impress with his knowledge of the effect of enemy weapons, and would quote exact figures of our own and of enemy production ... There is no doubt that he had shown considerable understanding and a great amount of energy in advancing our rearmament.[75]

In his world-wide bestseller *Anmerkungen zu Hitler* (Comments to Hitler), Sebastian Haffner wrote:

> That Hitler was not the 'greatest commander of all times', hardly requires lengthy comments. (The slogan *'Gröfaz', grösster Feldherr aller Zeiten,* was coined by Keitel after the victory over France). In fact, one has to come a little to his defence against his generals. According to their memoirs, they could all have won the Second World War, had Hitler not prevented them from doing so. But this is likewise not the truth. True, the concept of an independent tank force was Guderian's. The brilliant strategic plan for the victory over France, a much better plan than the Schlieffen plan, was Manstein's creation. But without Hitler, neither Manstein nor Guderian would have prevailed against the senior, traditional and narrow-minded Army generals. It was Hitler who understood their ideas and turned them into realities. Hitler was not the military genius that he saw himself, but neither was he the hopeless ignoramus and bungler whom his generals made the scapegoat for their failures.[76]

After Hitler and Manstein had met for the first time in 1940, Hitler said to Schmundt: "Clever brain, but I don't trust him."[77] Rüdiger von Manstein says that his father never came to grips with Hitler's personality. One should add that Manstein never understood the nature of Hitler's dictatorship. The German *Spitzengliederung,* ie highest command structure, was an absurdity.

---

74   *Verlorene Siege,* p. 313
75   Ibid., p. 305 ff
76   S. Haffner, *Anmerkungen zu Hitler,* Frankfurt 2000, 22nd edition, p. 80 f.
77   Knopp, p. 177

OKW had developed into a second General Staff with authority over all 'theatres' except the Eastern front which remained subordinate to *OKH*. *OKW* now superseded *OKH* in importance. Its head, Keitel, and his deputy Jodl, were personally closer to Hitler than the heads of *OKH*. However, *OKH* continued to have control of centralised weaponry, such as motorized artillery and heavy engineering equipment. When a unit operating in an *OKW* theatre was in temporary need of such weaponry, it still had to turn to *OKH*. The personnel department of the Army had remained with *OKH*. It would continue to appoint commanders in *OKW* theatres, and remain solely responsible for the training and selection of *Generalstab* officers.

The historical division was with *OKW*, which also issued the daily war communiqués. The *Waffen-SS* was operationally subordinated to *OKH* and *OKW*, but appointment, promotion and dismissal of its commanders was the authority of its own personnel department. This confusion was indispensable to Hitler whose power was built on *divide et impera*, divide and rule. When Manstein requested freedom in operations from Hitler, he had logic on his side, since operations in a war of movement always entail withdrawals from some areas in order to establish new centres of gravity. However, Manstein overlooked that voluntary retreat from anywhere was a taboo for Hitler after he had issued his 'stay put' order in 1941. When Manstein urged Hitler to appoint a real head of the *Generalstab*, or a commander in chief East, Hitler understood immediately that this was not selfless, but Manstein knew that only he was capable of filling either position.

Stahlberg wrote of an encounter between Manstein and *Feldmarschalls* von Kluge and Rommel on 13 July 1943, after operation 'Citadel' had to be broken off. It was Manstein's first personal meeting with Rommel:

> Kluge said, the end will be bitter. I repeat what I have already told you earlier. I am prepared to place myself under your orders. Rommel added: This war will end in total catastrophe. If the Allies succeed in landing in the Balkans, and later in the West, everything will crumble. Manstein countered: This is still far away. Hitler will give up his command before it is too late. Rommel remained hard: He will never give up his command. Apparently I know him better than you do, *Herr* von Manstein. I am also ready to subordinate myself to you. After Manstein had left, Rommel said to Stahlberg: Your *Feldmarschall* is a strategical genius. I admire him. But he is an illusionist.[78]

On 4 January 1944, Manstein made a last attempt to convince Hitler of the necessity of making a change in the supreme command structure. The description is Manstein's:

> After everyone except Zeitzler had left the room, I requested Hitler's permission to speak without inhibition. In an ice-cold and totally uncommunicative manner he replied: 'if you please.' I then began: 'It has to be clear, *Mein Führer*, that our present critical situation is not solely due to the uncontested superiority of the enemy. It is also a consequence of the structure of our command.' As soon as I had pronounced those words,

---

78 Stahlberg, p. 339

Hitler's expression hardened. He looked at me in a manner that made me feel that he now wanted to bring me to my knees. I cannot recall a single instance where a man could look at someone in a manner that would totally express the power of his will. ("In his post-war recollections, the ambassador of a foreign power recalls the impression that Hitler made on him at their first encounter. He emphasises the effect of Hitler's gaze. In the instance mentioned by him it was 'engaging'. Undoubtedly his eyes were the only expressive even attractive part of his rough face.")

Manstein continued:

Now, Hitler stared at me as if he wished to force his opponent to his knees with one look of his eyes. I suddenly thought of an Indian snake charmer. It had turned into a silent encounter of a few seconds between us. I understood that Hitler had often been able to intimidate many men with a simple look of his eyes, or to use somewhat vulgar but adept words, 'punch them groggy.' I decided to proceed and said that the present military leadership simply could not continue. I had to revert to a proposal that I had made twice already. I told Hitler that, for the overall conduct of the war, he needed one Chief of the *Generalstab*, but one invested with authority, upon whose advice he would have to rely for his military decisions. The consequence of such an appointment would then be the appointment of a Supreme Commander East who, as in the West and in Italy, would enjoy full independence in his decisions while remaining under his authority.

As on previous occasions when I had attempted to convince Hitler to make fundamental changes in his exercise of military command, practically, if not formally, to abandon it, he was totally negative. He said that only he was in possession of all the means of the *Reich* to exercise effective military command. Only he could judge the number of units required by every theatre and thus how they would have to operate. Furthermore, Göring would never agree to subordinate himself to another commander.

As to my suggestion to appoint a Supreme Commander East, he repeated, as he had done on previous occasions, that no one else could enjoy an authority comparable to his own. 'The *Feldmarschalls* don't even obey me! Do you think that they would be more willing to obey you? I can at least dismiss them, no one else would have such authority.' Hitler did not react to my reply, that orders given by me were always followed. He simply broke off the conversation. Once again, I had failed in my attempt to convince him of the necessity to change our supreme command structure, without infringing on his personal prestige.[79]

After that encounter, Manstein resigned. A few weeks later, Zeitzler requested Manstein's assistance in convincing Hitler to evacuate the Crimea and received the reply: "Leave me out of this, I simply cannot cope with his diatribes."[80]

---

79   Ibid., p. 572 ff
80   Meyer, Heusinger, p. 205

"This will indeed be so, *Mein Führer*" – the interruption incident

All the commanders of Army Groups and Armies in the East, together with a number of other senior officers, had been called to Hitler's headquarters, the *Führerhauptquartier*, on 27 January 1944. They had to listen to an address by Hitler, on the necessity of increasing the education of the Army in the National-Socialist spirit. During his address, Hitler said:

> Things hinge on strong and consequential leadership only if it cannot be shaken. Leadership decisions may not be criticized. This is a prerequisite of the struggle for our existence. I will not brook any criticism. Criticism is only permitted from above. Measures and decisions may never be criticized from below. I have the unfortunate feeling that most criticism comes from within the *Wehrmacht*. Should it come to the worst, I have to be surrounded by the whole Officer Corps, just as every *Feldmarschall* will expect to have his generals and his officers stand with their drawn swords at his side.[81]

At that point Manstein interrupted Hitler. Testimonies from eyewitnesses differ. Firstly Manstein's own account:

> I was never ready to swallow insults. However, Hitler's words were an intended snub against his commanders, since his rhetorical question showed that he doubted their courage and their will to fulfil their duties to the end. All the officers present remained silent, since as soldiers we knew that it was not permitted to interrupt an address by a superior. However, I resented Hitler's insult to such a degree that the blood rushed to my head. When Hitler repeated his words, I interrupted him: 'This will indeed be so, *Mein Führer*.'
>
> My words were certainly not a testimony of my personal attitude towards the regime or towards Hitler himself. They would simply show him that we were not prepared to have such a moral challenge thrown in our faces. My comrades who were present, told me afterwards that they had breathed a sigh of relief, since they had also felt the insult in Hitler's words. Hitler had never experienced an interruption of an address by him, as Head of State and as Supreme Commander of the armed forces. The times when he had to face cat-calls at political meetings had long gone. He was obviously put off. I was sitting close to him, and he replied with an ice-cold look in his eyes: 'Thank you, *Feldmarschall* von Manstein.' He then finished his speech in an abrupt manner.
>
> While I was having tea with Zeitzler, I was called to the phone and told that Hitler wanted to see me in Keitel's presence. He received me with the words: '*Herr Feldmarschall*, I will not stand for your interruption when I am addressing the generals. You would likewise not accept this on the part of your subordinates.' Of course, there was nothing I could reply to this and I simply acknowledged his remark. But, because he was angry,

---

81 Below, p.359

he went too far. He continued: 'A few days ago you sent me a report about the situation of your Army Group. You obviously had the purpose to vindicate yourself in future history by entering it in your war diary.' This was the last straw. I replied: 'Copies of my personal letters to you are never put into the war diary. They are transmitted through courier by my Chief-of-Staff. Please excuse me if I now use an English expression: 'I am a gentleman'. Short silence and then: 'Thank you very much.' During our meeting in the evening, Hitler treated me with benevolence. However, it was obvious that he would not forget the incident, but I had other worries than to think about his personal feelings for me.[82]

Accounts from other officers present are different. After mentioning the interruption, Colonel von Below wrote:

Hitler replied: 'This is really good, *Feldmarschall* von Manstein. If it will indeed be so, we cannot lose the war. I am happy to hear your words.' Manstein may perhaps have felt that he had been insulted, however that was not my impression at that time. I felt that he simply expressed his honest opinion. Hitler's address continued for half an hour and ended with the words: 'I have no greater desire than to abide by the law of nature, that only he is rewarded with life who fights for it, and is prepared to put it at stake.'[83]

Professor Percy Schramm, who wrote the diary of *OKW*, was also present, and told Knopp that Manstein's intervention was hardly noticed. Manstein was seated close to Hitler, most of the officers present only heard a humming.[84]

General Heusinger viewed Manstein's interruption with undisguised contempt, therefore he decided not to hide it from his subordinates. On the day following the incident, he wrote to his wife:

Manstein is simply a 'small' man. Now I have another example of his eagerness to stick to his position, which leads him to betray himself. There was no necessity for Manstein to make such a declaration of faith since he knew quite well that Hitler did not view him with benevolence. Once again I am disappointed. Manly pride when standing before kings' thrones has become rare. There were times when this was considered to be natural. Today one notices more and more how such virtues have receded.[85]

An entry in Schmundt's diary, on 27 January, is evidence that Hitler took a serious view of the incident:

At the end of a meeting of the NS-leadership, the *Führer* delivered a most seriously worded address to the *Feldmarschalls* and Generals of all three *Wehrmacht* commands. During his speech, *Feldmarschall* von Manstein made an interruption. Given this interruption and the tensions in the

---

82   Ibid., p. 580 f
83   Below, p. 360
84   Knopp, p. 216
85   Meyer, Heusinger, p. 256

recent past, a relief of *Feldmarschall* von Manstein is again under consideration.[86]

The end was inevitable. Manstein had run his course. In 1942, he was looked upon as irreplaceable. In 1944, this was no longer the case. After Hitler dismissed Manstein, the two would never meet again.

---

86   *Tätigkeitsbericht des Chefs des Personalamtes General der Infanterie Rudolf Schmundt, fortgeführt von General der Infanterie Wilhelm Burgdorf, 1.10. 1942– 29.10.1944*, herausgegeben von Dermot Bradley und Richard Schulze-Kossens, Osnabrück, 1984, p. 126

Chapter 2
The Battle for France 1940

Blitzkrieg Legend

The rout of the French Army, in 1940, was accomplished in less than six weeks. It created the term *Blitzkrieg*, that was then used, world-wide, without translation. By 25 September 1939, it had already appeared in English, in an article on the war in Poland in TIME magazine: "This was no war of occupation, but a war of quick obliteration – *Blitzkrieg* … "

However, the Polish campaign cannot be called a *Blitzkrieg*, perhaps not even a war. The die was cast before the first German soldier stepped across the Polish border. Poland was surrounded by two hostile powers, Germany and the Soviet Union. The Polish Army was weak, its equipment was antiquated. On several occasions the Polish cavalry attacked German *Panzer* with spears and swords.

(The term 'tank' does not exist in German military terminology, a German tank is a *Panzer*. The term *Panzer* covers all armoured vehicles, even those which were not tanks. Since there will be numerous references in this book to *Panzer* divisions, *Panzer* corps and *Panzer* armies, the term *Panzer* will be used throughout, to permit an exact understanding of German documents.)

The battle for France turned into a *Blitzkrieg* without it having been planned as such. Even Manstein's operational plan, which was adopted, did not foresee a total collapse of France in a few weeks. Its main element was to attack the much stronger French Army at a location where it was hoped that they would not expect the Germans to place the *Schwerpunkt*, ie the centre of gravity, in the main area of their offensive. By achieving a decisive breakthrough, they hoped to reduce the strength of the French Army to a state where it could no longer threaten the Germans. Churchill gave the German plan the German name *Sichelschnitt*, because its implementation had the appearance of a scythe cutting through the centre of a field of wheat. German military terminology did not use this expression during the war. The only German campaign that was planned as a *Blitzkrieg* was the attack on Russia, and it turned into the opposite.

In 1996 the German historian, Colonel Karl-Heinz Frieser, wrote probably the final book in the series about the campaign for France, to which he gave the title *Blitzkriegs – Legende*, ie 'The legend of the *Blitzkrieg*'.[1] Frieser's book is part of the series that continues to be published by the *Militärgeschichtliches Forschungsamt* –MGFA, in Potsdam (German institute for military history research) on the history of World War II.

Most comprehensive books on the battle for France were written by British and American authors. There were fewer by French writers who tended to concentrate on French politics during the immediate pre-war years and in the months of the campaign. Relatively little was written by German historians. Most of those

---

1   K-H. Frieser, *Blitzkriegs – Legende, Der Westfeldzug 1940*, Munich, 1996, (henceforth Frieser)

books were brought to the market during the twenty years following the end of the Second World War and reflect the purported superiority in numbers of German equipment. Memoirs by German and French generals are limited to their personal experiences during the campaign, without attempting any global analysis.

The renowned British military historian, John Fuller, wrote in his analysis of the campaign in the West:

> *Blitzkrieg* consists in turning mobility into a psychological weapon. Not in order to kill, but to create confusion and stupefaction at the front, and shock, uncertainty and chaos in the rear. Rumours will get wilder by the day and finally create panic.[2]

Even many years after the war, military historians in many countries wrote about a purported German superiority in troops and equipment. On 16 May 1940 Churchill asked the French commander in chief, General Gamelin, when and where he intended to attack the German 'bulge'. In the first French communiqués, the German breakthrough was described as a 'bulge' that had to be sealed off. With a hopeless shrug, Gamelin replied that this was impossible because of French inferiority in number of troops, equipment and methods. Only the last point mentioned by Gamelin was correct. In numbers of troops and divisions the Allies enjoyed superiority.

Prelude

In 1930, General Debeney, Chief of the French General Staff, wrote in an article for a military journal that

> France might well be invaded once more. The French Army could again be compelled to retreat to the Marne, as it had done in 1914, and perhaps even to the Seine. War would again be fought on French soil. This should be no cause for concern, since France had been victorious in 1918.

The same year, shortly before his death, Georges Clemenceau published his recollections of the years 1917 and 1918 when he was Prime Minister. Marshal Foch had during his last years had a series of talks with the journalist Raymond Recouly, who published his notes after the Marshal had died. Part of the book contained 'poisoned darts' against Clemenceau, to which Clemenceau replied in his own book. One paragraph reads like a prophecy: "Risks? Yes, there are always risks and there will always be risks. Perhaps we will receive help at the right moment. Perhaps not, who can foresee it? France will have the fate her citizens deserve." (*La France sera ce que les Français ont mérité.*)[3] A number of chapters in Clemenceau's book show that the '*père de la victoire 1918*' was aware of the impending doom.

From the day Britain and France declared war, on 3 September 1939, until the German attack on 10 May 1940, the campaign in the West was a mutual 'comedy of errors.' Both sides grossly overestimated each other. The German command was frozen in its memory of the First World War when the French Army had shown

2   J. Fuller, *Die entartete Kunst Krieg zu führen 1789-1961*, Cologne 1964, p. 282
3   G. Clemenceau, *Grandeurs et Misères d'une Victoire*, Paris, 1930

itself the equal of the German. A similar respect was accorded to the French high command. During the Paris world exhibition in 1937, General Beck, Chief of the German *Generalstab*, paid a visit to Paris and met with the Commander in Chief of the French Army, General Gamelin. Gamelin made a strong impression on him. Beck was an intellectual general and an intellectual like Gamelin, who had great gifts of expressing himself, would certainly have impressed a highly educated interlocutor.

Two totally contradictory versions remain of the conversation between the two generals. In his memoirs, Gamelin wrote that Beck told him: "When all is taken into account, we could be the masters of the universe, if the French and German Armies would unite."

Gamelin purports to have answered: "But we have no such ambition. We don't want anything which belongs to others. I was tempted to add, and what will be our respective fate? Undoubtedly, we would only play a secondary part to you."

He quotes Beck as having replied: "Belgium is an anomaly. The French speaking provinces are really part of France, the Dutch speaking parts belong to the German sphere. The existence of smaller nations stands in contradiction to modern civilization which calls for greater unions."

Gamelin then indulged in self-reflections and questioned the background of Beck's supposed statements:

> Once again, one meets the German aspiration of a sovereign ruler of the universe. Either they would use us for the purpose of later ruling us, or we would agree to be the junior partner, and not cast our shadow on the *Reich*.[4]

General Dr Speidel, who at that time was a major, and deputy to the German military *attaché* in Paris, *Generalleutnant* Kühlenthal, strongly contradicted that account:

> I was present at all the meetings between the two generals. The sentence, 'United we would be the masters of the universe,' was never uttered. Neither its content nor its language reflects Beck's style. I can recall a statement by him to Gamelin, that peace in Europe, and beyond it in the world, could be secured if Germany and France were to bury their old quarrels and thus have their Armies act together as a bronze rock, ie *rocher de bronze*, for preserving peace. Gamelin's purported reply did not take place in my presence. I know nothing of a conversation about Belgium. At that time, General Beck already thought as a European, and considered local nationalism as a thing of the past. All our French discussion partners, among them Marshal Pétain, said to me that General Beck was in no respect a representative of a militaristic Germany thirsting for revenge, rather he was the embodiment of the best German tradition.[5]

---

4   M. Gamelin, *Servir*, Paris, 1947, 3 volumes, vol. 2, p. 283 ff, henceforth: Gamelin. All further quotations come from vol. 3.

5   W.Foerster, *Generaloberst Ludwig Beck, sein Kampf gegen den Krieg*, Munich 1952, p.66 (henceforth Foerster)

There is little reason to doubt Speidel's account. General Beck's thoughts were always distanced from any idea of German dominance, whereas Gamelin's memoirs are full of inventions and factual distortions with which he attempts to explain his ultimate failure.

One is entitled to express some amazement as to how the decay of the French State, and the deterioration of the French Army, took place in broad daylight, yet remained unnoticed by the Germans. German military *attachés* in Paris were guests at all French Army exercises. They could at least have noticed that the French doctrine had remained static, and that the troops were of poor quality. When Germany was already at war with France, the French were still receiving enlightening reports from friendly nations such as Italy, Spain, and Japan. Even if this had escaped their attention, the behaviour of the French Army during the 'phoney war' of the first eight months of the war, should have shown the German Command that they faced an opponent that was defeated in advance.

Yet strangely, the commander in chief of Army Group C, *Generaloberst* Ritter von Leeb, addressed a memorandum in September 1939 to the Army's Commander in Chief, *Generaloberst* von Brauchitsch: "I consider it impossible at this time, to vanquish Britain, France and Belgium in a military way."[6]

That statement is the more surprising since it was Leeb's Army Group that had remained in the West during the Polish campaign. It had encountered the absurd French 'offensive' in the Sarre region in September of 1939. Leeb was obviously aware of the friendly encounters between German and French soldiers in no-man's-land, and the mutual waving at each other over the Rhine.

Meticulous post-war research by the Dutch historian, Louis de Jong, established that the purported 'fifth column', to which some French historians ascribed a decisive part in the defeat of France, never existed.[7] Like any nation at war, Germany had some agents in enemy territory and they were well aware of French troop movements. Whenever a French regiment was relieved on the front, the French speaker at Radio Stuttgart, Paul Ferdonnet, broadcast German greetings to the newly arrived soldiers and always gave the number of their regiments. Ferdonnet was a *Nazi* sympathiser, who had fled to Germany before the outbreak of the war. After the war, the French executed Ferdonnet whom they had labelled the 'Stuttgart traitor'.

One can mention further statements by German generals. Again Ritter v. Leeb: "Surprise is impossible. We will suffer heavy casualties and still the French will not be vanquished. An offensive against France cannot be conducted like the attack on Poland, it will take much longer and lead to heavy losses."

General von Sodenstern, Manstein's successor at Army Group A: "With all consideration given to our successful armoured operations in Poland, we have to admit that they can hardly be employed in such a manner against the fortifications in the West."[8]

On 29 September, while the absurd French 'offensive' in the Sarre was in progress, General Halder noted in his diary: "Polish methods are not a recipe for the West and cannot be put to use against an Army protected by fortifications."

---

6   W. Ritter von Leeb, *Tagebuchaufzeichnungen*, Diaries, p. 184 f
7   L. de Jong, *Die deutsche fünfte Kolonne im Zweiten Weltkrieg*, Stuttgart 1959
8   BA – MA, RH 19 I/38, p. 310

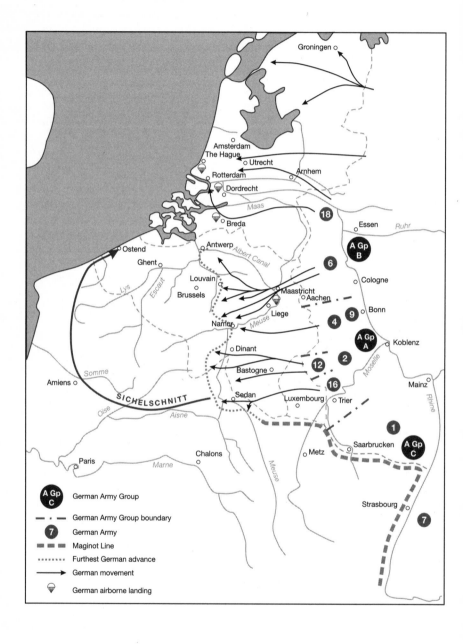

The German Invasion of the Low Countries May 1940 (substantially embodying the *Sichelschnitt* plan drawn up by von Manstein).

In a memorandum of September 1939, General Carl-Heinrich von Stülpnagel, at that time *Oberquartiermeister* I, wrote: "The *Wehrmacht* is not armed for a campaign against fortifications. One cannot think of a successful offensive earlier than spring 1942."[9] All those statements could well have been taken from a French Army manual.

Frieser believes that, given the German inferiority, it was lucky for the *Wehrmacht* that the attack was postponed until 10 May 1940. I hold the contrary opinion. I am convinced that, given the state of the French Army and the frame of mind of the population, an attack at the time Hitler wanted, ie early winter, would likewise have achieved rapid and complete success. In this view I am supported by competent authorities.

The British General Brooke commanded a Corps in France, and later became the British Army's Chief-of-Staff. When questioned by his biographer Bryant after the war, he stated that only the harshness of the winter prevented Hitler from attacking in the winter of 1939.

The *Wehrmacht* would have reached the channel coast five months earlier, at a time when we were still short of 20 Royal Air Force squadrons. Even now, after the final victory, I still tremble at the thought as to what would have happened if Hitler had attacked in winter.

Arthur Bryant also recalled a conversation with General Gort, who commanded the British Expeditionary Force in France, the BEF. He met him in January 1945, after the Battle of the Bulge, and asked him if his force and the French would have been able to put up more resistance if the Germans had attacked in November 1939. He received the reply: "Much less."[10]

The French General Menu thought,

our units were scarcely better in May 1940 than in September 1939. Some would even say, with sadness in their heart, that they were worse. In 1914, during the first months of the war, General Joffre dismissed 47 Generals. How many Generals did our 1940 Commander in Chief relieve from their post for inefficiency during the phoney war?[11]

The Germans overestimated the French strength, and the French likewise erred in their assessment of the Germans. Gamelin was simply awestruck by the 'Siegfried' fortifications which he considered to be the equal of the French Maginot Line. (The 'Siegfried Line' was the Allied term for the German fortifications in the West, the German term was *Westwall*). Senior German commanders had deprecated the German fortifications. However, by 1938, *Generaloberst* Adam had already been relieved from his command in the West, after he told Hitler face to face that the line was not worth the concrete poured into it. After the initial reverses, Gamelin estimated there were 7,000 German *Panzer*, but later corrected that figure in his memoirs. Daladier knew the exact German figures in 1940 and

---

9   War diary *OKW*, vol.I/2, p. 950

10   A.Bryant, *The Turn of the Tide, A Study based on the Diaries and Autobiographical Notes of Feldmarschall the Viscount Alanbrooke*, London 1957, p.66 (henceforth Bryant)

11   A.Goutard, *The Battle of France 1940*, London 1958, p.85 (henceforth Goutard)

required a correction, but Gamelin said to him: "Better let it stay, perhaps we will need it for an alibi."[12]

The commander in chief of the French air force, General Vuillemin returned from a visit to Berlin literally reeling. Göring had treated him to a red carpet welcome and staged a 'bluff' with a *Luftwaffe* display, by simply turning the same squadrons around and returning them, once they were out of sight. In his report after his visit, Vuillemin stated that the French air force could at best resist for a few days.

Gamelin was convinced that whoever attacked first, would certainly be defeated: "Whoever will first come out of his 'snail-shell' will certainly be crushed." In February 1940, Gamelin said to a guest that he would be happy to make the Germans a gift of one billion francs, if they would do him the favour of attacking.[13] In his memoirs, de Gaulle recalled a conversation with Léon Blum in January 1939. Blum had asked him about his forecast, and he had replied that the Germans would either attack Russia in the East, or France in the West. Blum had replied that this was unthinkable. In the East, they would drown in the spaces of Russia, in the West they would be broken by the Maginot Line.

When the war had already started, de Gaulle talked to the President of the French Republic, Albert Lebrun, who told him that he was aware of his ideas, but that it was far too late to implement them. De Gaulle had been a proponent of armoured divisions, and of an offensive push with tanks.[14] On 10 May, the controller general of the French Army, Pierre Jacomet, told a friend:

If you had been with me when I saw the broad smile on General Gamelin's face this morning, as he showed me the direction of the German attack, you would sleep soundly to-night. The Germans have provided him with the opportunity he had hoped for.[15]

Spears felt that Gamelin and Georges should be happy since the Germans had done what he had expected.[16]

Against that background of opinions and ideas, one can understand Gamelin's joyful mood, when he heard of the German attack on 10 May 1940. General Beaufre, who was a junior officer of his staff, and who would later become a renowned military historian, recalled that Gamelin was strolling martially across his room, humming a song. Now 'his battle' had started and the Germans had walked into his trap. He would now successfully carry out his 'Dyle river plan.' Beaufre added that he had never seen him so happy.[17] It took Gamelin only a few days to realise that the Germans had not walked into his trap, but that he had fallen into theirs. Colonel Minart visited him at his headquarters on 16 May: "The winds

---

12   Ibid. p. 35
13   *Ciano Diaries 1939–1943*, H. Gibson (ed) New York 1946, p.201
14   C. de Gaulle, *Mémoires de Guerre,*vol. 1, *L'appel*, Paris, 1954, p. 23, (henceforth: de Gaulle)
15   Frieser, p.110 and Horne, *To lose a battle – France 1940*, Boston 1969, p. 70(henceforth Horne)
16   E. Spears, *Assignment to Catastrophe*, London 1957, p. 137 (henceforth Spears)
17   General Beaufre, *Mémoires 1920 – 1940 – 1945*, Paris, 1965, p. 209, (henceforth: Beaufre)

of panic were blowing through Gamelin's headquarters. The Commander in Chief walked sadly around. No one dared to approach him. Everyone knew that the battle was lost."[18]

German and Allied forces on 10 May 1940

Frieser is the only author who, through meticulous research, has succeeded in presenting the exact figures for the opposing armies.

By the end of the campaign in Poland, shortage of ammunition brought the *Wehrmacht* close to a debacle. Only one third of its divisions were left with any ammunition, and that would last for two weeks at the utmost. Production of steel was short of a monthly 600,000 tons. The *Luftwaffe* stock of bombs was sufficient for only two weeks. However, a rapid increase of production turned the *Wehrmacht* into operational strength in 1940.

Soldiers in total:
* *Wehrmacht,* including Army, Air Force, Navy and *Ersatzheer* (central reserve army): 5.4 million men, of which 3 million available in the West.
* France: 5.5 million men, of which 2,240,000 on the Northeastern front.
* British troops already in France (BEF) and including the ones in the process of being shipped: 500,000 men.
* Belgium: 650,000 men and the Netherlands 400,000 men.
* Thus 3 million Germans opposed to 4 million Allied soldiers.

Artillery:
* *Wehrmacht:* 7,378 guns of all calibre
* France: 10,700 guns; BEF: 1,280
* Belgium: 1,338; and Netherlands: 656

Thus a two to one Allied superiority.

Panzer:
* *Wehrmacht:* 2,439
* France on the front facing the Germans 3,254 out of a total 4,111. The quality of the French SOMUA and Char B tanks was superior to all German *Panzer.* However, they were not equipped with radio communication equipment.
* BEF: Already in France 320, and a further 330 ready for shipment.
* Belgium: 270 and the Netherlands: 40.

Thus 4,204 Allied tanks opposing 2,439 German *Panzer.* Most of the German *Panzer* were of the models *Pz 1* and *Pz 2.* Neither can be called *Panzer,* they were simply lightly armoured vehicles equipped with two machine-guns (*Pz 1*) or a small artillery gun (*Pz 2*). German *Panzer* officers called the *Pz 1* a 'tin.'

Air Force:
General Vuillemin was still under the shock of his visit to Berlin. After the war, he stated that he faced a German superiority of 5:1 in the air. He failed to mention

---

18   J. Minart, *P.C. Vincennes, secteur 4,* Paris 1945, vol. 2, p. 163

that the majority of the French planes never took to the air while, at the same time, the French were increasingly imploring the British to send more Royal Air Force fighters to France. Nor did he reveal that a large number of French planes were located without damage after the armistice. A control commission, established immediately after the armistice, found 4,268 undamaged planes in un-occupied France and a further 1,800 in French North Africa.

- The *Luftwaffe* had 2,598 planes ready for action on 10 May 1940.
- The French Air Force numbered a total of 5,026 planes, of which only 879 were ready for action.
- The Royal Air Force had 384 planes in France.
- The Belgians had 118 and the Dutch 72 planes ready for action.

In terms of planes ready for combat, the *Luftwaffe* thus enjoyed superiority. The German fighter plane Me 109 was superior to the French Morane and Potez 63, the later French models Bloch 152, and Dewoitine 520, were equal to the Me 109, as was the Curtis Hawk purchased in the USA. In the Royal Air Force, the Hurricane was the equal of the Me 109. The Spitfire was perhaps superior. The German Air Force had neglected the production of bombers and had no long distance bomber planes. The most efficient German bomber was the somewhat primitive dive bomber *Stuka Ju 87*. It was often unable to hit located targets, but it was fitted with sirens which were switched on while diving and which caused a panic among French soldiers, many of whom simply fled when they heard the noise and shouted to their comrades: "The *boches* are coming. Bolt!" Often the Germans were not even close. The successes of individual German fighter aces during the war created the myth of superior German pilots. In reality most of them did not come up to the average standards of their French and British counterparts. During the ten weeks preceding the outbreak of the war, 281 German pilots crashed to their death, an additional 287 were severely wounded.

Frieser limits himself to statistics that are now fully recognised, but he does not examine the defects of some individual French arms. Beaufre emphasises that the light machine-gun, the *Fusil-Mitrailleur* 1924, was delivered first in 1926 in small numbers and that its quantity had only first become adequate in 1932. Its ammunition was not ready before 1936. The heavy machine-gun dated from 1916. It was so heavy that its transport was very cumbersome in troop movement. Most front line soldiers were equipped with the rifle 07/15, created in 1907 and modernised in 1915. Only a few troops had the 1937 rifle. On paper the French Army had four motorized divisions, but when the war began, none was yet ready for combat. On 10 May 1940 only the first division could be put into action. However, in accordance with French manuals, its tanks were distributed in small packages to infantry battalions. The only real armoured division during the French campaign was the small fourth under de Gaulle, which was put into action in May 1940.

A comparison between manpower strength of the French and the German Armies is not sufficient, if only figures are taken into account. 80% of all French soldiers, and 100,000 of 128,000 officers, belonged to the reserve. In the B divisions of the second tier, the average age of soldiers was 35. Officers and non-coms often skipped the routine exercises that were of short duration, and went without any instruction in modern equipment technology, or in unit combat. While the *Wehrmacht* had fewer troops, many of its soldiers had been trained in 1935 and the years thereafter.

Some of Frieser's conclusions can also be questioned. While he is critical of the French military command, he takes small account of the political decay which was its main cause. He blames neither French society nor the common French soldier. He believes the French high command was the sole cause of the French failure. Beaufre contradicted the version of the Vichy government, which was established after the armistice, that the Parliament was to blame for such shortcomings.:

> Parliament had agreed to every demand for defence funds. The cause for the insufficiencies was our paralysis, our inability to get things done. This concerns not only the Army. We are an old nation with tradition going back to the horse and the 'goose quill'. We have never been able to adapt ourselves to changing circumstances.[19]

The German plan

Any description of the first German plans must take into account that the *Wehrmacht* did not intend to launch a major offensive in the West. Thus the first plan, 'Yellow', was developed on 15 October 1939, after Hitler had already insisted on attacking in the West in autumn, against his commanders' advice. The American historian, Brigadier General Telford Taylor who headed the US prosecution team during the trial of the major *Nazi* war criminals at Nuremberg after the war, emphasizes that *OKH* never intended to submit a plan for victory that it considered to be impossible.

> Military plans are not composed for the intrinsic beauty of their pattern, like a Bach fugue, they are shaped to achieve specific objectives. It is especially important to bear this in mind when analysing the original German plan of attack in the West. Only in this way can one understand the much criticized limitations of the plan that the highly competent staff of *OKH* produced in October 1939.[20]

The thoughts behind the first 'Yellow' plan did not go in the direction of an offensive, their main objective was to prevent it. Many compared 'Yellow' to the German 'Schlieffen Plan' of 1914, because it also called for a march through Belgium with the possible addition of the Netherlands. But there the comparison ends. The Schlieffen Plan aimed at total victory over France, while 'Yellow' only attempted to advance to the Channel coast. Some German commanders also saw 'Yellow' as a repeat of the Schlieffen plan. General Guderian wrote that it was simply a repetition of a former plan, with the advantage of simplicity, and the disadvantage of lack of novelty.[21] Generals Blumentritt and Westphal advanced similar opinions.

---

19   Ibid., p. 79
20   T. Taylor, *The March of Conquest – The German Victory in the West 1940*, London, 1959, p. 17
21   H.Guderian, *Erinnerungen eines Soldaten*, Wels 1951, p. 89 (henceforth Guderian)

Taylor criticizes other foreign historians, among them Liddell Hart, Bullock and Wilmot, for advancing similar views. He emphasizes that Hitler himself had given the original order to advance to the Channel and therefore the first versions of 'Yellow' were to conform to his directives. When the first draft for 'Yellow' was presented to him, Hitler was dissatisfied and on 29 October, Brauchitsch submitted a second version. There was little difference between the two plans and the advance to the Channel coast remained the aim. Hitler was again dissatisfied. The element of surprise was lacking and on 30 October, he mentioned the Sedan for the first time.

Contrary to his traditional-minded generals, Hitler never wavered in his conviction that the France of 1939 was unable to put up the resistance of the First World War. However, he had not yet a new operational plan at his disposal, and he may have recalled the French disaster at Sedan in 1870. The French parliamentarian Taittinger, who visited the Sedan area and its defences, shortly before the beginning of the German offensive, stated in his report that there are names which have a sound of doom for our Army. (*Il semble qu'il y ait des terres de malheurs pour nos armes.*)[22]

On 21 October 1939, Manstein, on his way to Rundstedt's Army Group A headquarters at Koblenz, stopped at *OKH* headquarters at Zossen. He received a copy of the first version of 'Yellow', and noted in his diary: "Accompanying 'music' by Halder, Stülpnagel and Greiffenberg rather depressing." Stülpnagel was *Oberquartiermeister* I and Greiffenberg was an officer in the *Quartiermeister* I department. He would later become a *General der Infanterie.*[23] He was also dissatisfied with the second version. After arriving at Koblenz, he laid out his his ideas about *Sichelschnitt* to Rundstedt

Rundstedt agreed, and on 31 October forwarded Manstein's ideas to Brauchitsch under his signature. Since Halder knew that the idea had been developed by his opposite, Manstein, he discarded it. On 1 November he simply wrote in his diary that it contained no positive ideas. He apparently did not transmit Rundstedt's letter to Brauchitsch. The war diary of *OKW*, which was meticulously kept by Jodl, shows no mention of such a transmission. Halder wrote in his diary that it might be more circumspect not to communicate Rundstedt's letter to *OKW*. The rivalry between *OKW* and *OKH*, which later became the plague of the German command structure, had already begun. Taylor claimed that Brauchitsch had maintained his original idea to advance to the Channel and from this perspective 'Yellow' had been preferable since it covered a shorter distance.

On 5 November, Hitler and Brauchitsch met in Berlin. As usual, their conversation was unsatisfactory. Brauchitsch, in his effort to oppose an offensive in France had told Hitler that the German troops in Poland had shown themselves not totally reliable. Since Hitler saw the *Wehrmacht* as 'his army', he flew into an uncontrollable rage and shouted at Brauchitsch and Halder that he would crush the 'spirit of Zossen.' As often after encounters with Hitler, Brauchitsch returned a broken man to *OKH*. On 28 November, Hitler reverted to the idea of Sedan and talked about a *Panzer* attack against Sedan through Arlon and Trintigny. At *OKW*, Jodl noted in his diary that the "Führer has a new idea, to attack Sedan with a

---

22   Frieser, p. 178
23   *Verlorene Siege*, p.67 f and 90

Panzer division and support this with a motorized division through Arlon." That was Hitler's first intervention on division level. As of that day, the irritated *OKH* added a prefix to every directive to Army Groups, "The *Führer* has now decided."

As a first step, the staff of Guderian's motorized XIX Corps was now transferred to Army Group A. Rundstedt simply transmitted Manstein's ideas and they began to gain support. Guderian was strongly in their favour. On 31 November, Brauchitsch and Halder visited Army Group A. Manstein submitted a memorandum requesting that an additional Army be transferred from Bock's Army Group B to Army Group A. In his memoirs, Manstein wrote that his memorandum to General Schundt had been forwarded by General Blumentritt. But he did not know if Schmundt had passed it on to Hitler and Jodl.[24] When Manstein met Hitler for the first time, after being relieved as Rundstedt's chief-of-staff, and appointed a Corps Commander. Hitler gave no indication of having received Manstein's memorandum, or the previous communications from Army Group A. However, Rundstedt and Manstein then believed that they were on the way to obtaining Hitler's consent, and so they wrote a new series of memoranda. On 30 November, Rundstedt again requested an additional army. On 6 December, Manstein wrote a long letter to Halder with a summary of all his ideas. Halder did not react. On 22 December, another meeting between Brauchitsch and Rundstedt produced no results.

After his relief as Rundstedt's chief-of-staff, Manstein, together with the other newly appointed corps commanders, was received by Hitler on 17 February 1940. Tresckow had arranged with Schmundt for a conversation between Hitler and Manstein. Schmundt immediately agreed. Tresckow had shown him Manstein's memoranda and Schmundt saw that they were in line with Hitler's thoughts. At personal meetings, Hitler would usually engage in monologues without allowing his visitor to speak. This time he remained silent and listened to Manstein's arguments with attention. Manstein gave Hitler a detailed description of his plan. A war-game, which took place between 7 February and 17 February had already shown that Manstein's ideas were sound.

On 18 February, Halder, finally relieved of his 'troublemaker' Manstein, made an immediate turn around and proposed his own plan, which followed Manstein's guidelines but went even further in some of their conclusions. To be fair to Halder, one must recall that he was faced with a dilemma that could have broken stronger men. As chief of the *Generalstab*, he was duty bound to develop the best possible plan for German victory. However, in 1938, he had headed a conspiracy of generals who intended to arrest Hitler, and possibly kill him if Hitler decided on war during the Czech crisis. Halder's plan had been meticulously prepared but came to naught, after Britain and France signed the Munich agreement.

It then became Halder's turn to encounter opposition at *OKH*. *Generaloberst* von Bock, unhappy with the reduction in size of his Army Group, told Halder that he was playing *va-banque*. Undoubtedly the final plan contained many *va-banque* elements. Halder replied:

---

24   *Verlorene Siege*, p. 108

Others already label me the grave-digger of the German *Panzer* arm. Even so! If this plan had only 10% chances of success, I will remain with it. Only this operation can lead to an annihilation of the enemy, unlike the old Schlieffen plan, that mainly pushed the enemy backwards! I firmly believe in this plan.[25]

As often happens after a successful campaign every participant claims that he was the determining factor. After the French Marshal Joffre had won the battle of the Marne, in 1914, he is reported to have said: "I don't know who won the battle, but I know who would have lost it." In 1940, after France had collapsed, Hitler said: "Manstein was the only general who understood me."[26] In his 'victory' speech to the *Reichstag* on 19 July, which named twelve new *Feldmarschalls*, Hitler declared that putting the *Schwerpunkt* on the left wing was his sole idea. Halder would also claim that he was the decisive factor. Manstein's voice was clearly audible. On 20 June, General Heusinger wrote to his wife: "From far away, Manstein is heard to proclaim that the authorship of the plan was solely his work. In reality, the plan was not the creation of a single brain, but the result of months of work at Zossen."[27]

Any objective assessment has to recognise that Manstein was the dominating factor. He was the first to put the new idea on the table and to develop it in every detail with his outstanding ability as a *Generalstab* officer. Conceivably it was his greatest achievement of the war. Historians, who label *Sichelschnitt* the 'Manstein Plan' are unquestionably correct. Curiously his plan rested on an illusion. In their overestimation of the French army, Manstein's thoughts did not differ from his comrades. But while these wrote endless memoranda about the impossibility of a successful attack, Manstein understood that only a totally new concept with an element of *va-banque* could bring success against an opponent, purported to be stronger. The *va-banque* element was that logic had to demand that the French expect an attack through the Ardennes, since the Germans had successfully attacked there in 1914. But in the years between the two wars, the notion *Les Ardennes sont impétrables*, the Ardennes are immune to penetration, turned into a firm belief. When a stronger Army is defeated in war, the loser is always showered with blame for having misunderstood the enemy's intention. But out of fairness to the French high command, it must be recalled that the senior German generals likewise failed to understand Manstein's thoughts. Only a decision by Hitler caused it to be adopted.

Thus, after months of discussions among senior commanders, between *OKH* and Army Group A, repeated postponements of the attack, and the 'relief' of a number of commanders, the final plan was adopted and quickly led to complete victory. Still, the question remains, were all those exercises really necessary? The following *excursus* attempts to provide an answer.

---

25   Heusinger, Befehl, p. 86
26   Knopp, p.181
27   Meyer Heusinger, p. 133

Excursus: The gradual deterioration of the Third Republic until the beginning of the World War I

Napoleon: "A great disaster always points to great culprits"

The Third Republic was born under an unhappy star. It became the official form of the French State through mere coincidence. After the defeat of 1870–71 and the abdication of Napoleon III, the state was given the provisional name of Republic, but the term was not anchored in a constitution. The constituent assembly had a monarchist majority, divided into three hostile groups. 1. Legitimists, who advocated a return of the Bourbons. 2. Orléanists, who had remained faithful to the house of Orléans. and 3. Bonapartists, who dreamt of a restoration of the Napoleonic empire. During one session, when temperaments clashed, the word *République* entered, unobserved, into a constitutional draft that was adopted and finalised in 1875. The Republic thus became the official form of the new state, simply through lack of attention by the majority in the constituent assembly.

During the years that followed, the Republic was no longer questioned. The monarchist groups quickly dwindled and were concentrated in the *Action Française* of Charles Maurras, which rose to new activities in Vichy France. A 'personality' was considered a Republican if his opinions leaned to the Left, if he advocated total freedom of opinion and speech, if he was basically anti-clerical, and if he had relations with freemasonry which wielded political power in France until the beginning of World War II.

The Right, with strong bonds to the Catholic Church, was deemed anti-republican. The Catholic newspaper *La Croix* was its main publication. Opposition between Republicans and Anti-republicans increased when a number of financial scandals, among them the 'Panama Canal affair' could be traced to the Left. Alongside *La Croix,* a number of reactionary daily papers and weekly journals gained increasing influence. The politician Paul Déroulède and the writer Maurice Barrès became spokesmen for the Right. Virulent anti-Semitic articles appeared in Edouard Drumont's *La libre Parole.*

Tensions between the two camps reached their height in 1895, when Captain Dreyfus, a Jewish officer, was falsely accused of espionage and sentenced to deportation for life. The 'Dreyfus affair' split the nation into two camps, *Dreyfusards* and *Antidreyfusards* and the heated disputes continued until 1906, when Dreyfus was officially rehabilitated. His innocence had become apparent years earlier and the real traitor, Major Esterhazy had fled to Great Britain. Most of the officers were staunch *Antidreyfusards* and simply closed their eyes to the exculpating evidence which emerged step by step. Union between Republicans and Anti-republicans could only be found in patriotism, in the restoration of the French *Grandeur,* and in hatred of the perennial enemy Germany. There was also the craving for the return of Alsace – Lorraine. Until the Allied victory in World War I, the Strasbourg statue on the *Place de la Concorde* in Paris remained covered with a dark cloth.

The French Army traditionally kept its distance from political quarrels. In less than a century, the form of the state constantly changed. The First Republic, the Directoire, Bonaparte's Consulate were followed by Napoleon I's Empire. Then came the restoration of the traditional monarchy, the 'bourgeois monarchy' of Louis Philippe. The Second Republic of 1848 was transformed by its President, Louis Napoleon, into the Second Empire, and finally came the Third Republic. Like most armies world-wide, the French Army was strongly conservative, but it kept away from the daily political problems and strictly observed the rule of serving every legitimate government.

After the rehabilitation of Dreyfus, political turbulences began to penetrate the Army. The minister of war, General André, compiled lists which classified the senior officers according to their purported political views. When Foch was appointed director of the *Ecole de Guerre* in 1907, he felt compelled to tell Prime Minister Clemenceau that one of his brothers was a Jesuit. Clemenceau replied that he could not care less. Matters came to a head when General Joffre was appointed Commander in Chief in 1911. Originally General Pau had been the main candidate. The official reason given for the preference of Joffre was that Pau had demanded the right to select commanders of armies in wartime. This was the prerogative of the government. In reality, Pau was suspected of strong clerical tendencies, whereas Joffre was a Freemason. For the fate of France, during the First World War, the choice of Joffre would prove to have been a stroke of luck.

The structure of the French High Command

The structure would remain basically unchanged until the defeat of France in 1940. The supreme body was the *Conseil Supérieur de la Défense Nationale*, the Higher Council of National Defence, which later was renamed *Conseil de Guerre*, War Council. The *Conseil* consisted of 12 to 15 generals. The minister for war was its president, the general who was to be Commander in Chief of the Army in war-time was the vice president. The other members held written letters of appointment, *lettres de service*, to command armies or corps if war broke out. In the second volume of his recollections, General Weygand pointed out an incongruity.[28] In peacetime, the future Commander in Chief had authority only over his staff and the other members of the *Conseil*. Only the chief of the General Staff had the authority to issue orders to army units and to sign on behalf of the minister and in his name. Until the outbreak of the war, no orders were signed by the designated commander in chief. The chief of the General Staff saw the minister practically daily, the vice president only occasionally. Thus the French Army in peacetime had two commanders in chief. This situation came to an end in 1935 when the chief of the General Staff, General Gamelin became the vice president of the *Conseil* and both functions were combined. Gamelin was therefore invested with direct command authority which, however, he never exercised, neither before nor during the war.

---

28   M. Weygand, *Mirages et Réalités – Mémoires*, Paris, 1957, p. 366

Continued decline interrupted by victory in 1918

In 1914, the French Army went to war sustained by a wave of patriotism and enthusiasm, as did the Germans. Its official doctrine had been established in 1911 by Colonel de Grandmaison, under the heading *Offensive à Outrance*, total offensive. During the first weeks of the war, Joffre, who followed this principle with his plan XVII, attacked in Alsace, although the *Schlieffen* plan had been known to the French some years before 1914, through the treachery of a German officer. Joffre's biographer, Pierre Varillon, wrote that the plan was communicated to the French by a German officer under the pseudonym *Vengeur*, the avenger, who had been passed over for promotion and who sold the plan for 60,000 Francs to the French *Deuxième Bureau*, the intelligence division of the French Army.[29]

At the beginning, Joffre had no inkling of what was taking place in the north. Communications in 1914 were mainly carried out by carrier pigeons. Joffre was embroiled in battles around Mulhouse, with heavy casualties, while the German Army steamrollered through Belgium and northern France. The defeat at Charleroi on 21 August was the eye opener. Joffre immediately reacted. He broke off combats, except for small-scale rear actions, accomplished an orderly retreat, with the help of newly formed strategic reserves, and then launched the successful counter offensive on the Marne. In 1940, Gamelin could not act in the same manner, since he had totally neglected the creation of strategic reserves. Also the speed of the German advances did not permit orderly retreat.

When the trench war began with its increasing casualties, enthusiasm in France and Germany quickly waned. In 1916, General Nivelle had replaced Joffre as French commander in chief. In 1917 he launched his disastrous offensive. It failed completely and led to mutinies in a number of French divisions. Draconian measures and the careful command of Nivelle's successor, Pétain, succeeded in restoring discipline.

In 1918, France bathed in the glory of victory. The fact that it was mainly due to the Allies was forgotten. France had suffered the highest casualties of all nations who took part in the war. The battles of the Marne and Verdun were fought under French command and by French soldiers. Finally, Marshal Foch was made Allied supreme commander in 1918. But disenchantment soon arose, and the effectiveness, of both the Republic and the Army, was rapidly degraded.

The French governments between 1918 and 1938 remained moderate with a leaning towards the left. A purely left wing government arose with Léon Blum's Popular Front in 1938. The majority of the Paris daily press was strongly reactionary, as were weeklies like *Candide, Gringoire* and the extreme *Je suis partout* of Robert Brasillach. The tendency of these media was at first anti-communist. When Mussolini and later Hitler came to power, the press would express growing sympathy for their movements and policies. In 1934, the perfume magnate Coty had already published an article in his privately owned paper *L'ami du Peuple* under the heading 'Together with Hitler against *Bolshevism*.' When Léon Blum became Prime Minister, the slogan arose, 'rather Hitler than Blum'. The deputy, Xavier Vallat, later to become commissioner for Jewish affairs in the Vichy govern-

---

29   P.Varillon, *Joffre*, Paris 1956, p. 15

ment, made a speech in Parliament: "For the first time in the glorious history of France, this Gallic country is governed by a Jew."

New reactionary groups arose, which were not represented in Parliament, such as the *Croix de Feu* under Colonel de la Roque and the extreme anti-Semitic movement of Jacques Doriot. Doriot had begun his career as a communist deputy, later he changed sides. During the war he joined the French units of the *Waffen SS* and was killed in an air raid. The veterans of World War I, the *Anciens Combattants* belonged to a number of diffuse organisations without determined political programs, but they regularly engaged in street demonstrations, wearing *Basque* berets and displaying their war decorations. In 1934, when the Stavisky financial scandal broke loose, they attempted to storm Parliament. On 6 February 1934, the police opened fire on them and they suffered casualties. The most extreme reactionary group was the somewhat mysterious CSAR, aptly given the nickname *Cagoule*, the hoods, who carried out bomb attacks against buildings in Paris.

Its full membership was never disclosed. Senior Army officers, among them Marshal Franchet d'Esperey and General Dusseigneur, are known to have been members. Other names were also known, but Daladier refused to disclose them to prevent a further decline in the army's prestige. Today it is known that at least one member of the *Conseil*, General Dufieux, belonged to it. Recent literature shows that the future president of the Fifth Republic, François Mitterand, had some links to the *Cagoule*. In 1939, little if any respect remained for the government or for parliament. When the war broke out, the Third Republic rested on feet of clay. General André Beaufre wrote that "the currents of history have drawn us into the abyss".

The development of the French Army between 1918 and 1939

Three names dominate those years, Pétain, Weygand and Gamelin. After the end of World War II, Marshal Pétain became vice president of the *Conseil* and remained in this post until 1931. Thereafter he was an adviser until 1934. He was then aged 78. Why did the government choose Pétain and not Marshal Foch, who had been supreme Allied commander in 1918? Pétain was probably the better commander of the two. Until he was invested with supreme Allied command, Foch's operations had mostly resulted in failures. In 1916, he was dismissed and left out in the cold, until his appointment of supreme commander in March 1918. Pétain could look back on uninterrupted success. His preference for defensive warfare appealed to the French postwar mentality, Foch's adherence to *Offensive à Outrance* did not. Pétain was looked upon as being a reliable Republican. Foch had strongly clerical and reactionary views and showed little respect for the government. During the negotiations for the Treaty of Versailles, he came into an increasing conflict with Clemenceau and, more than once, harsh words were exchanged between the two.

Pétain's influence was a forerunner of the future doom. Even after he had been restricted to an advisory rule, he continued to dominate the principles of combat doctrine. Several older generals of the war were exempted from normal retirement age limits. During the years from 1918 to 1930, the retirement age of generals had been raised from 60 to 65, and was later increased even further to 70 years. A number of French Army commanders in 1940 had already led divisions during the First World War and remained with their conceptions of their previous commands. In 1939 the French high command gave the appearance of a group of 'Methusalems', Gamelin was 68, and Weygand was aged 72.

The French military doctrine can be summarised in a few words. Hold on to the experience of World War I, allow no further development, give no thought to a war of movement and motorization, and rely on an uninterrupted front line, *front continu*. In 1921, Pétain ordered the following paragraph to be deleted from the general Army manual:

> The offensive is the major action, only attack permits decisive results. A local defence is a temporary decision of the commander, who feels that he cannot attack a given objective at a given moment. As soon as conditions change, one has to revert to the offensive. Only attack can obtain a final success.

In 1938, General Chauvineau, one of the most respected teachers at the *Ecole de Guerre*, published a book: "Is an invasion still possible?"[30] He wrote that "a war of movement belongs to the past. Everything speaks against offensive actions. If an opponent tries to attack our front line, he will quickly get a 'bloody nose'. Tanks are useless, it goes without saying." In a previous article in the Infantry Review journal, General Chauvineau had already stated that no tank could advance beyond 1200 metres.

Pétain wrote the preface to General Chauvineau's book. It was unusually long, 17 pages. There was a suspicion that Pétain contributed more to the book than merely his preface. Some of Pétain's comments read:

> General Chauvineau's views reflect complete wisdom, *plein de sagesse* ... They are based on historical experience and a profound knowledge of the value of a defensive front ... Tanks are very expensive, and difficult to put into action. Doubtless our troops can repulse any enemy that would cross our borders.

In 1928, the government decided to construct the Maginot line which was completed in 1934. The public believed that it extended over the whole length of the border, but in reality, it ended in the vicinity of the Belgian border. There its fortifications were weak. The high command argued that one "could not offend the Belgians by erecting fortifications along their borders and, after all, the Belgian Army is our Maginot line." All of a sudden, the weak Belgian Army became an 'impregnable' fortress and the much stronger French Army required additional protection. While minister for war in the 1934 government of Paul Doumergue, Pétain had stated that this part of the French border presented no danger.

The concept of the Maginot line arose from the experience of the battle of Verdun in 1916. Had it been put to use correctly, its concept and structure, with large underground facilities and underground rail connections between the fortifications, would have fulfilled the expectations of its creators. The 'impregnable' Maginot line quickly became a French myth. It would have fulfilled its purpose if

---

30   N. Chauvineau, *Une invasion est-elle encore possible?*, Paris 1938

only a limited number of troops had remained in the fortifications, and the remainder had become available for offensive operations. The opposite occurred. In one day, from the many units that had remained in the Maginot line, up to 500,000 men were taken prisoner by the Germans. Napoleon had already said that, "he who remains idle behind the cover of a fortification, will always be defeated".

In 1931, General Weygand succeeded Pétain as vice president of the *Conseil.* His appointment was greeted with protest in parliament, as he was suspected of planning a *coup d'état.* Weygand was very articulate, and totally devoted to his commander. During one of the clashes between Clemenceau and Foch in 1919, Weygand felt that Clemenceau had exceeded the boundaries of politeness. Since Foch had always had difficulty in expressing himself clearly, Weygand intervened angrily and left the room. Clemenceau is purported to have said later: "If ever a general will attempt a *coup d'état,* it will be Weygand." Weygand defended himself in parliament and was supported by the minister for war, André Maginot.

During Weygand's tenure, 'a voice arose from the desert', Charles de Gaulle. He had been a proponent of motorized warfare for years. In military journals, he had advocated the creation of an elite professional Army, alongside the regular Army. In the first edition of his book there was no mention of cooperation with the air force. When de Gaulle rose to supreme power after the war, he inserted *ex post facto* corrections, ie using hind-sight, in subsequent editions. The new Army would consist of volunteer soldiers with a service of six years. It would have six motorized divisions and a light division. His ideas were turned down by the General Staff, so he turned to the press. André Pironneau published a detailed description of de Gaulle's views in forty articles in the daily *L'Echo de Paris.* De Gaulle then turned to the future Prime Minister Paul Reynaud, who was immediately captivated, and proposed his ideas to parliament. However, they were turned down by parliament on 15 March 1935.

De Gaulle was now considered to be a politicising officer and his promotions were delayed. When, on 18 June 1940, he issued his historic appeal to continue resistance from London, he was still a temporary brigadier – *Général de Brigade à titre temporaire.* This rank had been conferred upon him when he assumed command of his armoured division. Until the mid-1930s, the French Army had only two generals' ranks, *Général de Brigade* (two stars) and *Général de Division* (three stars). The *Maréchal de France* was not a military rank but a *dignité nationale,* which was conferred by special decree, signed by the President of the Republic and the Prime Minister.

The old system permitted flexibility, since it made it possible to have a *Général de Division* switched from commanding armies down to divisions without encroaching on his personal prestige. Thus Pétain, who was a colonel in 1914, was able to rise to commander in chief of the French Army in less than three years. Shortly before the war, two additional ranks were introduced, the *Général de Corps d'Armé,* four stars, and the *Général d'Armée,* five stars. The new system came at the expense of previous flexibility. Thereafter, Commands were given according to individual ranks.

In his memoirs, de Gaulle recalled the reactions to his views of a number of senior commanders. General Debeney: "Every conflict will be decided on our northeastern borders. No changes to present measures are required." General Weygand: "On no account have two parallel armies. Perhaps the ideas offer some interest, but they can be implemented with our present organisation. Nothing has to be created, everything is already there." General Brécart: "Motorized divisions would endanger our beautiful horses." At a meeting of the *Conseil*, when de Gaulle acted as secretary, the minister for war, General Maurin, exclaimed: "*Adieu*, de Gaulle, where I am, there is no place for you". Later, to a group of visitors, he said, "He has found a pen *(Pironneau)* and a gramophone (Paul Reynaud). I would like to send him to Corsica."[31]

In May 1940, de Gaulle was entrusted with the command of the hastily formed 4th motorized Division and scored a local success. Newsreels presented him as the youngest French general, without mentioning his name. After he had flown to London in protest against the armistice, and had established the Free French movement, his appeal of 18 June 1940 in military journals remained unnoticed. At that time, hardly any Frenchman had the time to listen to foreign broadcasts. A few days later, the Vichy Government issued a short *communiqué*, stating that it had given no official mission to de Gaulle. It was the first mention of what would soon become a household name.

During his years as vice-president of the *Conseil*, Weygand did little. He replaced the paragraph deleted by Pétain the Army manual, but then was mainly passive. Cooperation with Gamelin, who had been appointed as chief of the General Staff, was rendered difficult by their mutual dislike. After leaving his post in 1935, Weygand engaged in lucrative business ventures and joined the supervisory board of the Suez Corporation. In July 1939, he made a speech at a horse show in Lille where he said, "I am convinced that today's French Army is stronger than ever. The fortifications are first class, morale is high and our commanders are remarkable. No one wants a new war, but if we are to be forced to win a new victory, we will do it."[32]

Of the three generals who dominated the French military scene between the two world wars, Gamelin is, without doubt, the most interesting. Certainly not however on the grounds of his achievements. But it will remain a riddle how a general with his character and dispositions could rise to the highest command and be unanimously praised by Allied propaganda before the first shot was fired. Walls in France and also in Britain were covered with posters, showing Gamelin full regalia and with the title, "One single chief—OUR Gamelin." *Un seul chef – NOTRE Gamelin*. Other posters showed a world map. France and Britain with their Empires coloured red, and Germany's blue. It had the inscription. "We will win, because we are the strongest". *Nous vaincrons parceque nous sommes les plus forts*. Some French newspapers suggested that Gamelin be made a Marshal of France on the first day of the war.

Before rising to the top, Gamelin could look back on a brilliant career. During the years 1914–1916 he was the operational head on Joffre's staff and had developed the detailed plan for the battle of the Marne. When Joffre was relieved in 1916, he asked Gamelin to go with him. Gamelin refused and said to Joffre that his desire to further his own career should be respected. He then became a successful division commander. In the 1920s he crushed the Druze uprising in Syria, and finally was made commander of XX Corps, which was traditionally the elite unit of the French Army.

Gamelin was an intellectual who maintained a regular correspondence with the philosopher Henri Bergson, a Nobel prize-winner. A diplomat who had

---

31   All quotations from de Gaulle, p. 6 ff
32   Weygand, p. 435

assisted at a dinner of honour for Gamelin at the French Embassy in London, recalls his surprise that Gamelin only talked about philosophy and Italian painting, without mentioning military matters. In politics he was moderate with slight 'left' tendencies. After he obtained senior commands, he increasingly sought close relations with parliamentarians and other political figures.

He was unpopular with his fellow generals. Weygand held him in open contempt and General Georges, number two on the seniority list of the Army and his designated successor, hardly spoke to him. Beaufre recalled that on his entry in the General Staff, his comrade Zeller received him with the words: "Do you know General Gamelin? Better be aware that *le général Gamelin est une nouille* (General Gamelin has no more spine than a noodle)."[33]

Beaufre recalled a meeting between Gamelin and the British Chief of Staff Deverell. Deverell had asked Gamelin specific questions and was treated to a lengthy speech that caused him to simply fall asleep. Gamelin complained to the British Secretary of War, Duff Cooper, who Deverell had relieved.[34] The British Air Chief Marshall Sir Arthur Barratt described Gamelin as a "pot-eyed, button-booted, pot-bellied little grocer."[35]

The politicians whom he courted had little regard for him. Paul Reynaud wanted to dismiss him on the day of his appointment as Prime Minister. However, he feared that he would not obtain a majority in parliament, given the opposition to such a move by his predecessor Daladier, who was a strong supporter of Gamelin. During the debate which followed the disaster in Norway, Daladier was asked why he considered Gamelin a suitable commander in chief. He found no better reply than "He is a very intelligent man and personally entirely devoted to me." Not a single word about Gamelin's capacity as a military commander.

On 12 April 1940 Reynaud told Paul Baudoin, who would become the first Foreign Minister in Pétain's government, that one simply could not keep this philosophical weakling at the top of the Army. Even Daladier ventured his frustration to Weygand: "When you say something, everybody knows what you mean. When Gamelin speaks, it is simply sand slipping through the fingers."[36] Georges Mandel compared him to a *préfèt*, who always adapts his decisions to the opinions of influential politicians."[37] Paul Reynaud again: "He may have become a good *préfèt* or a bishop but certainly not a leader of men." Gamelin was totally out of touch with less senior commanders and the soldiers. In his memoirs he admits that he knew nothing about troop morale since he had made it a principle to talk to Army commanders only.

During his tenure as vice president of the *Conseil*, Gamelin simply did nothing. When the Germans re-occupied the western Rhineland, he stated that he could only intervene if the government ordered a general mobilization. He claimed that he was faced by one million German soldiers. In reality, the German strength in this operation was limited to three battalions.

---

33 Beaufre, p. 61
34 Ibid.
35 Horne, page 109
36 Ibid
37 Ibid, p. 165

Among the population the prestige of the Army had reached its nadir. One general recalled a conversation with a son of a fellow general of his, whom he wanted to join the Army: "General, it is not my salary as lieutenant which prevents me from choosing this path, but yours." Many tried to avoid the draft and failed to show up at the few exercises. Reserve officers considered them to be a waste of time and simply excused themselves. When Daladier returned to Paris after signing the Munich agreement, he feared a hostile reception from the crowd and directed the pilot of his plane to lend at a distant military airfield. Contrary to his apprehension, he was received in triumph. Thousands acclaimed him when he drove down the *Champs Elysées*. Daladier, who had more brains than he is often credited for, is reported to have turned to an aide and said: "What a bunch of idiots."

When it became clear that Germany would attack Poland, the slogan "Die for Danzig?" became widespread. During the first weeks of the war, General Gransard, who commanded a corps stated: "There is nothing but nonchalance. The feeling is that France cannot be beaten and that Germany would lose the war without any fighting taking place."[38] There was however more than nonchalance. Frenchmen, who did not have far-reaching insight into world politics, could well ask themselves why they were called upon to fight, once Poland had been defeated. Since Poland had joined Germany during the Czech crisis in 1938 and annexed the Teschen area, fighting and perhaps dying for Poland, elicited no enthusiasm.

Neither the French nor the British governments had issued a declaration of war aims. There was an increasing feeling that France was supposed to pull Britain's chestnuts out of the fire. Given the disparity in numbers between the French and the British forces on the ground, the higher pay received by British soldiers, the better food and cigarettes available to them, such sentiments cannot be dismissed out of hands. German propaganda, under the masterful direction of Dr Goebbels, played increasingly the anti-British theme. German posters on the front line would send a French message across the lines: "*Les Anglais donnent leur machines, les Français donnent leur poitrines.*" (The British provide equipment, the French the bodies of their soldiers). The historian Fonvieille-Alquier wrote in his book about the French people in the phoney war: "In 1914, French mothers told their sons to, 'Do your duty.' In 1939, it became, 'Try to become a shirker.'"[39]

The phoney war between 3 September 1939 and 10 May 1940 seen through French eyes. "Thus vanished the roar that was the *Grande Armée*" – Victor Hugo after the battle of Waterloo.

Gamelin's memoirs are a priceless source for an understanding of how the French high command viewed the eight months of what had entered history as 'the phoney war'. They take the shape of a daily diary, in which he attempts to win on paper the battles that he lost in the field. Furthermore, they contain the most insig-

---

38   Ibid, p.161
39   F. Fonvieille-Alquier, *Les Français dans la Drôle de Guerre*, Paris, 1917 (henceforth Fonvieille)

nificant details of his life day by day. (All statements and orders by Gamelin are taken from the third volume of his recollections). For instance, he dwells with relish on the meals that he served his guests at headquarters. He adds that he always saw to the high quality of food that was served. This was an inheritance from his former chief, Joffre, who never departed from his sleeping and eating methods in times of crisis. However, Joffre had an iron grip on events and wanted to show his subordinates that he never panicked. Gamelin wrote: "Only champagne was proscribed, it had to wait for the victory celebration."[40]

As a first step, Gamelin set up a command structure which was so diffuse that until the present day no expert is able to determine who was entitled to give orders to whom. He established his headquarters in the Paris suburb of Vincennes. It was far in the rear of the combat zone, but close to parliament, which he wanted to visit at regular short intervals. In his memoirs, de Gaulle described Gamelin's headquarters as something close to a convent, a *Thébaide*, where Gamelin gave the impression of a research scientist mixing in his laboratory the chemical components of his strategy. There were no radio communications. Gamelin felt that they were not necessary, since every Army headquarters could easily be visited in person, without running the risk of enemy interception.[41]

Obviously the Germans knew where Gamelin's headquarters were located, just as the Allies knew the location of *OKW* and *OKH*. Furthermore an automobile drive from Vincennes to the headquarters of General Georges, who was his deputy, took at least two hours. Gamelin appointed General Georges, first as his 'deputy' for the northeastern front, and then on 6 January 1940 made him officially Supreme Commander Northeast. With this step he relieved himself of direct responsibility and whenever someone spoke to him about 'your battle' he immediately replied: "You mean the battle of General Georges."[42] From that day, Gamelin simply became short-circuited and received only few reports from the front.[43]

In previous years, Georges had the reputation of an able soldier. However, he was physically diminished by the wounds he had suffered, when King Alexander I of Yugoslavia and the French foreign minister Barthou were assassinated in Marseille, in 1934. Beaufre recalled that Georges suffered a complete breakdown when he heard on 13 May that the Germans had reached Sedan:

> The mood at headquarters recalled a room with people standing around the deathbed of a next of kin. General Georges was completely pale. He said that the Germans had broken through at Sedan and that everything was lost. He fell sobbing into his armchair. This was the first time I ever saw a man weep during battle. Later I would see many more. It was simply terrible. General Doumenc quickly regained composure. He said to Georges that it was war, and in every war unforeseen events will occur.[44]

---

40   Gamelin, p.118
41   Gamelin in an article in the Paris daily 'L'Aurore', November 8, 1949
42   Fonvieille, p. 100
43   Goutard, p. 98
44   Beaufre, p. 233

Gamelin told one of his staff officers, Colonel Minart, that he refrained from going to see Georges because he would have felt humiliated and upset at Georges' appearance.[45]

Napoleon threatened to resign when the *Directoire* wanted to split the Italian command between him and Kellermann.

In war there can only be one commander in chief. Better an incompetent commander than two able ones, who rival in the same command. Gaul was not conquered by Rome but by Julius Caesar. The Seven Years War was not the war of the Prussian Army, but the war of Frederick the Great.

How would Napoleon have judged a situation where two incompetent generals rivalled with each other in the same command?

The parameters of Georges' command were never defined. At first, there were two Army Groups, North under General Billotte, with 7th Army under General Giraud, 1st Army commanded by General Blanchard, 9th Army (General Corap), 2nd Army (General Huntziger) and the BEF (General Gort). Even the most capable Army Group commander would have found it difficult to lead five armies, and Billotte was far from capable. Moreover Georges and Billotte had no direct authority over the BEF which was subordinated directly to Gamelin. Its commander had the right to appeal to the British government, if he was dissatisfied with an order given to him.

During one of his inspections, Sir Edward Spears asked Gamelin exactly who had supreme authority over the BEF. Gamelin replied "General Georges", but added immediately that Georges received his instructions from him. Spears wrote angrily that since Gamelin turn received his orders from Daladier, the latter had become the highest authority for Gort, who in turn had the right to appeal to the British government if he disagreed with orders issued to him.[46] Army Group Centre, commanded by General Prételat, consisted of three armies, 3rd Army (General Bourret), 4th Army (General Requin) and 5th Army (General Condé). South of Army Group Centre was the 6th Army (General Garchery) and an Army Group staff, headed by General Besson. It would be activated during the German offensive and then commanded by General Touchon.

Confusion was increased when Gamelin set up an additional General Staff under General Doumenc, since he was unable to find a common language with Georges. "They are so busy fighting each other that neither has the time to fight the Germans."[47] Doumenc's task was to prepare combat orders and put them in final shape, but in reality he became a liaison officer between Gamelin and Georges. Since he had no staff of his own, he borrowed officers from the staff of Georges. Gamelin then saw fit to create yet a fourth General Staff of the Army under General Colson, which, in spite of its lofty name, functioned basically as a quarter-master department in the rear.

Gamelin had no authority over the Air Force, which remained under the command of General Vuillemin, and was put into action in accordance with the rules of the French military manuals. Planes ready for action were sent to the Army

45   Ibid, p.99
46   Spears, p. 75
47   A British General to André Maurois, quoted by Horne, p. 181

Groups which distributed them in accordance with a percentage key determined by the pre-war manuals. When a Front commander was in urgent need of planes, he had to make a number of written applications to several authorities that did not communicate with each other. Most Army commanders were unwilling to part with their planes which remained grounded, of course.

Gamelin's operational plan, 'Dyle River', foresaw that the Allied troops would advance to the Dyle river in Belgium and there wait for the Germans. Originally he had intended to stop at the Scheldt river. During the winter he added the 'Breda variant', which called for 7th Army to pass through Antwerp to the Dutch city Breda where it would join with the Dutch Army. As director of the *Ecole de Guerre*, Foch had developed the concept of *manoeuvre à posteriori* which called for the establishment of an operational plan only after the intentions of the enemy could be recognised. A *manoeuvre à priori* was excluded, since it fixed one operational plan before hostilities had started. The 'Breda variant' was an *extreme à priori*, 7th Army was the strongest Army at Army Group North. The Germans took Breda before 7th Army reached the city. During the ensuing encounter 7th Army was practically destroyed and Gamelin had wasted his last available strategic reserve. In his description of the 'Breda variant', Frieser calls Gamelin a new Terentius Varro,[48] an early Roman scholar.

No attack was planned and Gamelin was convinced that the Germans had no such intentions either. This may call for raised eyebrows. France had declared war on Germany and ought to have taken the initiative of operations. If France did not act, it was obvious that Germany would do so. Since the Ardennes were considered to be *impénétrables*, Gamelin paid no attention to them. A war-game conducted by General Prételat in 1938, however, foresaw that a German attack in the direction of the Meuse, would reach it within 60 hours and cross in less than one hour. Gamelin kept the war game secret from his commanders. He told Prételat that it was laughable and that he was an incurable pessimist, *jouer le pire*. Had the Germans obtained knowledge of this war game, their amazement at the French neglect of defense of the Ardennes sector would have been boundless.

Nevertheless, Gamelin could not entirely abstain from action. He had signed an agreement with the Polish General Staff to launch a limited attack immediately on the outbreak of war, and to increase it to full strength after two weeks. Therefore, General Prételat was given the order for an advance with nine divisions on a narrow sector in the Sarre region. It took place on 6 to 7 September and led to the occupation of 40 villages in no-man's-land which the *Wehrmacht* had previously evacuated. The French daily *communiqués* exulted. Every attack was *brillant*, every piece of ground conquered was *important*, every progress was *sérieux*.

The first German *communiqué* about the French 'offensive' was sober. On 10 September 1939 *OKW* announced: "In the West some French patrols have crossed the German border and come in contact with our outposts. The enemy lost a number of killed in action and prisoners, among them a French officer." After that day, and until the successful German counter-attack on 16 October, the German *communiqués* mentioned only small skirmishes, in the style of 'nothing new on the Western front.'

---

48 Frieser, p. 106

French newspapers ran enthusiastic headlines: "For the first time we fight on German soil". Newsreels showed French artillery firing, and included comments like: "With every shot, Germany feels the approach of doom." A few German soldiers had been taken prisoner and newsreels showed them in gym outfits, with the comment that Germany could not afford to provide sufficient uniforms for their army. Foreign correspondents in Berlin wrote that they became increasingly surprised at the asinine French propaganda that was an insult to their intelligence, particularly to those who felt sympathy for the Allies.

French papers printed a story by Clare Booth about a miracle spring in Lorraine that flowed on 8 August 1918, the 'black day of the German army' and started flowing again February 1940. One of the papers that reproduced the story ran a headline: "Will Germany collapse by the end of May?" Joseph Harsch wrote from Berlin that he had heard over *Paris-Mondiale* that Berlin was on the verge of starvation. He then went out and could eat a meal at any one of a dozen Berlin restaurants which were offering 'all a man could eat.'[49] Apparently the French station had recalled a speech by Göring when German rearmament began, that the *Reich* would rather produce guns than butter. But Germany produced both and much more.

One almost unbelievable story turned out to be true, by chance. During the spring of 1940, rumours started to fly in Paris that the Germans might conquer the capital on 15 June 1940. When the Germans entered Paris on 14 June, the few prophets of doom felt vindicated. After the war it became known that an officer on the staff of the German embassy at Belgrade had become slightly drunk at the Christmas party and boasted that he might be in Paris on 15 June.

As soon as the Polish campaign was over, Gamelin hastened to return his troops to the Maginot line. In his words, his retreat "was totally unnoticed by the Germans." When the Poles, already at bay, protested at the slow French progress, Gamelin sent a note to the Polish military *attaché* in Paris, for communication to the Polish Commander in Chief, Marshal Rydz-Smigly:

1. More than half of our regular divisions in the North-East are engaged with the enemy.

2. Our air operations have been linked up with operations on the land from the start. We know that we are keeping a considerable portion of the *Luftwaffe* engaged in front of us.

3. I have more than honoured my promise to take the offensive with the principal part of my forces, on the 15th day after the first day of mobilization. I could do no more." Colonel Goutard adds with irony: "If the Poles were not satisfied with that, they must have been difficult to please.[50]

A series of strange orders of the day from Gamelin then followed. On 14 October, two days before the *Wehrmacht* counter-attacked in the Sarre, Gamelin issued his first order of the day:

---

49   Quoted in Horne, p.101
50   Goutard, p. 69

At any moment a battle can begin and as often in our history the fate of our nation will be in cause. France and the whole world are watching you with expectation and hope. Lift up your hearts. Make good use of your weapons. Always remember the Marne and Verdun.[51]

On 16 October, the *Wehrmacht* launched a limited sharp counter-attack that immediately recaptured the *terrain* that had been evacuated and took a sizeable number of prisoners. On 25 November, Gamelin issued his second order of the day:

On 14 October, I ordered you to be on guard against an immediate major German onslaught. On 16 October, the Germans launched a preliminary offensive, which thanks to our measures, they failed to notice, and it led to nothing. Since then we have noticed that the German preparations continued, but they do not dare to pursue their attack. We can await coming events in total calm.[52]

On 23 December, Gamelin issued a New Year's order of the day in which he proclaimed that the brilliant actions of the Army were a guarantee of final victory. In his memoirs he admits that he was mistaken about the date, but since the war was finally won in 1945, he had ultimately been proved right. In their last chapter he wrote that he never committed a single mistake during his time as commander in chief.

After the German victory over Poland, the *Deuxième Bureau* issued a long document reviewing the methods employed by the *Wehrmacht* in Poland.

The success of the German methods are due to peculiar circumstances, a very long front line, lack of proportion between the opposed armies and the absence of Polish fortifications. The situation in the West is obviously different. But since the Germans are known to be a conservative people and tend to adhere to their traditional methods, we cannot exclude that they will attempt to use some of them against us. Since we know their methods, we have ample time to prepare counter measures.[53]

On 10 May 1940 the Germans attacked with their 'conservative' methods and the French resistance lasted hardly longer than the Polish.

The limited scope of the operations in the Sarre is evidenced by the casualties. The Germans had 196 killed in action, 144 missing, 356 wounded and a handful of prisoners-of-war. The casualties of the French Army were 1,954 killed in action, or severely wounded, and 714 prisoners-of-war.

Apart from local skirmishes there was no more action on the front line until 10 May 1940. The phoney war continued. The soldiers rested in the *Maginot Line* or assisted the farmers in the rear. Many officers left their posts and went home for days. German and French patrols would exchange friendly words if they happened to meet in no-man's-land. On Christmas Eve, German and French soldiers joined in a Christmas party. German power plants continued to supply French industry.

51 Gamelin, p. 92
52 Ibid, p. 134
53 H. Amouroux, *Le peuple du désastre 1939–1940*, Paris 1976, p.206 (henceforth Amouroux)

On 9 September, Lieutenant Lacombe shot down an Me 109. He was punished because he had not obtained previous authorisation.[54] Barter deals flourished. One day French soldiers brought a cow to the German lines and returned with radio sets.[55] Otto Abetz was a German journalist who had been expelled from France in 1938. He became German ambassador to the German military government in Paris after the armistice. He recalled that he witnessed a shooting contest between German and French soldiers, on a Rhine bridge, with a doll representing Neville Chamberlain as a target.[56]

British observers became increasingly apprehensive. Sir Edward Spears, a Tory member of parliament, had been sent by Churchill as his personal observer to the French Army. Spears had been given the same task during World War I. He spoke perfect French and had many personal friends among the French commanders. He consigned his daily worries to his book, 'Assignment to Catastrophe.'[57]

General Brooke, later to become the British Army chief-of-staff, was a Corps Commander in the BEF and recalled a visit to General Corap, commander of the 9th French Army. Brooke had been born and educated in France and spoke French like a native. Corap had asked him to attend a review of his troops:

> I can still see those troops now. Seldom have I seen anything more slovenly and badly turned out. Men unshaved, horses ungroomed, clothes and saddlery that did not fit, vehicles dirty, and complete lack of pride in themselves or their units. What shook me most, however, was the look in the men's faces, disgruntled and insubordinate looks and, although ordered to give 'Eyes left', hardly a man bothered to do so. After the ceremony was over, Corap invited me to visit some of his defences in the Forêt de St. Michel. There we found a half-constructed and very poor anti-tank ditch with no defences to cover it. By way of conversation I said that I supposed he would cover this ditch with the fire from anti-tank pillboxes. This question received the reply, 'Ah *bah! on va les faire plus tard – allons, on va déjeuner*'.[58] (We will do this later, let us first have lunch)

The lunch lasted for two hours and consisted of oysters, lobster, chicken, goose liver pâté, pheasant, cheese and fruit, coffee, liqueurs, all accompanied by a variety of wines. Thereafter any kind of work became impossible. Brooke wrote that the chief concern of the French generals seemed to be the culinary standards of their headquarters' messes and that the meals he was constantly served interfered with his work and his liver. The meeting with Corap was attended by an aged general, designated to become a liaison officer to the BEF. He told Brooke proudly that he was teaching himself English with the help of a gramophone, while shaving, and added that he had just learned a new sentence: "Why will you not dance with Helen? Because Helen will smoke cigarettes and I am wearing a celluloid collar."

54   Ibid, p. 216
55   Frieser, p. 406
56   O. Abetz, *Das offene Problem. Ein Rückblick auf drei Jahrzehnte deutscher Frankreichpolitik*, Cologne 1951, p. 113
57   E. Spears, *Assignment to Catastrophe*, London, 1957, henceforth: Spears
58   Bryant, p.70 ff

Brooke could not resist asking him if he had found this kind of conversation useful in contacts with the British troops.[59]

During the battle, language problems would at times create havoc. On 21 May 1940, General Sir Edmund Ironside, British chief of the general staff, requested a joint British French counter-attack. The French interpreter at Blanchard 1st Army translated 'on' with 'as of' *(à partir de)*. The French Corps under General Altmayer that was to lead the French attack was not yet ready for action on 21 May. The British attacked alone and were easily beaten back. On that day, General Altmayer joined the French generals, who wept. The liaison officer of 1st Army to the BEF, Major Vautrin, recalls: "General Altmayer looked tired and depressed. He sat on my campbed and wept silently. He told me that we have to look at things how they are and that his troops were finished."[60]

When the Soviet Union attacked Finland in December 1939, Gamelin suddenly advanced ideas which bordered on insanity. He would not consider attacking Germany with whom France was at war, but he advocated taking action against the Soviet Union. At first, he wanted to send a French expeditionary force to Finland, but quickly retreated from that idea "because our troops were not equipped to withstand the Scandinavian winter." Then, encouraged by General Weygand, who had been called back from retirement and appointed commander in chief in Syria and the Lebanon, he dreamt of launching air raids against Baku. Weygand had written him on 29 January 1940: "One has to break the back (*casser les reins*) of the Soviet Union, in Finland, but also elsewhere." [61]A. P. Herbert wrote a satire: "Baku, or the Map game.'

> It's jolly to look at the map
> And finish the foe in a day.
> It's not easy to get at the chap;
> These neutrals are so in the way.
> But if you say "What would you do,
> To fill the aggressor with gloom?'
> Well we might drop a bomb on Baku
> Or what about bombs on Batum? [62]

Fortunately, for the later course of the war, the armistice between Russia and Finland put an end to those delusions.

At home, life was unruffled by the war. During the first days, people would carry their gas-masks in the streets. Every time a German plane crossed the French border, alarm was sounded down to Paris and people ran for the shelters. When it became clear that nothing happened, the alarms were discontinued and the gas-masks put back into the closets. Theatres and movies played to sold-out audiences. Food rationing was introduced to a small extent during the winter, but the better restaurants paid no attention to it.

Until the very last days, no real fear arose in Paris. The flow of refugees which had set in from Belgium and Northern France was diverted from the centre of the

---

59   Ibid
60   Frieser, p. 353
61   Letter by Weygand to Gamelin, January 29, 1939, quoted in Gamelin, p. 199
62   quoted in Horne, p. 128

city and was not observed in the wealthy neighbourhoods. Paris fell on Friday, 14 June. On the preceding Sunday the café terraces on the *Champs Elysées* were full of people, even though the echo of artillery fire was already audible. 24 hours later panic suddenly set in. The city was covered by dense black fog after the petrol reserves had been blown up. Rumours started to fly and the word spread that Russia had declared war on Germany. In 24 hours the city was emptied of its population.

I had obtained my commission a few days earlier and searched for my commander, only to learn of his assignment elsewhere, and then found that all the officers had already fled. Together with a few comrades, I had decided to leave Paris on my own after the capital had been declared an open city during the night of Tuesday to Wednesday. We decided to take a last look at the *Place de l'Opéra* before leaving the city on foot, hoping to find some transport on the way. The square was entirely deserted, not a car, not a single person was in sight. A café was open and while we had a cup of coffee, a poster with a *swastika* and an inscription in German with the words 'German is spoken here' (*Man spricht Deutsch*) was fixed to the window. Apparently there was better preparation for the Germans than for the war.

During the spring of 1940, warnings about an impending German attack began to multiply. In March 1940, Pierre Taittinger headed a parliamentary delegation on a visit to Sedan and was shocked by the defences, 'in embryo'. In his report, he wrote that he trembled at the thought that a German attack might occur there. In his contempt for parliament, General Huntziger paid no attention and declared that he saw no reason to strengthen the Sedan sector.[63] Since Gamelin was always eager not to incur politicians' displeasure, he made a one day trip to Sedan. He felt that no measures were required, but to please the Taittinger delegation, he dispatched one additional battalion to Sedan.[64] One week before the Germans attacked, Huntziger gave orders to pull down part of the defences around the city.

When questioned by Jacomet, the chief comptroller of the Army, if the Taittinger report had caused him to expect an attack against his army, Huntziger replied: "Certainly not, the Germans are dead afraid of attacking".[65] On 9 May, General Colson wrote that there was no reason to recall soldiers on leave, since no action could be expected on the following day.[66] General Billotte told Spears that an attack could not occur before 1941. On the same day, Huntziger addressed his staff officers: "The German preparations which you have observed are only an exercise. The Germans are not crazy enough to take the additional risk of facing 27 Belgian divisions."[67]

Two written warnings from an agent of the *Deuxième Bureau* in Switzerland were simply ignored. The first message from 1 May read: "The Germans will attack on the whole front between 8 May and 10 May. The Netherlands, Belgium, and the Sedan sector will be overrun in ten days and all of France will be defeated in one

---

63   Frieser, p.175
64   Beaufre, p. 203
65   J.Williams, *The Ides of May-The Defeat of France May-June 1940*, London 1968, p. 137
66   Fonvieille, p. 357
67   Frieser, p. 247

month." A second message arrived on 9 May: "Attack begins tomorrow, 10 May."
Goutard wrote that on 10 May 1940, the French Army had become a soulless
body, a house of cards, which collapsed at the first blow.[68]

The German attack

On 10 May, at daybreak, the *Wehrmacht* attacked in full strength through the
Netherlands and Belgium. The Dutch and the Belgian Armies were not under
Gamelin's command, thus additional confusion arose even on the first day.
Gamelin issued an order of the day: "The attack which we had expected since
October, has begun today. Germany has engaged us in a life or death struggle.
France and her Allies have now one duty: 'Courage, energy and confidence'. As
Marshal Pétain said at Verdun: We will get them. *On les aura.* "

On the first day, Corap's 9th Army suffered the brunt of the German
onslaught and simply evaporated, with many of its officers abandoning their
troops and driving away in private cars. Its units dissolved, and soldiers ran back in
smaller groups in the direction of Paris. Corap was immediately dismissed and
General Giraud, whose 7th Army had been beaten in the Breda area, succeeded
him.

When Giraud arrived at his new headquarters, the Germans were already there
and he was taken prisoner. By 13 May, the Germans had already reached the
Meuse at Sedan, and for all practical purposes the campaign was over. When
Huntziger heard that small advance units had crossed the Meuse and established
the first bridgehead, his first reaction was: "Fine, this will mean more prisoners-of-
war."[69] The next day his 2nd Army was in turn destroyed.

No army consists of good divisions only, but common sense demands the
spread of weaker divisions over as many corps as possible. The French high
command had concentrated their bulk in 2nd and 9th Armies, and they were to
defend the sector that the Germans had chosen for their *Schwerpunkt*. General
Huntziger became the head of the French delegation which signed the armistice
with Germany and Italy. Thereafter, he became minister for war in Pétain's
government and made frantic efforts to destroy all compromising papers about his
statements prior to the German attack, but a sufficient number were recovered.

At first, neither Gamelin nor Georges, who had recovered from his first shock
after hearing about the German breakthrough, failed to realise the gravity of the
situation. Georges reported that a serious but small setback, *un sérieux pépin*, had
taken place, and Gamelin felt that it was only a local interruption. On 15 May,
Gamelin panicked.

Since he did not know in which direction the Germans would advance, he told
Daladier, over the phone, that he had no additional troops available between Laon
and Paris and that the Germans could be in Paris on the following day. In his
shock, Daladier felt at first that he had misheard and said to Gamelin: "What I just
heard would mean the end of the French army!" Gamelin replied that the French
Army was indeed finished. On 16 May, Churchill flew to Paris. He asked Gamelin
where he had placed his strategic reserve. When Gamelin replied that there was

---

68   Goutard, p. 84
69   Frieser, p. 247

none, Churchill was flabbergasted, to the point that he repeated his question in French and received the same reply, '*aucune*'.[70]

On 19 May, Gamelin was dismissed and General Weygand was appointed commander in chief. On the day before, Doumenc had urged Gamelin to finally pay a visit to Georges. After some hesitation, Gamelin agreed. He went into Georges' office, left him a note, and told him to read it after he left. In typical manner, the note began: "Without desiring to interfere in a battle, which is the responsibility of General Georges, I offer the following opinions ... " Gamelin suggested an attack from North and South against the German forces which had broken through, and finished his note with the sentence: "Action must begin the next few hours." *Le tout est une question d'heures.*

Conceivably this was the only sensible directive issued by Gamelin during the war, since the operation suggested by him hinged upon a few hours. If the attack could have succeeded is somewhat doubtful, but it had at least to be attempted. Napoleon had written that the two elements of strategy were space and time. Lost space could be retaken, but the worst possible scenario was waste of time, because lost time could never be regained. Weygand wasted much time. At first he did nothing and after four days he issued an order which differed from Gamelin's note only in words, not in content. But four days had been wasted.

The call for Pétain as deputy prime minister and Weygand as new commander in chief was a return to the age old French tradition in times of national danger, to call upon the glorious ancestors, *les grands ancêtres*. Pétain was the victor of Verdun. Weygand was Foch's right hand and Georges Mandel had been Clemenceau's close associate in 1918. The appointments were made, but not without incident, as little sympathy was lost between *la maison Foch* and *la maison Pétain*. Reynaud had to soothe Pétain's anger at his call of Weygand. Pétain said to him:"Weygand! I can't stand him". Pétain had not forgotten that in 1919, during the ceremony awarding him his Marshal baton, Weygand had audibly said to Foch: "We have brought him here with a kick in the "arse"! *Dire qu'on l'a amené ici à coups de pieds dans le cul.* Mandel exploded when Pétain told him that if communications were bad, one had to revert to carrier pigeons.

Weygand was not more qualified for his command than Gamelin had been. De Gaulle held the opinion 'even less', although he viewed him as the stronger personality of the two.[71] Weygand was already aged 73. Since his appointment as Foch's chief-of-staff, in November 1914, he had never held a troop command. Spears wrote that the difference between a commander and a staff officer was like the difference between a rider at a Grand Prix and a photographer who takes his picture.[72] Weygand arrived by plane from Beirut in the early morning hours of 19 May. On landing he said that he was tired and needed some sleep. He slept until late afternoon, and spent the rest of the day calling upon ministers and parliamentarians.

During the next three days he went from one part of the front to another with whatever means were at his disposal, to inform himself of a situation that required no additional information. He wanted to meet the top Allied Commanders in

70   W. Churchill, vol. 2 of his memoirs, *Their finest hour*, Boston 1949, p. 46
71   P. de Gaulle, *De Gaulle mon père*, Conversations with M. Tauriac, vol.1, p. 158
72   Horne, p. 475

person, but found none except Billotte. Due to a partial breakdown of communications, he was informed only after his return to Paris, one day later, that Billotte had died in a car accident immediately after taking leave of him.

For a few days, Army Group North, in which the better French troops were concentrated, had no commander in chief, then Blanchard was named its commander. Spears recalled that a major Fauvelle, an officer on Blanchard's staff, when reporting on the change in command, told him: "We have staff without a commander, and a commander without a staff."[73] Blanchard had not yet taken over Billotte's staff, and his own staff had been reduced. Spears told Churchill that he had never met Blanchard. He had however been told that Blanchard was a "very charming, rather shy man, typical of the military professor type, more at home in a lecture hall than on a battlefield".[74]

Spears wrote that Billotte, whom he had known in the First World War, "then appeared as a big, cheerful, if not particularly intelligent man. Now he seemed to have aged greatly. He had the appearance of one whose vitality had evaporated in over-heated offices. He looked very soft, worried, a great big flat-footed man."[75] The French historian Marc Bloch served as captain on Blanchard's staff and was murdered in 1944 by the Gestapo. He wrote in his book, published after the war, that on 26 May he had overheard a conversation between Blanchard and one of his corps commanders. The latter said to Blanchard: "General, do whatever you like, but at least do something". Blanchard replied, "I can see two total surrenders looming."[76] Spears wrote that Weygand's main preoccupation at their meetings was to loudly blame the British for the disaster.[77]

While it is true that the British gave preference to their own interests when the catastrophe was clear, they could certainly not be blamed. They had trusted the French high command and had subordinated themselves to it. When the incapacity of the French generals became apparent, and the French troops increasingly unreliable, they had to save as many of their own troops for a defence of the British Isles. However, they still succeeded in evacuating 123,000 French soldiers from Dunkirk.

For some days the French public remained ignorant of what had occurred. The first communiqués mentioned the German breakthrough at Sedan as a minor bulge, *une brêche*, which our troops were in the progress of sealing off, *colmater*. Since someone had to be found guilty, Reynaud, in a speech to the nation, tore General Corap to shreds. Corap was looked upon by the public as having been a member of the 'fifth column'. Reynaud had accused him of having neglected to blow up the Meuse bridges. This turned out to be false and Corap was later rehabilitated. On 16 May, the Paris daily *L'Epoque* published a lead story:

> The enemy has not succeeded in breaking through our front line. He has been halted in the area of Sedan-Mézières. He has thrown wave after wave, divisions after divisions into our blast furnaces. Our valleys, our fields, our roads are covered with his bodies. We have to claim, repeat and

---

73 Spears, p. 194
74 Ibid. p. 165
75 Ibid
76 M. Bloch, *L'étrange défaite – Témoignages écrits en 1940*, Paris 1946, p. 168 f
77 Spears, p. 317

shout to heaven, as at Verdun, the enemy has attempted to break through and he has failed.

When the Germans reached the Channel coast on 20 May and captured Abbeville and Amiens, there was an awakening. Amiens had a connotation of doom from World War I. In March 1918, the Germans had closed in on Amiens. The British and French high commands had been in confused disagreement about the necessity of holding the town. Foch, who held no active command, and as chief of the General Staff was basically only a military adviser to the government, had vociferously claimed that Amiens had to be held at all costs, and he was appointed commander in chief of the Allied forces.

A hastily convened service at *Nôtre Dame* Cathedral was not free of the comical. The anti-clerical ministers had never attended a church service and did not know when to kneel and when to make the sign of the cross. Weygand had left Paris with the government. Since there was nothing left for him to command, his main activities centred around increasingly vociferous discussions with Paul Reynaud about the alternatives of capitulating, or approaching the Germans for an armistice. Weygand had established his new headquarters in a castle at Briare in central France. There was only one telephone and it did not function between noon and 2 pm, because the lady operator took time out for lunch. Spears recalled with some amusement that he observed an increasingly agitated Weygand in a telephone booth, desperately trying to obtain a communication.[78] It was a fitting epilogue to the failure of the French command.

Wehrmacht operations in France

Since the participation of Manstein's corps during the battle was relatively insignificant, this chapter could end here. However, Manstein's plan became the decisive factor in German victory, even after his relief, and it is necessary to outline how it worked during the battle. Manstein's plan owed its success to the incompetence of the French command, and to the daring of the German *Panzer* Generals. They pushed their freedom of action in the field, a traditional feature of German military doctrine, to the utmost limit. Most of the senior German generals, with the exception of Halder, continued to have a sceptical view of Manstein's idea. They issued orders during the battle that may well have led to failure. German generals were not less conservative in their thoughts than their French counterparts, and remained captives of the logic that had been taught to them during their service at the *Generalstab*.

The element of genius in Manstein's plan was its contradiction of traditional logic. It was basically illogical. Manstein was no gambler, he was a *Generalstab* officer of unrivalled competence. However, he was the only German general who understood what his seniors were unable to comprehend. Manstein, like all German generals, felt that the French Army was stronger than the *Wehrmacht*. He understood immediately that the only chance of vanquishing an enemy who was purported to be stronger, consisted in finding an 'Achilles' heel' ie a vulnerable

---

78   Spears, p. 309

point, and concentrating everything on an attack there, even at the risk of *va-banque*.

His calculations were proved entirely right. The German generals could not believe their eyes, when they saw that the French Army was sending its strongest units into Belgium. Orders were immediately issued to the *Luftwaffe* not to interfere. When von Bock heard of the breakthrough at Sedan on 13 May, he wrote in his diary: "The Frenchman has apparently taken leave of his senses. He could have prevented this and ought to have prevented it."[79] One can only prevent matters which one recognises, and the French simply had not recognised them.

On 13 May, after the Germans had already broken through at Sedan, Gamelin wrote a situation report that ended with the sentence: "It is still impossible to determine the *Schwerpunkt* of the German attack." General Koeltz, chief of the operations department at Gamelin's headquarters, added in handwriting: "Overall impression very good." Frieser attempts to solve the riddle of the absurd French views, and believes that it can be explained in four different phases:

1. Apparent confirmation of the French expectations: The first reports that reached Gamelin could give the distinct impression that the German *Schwerpunkt* was in northern Belgium. In reality, such reports sounded too good to be true. The Germans simply did their best to play the part attributed to them in Gamelin's script. Perhaps they were even excessive. Colonel Villelume, Reynaud's adc, asked Gamelin if there was not a trap, and why had the *Luftwaffe* not attacked the Allied troops? The best reply Gamelin could find was, "They are probably busy elsewhere."

2. First doubts: An increasing number of German *Panzer* columns suddenly appeared in the Ardennes. Since this did not fit the prefabricated picture, they were either ignored or dismissed with irony. Reports from a reconnaissance plane, that it had noticed endless columns of German vehicles with all their lights turned on, were termed " a nightly illusion."

3. Self deception: When it became clear that the reports were confirmed by reality, the German *Panzer* advance through the Ardennes was considered to be a malicious deception that would fool no one. But even when it became clear that the German *Schwerpunkt* was real, there was no feeling of crisis since it was felt that the German attack would certainly be blocked on the Meuse.

4. Disaster admitted: When Gamelin finally came to understand the reality, the moment of truth had come, but it was too late. The *Panzer* Divisions had already crossed the Meuse and were on their way to the Channel coast, where they would close the trap. Gamelin's main, and fatal mistake, was his continued insistence on his Dyle-plan. He could still have withdrawn all his armies, which later became encircled, from Belgian and Northern France, and then regrouped them in a new defensive front at the Somme river." [80]

I strongly disagree with Frieser's conclusion in the last item, since I am convinced that by then, four days after the German offensive, the French Army was no longer capable of a massive organised operation of retreat. Frieser likens the

---

79   BA-MA, Study P-210, vol. 1, *Diary von Bock in the West*, May 13, p. 9
80   Frieser, p. 171 f

collapse of France to a Greek tragedy, in which the act of 'Ate', blindness, always precedes the act of catastrophe.[81]

Among the German high commanders Rundstedt would become the main obstacle in the implementation of a plan that he had previously nurtured. In 1940 he would begin to show the weaknesses which would increasingly impair the qualities of his leadership during the remainder of the war. As long as Manstein was his chief-of-Staff, Rundstedt came out in support of his plan. When the plan was put into action, it became apparent that Rundstedt had been impressed by Manstein's ideas without understanding them. Manstein was succeeded as chief-of-staff of Army Group A, by General von Sodenstern, who had been in strong opposition to his idea. Rundstedt immediately agreed with Sodenstern's objections and turned into a brakeman. During the march into Austria in 1938, Guderian had described von Bock, who commanded the 8th German Army, as a *Panzer* amateur. The same appreciation would hold true for Rundstedt, even before the beginning of the offensive. Guderian had complained that Rundstedt understood practically nothing about *Panzer* tactics.

Curiously, Rundstedt's reputation remained unimpaired with the Allied military commanders and historians. Eisenhower called him 'the most capable German general', and Montgomery described him as 'the best German general' he encountered during the war.[82] General Bradley wrote in his recollections: "When we launched our November 1944 offensive, we knew from *Ultra* that the professional soldier von Rundstedt had reassumed command of Hitler's Western Front ... We expected a textbook defence against our offence." [83]Bradley had apparently not noticed that Rundstedt had remained on the sidelines during his last command in the war. The German operations against Bradley were commanded by the far superior *Feldmarschall* Model.

Another 'brake shoe' was the *Panzergruppe* Kleist that contained most of the *Panzer* units of Army Group A. It was originally a corps, but grew to Army strength without being officially formalized as an army. It remained with the insufficient staff of a corps, headed by the then Colonel Zeitzler who, two years later was to become Halder's successor as chief of the *Generalstab*. General Kleist was a cavalry officer, with only limited understanding of *Panzer* warfare, who continuously wavered between temerity and sudden fear. Bouts of temerity would cause him to spur on his *Panzer* commanders beyond their capacity while, when replaced with sudden fear, he would order them to halt, even when their progress was unimpeded.

On 12 May, Guderian was ordered by Kleist to cross the Meuse with his corps, at all costs, on the following day. After he succeeded in crossing, his advance became rapid beyond expectation. On 16 May, Kleist panicked, arrived by plane and told Guderian to halt until he could bring forward new reserves. The hot-tempered Guderian resigned his command and passed it on to his senior divisional commander, *Generalleutnant* Veiel. A few hours later, *Generaloberst* List appeared.

---

81   Frieser, p. 172

82   C. Messenger, *The last Prussian, A Biography of Field Marshal von Rundstedt*, London 1991, p. 222

83   O. Bradley/C. Blair, *A General's Life, an Autobiography by General of the Army Omar N. Bradley*, New York 1983, p. 350 f

His 12th Army included the *Panzergruppe* Kleist. He cancelled Kleist's instructions, ordered Guderian to resume his command and told him, with a twinkle in his eyes, to take 'advance reconnaissance movements.'[84]

The first German division to reach the Channel coast was Rommel's 7th *Panzer*, which was part of Hoth's *Panzerkorps* belonging to *Generaloberst* von Kluge's 4th Army. Rommel had never been a *Generalstab* officer. Before the war he was an opponent of armoured warfare, but changed his mind after the Polish campaign. Frieser wrote that Rommel obtained his successes not because he led according to *Panzer* rules, of which he knew little, but because he simply relied on his intuition.[85] Rommel's success in France laid the foundation stone of the 'Rommel myth.'

Thanks to his uninhibited bragging he soon became Hitler's favourite general. His boundless ambition caused him to write daily reports which grossly exaggerated the dangers he faced, in order to increase his glory. He sent his superiors accounts of impending catastrophes and wrote about 'hundreds' of enemy tanks that were assembling to attack him. The 'Rommel Album', which he sent to Hitler after the conclusion of the battle for France, contained a horror picture, with red arrows, purporting to represent nine British tank divisions that were assembling to attack him. In reality, the BEF had only a total of five divisions and not a single tank division. Rommel then became a household name in Germany, popular cabaret songs had their text rewritten to mention his name.

In many places the German advance turned into a pleasure ride. German commanders had given up their staff maps and found their orientation by using ordinary Michelin tourist maps. *Panzer* officers and soldiers sat on top of their vehicles and waved to the civilian population. German infantry advanced singing, dressed in open shirts and without helmets. On both sides of the roads French prisoners-of-war walked with their cumbersome equipment. Many roads were clogged by up to 10 million refugees, about one quarter of the total French population.

Sichelschnitt did not function like clockwork. During the first days chaos arose on the roads, many of which were unable to accommodate the mass of *Panzer*. Infantry units were unwilling to give up roads that had been reserved for them. Whenever an obstacle arose Hitler panicked. On 17 May, Halder wrote in his diary: "A most unpleasant day. The *Führer* is extremely nervous. He is increasingly afraid of his own success and would prefer to hold the advance. He pretends to be worried about his left flank."[86] Another entry on the next day: "The *Führer* has an incomprehensible fear for his southern flank. He raves and screams that we are spoiling his whole operation which may well turn into defeat."[87] On the same day, Jodl made an entry into his diary that Hitler had had a fit of rage and ordered *OKH*, in the sharpest possible manner, to immediately issue orders to cope with the situation that had arisen.[88]

84   Guderian, p. 99 ff
85   Frieser, p. 278
86   Halder, War Diary, vol. 1, p. 302
87   Ibid
88   Jodl Diary, May 18, 1940, BA-MA, RW 4/32, p. 50

The 'Miracle of Dunkirk' – why did the *Panzers* suddenly halt their advance? – The 'Halt-order'

Facts

On 23 May, the Germans had advanced to a point 15 kilometres from the centre of Dunkirk. On the same day they were halted by an order of Rundstedt and remained in place for four days, thus permitting the British to prepare the evacuation of Dunkirk, Operation 'Dynamo'. It permitted the rescue of 247,000 British and 123,000 French troops. On 24 May, Hitler confirmed Rundstedt's order. The German advance was resumed on 26 May. Rundstedt had issued his order after receiving a panic-stricken message from Kleist that his *Panzer* units were too weak to face a massive British counter-attack, and that other German troops had to be brought from the rear (*Aufschliess*). Halder mocked Kleist, "who was simply not up to his duties". However, *Generaloberst* von Kluge agreed with Rundstedt and was the first to mention the term *Aufschliess*. Rundstedt's order resulted in uncontrolled anger at *OKH*. Until that day, Brauchitsch had given Halder a free hand in the conduct of the battle, now he decided to intervene in person. On 24 May he ordered all of Rundstedt's *Panzer* units to be transferred to Bock's Army Group.

On the same day, Hitler visited Rundstedt's headquarters and heard to his surprise, that *OKH* had ordered Kluge's 4th Army, which contained all the *Panzer* of Army Group A, to be placed under Bock's command. *OKH* had not even bothered to inform him. Hitler was furious, rescinded the *OKH* order, and declared himself in full agreement with Rundstedt's pessimistic views.[89]

Later, on the same day, Kleist and Kluge turned around and asked for a resumption of the offensive. All front and *Luftwaffe* commanders joined in. During the afternoon, Hitler ordered Brauchitsch to appear before him. Brauchitsch had hoped that this meeting would enable him to convince Hitler that the 'Halt-order' was irrational. Hitler did not let him utter a word. He shouted at him, insulted him repeatedly, refused to talk about the Dunkirk operation and ended the conversation by forbidding Brauchitsch to issue orders to the armies without his prior consent. As often, after a meeting with Hitler, Brauchitsch returned to his headquarters a broken man.

OKH, under the guidance of Halder, then felt that they had found a way out, by issuing a directive to Army Groups A and B which left it to them to give a 'free hand' to their commanders. Any mention of the 'Halt-order' was carefully avoided. *OKH* was confident that Rundstedt would simply transmit this directive to his *Panzer* commanders who needed no more instructions to resume the attack. But then an unprecedented event in German military history occurred. Rundstedt

---

89   HGr.A, KTB, BA-MA, RH 19 I/37, p.140 and diary Jodl, May 25, 1940, BA-MA, RW 4/32, p. 54

simply refused to transmit the *OKH* directive and made a point in entering his refusal in the diary of his Army Group.[90]

During the morning hours of 25 May, Brauchitsch paid another visit to Hitler, who again refused to discuss anything with him. Jodl noted in his diary: "*Führer* opposes any change in his order and leaves it to Army Group A to decide. Rundstedt refuses to alter his order, since he feels that his *Panzer* need a rest." The commander in chief of the Army and *OKH* thus became the subordinates of one Army Group commander. Never before had a Commander in Chief of the German Army suffered such a humiliation.

During the morning of 26 May, Rundstedt became nervous. He visited his *Panzer* commanders, all of whom urged him to grant them freedom of movement. He had to inform Hitler who rescinded the 'Halt-order' at 1.30 pm, while making it a point that he had reached his decision only after obtaining Rundstedt's approval.[91]

Motives of the Halt-order and effects of the Dunkirk rescue

The facts that lay behind the 'Halt-order' are known world-wide. The motives that prompted the order, and the effects of the rescue at Dunkirk, continue to be in dispute among historians to this very day.

True to their post-war tradition, the memoirs of the German generals describe the Halt-order as yet another folly of the 'bungler' Hitler. Guderian heads the relevant chapter as 'Hitler's fateful order.'[92] Although at that stage in the battle he himself had displayed an astonishing lack of interest in a continued German advance. He had stated that the swampy ground conditions were an obstacle to *Panzer* progress and entered that in the war diary of his corps.[93] In his memoirs, Guderian denies having made this statement, in spite of having signed the relevant page in the war diary.[94]

Of all people, Rundstedt saw fit to join this chorus. He wrote: "Hitler is the sole guilty party and not myself, as 'Mr' Churchill endeavours to show in his memoirs. I finally had no choice but to obey Hitler's repeated orders".[95] Since the *Panzer* had already been stopped, a full day before Hitler confirmed Rundstedt's order, such statements require no further comment.

German historians, among them names of repute, attribute Hitler's decision to allow the BEF to leave, as part of his purported 'anglophilia,' which caused him to bend over backwards in permitting the British to rescue what was left of their army. This argument is supported by Hitler's repeated declarations of his admiration for the British Empire, which he repeated even in his political testament, a few hours before he committed suicide in the Berlin bunker.

90   HGr.A, Anl. 37 zum KTB, BA-MA, RH 19 I/38, p. 97
91   Halder, War diary, vol.1, p. 320, May 26. Also Diary Jodl, BA-MA, RW 4/32, p. 56 and Hgr. A, KTB, RH 19 I/37, p. 146 f.
92   Guderian, p. 104.
93   PzKorps Guderian, KTB, BA-MA, RH 21-2/41, p. 163
94   Guderian, p. 107
95   Rundstedt, *Feldzug im Westen*, BA-MA, Study C-053, p.4

Are such words of Hitler worthy of credence? Hitler had always praised countries before he attacked them. Only a few days before entering Austria, he expressed his gratitude to Chancellor Schuschnigg in a speech before the *Reichstag*. Until 1939 he repeatedly expressed friendly feelings for Poland, and said that he always recalled with great pleasure his co-operation with Marshal Pi³sudski. When he demanded the incorporation of the Sudeten province into Germany, he repeatedly stated that this was his last territorial demand in Europe. In a speech before the *Reichstag* he said: "We don't want any Czechs." Hitler had always lied and did not shrink from cynically acknowledging this. In a closed meeting with representatives of the German press, in Munich, he stated: "Circumstances have compelled me to talk about peace for tens of years. Obviously this kind of propaganda, repeated over such a long time, has risky aspects, since it can easily lead many men to believe that the present regime is bound to a wish, and to a decision to preserve peace under all circumstances."[96] Is there any reason to take a statement by Hitler at face value, for the sole reason that it suits the thesis of some historians?

Frieser holds the opinion that "Hitler's 'anglophilia' appears as a kind of love-hate relationship which, with him, suddenly turns into a will to destroy."[97] He believes that Hitler himself launched the idea of his wish to spare the British troops as an *ex post facto* justification of a military mistake, that is with hind-sight. He quotes a statement by Göring during the days when the *Panzer* were halted at Dunkirk: "The Army suddenly wants to be gentlemen ... The knights in chivalrous suits of armour simply want to take the British prisoners. The *Führer* wants to teach them a lesson that will take a long time to forget."[98] Halder noted that while the British troops were standing on the shores to wait for their embarking, Hitler wanted a massive bloodbath. When he was told that artillery was not effective on beaches of sand, he ordered the use of anti-aircraft grenades equipped with time fuses.[99] His Army adc at that time, Major Engel, recalls that he had insisted on employing special *SS*-units to ensure that none of the British troops survived.[100]

Frieser advanced the opinion that the reason for the 'Halt-order' should not be searched for in objective considerations, but rather in the subjective thoughts of an egomaniac dictator. In his view, the 'Halt-order' was Hitler's wish to assert his total authority over his generals. This is a hypothesis and thus lacks final proof.

However, to me, Frieser's analysis appears reasonable when seen against the background of Hitler's personality:

> In reality, there was a motive which was far more important to him than any tactical, operative, strategical, or political-ideological considerations, namely his undisputed authority as the military *Führer*. To put it bluntly, it was not the *Panzer* that Hitler wanted to stop at Dunkirk, but the *OKH* generals. He was only concerned with one principle, the *Führer* principle. The Third *Reich* was viewed by him as a *Führer* state, in which everything

96   *Es spricht der Führer, 7 exemplarische Hitler-Reden*, H.von Kotze/H.Krausnick (ed), Gütersloh 1966, p. 269
97   Frieser, p.390
98   Ibid
99   H. Meier-Welcker, *Der Entschluss zum Anhalten der deutschen Panzertruppen in Flandern 1940*, in Vierteljahreshefte für Zeitgeschichte , 2. Jahrgang (1954), p. 286
100 Frieser, p. 390

had to be concentrated around him alone, and above all he had complete military authority. The war in the West was unequivocally 'his war'. All his military advisers had told him that it could not be won. In the end he had had to practically force it on his hesitating generals. Then it became clear that he had, apparently, been right, since this campaign turned into one of the most spectacular victories in military history. But now it suddenly appeared that the generals and not himself were the famous victors. Even Halder, who had been repeatedly scorned as 'over cautious' and 'timorous', suddenly brimmed with self-assurance. The *OKH* generals were about to reduce him to an 'also-ran'.

On 24 May, when arriving at Charleville, he discovered that Rundstedt, his most trusted subordinate, had been practically stripped of power. *OKH* had decided to take the *Panzer* away from Rundstedt, without even bothering to inform him. Hitler found himself assailed in his most sensitive point, his prestige. Now his instinct for power rebelled. Never before had a General dared to ignore him and make him lose face. It was the moment when the explosion occurred. In his desire for vengeance, which often took irrational aspects, Hitler decided to restore the former order, and demonstrate who held final and sole military authority. He now turned matters around. He degraded Brauchitsch and Halder to 'also-rans' and let Rundstedt decide how much longer the *Panzer*, which were already halted, should remain without moving further. Hitler savoured his vengeance when *Generaloberst* von Brauchitsch appeared and asked him to cancel the 'Halt-order'. He sent him to Rundstedt and the commander in chief of the Army had to go to his subordinate like a petitioner.[101]

The operations of Army Group B – was *Sichelschnitt* perhaps superfluous?

Military history pays only small attention to the operations of Army Group B. Most accounts of the battle for France begin with the German break-through at Sedan by Army Group A. It is logical, since that was where the decision was obtained. Among German historians only Frieser gives a detailed account of Army Group B activities. However, the successes achieved by this smaller Army Group have led me to the opinion that *Sichelschnitt* may have been superfluous.

After Army Group B had been reduced in size, it consisted of 2 armies, 6th Army under von Reichenau, 18th Army under von Küchler and Hoepner's XVI motorized Corps. It was soon diverted to Army Group A, which had 5 armies and 3 motorized corps.

During the first days, Army Group B faced the Belgian and the Dutch armies and when the Allies had walked into the German trap, it encountered the best French units and the BEF. It advanced in *Blitzkrieg* fashion. The strong fortification of Eben Emael at Liège was taken in one day by German parachute and glider troops. Two days later all of Liège was in German hands. In 1914, Ludendorff, who commanded the assault, had needed close to two weeks to conquer the city.

---

101   Frieser, p. 391 f

The only tank battle of the French campaign began on 12 May when Hoepner's Corps encountered the French Cavalry Corps of General Prioux. Prioux had more and better tanks than Hoepner, but his corps was soon decimated by the combined efforts of Hoepner's unit and the *Luftwaffe*, and could never be redeployed. Prioux then succeeded Blanchard as commander of the French 1st Army. The Belgian Albert-canal, which until then had been viewed as a strong defence position, was easily overcome. Brussels and Antwerp fell on 18 May. The Dutch Army had capitulated four days earlier. Belgium surrendered on 27 May, providing Paul Reynaud with a welcome opportunity of castigating yet another man as guilty, the "treasonous Belgian king."

After reaching the channel coast and completing the occupation of Dunkirk both German Army Groups joined forces and on 6 June began their second offensive, 'Red'. The French press reported about a new 'Weygand line' which only existed on paper. Some French units fought courageously but where rapidly overwhelmed.

At that time, I was still sufficiently naive to believe that the Germans could be halted somewhere. I dropped my last illusions when the Germans took *Forges-les-Eaux* on the Seine on 9 June, and the first rumbles of artillery fire became audible in Paris. The German advance reached such a pace that *OKH*, when receiving reports about a captured city, wondered if perhaps confusion between resembling names had occurred and they requested the commanders' confirmation. Bock, who had been disappointed that Army Group A had been instrumental in the battle at the expense of his own Army Group, could draw comfort from the capture of Paris by his 18th Army under Küchler.

Because the strongest units of the French Army were unable to resist the advance of Army Group B, there may be some ground for the substance of the opinion that *Sichelschnitt* may well have been superfluous and that the original plan 'Yellow' would likewise have achieved total victory. True, 'Yellow' was a plan with a limited purpose, inspired by a mistaken appreciation of the French Army. But the weakness of the French Army became quite obvious after a few days of fighting and the original plan would have undoubtedly have been altered. The elder Moltke had already written a century earlier: "No operational plan extends further than the first encounter with the opposing Army." 'Yellow' would certainly have proceeded with the new aim of total victory. *Sichelschnitt* was a plan of genius but it had a *va-banque* element that events showed to have perhaps been unnecessary.

Conclusion – a victory into the void

After the battle was lost, France concluded an armistice agreement with Germany. Uhle-Wettler calls the battle of France a brilliant 'victory into the void'.[102] Every military success will remain a 'victory into the void' if it is not followed by a reasonable political settlement. The 'void' of the victory over France could have been avoided. Hitler could have followed the armistice with a peace treaty which the French government, at that time not yet a German puppet, longed for. A reasonable peace treaty with France could have paved the way for similar treaties with the other

---

102   Uhle-Wettler, p. 171

nations in German-occupied Europe. Britain may well have felt that it was not worth while to continue the war. Such a policy would have required a statesman like Bismarck at the helm of Germany, but in 1940 the *Führer* was Adolf Hitler.

Wars are fought in order for the victor to make a favourable peace, but peace has to be offered to the vanquished. Instead of offering peace to the vanquished France, Hitler made his nonsensical peace offer to Britain, which not only was unvanquished, but which was increasing her military strength behind the cover of the Channel.

The armistice agreement with France was violated by the Germans before the ink had dried on the document. Alsace and Lorraine were annexed and the men in both provinces were conscripted into the *Wehrmacht*. The northern provinces of France were removed from the authority of the military governor of France and came under control of the military governor of Belgium and Northern France. In the official documents of the Vichy government these provinces were not part of the *zone occupée* and were designed as *zone interdite*. In *Mein Kampf* Hitler had already used the word annihilation when writing about France. Hitler's intentions for France, after her defeat, are described in a number of mentions full of venom, in the diaries of Dr Goebbels. Two examples are sufficient:

> 7 March 1942: "The Vichy-French are perhaps prepared to give up their neutrality and enter the war on our side, if we offer them an acceptable peace. But the *Führer* is right in his refusal to consider such a solution. France will always remain an enemy up to her last breath. We have to remove any trace of French political and military power from future Europe."

> 30 April 1942: "Of course, Vichy would like to conclude a separate peace treaty with us. Bu the *Führer* is right in his rejection. France will never consider such a treaty as binding upon her, should we lose. If we win, she will insist on the validity of the treaty. In other terms, we would never be able to complete the 'amputation' of France. The French may perhaps agree to cede Alsace to us, but would strongly object to parting with Lorraine. One could ask oneself why we ever waged a war against them. If the French knew what the *Führer* really has in store for them, they would not believe their eyes."

This attitude went far beyond France. During the whole war Hitler never took a single step in the direction of a political act with an objective of peace. Authors who have made in-depth analyses of Hitler's mind, voice the opinion that he was simply unable to conceive a world without war. Even in 1938, at the signing of the Munich agreement, he complained to his *confidant* that the stupidity of the British and the French had prevented him from beginning the war, even back then. In his eyes, every nation conquered by him was only a bridgehead for another war. Even when a major battle was nearing, he dreamt of new battlegrounds.

On 30 November 1942, after 6th Army had already been encircled and came daily closer to total destruction, he phoned Manstein the midde of the night. He told him he was considering a new offensive in the Middle East, in the coming spring, with Manstein's Army Group joining hands with Rommel's troops in

Palestine, and then marching jointly on towards India.[103] In his recent book about Hitler's last days in the Berlin bunker, Joachim Fest voices the opinion that Hitler's military successes gave him no real pleasure, since a situation without continued war was looked on by him as insufferable.[104] Sebastian Haffner feels that Hitler's repeated references, even during his early years, to his end by suicide, show that he was unable to conceive of anything brought to a 'normal' ending.

Thus *Sichelschnitt*, which Alistair Horne labels as "one of the most inspired blueprints for victory that the military mind has ever conceived,"[105] was not only perhaps superfluous but ultimately only a 'victory in a void'. Defeat always looms close to victory. The defeat was the underrating of the strength of the Red Army, after the easy rout of the French. No German high command would go further than Manstein berating the quality of Russian military leadership. The Tarpeian Rock is always close to the Capitol. In 'antiquity', traitors were thrown off the Tarpeian Rock in Rome.

German and Allied casualties in the West 1940

* Germany: 49,000 killed in action and missing, 110,000 wounded
* France: 120,000 killed in action and 2 million prisoners of war
* BEF: 70,000 killed in action, wounded and prisoners of war
* Belgium: 7,500 killed in action
* Netherlands: 3,000 killed in action

The *Luftwaffe* lost 1,236 planes, a further 429 were damaged. The French air force lost 892 planes and the Royal Air Force lost 1,029 planes. The Dutch and Belgian airforces were destroyed on the ground on 10 May 1940.[106]

Excursus: *Sichelschnitt* and the German plan for the Ardennes offensive in December 1944 – a comparison

Frieser shows two maps that point to an amazing similarity in concept.[107] The plans for the Ardennes offensive likewise called for a crossing of the Meuse, a march through the Ardennes, to be followed by an advance to the channel coast and the capture of Antwerp. But here the similarity ends. Manstein had carefully planned his operation and paid particular attention to the availability of supplies. The Ardennes offensive was directed against an enemy superior in all areas, who had

---

103   Stahlberg, p. 249
104   J. Fest, *Der Untergang. Hitler und das Ende des Dritten Reiches. Eine historische Skizze.* p. 157
105   Horne, p. 157
106   German losses recorded at the military archives of the Federal Republic, *Bundesarchiv-Militärarchiv*, BA-MA, RW 6/180, RW 19/1381, RM 7/808, RW 4/170. Allied losses vary slightly in national secondary literature.
107   Frieser, p. 439

total control of the airspace. The Germans had fuel reserves for an advance of 60 kilometres only. Whatever additional fuel was required, was ordered to be taken from Allied stocks 'to be captured during the advance'. Karl Marx had written: "Somewhere Hegel says that many historic events tend to occur twice. He forgets to add, the first time as a tragedy, the second time as a farce." [108]

On 16 December 1944, Manstein was shown the situation map of the Ardennes offensive. When it was evident that no strategic reserve had been put in place for the battle, he said to Stahlberg: "*Effendi* has a fertile imagination, he wants to attack an enemy in depth without having reserves." (In private conversations, Manstein called Hitler *Effendi* after a delegation of Crimean Tartars had brought him gifts for 'Adolf *Effendi*'.) When the German offensive ground to a halt, Manstein told Stahlberg: "If Eisenhower now attacks, he can finish the war in a few weeks." [109]

---

108   K.Marx/F.Engels, *Werke*, vol. 8.
109   Stahlberg, p. 411

Chapter 3

Manstein and the Battle for Stalingrad

Stalingrad was not the decisive battle of the Russo-German war. The war in the East continued over an additional two and a half years. For Germany's European allies, Stalingrad was a deadly blow. The Romanian and Hungarian units that participated in the battle, rendered the Armies of both countries increasingly unfit for further efficient deployment. The Italian Army in the East had been sent to Stalingrad. Both it and the Croatian regiments were destroyed. The *Wehrmacht* remained an efficient fighting force. True, in the *Kessel* it lost a whole Army of some 22 Divisions, its largest loss in the East. 6 additional Divisions were destroyed during the relief attempts. But prior to Stalingrad entire French and Russian armies had been obliterated. During the years following Stalingrad, more German armies would suffer a similar fate. In the summer of 1944, the huge Russian offensive, *Bagration*, against the German Army Group Centre, would wreak far greater havoc. If a battle had to be labelled as decisive, it would probably be the German defeat at Moscow in December 1941.

But in many respects Stalingrad was unique. For the first time in the Second World War, the Red Army defeated the Germans by employing and improving on the methods which the Germans themselves had developed in their previous victorious battles. In 1937, when the Great Terror hit the Red Army, most of its high command were executed. However, some outstanding instructors at the war academy had been spared. They succeeded in developing a new high command in a relatively short time. It is not difficult to turn good regimental commanders into good generals. Clausewitz had previously written that the art of war is a 'simple thing,' easily understood by 'common sense'. For Clausewitz the difficulty resides in the art of command. The new Russian generals showed themselves to be brilliant commanders, at least equal to their German counterparts.

Outstanding Russian military scientists, among them the father of the rocket programme, Koralev, and the aircraft designer Tupolev, had been arrested in 1937. They were not sent to the *Gulag* but to closed research institutes under NKVD control, the *Sharashka*, where they pursued their research. Even before the war they succeeded in developing armaments which, by 1941, proved superior to most German military equipment. As the war progressed, the Russian advantage in quality increased.

However, Stalingrad had a unique symbolic significance, because of the city's name. Both Hitler and Stalin recognised it. In a recording of his speech on 8 November, when the German offensive had already failed, Hitler's speech showed an unusual edginess, with him tapping his pencil continuously on his desk. He said:

> I always consider what others expect me to do, and then I do the contrary.
> Mr. Stalin expected me to attack in the Centre. I never had such intentions, not because Mr. Stalin thought that I had, but because it was not

important to me. I wanted to reach the Volga River, at a certain place, at a certain city. It is chance that it is named after Stalin. But don't think for a moment that I was prompted by that, it was because of its great strategic importance. As far as I am concerned the city could just as well have another name. Here one can cut off 30 million tons of shipment, including 9 million tons of oil. All shipments of wheat, from the Ukraine and the Kuban region to the North, pass through here. It is a centre for the shipment of manganese ore, in short a gigantic transhipment centre.

At that point Hitler's nervousness overcame him. His voice cracked repeatedly. Less than two weeks later and he would regret his subsequent words:

I wanted to take this place and, you know, we are modest. We have it already. Only a few isolated pockets of resistance remain. Then some people ask, 'why don't you finish it off faster?' Because I don't want a second battle of Verdun, and I prefer to operate with small assault units. Time is of no importance. No ship can pass the Volga anymore. And this is decisive.

They did not 'have it'. Ships continued to pass the Volga. The slogan "Trains are rolling for victory" (*Räder müssen rollen für den Sieg*) was no longer valid on the Eastern front. To the bitter end, trains rolled unimpeded, but only to the extermination camps.

Hitler had an obsession for symbolism. In 1918, Marshal Foch had convened the armistice talks with the Germans in his railway carriage in the forest of Réthondes, near Compiègne, as he wanted to spare the German delegations the hostile demonstrations by the French population. In 1940, Hitler chose to humiliate the French by having their armistice delegation received at the same location and in the same railway carriage.

Stalingrad had no less symbolic value for Stalin. After 1917, many cities in the Soviet Union were renamed after famous revolutionaries. When they fell victim to the Great Terror, their names were replaced by other political personalities. There was no lack of Soviet cities named after Stalin—Stalino, Stalinabad, Stalinogorsk, simply Stalin, and many others. But Stalingrad was the first, and the largest, and it had a special significance for Stalin. Before the revolution it was called Tsaritsyn. During the Civil War, Stalin was the Political Commissar of the Red Army units that had successfully defended the city, and Tsaritsyn was the first city named after him.

Hitler was convinced that the capture of Stalingrad would deal Stalin a mortal blow. As usual, he failed to understand the mentality of his great enemies. Stalin was no less obsessed with power than Hitler. But he was a far cleverer tactician and did not lose his sense of reality. His order, "not a step backwards", when the Germans approached Stalingrad was not due to the name of the city. Previously, a number of cities named after Stalin had been given up. Stalin felt that the Volga had to be secured in order to bring reserves to the areas that had not yet been taken by the Germans. The major Russian armament plants had already been set up behind the Ural mountain range in the 1930s. Others had been transferred beyond German reach when the Soviet Union was attacked. However, some sizeable plants had remained at Stalingrad and they were sorely needed.

Selection of sources in literature

World-wide, more books have been written about Stalingrad than about any other battle of the Second World War. In 2003, the year of the 70th anniversary of the destruction of 6th Army, a number of TV series were made in Germany, in which both German and Russian survivors recalled their experiences. For the purpose of this book, a narrow selection had to be made. The most complete collection of German archive documents is compiled in Manfred Kehrig's book, which was his doctoral thesis and later turned into a book.[1] Until his recent retirement, Dr Kehrig was the director of the German military archives. (*Bundesarchiv-Militärarchiv* in archive documents labelled BA-MA.) Kehrig published his book in 1974. He had no access to Russian documentation and his account is thus incomplete. It could best be described as a vastly expanded war diary of 6th Army and Army Group Don.

Among German Generals' memoirs, General Doerr's book is significant.[2] Doerr was the head of a liaison staff with the Romanian troops engaged at Stalingrad. He was a *confidant* of *Generaloberst* Zeitzler, who had succeeded Halder as head of the *Generalstab*. His post-war correspondence with Zeitzler contradicts a number of statements in *Verlorene Siege*.

The recollections of Paulus' adc, Colonel Wilhelm Adam, were written in 1963 at a time when Adam had become the commander of the East German armed police force. (*kasernierte Volkspolizei*) It was the forerunner of the new armed forces. (*Nationale Volksarmee – NVA*) The communist overtone is only found in the last part of the book that deals with his years in captivity, and his later role in East Germany. The part of his work that deals with Stalingrad shed a light on the Byzantine conditions prevailing in 6th Army's staff.[3]

The German offensive 'Blue', in the summer of 1942, finally led to the disaster at Stalingrad. The best account is in the Stalingrad chapter in Uhle-Wettler's *Höhe und Wendepunkte deutscher Militärgeschichte*. (High points and turning points in German military history)[4]. It is written in the same concise manner as the other eight chapters of that book. Uhle-Wettler never gets lost in the endless compilations of details that are common to many German military historians. Such books are rendered practically unreadable for people who are not themselves experts. We are in regular contact in exchanging opinions and advice about our respective works. Often our conclusions differ strongly, in particular about the responsibility of the German commanders at Stalingrad. Uhle-Wettler tends to absolve Manstein and put all the blame on Paulus. I hold the opposite view.

Among the recollections of younger officers at Stalingrad, the book by Joachim Wieder, *Stalingrad und die Verantwortung des Soldaten* (Stalingrad and the soldier's responsibility) is in my view, the most valuable source. Wieder was intelli-

---

1 M. Kehrig, *Stalingrad, Analyse und Dokumentation einer Schlacht*, Stuttgart, 1967 (henceforth Kehrig)
2 H. Doerr, *Der Feldzug nach Stalingrad*, Darmstadt, 1955, henceforth: Doerr
3 W.Adam, *Der schwere Entschluß*, Berlin East 1963 (henceforth Adam)
4 F. Uhle-Wettler, *Höhe-und Wendepunkte deutscher Militärgeschichte*, Hamburg 2000, pages 249-279 (already quoted as "Uhle-Wettler" in the Introduction and the chapter about the Battle for Fance).

gence officer Ic, on the staff of 6th Army's VIII Corps under General, later *Generaloberst,* Heitz. He was made a prisoner-of-war at Stalingrad. After his return from captivity he became a historian of repute. He emphasises that Manstein's Army Group South kept 6th Army ill-informed of the situation. He stresses the degree to which he, and his fellow officers, became increasingly desperate when Paulus' repeated appeals to Manstein remained unanswered.[5] Most memoirs by German survivors are highly critical of Manstein. They charge him of having failed in his overriding duties. When Manstein was made commander of Army Group Don, his name had become a symbol of hope for the soldiers in the *Kessel.* "Manstein is coming" was a common slogan.

Janusz Piekalkiewicz's *Stalingrad – Anatomie einer Schlacht* (Stalingrad – anatomy of a battle) is a unique day-by-day compilation of 700 pages of German and Russian *communiqués,* press releases and accounts by survivors. The author adds no personal comments.[6]

The most important book about Stalingrad, possibly the final account, is Anthony Beevor's *Stalingrad,* which was published in 1998 and translated world-wide.[7] Beevor had access to Russian archives, and was able to meet with numerous German and Russian survivors. Beevor sticks closely to facts, but he writes in the vivid style of other British and American historians such as Cornelius Ryan and John Toland. That style makes his book easily accessible to the lay reader.

Another valuable recent source is the TV-series 'War of the Century' and its accompanying book, under the direction of Laurence Rees. He had the co-operation of reputed historians, among them Ian Kershaw, author of the latest two-volume biography of Hitler. The movie is a compilation of newsreels, and inter-views of survivors on both sides.[8] It is intended to show the boundless cruelty of the war in the East, on both sides. In the part dealing with Stalingrad, a number of NKVD officers recalled how they terrorised their own troops, as well as the civilian population that had remained in the city. Male and female officers of *Smersch,* a special NKVD controlled unit, set up for the purpose of dealing with espionage, described how they interrogated German prisoners-of-war, and after questioning, shot them.

The two highest Red Army Commanders at Stalingrad, Marshal Zhukov, who headed the 'theatre,' and Marshal Rokossovsky, who commanded the 'Don Front', devoted only a small part in their memoirs to the battle. In Zhukov's memoirs of 749 pages, only 33 cover Stalingrad. In the 340 pages of Rokossovsky's recollec-tions, only 46[9] cover Stalingrad. In their eyes the two decisive battles of the Russo-German war were Moscow and Kursk. Both battles are treated in great detail.

Both Marshal Yeremenko and Marshal Chuikov are far more explicit. Yeremenko commanded the 'Stalingrad front'. Chuikov defended the city centre

5   J. Wieder, *Stalingrad und die Verantwortung des Soldaten,* Munich, 1962, (henceforth Wieder)

6   J. Piekalkiewicz, *Stalingrad – Anatomie einer Schlacht,* Munich 1977 (henceforth Piekalkiewicz)

7   A. Beevor, *Stalingrad,* London, 1998, henceforth: Beevor

8   L. Rees *War of the Century,* accompanying book with the same title, London, 1999, (henceforth Rees)

9   K. Rokossovsky, *Soldatski Dolg,* Moscow, 1970, henceforth: Rokossovsky

during the German onslaught. Rokossovsky was preferred when dealing the final blow. Chuikov's recollections are the most candid memoirs of any Red Army commander. His book is outspoken in his personal hatred of Zhukov. As 'Southern Generals', who were denied promotion to the highest ranks, until the death of Stalin, both Yeremenko and Chuikov had 'old accounts' to settle.[10]

The German offensive 'Blue'– a short summary

Uhle-Wettler begins his chapter on Stalingrad with the following sentence: "Some Commanders and some Armies were already doomed to destruction, before the first shot to decided their fate was fired."[11] Indeed, the whole plan for 'Blue' was based on mistaken assumptions. It was bound to turn into an unmitigated disaster.

In 1942, the Campaign in the East began with a major Russian debacle. It would be the last time that Stalin overrode the advice of his Generals. His closest advisers understood that the Red Army was not yet capable of offensive actions on the whole front. They implored Stalin to fortify positions around Moscow, and then await German initiatives. Stalin disagreed. He felt that, after the Russian victory at Moscow, he could attack wherever he pleased. He gave way to the entreaties of Marshal Timoshenko, one of the few major names who had survived the Great Terror. When the war began, Timoshenko commanded the central theatre and suffered a series of crushing defeats. Stalin knew that Timoshenko was not up to his task. He hurriedly replaced him with Zhukov, who halted the German attack on Moscow and launched the first successful Russian counter-offensive. But Timoshenko had not fallen into disgrace, and Stalin followed his suggestion to launch a major attack on Charkov on 12 May. All the Russian units were destroyed and the Red Army lost 250,000 prisoners-of-war.

A Ukrainian *Hiwi* Boris Witman, (*Hiwi, ie Hilfswillige,* was the designation of close to 1 million prisoners-of-war, who had volunteered for service with the *Wehrmacht* without engaging in combat) an interpreter at German headquarters, told Rees that he had overheard a conversation between two high- ranking *Waffen-SS* officers at the end of the battle. "What a pity that Marshal Timoshenko is not here. The *Führer* wants to hand him a high decoration, the Knight's Cross of the Iron Cross with Oak Leaves, as a token of gratitude for his contribution to the German victory.

After the completion of the conquest of the Crimea, the *Wehrmacht* battle plan for 1942 foresaw a major operation in the south, 'Blue'. By then the Germans no longer had the strength to attack on the whole front. In 1941 they had suffered the loss of 1.3 million soldiers, either killed in action, wounded, or missing. That amounted to 40% of their total manpower in the East, on 22 June 1941. Up to the beginning of the war against Russia, total German casualties on all fronts had been

---

10 A. Yeremenko, *Tage der Entscheidung – Als Frontenbefehlshaber an der Wolga,* German translation, East Berlin, 1964, henceforth: Yeremenko, *Stalingrad,* and V. Chuikov, *The Beginning of the End – The Battle for Stalingrad,* English translation, London, 1963, henceforth: Chuikov

11 Uhle-Wettler, p. 249

around 100,000. *Panzer* strength had been reduced from 3,600 to 3,000. Reserves were not available in sufficient numbers. Replacements in manpower were less than 30% to 35% of the requirements.

The original plan called for 'Blue' to be launched by Army Group South under *Feldmarschall* von Bock. A few days after the offensive started, von Bock was dismissed and Army Group South was split into two Army Groups, Army Group A, under *Feldmarschall* List, and Army Group B, under *Generaloberst* von Weichs. One Army Group would cross the Don in the area of Voronezh, the other would head out of Charkov. Thereafter the two Army Groups were to proceed towards Stalingrad and take the city. One Army Group would then drive into the Caucasus with the objective of capturing the Baku oil fields.

The Russians had early awareness of 'Blue'. A German plane had made a forced landing behind the Russian lines. One of its officers, Major Reichel, carried the complete battle-maps. The attack began on 28 June, and at first proceeded as planned. But the Germans had an initial surprise. The Russian Generals had learned their lessons from the *Kessel* battles of 1941 that had cost the Red Army nearly 4 million men taken prisoner. Everywhere operational retreat had replaced the former resistance and the Germans were only able to take a few prisoners.

Gradually the attack ground to a halt. The *Wehrmacht* committed the fatal mistake of separating the two Army Groups, and attacking in the Caucasus before having secured their positions on the Volga. The Germans approached Stalingrad in August and started to penetrate the city in early September. At that time, the Russians had already developed the plan for their *Uranus* counteroffensive. During the following weeks, most of Stalingrad was taken. However, a small area of this city, a waterfront of nearly 50 kilometres length along the Volga River, remained in Russian hands. Skirmishes in Stalingrad turned into fierce house-to-house fighting. At times the Russians would occupy the ground floor of a building, the Germans would be on the second floor, and the Russians on the top floor. German survivors told Rees of their despair that they had not been trained for such fighting. They were no match for the Russians, who succeeded in developing an increasing number of very efficient snipers. German infantry arms were not suitable for hand-to-hand combat. Their stem hand-grenades took ten seconds before exploding. The Russians often succeeded in throwing them back into the German lines, where they then detonated.

NKVD and *Smersch* presence was strong in the city. German prisoners-of-war were immediately interrogated and then summarily shot. A female *Smersch* officer, Zinaida Pytkina, appeared in Rees' movie. She told how she conducted her interrogation, and followed it by shooting the German officers who she had just questioned. When asked how she, now an old woman, felt about her actions today, she replied that, at her present age, she would perhaps not do it. But it gave her total satisfaction at the time. She certainly had no regrets.

The offensive in the Caucasus managed to cross the mountains, but could not make a sizeable advance on the plains. Hitler was furious when he heard that the mountain troops had wasted time in climbing the highest peak, the Elbrus, in order to plant a *swastika* banner on the summit.

When the offensive in the Caucasus slowed down, Hitler decided to relieve *Feldmarschall* List from his command of Army Group A. On 9 September, he made himself Direct Commander of the Army Group. An unprecedented, literally unbelievable hierarchy arose. As Commander in Chief of Army Group A, Hitler reported to the Commander in Chief of the Army, ie Hitler. The Commander in Chief of the Army reported to the Supreme Commander of Germany's armed forces, ie Hitler. The Supreme Commander reported in turn to the Chancellor of the Reich and Head of Government, ie Hitler. Above the Chancellor was the position of the *Führer*, once again Adolf Hitler. Even the greatest genius could not handle such an accumulation of power, since a day consists of only 24 hours. Hitler was a lazy man and slept during part of every day.

On 19 November, operation *Uranus* broke loose. Three days later the whole 6th Army was encircled. On that day, Hitler had made one of his periodic retreats to the *Berghof*, his Bavarian residence at Berchtesgaden. He slept until midday, no one daring to wake him up. A similar situation would occur when the Allies landed on 6 June 1944.

Uhle-Wettler wrote that "the final battle of 6th Army is, strictly speaking, of no interest to military history."[12] Indeed, after the *Kessel* was closed, there was no doubt about the end. The fate of 6th Army was sealed.

When the Russian offensive began, 6th Army could still have broken out. But Hitler ordered it to become a *Kessel*, relying on Göring's assertion that the Air Force could ensure its supply. Manstein launched a relief offensive, *Wintergewitter*. According to the plans, it was to be followed by a break-out of 6th Army, *Donnerschlag*, as soon as the distance between Army Group Don and 6th Army had been sufficiently reduced. *Wintergewitter* was undertaken with insufficient forces. It had to be broken off when Hoth's 4th Army, which had progressed to a point some 50 kilometres from the *Kessel*, was in turn at risk of being encircled.

For two months, the *Kessel* was kept secret from the German public, although rumours began to flow. The *Wehrmacht communiqué* of 24 November only mentioned that

> Southwest of Stalingrad, and in the large Don bend, the Soviets have succeeded, without any consideration of losses in troops and equipment, in creating a breach in the Front along the Don River. Counter-measures have already been initiated. In the bitter and alternating combats of the past two days, several hundred enemy vehicles have been destroyed. German and Romanian aircraft intervened, in spite of bad weather. In Stalingrad only local encounters.

German *communiqués* were generally worded in a sober manner, but it was easy to read between the lines. 'Alternating combats' meant that the Germans had suffered a set-back. The secret daily *OKW* report of the same date was more to the point:

> The northern front of VII Corps has been pushed back by strong enemy forces, towards the hills of Ssadogoye. The VI Romanian Corps has been destroyed, its troops are in a state of dissolution. Reception posts have been established to help assembling the fleeing troops. Weakened German rear-

---

12   Uhle-Wettler, p.274

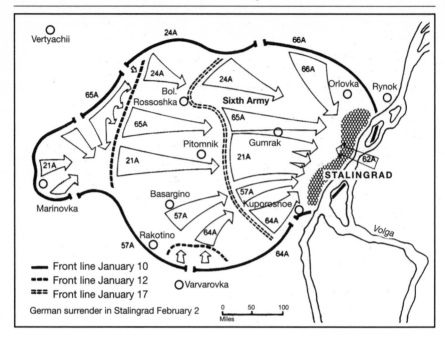

Stalingrad, January–February 1943

guards have retreated to the southern bank of the Yeshalouvsky sector, from Aksya to the West, after difficult defence actions.[13]

Thereafter, the daily bulletins would only mention bitter fighting in the region of Stalingrad, and within the city. The whole truth was revealed in the *communiqué* of 16 January 1943:

> In the area of Stalingrad our troops, who for weeks have heroically resisted an enemy attacking from all sides, succeeded in beating back strong enemy attacks, conducted with infantry and tanks, and caused the enemy heavy losses. Command and troops have once more shown a shining example of German soldiers' virtue.

When a German *communiqué* included words like 'heroic', 'shining example', 'exceptionally brave', it was immediately clear that a catastrophe had occurred.

The *Kessel* was gradually reduced. On 8 January 1943, Russian parliamentarians brought a formal request for surrender to 6th Army's headquarters. It was turned down. Two days later, the final Red Army's offensive *Koltso* began. The fighting came to an end on 2 February 1943.

---

13   *Die geheimen Tagesberichte der deutschen Wehrmachtsführung in Zweiten Weltkrieg 1939–1945*, Osnabrück 1991, vol. 5, p.299 (henceforth *Geheime Tagesberichte*).

German and Russian
commanders at Stalingrad

Feldmarschall Friedrich Paulus

Fate turned Paulus into one of the most interesting and controversial of top German commanders. His final rank was *Feldmarschall*. However, his last two promotions did not follow the usual pattern, and occurred through the unusual circumstances at Stalingrad. Paulus was promoted to *Generaloberst* on 30 November 1942, when his Army was already doomed. He was made a *Feldmarschall* on the eve of being taken prisoner, in the expectation that he would either die while fighting to the last bullet, or commit suicide.

Paulus was born in 1890, the son of a minor official at a re-education home for juvenile delinquents. His intention was to enter the Imperial Navy but he was turned down because of his family background. After that refusal he entered university and studied law, but then applied for admission into the Army. The Army accepted him and he became an officer candidate in 1910. He was a good-looking man, of elegant appearance, except for a nervous 'tic' in his face that increased rapidly under the stress at Stalingrad. He had impeccable manners. In the *Generalstab* he was saddled with the nickname *Fabius Cunctator*, the delayer, because of his endless hesitations before finally coming to a decision. His private diary had his motto on its first page, a poem by an unknown author.

> If you feel that everything appears clear,
> Do not rest and continue to doubt.
> Doubt everything which appears beautiful and clear,
> Always ask yourself for what purpose.
> Never believe that anything is straightforward.
> Straight is not straight and twisted not twisted.
> If someone tells you a value is final,
> Ask him softly: How?
> Truth of today can be tomorrow's lie.
> Follow the river down from its source.
> Never accept single steps of the path.
> Ask yourself always: Since when?
> Search for the reasons, connect them, and solve.
> Always dare to look behind words.
> If someone tells you, this is good or bad,
> Ask him quietly: Why?

While this is not great poetry, no one will say that it is a bad motto. But is it the motto of a troop commander? Clausewitz had written:

> War is uncertainty. More than three-quarters of events, which prompt action during war, are buried in the fog of uncertainty. The common man, not to speak of weak and undecided characters, will only arrive by chance at the right solution, based on premises imagined in a closed room. But, if suddenly confronted with danger and responsibility, he

loses overview. If he has to rely on the views of others, a decision taken by him would not be his own, because in the solitude of his command no one is there to assist him. Therefore we are convinced that no man who lacks audacity can become a great commander. No one, who was not born with audacity, can grow into such a man.[14]

Paulus would always remain a perfect 'number two' man, but never became a commander in his own right.

In 1912, Paulus married Elena Rosetti-Solescu, who belonged to the high Romanian aristocracy. Paulus then gained entry into the highest spheres of society. During the First World War he saw no troop service and was employed only in staff positions. He was accepted into the *Reichswehr* and served initially in the *Grenzschutz Süd*. His troop commands, in the *Reichswehr* and the *Wehrmacht,* were limited to short spans as commander of a company, and of a *Panzer* battalion.

In 1922 he attended a course at the *Truppenamt*. His teacher, the future *Generalleutnant* Heim, later became his subordinate as one of 6th Army's corps commanders. He gave Paulus a 'doubtful' performance evaluation: "Lack of decisiveness in precarious situations" [15] *Generaloberst* von Hammerstein-Equord was later more blunt: "He was a good worker at the *Generalstab*, but he lacked every element of independence. He should never have been given command of a large unit."[16]

He was accepted into the *Generalstab*, where he supported the modernisation of the Army, and pushed for the creation of *Panzer* divisions. In Poland, he became chief-of-staff of General von Reichenau's 10th Army, and succeeded him when Reichenau took over 6th Army in the West. Reichenau and Paulus were an ideal team.

Reichenau was ambitious, politically active and an enthusiastic sportsman. He spent hours every day on the tennis court, he was a keen rider, practised shot-putting, and jogged daily. During the Polish campaign he swam across a river at the head of one of his units. Such a man would always need a chief-of-staff who relieved him of the many routine chores, and Paulus was the ideal man for that task. After the battle of France, Paulus returned to the *Generalstab* as *Oberquartiermeister* I. He drew up the final plan of attack against the Soviet Union, *Barbarossa*. An earlier plan had already been submitted, in July 1940, by General Marcks.

In 1941, *OKH* had become increasingly irritated with Rommel's independent actions. On 25 April, Halder sent Paulus to North Africa, to "correct matters which had got out of hand". On 23 April, Halder had noted in his diary:

Things have finally to be cleared up in Africa. I have thought of flying down there myself, but after having carefully thought things over, decided against it. I can't appear there as an investigator. If I go to North Africa, I must have command authority. Brauchitsch has reservations, and mentions difficulties with the Italian High Command. I know that this is only a pretext, but perhaps it would be preferable to send *Generalleutant*

---

14   Clausewitz, p. 244 f
15   Knopp, p. 236
16   K. von Hammerstein, son of the *Generaloberst, Manstein* in Frankfurter Hefte 11, 1956, p. 425

Paulus. He is on friendly terms with Rommel, from former times, and may be in a position to use his personal influence to put an end to the initiatives of this lunatic.[17]

Paulus remained in Africa for two and a half weeks. Rommel had never belonged to the *Generalstab*, and Paulus viewed him with condescension, feeling that he himself might be a suitable replacement. In a report to Halder he wrote: "The situation in North Africa is unsatisfactory. By constantly disobeying orders, Rommel has created a situation where arrival of supplies is no longer assured. Rommel is simply not up to his command."[18]

Others report Paulus as having said: "This Swabian pig-head acts as if no one can give him any order." Ms Paulus is reported to have warned her husband: "Just keep your fingers out of this pie, do you want to end up by having them catch you down there?"[19] At that time the Rommel legend was already blossoming, Rommel was increasingly praised in propaganda, therefore his 'relief' was out of the question.

Paulus was then considered as a successor to Jodl at *OKW*. When List was dismissed from his command of Army Group A, Jodl had been sent on an inspection to the Caucasus front. On his return, he told Hitler that he agreed with all the steps taken by List. Hitler lost his temper. Jodl was barred from attending the daily luncheons at Hitler's headquarters, and Hitler decided to replace him at the earliest possible moment.

On 1 December 1941 Reichenau succeeded *Feldmarschall* von Rundstedt as Commander in Chief of Army Group South. Paulus was given the command of 6th Army, which at that time, with 330,000 men, was the strongest of the *Wehrmacht*. To Paulus' later misfortune, his Army was the strongest unit during the destruction of the Russian forces at Charkov in spring 1942. Suddenly he was looked upon as a capable Army Commander in his own right.

His appointment caused more than surprise. It was contrary to all established rules of seniority and was one more of Halder's incomprehensible mistakes in the war against Russia. As *Oberquartiermeister I*, Paulus had been Halder's direct and trusted subordinate. Paulus was only a *Generalleutnant*. All the corps commanders of 6th Army were senior to him in rank and had considerable experience of troop command. Therefore Paulus had to be quickly promoted to *General der Panzertruppe*. His promotion was backdated to 1 January 1942, in order to coincide with his appointment as Commander of 6th Army.

To this day, apart from Halder's caprice, no logical explanation has been found for his appointment. Since Paulus was considered to succeed Jodl as deputy head of *OKW*, Uhle-Wettler feels that some high command experience was a requirement for that promotion.[20] However, this is not borne out by history. Halder and Zeitzler had become Chiefs of the *Generalstab* without any previous notable troop commands. Jodl had reached his position at *OKW*, in 1938, in a similar manner.

---

17 Halder Diary, this passage in Knopp, p. 243 f
18 Knopp, p. 248
19 Ibid
20 Uhle-Wettler, p. 250

Uhle-Wettler wrote that the appointment of Paulus recalls the Imperial court of Byzantium, where commanders were often chosen according to their popularity with the ruler.[21] But now the 'emperor' was not Justinian but Reichenau. A possible explanation of Paulus' appointment was that the ambitious Reichenau wanted to continue commanding 6th Army directly, alongside with his Army Group. Reichenau is said to have favoured Paulus for the very reason that Paulus was not suitable for independent command. He himself would see to it that matters remained on course. His letter of congratulations to Paulus, on assumption of 6th Army's Command, seems to confirm this. Reichenau wrote: "I cannot imagine the Army to be in better hands than yours. Perhaps one day?"[22] Reichenau died of a stroke on 17 January 1942, and Paulus was left on his own.

OKH was aware of Paulus' weaknesses and felt that he had to be assisted by an energetic chief-of-staff. On 20 June 1942, *Generalmajor* Arthur Schmidt was appointed. Von Bock was convinced that he would bring more firmness to 6th Army.[23] Soon an increasingly grotesque situation arose. Paulus was Commander in Chief in name only, while being dominated by his more energetic and capable chief-of-staff. Doerr gives a description of the relationship between the two men:

> The relationship between the two was correct in form, but void of any human warmth. Paulus was intelligent, he had operative talent, he was a generous man, very sensitive and easily impressed, but simply not a strong personality. His chief-of-staff was a bachelor, of an aesthetic nature, clever, energetic, a thoroughly capable tactician, a man hard to the core, to the point of inflexibility.
>
> Both commanders might well have complemented each other, but Schmidt was the stronger man and dominated. There was no basic disharmony at the top. Nor did the different characters of the two men, and their formally correct relationship, have a negative influence on 6th Army's Command. The fateful element that bound them together was something common to both. It was their belief in Hitler and their trust in him, which many shared. It did not permit them even to imagine that their supreme commander could lie to them, or make solemn promises that he knew could not be kept.[24]

Absurd situations arose by the day. Schmidt could never stand fools, and held Adam in contempt. In his eyes, Adam was a mixture of *Kommisskopf*, a German military slang expression for 'small-minded barracks brain", and of *Briefträger,* another slang expression describing a man with the mind of a small village mailman.[25] Colonel Wilhelm Adam was adc to Paulus. Behind Paulus' back, Adam turned to *OKH*. On a visit to Hitler's temporary headquarters, at Vinnitsa in the

21 Ibid, p. 272
22 W. Görlitz(ed), *Paulus, Stalingrad. Lebensweg und Nachlass des Generalfeldmarschalls,* Bonn 1964, p.49 (henceforth Görlitz)
23 Piekalkiewicz, p. 20
24 Doerr, p. 53
25 Told by Winrich Behr to this author. Behr's and Schmidt's families were friends and Behr met general Schmidt repeatedly after the war.

Ukraine, he asked for a 'relief' of Schmidt who constantly "lectured Paulus like a disobedient pupil, in the presence of his staff officers."[26] An energetic commander would have meted out a severe punishment to Adam and thereafter sent him to a minor post. Paulus only issued a mild reprimand. Paulus would rely on Adam, when he had to communicate unpleasant messages to subordinate commanders.

His most experienced *Panzer* commander, General von Wietersheim, had warned him in September 1952 not to engage *Panzer* in the street fighting at Stalingrad. Paulus disagreed and felt that Wietersheim had simply lost his nerve. He 'relieved' him but did not have the courage to tell him so, face-to-face, and had Adam communicate his decision. When Wietersheim received Paulus' letter, he shrugged and said to Adam: "It is not always easy to be an adjutant."[27] Wietersheim had been Manstein's predecessor as *Oberquartiermeister* I. Adam would 'pay Schmidt back' in his post-war recollections and malign him as the man responsible for the plight of 6th Army.

All this occurred before the Russian counter-offensive and the closure of the *Kessel.* But even at that stage, it was evident that Paulus was not the man to disobey an order by Hitler, unless totally covered by an unambiguous order issued by Manstein. 6th Army would have required an exceptionally strong and energetic commander. There is little doubt that a general such as Model would have broken out on his own initiative. He would have told Hitler, in his usual manner after such disobedience, that a new and unforeseen situation had arisen. Then he was sure to have handled it according to Hitler's wish. Even Reichenau, a commander far less independent and of smaller talent than Model, had defied an order, by Hitler, to stay put. That was in December 1941 when he had retreated across the Mius line.

When Adam told Paulus how Reichenau would have acted, Paulus answered him in resignation: "I can imagine that the daredevil Reichenau would have broken out on 19 November. Then he'd tell Hitler, do with me whatever you like. But you know, Adam, I am not a Reichenau."[28]

On 30 January 1943, Paulus had sent his last message to Hitler:

> On the anniversary of your assumption of power, 6th Army salutes its *Führer*. The *swastika* banner still flies over Stalingrad. World history has shown that no sacrifice is in vain. May our fight serve as an example, to today's and future generations, never to surrender in a hopeless situation. Then Germany will be victorious. *Heil, mein Führer.* Paulus, *Generaloberst.*

One can be tempted to show contempt for the devotion of this message, but this would not be fair to Paulus. Other generals, who after the war described themselves as bitter opponents to Hitler, had sent messages and issued orders of the day which were no less subservient. Hitler replied,

> My *Generaloberst* Paulus! Today the German people already look with deep emotion upon its heroes in this city. As always in world history, this sacrifice will not be in vain. The legacy of Clausewitz is confirmed. Only

---

26 Adam, p. 42 ff
27 Ibid, p. 102
28 Ibid, p. 238

now the German nation understands the total gravity of the fight and will be ready to make the highest sacrifice. My thoughts are with you and your men. Your Adolf Hitler.[29]

On 31 January, Paulus was promoted to *Feldmarschall* and on the following day he surrendered to the Russians together with his staff. After the war a number of officers wrote that they had informed Paulus of his promotion. Adam wrote that he had woken Paulus up, informed him, and entered the promotion in Paulus' service record book. Others had Schmidt as the message bearer.

Rees talked to a battalion commander, Werner Hindenlang, who told him that he had received the radio message and been ordered to convey it to Paulus:

I went over to his headquarters, reported to the general and told him that I had been informed by radio of his promotion. I congratulated him, and then added that we had to surrender next day, because the Russians had surrounded his headquarters and no further defence was possible. Then he said to me: 'Hindenlang, now I am the youngest *Feldmarschall* of the German Army and I will become a prisoner-of-war.'

I was puzzled, since this was unexpected. He noticed my reaction and asked me: 'Hindenlang, what is your opinion about suicide?' I replied: *Herr Generalfeldmarschall*, I command a troop and have to stay at its head until the last moment. If necessary, I will follow it into a prison camp. But you have no longer any troops.' He answered: 'Hindenlang, I am a believing Christian and I reject any notion of suicide.' I simply turned round and left.[30]

Paulus had General Roske negotiate his personal surrender with the Russian general Laskin. He was first taken to the commander of the Russian 62nd Army, General Shumilov. Thereafter he saw Air Marshal Voronov who acted as representative of the Soviet Supreme Command, and the commander of the 'Don front,' Colonel General Rokossovsky.

Reports of his questioning differ, some are anecdotal. Many Russian officers were present and were eager to recount their story to the numerous American and British war correspondents who had been invited to the city, and in turn reported to their newspapers. The capture of a German *Feldmarschall* before the fighting had come to a close, was a unique event of the Second World War. The northern part of the *Kessel* under the *Generaloberst* resisted for two more days. The Russians expressed surprise that Paulus had stayed with his troops, since their own high commanders were usually flown out in similar situations.

One account purports that Paulus made the *Nazi* salute, and said *Heil Hitler*, when brought before Shumilov and that the Russian General asked him to desist.[31] Adam recounts that Shumilov had treated both to a fine dinner, and had proposed a toast to the brave of both armies.[32] Another story had Shumilov asking Paulus about his rank, whereupon Paulus presented his service record book into which Adam had entered his promotion to *Feldmarschall.*

---

29   Knopp, p.261 f
30   Rees, p. 185
31   Piekalkiewicz, p. 667
32   Ibid, p.350 ff

Beevor writes that Voronov had addressed Paulus as *Herr Generaloberst* whereupon Paulus interrupted him and said that he had been promoted to *Feldmarschall*. He added that under the circumstances he had not been able to obtain the shoulder straps of his new rank.[33] Voronow and Rokossowsky exchanged amused smiles, since Shumilov had already informed them of Paulus' new rank. After Paulus was brought into a generals' prison camp, he immediately requested the German military *attaché* in Ankara to send him six pairs of a *Feldmarschall*'s shoulder straps. It was a new uniform of the kind he had had tailor-made in Paris, his wife would provide the details.[34] On every photo taken in captivity, he would display the shoulder straps. However, the military *attaché* had omitted, perhaps out of malice, to send him *Feldmarschall* collar patches.

The Russians were eager to forward this letter, since they wanted to display Paulus in *Feldmarschall* uniform on their photos. The two Russian Generals told Paulus that it was unworthy of a supreme commander, having been taken prisoner, to then have his troops continue fighting. He is reported to have replied that he had not been taken prisoner, but fallen into Russian hands 'by surprise.'[35] Junior German officers to whom his words were reported, laughed bitterly when they heard the word 'prisoner,' since Paulus was immediately taken to a de-luxe sleeping-car while they had to march through snow and ice until they reached their prison camps. Lieutenant Joachim Stempel told Rees:

> This is simply laughable, ten minutes later the *Feldmarschall* was no longer with his troops. He sat in his sleeping-car, with clean sheets on his bed, and a clean tablecloth on his eating table, and was on his comfortable way to a generals' camp near Moscow.[36]

Joachim Stempel was the son of *Generalleutnant* Stempel, who shot himself on 15 January, when his division had been destroyed. Stempel had been present at his father's last talk with Paulus. Paulus had told General Stempel:

> My proud 6th Army suffers an undeserved fate. You know what you have to do as a German General. All my staff and myself will defend our headquarters with our last bullets and then we will blow ourselves up. I wish you all the best on your last path.

When he heard of Paulus' surrender, Joachim Stempel was very bitter: "I was simply disappointed and asked myself what the word of a high commander was worth. Had my father suspected that Paulus would give himself up, he would still be alive."[37]

The photographs of Paulus' questioning by Rokossovsky and Voronov, which were published in the Soviet press, resulted in "one of the grotesque farces of the Stalinist era." According to Beevor, General Telegin, Rokossovsky's political commissar attended, but he was removed from the published photo because Stalin did not consider him important enough. Telegin was terrified, since it was stan-

---

33 Bevor, p. 290
34 Knopp, p. 246
35 Knopp, p.264
36 Rees, p. 187
37 Ibid, p. 188 f

dard Soviet practice to doctor photos, and remove people who had been declared 'enemies of the people." Since nothing happened to Telegin, he felt that he was safe. However, he was to be arrested in 1948.[38]

Regardless of the variations in many accounts, the fact remains that Paulus' surrender lacked any dignity. In his book, *Freies Deutschland*, the historian Bodo Scheurig wrote:

> Although Paulus had extolled the faith and devotion of 6th Army to the bitter end, in his many messages to higher levels, he did not choose death for himself. His surrender took place without formality. 'Fighting unto death, which had been ordered unscrupulously from above, was only valid for the soldier at the front. A Command, which had at first chosen to obey, and then acted bereft of any dignity, chose an inglorious exit for itself. Far too often, the Command had made a mockery of actions that it had demanded from others, and thus lost what was left of its 'face'.[39]

Hitler reacted to the news of Paulus' surrender with an outburst of uncontrolled rage. The document that recorded his tirade is partly damaged:

> They have simply surrendered. Otherwise they would have formed a 'hedgehog' and shot themselves with their last bullets ... I have no respect for a soldier who prefers to be taken prisoner ... The Russians will take them to the Lubyanka and Schmidt will sign everything requested from him. If one does not have the courage to do what one should, one will not be able to resist their pressure ... They will be taken immediately to Moscow and worked over by the GPU ... Schmidt is going to sign everything ... We have paid far too much attention to intellect and not enough to character ... How easy he has made it for himself ... My first doubts arose when he asked me what he should do. Why does he have to ask at all? So, in the future, whenever a fortress is under siege and is told to surrender, the Commander will ask what he has to do ... What hurts me most is that I have promoted him to *Feldmarschall*. There will be no more *Feldmarschalls* in this war. [The following day Kleist, Busch and Weichs were promoted to *Feldmarschall*] ... He will immediately talk on the radio, you will see. Seydlitz and Schmidt will both talk. They will lock them up in 'the rat's cave', after two days they will have softened them up and they will immediately talk ...[40]

The captured German Generals were treated in a wholly different manner from the other officers and soldiers. Marshal Rokossovsky wrote in his memoirs that the preferred treatment, which the Generals enjoyed, went to their heads. "They began to act like 'big shots', were impolite, and would continuously demand

---

38   Beevor, p. 388

39   B. Scheurig, *Freies Deutschland. Das Nationalkomitee und der Bund Deutscher Offiziere in der Sowjetunion 1943–45*, Frankfurt 1984, p. 28 f

40   *Hitlers Lagebesprechungen. Protokollfragmente seiner militärischen Konferenzen 1942–1945*, H. Heiner (ed.), Stuttgart 1962, p. 120 ff (henceforth *Lagebesprechngen*).

new privileges. We had to remind them politely that they were prisoners, and to behave themselves accordingly."[41]

Generalleutnant Sixt von Armin had a conversation in German with the British author Alexander Werth: "The Russian officers are correct, but the soldiers are thieves and rascals. (*das sind Diebe, das sind Halunken. So eine Schweinerei!*) Impudent thieves! They stole all my things. Four suitcases, and they stole them all. What obscene behaviour (*Schweinerei*)."[42] General Heitz, who until the last day had threatened to shoot anyone who talked of surrender and was rewarded with a promotion to *Generaloberst* on the day on which Paulus was made a *Feldmarschall,* quietly gave himself up and had dinner with General Shumilov. After spending the night at Shumilov's headquarters he joined his fellow Generals, with a number of suitcases in his car. He told his outraged comrades that he had intended to commit suicide but that his chief-of-staff had prevented him.[43]

In his residence as a prisoner-of-war, Paulus had been given a comfortable house with a garden for himself. Paulus' behaviour became increasingly weird. The Austrian communist emigrant, Ernst Fischer, after the war became the Austrian Communist Party's chief ideologist. His aristocratic wife, Ruth von Mayenburg, wrote about a meeting with Paulus. Paulus had suddenly asked for her assistance in getting a riding-horse. Ruth von Mayenburg was outraged that he had not asked to visit a prisoner-of-war camp, even if he had only been shown a Potemkin type village.[44]

Before Stalingrad, the Russians had made strong efforts to woo German prisoners-of-war. Those who showed themselves amenable were sent to 'anti-fascist' ie *Antifa* schools that were controlled by *NKVD* officials. The schools were headed by General Melnikov, and by German Communist politicians who had emigrated to the USSR. East Germany's future leader, Walter Ulbricht, was the most prominent. Until the Stalingrad surrender, the Red Army had taken only relatively few German prisoners. When the fighting at Stalingrad ended, they suddenly had more than 80,000 officers and soldiers, and 23 Generals. To pursue their efforts, the Russians needed an organisation. On 13–14 July 1943, they established the *NKFD, Nationalkomitee Freies Deutschland,* a National Committee for a Free Germany, at the prisoner-of-war camp at Krasnogorsk. Since they saw that the somewhat primitive Communist flavour of the *NKFD* would not attract senior officers, by the end of August a new body was established at Lunyovo, the *BDO, Bund deutscher Offiziere,* the League of German Officers, which admitted officers of all ranks. The *BDO* adopted a national German style and the black, white and red Imperial flag.

Half of the Generals who were taken prisoner at Stalingrad joined the *BDO.* Some would succumb to Soviet propaganda, become Communist sympathisers and remain East Germany after the war. General Vinzenz Müller, before 1933 a close associate of Schleicher, became deputy chief-of-staff of the *NVA* and deputy minister of defence of the GDR. General von Lenski, who prior to being sent to Stalingrad had been an assistant judge at one of the 'Popular Courts' ie *Volksgerichtshof,* would be rewarded with a candidate seat on the Eastern German

41 Rokossovsky, p.173 f
42 A. Werth, *Russia at War,* New York 1964, p.549.
43 Wieder, p. 246 f
44 Kosthorst, p. 38ff with quote from R. von Mayenburg, *Blaues Blut und Rote Fahnen. Revolutionäres Frauenleben zwischen Wien, Berlin und Moskau,* Munich 1969

Politburo. General Bamler was later suspected of having been a Soviet agent since before the war.

The much maligned General Arthur Schmidt behaved differently. When high ranking NKVD officers invited him into a luxury railway coach, and served him a sumptuous meal with caviar and champagne, he replied to their entreaties that he would behave in the manner which he expected from Russian Generals, who might find themselves in a similar situation. This was the end of the festival, Schmidt was immediately sent to the *NKVD* Lubyanka prison in Moscow. There he remained incarcerated until Adenauer's visit to the USSR in 1955 which led to the liberation of the remaining German prisoners-of-war.[45]

After 20 July, and the execution of *Feldmarschall* von Witzleben and his fellow generals on the gallows, Paulus joined the *BDO* and became its president. At the Nuremberg trial he testified for the prosecution. Allied observers were shocked when he referred to his former comrades as 'accused'.[46] Jodl's attorney cornered him, when he labelled the *Barbarossa* order as having been criminal, by forcing him to admit that he himself had drafted it. When Paulus entered the hall, Göring shouted: "Ask this dirty swine if he knows that he is a traitor."[47]

Keitel said to the American psychologist Dr Gustave Gilbert who talked with every accused at the end of each day of the proceedings: "Suddenly it occurred to me that if the plan of having Paulus succeed Jodl, he and not Jodl would be sitting on this bench."[48] Gilbert wrote that Paulus' appearance in the court hall turned the place into a madhouse, and that the other accused among the military joined Göring in his invectives. However, Fritzsche, Neurath, Seiss-Inquart, Schacht and Funk told him that they simply felt pity for him.[49] Some German spectators expressed outrage when Paulus, after being asked about the health of his soldiers who had been taken prisoner, replied: "Tell the mothers that their sons are fine". Only 5,000 of the more than 80,000 German prisoners-of-war returned alive.

After his release from captivity, Paulus settled in East Germany. His wife had refused a party request to divorce him. After 20 July 1944 she was arrested, sent to the Dachau concentration camp and freed by the Americans. After her last encounter with her husband, prior to the closure of the *Kessel*, she never saw him again. Paulus lived out his life in luxurious conditions at Dresden. He gave lectures at the war academy of the *NVA*. In official East German documents he was never mentioned by his name but only as 'the object' or 'the object *Terrasse*.' He never returned to West Germany but was allowed to receive regular visits by his son and other close relatives and was provided with Western newspapers and magazines.

---

45   The fate of General Schmidt in captivity is public knowledge and widely reported in all books dealing with Stalingrad, as is his refusal to cooperate with the Russians. He described his conversations with his captors after his return home with Winrich Behr, who communicated his notes to this author.

46   Georges Vassiltschikow in a letter to Winrich Behr, which Behr communicated to this author.

47   G. Gilbert, *Nürnberger Tagebuch, Gespräche der Angeklagten mit dem Gerichtspsychologen*, Frankfurt 1962, p. 147

48   Ibid, p. 148

49   Ibid

He died of a brain tumour in 1957. The authorities permitted his burial in his family grave in West Germany.

Many aspects of his personality still remain unknown. A number of his personal papers have been assembled by Walter Görlitz. The book came in for criticism, because of its arbitrary selections of documents. They were also altered by splitting one document into separate sections, and appearing in different parts of the book with the purpose of rendering credence to the author's opinions. A serious biography of him remains to be written.

General Walter von Seydlitz-Kurzbach

General von Seydlitz was a direct descendant of the famous cavalry commander of Frederick the Great. His ancestor had risen to fame in history, when he three times disobeyed a direct attack order from Frederick during the battle against the Russians at Zorndorf in 1757. The third time, the king told him that his disobedience would cost him his head and received the reply: "After the battle, Your Majesty. While the battle still proceeds, I need my head to serve Your Majesty." Seydlitz attacked later, at the moment of his choice, and won a decisive battle. The king congratulated him. His descendant commanded 6th Army's LI Corps. A few months earlier, Seydlitz had taken part in the relief of the Demyansk *Kessel*, which was smaller in size than Stalingrad. He was awarded the Oak Leaves and was regarded as Paulus' outstanding Corps Commander.

On the day of the closure of the *Kessel*, 6th Army's headquarters were outside the area. On 22 November, Hitler ordered Paulus to immediately transfer them inside. On 23 November, Paulus sent an urgent message to Hitler:

> *Mein Führer!* Since receiving your message on the evening of 22 November, things have started to happen at a rapidly increasing pace. Although the *Kessel* is not yet entirely closed in the West and the Southwest, new enemy breakthroughs are expected. Ammunition and fuel are coming to an end. Many artillery batteries and anti-tank guns are no longer performing. Possible arrival of sufficient relief must be excluded.
>
> The Army faces certain annihilation, unless all available forces are concentrated on an attack against the enemy, advancing in the south and the west. This requires an immediate withdrawal of all divisions from Stalingrad and the northern front, to permit a breakthrough towards the Southwest, since the northern and eastern parts of the front are no longer defensible.
>
> I remain solely responsible for this most serious report, but I must add that my corps commanders, Generals Heitz, Strecker, Hube, von Seydlitz, and Jaenecke share my opinion. I request once more your permission to act according to my judgement.[50]

On the same day *Generaloberst* von Weichs, commander in chief of Army Group B to which 6th Army was subordinated, sent a lengthy message to *OKH*, which began with the sentence:

---

50   Piekalkiewicz, p. 413 ff

Not withstanding the difficulty of reaching a decision of such far-reaching consequences, I feel bound to report that I consider the request of General Paulus to withdraw 6th Army to be justified ... If parts of 6th Army can be saved, its units will be indispensable for building up new defence positions ... While I am aware that my suggestion will lead to heavy losses, particularly in equipment, these will however be even heavier if the inevitable destruction of 6th Army occurs.[51]

Hitler sent a short reply that the Army had to stay put in the *Kessel*, that relief by air would be forthcoming, and that he had faith in the brave soldiers of 6th Army and their commanders.

On 25 November, General von Seydlitz dictated a lengthy memorandum to his chief-of-staff, Colonel Clausius, to be forwarded to Paulus. It ended with the following sentences:

If *OKH* will not immediate cancel its order to remain within the *Kessel*, our conscience towards the Army, and the German people, dictates us to take liberty of action in our own hands, and to use all remaining possibilities to avoid the catastrophe, by breaking out. The total annihilation of 200,000 men and all their equipment is at stake. There is no other choice.

Schmidt transmitted the memorandum to Army Group Don with the handwritten comment: "We don't have to rack the brains of the *Führer*, and General von Seydlitz does not have to rack the brains of the *OB*."[52] (*OB-Oberbefehlshaber* was the official German military term for commanders-in-chief of Armies and Army Groups. A corps commander was a *Kommandierender General*, a division commander a *Kommandeur*).

Stahlberg recalls that Manstein was outraged at Seydlitz' initiative:

Seydlitz' memorandum had not passed my desk. Apparently Manstein had received it from his chief-of-staff, General Schulz. The door leading from my room to his was always open and I heard him breaking into loud shouts. I went into his room and asked him if I could do anything for him. He looked at me and said, in a state of great agitation: 'General von Seydlitz has written a memorandum of which I totally disapprove. It is simply incredible that Seydlitz dares to meddle in such matters as this.'

I returned to my room to prepare the situation map. When I returned to Manstein with my report, I saw that the memorandum was on his desk. I asked him if I could read it. Manstein was still agitated and replied with a curt 'No'. This was the first time that the *Feldmarschall* would not show me a document that had been communicated to him. I first read it after the war.[53]

Why such outrage? Was a corps commander suddenly a roly-poly? What does Manstein mean by 'meddling'? Had Manstein, while a junior officer at the *Generalstab,* not constantly meddled in others' departments? Had Manstein, who was well versed in German military history and tradition, suddenly forgotten the

51   Ibid, p. 411 f
52   Ibid, p. 432
53   Stahlberg, p. 252

famous dictum by Prince Friedrich-Karl of Prussia: "Sir, His Majesty has made you a staff officer in order to have you know when you don't have to obey." King Friedrich-Wilhelm I of Prussia had said that "a Prussian officer owes obedience unless it infringes upon his honour."

Seydlitz' action followed the best Prussian tradition, a tradition that Manstein knew only too well since he once had to personally experience the consequences of its breach. In 1924 he had complained about the quality of a service apartment allotted to him in Berlin. *Generaloberst* von Seeckt, a strong believer in the traditional dictum that *Generalstab* officers have to remain nameless (*Generalstabsoffiziere haben keinen Namen*) was outraged and simply struck Manstein from the list of officers who received the customary two years' backdating of their rank on being accepted in the *Generalstab*. Manstein had to wait thirteen years before the two years were retroactively credited to him.[54] Manstein would have been well advised to give Seydlitz' memorandum careful consideration. Seydlitz had personal *Kessel* experience that Manstein lacked. Conceivably a careful review of Seydlitz' arguments could have led Manstein to depart earlier from his first optimistic view of the situation.

However, two days later, Seydlitz would show that he could pass the responsibility on to his commander, but that he was not prepared to act himself. Paulus had told him that he expected to be relieved, and since Seydlitz was *persona grata* with Hitler, he could be expected to receive command of 6th Army. Would he then act on his own? Seydlitz remained silent for some minutes and replied: "No, I would have to obey."[55]

On 26 November, a special order from Hitler arrived, giving Seydlitz command of the northern and eastern sectors of the *Kessel*, with direct reporting to Hitler. Paulus said to Seydlitz, "Now you are free to act as you choose." Seydlitz issued an order to his troops: "Not a single step backwards! Whatever is lost must be immediately recaptured. Relief is on the way, supply by air has begun. All divisions have to hold their positions to their last bullet."[56]

When Stalingrad surrendered, the Russians looked at Seydlitz as their prize capture. He was the bearer of a name surrounded by generations of fame, and the Russians had obtained knowledge of his memorandum. After consultations with Generals Lattmann and Dr Korfes, the NKVD general Melnikov approached Seydlitz. He asked him to assume the presidency of the *NKFD* and the *BDO*. *Generalmajor* Lattmann had commanded 14th *Panzer* division at Stalingrad. Until his capture he had been an enthusiastic National-Socialist, thereafter he underwent a change.

Dr Korfes can be described as an unimportant 'random general'. From 1920 to 1936 he was the head of the German military archives. In 1937 additional officers were rapidly needed and Dr Korfes was given a Major's commission with backdating to 1935. He was the brother-in-law of Colonel Mertz von Quirnheim, one of the leading figures during the attempted *coup* on 20 July 1944. After the war, both Lattmann and Dr Korfes remained in the GDR and obtained senior *NVA*

54   *Soldatenleben*, p.90 f
55   Adam, p. 285
56   Piekalkiewicz, p. 432

commands. Seydlitz agreed to Melnikov's proposal.[57] The politically naive Seydlitz was obviously no match for an experienced NKVD general like Melnikov. Seydlitz asked Melnikov what was expected from him and received the reply that the *BDO* could become a useful instrument for the termination of the war across the front lines.

Sedlitz wrote in his memoirs that Melnikow gave him assurances, "upon direct instructions of the Soviet government":

> Should the *BDO* succeed in convincing the *Wehrmacht* High Command to spearhead an action against Hitler, which would end the war before the Red Army penetrates into Germany, the Soviet Union would support a peace settlement that would leave Germany with its 1937 borders. The Soviet Union will likewise allow Germany to maintain a *Wehrmacht*. Our only condition is the establishment of a civil-democratic government that would conclude pacts of mutual friendship with the East. You will be able to talk to German troops by loud-speaker and enlighten them about your objectives. You may likewise write letters to German commanders, we have reliable ways to make them reach their addressees. You can thus make a valuable contribution to an overthrow of Hitler and an ending of the war in good time. The Soviet Union will give you every support.

> When I voiced carefully worded doubts about the honesty of the Soviet assurances, Melnikov referred to the good relationship in the past between the Red Army and the *Reichswehr* in Seeckt's time.[58]

Seydlitz wrote to Generals Model, Mattenklott and Lieb. *Generalleutnant* Edler von Daniels wrote to Manstein, and many more letters were sent. Messages from the *BDO* were transmitted by loud-speakers. The letters remained unanswered and the appeals fell on deaf ears. The German Front Commanders continued to live in the illusion of a successful defence of the fatherland. However, at the *Führerhauptquartier* the increasingly unfavourable war situation caused fear that the *BDO* appeals might receive attention. Schmundt wrote the 'declaration of loyalty', the *Treuegelöbnis*, in which Seydlitz was showered with the worst terms of *Nazi* propaganda. The declaration was signed by all *Feldmarschalls* in the East and, not surprisingly, presented to Hitler by Rundstedt.

Worries also arose at *OKH*.

After 20 July 1944 Guderian wrote an appeal, distributed as a circular to the troops. It contained the most obscene expressions ever used by a chief of the German *Generalstab*:

> The leaders of the committee are emigrated Jews and Communists like Wolf, Weinert, Pieck and Hörnle. All of them are swine (*Schweinehunde*). They have been joined by the former German General von Seydlitz, who deserted in cowardly fashion after Stalingrad, and went over to the *Bolsheviks*. The other members of the committee are a handful of deserters.

---

57   Details about Seydlitz' activities in Kosthorst, p. 27 and 36 and his own memoirs, W. Seydlitz, *Konflikt und Konsequenzen. Erinnerungen.*, Hamburg 1977 (henceforth Seydlitz) Also K-H Frieser, *Krieg hinter Stacheldraht, die deutschen Kriegsgefangenen in der Sowjetunion und das Nationalkomitee Freies Deutschland*, Mainz 1981

58   Seydlitz, p. 285 ff

Some prisoners-of-war have been turned around by Soviet propaganda. The committee is just a bunch of traitors who carry no weight ... Men like Stauffenberg have come from the *NKFD*. There is no room for traitors and deserters in the *Wehrmacht*, no soldier of honour will lend them his ear. They belong to the gallows and will be hanged like all the accomplices in the plot against our *Führer*. We remain loyal to our oath and will continue to fight for our *Führer*, our people and our fatherland.[59]

Likewise, the appeals did not remain unheard in the military 'resistance' movement. In a post-war affidavit under oath, Ms Korfes wrote about a talk with her brother, Colonel Mertz von Quirnheim on 25 June 1944. Her brother told her that he was well informed of the activities of the *NKFD*. He agreed with Stauffenberg, that they were a useful instrument in the attempt to save Germany from a catastrophe.[60]

General Röhricht had been a close associate of Schleicher in the early 1930s. At that time he was a major. He recalls in his memoirs a conversation on 20 January 1944. It was with Tresckow, when the latter tried in vain to gain his active participation in the 'resistance' movement. Tresckow told him: "The victor will be Russia, with some help from the Allies. All the talk from across the Atlantic Ocean is simply mist and waffle. What remains is a field of ruins from the Danube to the Biscay. What else can we do but to seek an alliance with the other side while there still is time?" Röhricht questioned: "In other terms, an alliance with the Soviet?" Tresckow said: "If an exemplary officer like Seydlitz, a nobleman without fear nor blemish, has chosen this path, it should be possible for us to join and to save what can still be saved." Röhricht then asked him:" Is this a vague hope or do you have something substantial at hand?" Tresckow replied: "Not yet, but we will find a way."[61]

Röhricht was an opponent of national-socialism, but he viewed an attempted *coup* as being hopeless. His foster son, Major Hans-Ulrich von Oertzen was an active participant in the *coup* attempt, and blew himself up with two hand-grenades when he was about to be arrested. Tresckow's remarks about the Allies must be seen against his disappointment that the 'resistance' movement never found an echo with the Western Allies.

After Paulus joined the *BDO*, Seydlitz's star gradually waned, at times in a petty manner. Both Paulus and himself were in need of dental treatment. Paulus was fitted with a golden crown. Seydlitz had to be content with crown of steel. The *NKFD* and the *BDO* had been dissolved after the German surrender in 1945. In May 1950, unpleasant incidents occurred between Seydlitz and Paulus. Even a year before, Seydlitz had refused to send Stalin a letter of congratulations on his 70th birthday. On 20 May 1950 Paulus was requested to send a letter of thanks to Stalin for the good treatment of German prisoners-of-war. Seydlitz told Paulus that he simply could not do this. Paulus could thank Stalin for his own treatment

59   Kosthorst, p. 80 f. The complete text of Guderian's appeal in P. Steinbach, *Widerstad im Widerstreit. Der Widerstand gegen den Nationasozialismus in der Erinnerung der Deutschen*, Paderborn 1994, p. 263 f

60   E. Zeller, *Oberst Stauffenberg. Ein Lebensbild*. Paderborn 1994, p. 227

61   E. Röhricht, *Pflicht und Gewissen. Erinnerungen eines deutschen Generals 1932–1944.*, Stuttgart 1932–1944, p. 206

but he could not talk in the names of all prisoners for whom he had never shown any interest and whose fate was unknown to him. "I don't know which diplomatic solution Paulus has found here. He never mentioned the matter again to me. Somehow he must have satisfied the Russians, since he remained in their favour, while I was given clearly to understand that I was written off."[62]

On 23 May 1950, Seydlitz and a number of senior officers of the *BDO* were arrested and arraigned as war criminals. On 8 July 1950 he was sentenced to death, but on the same day, his sentence was reduced to 25 years. He remained in prison until his repatriation on 4 October 1955. A General Schulz, who was in charge of distributing seats in the train, refused him a seat in the officers' car and relegated him to the soldiers and non-coms. When he arrived at the West German repatriation reception camp at Friedland, he encountered his old friend, General Hossbach. As a Colonel, Hossbach had been Schmundt's predecessor as Hitler's *Wehrmacht* adc. He was dismissed in 1938. He had contravened an explicit order by Hitler not to reveal to Fritsch the charges that had been brought against him, prior to the General's visit to the chancellery. Seydlitz turned to Hossbach and asked him, "Do you also despise me?" Hossbach shook his hand and replied, "I was not in your situation." Seydlitz burst into tears.[63]

Seydlitz had been sentenced to death in Germany. The sentence was not quashed until 1956. The *Bundeswehr* did not restore his rank.

The opponent – General Vassily Chuikov

On 11 September 1942, Lieutenant General Lopatin was relieved as commander of 64th Army that held the centre of the city. Colonel General Yeremenko, commander of the 'Stalingrad front', felt that Lopatin could not cope with this task. Lieutenant General Vassily Chuikov replaced him. During the first six months of the Russo-German war, Chuikov had served as military attaché to the government of Chiang-Kai-Check. Upon his return to Russia he received command of a small reserve Army at Tula. He sustained back injuries in a car accident and when he came to Stalingrad he still needed a walking stick. Krushchev and Yeremenko asked him how he viewed his new command. Chuikov wrote that he had not expected such a question, but immediately found the answer: "We may not abandon this city. I will never leave it. Either we hold Stalingrad or we will die."[64]

The Soviet High Command could not have made a better choice. Chuikov was the most brutal Russian commander. Brutality was not an uncommon aspect of many Red Army Generals, but none would equal Chuikov. One of his staff officers, Anatol Mereschko, told Rees:

> Chuikow could literally feel a battle. He always reached his decision at the right time and overcame every obstacle. He embodied a Russian proverb: 'If you shoot, simply shoot. If you feel merry and cheerful, just be merry and cheerful'. With him shooting was always paramount. He possessed a

---

62   Seydlitz, p.360 f
63   Told by Georg Meyer to the author with reference to a conversation with Seydlitz
64   Chuikov, p. 104

colossal energy that he transmitted to his commanders and his soldiers. Had Chuikov been a different man we could never have defended Stalingrad.[65]

Chuikov was scruffy in appearance, used gutter language, and he often got drunk. When inebriated he engaged in fist-fights with his 'front' commander Yeremenko and General Rodimtsev, who commanded 13th Guards Infantry Division. If he was dissatisfied with one of his staff officers, he would rain blows on him with his stick. Mereschko told Rees that he had once appeared at Chuikov's command post and seen one his comrades with blood streaming from his nose. He asked another officer what had happened and was told that he had been lucky not to have been present, because he would likewise have received a beating. In 1955, Chuikov had become a Marshal of the Soviet Union. He would no longer beat officers, but there were constant complaints about his rude behaviour.

General Grigorenko, who became a dissident in Breshnev's time, was allowed to leave for the West after having been confined to a psychiatric hospital. He had had to suffer under him when serving at Kiev:

> The meeting at party headquarters at Kiev saw heated exchanges. During two days many officers spoke and there was only one subject, the crudeness, the loutish behaviour and the vindictiveness of the military district commander, Marshal Vassily Ivanovich Chuikov.[66]

For the merciless battle and the house-to-house fighting which occurred in Stalingrad, no commander was more suited than Chuikov. Paulus sat out the battle in a comfortable department store. Chuikov's headquarters were constantly in the advanced front line and he was repeatedly compelled to move his staff post from one location to another. He ordered that there should never be more than 50 to 100 metres distance between the two armies' advance positions. On three occasions his Army was practically destroyed. At one time it numbered only 20,000 men and 60 tanks, only his artillery with its 700 guns was of sufficient strength. Many desertions occurred. Some reports have it that Chuikov had more than 30,000 of his soldiers shot. An analysis by Beevor and Rees puts the figure at 13,000.[67]

When he was in immediate need of additional troops, he would empty the city jails of political prisoners who had been sentenced for minor offences and form them into penal battalions that were sent on suicide missions "to atone with their blood for their crimes against the motherland".[68] If a soldier in a penal battalion was wounded, he was only allowed to withdraw if he could prove that his wound made him unfit for further combat. Vladimir Kantovsky, 18 years old at that time, had been sentenced to a short prison term after objecting to the arrest of his teacher. He told Rees that he was wounded in his arm and his shoulder but was

65   Rees, p. 153
66   P.Grigorenko, *Erinnerungen*, Munich 1981, p. 295
67   Beevor, p.473 and Rees, p. 154
68   Rees, p.85

frightened to death if this would be considered as sufficiently severe or if he would be treated as deserter.[69]

Chuikov's commissars Abramov and Gurov assisted the NKVD in their 'terror'. In his novel *Zhysn i Sudba* (Life and Fate) Vassili Grossmann has a colonel tell how Abramov invited him to his headquarters, on a phoney pretext, and had him arrested upon entering. On 19 December, Chuikov came close to an inglorious death. He had crossed the Volga to attend a party given by the NKVD, in celebration of the twenty-fourth anniversary of the founding of the secret police. He returned completely drunk, the ice was brittle, he fell through a hole and had to be fished out.

Chuikov was a 'Southern general' and would receive no promotions and never command more than an Army during the remainder of the war. Seaton was oblivious to the reasons that halted Chuikov's promotion and described him as "a relatively unimportant General, who never commanded more than an army."[70] During the final battle for Berlin, Chuikov commanded 8th Guards Army and had at least the satisfaction of receiving the surrender of the Berlin garrison.

After Stalin's death he rose quickly. He became a Marshal of the Soviet Union in 1955 and ended his career as Commander in Chief of the Red Army's ground forces and Deputy Minister of Defence.

"Manstein's letter to Paulus in the *Kessel* shows the mentality and the thoughts of a corporal and not of a *Feldmarschall*" General Heusinger in a conversation with Lieutenant-Colonel Heinrich Bücheler on 27 November 1976.[71]

Stalingrad in *Verlorene Siege*

Heusinger refers to a letter by Manstein to Paulus of 24 November 1942, after he had transmitted and endorsed Hitler's order to have 6th Army remain the Pocket: "The *Führer's* order relieves you of any responsibility beyond what has already been ordered by the *Führer*. What may happen when the army has fired its last bullet, is not your responsibility."[72]

The same exasperation could be levelled at other orders of Manstein, and also against many of the 78 pages of the Stalingrad chapter in *Verlorene Siege*. The chapter begins with the Thermopylae verse: "Stranger, tell the Spartans, thou that passest by, that here obedient to their laws we lie." Manstein continues: "Those verses which remind us of the Thermopylae heroism and which are the highest

---

69   Ibid, p.
70   A. Seaton, *Stalin as Warlord*, London 1967, p. 367 f
71   Meyer, Heusinger, p.204
72   Wrochem, p.38

praise of bravery, loyalty and obedience, will never be carved into a rock in the city of Stalingrad as a reminder of the sacrifice of 6th Army.[73]

This quote is out of place. No one can challenge the courage of the German soldier in a battle that turned desperate, but the Russian soldiers were no less brave and the cause for which they fought was worthier. The Germans waged a war of aggression against the 'Jewish-Bolshevik subhuman', the Russians defended themselves in the 'Great Patriotic War'. Such a war can also be cruel, and cruelty was not lacking in the Russian treatment of its own people, nor of captured German soldiers. 6th Army was no 'Leonidas defending Sparta against the Persians'. During its advance, 6th Army had committed heinous crimes.

The three armies of Army Group South, 6th Army under Reichenau, 17th Army under Carl-Heinrich von Stülpnagel and Hoth, and 11th Army, then under Manstein, were more involved than other German armies in the murders of the *Einsatzgruppen*. Their commanders-in-chief, Reichenau, Hoth and Manstein had issued orders of the day that were direct appeals for murder. On 18/20 August 1941 a massacre occurred at Belaya Tserkov. All adult Jews were slaughtered, 90 children were spared. Lieutenant-Colonel Groscurth tried in vain to obtain Reichenau's agreement to spare the children. Reichenau ordered their execution and since Groscurth's appeal had reached him through official channels, he added in his refusal: "This report had better not been written."[74]

The largest single massacre of Jews during the whole war in the East was carried out in September 1941, at Baby Yar near Kiev. 30,000 Jews were shot in under 48 hours, with units of 6th Army actively participating. The town commander, *Generalleutnant* Eberhardt, directed the preparation and the supervision. Eberhardt committed suicide in prison after the war. The massacres continued after Paulus had taken over from Reichenau. Beevor mentions the slaughter at Komsomolsk on 29 January 1942.[75] In captivity Paulus said to Ruth von Mayenburg: "During my time the *Wehrmacht* had nothing to do with such horrors. But later it will be held against us."[76] His first sentence was a lie, the second was the truth.

In his criticism of Manstein's Stalingrad chapter Wieder wrote:

In the *Feldmarschall's* command, everything purports to respond to what is required in a strategic situation, which has to rely upon what can somehow be achieved with limited means. The technical virtuosity, that attempts to overcome the difficulties forced upon an unwilling commander, does not allow for any criticism of the chain of decisions that irrevocably ended in the destruction of a whole army. The reader gets the impression that a grandiose chess game is being played out, during a fateful period of the war, with daring combinations and impeccable positional play, subject to the meagre means at disposal.[77]

---

73   *Verlorene Siege*, p. 309
74   H. Groscurth, *Tagebuch eines Abwehroffiziers*, H. Krausnick (ed), Stuttgart 1970, p. 538 ff (henceforth Groscurth
75   Beevor, p. 57
76   Kosthorst, p. 42
77   Wieder, p. 148

Manstein's chapter about Stalingrad could have been an important contribution to the history of the war. It could have shown how the most senior commander of the battle viewed his assignment, and how he reached his decisions in his attempts to redress the situation. However, the chapter fails to rise to that level. Manstein is mainly concerned with attempts to justify every decision taken by him, while absolving himself of any responsibility for failure, and simply putting the blame on others. The overblown pathos of the chapter has led some of Manstein's critics to put additional and sometimes excessive blame on him.

Manstein assumes command of Army Group Don

Criticism of Manstein has to remain within boundaries. When Manstein took over Army Group Don, 6th Army was already lost. Unless it could have had a strong minded and forceful commander at its helm, who had broken out immediately upon the closure of the *Kessel* in disobedience to Hitler's order, it was doomed. The fate of 6th Army was also doomed by the faulty planning and execution of 'Blue'. The plans for the Russian counter-offensive *Uranus* were already laid, before the Germans had begun to penetrate the city. The many orders, counter-orders and disputes between Hitler, Manstein and Paulus did not aim at a rescue of 6th Army. Although Manstein heads a section in his Stalingrad chapter, "The chance of salvaging 6th Army was neglected" (*Die Chance einer Rettung der 6. Armee wird nicht genutzt*), 6th Army's fate was doomed when Hitler and Manstein issued their first 'hold' orders. [78]

Army Group Don was a relatively weak formation. 6th Army was its strongest unit but it was already surrounded in the *Kessel*. Besides 6th Army, it comprised Hoth's 4th *Panzer* Army, the *Armeeabteilung* Hollidt, the 3rd Romanian Army under General Dumitrescu, and a small Romanian *Armeeabteilung*. An *Armeeabteilung* had an Army staff and consisted of up to two corps, but it did not have the manpower and the equipment of an army. It was always designated by the name of its commander. The Romanian units had antiquated equipment and the soldiers were already demoralised. Parts of the Romanian Army were annihilated on the first day of the Russian counteroffensive

Manstein had been informed by cable of his new appointment on 20 November 1942. He arrived at Weichs' headquarters on 24 November, having made a comfortable journey in the deluxe train of the former king of Yugoslavia. Manstein wrote that he decided to travel by train because of bad weather conditions and danger from partisans. [79] In a situation of catastrophe he had other means of transportation, at his disposal, such as planes. However, at that moment Manstein was not yet aware that a catastrophe had arisen.

During his journey, he stopped for a few hours at Kluge's headquarters at Smolensk. Kluge was two years his senior as *Feldmarschall* and had commanded an Army Group from December 1941. Since an Army Group Commander was directly subordinated to Hitler, Kluge could provide Manstein with his experience. He warned him that Hitler was more interested in details than in fundamental operative thoughts. He would often intervene in actions down to battalion level. If

---

78   *Verlorene Siege*, p.368
79   *Verlorene Siege*, p.302

Manstein could not manage to block this, he would soon become inefficient. Kluge asked Manstein to bear in mind that Hitler ascribed the overcoming of the crisis during the winter of 1941 solely to his own genius and not to the capacity of his commanders and the bravery of the troops.

On his arrival, Manstein at first displayed strange optimism. When Weichs attempted to show him the seriousness of the situation, Colonel Winter, Ia of Army Group B, recalls that Manstein replied: "We will show you 'old papas' how we handle this."[80] Manstein was supported by his always optimistic Ia, Colonel Busse, later to become his chief-of-staff, who told him: "It's a bad situation, but somehow we will cope with it."[81] Schmidt wrote to Manstein's chief-of-staff, General Schulz, with whom he would be in constant touch during the battle: "6th Army will hold out, you just have to see that it is supplied." Manstein's arrogant statement to Weichs was certainly out of place. Whether his favourite, Busse, who would often display unwarranted optimism, was his best adviser can be doubted.

On 24 November, at 1 pm, Manstein sent his first order by telex to 6th Army:

> I will assume command of Army Group Don on 26 November. We will do our best to get you out. It is imperative for 6th Army, in obedience to orders by the *Führer*, to hold firm in its positions north of the Volga, and to prepare the strongest possible units for the opening of a supply route towards Southwest.[82]

As already intimated, this first order by Manstein sealed the fate of 6th Army, the remainder of the Stalingrad chapter in *Verlorene Siege* is meaningless talk. On the same day, Manstein talked to *OKH* over the phone:

> 6th Army can still break out towards the Southwest. To have it remain its present position, given its reserves in ammunition and fuel, represents an extreme risk. Nevertheless, I cannot agree to Army Group B's proposal for a breakout, as long as supply by air is assured. This is however essential.[83]

This message was not communicated to 6th Army, which thus was not aware that Manstein considered sufficient supply by air as essential. Uhle-Wettler feels that Manstein could not judge by himself that supply by air was more than problematic.[84] Manstein wrote: "A soldier could certainly not foresee that Göring would give frivolous assurances of required supply by air, and thereafter do nothing to at least provide the necessary minimum."[85]

I disagree with both statements. During the train journey to Manstein's new headquarters, Stahlberg had asked him what he thought of Göring, and Manstein had replied, "He is just a figure of operetta. He does not count."[86] Manstein had been close to the highest *echelons* during his pre-war years at the *Generalstab*. He

---

80   Kehrig, p. 223 f. also at BA-MA, Estate Weichs
81   Stahlberg, p. 236
82   Piekalkiewicz, p.
83   Kehrig, p. 22, footnote 24
84   Uhle-Wettler, p. 266
85   *Verlorene Siege*, p. 322
86   Stahlberg, p.235

knew Göring well and had first-hand experience of Göring's incapacity as a commander and of his tendency to bluff. He had been a witness to Göring's empty promise to destroy the British Expeditionary Force at Dunkirk, and to wipe the Royal Air Force from the skies during the Battle of Britain. Manstein was certainly aware that the fate of an entire Army could not hinge on Göring's personal assurance. No German high commander took Göring's promises seriously.

On 24 November, the day on which Manstein sent his first order to Paulus, a violent incident occurred at the *Führerhauptquartier*, first between Zeitzler, Hitler, Keitel, and Jodl, and then with Göring. Zeitzler made stenographic notes and published them in a post-war British anthology *The Fatal Decisions*, published in 1956:

> I told Hitler that since the operations proposed for a relief of 6th Army are doomed, an order for an immediate breakout is the only solution. This order must be issued without delay. We have arrived at the last possible moment. While I was talking, Hitler became increasingly angry, he tried to interrupt me several times, but I pursued, since this was my last chance and I simply had to speak. When I finished, Hitler shouted: '6th Army will remain where it is. It is the garrison of a fortress and every garrison has the duty to resist a siege. If necessary, they will endure until spring and then I will liberate them with a spring offensive.' This was pure fantasy.

Zeitzler continued:

> I replied: 'Stalingrad is not a fortress. Furthermore, there is no way to bring supplies to 6th Army.' Hitler's anger increased and he shouted even louder: 'Göring has said that he can supply the Army by air.' I shouted back: 'This is nonsense,' Hitler insisted and said, 'I will not retreat from the Volga.' I said loudly: '*Mein Führer!* It would be a crime to leave 6th Army at Stalingrad. It will result in the death or the capture of 250,000 men. Every attempt to liberate them will be in vain. The loss of this Army will break the backbone of the whole Eastern front." Hitler paled but said nothing. He looked at me with an ice-cold glance and pressed a bell on his desk.
>
> When his *SS*-orderly appeared, he ordered: 'Call *Feldmarschall* Keitel and General Jodl' When they entered the room, Hitler said in a calm voice: 'I have to reach a very difficult decision. Before I decide, I want to hear your opinion. Shall I give up Stalingrad' ... Keitel stood at attention and said with gleaming eyes: '*Mein Führer!* Stay on the Volga!' Jodl was more to the point. After giving his overall view, he concluded: ... ' After carefully weighing all considerations, I feel that we have to stay on the Volga.' Hitler said: 'Now it's your turn ... ' I stood at attention and said: 'My opinion remains unchanged ... ' Hitler kept a calm appearance but I sensed that he was boiling with rage. He said: 'As you see, General, I am not alone with my opinion. Two officers, who are senior to you, share my view. I will thus remain with my decision ... '
>
> Hitler called Göring and asked him: 'Can you supply 6th Army by air'? Göring raised his right arm and said with solemn emphasis: 'I promise that the *Luftwaffe* will ensure 6th Army's supply'. Hitler cast a triumphant look at me but I said simply: 'The *Luftwaffe* can't do it.'

Göring looked angrily at me and said: 'You are not in a position to make such a judgement.' I turned to Hitler and asked him: 'May I put a question to the *Reichsmarschall?*' 'Yes, you may!' 'Do you know, *Herr Reichsmarschall,* the daily amount of tonnage required?' Göring became visibly embarrassed and frowned. He replied: 'I don't know, but my staff officers do.' I replied: 'The minimum daily need required is 500 tons, weather permitting.' Göring replied: 'I can do this.' I lost my temper and shouted: 'This is a lie.' Göring was white with fury, like a ghost … I then asked Hitler for permission to submit him a daily report of the supplies which must reach 6th Army. Göring said that this was none of my business, but Hitler turned him back and allowed me to submit the reports.[87]

Manstein was not present at that meeting, but he was in daily phone contact with Zeitzler who never left him in the dark. Although Manstein wrote in V*erlorene Siege* that Zeitzler had never been his friend, he admits that Zeitzler had spared no effort to support both Paulus and him during the Stalingrad campaign.[88] Zeitzler reduced his own food rations to the level that was available to the soldiers of 6th Army, to give Hitler a vivid image of their plight. When Manstein was dismissed, Zeitzler had submitted his own resignation in protest.[89]

An entry in Manstein's diary on 25 November can cause raised eye-brows: "If I decide to stay put at first, although an attempted breakout is possible, he, Hitler, will become more inclined to listen to me than if I had changed my orders immediately. Anyway, a breakout cannot take place before 28 November."[90] Hardly the words and thoughts of a *Feldmarschall.* In his memoirs Manstein admits that he made a mistake and that he should immediately have requested a breakout.[91]

Was 6th Army subordinated to Army Group Don?

Manstein wrote:

Someone like myself who has participated in the battle in a responsible position, even if only from the outside, practically as a stand-by, *Mithandelnder,* can be deprived of any influence on its course.[92]

He adds:

The subordination of 6th Army to Army Group Don was more or less a fiction. Before that the Army had already been practically subordinated to *OKH.* [However, there is not such a thing as a 'practical' subordination, one is either subordinated or one is not]. Hitler had nailed it down at Stalingrad at a moment when it had still a chance to free itself with its own

87   *The Fatal Decisions,* New York 1956, essay Zeitzler, p. 129-189 (henceforth *Fatal Decisions).*Excerpts quoted in Wieder, p. 306 ff
88   *Verlorene Siege,* p. 327
89   Ibid, p. 615
90   Knopp, p. 193
91   *Verlorene Siege,* p. 337
92   Ibid, p. 320

means. By then it had been reduced to operative immobility. Army Group could no longer lead. It was reduced to providing assistance.

Furthermore, Hitler maintained direct command of the Army through his personal *Generalstab* liaison officer, [at first Major Menzel, then Major von Zitzewitz], with whom he was in direct radio communication. Even supply remained in Hitler's hands since only he had authority over the *Luftwaffe*. In a formal way it would probably have been preferable if I had declined the allocation of 6th Army to Army Group Don, since it would not have altered its chain of command to *OKH*. I refrained from this step, since I felt that with the units of my Army Group I could give better assistance to 6th Army than *OKH*.[93]

A fiction? Manstein simply a stand-by? Was Manstein again the *Schlachtenbummler* of the first weeks of the battle for France? In this case he could have saved himself the trouble of writing a lengthy chapter about Stalingrad and contented himself with a few short paragraphs, such as his descriptions of the actions of his corps in France. The real fiction is Manstein's account. 6th Army had never been subordinated directly to *OKH*, initially it was under the authority of Army Group South, then Army Group B and finally Army Group Don. Major von Zitzewitz had not been sent by Hitler, but by Zeitzler, who wanted to have his own liaison man in the *Kessel*. Zeitzler would confirm this himself in a letter to General Doerr after the war. He added that there was never any doubt that the Army Group had full authority over 6th Army.[94] He had had Zitzewitz flown into the *Kessel* on 23 November, with the written instruction: "I want you to report to me immediately, as soon as possible. You have no command authority. Don't worry, everything Paulus is doing is fine. ("*Der General Paulus macht alles sehr schön*") [95]

Wieder states that 6th Army never received a direct order from Hitler. He writes:

> Contrary to Manstein's assertions, the liaison officer in the *Kessel* has never encroached upon the authority of the commands of Army Group Don and 6th Army. Major von Zitzewitz was not the *OKW* spy, he was the vigilant and well-meaning liaison officer of *OKH*. All his messages were shown to General Schmidt, who added his initials. But soon Schmidt felt that while Zitzewitz's messages left no doubt about the seriousness of the situation, he looked at them as being worded in a too pessimistic manner, at too early a date. After that Zitzewitz reached an agreement with 6th Army's Ia, Colonel Elchlepp, that he could convey his messages to *OKH* without showing them to the Army's chief-of-staff.[96]

It stands to reason that Hitler would have sent an officer of higher rank than a major into the *Kessel* if he really had intended to exercise direct command over 6th Army. Zitzewitz was flown out on 20 January, and reported to Hitler in the pres-

93 Ibid, p. 331
94 Doerr, p. 96
95 C.von Zitzewitz, *Am Wendepunkt des 2.Weltkrieges. Ein Erlebnisbericht. Als Verbindungsoffizier beim AOK 6 in Stalingrad vom 23. November 1942 bis 20. Januar 1943*, unpublished manuscript.
96 Wieder, p. 235

ence of Keitel and Schmundt. He told Hitler that one could not order the soldiers at Stalingrad to fight to the last bullet, since they were no longer in a state of mind to fight, and no bullets were left. Hitler was at first taken aback and then replied: "Men regenerate themselves quickly."[97]

Manstein's statement that he should have declined the 'allocation' of 6th Army does not stand to reason. Army Group Don was established for the sole purpose of a direct command over 6th Army and providing assistance with its other units. Manstein had been urgently appointed to his new command since he was looked upon as the only German high commander capable of redressing the situation.

Paulus was never in doubt as to who his commander was. At that time his admiration for Manstein came close to veneration, and he felt gratified when Manstein was appointed. He wrote to Manstein a hand-written letter of 26 November: "Since I am increasingly snowed under with questions as to the future, I would be grateful if I can be provided with more knowledge than hitherto, to enable me to raise the level of confidence of my men." He would then conclude his letter with the following sentences: "I may report, *Herr Feldmarschall,* that I view your assumption of command as a guarantee that everything will be done to help 6th Army. My commanders and my brave men join me in doing everything to justify your trust in us."[98]

If Manstein had no authority over Paulus, why did he not reply to him accordingly? And how could he issue repeated orders to Paulus if he was not invested with direct command?

The flight into the *Kessel* which never took place

Manstein would never fly into the *Kessel.* This was probably his major failure at Stalingrad In *Verlorene Siege* he wrote:

> I decided to fly into the *Kessel* and consult with Paulus. After pressing entreaties by my chief-of-staff and my Ia, I desisted. Under prevailing weather conditions, I could well have been kept there for two or more days. An absence of such duration from my headquarters could not be tolerated, in view of the tense situation of our other armies, and my necessity to continuously inform *OKH* of the views of the Army Group. I therefore sent my chief-of-staff, General Schulz, and at a later date, my Ia, Colonel Busse.[99]

Manstein added that neither Schulz nor Busse viewed the situation of 6th Army unfavourably, provided adequate supply was available. Schmidt contributed his optimism: "It simply must work. We can start by eating all the horses in the *Kessel.*" Manstein admitted that this attitude could also develop into a danger, and that subsequent events would confirm it.[100]

---

97   mentioned in Zitzewitz without indication of page number.
98   Kehrig, Document 34
99   *Verlorene Siege*, p. 345
100   Ibid., p. 346

At a later date, Manstein sent Major Eismann on short visits to the *Kessel*. When Eismann arrived, Paulus said to Adam: "I simply fail to understand how Manstein can send a major to report about the growing catastrophe instead of coming himself." Beevor comments:

> *Feldmarschall* von Manstein sent Major Eismann, one of his intelligence officers, into the *Kessel* by air, on 19 December. His mission, Manstein claimed later, was to brief Paulus and Schmidt to prepare the 6th Army for operation Thunderclap, ie *Donnerschlag*. Different versions and different interpretations of what was said at this meeting will never be resolved.
>
> However, it is clear that Manstein still avoided taking the responsibility for disobeying Hitler. He would not give Paulus a clear lead and refused, no doubt for sound reasons of security, to fly into the *Kessel* to discuss the matter with him face to face. ('Sound reasons of security' is unfair to Manstein. Manstein showed himself to be a moral coward at Stalingrad, but he never feared for his life in battle). Yet Manstein must have known from the start that Paulus, a firm believer in the chain of command, would never have broken out without a formal order from higher command. Manstein's efforts in his memoirs to absolve himself from any blame for the fate of 6th Army are curiously exaggerated, as well as unfair to Paulus.

It would appear that he suffered from an uneasy conscience, yet no one blamed him. Beevor should have added "at that time" …

> The whole 'Breakout or Defence' debate is thus a purely academic diversion from real issues. In fact, one suspects that the formidably intelligent Manstein recognised it, at that time. He made a great show of sending Major Eismann, his intelligence officer, into the *Kessel* to prepare 6th Army for operation Thunderclap. Yet Manstein knew that Hitler, who had again reaffirmed his determination not to move from the Volga, would never change his mind.[101]

Manstein's arguments in justifying his decision to dispatch Schulz and Busse in his stead are not convincing. There was as yet no danger for his 'other armies,' since the size of Army Group Don was increased only after the end of Stalingrad. All troops under his command at that time were either in the *Kessel* or engaged in relief attempts. Even if weather conditions had kept Manstein the *Kessel* for a few days, no crisis would have arisen. Communications between Army Group headquarters and 6th Army were still unimpaired.

Manstein had a very competent staff to whom he could transmit his instructions. He was certainly able to follow operations at his headquarters with his situation map and the daily reports of 6th Army. Schulz and Busse were well qualified to convey the views of Army Group Don to 6th Army. Surprisingly, they did not do it.

Wieder emphasised that 6th Army was never informed of the intentions of Army Group Don. He recalls a conversation with Captain Toepke, the first quarter-master of 6th Army, who complained:

101   Beevor, p. 299 and 309

... about the total lack of content in the exchanges between Army Group Don and 6th Army. Precise questions put by Paulus to Manstein about the general situation and, in particular, the availability of air supply, were only answered with vague promises. I had expected Manstein to convey comprehensive replies to our Army commander, in particular with indications of dates on which supplies could be expected. This never happened.[102]

However, there was an overriding necessity for Manstein to make a personal flight into the *Kessel*. Manstein had to judge if Paulus was up to the demands of his command, in particular under the circumstances that had arisen. Manstein knew Paulus well from their time in the *Generalstab* and he was aware that Paulus was named a *Fabius cunctator*, ie a great delayer. During the war he could add personal experiences to Paulus' lack of decisiveness. On 5 June 1941 he wrote a personal letter to Paulus, who was at that time *Oberquartiermeister* I, and complained about the insufficient equipment given to his LVI Motorized Corps:

> Dear Paulus, I have sent my enclosed request through channels. I am not convinced that it will ever reach you. Perhaps you will find it possible to give my corps the equipment requested by me. Maybe you will recall that the availability of assault guns is solely due to me during my time as head of operations at the *Oberquartiermeister* I department. I think I am entitled to at least receive some.[103]

Paulus never replied and Halder's refusal has already been mentioned. Only a personal visit to 6th Army could have permitted Manstein to get a picture of the Byzantine situation which had arisen within the Army's staff and which can be likened to a Kafka novel. Manstein would then have to judge if Paulus should be replaced. An Army Group Commander could not relieve an Army Commander on his own authority, but he could request his 'relief' if he felt that he could not cope with the situation. Paulus was never a favourite of Hitler and although Hitler had little sympathy for Manstein, he was aware of Manstein's unique capacity and it can safely be assumed that he would have acceded to such a request. It would have been easy to find a successor for Paulus within 6th Army. Corps commanders like Hube, Seydlitz or Strecker were certainly up to the requirements of Army Command. Had Manstein met a refusal by Hitler, he could have requested his own 'relief'. If confronted with a choice between Manstein and Paulus, Hitler would certainly not have given preference to the latter.

Did Manstein issue an order to launch Operation *Donnerschlag*?

A statement that he never issued such an order would be a gross simplification. In fact there were two orders by Manstein with explicit reference to *Donnerschlag*. One was not communicated to 6th Army, the second was passed on with an

---

102   Wieder, p. 148
103   Görlitz, p. 141

explicit *reservatio mentalis*, that is, a 'silent disagreement,' when it would be unwise to 'openly disagree'.

Manstein's first order of 18 December, which was not communicated to 6th Army, read in excerpts: " … As soon as the supply situation permits, 6th Army is to break out in the direction of Donskaya Tsaritsa on both sides of Buzinovka … Date and hour of the attack to be communicated on the same day and hour … " [104]

The second order was sent on 19 December to *AOK* 6. *AOK*, *Armeeoberkommando*, is the term for the whole staff of an army, followed by the army's number. It has to be reproduced in full, since it was a bone of contention among military historians, over a number of years, in their dispute about Manstein's responsibility at Stalingrad. All readers must be given the opportunity to judge this order for themselves:

- 4th *Panzer* Army and its XLVII Corps have beaten the enemy in the sector Verchne-Kimsky and have reached the Mychkovka sector at Nish-Kimsky. Further attacks against strong enemy forces have been started in the area of Kamenka and further north. Difficult combats to be expected. Situation on the front along the Tchir does not permit an advance towards Kalatch, west of the Don River. (Kalatch was the city where the two pincers of the Red Army made their junction and closed the *Kessel*.) The bridge over the Don at Tchirskaya continues to be held by the enemy.
- 6th Army launches the offensive *Wintergewitter* at the earliest possible date. It has to foresee the possibility, if required, to establish a connection with XLVII Corps over Donskaya-Tsaritsa, in order to permit the arrival of supplies.
- Developments can lead to a situation which expands the attack, mentioned under 2. to Mychovka. Code word *Donnerschlag*. In such a case, it becomes necessary to establish the connection to XLVII Corps with the assistance of *Panzer* units. Thereafter, they must cover the flanks at lower Karpovka and along Tcherwlenaya, taking a step-by-step withdrawal from the fortress. Circumstances may demand that *Donnerschlag* immediately follow *Wintergewitter*. Supply by air will be continuously provided, with no sizeable reserves available. Continued defence of the airstrip at Pitomnik is important. All light weaponry must be withdrawn from the fortress. Artillery guns which are combat-ready, and with available ammunition, are likewise to be withdrawn, as well as other equipment which is difficult to replace. Such equipment to be assembled in good time in the South-West.
- The operation foreseen in 3. above, has to be prepared. Execution only after express order *Donnerschlag*.
- Day and hour of operation in 2. to be reported. [105]

A glance at the situation map shows that this was an order with considerable daring, since Manstein foresaw the possibility of giving up Stalingrad (named 'the fortress' in his order), in contradiction of Hitler's order to hold on to the city. Uhle-Wettler is the only German military historian of high standing, who remains adamant in his opinion that no blame can be directed against Manstein. He insists

---

104   Hgr. Don/Ia 39 694/5
105   Ob.Kdo Heeresgruppe Don, Ia, Nr. 0396/42. Also *Verlorene Siege*, p. 656

that Paulus was solely responsible in preventing Manstein's order being carried out. He wrote:

> Since Hitler would not agree to a breakout, Manstein had to act ... He could not issue a clear order to 'break out' that Hitler would immediately have repealed. However, he could order an operation that gave the appearance of assisting a relief attack, while simultaneously rendering it impossible to remain the *Kessel*, thus forcing a breakout. That was exactly what Manstein ordered, and none of the many who criticize him have been able to suggest a better alternative.[106]

I happen to be one of the 'many who criticize Manstein' and feel that there was an alternative. Manstein's order is simply total confusion. Kehrig writes that it cannot even be called an order and that Paulus and Schmidt could not be expected to guess Manstein's 'intentions' in such unclear wording. He adds that it is, mildly speaking, strange that Manstein issued his 'order' with a *reservatio mentalis*, ie a silent disagreement, in the purported expectation that *AOK 6* would notice that he wrote about *Wintergewitter*, while meaning *Donnerschlag*. He concludes that Manstein simply engaged in an exercise of 'dialectics', which neither Paulus nor Schmidt could be expected to comprehend.[107]

Wintergewitter was a relief attempt, to be undertaken by Army Group Don. 6th Army was to attempt to link up, if it had sufficient fuel reserves, and reach the same location as the troops of Army Group Don. However, the fuel reserves of 6th Army were barely sufficient to cover a distance of 30 to 40 kilometres. That was not enough for an assembly in the locations required for *Donnerschlag*. Nor was it sufficient to attack and join up with the troops of Army Group Don which were 50 kilometres away.

An assembly, not to speak of actions thereafter, was only possible if the *Luftwaffe* could immediately supply 1,000 tons of fuel and 500 tons of food rations. At that time, its capacity did not exceed 100 tons a day. Paulus sent daily reports to *OKH* about his fuel reserves. Since Hitler had reached the decision not to abandon Stalingrad, their insufficiency was welcome news to him. When Manstein remonstrated with him, he received the reply: "Why are you pestering me? Paulus has fuel for 20 or 30 kilometres only, he tells me himself that he is unable to break out."[108]

Most of the horses required for artillery guns had already been slaughtered and without artillery support combat was impossible. Many of the soldiers had suffered wounds, most were already undernourished. But then they were required to proceed, through steppes covered with ice, against massive Russian tank concentrations, without support from *Panzer* and artillery, clearly a mission impossible.[109] *Wintergewitter* was a desperate attempt that had to be rapidly halted when the units of Army Group Don were on the verge of becoming encircled. In *Verlorene Siege*,

106   Uhle-Wettler, p. 270
107   Kehrig, p.394 f
108   *Verlorene Siege*, p. 371
109   Uhle-Wettler, p. 270 ff

Manstein describes *Wintergewitter* as a race for life or death and added that its fate was sealed on Christmas Eve.[110]

General von Senger und Etterlin, commanded the 17th *Panzer* Division which was the only division at full strength during the operation. He wrote:

> It is striking that the attempt to free Stalingrad was made with such inadequate resources ... One full strength and two only half strength divisions had to launch an offensive over a distance of 100 kilometres! ... The elements of surprise had long disappeared. For more than two weeks the divisions had already faced a stronger opponent. Even if surprise had been achieved, they would not have been able to hold the large area that still remained to be conquered. It was obvious to us that the enemy would use all means available to him to prevent any relief operation and that he would not allow victory to slip through his fingers. The weakness of our own troops showed that no adequate reserves were available.[111]

Manstein's order put the inititiative for *Wintergewitter* on to 6th Army, at a moment when it was increasingly pushed back into the city. It had previously been ordered to engage only such forces in *Wintergewitter* as could be spared from the defence of the city centre.[112] The 'earliest possible date' mentioned in point 2 of Manstein's order lacks precision. It left the date of the action to the discretion of the Army Commander. Under normal circumstances this is logical, since only the Army Commander knows when his Army is ready for action. But Manstein knew the *Fabius cunctator* Paulus well enough to realise that he would only act if he received an order with a precise date. Manstein should have added to his order: "Report to me immediately when your Army is ready for action", and then determined the date on his own responsibility.

Donnerschlag is defined as an auxiliary operation, with the express reservation that it could only be launched after a separate order by Army Group Don. In Paulus' eyes, which Schmidt confirmed in an affidavit after the war, *Donnerschlag* was a separate action with the sole purpose of permitting a break-out attempt. This is clearly evident from a conversation between Manstein and Paulus, over the phone on 23 December, which is reported by Stahlberg: "Paulus said to Manstein: '*Herr Feldmarschall,* I beseech you to order me to break out.' In spite of the defective voice connection, since conversations had to be conducted through 'mincing' equipment, I clearly heard the imploring tone in Paulus' voice.

Manstein had replied: "Paulus, I can't give you such an order. However, should you decide to act on your own, I will do all I can to assist you."[113] Paulus then asked Manstein if he could give him authority to take preliminary steps for *Donnerschlag*.

---

110   *Verlorene Siege,* p. 360
111   F.von Senger und Etterlin, *Krieg in Europa,* Cologne 1960, p.74
112   Details in Kehrig, p. 394 ff
113   Stahlberg, p. 250

Manstein replied: "I can't give you authority today, I hope to be able to reach a decision tomorrow."[114] Paulus then asked Manstein if he could at least mentally prepare his corps for *Donnerschlag*.

Manstein told him: "Wait for a later call from General Schulz to General Schmidt."

The conversation then continued and, at the end, Paulus asked: "Will the call from General Schulz to General Schmidt come now?"

Manstein replied: "No further calls to be expected."[115] On that day Manstein spoke to Heusinger and made a surprisingly positive comment about the Red Army: "The *Führer* had better realise that the Russians also have tank corps and are as good as ourselves in their command."[116]

Breithaupt criticized Stahlberg's account, which he labelled as one of his 'stories'. He wrote that communications between an Army Group and an Army could no longer be conducted by voice after 10 December, but only by means of 'decimetre equipment.' Breithaupt is only correct as far as the date of 23 December is concerned, because phone communications between Army Group Don and the *Kessel* had been broken off the day before. Therefore Stahlberg cannot have heard the 'imploring tone' of Paulus, probably this is one of his inventions in his attempts to paint a vivid picture. With his other comments, Breithaupt shows that he has simply not done his homework, since 'decimetre equipment' was an instrument that was designed to permit voice communication under the most unfavourable conditions and without the danger of being overheard. Colonel Arnold, the staff officer who installed the decimetre equipment at 6th Army wrote in a report that is kept at the BA-MA:

> ... I tried at first to install decimetre equipment on the heights along the Don River. However, the altitude was insufficient, and we could not obtain voice communication. Then I had a wooden tower erected. The first two were destroyed by Russian artillery fire, but the third did function. Suddenly, I heard the voice of *Feldmarschall* von Manstein who asked to speak immediately to Paulus. I ran into Paulus' bunker. He was sitting at his desk, with his head buried in both hands. I gave him the receiver and said, 'Manstein is on the line.' Paulus said: 'Arnold, stop making silly jokes.' Then he heard Manstein's voice and was simply electrified. A long conversation ensued.
>
> From that day on, six to eight hours of conversations would take place every night, both between the two commanders in chief, the quartermasters and other staff officers. The last two hours were reserved for conversations with families in Germany. During the day, the tower would be taken down. News that it was possible to phone home spread like wildfire through the *Kessel* and improved morale. I even recall one marriage ceremony over the phone between a soldier in the *Kessel* and his bride in

---

114 BA-MA, RH 19 VI/42 + RH 19/44. Attachment to war diaries of Army Group Don and 6th armies. Also *Geheime Tagesberichte*, vol. 6, p. 464 ff

115 Kehrig, p. 602, Document 39

116 BA-MA, RH 19 VI/42 and RH 19 VI/44. Annex to war diaries Army Groups Don and South. Also *Geheime Lageberichte. vol. 6*, p. 464 ff

Germany. We lost this communication on 22 December 1942, when we had to retreat from the Don heights.[117]

This passage shows how easy some historians, in this case Breithaupt, make it for themselves when they intend to deprecate a colleague. The 'imploring tone' is without relevance since the conversation was recorded fully in the war diaries of Army Group Don and 6th Army.

Other means of voice communications were apparently still somehow available after that date. In a letter to the *Frankfurter Allgemeine Zeitung* of 22 February 1988, the daughter of Colonel Selle, the chief engineering officer of 6th Army, wrote:

> … My father's diary records a letter to his wife which mentions a phone conversation with her around 16 January 1943. … My father never expected this call to come through, but he succeeded again on 23 January. Thus, the possibility of isolated communications remained at least until this date.

Finally, if as Manstein wrote, 6th Army was not subordinated to his Army Group, how could he promise an authority to Paulus that he himself did not possess? Furthermore, if he intended to cover an independent action by Paulus, a simple intimation at the end of a phone call was insufficient. A face-to-face conversation with Paulus was required which would have provided him with full information about the Army Group's intentions and possibilities, and permitted him to reach a decision.

When General Schmidt returned from captivity in 1956, Manstein's past caught up with him. General Schmidt was adamant that Manstein's 'break out' order had never reached 6th Army and he engaged in increasingly sharp polemics with *Verlorene Siege*. He received support from General Friedrich-Wilhelm Hauck who went on record with a statement that the war diary of 6th Army showed no record of the purported order. (As a colonel, Hauck had been the quartermaster of Manstein's 11th Army). Hauck was supported by General Heim, who referred to the 'decimeter' tapes and said that "Manstein simply can't get away with his statements. He simply wants to shed any responsibility." Manstein refused to enter personally into any discussion or to take part at round table conferences where both opinions were discussed, stating that such meetings were "below his dignity".[118]

Could *Donnerschlag* have succeeded?

Without doubt Hitler would have issued a counter-order. Kehrig feels that an order by Manstein, in direct contradiction to previous orders by Hitler, could only have succeeded if radio communications to the outside had broken down.[119] This can be questioned. An order by Manstein given in agreement with the Commander in Chief of 6th Army and all its Corps Commanders, is carried out

---

117   Copy communicated by Winrich Behr to the author, April 5, 2003
118   Wrochem p.303 ff
119   Kehrig, p. 358

without delay. The first step would have been to cut off all radio communications to the outside. New commanders, down to division level, would have had to be appointed, and they had to put new staffs together. This takes time while the breaout proceeds. Kehrig wrote that Manstein had two possibilities, either resign his command without having given an order to break out, or simply issue such an order with the risk of being dismissed.[120] Manstein did neither. Kehrig felt that his account in *Verlorene Siege* is simply an *ex post facto*, ie an 'after the event' attempt to put responsibility on others.[121]

Chuikov on *Donnerschlag*

Chuikov wrote that an outbreak attempt by Paulus would have served no purpose:

> Had Paulus broken out, he would have been compelled to leave all his mobile equipment, his artillery and all his heavy weaponry behind. Our fire-power was so intense that only few men could have left the ruins of the city. Not all of 6th Army was encircled at Stalingrad. Some units had remained in the outskirts. It would have been possible to concentrate them in a narrow sector and to attempt a breakout on 23 or 24 December. Supposing that it had succeeded, all equipment would have had to be abandoned before they could reach open territory and fuel was at its end. 6th Army would have been exposed to our blows in frost and snow-storms. Napoleon lost his Army during his retreat from Moscow to the Berezina. Paulus would have lost his army much earlier in the steppe.[122]

> Chuikov's statement is simply common sense. His strong defence of Manstein not withstanding, Uhle-Wettler sides with Chuikov and writes that only 'debris', *Trümmer*, could have gone through.[123]

Should 6th Army have accepted the Russian offer of surrender of 8 January 1943?

Manstein denies it. In the relevant passage in *Verlorene Siege* he reverts to his 'draw theory' which became an obsession as the war progressed:

> I can certainly not be reproached for never having criticized Hitler's military decisions and actions. However, in this instance I fully share his decision. It was necessary at that time, even if it had harsh human consequences.
>
> I will not dwell on the principle that an Army cannot be allowed to surrender if it is still able to fight. To negate this rule would mean the end of every military code of behaviour. Until better times come, when states can dispense with Armies and soldiers, laws of military honour have to be preserved. Even a hopeless fight does not justify surrender. If every commander were to surrender when he considered his situation to be

---

120 Ibid
121 Ibid
122 Chuikov, p. 365 f
123 Uhle-Wettler, p.273

without issue, a war could never be won. In many situations that appeared desperate, salvation could still be found. Paulus had the soldier's duty to refuse surrender, unless further combat had been useless.

This brings us to the central question, 'if Hitler's refusal to permit surrender, in which Army Group had concurred, was justified.' Even if further resistance was hopeless in the long run, 6th Army still had to play a decisive role, within the context of the general situation, by binding the forces that opposed it. At that time it was not yet certain that Germany would lose the war. A military draw that would have led to a political draw was still within the realms of possibilities.[124]

Yeremenko voiced a contrary opinion:

Anyone who makes an objective analysis, will come to the opinion that further resistance was meaningless in mid-January ... Manstein must have realised this, since he knew that the German units, which had been earmarked for relief, had been beaten far back in the direction of Rostov. At that time, the troops in the *Kessel* had already fulfilled their strategic and operative task of binding the Russian units on the Volga, and they had no fighting strength left. If Manstein had not shared Hitler's opinion and had had the courage to permit Paulus to surrender, 6th Army would not have lost 90,000 prisoners but as many as 150,000 to 200,000 solders would have survived. 6th Army suffered its heaviest casualties during the days between 15 January to 2 February. Furthermore, a simple calculation can evidence that our troops around Stalingrad would not have been able to participate in the battle against the Germans retreating from the Caucasus since they would have needed two to three weeks before regrouping. They were never intended to be used on the Caucasus front. After a period of rest they were destined for another area of the front.[125]

One has to concede, that the Soviet general who commanded the 'Stalingrad front', had better knowledge of the assignment of his troops than Manstein. General Doerr agrees with Yeremenko's 6th Army's casualty figures during the final phase and puts the numbers of killed in action, in the last two weeks, at not less than 100,000.[126]

Soon after, Manstein would show at least part of the courage which Yeremenko denies him. He made repeated requests that Hitler permit 6th Army to surrender. Army Group's Don war diary of 22 January has an account of a conversation between Manstein, Hitler, Zeitzler, Heusinger and Schmundt, It lasted for several hours because of repeated interruptions due to the weather conditions:

22 January, 10.23 am. Call from *OB* Manstein to Zeitzler: Have you communicated my yesterday's views about possible negotiations by 6th Army to the *Führer*?

124   *Verlorene Siege*, p. 384
125   Yeremenko Stalingrad, p. 448
126   Doerr, p. 116

Zeitzler: Yes. *Führer* has refused for the time being. Army has to continue to fight.

3.15 pm *OB*: Have you spoken again to the *Führer?*

Zeitzler: Yes. *Führer* does not trust any promises by the Russians. Army must continue to hold out.

5.40 pm. *OB*: *OKH* has to decide if Paulus shall be permitted to nego-tiate. If he agrees, observance of the Geneva convention must be a condi-tion. Either *OKH* has to wire the Russian directly or Paulus has to do it himself. Paulus has to get a reply to his last radio message.

Schmundt: *Führer* has just dictated his reply. Army has to fight until the last bullet, even if the *Kessel* is increasingly reduced. *Führer* feels that surrender will not improve army's condition.

OB: One can insist upon observance of the Geneva convention. The Russian can't refuse this. Schmundt: *Führer* says that the Russian can't feed 6th Army's troops.

OB: We could propose to supply 6th Army with food by plane during the fourteen days.

Schmundt: I connect you with the *Führer*.

Hitler: *Heil, Herr Feldmarschall.*

OB: *Heil, mein Führer.* I respectfully ask for a reply concerning Paulus.

Hitler: My reply is on the way.

Here communications are interrupted. Thereafter Schmundt picks up the phone:

Do you really believe, *Herr Feldmarschall,* that the Russian will observe the Geneva convention?

OB: I don't believe that he can refuse. Will he adhere to it? This cannot be affirmed with certainty.

Hitler picks up the phone: Russian promises will only serve as a pretext. I know how difficult things are with 6th Army. I suffer myself ... history of hundreds, nay thousand years (parts of his sentence not audible because of bad communications). The Russian offer can't be accepted. Army has to fire until the last bullet.

OB: And if no last bullet remains?

Hitler: This will not change 6th Army's condition. Paulus has to hold, even if the *Kessel* is reduced. He is still binding important enemy units. I am looking into the possibility of strengthening the defence with 1st *Panzer* Army, it can be brought there from the North.

OB: We have to face the fact that 6th Army will collapse anyway. Enemy units will then become available at other fronts held by Army Group. Probably they will reach Starobielsk within three to four weeks.

Hitler had not heard the last sentence due to bad communications. Then he continued;

Even if Paulus can only hold out for a few more days, this is helpful, especially for your Army Group, *Herr Feldmarschall*. I am now looking into the possibility to strengthen you with 1st *Panzer* Army. We will then establish a small bridgehead on the Taman peninsula. Honour forbids any surrender and, besides, the Russian will not keep his promises. *Heil*

5.55 pm: End of the conversations.

Now Manstein was the *Fabius cunctator*, the great delayer. He asks for permission to surrender but refrains from ordering it.

Captain Behr's mission

Fate had it that Winrich Behr and I were schoolmates at the Berlin French Gymnasium from 1934 to 1936. The French Gymnasium had been founded by the Prussian Prince Elector when Louis XIV expelled the Huguenots from France. Tuition continues be in French until this day. We did not meet at school as Behr was four years older. Our first personal meeting took place in 1998, when I was engaged in research for my Model biography.

The mission is mentioned in detail in every book dealing with Stalingrad. 2003 was the sixtieth anniversary of the fall of the city and Behr appears in every movie produced by German television to commemorate this event. His mission had no direct impact on the battle, but his account conveys an interesting and vivid picture of the prevailing situation at 6th army, and at Hitler's and Manstein's headquarters.

Behr had been decorated with the Knight's Cross in North Africa, in 1941, when he was a lieutenant in *Panzeraufklärungsabteilung* 3. It was the reconnaissance unit of a *Panzer* Division that consisted of five companies, one of which was equipped with anti-tank guns. On 29 April 1941, he was mentioned by name in the daily *Wehrmacht communiqué* for exceptional bravery. At Stalingrad, he served as O4 on 6th Army's staff. He had already completed his training as a *Generalstab* officer, but was not yet a formal member. He did not yet wear the uniform of a *Generalstab* officer with its distinct shoulder straps, collar patches and the carmine-red trouser stripes, but was clad in the black *Panzer* battle dress.

As the battle neared the end, Paulus was growing increasingly desperate. A number of senior officers had been sent out of the *Kessel*, in an attempt to convince Hitler of the gravity of the situation, and to implore him to take whatever steps were still possible. All failed, some took advantage of the occasion not to return. Paulus hoped that perhaps a young and highly decorated front-line officer, appearing in black combat dress, might appeal more to Hitler than his previous General emissaries. Behr was to stress the urgent need for an immediate relief operation and for adequate supply. If neither was possible, 6th Army should receive permission to take action under its own responsibility. The real intention was to obtain permission to surrender.

Behr was flown out on 13 January 1943 and reported to Manstein. He was well received, and Manstein listened carefully to his description of 6th Army's plight. He then ordered Behr to repeat every word he had told him to Hitler. He warned that he would be surprised if Hitler could be convinced. Manstein phoned Zeitzler to make sure that Behr would be immediately received upon arrival. Behr attended two situation meetings. The first was in the evening of 14 January, and the next on the following day.

Before going into the first meeting, Behr had been warned by his brother-in-law, Hitlers's *Luftwaffe* adc von Below, of Hitler's tactics when receiving unpleasant news. Hitler would engage in a long monologue and then break off the conversation. Hitler met Behr in the ante-room, greeted him with: *"Heil, Herr Hauptmann,"* shook his hand, and took him to the situation room, where around twenty senior officers were present. Zeitzler did not attend and Jodl presented the daily situation report.

As expected, Hitler followed Jodl's presentation with a monologue that lasted one and a half hours. During it he told Behr several times: "Report this to your *Generaloberst*." When Hitler finished and was preparing to leave, Behr asked for permission to speak and said that he had been ordered by Paulus to present a totally candid report to Hitler. Hitler then listened to him without interrupting, even when Behr reported on the increasing number of desertions by German soldiers. Generals Keitel, Jodl, Warlimont and Schmundt stood behind Hitler's back and made angry gestures to have Behr shut up. Keitel repeatedly wagged his finger at him. The meeting lasted for three hours and Behr was ordered to appear again on the following day, 15 January.

When Zeitzler returned, Behr reported to him. Zeitzler reprimanded him for having gone into the meeting without first having reported to him, but added that he agreed with every word that Behr had said to Hitler. He asked Behr to carry a detailed letter from him back to Paulus, in which he intended to give Paulus a detailed review of the situation on the Eastern front.

In his post-war accounts, Behr would say that he felt that only Keitel, Jodl, Schmundt, and Warlimont believed that Stalingrad could somehow be rescued. But, while it was evident that Hitler had already written off the *Kessel*, he thought in terms of a 'heroes' epic.' Hitler made great case of immediate relief, a *Panzer* Corps, which had been transferred from the West and which was in the process of being unloaded at Charkov, some 600 kilometres away from Stalingrad. Manstein had already informed Behr that the Corps had been nearly destroyed by Russian T–34 tanks while being unloaded. Furthermore, Hitler promised increased air supply by bringing *Luftwaffe* transport planes over from North Africa and Italy. It was obvious to any officer that a number of weeks would be required for them to arrive and become equipped for the Russian climate.

Behr would write that he was shocked at Hitler's unrealistic shuffling around of divisions, regiments, and battalions on the situation maps, as if they were fresh units with prescribed strength. As of that moment, he had lost all his previous respect for Hitler and the Generals surrounding him. In a recent magazine article, he repeated that, as of that day, he had simply written Hitler off.

On 15 January, Behr made his report to Zeitzler. Then Schmundt requested that Behr remain. After a two-hour discussion, Schmundt asked him what he would tell Paulus. Behr replied that he would have to report that there was no hope of relief, nor of permission to take independent action. Schmundt then said in an abrupt manner: "There are no more possibilities for you to fly back into the *Kessel*. I am transferring you to the special staff of *Feldmarschall* Milch." Milch was a *Luftwaffe Feldmarschall* and had been made responsible for air supply of the *Kessel*.

Behr decided to attempt to fly back into the *Kessel* in spite of Schmundt's order. When he arrived at the airfield at Taganrog, the transport officer in charge told him that Schmundt had phoned him with express orders to prevent Behr's return and his plane was grounded.

While still at Hitler's headquarters, Behr was approached by Colonel Stieff and Lieutenant Colonel Klamroth, both of whom would be hanged after the 20 July plot. Klamroth had been Behr's tutor, his *Fähnrichsvater* at his first officer course in 1938. Both asked him in what Beevor called 'a coded manner'[127] whether he would join a movement to oust Hitler.

Behr confirmed to me that this conversation took place as described by Beevor. Beevor had obtained the details from him when interviewing him for his book on Stalingrad. Behr believed that Stieff and Klamroth were very discreet, since they did not know how close he was to Below, who was very devoted to Hitler. Behr replied that he had just experienced a shock, after his report to Hitler, and felt that he could not yet make a complete about-turn. Klamroth then warned him to be careful with Manstein: "At table, he is very much against Hitler, but he just shoots his mouth off. If Hitler were to order him to turn left or right, he would do exactly as he was told."[128]

Manstein would indeed engage in jokes about Hitler when talking with his staff officers. He often called Hitler a *Pinkelstratege*, literally a 'peeing' strategist. He had a dachshund that he had coached to raise its right paw in the *Nazi* salute.

Behr told me that he took Klamroth's advice but added that Manstein received him upon his return with utmost politeness, listening carefully to his report. Stahlberg wrote that Behr was irritated and added:

> Hitler had given him a most optimistic account. 6th Army had to stay at Stalingrad, which was of decisive importance for the war. Then the greatest *Kessel* offensive in world history would be launched under the command of *Feldmarschall* von Manstein. Army Group Don, and Army Group A would join with 6th Army and launch an offensive which would lead to the annihilation of all Russian units in the South. Manstein was simply speechless. 'Behr, do you really believe this nonsense?' Behr replied: '*Herr Feldmarschall*, I must believe what I am told by the Supreme Commander. Whom else can I believe if not the Supreme Commander?' [129]

In a thirteen-page letter to Stahlberg on 26 October 1987, Behr took exception to this account. He wrote that, after more than forty years had gone by, he was not able to remember every word that was said. But he thought it was somewhat improbable that Manstein would have questioned him about Hitler's credibility in Busse's presence. If this had taken place, however, Behr could not exclude that he

---

127 Beevor, p. 345

128 Beevor, p. 345. Behr confirmed this conversation to this author.

129 Stahlberg, p. 260

had used the words which Stahlberg attributes to him, since the conversation would have had an official character.[130]

While Behr's mission did not change the course of events, it led to repercussions within Germany. Until 15 January, the German press had only reported somewhat casually about Stalingrad. The German public at home had little knowledge of the suffering that the soldiers of 6th Army endured. Behr says that the soldiers in the *Kessel* had an increasing impression that 6th Army was simply forgotten at home, and that wild rumours were in abundance.

When Behr told Manstein that *OKH* seemed to have little awareness about the situation in the *Kessel*, Manstein was irritated and phoned Zeitzler: "Captain Behr, O4 of 6th Army told me that the *Führer* was impressed with his report and that he was not aware of the seriousness of the situation. How is this possible? I have never left any doubts about this." [131] Zeitzler replied: "I have always reported this to the *Führer*. The O4 of 6th Army was here and has given a totally clear account. I have always foreseen that it would come to this." [132]

Generalleutnant (Bundeswehr) Freytag von Loringhoven was one of the last officers to be flown out with letters from the soldiers to their relatives. At Stalingrad he was a major and commanded a *Panzer* Battalion. He reported to Manstein before he could wash and change his clothes. He was received by Stahlberg, who was startled, and did not shake his hand, because he feared that Freytag von Loringoven could be covered with lice. Freytag von Loringhoven told me that this was certainly possible. He was then brought to Manstein who received him politely, but conveyed the impression of a cold and distant man. He then reported to *Generaloberst* von Richthofen who received him surlily in his sleeping-car and told him that he had no time to spare. *Feldmarschall* Milch then took care of him, arranged a sleeping-car compartment, and provided him with meat, butter and honey.[133]

During the last days, Manstein would become unnerved during the discussions among his officers about the responsibility for the disaster. He had Schulz issue an order that they had to cease, since they could do nothing to change the facts of the matter and could only cause damage by undermining confidence. Officers were also forbidden to discuss the causes for the destruction of 6th Army in their personal correspondence.[134]

The Stalingrad chapter in *Verlorene Siege* ends with the same pathos as its beginning:

> Officers and soldiers of 6th Army have by their courage and their sacrifice erected a monument which, while not sculpted in marble or rock, will remain over the years as a memory. An invisible document engraved with the words written at the beginning of the description of this greatest soldierly tragedy.[135]

---

130   Copy of the letter handed by Winrich Behr to this author
131   BA-MA, RH 19 VI/42 and RH 19 VI/44. Also in *Geheime Lageberichte*, p. 475
132   Ibid
133   Told by *Generalleutnant* Freytag von Loringhoven to this author
134   Beevor, p. 347
135   *Verlorene Siege*, p. 398

On 30 January, Göring made a speech in Berlin that was listened to at Stalingrad over radio. He quoted the Thermopylae verse and added that it was indifferent to the German soldier if he fell at Rshev, at Stalingrad, or in Africa. This speech caused an uproar among the soldiers of 6th Army, some yelled 'switch it off'. Survivors told Beevor "that it was Göring, of all people, who was delivering their own funeral speech. He heaped insult on injury. Some officers joked bitterly that the suicide of the Jews on the top of Masada might have been a more appropriate comparison than Thermopylae. They did not realise quite how accurate they were. Hitler was indeed counting on a mass suicide, above all of senior officers."[136]

However, at his first meeting with Manstein after the surrender on 5 February, Hitler would cut short any recrimination:

I bear the sole responsibility for Stalingrad. I could perhaps say that Göring has given me an erroneous view about the *Luftwaffe* capacity, and thus shoulder him with part of the blame. However, I have myself appointed him as my successor, since 1 September 1939, and therefore I cannot let him assume a share of my responsibility.[137]

Manstein adds: "It is certainly commendable that Hitler admitted his responsibility and did not search for a scapegoat."[138] Manstein may well have feared that Hitler would make him the scapegoat.

Excursus: Operation *Uranus*

The Russian counteroffensive, *Uranus*, ranks unique among the major strategic operations of World War II. It was the only operation of its kind where planning and execution were left exclusively to the military commanders, without interference from the political side. Stalin retained supreme control, but only after approving the basics of the plan. Stalin limited himself to deciding on the choice of the commander for the final assault *Koltso*.

The *Kessel* and the subsequent destruction of 6th Army was planned in detail two months after the beginning of operation 'Blue', before the German troops had even penetrated into Stalingrad. The original plan remained unaltered apart from insignificant changes during the fighting. The myth of the superior German *Generalstab* was laid to rest. The rivalry between *OKW* and *OKH* had already taken its toll. The views put forward by the *Generalstab* at Stalingrad were simply laughable. No major Red Army actions were considered possible, instead the evaluations contained sentences like: "No possibilities of an enemy offensive can be foreseen in the near future", "The Red Army's forces are obviously too weak for wide reaching operations." "At present, the Russian is unable to launch an offensive with far reaching objectives."

The Soviet Union's production of war equipment exceeded the German output in every field. More importantly, they produced better weapons in mass production. In 1942, Russian tank production came to 24,000 tanks. 12,000 were of the T–34 type that out-performed all other tanks of the Second World War.

136 Beevor, p. 380
137 *Verlorene Siege*, p. 395
138 *Verlorene Siege*, p. 394

German *Panzer* production amounted to 6,400 during 1942 and consisted of many different models. Of the 307 *Panzer* assigned to 6th Army, only 96 were *Panzer* IV models. It was the only German *Panzer* that stood a slight chance against the T–34. A Russian tank gunner produced a rhyme which became a hymn at the Ural Tchelyabinsk combinate where most T–34 were produced:

> For the death of enemies,
> For the joy of friends,
> There is no better machine
> Than the T–34.[139]

4,364 production-line workers at Tchelyabinsk, among them 1,253 women applied for service in the 'First Ural volunteer tank regiment.[140]

In 1942 the Soviet Union produced 24,000 aircraft, German industry only 12,000. *Stavka* performance improved greatly with the appointment of General Antonov as its deputy chief. Vasilevsky would nominally remain Chief of the General Staff. However, he was constantly sent to command 'theatres' and Antonov became Stalin's closest military adviser until the end of the war.

As the war progressed, more and more inheritance from the past was dug up. 'Great Patriotic War' superseded Communist slogans. After Stalingrad, the Imperial Army's shoulder straps replaced the former rank collar patches. New decorations would bear the names of past national heroes such as Suvorov, Kutuzov and Alexander Nevsky. Privileges were restored to the Church. At the victory banquet after Germany's surrender, the Georgian Stalin extolled the superiority of the Russian people over all other nations of the Soviet Union. Beevor wrote that "Stalin's great advantage over Hitler was his lack of ideological shame". After the disasters of 1941, he was not in the slightest bit squeamish about reviving the disgraced military thinking of the 1920s and the early 1930s."[141]

A number of the new high commanders, who had been arrested during the purges, were released in 1940 and rose to the highest ranks, among them the future Marshals Rokossovsky, Meretskov and Army General Gorbatov. Rokossovsky had all his teeth knocked out during his NKVD interrogation and he wore a steel denture. Stalin forgot nothing and saved his vengeance for the day of victory, when he wanted to appear as the sole supreme victor. He sent his high commanders to unimportant posts. Zhukov was summarily sent to command the Odessa military district and later the Ural district, "because he claimed too large a share in victory for himself". Stalin told him that suspicions had arisen against him when the Red Army was 'purged' in the late 1930s. Apparently they had somehow remained unnoticed, but, since they were in the files, it would be better if Zhukov would step aside for a while. The Pole, Rokossovsky,was dispatched to Poland as a member of the Polish Politburo with the rank of a Polish Marshal. The 'Southern commanders' were not promoted. Antonov was already Army General when he was appointed at the *Stavka*, but he never rose above this rank, and received only a minor command in the Caucasus.

---

139   Beevor, p. 224
140   Ibid
141   Beevor, p. 221

The planning phase

On 12 September 1942, Zhukov had been ordered to Moscow to report to Stalin and Vasilevsky. The *Wehrmacht* daily *communiqué* of 12 September mentions Stalingrad in a cursory manner: "Outside Stalingrad hard combats along fortress lines." On the next day: "Outside Stalingrad our troops are approaching the city limits and are endeavouring to penetrate into the southern parts of the city."

Stalin gave Zhukov one of his usual dressings down for a failed attack of his 'front' against the northern flank of 6th Army. He paid no attention to Zhukov's explanations and retreated to a corner of his large room where he looked at a situation map. The two Generals moved to another corner and started whispering about the need for another solution. Stalin had exceptionally sharp hearing and asked the Generals what they had in mind with 'another solution.' Before either could reply, Stalin ordered them to first go to *Stavka* and review their idea there, then immediately report back to him.

Zhukov and Vasilevsky returned on the following evening. Zhukov was still smarting under the reprimand of the previous day and expected to be once more taken to task. Stalin greeted both Generals cordially and asked who would make the report. Vasilevsky replied that either of them could present it since they were in total agreement. Zhukov made the presentation. Vasilevsky and he had looked at the map of 6th Army's salient and noticed that it became increasingly vulnerable on both flanks. Their solution aimed at a major operation that would decisively shift the strategic situation in the South. The city of Stalingrad should be held in a war of attrition, with just enough troops to keep the defence alive. No formations should be wasted on minor counter-attacks, and efforts should be limited to keep the Germans from seizing the whole west bank of the Volga. Zhukov knew that the Germans would focus entirely on capturing the city. *Stavka* would in the meantime secretly amass fresh armies behind the lines for a major encirclement of the entire 6th Army and its ultimate destruction.[142]

At first Stalin was hesitant. He feared that Stalingrad could be lost if the Red Army were to wait until the date foreseen by Zhukow and Vasilevsky. Zhukov remained adamant. Everybody in Russia feared Stalin, Zhukov no less than the other Red Army Generals, but this time Zhukov knew that he held a strong hand. In September 1941 he had warned Stalin to defend Kiev. Stalin told him that he was talking 'rubbish', *chipucha*. Zhukov said: "If you feel that the Chief of the General Staff talks only rubbish, my place is not here. Better to give me a command at the front where I can be of better use." Stalin replied: "We'll manage without you."[143]

He did not 'manage without him' for long. Zhukov was urgently recalled to replace the incompetent Voroshilov and to assume command of the defence of Leningrad. When the Germans approached Moscow, Stalin asked him if he could hold the city. Zhukov replied that he had no doubt, and he was immediately asked to relieve Timoshenko in command of the central front area. He not only defended the city, but he prepared and led the masterful Russian counter-offensive that inflicted the first major defeat upon German ground forces during the war. He felt

---

142   Ibid., p.220 f
143   Zhukov, p. 311

that Stalin would now listen to him. Stalin was finally convinced and gave his two commanders the green light.

The preparations on the ground

During this phase, the Russians would display their unsurpassed mastery in camouflage, *Maskirovka*. Strict secrecy was ordered. All principal actors were given code names. Stalin became Vassilev, Vasilevsky-Michailov, Zhukov-Konstantinov, Rokossovsky-Dontsov, Yeremenko-Ivanov, Vatutin-Fyodorov, etc. Two new 'fronts' were established. The 'Stalingrad Front' was under Yeremenko, and was incorporated into a 'theatre' commanded by Zhukov. The 'Don Front', under Rokossovsky, was part of a second 'theatre' under Vasilevsky. Later, a third 'South-Western Front', under Vatutin, was added.

Postal service between the front line and the homeland was entirely suspended. Troop movements were only permitted during the night. Communication centres, of divisions that had been moved, were left at their former location and continued to send fictitious messages from there. Orders related to *Uranus* were only given verbally. No written communication was allowed. In order to create a feeling of an impending offensive in the Centre, sizeable reserves were sent into this area and local attacks took place around Velikiye Luki.

Halder fell into the trap and kept Manstein's 11th Army with Army Group Centre. To increase deception of the Germans, an order to the 'front' commanders was openly broadcast in mid-October: "Begin to organise yourselves for defensive." An entire tank corps was built up with dummies. Dummy airports were set up and thereafter camouflaged as if they were genuine. Dummy bridges were erected over the Don River. The real bridges were underwater.

In spite of these measures, Russian preparations did not remain entirely unnoticed. On 2 October, a captured Red Army officer had disclosed such elements of the Russian plan as were known to him. When Winrich Behr arrived at 6th Army, the Ic, Lieutenant Colonel Niemeyer, showed him the situation map where he had inserted the Russian troop movements. He warned that a pincer offensive was to be expected very shortly.[144] Paulus and Schmidt dismissed his report as too pessimistic. After the war, Paulus confirmed that he had immediately recognised the danger, while Schmidt admitted that he had failed to grasp it.[145]

Chuikov had not been informed of *Uranus* in advance. In his recollections, he wrote that he received his first official notification on 18 November, the eve of the attack. He must have had some suspicion, because on 18 October he had requested more artillery. It was denied him.[146] The Russian attack broke loose with fury on 19 November. In the early morning hours a personal message from Stalin was read to the troops. It began with the words: "Dear generals and soldiers, my brothers. Today you will launch an offensive that will decide the fate of our country. Will it remain an independent nation or be destroyed." [147]Ivan Golokolenko told Rees: "I

---

144   Beevor, p. 227
145   Ibid. p. 228
146   Chuikov, p. 280 and 341
147   Rees, p. 176.

was deeply moved by these words. When the meeting ended, I was close to tears. I felt an internal urge, a spiritual urge."

Mereschko said:

> Today people talk about Stalin and say that he had murdered millions. At the time we did not know that. When we went into battle, we shouted "For the motherland, for Stalin". Now we have no more ideology. No words like "everything for the front, everything for victory" remain. At that time. many women and children worked in the factories under this motto. This was not hot air, people really felt that way.[148]

During the war 'Stalin's Terror' was forgotten, his person became a focus for the people. Boris Pasternak wrote in his novel 'Doctor Zhivago,' that the Russians saw the victorious war as a beacon of hope that terror would not return. Ilya Ehrenburg wrote that had Stalin died in 1945, the war might have obliterated a great deal. People would have clung to the illusion that it was owing to Yagoda, Yeshov and Beria that millions of innocent people had perished. The memory of those who took part in the war would have preserved the image of Stalin a soldier's greatcoat, symbolising the arduous days of the battle of Moscow.[149] The Russians were to suffer bitter disappointment until Stalin's death. Large-scale 'Terror' resumed immediately after victory.

The first Russian strike hit the Romanian units and simply pulverised them. They fled in panic, abandoning most of their equipment. The Germans' turn would come on the following day and they were completely taken by surprise. XLVIII *Panzer* Corps under the command of *Generalleutnant* Heim, Paulus' former teacher, was ordered to launch an immediate counterattack. His Corps was not ready for combat and could make no progress. Heim was dismissed and reduced in rank to private soldier, but he would be reinstated in 1944. On 22 November, the *Kessel* was closed and 6th Army had become encircled.

Stalin's only intervention occurred when a commander for the final assault had to be decided. Zhukov recalled the *GKO* meeting that decided on the appointment. *GKO, Gossudarstvennyi Komitet Oborony*, a state control committee, was the supreme body for the conduct of the war. It consisted of seven permanent members, headed by Stalin, and six political personalities drawn from the highest echelons. High ranking commanders attended its meetings as consultants. Zhukov wrote, "Someone mentioned the name of Rokossovsky as commander for the final assault. Stalin looked at me and said. "You remain silent?" I replied that both Yeremenko and Rokossovsky were outstanding commanders, however Yeremenko, who had born the major weight of the battle, would be hurt. Stalin said angrily that there was no time for sentiment. "Phone Yeremenko immediately and tell him that he has to put his armies under Rokkossovsky's command."

As I had expected, Yeremenko was desperate and asked for my help. I could only suggest to him to call Stalin directly. After fifteen minutes Yeremenko phoned me and said that Stalin refused to take his call. He had been told that he could discuss this matter with me only. Yeremenko continued to press me and I had to phone Stalin again. As I expected, I received a tongue-lashing and was ordered to

148 Ibid
149 I. Ehrenburg, *The war: 1901–1945*, New York 1964, p. 45

inform all commanders about Rokossovsky's appointment without delay." [150]At that time Rokossovsky was still a Lieutenant General and junior in rank to Yeremenko, who was a Colonel General. Rokossovsky would soon receive three successive promotions and rise to become a Marshal of the Soviet Union in 1944. As one of the 'Southern generals,' Yeremenko would have to wait for Stalin's death before becoming a Marshal of the Soviet Union in 1955.

German and Russian casualties at Stalingrad

Surprisingly, exact figures are still not available. Not even the number of troops encircled in the *Kessel* has been established. Uhle-Wettler believes that they amounted to a total of 275,000, of which around 230,000 Germans, 20,000 *Hiwi*, 10,000 Romanians, a Croatian regiment, and some Italian troops. [151]Rüdiger Overmans arrives at a total figure of 250,000, comprising 190,000 Germans, 52,000 *Hiwi* and 5,000 Romanians. [152]Peter Hild gives a total number of 286,900, comprising 19,300 *Hiwi* and 13,000 Romanians and Italians. [153] Hild's figures clash with the estimations of 6th Army's quartermaster. Up to 6 December 1942 he prepared 275,000 food rations for the *Kessel.* Beevor wrote that historians are unanimous that a total of 25,000 men were flown out during the battle.

After the Red Army launched *Koltso,* chaos increased by the day, and no precise figures are available for the last two weeks. Beevor arrived at a total of 52,000 killed in action between 22 November 1942 and 7 January 1943. How many of them were *Hiwi* cannot be ascertained. [154] Doerr estimated that an additional 100,000 were killed between 27 January and 2 February. [155] Beevor arrived at a similar figure. [156] The Russians claimed to have taken 111,496 combat-ready soldiers as prisoners-of-war and a further 8,925 picked up in field hospitals. [157] There is little doubt about the ultimate fate of the *Hiwi.*

Russian casualties were staggering. Rees arrived at a total figure of 1 million killed in action and estimates that the life expectancy of a Red Army soldier in the *Kessel* to be, at most, 24 hours after coming into combat. More than 2 million Russian civilians lost their lives in the city and its suburbs. Unknown graves continue to be discovered.

150   Zhukov, p. 456 f
151   Uhle-Wettler, p.274
152   R. Overmans, *Das andere Gesicht des Krieges: Leben und Sterben der 6.Armee* in J. Förster (ed.), *Stalingrad: Ereignis, Wirkung, Symbol,* Munich 1992, p. 442
153   P. Hild, *Partnergruppe zur Aufklärung der Vermißtenschicksale deutscher und russischer Soldaten des 2. Weltkrieges* in A.Efipanow/H.Mayer (ed.) *Die Tragödie der deutschen Kriegsgefangenen in Stalingrad von 1942 bis 1956,* Osnabrück 1996, p. 29 (henceforth Epifanow)
154   Beevor, p. 439 f
155   Doerr, p. 116
156   Beevor, p. 440
157   Epifanow, p. 397

Manstein's responsibility

Uhle-Wettler describes Stalingrad as the all-time low in German military history.[158] The loss of the battle can be charged neither to Manstein nor to Paulus. It was the result of the disastrous planning of 'Blue'. Even more so, it was the simple consequence of the Red Army having become much stronger than the *Wehrmacht*. During the advance on Stalingrad, Paulus only carried out Army Group B's order, which in turn followed the master plan of *OKH*. When Manstein took command of Army Group Don, the *Kessel* was already a *fait accompli*. His operational decisions during the battle could not be faulted, even if they were doomed to failure. He could not achieve more with the strength left at his disposal and no alternatives were left to him.

The responsibilities of both commanders must be searched for elsewhere. When both understood that the battle was irretrievably lost, did they do their utmost to save as many of their soldiers from death or captivity? Neither did, but Manstein's share of this responsibility is far greater. Paulus was given a command way beyond his aptitudes. No man can jump over his shown shadow and Paulus cast a very large shadow. No German general was more apt for the command at Stalingrad than Manstein, who was the most outstanding *Wehrmacht* commander of the Second World War. He was certainly capable of independent action, but he was simply unwilling to take that step.

After relieving General Sponeck on the Crimea, Manstein had written:

> The case of General Sponeck shows the tragedy of a commander when he is torn between his duty to obey orders, and his own understanding about required operative steps. He knows that he risks his head if he disobeys. But still he can find compelled to act contrary to orders.[159]

Sponeck had risked his head at Kertch, *SS-Obergruppenführer* Hausser had risked his head at Charkov. Manstein never risked his head, because he believed himself to be irreplaceable and chosen by fate to the highest command. No man is irreplaceable. Manstein could have suffered a sudden stroke. Would that have meant the end of his Army Group? When he was dismissed, he said to Hitler that he hoped Hitler would never regret this decision. Hitler hardly had any strong regrets, since he had found a competent successor in Model.

At Stalingrad, Manstein simply made it easy for himself. He never flew into the *Kessel* to obtain a personal insight into the conditions at 6th Army's staff. He did not request the relief of Paulus. If he felt that such a step was not required, he should have intervened directly in the command of 6th Army and made Paulus a stand-by who had to carry out his daily orders. As an Army Group Commander, *Feldmarschall* Model was often unhappy with the performance of his Army Commanders. Given his impossible temperament and his frequent outbursts, this occurred at regular intervals. He would then take over direct command of the Army concerned. The Army commander, who was victim of his frequent outbursts, became a stand-by. Manstein refused to give Paulus a clear and direct order to break out, although Paulus had repeatedly implored him to do so. Manstein knew that Paulus would

---

158 Uhle-Wettler, p. 249
159 *Verlorene Siege*, p. 244

have obeyed him, notwithstanding that this was in direct contradiction to Hitler. No one can doubt Manstein's suffering at the bereavement of 6th Army and his constant attempts to convince Hitler to save what could still be saved. But it is easier to act by phone from the comfortable surrounding of headquarters than to take direct responsibility inside the *Kessel* or to personally disobey Hitler.

At the end he pleaded for a surrender, but refrained from taking it upon himself to order it. Manstein saw fit to blame Paulus rather than acknowledging his own responsibility. His posthumous fame would have been served better, had he abstained from writing in *Verlorene Siege*:

> I have decided to give a detailed account of the reasons which led the commander in chief of 6th Army to abstain from seizing the last opportunity of saving his army. This is my duty towards the soldiers, regardless of Paulus' personality and his behaviour in later years. It is easy to criticize the actions of *Feldmarschall* Paulus during those decisive days. Undoubtedly, Paulus was facing a grave conflict of conscience when he had to launch an operation that, contrary to explicit orders from Hitler, would have him abandon Stalingrad. However, it must be understood that such an abandonment, under irresistible pressure from the enemy, would have justified him in acting contrary to Hitler's order. But the Army Group had ordered him to do so, thus assuming responsibility. [160]

From that day Manstein became his direct superior, Paulus suffered no conflict of conscience. He only waited for a direct order by Manstein and would have obeyed it without qualms. Paulus' conduct in captivity was certainly bereft of dignity. However, Manstein was not entitled to preach morality to others, after having issued his infamous order of the day of 20 November 1941 and participated in the heinous German crimes in the Crimea.

One can show understanding for Paulus' outrage when he read *Verlorene Siege*. He said to Adam:

> You have to read this. Suddenly Manstein appears without blame for the disaster of 6th Army. This man writes blatant lies. He puts all the blame on Hitler and me. You have listened in to all my conversations over decimetre with him. You know that he never informed me about the situation and how he practically paralysed me. Now he turns everything upside down. And this is a man whom I once held in the highest esteem. A man, who at that time did not see fit to give me an order, or at least permission to break out, has no right today to write that he had wished me to break out and would have covered me. [161]

At Stalingrad, Manstein did not conduct himself like a *Feldmarschall*. *Generaloberst* von Richthofen, who commanded the Air Fleet attached to Army Group Don, wrote in his diary: "As things are now, one is at best a highly paid sergeant." This would have been a fitter conclusion to Manstein's Stalingrad chapter than the Thermopylae quote.

---

160   *Verlorene Siege*, p. 371
161   Adam, p. 482 ff. Also in Knopp, p. 200

Lidell Hart described the German commanders of the Second World War as prototypes of a modern Pontius Pilatus, who washes his hands of responsibility for all orders that he carried out."[162]

Finally, a conclusion by General Doerr:

> Stalingrad was no sacrifice, such as the combat of Leonidas and his Spartans at Thermopylae. Nor was it such as the self-sacrifice of the Spaniards at Numantia. Stalingrad will be known in history as the greatest military error ever committed by a Supreme Commander, and as the greatest abuse ever by the leadership of the soul and strength of its people.[163]

162   Quoted in H. Herzfeld, *Das Problem des deutschen Heeres 1939–1945* in *Geschichte und Politik. Eine wissenschaftliche Schriftenreihe*, Heft 6, H. Dahms (ed.), Laupheim 1952, p. 10

163   Doerr, p. 119

Chapter 4

The Battles for Kursk

German military archives contain a wealth of documents on Kursk, probably more than on any other battle of the war in the East. Surprisingly, only a few German military historians have written books or lengthy essays on it. However, it is considered to have been one of the most decisive encounters of the Russo-German war. In the view of some historians it was the most decisive. German literature tends to concentrate on the battles of Stalingrad and Berlin. Stalingrad was the most spectacular encounter. Berlin saw the 'Twilight of the Gods', with Hitler's final days in the Bunker, and his suicide, symbolising the downfall of the Third *Reich*. However, Kursk had more significance than any other major battle in the East as it marked the end of any further German initiative on the Russian front.

Russian military history is much more comprehensive about Kursk, but until recent years, it was strongly subject to political constraint. Nevertheless, until recently, it could be assumed that at least the relevant facts about a battle of such importance are known to experts, and to readers who take a more than superficial interest in the Second World War.

Yet surprisingly, Roman Töppel, a young and still little known historian, submitted a thesis for his MA to the University of Dresden in 2001, *Die Offensive gegen Kursk 1943 – Legenden, Mythen und Propaganda* (The offensive at Kursk – legends, myths and propaganda)[1]. It shows that, up to now, most of what has been written about Kursk is not consistent with the facts. Töppel has had access to recently released (1993) Russian military archive documents (CAMO-*Centralnyi Archiv Ministerstva Oborony Rossiskoy Federacyi*) and to statements by Russian historians who could only go public after the breakdown of the Soviet Union.

A summary of Töppel's findings has been published in number 2 (2002) of *Militärgeschichtliche Zeitschrift*, the bi-annual publication of the *MGFA*. The title of the article is: *Legendenbildung in der Geschichtsschreibung – Die Schlacht bei Kursk*. (How legends enter history – the battle of Kursk).[2] Both these titles are well chosen, since few military operations have been subject to so many legends. Töppel's thesis has yet to be published, but I have been privileged to receive a typed copy. I can only express the hope that Töppel's findings will soon become available as a book, since no future historian will be able to ignore them.

---

1 R. Töppel, *Die Offensive gegen Kursk 1943, Legenden, Mythen und Propaganda*, MA thesis submitted to the Technical Univesity, Dresden 2001 (henceforth Töppel)
2 R. Töppel, *Legendenbildung in der Geschichtsschreibung – Die Schlacht bei Kursk*, in *Militärgeschichtliche Zeitschrift*, Potsdam, 61 (2002), Heft 1, p. 369-401

Operation 'Citadel' or 'Battles for Kursk'?

'Citadel' was the German code name for the initial German offensive. It turned into a fiasco and petered out after one week. German writers, and parts of Western military history, limit accounts of Kursk to 'Citadel'. What followed 'Citadel' is viewed by German generals in their memoirs, and by historians, as separate individual actions. Russian historians use the term 'Battle of Kursk' (*Kurskaya bitva*) which is more appropriate, since 'Citadel' was only one of three interconnected major actions. First came the German offensive in the north of Kursk, lasting from 5 July to 11 July 1943. It was followed by the Russian counter-offensive at Orel, between 12 July and 18 August. Finally came the counter-offensive at Charkov, between 3 August and 28 August. All of that was followed by the recapture of most of the Ukraine, and by the fall of Kiev in the November.

British literature adapts the Russian terminology in words only. Albert Seaton heads the relevant chapter in his book about the Russo-German war, 'The battle of Kursk', but limits his account to the 'Citadel' phase. The Russian offensives which followed the failure of 'Citadel' are described in his following chapter, 'The Russian autumn offensives 1943'.[3] In their recent works, the American historians David Glantz and Jonathan House adopt the Russian definition. They treat the three phases of Kursk as an entity.[4] Glantz is the first author to translate a study of Kursk, by the Russian general staff, that had been written during the war.[5] This chapter adopts the correct Russian heading.

However, a book about Manstein need only dwell in detail on 'Citadel', since the plan for the offensive originated with him. His Army Group was the larger of the two Army Groups engaged in the battle. After the German breaking off the offensive, Manstein was no longer the pre-eminent commander in the East and acted on a par with the other heads of Army Groups. Hitler became increasingly impatient with his lectures.

In a talk with Zeitzler in July 1943, Hitler said: "Manstein is a good commander when he can draw from plenty. But he does not know how to cope with a crisis."[6] Zeitzler then suggested giving Manstein part of Kleist's Army Group as far as the shores of the Azov Sea. Hitler immediately rebuked him:

> So, we should let *Herr* von Manstein free to do what he wants? If he feels like it, he will withdraw from all of Ukraine, just because he wants to operate. He couldn't care less where I will then get the necessary food for the German people. No Zeitzler, we have to remain control. If Manstein has his way, he will only confront us with a *fait accompli*.

When Zeitzler replied that one could put limits on Manstein's freedom of action, Hitler said angrily:

---

3   Seaton, *War*, p.353–368.

4   D.Glantz/J. House, *The Battle of Kursk*, Lawrence 1999 (henceforth Glantz)

5   D.Glantz/H.Orenstein (ed), *The Battle for Kursk 1943. The Soviet General Staff Study*, London 1999 (henceforth Glantz General Staff)

6   A. Heusinger, *Befehl im Widerstreit, Schicksalsstunden der deutschen Armee 1923–1945*, Stuttgart 1950, p. 265 (henceforth Heusinger Befehl)

I know what will happen. He will write his reports in a manner that only the solution preferred by him remains. I have experienced this many times. If one could at least rely on reports. But every commander thinks only about himself and his sector. The overall situation is of no concern to him. We are the ones who have to take care of this.[7]

Eight months latter Manstein was dismissed from his command.

Was Kursk the decisive battle of the war in the East?

The Russian Generals viewed the battles of Moscow and Kursk as the two decisive encounters of the Russo-German war. The ideological overtones, which are common in Soviet historical works up to the emergence of *Glasnost*, were greatly exaggerated in their accounts of Kursk. General Shtemenko, Antonov's deputy at *Stavka* at that time, wrote:

The high moral values that distinguished our soldiers, from the first day of the war, were now strengthened. Our people became increasingly mature, their confidence in the wisdom of the party and the unshakeable Soviet organization, grew by the day.[8]

Marshal Vasilevsky saw, in the battles for Kursk, "above all, the proof the superiority of the Soviet high command."[9]

The Soviet historian Boris Solovev added:

The battles of Kursk were not only evidence of superior Soviet military art but, even more, they showed evidence of the indisputable superiority of the military and economic elements of socialism that would turn the Red Army's victories at Kursk into an iron clad law of world history.[10]

The first Artillery Salute, fired in Moscow during the war, was a sign of the symbolic value that the Russians attached to Kursk. It was fired after the capture of Orel during the first phase of the Red Army's counter-offensive. The Salute was then repeated after every capture of a major city.

After the collapse of the Soviet Union, the Russian military began to distance themselves from their former ideological historiography. In 1996, on the battle-field of Prokhorovka, at a meeting of military historians from a number of coun-tries, the Russian historian Grigoryi Koltunov admitted: "I have committed forgeries, and I have lied. I was ordered to exaggerate German losses and to mini-

---

7 Heusinger Befehl, p. 267
8 S. Shtemenko, *Generalnyi Schtab v Gody Voiny*, Moscow 1968 p. 156 (henceforth Shtemenko)
9 A. Vasilevsky, *Sache des ganzen Lebens*, East Berlin 1977, p. 310
10 B. Solovev, *Wendepunkt des Zweiten Weltkrieges – Die Schlacht bei Kursk*, Cologne 1984, p. 13f, 30, 93, 111

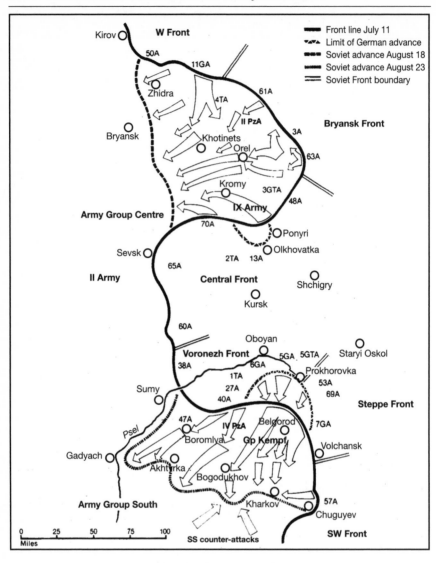

Kursk, July–August 1943

mise Red Army casualties way below genuine figures. My works cannot be taken seriously."[11]

German historians and generals could have been expected to voice their customary denials at Soviet figures and accounts. But in that instance they would concur, without adopting the ideological overtones of course, The reason is obvious. Given the disaster of the battle, the German generals were eager to

11 W. Will, *Wo Panzergeschichte geschrieben*, article in *Berliner Morgenpost*, July 20/21 1996, supplement, p. 2

distance themselves from any connection with it. The high commanders, who had opposed the 'Citadel' plan from the outset, intended to show in their post-war accounts that their doomsday prophecies had been confirmed by events. Whether any battle in the East can be called decisive is open to doubt. One could just as well say that the fatal decision had already occurred on 22 June 1941 when Germany attacked Russia. But after 'Citadel', Germany's military situation took a dramatic turn for the worse. A new *Schwerpunkt* of the war arose in the West after the landing of the Allies in North Africa, then the German defeat at El-Alamein, the surrender of the *Afrika Armee* at Tunis, and the landing on Sicily, that was soon to be followed by the invasion of mainland Italy. Carpet-bombing of German cities increased by the day.

After the failure of 'Citadel', the *Wehrmacht* was unable to launch further offensive actions in the East. Manstein wrote:

> Once 'Citadel' was broken off, all initiative in the East passed to the Soviet side. We had failed to encircle the strong enemy forces in the Kursk salient. We had broken off any action against the reserves brought forward by the Russians, before there could be a favourable outcome. After that, it was evident that the enemy could then avail himself of his superiority in numbers and equipment. His counter-attack in the Orel salient was only the beginning of a major offensive.[12]

Only the first and the last sentences are true, the remainder is yet another variation of Manstein's 'draw theory'. An encirclement of the Red Army units in the Kursk salient was never on the cards. 'Citadel' was not broken off just ahead of a favourable outcome for the *Wehrmacht*. Hitler ordered an end of the offensive when it had become totally bogged down.

Kursk had far-reaching political consequences. Mussolini was overthrown, and Italy declared war on Germany. Antonescu wanted to pursue the war against Russia, while at the same time searching for contacts with the West. A year later, he was overthrown by a *coup*, and Romania declared war on Germany. Through secret channels, Hungary made careful approaches to the Allies. Finland abstained from further military actions.

Kursk in German literature

The first lengthy and, in its comments, totally misleading account, was written by Paul Carell.[13] Carell devotes more than 100 pages to Kursk, but the historic value of his book is nil. Carell was the pseudonym of Paul Schmidt, the former head of the foreign office's press office. He chose a pseudonym, to avoid confusion with the chief interpreter of the German foreign office, who was also named Paul Schmidt. He published his recollections before Carell wrote his books. Carell wrote in the journalistic style of his former occupation. Not unusually, for a journalist turned historian, Carell's account is a mixture of veterans' tales, legends, myths, and accounts of mysterious 'purported' traitors who were alleged to have caused the

---

12 *Verlorene Siege*, p. 507 f
13 P. Carell, *Verbrannte Erde. Schlacht zwischen Wolga und Weichsel,* Frankfurt 1966 (henceforth Carell)

German effort to fail. Blends of facts and fiction are well received by the public, and Carell's many books became best-sellers.

A serious account of the opposing forces is given by the historian Ernst Klink.[14] However, his book was published in 1966. It suffers from the insufficiency of archive material available at that time. In particular is the absence of Soviet archive sources that were inaccessible to foreign historians. A relatively objective account, if one omits the unavoidable political sidelines, appeared in East Germany, under the auspices of its Academy of Science in 1979.[15] Some elements of myth and fiction were put right, by Karl-Heinz Frieser, in a memorial book honouring the historian Gerhard Ritter. It was published in the mid-1990s.[16]

Operation 'Citadel' – Planning and postponements

The state of the German Army in 1943

Albert Seaton drew up a general summary that found its way into a number of Western accounts. However, it was totally erroneous:

> It was at the beginning of 1943, during the Soviet offensive, that a change first became apparent in the composition and relative strength of the German and Soviet Armies. Germany entered the war with highly efficient and very well equipped *Panzer* and motorized forces. They were the best in the world, although they represented only a minor part of the German Army as a whole. German tactical air support was excellent. The Red Army at that time did not lack for tanks, aircraft or equipment, but it was in no way a modern motorized Army. It was not even a match for the German marching Infantry Divisions, with their horse-drawn guns and wagons. However, by 1943, German organisation and the quality and scale of equipment, instead of being improved to keep ahead of those of their enemies, had fallen far behind.
>
> In March 1943, the Eastern Front was short of their establishment of 470,000 men. The German High Command tried, through necessity, to make a virtue of going without. Hitler, with his obsession for divisional numbers, was continually raising new formations. He refused to maintain, reinforce or re-equip existing divisions, so that they became little more than *cadres*. So-called *Panzer* divisions numbered only thirty or forty tanks. The German Army had gone into Russia with 3,300 *Panzer* in 1941. On 23 January 1943, it had only 495 *Panzer* fit for battle, over

---

14 E. Klink, *Das Gesetz des Handelns. Die Operation 'Zitadelle' 1953*, Stuttgart 1966 (henceforth Klink)

15 *Deutschland im Zweiten Weltkrieg, Der grundlegende Umschwung im Kriegsverlauf (November 1942 bis September 1943)*, W. Schumann (ed.), Berlin East 1973

16 K-H. Frieser, *Schlagen aus der Nachhand-Schlagen aus der Vorhand* in *Politik, Geschichte, Recht und Sicherheit, Festschrift für Gerhard Ritter*, p.247 (henceforth Frieser, Citadel)

the whole of the Eastern Front. Except for a handful of 'Tiger' model *Panzer*, no new *Panzer* were in service. The *Panzer* 2 and 4 had been improved by the addition of skirting plates, re-enforced armour-plating, and longer guns that had an increase of muzzle velocity. Divisional organisations began to be altered. The divisional title remained, but the number of regiments in the divisions, and of battalions in the regiments was reduced. It resulted in a further reduction in the fighting strength of formations.

The Red Army's transformation, on the other hand, had been for the better. The Red Air Force, although still inferior to the *Luftwaffe* in performance, had made great strides in the development of the quality of its aircraft. The KV [*Klement Voroshilov*] and T–34 tanks were superior to the German *Panzer* 3 and 4 and were being manufactured in large numbers, From mid 1942 onwards, tank and mechanized corps were being grouped as tank armies. But in 1943, one of the most significant changes to be observed in the Red Army was the rapid motorization that was to enable the Soviet High Command to undertake deep penetration in the depths of winter, and also at the time of the thaw. It was achieved largely by the introduction of United States trucks.

Once the best equipped in the world, the German Army, within a space of two years was relegated to the position of an out-of-date force, indifferently provided with obsolescent equipment. The German equivalent to the Red Army quarter-ton jeep, for a commander or messenger, remained the horse. The counterpart of the Studebaker or Dodge six-wheeled drive truck was the horse-drawn *panje* wagon. The efficiency of German field formation staffs and the quality of the German fighting soldier were still superior to those of the Red Army. Yet for all of that, the German Army, once the pride of the *Reich*, had become one of the poorer armies of the world.[17]

Seaton's book ranks among serious writings on the Russo-German war, however the paragraphs quoted above are wide of the mark. The *Wehrmacht* had not *become* (my emphasis) 'one of the poorer armies of the world'. Even by 1939 it 'was the poorest' of all major European armies. At its best, it could only be described as a 'semi-modern' army.[18]

Frieser elaborates:

The *Wehrmacht* of 1939 consisted of two distinct Armies. Only 10 *Panzer* divisions and 6 motorized divisions could be called élite units. The remaining 90% were old-fashioned, with low-grade equipment, suitable for defence only, and certainly not suitable for offensive purposes. Only the first two Division 'waves', with soldiers on active duty in 1939, and fully trained soldiers of the first reserve, could be considered as fully combat worthy. The Divisions of the third and fourth 'waves' consisted of soldiers of the second reserves. They belonged to the age groups that had

---

17 Seaton War, p. 351 f
18 T.Ropp, Preface to L. Addington, *The Blitzkrieg Era and the German General Staff 1865–1941*, New Brunswick 1941, p. XV

been bled 'white' during the First World War. Their training period had not exceeded three months at most. A number of their soldiers were veterans of the First World War, aged 40 or over. Apart from the *Panzer* and motorized divisions, the Army was basically suitable for defence only. Perhaps, at most, it was suitable for individual limited offensive actions.[19]

The *Panzer* and motorized units of the *Wehrmacht* were neither the 'best in the world' nor were they 'highly efficient'. The *Wehrmacht* was in no way motorized. On the contrary, a 'de-motorization' had been ordered before the outbreak of the war. Frieser described the motorization of the *Wehrmacht* as 'simply pitiable':

A typical aspect of the purported *Blitzkrieg* army of 1940 was its lack of vehicles. In contrast, the BEF was highly motorized. The French Army had 300,000 vehicles of all types in 1940. The *Wehrmacht*, even after requisitioning all available private property, had only 120,000 lorries. Monthly production amounted to around 1,000 lorries, only 1% of the stock in 1939. Meanwhile, monthly wear and tear put twice this figure out of action. This misery led Halder to order a 'programme of de-motorization'. The horse was to replace the vehicle. During the First World War, the German army had 1,400,000 horses, during the Second World War their number increased to 2,700,000.[20]

Both in numbers and in quality the German *Panzer* were inferior in quality to the tanks of their enemies. Germany never succeeded in mass production of a *Panzer* model that could equal the quality of the Russian T–34. The successes of the *Panzer* units, in the first battles in the East, were solely due to the methods of their employment that the Red Army had not yet adopted. In 1941, the Red Army was far more motorized than the *Wehrmacht*. Its number of tanks in June 1941 has been estimated at 30,000. In a conversation with Marshal Mannerheim during the war, which was secretly recorded by the Finns, and which is available on gramophone records, Hitler said that he had not been aware of that number. Had he known about it, his decision to attack Russia would have been much more difficult to reach, although, in the end, he would still have decided upon war.

The modern 'doctrine' of tank deployment was developed in Russia in the early 1930s by Marshal Tukhatchevsky and General Uborevich. Both were shot in 1937. Their doctrines were labelled as 'criminal'. After the Red Army's setbacks during the summer of 1941, the doctrines were simply brought out again. In 1941, the T–34 was already the core of the Russian tank forces. Russian infantry was not inferior to the German. Even in the first days of the war, Russian infantry soldiers put up a resistance that the Germans had not encountered in their previous campaigns. The destruction of entire Russian Armies in the first *Kessel* battles was not due to inferiority of the Russian infantry soldier, but was a consequence of Stalin's first order, to 'defend every inch of Russian soil'.

German tactical air support was no longer excellent. The number of planes was insufficient. In 1939, the *Luftwaffe* was not yet ready for war. While it was the most modern of its kind, it was simply the wrong air force for the war that Hitler

---

19   Frieser, p. 37 f
20   Ibid, p. 37 f

had in mind. It had been built up with an erroneous concept. Production of bombers was neglected and when the war turned into a 'world war', it was too late for changes. During the Battle of Britain, the *Luftwaffe* lost more than 900 of its elite pilots, and was never able to replace them. The Battle of Britain had shown that most German aircraft lacked the 'reach' required for a modern war in the air. By 1943, the Russian Air Force was equal in quality to the German. Russian aircraft production was twice that of Germany.

Hitler had no obsession to create new Divisions by reducing the equipment of existing ones. In fact, he held the opposite opinion. On 10 May 1943 he said to Keitel:

> Unfortunately I no longer believe in the possibility of creating new divisions by making use of *'Gerippe'* ie skeletons. Existing divisions that had been reduced to minimal numbers. No commander is ready to part with them. This is a shame. I am always told that it would be more practical to replenish them. Of course, it would be more practical. But it can't be done because no one wants to part with them.[21]

Helmut Heiber, the editor of the records of Hitler's situation meetings, elaborates in a footnote:

> Both the *Generalstab* and Hitler held the opinion that the best way of creating new combat-worthy Divisions was to replenish existing units. The war situation made it increasingly incumbent upon commanders to establish fresh reserves. Such reserves were only available to Germany in Polish provinces that had been annexed by Germany, or in the German occupied countries of Western Europe. Divisions, that had lost most of their equipment in the East, should have been sent there to be replenished with new equipment. Although this was carefully planned over periods of weeks, it could never be done because the Commanders in the East never agreed to part with what remained of their own divisions. Under such conditions, Supreme Command had no choice but to resort to the creation of new divisions.[22]215

At the beginning of the war against Russia, Hitler had indeed doubled the number of *Panzer* divisions, by halving the number of *Panzer* in every unit. Guderian wrote, with some frustration, that nominal increases in numbers came at the expense of efficiency.[23] This decision by Hitler was not unreasonable, since the huge space of the territories invaded could not be covered by the existing Division numbers. Hitler had hoped that lack of numbers would be compensated for by the surprise factor, which could then turn out to be successful.

The number of *Panzer* available in the East in 1943 was not 495, as indicated by Seaton. At the beginning of the year it had already risen to 3,000, after Speer had

---

21 H. Heiber (ed). *Hitlers Lagebesprechungen. Die Protokollfragmente seiner militärischen Konferenzen 1942–1945,* Stuttgart 1962, p. 215 (henceforth *Lagebesprechungen*)

22 Ibid, p. 215 f

23 Guderian, p. 124 f

succeeded in giving a strong boost to the German war production.[24] During 1943, Germany produced 5,966 *Panzer* and 3,406 assault guns.[25] German production's main drawback was the typical German urge for perfection. That led to endless attempts at improving existing models, instead of deciding on mass production of arms that had served their purpose. During the battle of Prokhorovka, in the second phase of Kursk, II *Waffen-SS Panzer* Corps alone had 236 tanks, 58 assault guns and 43 *Panzerjäger* vehicles of the *Marder* type, ie self propelling anti-tank vehicles equipped with anti-tank guns.[26] Töppel established, after careful research of all available sources, that the total number of *Panzer* and other motorized vehicles engaged by the Germans at Kursk, was 2,829 with an additional 541 in process of being shipped to the front after repair.[27]

Like many Western authors, Seaton fell victim to a clever propaganda trick by Dr Goebbels. Frieser writes:

A guiding principle of war propaganda consists in exaggerating the strength of the enemy while deprecating one's own. Thus victory becomes more brilliant and defeat easier to forgive.

Why then did the official German propaganda not deny the grotesque exaggerations of the *Wehrmacht* strength that made headlines everywhere abroad? Why did German propaganda, under the masterful direction of Dr Goebbels, engage in spreading shameless exaggerations which confirmed, even surpassed the horror visions put forward in the West? The explanation is obvious. The foremost aim of German propaganda was to prevent Britain from continuing the war alone, while at the same time frightening America from entering it. What could be more suitable for such a purpose than the myth of the invincible *Blitzkrieg-Wehrmacht* which would crush every enemy with an avalanche of steel?[28]

Given such obvious inferiority, one may well ask how Germany was able to achieve spectacular victories during the first two years of the war. After the first disasters in the East, how did Germany manage to hold out for another three and a half years against both the Russians and the Allies before surrendering. It cannot be ascribed to the courage of her soldiers. Soldiers in opposing armies were no less brave. In his classic 'Fighting Power', Martin van Creveld emphasised German morale, vigour, team spirit and flexibility.[29] In another book he added: "Never before have so few scantily-equipped soldiers fought so hard and so persistently against overwhelming superiority. The *Wehrmacht* embodied the combination of

24   H. Jacobsen, *1939–1945. Der Zweite Weltkrieg in Chronik und Dokumenten*, Darmstadt 1959, p. 31. For details of German war production 1942–1945, A. Speer, *Erinnerungen*, Berlin 1969, Parts II and III.

25   Töppel, p. 66 with reference to B. Müller-Hildebrand, *Das Heer 1933–1945. Entwicklung des organisatorischen Aufbaus*, 3 volumes, Darmstadt 1954–1969, vol. 3, tables after p. 274

26   *Beilage zum Kriegstagebuch Nr.6, II. Waffen-SS Panzerkorps*, June 1- August 2, 1943, BA-MA, RS 2-2/18, p. 228–258

27   Töppel, p. 26

28   Frieser, p. 41

29   M. van Creveld, *Fighting Power, German Military Performance 1914–1945*, Potomac. Md. 1981, p.4.

initiative and discipline better than any other army of the twentieth century."[30] One could elaborate further.

The quality of German Command at its highest level was not decisive. While British and American Commanders of ground forces were often mediocre, the top Commanders of the Red Army had become at least equal to their German counterparts. But German Corps and Division Commanders maintained their superiority over their opponents until the very end. Relations between officers and soldiers were very close, formalities such as saluting superiors were often dispensed with, and all ranks shared the same food. A further important, and perhaps the most decisive feature of the German Army's eminence, was the *Auftragstaktik* or the mission tactics. There was no equivalent in other armies. 'Mission tactics' turned the German Army into the best fighting force world-wide, during the 150 years following the Napoleonic wars.[31]

The concept was fathered by Scharnhorst, in his reform of the Prussian army after the defeat of Napoleon. It was further developed by Ludendorff during the First World War and pushed to extremes by the *Wehrmacht* during the Second World War. It can be roughly described as a system where Commanders, at all levels, were only given a final mission. Meanwhile their subordinates, down to sergeant, were left entirely free to determine the means by which they would reach the prescribed aim. Thus two Regimental Commanders in a Division, who were given the same mission, could use totally different means of execution in reaching the prescribed target. If unforeseen circumstances arose, the Commander was left free to deal with them according to his own judgement, without referring to his superiors. If circumstances arose which permitted him to go further than the original order, he would proceed without asking for authorisation from above.

In all other armies, a commander was not allowed to act on his own, without having first referred to higher level and obtained permission. Independent thinking down to the lowest level had always been imbued as a rule to the Prussian soldier. Previously, Frederick the Great had stressed the necessity for the 'ordinary' soldier to think independently. He made a mockery of high commanders who immersed themselves in every detail. He demanded that every soldier be totally familiar with all aspects of the 'arm' in which he served.

Aimez donc ces détails, ils ne sont pas sans gloire,
c'est le premier pas qui mène à la victoire

(Always take care of the smallest details, they don't lack glory, they are the first step towards victory).[32]

The King had a preference for expressing himself in French. To him, the French language was the embodiment of culture. He once expressed the hope that one day in the future the German language would rise to the same level. The Prussian army manual of 1806 stated that high commanders should not give far-reaching orders of detail before the beginning of the battle. Division commanders

---

30   M. van Creveld in R.-D.Müller/H.-E. Volkmann (ed), *Doe Wehrmacht – Mythos und Realität*, Munich 1999, p. 331 ff

31   For details, A.Harvey/F. Uhle-Wettler, *Kreta und Arnhem. Die größten Luftlandeoperationen des Zweiten Weltkrieges*, Graz 2004, p. 97 ff

32   C. Duffy, *Frederick the Great. A military life*, London 1986, p. 24

were to receive basic outlines and then reach their own decisions. After the Franco-Prussian war of 1870 to 1871, a teacher at the French *Ecole de Guerre* wrote that the German officer was instructed

> to keep the initiative, while soldiers were encouraged to develop individual ideas, and not rely on previous examinations of a given situation by their direct commanders. They had to reach their own conclusions. The non-commissioned officers were the backbone of the Prussian army, which was rightly proud of them.[33]

Thanks to the *Auftragstaktik*, the German Army had an officers' and non-commissioned officers' corps which no other army could match.

The absence of a similar doctrine could at times spell disaster. One such example from the battle of France 1940 can be quoted. On 14 May 1940 the French Army had the last possibility to cut off and destroy the German *Panzer* spearhead. General Flavigny, who commanded XXI Corps and was viewed as the foremost French tank expert, was ordered by General Huntziger to attack. His 3rd Division, under the command of General Brocard, had 138 tanks, half of them Char B. and Hotchkiss. Against those tanks, Guderian's 30 *Panzer*, which had crossed the Meuse, were unable to offer resistance. General Brocard had already been ordered on 12 May, at 4 pm, to bring his division to the front line. He wasted two days, and his Division only arrived on 14 May.

During the two days, General Flavigny had watched the flight of 2nd Army's Infantry and panicked. He hesitated, back and forth, and postponed the time prescribed for his attack. Then he decided to transfer Brocard's Division to another Corps because he was no longer willing to command the attack himself. He was unable to reach the commander of 2nd Army, General Huntziger. He was busy transferring his headquarters to Verdun, some 50 kilometres behind of what remained of the front. In the end, no attack took place because Brocard felt that he had not sufficient fuel.[34] There is little doubt that a German Commander, after becoming aware of the weakness of Guderian's troops, would have attacked them immediately, without referring to higher level.

Zeitzler's appointment as chief of the *Generalstab*

At the end of August 1942 a violent incident occurred between Hitler and Halder which was witnessed by Heusinger:

> Halder: "The situation at Rshev is becoming untenable. The main supply road is under enemy artillery fire. Other roads cannot be used because of danger from partisans. Parts of 9th Army will soon be cut off and can only be supplied from the air. Demyansk has shown us how difficult this will become. I have to repeat my suggestion to retreat towards a shortened front line or let 9th Army free to act."

> Hitler: "As usual, you have no better proposal than retreat. What will we gain? We withdraw to a new position that has not even been prepared.

---

33   L. Rousset, *Histoire générale de la guerre franco-allemande*, Paris 1886, p. 21 and 34
34   Frieser, p. 248 ff

The enemy will quickly reach it, break through and, as a result of your genius, we will once more give up a few dozen kilometres. Slowly and safely we will retreat ourselves out of Russia. This is the main element of your purported operative genius."

Halder: "No! I intend to consolidate the front, create additional reserves and establish better positions for the divisions. What we are doing at present makes no sense."

Hitler: "Stop telling me fairy tales. I know what this will lead to. We have to remain firm. I expect the generals to be just as firm as the troops."

Halder: "I am firm enough. But at the front, thousands of brave officers and soldiers lose their lives because my hands are tied by orders of Supreme Command."

Hitler was at first speechless and stared at Halder with increasing fury. Then he exploded:

Generaloberst Halder, how dare you speak to me in such a tone! You want to tell me how the front soldier feels? What do you know about the front? Where were you during the First World War? All that time you sat at some comfortable staff headquarters. And you dare tell me that I don't understand how the front soldier feels? I will not stand for that! This is simply outrageous![35]

Manstein happened to be present and could not have been blamed if he had felt satisfaction that Halder now received a pay-back for the many grievances he had caused him. But he did not sink to that level:

The scene was so disgraceful that I withdrew ostentatiously to a corner of the room. I returned to the situation map-table only after Hitler had calmed down and requested me to join the meeting. After it ended, I took Schmundt aside. I told him that such a relationship between the Supreme Commander and his chief of the *Generalstab* was simply impossible. Either Hitler had to listen to Halder and observe obvious forms of polite behaviour, or Halder had to take the consequences and offer his resignation. Unfortunately neither occurred and it took six more weeks before Halder was dismissed.[36]

General Zeitzler was appointed Chief of the *Generalstab* on 24 September 1942. 'Citadel' thus became the first major operation that was planned under his authority. His appointment caused surprise. When the war began, Zeitzler was a 44-years-old Colonel. He was promoted to *Generalmajor* on 1 February 1942. When appointed chief of the *Generalstab*, he was still a *Generalmajor*. On the day following his appointment, he was promoted directly to *General der Infanterie*. The usual rank of the chief of the *Generalstab* was *Generaloberst*. Zeitzler had to wait until 30 January 1944 for that promotion. During the Second World War he

35 Heusinger, Befehl, p. 201
36 *Verlorene Siege*, p. 292

held no troop command and served as chief-of-staff of corps, armies and army groups.

Hitler was aware of Zeitler's lack of experience. On the day of his appointment he told Heusinger:

> I have decided to relieve *Generaloberst* Halder as chief of the *Generalstab*. He lacks National-Socialist conviction, and the belief in my ideas that I expect from my chief of the *Generalstab*. He is unable to convey them without reservation to his subordinates. I have appointed General Zeitzler as his successor. I request you to stay and work with him. He is somewhat new and is not yet familiar with the major elements of warfare. I know that you would prefer a troop command but I need you here. Help General Zeitzler, and see to it that he can quickly become familiar with his new duties.[37]

The appointment of a chief of the *Generalstab*, "who is not yet familiar with the major elements of warfare", is somewhat surprising. Zeitzler's appointment was at first viewed with apprehension. Hitler had indicated that he wanted an *OKH* imbued with National-Socialist spirit. Zeitzler's first address to his officers on 25 September 1942 seemed to respond to his wish:

> I request from every officer of the *Generalstab*:
>
> He must be a devoted and reliable *aide* to his commander, in every situation, and he must be thoroughly knowledgeable in all his duties.
>
> He has to be in close touch with the troops and never lose contact with the front.
>
> Even in difficult situations he has to be candid and honest in his reports to higher authorities.
>
> He must believe in the *Führer* and his leadership. He has to radiate this belief on every occasion to his subordinates and his fellow officers.
>
> In the *Generalstab* I have no use for an officer who does not respond to these criteria.[38]

However, Heusinger knew Zeitzler well from former times and felt that the people who had recommended him, Göring and Himmler, would soon be disappointed. Hitler repeated the mistake he made, when he appointed Brauchitsch to succeed Fritsch, as commander in chief of the Army in 1938. He had told Brauchitsch that he expected him to create a true National-Socialist *Wehrmacht*, but was soon to find out that Brauchitsch was less amenable to his views than his predecessor Fritsch. Heusinger viewed Zeitzler as a bulldog that would bite anyone who would 'tread on his toes'. He was thus not surprised when Zeitzler soon showed that he was a representative of *Generalstab* tradition to the core. His altercations with Hitler would reach proportions that never occurred in Halder's time. His own co-operation with Zeitzler soon became better than his former work with Halder.[39] Hitler was quick to notice it. When Zeitzler reported the beginning of

---

37   Heusinger, Befehl, p. 210 f
38   Ibid., p. 212
39   Meyer, Heusinger, p. 191 ff, under the heading '*Der neue Chef*'

the second phase of the battle with the Russian offensive at Orel, Hitler said to Schmundt: "Zeitzler also begins to think too much." [40]

Was 'Citadel' Hitler's battle, Zeitzler's battle, or Manstein's battle?

No battle is the creation of one man. A number of commanders develop it and more are involved in the execution. If the battle is lost, there will always be a tendency to search for one individual to name as the one responsible. Thus, the disastrous French offensive in 1917, which led to widespread mutinies in the French Army, was named the Nivelle offensive, and the failed German offensive of 21 March 1918, the Ludendorff offensive.

Hitler's battle?

Once 'Citadel' turned into a catastrophe, the search for a guilty party was automatic. Obviously Hitler was the prime candidate. Carell wrote:

> The Generals, Manstein, Guderian, Kluge, Model and many others had strongly objected to Hitler's plans to launch a new offensive in the East, as soon as possible after Stalingrad. They felt that it was much too early to engage the fresh reserves and, in particular, the new *Panzer* 'Tiger' and 'Panther' into a dangerous offensive battle of major proportions.
>
> *OKW* had likewise warned, and pointed out, that a new danger had arisen in the Mediterranean. Eisenhower was about to land on the Italian mainland. If he succeeded, *Panzer* had to be transferred from the East. But Hitler had pointed out the danger of the Kursk salient where the Russians had assembled huge forces for an offensive of their own. 40% of all the Red Army ground forces and all of its tanks had been brought into the salient. It was a most dangerous concentration. But it was also a tempting objective for a preventive attack. If it succeeded, the Red Army would be dealt a mortal blow. Hitler was fascinated by this idea.[41]

All this is mere fiction. Manstein and Kluge were the two main advocates of Citadel. Model never objected to 'Citadel'. As commander in chief of 9th Army his opinion was not even requested. His objections, which played a major part in the decisions to postpone the offensive, were limited to the strength of his army that he viewed as insufficient for the task given to it.

Guderian did indeed fear that his new *Panzer* models were not yet ready for a major battle. However, his objections were not as unambiguous as he would attempt to make them appear in his memoirs. In his account of the Munich conference, where the first postponement was decided on, he wrote: "I got up, and stated that the offensive lacked purpose ... Speer supported me and pointed out the deficiencies in war production."[42] The stenographic minutes of the Munich confer-

---

40   Heusinger, Befehl, p. 212
41   Carell, p. 15
42   Guderian, p. 278

ence show no mention of the sentence "the offensive lacked purpose." Speer did not attend the Munich meeting.

'Citadel' cannot be labelled Hitler's battle, unless one attaches the name of the Supreme Commander to every major operation of the war. Prior to the conclusion of the battles of the winter of 1942, and while Manstein's counter-offensive at Charkov and Belgorod was still in progress, Hitler had issued a directive (*Weisung*) ie an operational order No.5. It called for a smaller offensive in the spring of 1943, with the objective of preventing the Russians from dictating the course of events. (*Gesetz des Handelns*).[43] The directive made no mention of a major attack against the Red Army forces assembled in the Kursk salient.

Before deciding upon 'Citadel', Hitler had ordered two attacks of limited scope, 'Habicht' and 'Panther', south of Charkov. Klink views both those operations as simple auxiliaries for 'Citadel'.[44] Töppel's analysis showed that 'Panther' was viewed by Hitler as a genuine alternative to 'Citadel'.[45] During the months of planning 'Citadel', Hitler kept a remarkably clear head, he postponed the beginning several times and decided to break the battle off when its failure was apparent.

Zeitzler's battle?

Zeitzler was the obvious second choice for a culprit. He had developed the original plan and 'Citadel' was his first major operation, after his appointment as chief of the *Generalstab*. He was obviously eager to show that he possessed the required talent at the highest level. His original optimism soon turned into scepticism, and he devoted much of his time after the war trying to remove that stain on his reputation. He wrote: "It was Hitler's obsession to resume the offensive in the East. He had reached this decision on his own, without taking any advice and no one was able to move him. Perhaps it remained possible to influence him in points of details, only time would tell."[46] In a study for the History Division of the US Army, Zeitzler wrote that he never supported any of Hitler's decisions.[47]

---

43   *Kriegstagebuch des Oberkommandos der Wehrmacht (Wehrmachtführungsstab) 1940–1945*, vol.3/2, p. 1,420 ff

44   Klink, p.71

45   Töppel, p. 11 f

46   K. Zeitzler, *Das Ringen um die grossen Entscheidungen im Zweiten Weltkriege. Die Abwehrschlachten in Russland nach dem Wendepunkt im Kriege*, BA-MA, ZA 1/1734 (Zeitzler estate), Study D-406, p. 56–81 (henceforth: Zeitzler study)

47   BA-MA, P-041 ii, part B, p.46-117. The complete text of Zeitzler's study is reproduced in O.Hackl, *Generalstab, Generalstabsdienst und Generalstabsausbildung in der Reichswehr und in der Wehrmacht 1919–1945. Studien deutscher Generale und Generalstabsoffiziere in der Historical Division der US Army in Europe 1946–1961*, Osnabrück 1999, p. 67–100

For a number of years after the war, 'Citadel' continued to be named Zeitzler's battle. Generals Warlimont,[48] and Von Mellenthin[49] supported this misnomer in their post-war recollections. Once the label was attached to Zeitzler, some competent Western authors, such as the French historian Pierre Masson, who has written most comprehensively in French about the German Army, also adopted it.

He wrote that, "*OKH* had been guilty of grievous miscalculations in its overconfidence in its own forces, and in its inexcusable underestimation of the enemy's reserves."[50] *Bundeswehr* General Count von Kielmansegg, who wrote the foreword to the German edition of Masson's book, and corrected a number of his statements in footnotes, contradicts him:

> This description is not correct. Hitler's objections concerned mainly the equipment available, but not the operative idea. Insufficiency of equipment caused him to postpone the original *OKH* plan that called for a date in early May. Zeitzler was in favour of the offensive only until mid-June. After that date he began to oppose it, and voiced his objection with strong support by Heusinger. It was Manstein and Kluge who insisted on going forward with the original plan. They were the ones whom Masson labelled the 'sinners', and who were guilty of overconfidence in their own strength, and the inexcusable underestimation of the enemy's strength.[51]

Hitler was quick to notice that Zeitzler distanced himself from any responsibility. General Heusinger reported a conversation between himself and Colonel Walter Scherff who was Hitler's writer for recording war history. Scherff was a fanatical *Nazi*. He became a *Generalmajor*, and shot himself after the German surrender. As chief of operations at *OKH*, General Heusinger was present at all situation meetings. His book, *Befehl im Widerstreit*, is written in the form of dialogues, mainly between himself and fellow officers between the years 1923 and 1945. The authenticity of the conversations at the *Führerhauptquartier* was corroborated by the stenographic transcripts of the meetings. After his temporary fallout with Jodl in 1942, Hitler had ordered two stenographers to take down every word uttered at his situation meetings and his table talks, to avoid having them 'altered' in later accounts. Conversations that took place elsewhere have been corroborated by survivors.

Heusinger's conversation with Scherff quickly focused on the responsibility for 'Citadel':

> Heusinger: "Don't you see how the situation becomes more and more untenable, by the day, because they are unable to reach necessary decisions in time. This has already happened at Stalingrad and at Tunis. And now were are faced with the same hesitations about the Donets region."

48 W. Warlimont, *Im Hauptquartier der deutscxhen Wehrmacht 1939–1945, Grundlagen, Formen, Gestalten,* Augsburg 1990, vol.2, p. 348

49 F. von Mellenthin, *Panzerschlachten. Eine Studie über den Einsatz von Panzerverbänden im Zweiten Weltkrieg,* Neckargmünd 1963, p.142 ff. (henceforth: Mellenthin)

50 P. Masson, *Die deutsche Armee. Geschichte der Wehrmacht 1941–1945,* Munich 1996, p. 269 (henceforth: Masson)

51 Ibid, p. 269, footnote Kielmansegg

Scherff: "You must not forget that the *Führer*, as Head of State, cannot limit himself to military matters. He must also take politics, economics and propaganda into account. He recognises the validity of your proposals and torments himself with them more than you think. But he has good reasons to discard them."

Heusinger: "Does he not, at least belatedly, recognise that his decisions were erroneous? Why will he never admit a mistake, why does he always search for the guilt of others?"

Scherff: "You don't understand the greatness of this man. He suffers the fate of all great men. If he were to admit to mistakes, he would become unsure of himself and lose strength."

Heusinger: "This may well be so. But we can't lose the war, simply because one man, despite all evidence to the contrary, continues to believe in the infallibility of his intuition."

Scherff: "Again, this contemptible doubt which gains increasing strength among the senior generals. The same doubts have been voiced at men of genius of the past, only remember Frederick the Great and Napoleon. They undermine trust, destroy unity of will and damage our cause. One has to believe the genius and put doubts aside."

Heusinger: "This is what Zeitzler did at first. But you can see for yourself that he can no longer remain blind if he does not want to abandon himself."

Scherff: "And the obvious consequence of such an attitude is that the *Führer* is blamed for mistakes by others. Hitler did not request the attack upon Kursk, Zeitzler convinced him. And now the *Führer* is held responsible for the failure."

Heusinger: "This is not true. Zeitzler was in favour of the attack, if it had started in mid June. After that date had passed, he no longer favoured it."

Scherff: "Once again the interpretation of the *Generalstab*. The usual method to shift responsibility to others. *Herr General*, I will report your words to the *Führer*."[52]

A few days later, Heusinger would be taken aside by Schmundt. Schmundt's devotion to Hitler was close to childish, however he always tried to protect fellow officers. The wife of *Feldmarschall* Ritter von Leeb had been reported to the Gestapo for offensive remarks about Hitler during a visit to her dentist. This was immediately reported to Schmundt who quashed further investigation and told von Leeb: "If your wife can't keep silent, tell her to beware at least of her dentist."
Schmundt said to Heusinger:

Some time ago, an officer who visited you made a negative report on the mood of your officers. They criticized the highest leadership in a manner that bordered on defeatism, and they quoted you personally. He has not

---

52 *Heusinger Befehl*, p. 269 ff

only reported to me, he has also mentioned it to Himmler whom he visited yesterday. I wanted to warn you so that you can take steps to protect yourself. I don't know what Himmler intends to do.[53]

After the war, Zeitzler wrote that Scherff had purposely shouldered him with the responsibility for 'Citadel.'[54] In one of his numerous post-war justification attempts, Zeitzler wrote that "the wish to attack in the spring of 1943 had been Hitler's obsession. He had reached this decision on his own and no one could dissuade him. Perhaps it might have been possible to influence him in some details. Time would tell."[55]

Manstein's battle!

If 'Citadel' can be identified with one commander, it would have to be called Manstein's battle. Manstein had developed the first plan and presented it to Hitler on 10 March 1943, during a visit to the *Führerhauptquartier*. Manstein wrote:

> After the battle for Charkov, Army Group South [army group Don had been renamed South] intended to take advantage of the weakness of the enemy to launch a new offensive before the 'mud' period set in. The purpose was the eliminating of the Kursk salient. This idea had to be abandoned because Army Group Centre had declared itself unable to participate in a major assault. Although the enemy had become soft after his defeat at Charkov, Army Group South lacked the necessary strength to take on the whole operation alone. Therefore a first attack against the salient had to be launched alone, from the *forehand*. [author's emphasis][56]

The word 'forehand' ie taking the initiative, is emphasised because Manstein would write in *Verlorene Siege* that he had always favoured an operation from the 'backhand', ie leaving the initiative to the enemy and then launching a counterattack. He had proposed this idea to Hitler, on 10 March 1943, but Hitler had turned him down. It would have meant a temporary abandonment of the Donets area that Hitler considered essential for maintaining war production, at least at its current level. Manstein admitted that he was unable to judge the economic importance of the Donets basin and added one of his strange comments: "Hitler lacked daring and trust in his own operative knowledge and in that of his generals."[57] The reader will have to judge if there is any relation between Manstein's statement and the economic importance of the Donets Basin.

Manstein's plan defied comprehension. Had all his military knowledge suddenly deserted him? That was unthinkable. Other explanations need to be searched for. His plan was based on a cardinal error, one that has been rejected by all creators of strategic thought, namely to attack an enemy in his *Schwerpunkt*.

---

53   Ibid.
54   Zeitzler study, p.80
55   K. Zeitzler, *Das Ringen um die grossen Entscheidungen im Zweiten Weltkriege. Abwehrschlachten in Russland nach dem Wendepunkt im Kriege*, Zeitzler Estate, BA-MA, ZA 1/1734, D-406, p. 56 f
56   *Verlorene Siege*, p. 484
57   Ibid, p.463

Manstein knew the methods that Hannibal had employed in his defeat of the Romans at Cannae. He knew that Napoleon had summed up the art of war in one sentence, namely that one could only attack at a point where one was stronger than the enemy. Almost 2,000 years previously, Sun Tsu had written: "If you only know your own strength but not that of the enemy, you will be defeated. But if you know both your own strength as well as that of the enemy, you will always be victorious."[58]

Manstein had read all the books by Clausewitz, Moltke the elder and Schlieffen. Clausewitz mentions the *Schwerpunkt* but writes only that 'an attack against a strong enemy in a good position is always a doubtful idea.' (*missliches Ding*).[59] In his lectures, Clausewitz never touches on matters that are simply contrary to common sense.[60] In Clausewitz's eyes, 'one may never attack an enemy frontally in his *Schwerpunkt*, as it is the place where he expects an offensive against him.' That was one of the obvious elements of common sense to require absolutely no detailed comments. (*Selbstverständlichkeiten eines gesunden Menschenverstande, über die man keine langen Ausführungen zu machen braucht.*)

Moltke's writings are full of warnings against frontal attacks. Schlieffen wrote:

> How to conduct an offensive against the destructive power of modern arms is a problem over which all military thinkers constantly argue. (*An der Frage, wie gegen die verheerende Wirkung moderner Waffen der Angriff zu führen ist, müht sich der Scharfsinn der führenden Geister ab.*)[61]

All that led to Schlieffen's rule, to 'attack the enemy only on his flanks and thus bypass him.' As a result, the Schlieffen plan of the First World War was developed. Had a pupil of Manstein at the *Truppenamt* submitted such a paper to him, he would have been sent packing. The only explanation possible for Manstein's aberration is that his *hubris* had reached such proportions that he became convinced that any operation in which he was given freedom of action would lead to success, even if it was contrary to all principles of strategy.

Manstein's comments are likewise absurd. To describe an enemy, who had inflicted defeat on the *Wehrmacht* at Stalingrad, who had inexhaustible reserves, and who out-produced Germany in every area of war production, as having become 'soft' after the short backlash at Charkov and Belgorod, defies imagination. Frieser labels 'Citadel' as the most adventurous operation undertaken in the Second World War.[62] In *Verlorene Siege*, Manstein wrote repeatedly that the flexibility of German troops was at its best mainly in the summer.[63] Then he suggested an attack in the winter, although the campaigns of 1941 and 1942 had shown how little the *Wehrmacht* was equipped for combat in the winter months.

---

58 Tao Han Zhang: *Sun Tsu's art of war*, translated by Yuan Shi Bing, London 1987, p. 35 f

59 Clausewitz, chapter 27, p. 603

60 C. von Clausewitz, *Übersicht des Sr. Königl. Hoheit dem Kronprinzen in den Jahren 1810, 1811 und 1812 vom Verfasser erteilten Unterricht: Die wichtigtsten Grundsätze des Kriegsführen.*

61 Summary of Schlieffen's yearly examination of his pupils after completion of the three years of their *Generalstab* course, in this instance the year 1901

62 Frieser, Citadel, p.195

63 For instance, *Verlorene Siege*, p. 475

The postponements

For the number of postponements of the date originally foreseen for the launching of the offensive, 'Citadel' ranks second only to the attack upon France in May 1940.

A 'fateful postponement' – Generaloberst Model had made a direct report to Hitler

It is with these words that Manstein heads the relevant paragraph in *Verlorene Siege.*[64]

Model's first Troop Command during the Second World War was the 3rd *Panzer* Division at the beginning of the war against Russia. At that time he was a *Generalleutnant.* Six months later he was already a *Generaloberst* and *OB* of 9th Army. Hitler had no direct part in this rapid promotion. Before Model received his Army Command, the two had never met. The personnel department of the army had quickly become aware of Model's talent. They felt that he was needed for high commands. As *OB* of 9th Army he conducted a series of successful defensive battles around Rshev during the winter of 1942 and the spring of 1943. He was then considered to be part of the elite among German Commanders. Model always led from the front line. Whether that was the best method for an army commander is somewhat doubtful. However, it appealed to Hitler, who always looked back with nostalgia on his own experiences as a front line soldier of the First World War.

Model was among the few commanders who, in a particularly sharp manner, dared to contradict Hitler on tactical decisions. Model was highly unpopular with his fellow officers because of his rude behaviour. His lack of self-control could be humiliating to senior officers, robbing them of their personal dignity. Dislike of him increased when he selected an officer from the *Waffen-SS* as his personal adc after his rise to Army Group *OB*. Little sympathy was lost between him and Manstein. During their joint time at the *Truppenamt*, Manstein was Model's direct superior and repeatedly had to call him to order when his behaviour exceeded bounds.

Later Manstein, after his dismissal, would never forgive Model that Hitler had picked him as his successor. In *Verlorene Siege* Model repeatedly became the victim of Manstein's skilfully launched 'poisoned barbs.' Many attacks were directed at Model after the war, some were unfair. He could not defend himself since he was the only *Feldmarschall* who had chosen suicide rather than captivity. Model shot himself on 21 April 1945 after he had simply dissolved his encircled army group in the Ruhr *Kessel* and told his officers and soldiers that they were free to attempt to go home. Winrich Behr was at Model's side until one hour before the *Feldmarschall* shot himself. Behr told me that Model suddenly exploded in a fit of temper. He yelled about the 'swine' in Berlin. Then he said to Behr that he could not forgive himself for having demanded sacrifices from his soldiers for what tuned out to have been an unworthy cause.

Model had not informed his Army Group Commander, von Kluge, of his intention to present a report to Hitler. Relations between Model and Kluge were

---

64 *Verlorene Siege*, p. 488 f

tense. Model considered Kluge to be unreliable and feared that he would not fully transmit his concerns to Hitler. Model was no operational genius, he was basically a 'stayer' and was known as the 'lion of defence'. He always made a careful study of the forces opposing him, insisted upon the availability of adequate reserves and never acted without thorough preparation.

Unlike Manstein, he never denigrated the Red Army, not its combat value, nor the talent of its commanders. Model felt that 9th Army had not sufficient strength to penetrate the particularly deep defence system of the Russian forces in the Kursk salient. He feared that not sufficient account had been taken of new Russian anti-tank weapons. As a reward for his success at Rshev, Model had been awarded the Swords to the Knight's Cross. Hitler would usually confer, in person, the higher degrees of the Knight's Cross, Oak Leaves, Swords and Diamonds. Model was thus provided with the opportunity of a personal meeting with Hitler and he took advantage of this opportunity on 27 April, to request a postponement of the date foreseen for the beginning of 'Citadel'.

In his account of Model's presentation to Hitler, Klink wrote;

> The behaviour of *Generaloberst* Model, *OB* of 9th Army, is an example of the dichotomy prevailing at the highest levels of the military command. In his talks with Hitler, and in his memoranda, Model always asserted that the offensive would lead to success. At the same time, he constantly requested additional troops and equipment. That was the decisive element in Hitler's decision to postpone the date originally foreseen. An examination of all the steps taken by Model, during the planning stage, shows clearly that he was not only not convinced of a success of the offensive, but that he used all his endeavours to delay it as long as possible. His ultimate aim was simply to abandon it, while avoiding having to face Hitler directly.[65]

That comment is unfair and a typical example of the many post-war attacks directed at Model. Model's overall opinion about 'Citadel' was never requested. As one of the Army *OB* he lacked an overall view of the situation. He was not even invited to the conference at Munich that Hitler convened after having received his report. His only concern was his 9th Army that he knew inside out and which, in his judgement, lacked the necessary strength for the task assigned to it. Model certainly never feared a direct confrontation with Hitler. Before his direct report to him, he had made several appeals to Army Group Centre, first on 8 April, then on 15 April, and finally on 17 April. In all of them he repeatedly stressed that the forces at his disposal were insufficient to launch an attack on the date originally foreseen. Army Group Centre paid no attention.

Brett-Smith was certainly no admirer of Model. He was one of the historians who had pinned the label '*Nazi*-General' on him, but included him among the 'near greats' in command ability. He wrote that "Model's objections should have been taken seriously, for Model was not the man to complain idly, but they did not prevail."[66] Even after Hitler had decided on a first postponement, Model issued further warnings. On 21 June he ordered his Ia, Colonel Günther Reichhelm, to draw up a seven-page memorandum in which he summed up his concerns. He had

---

65   Klink, p. 469
66   Brett-Smith, p. 199

it signed by his four Corps Commanders, Generals Friessner, Gollnick, Lemelsen and Harpe, in order to confer additional emphasis on it. The memorandum stated clearly that his Army, if provided with the additional troops and equipment required by him, might possibly complete its task, provided the overall situation had developed favourably.[67]

A somewhat curious comment by Masson must be mentioned: "Kursk was forced upon a reluctant Hitler by Zeitzler, Manstein and Model."[68] Again, Kielmansegg contradicts:

> This is totally wrong. Hitler had finally come round to accepting the concept of 'Citadel'. No one could ever force anything on him. In June, Zeitzler wanted to cancel the whole operation. Strongly prodded by Manstein and Kluge, Hitler refused. He felt that he was bound to take the initiative and that the increasingly unfavourable war situation made it incumbent on him to score at least some success.[69]

Liddell Hart, to whom every word of Manstein comes close to 'gospel,' wrote that 'Citadel' failed because Model had requested its postponement.[70]

Töppel mentions Klink's opinion, while not subscribing to it. He viewed it as a hypothesis and quoted an extract from the 9th Army's war diary:

> The dice are finally cast. Around 6 pm we are informed by a written message from army group that the *Führer* has finally reached a positive decision about 'Citadel'. *Gruppe Weiss*, the code name for 9th Army, is overjoyed. Our careful preparations over the past months will now come to fruition.[71]

Some care is called for when quoting from war diaries. The commanders had to sign them but hardly ever took the time to read them. War diaries were frequently written in a superficial manner, and some time after the event described. Their editing was often given to officers who had nothing more important to do. Since copies of the war diaries of large units were always shown to Hitler, words like 'enthusiasm', 'joy', 'conviction of success', were often included.

Given Model's outrageous manners, he seldom had a competent staff at his disposal. Whenever he arrived at a new command, a number of staff officers, who had served under the preceding commander, requested an immediate transfer. The few capable staff officers who remained with him could not be bothered with keeping war diaries. Colonel Reichhelm told me that 9th Army's war diary was kept at that time by a reserve officer, Lieutenant Wendtlandt, whom he described as a totally convinced *Nazi*, and a less than capable officer. Wendtlandt was later sent to the front and was killed in action.

---

67   Memorandum in facsimile in the album *Generalfeldmarschall Walter Model (1891–1945), Dokumentation eines Soldatenlebens*, H.-G.Model (the son of the *Feldmarschall*)/D. Bradley (ed), Osnabrück 1991, p. 65-71
68   Masson, p. 351
69   Ibid, footnote Kielmansegg.
70   Liddell Hart, p.101
71   AOK 9, Ia, KTB Nr.8. Annex IV, vol.1, Orders and reports by AOK March 20. 1943–May 5. 1943 (35883/12) BA-MA RH 20–9/134

'Citadel' had originally been planned for the first half of May. On 6 April, Hitler signed his operational order No.6 which ended with the words." The best units, the best arms and the best commanders will lead the battle. 'Citadel' must appear like a beacon in the eyes of the whole world."[72]

After having listened to Model, Hitler ordered a first postponement. He had 10 June in view, but did not yet reach a firm decision because he wanted first to hear the joint opinions of all the commanders involved. They were ordered to attend a joint conference in Munich on 5 May. Manstein labelled that postponement as 'fateful'. However, the delay permitted the bringing forward of additional equipment, in particular more *Panzer*. But this did not keep 'Citadel' from developing into a fiasco that had to be broken off after a few days. The word 'fateful' calls for a query. It is easy to imagine what would have occurred, had the attack taken place on the date suggested by Manstein.

The Munich conference

Manstein had returned from a brief sick leave on 3 May, after receiving treatment for his cataracts. He had gone to rest at his home at Liegnitz where his chief-of-staff informed him that he was to attend a meeting of high commanders at Munich two days later. Manstein's chief-of-staff *Generalmajor* Busse, Kluge, the chief quartermaster of Army Group Centre, Zeitzler, Guderian, Schmundt, the *Luftwaffe* chief-of-staff, *Generaloberst* Jeschonneck and Scherff were also present. Manstein had no previous knowledge of Model's report.

The only reliable accounts, of what was said at Munich, are Busse's stenographic minutes. They will be reproduced in full. The memoirs and verbal accounts of the other participants serve mainly to show how right they were in their objections, while casting aspersions on those who did not share their view. Thus Guderian wrote that Manstein, as usual, was not at his best when confronting Hitler.[73] Coming from Guderian, such a statement makes strange reading, since it will be a difficult to find an occasion when Guderian was at his best when facing Hitler.

Some historian accounts contain fiction. David Irving quotes Jeschonnek as having advanced the opinion that Manstein and Kluge had initially agreed to a postponement. When they heard that this was also Hitler's view, they suddenly urged an immediate launching of the offensive, to avoid later blame.[74] Any statement by David Irving must be viewed with considerable caution. At his recent lawsuit in London against Professor Deborah Lipstadt, Irving was shown to be a Holocaust denier. No publisher of repute any longer accepts his book and a number of countries do not grant him entry visas. Irving has amassed one of the most extensive archives about Hitler in private possession. However, he often manipulates his documents to adapt them to his views. In this case, he contends that his statement was taken from a page from Jeschonneck's diary which

---

72   Operationsbefehl Nr.6-OKH/Gen.Std H/Op Abt (1) Nr. 430/426/43, g.Kdos./ Chef, 15.4.1943 (henceforth Operationsbefehl 6)
73   Guderian, p. 278
74   D. Irving, *Hitler's War 1942–1945*, London 1977, p. 501

Richthofen had pasted into his own. But he gives no clear identification of either.[75] Jeschonnek was already depressed, since he had been shouldered with the blame for the insufficient air supply at Stalingrad. In August 1943 he shot himself. Irving also writes that no minutes from the conference exist, although Busse's account was available to him at the BA-MA.

The atmosphere at Munich was stormy. Old personal quarrels were revived. Kluge and Guderian had not met since Guderian's relief as *OB* of 2nd *Panzer* army in December 1941. Guderian believed that was due to an intrigue by Kluge. When Kluge entered the room and extended his hand, Guderian refused to shake it. Kluge then requested Guderian to step outside and queried him about the reasons for his behaviour. Guderian replied that Kluge had seriously damaged him in December 1941, that his health had been impaired as a result, and that he was owed satisfaction. Kluge broke off the conversation and the two would not address each other during the meeting. A few days later, Schmundt visited Guderian and brought him a letter from Kluge with a challenge for a duel in which he had asked Hitler to act as his 'cartel bearer'. Hitler did not brook this nonsense and had Schmundt convey an order to Guderian to apologise to Kluge. Guderian wrote Kluge a reluctant letter in which he regretted having insulted him at Munich, while emphasising that he was unable to forgive or forget the injustice he had suffered in 1941.[76]

The following is the complete text of Busse's minutes. The stenographic style remains unaltered:

> Discussion between *OB* [Manstein] and Chief *Generalstab*:
>
> Chief *Generalstab* informs *OB* about the matters to be discussed and develops his views. *Führer* has become hesitant after having listened to the report by *Generaloberst* Model. He is no longer convinced that the attack will break through. *Führer* is mainly impressed by maps showing a Russian defensive system, with a breadth exceeding 20 kilometres and very close firing positions. *Generaloberst* Model has submitted a six-day plan for an attempt at breakthrough. *Führer* has reached the conviction:
>
> 1. that it is doubtful if 9th Army's Infantry can succeed if *Panzer* are held back.
>
> 2. that it is more than questionable if a *Kessel* can be established. He feels that the enemy, supported by his large size defensive system, will have sufficient time to withdraw from any encirclement.
>
> Since *Führer* feels that, given the overall military and political situation, this first offensive of the year has to result in a conclusive success. He has the opinion that, in particular, Army Group Centre has to be strengthened with additional *Panzer* and anti-tank weaponry. This should be done by means of more 'Tiger' *Panzer*, strengthened armour of *Panzer* 4, *Hornissen*, *Ferdinand*, an extra heavy Porsche-*Panzer*, and anti-tank guns. Since all this can only be available on 10 June at the earliest, *Führer* intends to postpone the date of attack accordingly. *Führer* is supported in his views by *Generaloberst* Guderian.

---

75   Ibid, annex, no page number indicated
76   Guderian, p. 280

Chief *Generalstab* then developed his view:

He is against a postponement, since preparations are already advanced. The troops are mentally ready for battle and look forward to it with optimism. Therefore any postponement will be to the enemy's advantage. We will only lose the advantage of striking against an enemy not yet fully prepared, to beat him and thus become able to build up new reserves for other purposes. He doubts if the additional *Panzer* and other equipment will arrive in good time, recent experience points to the contrary. The new *Ferdinand* still suffers from children's sickness, even *Generaloberst* Guderian doubts if they can become combat-ready in June.

[Guderian wrote about the *Ferdinand Panzer*:

They were a variation of the 'Tiger', designed by Professor Porsche, equipped with electric propulsion and a 1.70 metre long 8.8 cm calibre gun, similar to an assault gun. Apart from this gun, the *Ferdinand* had no other weapons and was thus useless in close combat, in spite of its heavy armour and the good quality of the gun. Since production had already begun and 90 *Ferdinand* were available, I had to use them although I could not share Hitler's enthusiasm for the latest 'toy' from his favourite constructor Porsche.][77]

Chief *Generalstab* has therefore asked *OB* and *Feldmarschall* von Kluge to come to Munich, to get their views about *Führer's* opinion and to assist him in his presentation to *Führer*. *Generalfeldmarschall* von Manstein said that he was in basic agreement with the views of Chief *Generalstab*. He was concerned with the increasing risks at the Eastern and Donets sectors facing his army group. While he did not dispute that additional reserves had to be brought to the battle, he doubted if they could compensate corresponding increases by the enemy and a further strengthening of Russian defensive positions. As far as he was concerned, the only advantage of a postponement would consist in not limiting reinforcements to equipment, but also bringing in additional infantry divisions. When it was reported to Hitler, he was happy to throw one of his usual barbs at Manstein, that he always asked for more troops than were available. He was unable to judge if this was possible, since his overall view of available troop reserves was not sufficient.

All participants then went into Hitler's situation room. *Führer* gave a lengthy outline of the reasons that led him to consider a postponement. He insisted on the following points:

1. He had been impressed by the maps of enemy defensive positions given to him by *Generaloberst* Model.

2. He increasingly doubted if he had sufficient strength available.

3. The failed attack at Novorossisk had shown that, without strong *Panzer* support, the infantry could not penetrate a strong defensive position that was doggedly defended.

---

77   Guderian, p. 271

He had the same fear for 'Citadel', where Model's 9th Army was to attack with infantry only, but with its *Panzer* kept in reserve. Meanwhile, Army Group South had only few Infantry Divisions and had already used its *Panzer* during the first attempt. Since Army Group South's Infantry was not sufficient, its *Panzer* would be already decimated during the first breakthrough attempt and would then be unable to force the final breakthrough. *Führer* then explained at some length that reinforcements could be made available by 10 June. In particular, the *Ferdinand* would reduce casualties in attacks of enemy fortified positions. He then requested the *OB* of the two Army Groups to present their views about a postponement.

Generalfeldmarschall von Manstein commented: He could not judge the extent to which an early success in the East was necessary, even desirable, against the overall political and military situation. His army group was too weak for the assault, in particular the infantry. Success was only possible if he was given additional infantry divisions. In particular:

1. I feel that a success in the East must be obtained before the fall of Tunis, and before the establishment of a new front by the Western Allies. [Tunis had fallen two months earlier!]

2. To wait means an increased risk at the front Mius-Donets. At present, the Russians are not ready to attack there, in June they will certainly be ready.

3. It is doubtful whether our reinforcements will be able to compensate for the additional units that the Russians will bring forward. There has been one additional month of Russian tank production, new defence lines, and recovery from the first mortal blow of German success.

Führer replied that additional infantry divisions for Army Group South are out of the question, and that *OB* had to keep in mind that additional *Panzer* would more than compensate for insufficient infantry.

Generalfeldmarschall von Kluge strongly objects to any postponement. The information given by *Generaloberst* Model about the strength of enemy position is grossly exaggerated. His maps show a number of former positions that had remained from previous battles but which were no longer manned. He fears that we will be relegated into the rear. We will be compelled to withdraw forces from the attack divisions and become unable to offer any further offensive actions during the remainder of the year.

Führer replied that *Generaloberst* Model was quite optimistic during his presentation, but it was he himself who was the pessimist.

Generaloberst Guderian emphasised that no efforts should be spared in attempting to reduce human loss of life by bringing forward as much equipment as possible. He felt that all available *Panzer* had to be given either to Army Group Centre, or to Army Group South, to be totally powerful at any one point.

Generaloberst Jeschonneck agreed with the views of *Generaloberst* Guderian. The attack should concentrate on one single point, and all available air force be likewise concentrated there. Russian air concentration shows that they intend to direct their attack against Army Group

South. Sizeable German air reinforcements are not available, but two additional *Stuka* groups could be put at their disposal.

Führer closed the meeting without having reached a final decision. It is however apparent that he has already decided on a postponement."[78]

On the day following the conference Hitler decided to postpone 'Citadel' until 12 June. General von Mellenthin wrote: "Had 'Citadel' been launched in April or May it would have yielded a rich harvest. By June all favourable elements had vanished."[79] Such words belong to the typical post-war wisdom of German memoir writers. An attack in April was never on the cards, because in April the 'mud' period still prevailed. The operational order Nr.6 is unambiguous:

All units of both army groups have to make the necessary preparations far in the rear of the lines earmarked for the launching of the offensive, and under cover of every measure of camouflage and deceit, so as to enable *OKH* to issue the final order six days after 28 April. Earliest possible date: 3 May.[80]

Further postponements

On 10 May, Guderian attended a meeting at the chancellery of the *Reich*, in Berlin. Hitler had ordered a review of delays in *Panzer* production and set new targets with higher numbers. After the meeting ended, Guderian requested a personal talk with Hitler. He asked him: "Why do you want to attack in the East at all this year?" Keitel said that there were political reasons and Guderian replied: "Do you really think that any person world-wide knows where Kursk is? It is totally indifferent to the world if we have Kursk or not. I repeat my question. Why attack at all in the East?" Hitler replied: "You are entirely right. The whole idea gives me an increasingly funny feeling in the pit of my stomach." Guderian said: "Then you have the right feeling. Simply keep your hands off the whole idea." Hitler assured him that he had not reached a final decision.[81]

Even lower ranks began to grumble. At a meeting at *OKH*, Colonel Helmut Staedke, chief-of-staff of XXXV Corps said to Colonel Heinz Brandt, the Ia at *OKH*'s operational department: "What is the purpose of the offensive? To conquer some more square kilometres of Russian territory? Surely we have enough of them." Manstein kept his illusions:

At Army Group South, we remained convinced that the offensive would be difficult, but end in success. We had some doubt if we could beat back a simultaneous enemy offensive in the Donets region, but we were convinced that, after a victory at Kursk, we could overcome any crisis in the Donets region and turn it into a great victory.[82]

Finally, 5 July was decided upon. Hitler issued an order of the day:

---

78   BA-MA, RH 19 VI/45
79   Mellenthin, p. 146
80   Operationsbefehl Nr. 6, item 3
81   Ibid. p. 280
82   *Verlorene Siege*, p.494

The German forces have to strike a decisive blow and bring about a turn around of the war. The operation has to be the final battle for German victory. A new severe Russian defeat will compound the breakdown of the already shaky Russian hopes of a final victory of *Bolshevism.*[83]

Russian intelligence was already unrivalled. The Red Army command had advance notice of every German step. Already, weeks before the German attack, Army General Vatutin, who commanded the 'Voronesh front', informed *Stavka* that the attack was expected between 3 July and 5 July. On 4 July, some German engineering soldiers were taken prisoner and revealed the exact hour, 5am, on which the offensive would start the following day. German intelligence measures were dilettantish. Black *Panzer* uniforms were exchanged for field-grey battle dress. On 3 July, Manstein flew to Bucharest and his departure by car, in full regalia and with the large *Feldmarschall's* baton, was shown in press photos and newsreels. The official purpose was to hand Antonescu the '*Krimschild*', a decoration created by Hitler after the capture of Sevastopol. The real intention was to create the impression that he was not required at the front and that no major action was impending. Paul Carell tried his hand at a 'humoresque'. He wrote that Manstein's visit was cancelled. In fact it was only postponed one day, and added:

> In Moscow, radios began to hum in the offices of *Stavka's* fourth floor department. Manstein comes to Bucharest to-morrow! The Russian officers nodded with satisfaction. If the commander in chief of army group South goes to Bucharest to drink cocktails, instead of being at his head-quarters at Zaporoshe, major operations will certainly not occur. This was what the Soviets were intended to believe. And this was what they did believe.[84]

Whoever listened to the German programme at *Stavka* headquarters probably had a good laugh.

Citadel – the battle

Wehrmacht and Red Army units

Wehrmacht

Two army groups were engaged in the 'Citadel' phase. Manstein's Army Group had been renamed 'South' after Stalingrad. The original army group South had been split into Army Groups A and B in 1942. Army Group Centre was under Kluge. Army Group South consisted of three Armies and one *Armeeabteilung*, 1st *Panzer* army under *Generaloberst* von Mackensen, 4th *Panzer* Army under *Generaloberst* Hoth, the new 6th Army under General Hollidt, which had been brought together out of *Armeeabteilung* Hollidt and *Armeeabteilung* Kempf. Army Group Centre comprised 2nd Army under General Weiss, 4th Army under

---

83   BA-MA, RH 20-9/138
84   Carell, p. 14

Generaloberst Heinrici, 9th Army under *Generaloberst* Model, 2nd *Panzer* Army under *Generaloberst* Rudolf Schmidt, and 3rd *Panzer* Army under *Generaloberst* Reinhardt. The brunt of the attack would be borne at Army Group South by 4th *Panzer* Army and *Armeeabteilung* Kempf, and at Army Group Centre by 9th Army.

The Red Army: Centre front under Rokossovsky, Voronesh front under Vatutin, Steppe front under Konev. Until 5 July, the three 'fronts' were subordinated to a 'theatre' commanded by Zhukov. On that day the 'theatre' was disbanded and Zhukov recalled to Moscow. Rokossovsky wrote that Zhukov had himself required his return because the 'front' commander, in this instance Rokossovsky, whose front was the strongest of the three with 16 Armies, was in full control of the situation and therefore Zhukov felt that he was of better use in Moscow.[85] That was not the whole truth. Relations between Zhukov and Rokossovsky were difficult. Before Rokossovsky's arrest, Zhukov had been his subordinate, when Rokossovsky was released from the *Gulag,* he served under Zhukov.

During the Russian retreat in the autumn months of 1941 a dispute arose between the two generals. Rokossovsky had ordered a retreat of his army. Zhukov had disagreed and Rokossovsky appealed to *Stavka. Stavka* sided with Rokossovsky, Zhukov simply tore *Stavka's* order up and told Rokossovsky that final authority was vested in him as 'front' commander.[86] In 1941 Rokossovsky felt that he had no choice but to follow Zhukov's order. In 1943 he was already an Army General, shortly after he was promoted to Marshal of the Soviet Union. He now felt that he was Zhukov's equal and he had a better relationship with Stalin.

Mention must be made of Lieutenant General of tank troops, Pavel Rotmistrov, who commanded 5th Guards Tank Army. Rotmistrov's army was defeated at Prokhorovka. His post-war description of this encounter was the main element in the creation of the Prokhorovka legend. After the war Rotmistrov rose to Marshal of tank troops, and chief inspector of the Red Army's tank forces.

The battle

After the interminable rotation of changed plans and postponements, the battle was a short final accord. Since Rokossovsky knew the hour of the German attack, he ordered the unleashing of a pre-emptive heavy artillery barrage at 2.20 am:

> On 5 July, at 2.20 am the roar of guns shattered the pre-dawn silence of the steppe, as the opposing armies faced each other south of Orel. As it turned out, on the 13th Army's sector and part of the 48th Army's, where the enemy's main effort had been expected, we had anticipated his artillery preparation by just ten minutes. The fire of more than 500 guns, 460 mortars and 100 M–13 rocket-launchers smote the enemy's troops poised for the attack, inflicting heavy losses, especially in artillery, and disrupting his system of troop control.
>
> The *Nazis* were taken completely by surprise and decided that *we* (Rokossosky's emphasis) were launching an offensive. This naturally

---

85 Rokossovsky, p. 195
86 Ibid, p.78

upset their plans and caused confusion in the ranks. It took the enemy a good two hours to marshal his troops, and it was only at 4.30 am when the artillery preparation finally began, at reduced strength and in considerable disorder.[87]

The war diaries of the German units make only scant mention of the barrage. They admit that a delay occurred at III *Panzer* Corps after destruction of a bridge. No further delay occurred and the offensive started at the prescribed hour.[88]

It is not unusual in descriptions of battles that the victor dwells with pride on all his achievements, while the vanquished attempts to play them down. The truth lies often in between. A massive barrage from more than 1,000 heavy guns was hardly without effect. Divisions need more than two hours to reach their positions. Since 'Citadel' immediately turned into a fiasco, no great importance should be attached to the Russian barrage.

The course of 'Citadel' can be summarised in a few lines. Model's 9th Army advanced around ten kilometres and suffered 20,000 casualties. After his short-lived success at Prokhorovka, Manstein progressed thirty-five kilometres. On 11 July, Kluge panicked and requested an immediate break-off. The following day, the Russians launched the first part of their massive counter-offensive at Orel ending in a German rout. On 13 July, Hitler ordered the offensive to be broken off.

The break-off of 'Citadel' – another 'lost victory'?

On 13 July, Hitler called Manstein and Kluge to the *Führerhauptquartier* to inform them of his decision to break off the attack. Again Manstein could not resist one of his superfluous comments: "It would have been appropriate if Hitler had, for once, decided to travel to his army groups, or if he felt unable to do so, he could have sent his Chief of the *Generalstab*."[89] The word 'once' is certainly out of place, Hitler paid frequent visits to the headquarters of army groups. On 17/18 February, he had flown to Zaporoshe for a meeting with Manstein. He left in a hurry on the morning of 18 February, because Russian troops had advanced to a point only 10 kilometres from the city's outskirts.

A further visit to Zaporoshe took place on 8 September, for a joint meeting with Manstein, *Feldmarschall* von Kleist, *OB* of Army Group A and *Generaloberst* Ruoff, *OB* of 17th Army.[90] Manstein conveniently forgets that he himself had abstained from flying into the Stalingrad *Kessel*, where his presence had been more than required. There was certainly no need for Hitler to displace himself to inform the two army group commanders, his decision had already been reached and nothing he could have seen on the spot would have altered it. For a communication of this kind, the *Führerhauptquartier* was certainly a suitable location.

In the diaries of *OKW*, 19 July is given as the date on which 'Citadel' was broken off: "In view of the strong enemy offensives, proceeding with 'Citadel' is no

---

87   Ibid, p. 195
88   BA-MA, RH 24-3/88, annex to war diary of III *Panzer* corps.
89   *Verlorene Siege*, p.501
90   Ibid, p. 526 ff

longer possible. Our own attack is broken off in order to create new reserves through a shortening of front lines."[91] Töppel explains the discrepancy in the dates after examination of entries in Kielmansegg's diaries. *OKW* refrained from immediate communication of the date of cancellation in order to give Manstein the possibility of pursuing an attack of limited scope, 'Roland'.[92]

When Hitler communicated his order to the two commanders, Kluge made a presentation of the reasons that had led him to request an immediate break-off. Manstein contradicted:

> I insisted strongly that, as far as Army Group South was concerned, the offensive had reached a point of decision. After our successful defensive operations against all reserves available to the enemy, victory was there for the picking. If we break off the offensive now, victory will be thrown away.[93]

Manstein searched for a scapegoat. He could not blame Hitler, since it was Kluge who had urged him to break off 'Citadel'. Zeitzler wrote that Hitler wanted to pursue the offensive and was therefore irritated at Kluge's sudden change of mind.[94] Manstein may have found it difficult to put the blame on Kluge. Kluge had been his main partner in advocating 'Citadel', while most other high commanders had opposed it from the beginning. 9th Army provided a convenient scapegoat:

> Supreme command broke-off 'Citadel' just before the decisive moment. Considerations of other theatres of war, Mediterranean etc, influenced this decision, as did the failure of 2nd *Panzer* Army in the Orel salient. 9th Army had become stuck. Just a few additional infantry divisions would have been sufficient to permit it to pursue its advance with success.[95]

The mention of 2nd *Panzer* Army is an indirect swipe at Model, to whom 2nd *Panzer* Army had been subordinated on 10 July. *Generaloberst* Rudolf Schmidt had been dismissed on that date. His brother had been arrested and during the search of his apartment the Gestapo had found letters from the *Generaloberst* which were highly critical of Hitler. Schmidt was immediately arrested and charges were brought against him before the Supreme Military Court of the *Reich*. The army's chief justice was Dr Karl Sack, who was hanged after 20 July 1944. He had succeeded in obtaining an affidavit to the effect that the general was somewhat mentally disturbed when writing the incriminating letters. Schmidt was acquitted but he was not given further commands. After the war, he paid a visit to his native city Weimar, in the Russian zone of occupation. He was arrested, and remained in prison until 1955 when he was released on grounds of severe illness. He died in 1957.

In his further comments, Manstein reverted again to his 'draw theory'.

All our reverses could have been foreseen and avoided, if Supreme Command had understood in spring 1943 that all efforts had to be

91   KTB OKW, vol. 2/3, p. 804
92   Töppel, p. 61
93   *Verlorene Siege*, p. 502
94   BA-MA, ZA 1/1734, p. 75 ff
95   *Verlorene Siege*, p. 504

concentrated upon obtaining a 'draw' in the East or, at least, a weakening of Russian offensive strength. But it totally failed to see the obvious.[96]

In its own report, 9th Army emphasised that the crisis at 2nd *Panzer* Army had grown with the speed of an avalanche. *Generaloberst* Model had received permission from the highest authority to withdraw his army to its original position, in order to create additional reserves of four Divisions through a shortened front line.[97]

Manstein's mention of 'other theatres', such as Mediterranean, are likewise not consistent with facts. Not a single unit that participated in 'Citadel' was sent to Sicily. They remained at first in the Belgorod region, and were then transferred to the Donets basin and the area of the Mius river. There a Russian offensive was expected to be launched, any day, against 6th Army and 1st *Panzer* Army.[98]

The Allies' landing in Sicily resulted in a not unusual post-war quarrel between Soviet and Western historians. Those kinds of opposed views increased in number as the war progressed both in the East and in the West. Western authors contended that the landings on Sicily were an important contribution to the Russian victories at Kursk. Soviet historians affirmed that it was the Russian victory at Kursk that facilitated the landings on Sicily. Conceivably both opinions contain elements of truth.

Manstein's subordinates did not share his optimism. On 13 July, *Generaloberst* Hoth reported to Manstein that his Army was unable to continue its progress.[99]

Not unexpectedly, Manstein wrote about yet one more 'lost victory':

> Thus Army Group had to break off the battle, before the decision, perhaps when close to victory at least in its operational area. It had succeeded in inflicting heavy blows upon the enemy. Not only the Russian rifle divisions and tank brigades that had opposed us at the beginning, but even the mass of mobile units that had been brought to the field from reserves, had been at least partly destroyed in the Kursk salient and around Charkov. Army Group had faced at least 11 tank and motorized corps, and 30 rifle divisions.
>
> We had taken 34,000 prisoners. 17,000 Red Army troops are estimated to have been killed in action. This means that at least twice the number of soldiers had been wounded. Thus the enemy can be supposed to have suffered a total of 85,000 casualties.
>
> Our Army Group had suffered a total of 30,720 casualties of which 3,300 killed in action. With the exception of one *Panzer* division all our units remained in shape for further attacks, even if some infantry divisions had absorbed heavy losses.[100]

Victory was never close.

Töppel quoted two entries from Kielmansegg's diaries:

96   Ibid, p. 505
97   BA-MA, RH 20-9/155, p.2 ff
98   BA-MA, RH 20-1/94, p. 86-92
99   BA-MA, RH 20-4/104, p.160
100   *Verlorene Siege*, p. 504

12 July: To-day is probably the turning point … South is stuck … At Centre, Russian attack against 2nd *Panzer* Army has led to breakthroughs of an amplitude that we had never been able to achieve in our previous operations. Whatever strength we still have must be sent there without delay. 'Citadel' is simply finished, after only one week. The Anglo-Americans progress in Sicily. All this is very sad.

July 13: Kluge and Manstein are here. 'Citadel' is officially buried. The situation of 2nd *Panzer* Army gets worse by the day. The Russians have practically broken through at Ulyanovo. On Sicily, general retreat. [101]

The Red Army losses were far in excess of Manstein's figures but they were easily compensated by reserves. This time, Manstein could no longer refrain from a positive mention of the Red Army:

The extraordinary organisational performance in bringing in fresh reserves, and expanding war production, had not been expected by us. We were faced with a *hydra* that immediately would grow two new heads after one decapitation. [102]

It would fall to Model to present a realistic view of the battle and the causes for its failure. On 13 July, the day on which the first phase was broken off, Model wrote a lengthy report about the Red Army's defensive tactics:

The enemy has operated from a very strong and deep defensive network, with heavy concentration of artillery and a particularly strong employment of new rocket launchers. His anti-tank weapons were particularly efficient. Tanks and other armoured vehicles remained hidden behind a careful camouflage, in positions well chosen and difficult for us to locate, and even more difficult to combat. The Red Army tanks have a reach that makes it possible for them to fire at our own tanks and assault guns, without fearing a reply from our side. The enemy embedded his tanks into the ground and camouflaged them, thus bringing them into action with surprise. Behind those tanks, he amassed further reserves which advanced in surprise, opened fire and quickly disappeared when we attempted to counter-attack, alternatively they would themselves simply continue to attack. [103]

In conclusion of his 'Citadel' chapter, Manstein wrote:

At our Army Group, we remained convinced that we would succeed in halting the enemy's onslaught. Apart from our trust in the superiority of the German soldier, we could recall the difficult combats of the winter of 1942/43. We had been able to finish them with a victory, our heavy losses notwithstanding. Calculations of *OKH* showed that Russians reserves must become gradually exhausted. If they could replace their losses with soldiers from only one single age group, the Russians could not be expected to mobilize new forces in major numbers. Admittedly, one Russian age group

---

101   Töppel, p. 509
102   Ibid. p. 509
103   AOK 9, Ia, Nr. 44038/43. August 8, 1943

was around three times the number of a German one. But this was a superiority in numbers which we were sure to overcome ...'[104]

Suddenly Manstein relied on *OKH* figures that he had often had to accept as unreliable. The Russian reserves never faced exhaustion. New large formations were set up without interruption until the war's end. The German successes of the winter of 1942/43 had turned from lost victories into faded leaves.

Foreign historians do not share Manstein's conclusions:

Pierre Masson: "Could 'Citadel' have been a success if it had been launched in May as urged by Manstein? Certainly not. Even if Russian counter-measures had not yet reached full strength, a first slow Russian retreat would have exhausted the German formations' strength."[105]

Matthew Cooper: "Whether or not the Germans were ever near to success at Kursk, as von Manstein thought they were, is open to debate. One thing is certain, even had the two German armies gained open country and completed the encirclement, they would have been so materially exhausted as to render any further advance impossible." [106]

John Erickson: "Stalingrad itself brought premonitions of disaster to the Germans. But the killing-ground at Kursk brought the full reality of vast destruction. After the frenzied mechanized jousting on the battlefields, in the salient at Kursk, the *Ostheer*, were fearfully mangled at the hands of the Red Army, and now began to wither."[107]

Albert Seaton: "'Citadel' failed because the plan for the offensive was badly conceived. Frequent postponements led to a loss of surprise. After the experiences of fighting in Stalingrad, the concept of attacking a strong enemy in well-prepared positions was of doubtful wisdom. Up to 1943, the Germans usually succeeded tactically but failed strategically. At Kursk they failed strategically because they were unsuccessful tactically."[108]

Legends and myths

The unknown traitor at the *Führerhauptquartier*

Since the Russians had advance notice of every step in the planning of 'Citadel', and moreover, had a network of agents in occupied Europe and neutral countries, suspicions of a traitor within Germany were bound to arise. A Russian spy-ring, *Rote Kapelle*, under Lieutenant Harro von Schulze-Boysen operated even within the German air ministry. *Rote Kapelle* was uncovered by the end of 1942 and its members executed.

---

104   *Verlorene Siege,* p. 510
105   Masson, p. 259 ff
106   M. Cooper, *The German Army 1933–1945. Its political and military failure.* London 1978, p.458
107   J. Eriksson, *The Road to Berlin,* London 1983, p. 134 f
108   Seaton, war, p. 367 f

Carell had a welcome opportunity to insert a cloak-and-dagger story into his book. He published his book in 1966. Rumours about a possible traitor had been spread during earlier years, but Carell was the first to put them into detail. He began his account with the pathetic sentence: "*Führer*, if you only knew"![109] He wrote about a purported Soviet spy ring, 'Werther'. Carell asked: "Who was Werther?" and then engaged in increasingly abstruse speculations. Did the Russian spy-master have a predilection for the great German poet Goethe? Did he choose the name 'Werther' out of admiration for Goethe's novel *Die Leiden des jungen Werther*? Was it perhaps a phonetic similarity with the Russian word *BEPTEP*, a den of brigands, which was intended to design the *Führerhauptquartier*? Carell leaves his question "who was 'Werther' unanswered". It had to remain unanswered, since there never was a spy with the name of 'Werther,' nor was any Russian spy-ring given this name.

A year after Carell's book came on the market, the German historian, Wilhelm Ritter von Schramm published his work *Verrat im Zweiten Weltkrieg* (Treason during the Second World War).[110] In June 1940, von Schramm was one of General von Küchler's delegates. He negotiated the surrender of Paris, with the French authorities in the capital, after it had been declared an open city. Later he served some time as Ic on the staff of one of Manstein's units. Von Schramm made a careful investigation into the 'Werther' story and arrived at the conclusion that it was simply fiction.[111]

His findings were supported by Leopold Trepper, a Polish Jew, who was the head of the central body of Soviet European 'spy-rings' in Paris. After the war, Trepper was arrested and spent some years in the *Gulag*. After Stalin's death he was set free and defected to the West. There he published his recollections. Trepper wrote that the 'rings' provided Soviet intelligence with valuable political information. The 'rings' had also contact with some members of the German 'resistance' movement. However, Trepper emphasised that military information conveyed by them was mostly useless. Trepper gave the names of all spy-rings and their leaders, but he is firm in stating that there never was a 'ring', nor an individual agent with the name of Werther. Possibly some messages sent by the Swiss 'spy-ring' 'Rado' had been signed 'Werther'.

Von Schramm then investigated other suspicions that had gained ground. A first track had led to the two heads of the German Intelligence Service, *Abwehr*, Admiral Wilhelm Canaris and his deputy, *Generalmajor* Hans Oster. Both were hanged in April 1945. Whether Canaris was an active member of the 'resistance' movement is still in doubt. It was not unusual for heads of espionage and counter-espionage bodies to play a less than transparent game. No doubts exist about Oster. He was consumed with hatred of Hitler, to the extent that he did not hesitate to give advance notice of every date foreseen for the German attack in the West to his friend, the Dutch military *attaché* in Germany, Colonel Sas. When the Austrian Lieutenant Colonel Erwin Lahousen joined the *Abwehr* in 1938, after the

---

109 Carell, p. 18
110 W. von Schramm, *Verrat im Zweiten Weltkrieg, Vom Kampf der Geheimdienste in Europa, Berichte und Dokumentation*, Düsseldorf 1967
111 Ibid p.178 ff

Anschluss, Oster received him with the words: "You really intend to serve the greatest criminal of all time?" [112]

The Canaris/Oster track had to be quickly abandoned. In the spring of 1943, Oster was already under arrest and Canaris' authority had become increasingly eroded by the *SD.* Von Schramm then investigated the name *Pakbo,* which General Gehlen had used. During the war, Gehlen was head of the department 'foreign armies East', and later was the first head of intelligence of the German Federal Republic. Gehlen had associated with Hitler's closest associate Martin Bormann. [113]

For a number of years, Bormann, who had disappeared during the battle of Berlin, was rumoured to have been a Soviet spy, who had managed to escape to the Soviet Union. Recently, DNA analysis of remains uncovered at Berlin showed that Bormann had been killed by Russian fire in his attempt to escape from the Bunker. Von Schramm established that *Pakbo* was an acronym of the Swiss cities Pontresina, Arth-Goldau, Kreuzlingen, Bern and Orselina and that the *Pakbo* agent was a Swiss social-democratic journalist Otto Prünter.

Von Schramm arrived at the conclusion that a traitor, had he existed, could only be found among the members of the *Sperrkreis I,* the inner sanctum of the *Führerhauptquartier.* Only the official members of the *Sperrkreis I* had unhindered access to it. They participated in the daily situation reports. Information, which was ascribed to 'Werther', could only come from one of the members of the *Sperrkreis,* since only they had access to such details. The membership of the *Sperrkreis* remained basically unchanged during the whole war. Hitler was averse to new faces in his surroundings. When von Schramm wrote his book, more than half of the *Sperrkreis* members were still alive and he questioned every one of them. He wrote that none voiced indignation at a suspicion directed at him, and that all simply burst out laughing.

Since all radio communications from the *Sperrkreis* were strictly monitored, information could only be conveyed by someone who left it at regular intervals. This was the case with only one man, Scherff's assistant, Captain Dr Wilhelm Scheidt. Scheidt commuted between the *Sperrkreis* and his Berlin office. He carried the minutes of the situation meetings that had to be taken by an officer. Scheidt came under suspicison because he was a somewhat shady person. He was the only *Wehrmacht* officer who was a member of the *SS.* His membership had come to light when he married a Slovak woman and had to obtain *SS* permission for marriage to a foreigner. Scheidt was in touch with many circles in Berlin. He was also acquainted with members of the 'resistance' movement, among them Beck and Dr Goerdeler. Von Schramm admitted that at first he shared the suspicions about Scheidt, but dropped them, because Scheidt talked too much and thus violated the iron-clad rule of silence of an agent.

Von Schramm also talked with Manstein. Manstein would undoubtedly have an interest in the existence of a traitor at highest level, since such a man could provide him with an excuse for his failures at 'Citadel', and could be viewed by him as an obstacle to his dream of achieving a 'draw'. However, Manstein told von Schramm that treason had no part worth mentioning in the whole war.

---

112   ÖStA (Austrian State archives) NL/B 1224

113   R.Gehlen, *Der Dienst. Erinnerungen 1942–1941,* Mainz 1971

Carell was obviously aware of the suspicions surrounding Scheidt. He wrote:

It would be tempting to give the name of a particularly suspicious cavalry captain, a man pointed out in many documents and in other circumstantial evidence. If he was not 'Werther', he was at least his most important aide at *OKW*. The stringent laws of the Federal Republic protecting the rights of the individual, and the absence of final proof, keep me from revealing his name. I do not intend to become a prosecutor. I content myself by including a 'mysterious traitor' in the description of 'Citadel'. 'Werther' was the masked producer of a grandiose play describing a decisive battle.[114]

Von Schramm did not fear the 'stringent laws of the Federal Republic' and named Scheidt. Carell could not name him, since that would have put his thesis of a 'decisive' treason to rest.

Reality is always simpler than mysteries. Soviet information about 'Citadel' was gathered from the usual military sources, air reconnaissance, large size patrols in the field, and interception of German radio communications. Moreover, the attack in the Kursk salient had become a subject of gossip in the homeland at an early date.

The German historian Antonius John wrote in his book on Kursk:

It was no secret in the German public that the *Wehrmacht* would launch a major offensive in the Kursk-Orel area in the spring or summer of 1943. From April 1943, it was a subject of widespread gossip all over Germany. I was on leave in spring 1943 and an *NS-Ortsgruppenleiter*, only a minor city party official, told me, in public, startling details about the plans.[115]

The two-volume history of 4th *Panzer* division, published in 1989, confirmed that the plans for 'Citadel' were already widely talked about, in trains bringing soldiers home for leave in the early spring of 1943.[116]

John developed a theory of 'treason by German order'. According to him, the Germans were eager to leak information to the Russians, in order to have them bring additional forces into the Kursk salient, which would then be destroyed by a successful attack.[117] This can be dismissed out of hand, the *Abwehr* was never capable of such an ingenious deception. During the Second World War, the *Abwehr* was an unmitigated disaster. It took no notice of most of the things that it should never have been allowed to miss. It had over-estimated the French army, under-estimated the Red Army, and it had paid no attention to the Russian preparations for the *Uranus* counter-offensive at Stalingrad. It had failed to notice the passage of the huge convoy carrying US and British troops through the straits of Gibraltar, for the landing in North Africa in November 1942. Its worst failure was the lack of attention paid to the coded broadcast on the French programme of the

---

114   Carell, p. 100 f

115   A. John, *Kursk '43, Szenen einer Entscheidungsschlacht*, Bonn, 1993, p. 24 ff (henceforth John)

116   Töppel, p.20

117   John, p. 24 ff

BBC, 48 hours prior to the Allied landing in France on 6 June 1944. The message consisted of two verses from a poem by Paul Verlaine:

Les sanglots long des violons de l'automne
blessent mon coeur d'une langueur monotone.

The first line was broadcast 14 days ahead of the landing, to inform the French resistance of an imminent landing. The second was broadcast 48 hours prior to it, to give the French sufficient time to blow up German railway tracks. The message had already been deciphered by the Germans weeks before. However, when the second line was broadcast on 4 June, no attention was paid to it, with the result that no senior German commander was at his post when the landing began.

The Prokhorovka myth

Conceivably, the Prokhorovka myth will never be laid to rest. At first it was the largest tank battle of the Russo-German war, then it became the largest tank encounter of all times. However, during the October war of 1973, between Israel and Egypt, many more tanks were deployed on both sides than at Prokhorovka. A recent movie about Kursk, on the American History Channel, deals only with Prokhorovka and labels it as the most decisive of all battles in the East.

The Prochorovka myth rests mainly upon the heroes' epic account of General Rotmistrov[118] and the recollections of Marshal Vasilevsky. Carell adopts Rotmistrov's account. He calls Prokhorovka the 'hour of Waterloo' and labels Rotmistrov's account "the most impressive account ever of a battle, and a most magnificent Soviet contribution to military history."[119] Contemporary Russian military historians have discarded Rotmistrov's book as 'pure fantasy'.

Vasilevsky wrote:

If one has to ask for the most important result of the defensive battle at Kursk, the destruction of the German *Panzer* units ranks foremost. Relative strength in this most important arm swung in our favour, mainly thanks to the great tank battle at Prokhorovka. I was an eyewitness to that truly titanic duel between two armies of steel. It took place on 12 July, in the Kursk salient. More than 1,200 tanks and other motorized vehicles participated.[120]

The historian Valentin Pronko added:

In the southern sector the German offensive likewise ended in failure. The high point was reached on 12 July, the day on which the largest tank battle of the Second World War took place at Prokhorovka. It ended in a victory for the Red Army.[121]

---

118   P. Rotmistrov, *Tankvoye zrashrenye pod Prochorovkoi*, Moscow 1960 (henceforth Rotmistrov)

119   Carell, p. 69

120   A. Vasilevsky, *Dyelo vsey zhisni*, Moscow 1977, p. 307

121   Töppel, p. 32

Until Töppel published his findings, the number of tanks engaged at Prokhorovka remained in dispute. Masson wrote of 700 German *Panzer* and assault guns that faced an overwhelming superiority. "It was the largest tank battle of the war, a merciless duel."[122] Kielmannsegg showed that Masson followed the numbers indicated by Rotmistrov, and indicates 237 German *Panzer* and 800 Russian tanks.[123] Töppel devoted 25 pages of his work to Prokhorovka and, thanks to his careful evaluation of all available documents, his figures may well be considered as being final.[124]

On 8 July, 1st Soviet Tank Army had launched a massive attack against 4th *Panzer* Army and was beaten back with heavy losses. The battle of Prokhorovka took place on 12 July, and for the second time Manstein owed his success to *SS-Obergruppenführer* Hausser, who commanded II *SS-Panzer* Corps.

The battle began on 12 July. On its eve, II *SS Panzer* Corps had 236 *Panzer* ready for action. Among them were 15 Tiger and 8 captured Russian T–34 tanks, 60 assault guns and 40 *Marder* vehicles. Only two of Hausser's divisions took part in the battle, with a total of 204 vehicles. The Red Army's 5th Guards Tank Army launched the offensive. Its total strength comprised 850 tanks and other motorized vehicles of which 550 were engaged. Thus, one is far distant from the greatest tank encounter of all times. The Germans were at first taken by surprise but quickly regrouped and counter-attacked. By noon, the 5th Guards Tank Army was forced on the defensive. A second attack was launched by the Red Army's 2nd Guards Tank Corps. It also had to retreat to its initial positions in the afternoon.

On the evening of 12 July, Manstein sent a message of congratulations to II SS-*Panzer* Corps: "The commander in chief of army group South, *Feldmarschall* von Manstein, conveys his gratitude and his appreciation to the division of II SS-*Panzer* Corps for its outstanding success and exemplary valour during the battle."[125] No mention of this message is found in *Verlorene Siege*.

The memory of some generals show surprising gaps. In August 1943, during the defence battles west of Charkov, commander Manstein had credited *Waffen-SS* division *Das Reich* with throwing back the Red Army troops which had broken through at Belgorod-Valki and thus enabling him to launch his counter-offensive. Memoir writer Manstein does not remember.[126]

German losses at Prokhorovka were insignificant. From 10 July to 13 July, Army Group South lost a total of 31 tanks and 3 assault guns. Rotmistrov wrote that German losses amounted to 350–400 German tanks out of which were 70 Tiger. Such a number of Tiger were not in action. Rotmistrov needed a scapegoat and found it in 1st Tank Army, which had been scheduled to participate in the battle but failed to do so. 1st Tank Army had indeed been held back by Vasilevsky

122 Masson, p. 267.
123 Ibid, footnote Kielmansegg
124 Töppel, p. 31-57
125 Ibid, p.55, with reference to S. Stadler (ed), *Die Offensive gegen Kursk 1943. Das II. SS-Panzerkorps als Stossteil im Grosskampf*, Osnabrück 1980
126 H. Höhne, *Der Orden unter dem Totenkopf, Geschichte der SS*, Hamburg, 1966, p. 405 (henceforth: Höhne)

and Vatutin, although Vasilevsky had urged Stalin a few days earlier to engage it. Rotmistrov admitted that he lost 420 tanks, out of which 112 only could be repaired in time. Stalin is purported to have said to Rotmistrov after the battle: "What have you done to your magnificent tank army?"[127]

The first appearance of the Tiger had caught the Russians by surprise. Some Tiger had been in action previously, both in other sectors of the Eastern front and in North Africa. But Red Army units at Kursk encountered them for the first time. Their size caused the Russians to fear that the Germans had finally built a tank that was more than a match for the T–34. They had not yet perceived the weaknesses of this model. They would soon find out that it was not more difficult for a T–34 to destroy a Tiger than for a Tiger to destroy a T–34.

At Prokhorovka, their first remedy was to embed their own tanks. Rokossovsky wrote:

> This order had been prompted by circumstances. I remembered only too well the time when our tank men had hastily launched a head-on attack against Tigers. They had suffered substantial casualties and been hurled back behind the infantry lines. The situation then had been saved by our artillery, which had stopped the enemy with well-aimed direct fire.[128]

The importance of Prokhorovka resides solely in the many legends written about it. It was not Carell's 'hour of Waterloo', nor had it any impact on the final outcome of the battle. Had the legends not been created, accounts of the war in the East would mention it only in a few sentences. It was a short-lived tactical success of the *Wehrmacht*, which was nullified the next day by the massive Russian counter-stroke at Orel, and the break-off of 'Citadel'.

The myth of the German *Panzer* swan song

The term 'swan-song' was employed for the first time by the Russian Marshal Konev.[129] Zhukov concurred and wrote that the elite units and the strongest forces of the enemy were destroyed at Kursk.[130] But the author of the myth is Guderian:

> The failure of 'Citadel' had resulted in a decisive defeat. Our tanks, that we had succeeded in rendering fit for battle, could no longer be employed after their heavy losses and the casualties of the troops. Their re-establishment in the East and even more so against the impending Allied landing in the West was then in doubt. Of course, the Russians took full advantage of their success. There was to be no more lull in the East. Initiative was then finally with the enemy.[131]

Guderian's views reflect his anger at the employment of his best *Panzer* in 'Citadel', an operation that he opposed. In his memoirs, this feeling was compounded when, in 1944 the best remaining *Panzer* Divisions were withdrawn from the East,

127 Töppel, p.56, with reference to Glantz, p. 428, endnote 31
128 Rokossovsky, p. 198 f
129 I. Konev, *Aufzeichnungen eines Frontenbefehlshabers 1943/44*, East Berlin 1978, p. 43
130 Zhukov, p.520 f
131 Guderian, p. 243

where a major Russian offensive was in the offing. They were transferred to the West to take part in the ludicrous Ardennes offensive. Since he was the creator of the German *Panzer* Arm, it is not surprising that other German generals and military historians shared his views about its final demise. General Warlimont wrote that all German troops engaged at 'Citadel' were burned to a cinder. (*zur Schlacke verbrannt*)[132]General von Mellenthin contended that all *Panzer* and *Panzergrenadierdivisionen* (the name given during the war to motorized infantry divisions) were bled 'white'. He wrote that the flower of the German army had been totally destroyed[133] and Görlitz added that 'Citadel' broke the neck of the German *Panzer* arm.[134]

Such opinions have found their way into the works of some contemporary Russian military historians. Boris Solovev wrote in 1998 that a determination of the exact German losses at Kursk was one of the most important tasks confronting Russian historians. Russian estimations of German losses would have to be revised upwards, but have to wait for the time when German archives would become accessible.[135] German archives had been accessible many years earlier and in 1998 Russians could already freely travel to the West.

In Soviet literature, German *Panzer* losses in the first days of the Kursk battle are given as 2,828 *Panzer* in total, out of which more than 700 Tiger. In reality, the total number of *Panzer* engaged during the whole battle for Kursk amounted to 3,147. Production of Tiger during 1943 was 350, of which 147 were given to army groups Centre and South.

At the end of 1943 the *Wehrmacht* had still more than 3,000 combat-ready *Panzer*. During July/August 1943 German *Panzer* losses on the whole Eastern front amounted to 1,337.[136] Most of the losses did not occur at Kursk but in the battles in the Donets and Mius areas. During 'Citadel' 2,374 *Panzer* were engaged, of which 270 were lost.[137] German war production continued to increase in 1944. There was no 'swan-song' until the end of the war, *Panzer* remained the backbone of the *Wehrmacht*.

The three Russian 'fronts' had a total of 5,130 tanks engaged at 'Citadel'. Sokolev estimated Russian casualties at Kursk at 1,677,000 killed in action, wounded and missing.[138] German casualties amounted to 200,000.[139] During the summer of 1943 Russian tank losses in the East were six times the *Panzer* losses of the *Wehrmacht*.[140]

All these figures can be called part of the statistical numbers game. After the 'Citadel' fiasco, the *Wehrmacht* can be likened to a groggy, beaten prize-fighter, who still manages to rise from a knock down, but who is unable to throw a further punch of his own.

---

132 Warlimont, vol.2, p.348
133 Mellenthin, p.165 and 171
134 W. Görlitz, *Der Zweite Weltkrieg 1939–1945*, Stuttgart 1952, vol. 2, p.288
135 Töppel, p.66, with reference to an article by Solovev in the *Voyenno-Istorichesky Zhurnal* Nr. 4, 1998, p. 11 f.
136 BA-MA, RH 10/64
137 Ibid
138 Sokolev, p 79–86
139 Töppel, p.71
140 Ibid, table 5 with detailed figures.

Chapter 5
Manstein and 20 July 1944

In 1943 Manstein was on three separate occasions approached by three leading members of the military 'resistance', Tresckow, Stauffenberg and Gersdorff. They tried to persuade him to join the movement. Manstein was adamant in his refusal. But he always left a door open for himself, in case a *coup* carried out by others might succeed. Manstein never reported those talks. He remained true to the age-old Prussian Officer Ethos never to denounce comrades. In the first edition of his recollections, Fabian von Schlabrendorff, a cousin of Tresckow, accused Manstein of having denounced Tresckow.[1] The renowned historian Joachim Fest later adopted Schlabrendorff's contention.[2] In the subsequent editions of his book Schlabrendorff retracted his charge.

In the first two decades after the war, the main criticism levelled against Manstein dwelt on his refusal to join the 'resistance'. Some of his antagonists contended that Manstein, by choosing to stay aside, compromised the success of a plot against Hitler. This does not stand up. Since the bomb planted by Stauffenberg on 20 July failed to kill Hitler, any attempt at a *coup d'état* against him was doomed to failure. Against a Hitler who had remained alive, no military commander carried any weight. Manstein's military standing would have been meaningless. Had Manstein participated in the plot, he would likewise have ended on the gallows.

German literature concerning 20 July is very extensive. There is no disagreement among authors in their accounts of the development of the 'resistance'. Only biographies of the military and civilian participants vary at times about the role played by their heroes. Peter Hoffmann's 1,000 pages *Widerstand, Staatstreich, Attentat* (Opposition, *coup d'état*, assassination attempt) is acknowledged as the standard work about the 'resistance'.[3] The main actors are the subject of biographies, Stauffenberg by Peter Hoffmann[4] and Wolfgang Venohr[5], Tresckow by Bodo Scheurig[6], Beck by Wolfgang Foerster[7] and Klaus-Jürgen Müller[8], Oster by

---

1   F.von Schlabrendorff, *Offiziere gegen Hitler*, first edition Zuerich 1946, second revised edition Berlin 1959 (henceforth: Schlabrendorff)
2   J. Fest, *Staatsstreich. Der lange Weg zum 20. Juli,* Berlin 1994 (henceforth: Fest)
3   P-Hoffmann, *Widerstand, Staatstreich, Attentat. Der Kampf der Opposition gegen Hitler*, Munich 1979 (henceforth: Hoffmann)
4   P. Hoffmann, *Claus Schenck, Graf von Stauffenberg und seine Brüder*, Stuttgart 1992 (henceforth: Hoffmann Stauffenberg)
5   W. Venohr, *Stauffenberg-Symbol der deutschen Einheit-eine politische Biographie,* Berlin 1968 (henceforth: Venohr)
6   B. Scheurig, *Henning von Tresckow*, Hamburg 1973 (henceforth: Scheurig)
7   W. Foerster, *Generaloberst Ludwig Beck. Sein Kampf gegen den Krieg,* Munich 1953
8   K.-J. Müller, *General Ludwig Beck. Studien und Dokumente zur politisch-militärischen Vorstellungswelt und Tätigkeit des Generalstabschefs des deutschen Heeres 1933–1938,* Boppard 1980

Count Thun-Hohenstein[9], and Halder by Christian Hartmann[10] and Gerd Ueberschär.[11] Gersdorff survived and wrote his memoirs.[12]

Manstein's views about a *coup d'état*

The events of 20 July 1944 are absent from Manstein's memoirs. Some passing mentions concern participants who had been close to him.

> General von Stülpnagel, military commander France, was a victim of the aborted *coup* of 20 July.[13]

> During the war, Tresckow became one of the heads of the military 'resistance', without my having any knowledge of it. When the *coup* of 20 July failed, he was chief-of-staff of an Army, and committed suicide at the front line.[14]

> Schulze-Büttger, a most gifted and noble-minded officer, unfortunately became one of the victims of 20 July.[15]

> Colonel Finck: As a participant in the conspiracy against Hitler, he was executed after 20 July.[16]

After his last talk with Tresckow, Manstein was obviously aware of the part played by him. When attacks directed against Manstein increased in number after the war, he took position against them in correspondence with his wife, and also in letters to those, both in Germany and abroad, who had intimated that he had betrayed comrades. Some of Manstein's arguments are convincing, others remain somewhat hollow.

In *Soldatenleben*, Manstein developed his general views about a *coup d'état*, without specific reference to 20 July:

> With a totalitarian regime, in particular under the dictatorship of a man like Hitler, the only way to topple him was a *coup d'état*, resulting in the fall of the regime and the elimination of Hitler and his closest associates. The German soldier's ancestry and his upbringing made him totally unsuitable for taking part in such activities.
>
> A *coup d'état*, headed by the military, could only be undertaken with success if all three *Wehrmacht* arms had agreed to participate, and if they could be certain to be backed by the German people. Apart from the very

9 R. Galeazzo, Grav von Thun-Hohenstein, *Der Verschwörer-Generalmajor Hans Oster und die Militäropposition,* Berlin 1982 (henceforth: Thun)
10 C. Hartmann, *Halder, Generalstabschef Hitlers 1938–1942,* Paderborn 1991
11 G. Ueberschär, *Generaloberst Franz Halder, Generalstabschef, Gegner und Gefangener Hitlers,* Göttingen 1991
12 R. Frhr. von Gerdorff, *Soldat im Untergang-Lebensbilder,* Frankfurt 1979 (henceforth: Gersdorff)
13 *Soldatenleben,* p. 225
14 Ibid, p. 265
15 *Verlorene Siege,* p. 534
16 Ibid, p.326

last weeks of the war, perhaps, such prerequisites never existed in all the years of the regime. After the reintroduction of nation-wide military service, officers could no longer be certain of the total obedience of their subordinates, as had still been the case during the *Reichswehr* years.

No military leader enjoyed a standing with the German people that could have permitted him to head an uprising against Hitler. There would have been no chance of success. One can understand that emigrants, who were unable to gauge conditions prevailing at the time, or politicians who no longer held positions of responsibility, appealed to soldiers, in claiming that it was their duty to replace a regime based on force, with one based on the rule of law. One can certainly sympathise with those to whom National-Socialism caused heavy personal suffering, if they blamed the *Wehrmacht* that it did not act while there still was time.

But the question that confronted German soldiers during those years was totally different. They had to choose between two alternatives. On one side was a man and his regime who had rescued the *Reich* from impotence, and put an end to the suffering and the inner conflict of its people. Admittedly, it was accompanied by acts of terror and perversion of justice. That it would develop into total terror could not have been foreseen at that time. On the other side, was the possibility of a civil war, the end of which could not be foreseen but that could well have led to the victory of *Bolshevism*. The German people would once more be torn apart. The *Wehrmacht* might have disintegrated and become an easy prey for hostile neighbours. Furthermore, soldiers were bound by their oath of allegiance.[17]

Manstein's side-swipe at emigrants and politicians was out of place. As a memoir writer Manstein knew well that emigrants had no part in the 'resistance'. The politicians, whom he always showered with contempt, had played an active part in the conspiracy. Manstein also knew that the attempt of 20 July was carried out by officers who, in his view, lacked the prerequisites for such action. Nineteen Generals, among them three *Feldmarschalls*, von Witzleben, von Kluge and Rommel, lost their lives, either by execution or by committing suicide, after the attempt had aborted.

The possible triumph of *Bolshevism* in a civil war is a fiction. Had a civil war erupted, it would have taken place between the *Wehrmacht* and fanatical supporters of Hitler. Neither was committed to *Bolshevism*. The former German Communist party had practically disappeared and had only a few remaining active supporters. The German Democratic Republic was not the result of a civil war, it was established by the Russians in their zone of occupation.

In a reader's letter to the *Frankfurter Allgemeine Zeitung* on 10 October 1988, Manstein's son Rüdiger gave an account of his father's convictions and his reasons for refusing any part in the plot:

- Obtain a 'draw' through a military stalemate. Therefore the *Wehrmacht* had to remain totally united.
- A successful *coup* will unavoidably lead to total military defeat.

---

17   *Soldatenleben*, p.267 ff

- Hitler was the only man who enjoyed the trust and faith of the soldiers and of the whole nation.
- A military commander cannot demand obedience from his soldiers over the years, and then lead them into defeat with his own hands.
- A successful *coup* would not affect the Allied demand for unconditional surrender.

Neither Manstein's own views, nor the opinions of his son are convincing. The renewed mention of Manstein's 'draw theory' is not surprising. Did a highly intelligent man like Manstein really believe in it? In *Verlorene Siege* he maintained it throughout. It was a comfortable apology for the many 'lost' victories. However, in his personal diary, in an entry of 8 August 1943 that was obviously not intended for third parties, he qualified it: "If we vanquish the Russians, or at least, succeed in halting and 'bleeding them white', we will always be able to finish off the Western Allies in Europe. If the Russians win, the war is lost."[18] Given the industrial potential of the United States, which was already fully developed in war production in 1943, that opinion was likewise divorced from reality. Germany's collapse was already accomplished in 1943, the absurd pursuit of a lost war, which the generals preferred to a *coup*, only delayed it at the cost of senseless additional loss of life.

It is true that Hitler continued to enjoy the trust of the German people, but would that trust have been devolved to his successors, had he been killed on 20 July? Hitler never had an official successor. The Third *Reich* had no constitution to replace the constitution of the Weimar Republic, and was solely concentrated on his person. In his speech of 1 September 1939, Hitler had designated Göring as his first successor. If Göring were to disappear, his place was to be taken by Hess and if "something were to happen" to Hess, "I will call the Senate into session, which will designate the most worthy, and that is the bravest". These were empty phrases. Göring was never taken seriously. Even before the war he was the target of underground jokes and in 1943 he was just an operetta figure. By 1943, "something had happened" to Hess, who was already in England. A Senate never existed. It is somewhat difficult to imagine a *Heil* Himmler, a *Heil* Bormann or a *Heil* Goebbels. History shows that a dead dictator is soon forgotten.

When Mussolini was overthrown in 1943, waves of joy swept through Italy. Three weeks after Stalin's death, his name had disappeared from the Soviet press. The fear of a civil war, a standing argument with the generals who opposed a plot, is also doubtful. It can safely be assumed that, in the event of Hitler's death, the troops would have obeyed the orders of their commanders.

High *SS* officers likewise participated in the plot. Those who were arrested for a few hours on 20 July, before the failure of the *coup* became apparent, remained quiet, and appeared to be unperturbed by the events. Major Remer quelled the uprising in Berlin, and admitted in the video *Operation Walküre* by Joachim Fest, that he had at first decided to obey the 'Valkyria' orders and arrest Dr Goebbels. But one of the officers of his battalion, the reserve Lieutenant Dr Hagen, warned him that matters looked suspicious and convinced him that he should go to Dr Goebbels, who immediately put him on the phone to Hitler.

---

18   Hoffmann, Stauffenberg, p. 313

The military commanders had indeed demanded the utmost sacrifice from their soldiers, but the defeat was not caused 'by their own hands', but by Germany's enemies. This truism need hardly be emphasised. The German Generals simply abandoned their soldiers to their fate. The fatality casualties after 20 July reveal staggering figures:

Fatal German casualties/missing, numbers from 1 September 1939 up to 6 May 1945:

- 1 September 1939 to 20 July 1944: Soldiers killed in action 2,335,000, civilian population deaths: 500,000. Thus a total of 2,835,000 fatal casualties over a period of 1,785 days, a daily average of 1,588.
- 20 July 1944 to 6 May 1945: Soldiers killed in action 1,976,000, civilian population deaths 2,850,000. Thus a total of 4,826,000 fatal casualties over a period of 290 days, a daily average of 16,641.[19]

Given such devastating figures, one might ask if the German Generals should not have been deferred to a German tribunal after the war, for crimes committed against their own soldiers. The soldiers decayed in their graves. The Generals were released after a few years from Allied imprisonment. They were received like heroes by veterans' associations and wrote their memoirs. Only *Feldmarschall* von Küchler abstained. When his friends beseeched him to write his memoirs, he refused and said to them: "The German generals should remain silent, since they had done nothing to avoid the catastrophe."[20] Küchler remained true to the dictum of the famous Prussian general of the 1870/71 war, Constantin von Alvensleben: "A Prussian general dies, he does not write memoirs."

Undoubtedly, the Allies should have kept to their demand for unconditional surrender, even if the plot against Hitler had succeeded. Ernst Jünger told General (*Bundeswehr*) Dr Günther Kießling after the war, that total surrender always followed total war. Extreme effort in war leads to total inactivity at its end."[21] The 'resistance' found little echo in the West. It was even viewed with a negative eye, after knowledge was gained of a memorandum by Dr Goerdeler. He had been considered as Chancellor of the *Reich*, only after a successful plot, in which he demanded that Germany should remain within its borders of 1938, including Austria and the Sudeten provinces. Obviously, the Allies would not allow a new Germany to keep territories that Hitler had incorporated by military force. The difference between a 'military surrender' and an 'armistice' is only semantic. In both cases the victor dictates the conditions and the vanquished has to accept

---

19   Letter by *Generalmajor(Bundeswehr)* Dr.Eberhard Wagemann, former commander of the *Bundeswehr* academy to Stahlberg, August 21, 1993, Stahlberg, p. 457. The final figures of German casualties during the second world war have never been conclusively determined, however the numbers indicated ibn all sources published to this day, show the same relation between the figures predecing July 20 and the months thereafter.

20   Told to the author by Dr, Georg Meyer who had heard it from some friends of Küchler.

21   G. Kießling, *Versäumter Widerspruch*, Mainz 1993, p. 336 (henceforth: Kießling)

them. Minor concessions are always obtained. On 8 May 1945, Jodl succeeded in obtaining a delay of 24 hours, before the surrender that he had signed took effect.

When questioned by the Gestapo after the failed *coup*, Stauffenberg's brother Berthold said:

> In our view, only a rapid end to the war would provide Germany with a tolerable future. But all of us knew that this could not be achieved as long as the present regime remained in power. Only an elimination of Hitler, by force, remained as a solution.[22]

Manstein's reference to the oath lacks relevance. Manstein had already sworn three oaths, he would also have sworn a fourth one. The oath is not one-sided, it also commits the state, or the man, to whom allegiance is pledged. Aristotle had pointed out that an 'oath could become invalid if its beneficiary violated his commitments'. Cicero, Thomas Aquinas, the 'Strassburg oath code' of 843 AD, the Magna Charta Libertatum of 1215, and many other codes have been expressed in a similar vein.[23] A dictum of the mediaeval Western Gothic kingdom stated: ' *Rex eris, si recte facies; si non facias, non eris.*'[24] Theodor Fontane wrote in his *Vor dem Sturm*: "If the sovereign departs from his oath, be it through insanity, crime or other reasons, my oath is no longer valid."

The first plots

The numerous attempts by the military to remove Hitler, either by a *coup d'état* or by simply killing him, were an uninterrupted sequence that moved from one *Wehrmacht* centre to another. At first, in 1938, the centre was at *OKH* in Berlin. Then, in 1941, it moved to the staff of Army Group Centre in the East. When that staff was dispersed in August 1943, the staff of the *Ersatzheer* became the new and final centre. The 'Replacement Army' was charged with raising reserves of troops and equipment, in Germany, to make up for deficiencies caused by casualties in the fighting unit,. The final *coup* attempt, on 20 July, was launched from its Berlin headquarters, the *Bendlerblock*. Hitler survived all direct attempts on his life through sheer chance.

Elser

On 9 November 1939, a carpenter, Georg Elser, had planted a bomb at the *Bürgerbraukeller*, the Munich beer hall where Hitler had launched his aborted *putsch* on 9 November 1923. It was the deed of a loner, the only such attempt ever, where only one man was involved. Hitler made a public speech at that location on every anniversary of the *putsch*. On that day, bad weather did not permit him to fly.

22   H. Jacobsen (ed.) *Spiegelbild einer Verschwörung. Die Kaltenbrunner-Berichte an Bormann und Hitler über das Attentat vom 20. Juli 1944. Geheime Dokumente aus dem ehemaligen Reichssicherheitshauptamt,* erweiterte Ausgabe, Stuugart 1984, vol. 1, p. 19 (henceforth: Kaltenbrunner reports).

23   A complete list in Kosthorst, p.288 ff, with the title: 'Traditions of ancient Europe of the right to resist the sovereign's abuse of power.'

24   Ibdid, p. 209

His personal railway coach was attached to a train to Berlin that had to leave at 9.35pm. Hitler left the hall at 9.07pm. The bomb exploded at 9.20pm, killing eight people in the audience and wounding sixty-three. The bomb had been placed in such a perfect place that Hitler could not have escaped death, had he stayed until the end of the meeting. The Gestapo refused to believe that it was the work of a single ordinary man. Elser tried to escape to Switzerland on the following night, but was arrested at the border crossing, near Konstanz. He confessed, and was sent to the Dachau concentration camp. There he was kept alive until the last weeks of the war. On 5 April 1945, the head of the Gestapo, *SS-Gruppenführer* Heinrich Müller, ordered the Dachau camp commander to have Elser shot.

Halder and Oster

Manstein had no knowledge of Halder's attempts in 1938. He was the last man whom Halder would have taken into his confidence. Oster likewise always kept Manstein at a distance. Manstein heard about Halder's plans for the first time at the Nuremberg trial of the major *Nazi* war criminals.[25]

Halder's first idea was to take advantage of a train journey by Hitler, to bring about an explosion and then claim that Hitler had perished in a train accident. He abandoned this idea after Beck discovered the plan and told him that he was opposed to bloodshed as a matter of principle.

Halder then planned to have Hitler arrested at the chancellery by *Wehrmacht* units, and then put him on trial, if he decided to go to war over the Sudeten crisis. He enlisted the support of General von Witzleben, at that time commander of the Berlin *Wehrkreis*, General Hoepner, who commanded the 1st Light Division in Thuringia, General von Brockdorff-Ahlefeld, commander of 23rd Infantry Division at Potsdam and Colonel Paul von Hase, who commanded a regiment in a Berlin suburb. On 20 July von Hase, then a *Generalleutnant*, was the Berlin city commander. He was hanged after the failure of the *coup*. Witzleben said to Hjalmar Schacht: "With Halder or without him, with an order from above, or in disobedience of one's direct superiors, this time we have to go all out."[26]

Halder's plan contained some quixotic elements. 1938 was not 1944. In 1938 Hitler stood at the zenith of his popularity. It is more than doubtful that soldiers would have obeyed their commanders in an action directed against him. Individual generals had no difficulty in entering the chancellery. Troops who approached with obvious intentions would have been met by arms fire from the guards that would have been quickly reinforced by *SS* and police units. It would have been difficult to find a tribunal prepared to try Hitler. Had such a trial taken place, Hitler's rhetorical genius would probably have had him emerge triumphant from the proceedings.

Major Friedrich-Wilhelm Heinz, one of the young officers who had joined the conspirators, quickly recognised the 'utopian elements' of Halder's plan. So he convinced some of his comrades to engage in an 'additional conspiracy within the

25   *Soldatenleben*, p.
26   Thun, p.206 with reference to Oster's questioning by the Gestapo.

conspiracy'.[27] During Witzleben's arrest of Hitler, they would provoke an exchange of gun-fire and kill Hitler. Heinz told Halder that a living Hitler was more dangerous than all the troops who had been assembled. Halder had also confided in *Generaloberst* von Hammerstein-Equord, who said to Rudolf Pechel: "Just give me a troop, I will not fail you."[28] When war broke out in 1939, Hammerstein commanded an *Armeeabteilung* in the West. Hitler had planned to visit his headquarters and Hammerstein had decided to arrest him the moment he appeared. Hitler cancelled his visit at the last moment and Hammerstein was retired from active service on 21 September 1939. When Hammerstein heard about the atrocities in Poland, he said to Pechel: "My former comrades have succeeded in turning even an old soldier like myself into an anti-militarist."[29]

Discussions about what to do with Hitler, in the event of a successful plot, continued among members of the 'resistance' until the very end. Dr Goerdeler remained adamant in his opposition to bloodshed. Beck always hesitated. In one of Knopp's videos, *Hitler-eine Bilanz*, General de Maizière, inspector general of the *Bundeswehr*, recalls that in 1943, when he was a major in *OKH* organisation department, he often discussed with close friends how to put an end to the war. Should Hitler be dismissed as commander in chief of the Army, and a supreme commander East be appointed? Should he be arrested and brought to trial? It is known that such discussions occurred between trusted friends. However, it is somewhat difficult to believe that highly intelligent men had thoughts totally divorced from reality. On the same video, Kielmansegg finds the only logical reply: "Hitler was supreme commander of the *Wehrmacht* and commander in chief of the army. He issued orders like every commander in chief and if one wanted to disobey him, one simply had to kill him. Voilà!"

When Britain and France surrendered to Hitler at Munich, Halder was shattered. An entry in Groscurth's diary purports that Halder had said, with tears in his eyes, that he carried a loaded pistol for a number of weeks, in order to kill *Emil* at a suitable moment.[30] That sounds somewhat doubtful. Halder often broke into tears. He was hardly a man for a single-handed deed. During all Hitler's years in power it would have been possible to kill him, since he often moved freely, surrounded by jubilant crowds. After Gersdorff had failed in his attempt to blow himself up with Hitler in 1943, he met the banker Waldemar von Oppenheim at the Berlin Union-Club. Oppenheim told him that he had just missed an opportunity to kill *Adolf*. "He drove by my suite on the ground floor of the Bristol Hotel, his car moved at walking speed. It would have been easy to throw a hand-grenade right into it."[31]

Oster

While Halder became passive after his failure, Oster made some more attempts. In November 1939, he was approached by Dr Erich Kordt, a senior official at the

27   Hoffmann, p. 125
28   Ibid, p. 147
29   Ibid.
30   Groscurth, p. 137
31   Fest, p. 199

Ministry for Foreign Affairs, who had free access to the *Reich* chancellery. Kordt proposed himself for an attempt to assassinate Hitler by planting a bomb in his study. But after the Elser attempt, control over all explosive stocks was severely increased and Oster was unable to procure the material required. Dr Kordt intended to pursue his attempts with other means, However, Oster feared that he would be uncovered in the Elser investigation and told him to desist.

Army Group Centre and the wooing of *Feldmarschall* von Kluge

Peter Steinbach began an essay about Kluge with the words:

> History records only few names of high military commanders, whose whole career and all their accomplishments are inextricably connected to a single event which furthermore turned into failure. *Generalfeldmarschall* Günther von Kluge is one such example.[32]

Steinbach added that Kluge's achievements as a troop commander and a staff officer were not particularly noteworthy. 'Not particularly noteworthy', but certainly not insignificant. Kluge commanded an Army in Poland and in France with significant success. On 19 July 1940 he was one of the nine Ground Forces *Generaloberst* who were promoted to *Feldmarschall*. In December 1941 he relieved von Bock as *OB* of Army Group Centre. He showed himself to be the equal of the other Army Group commanders, with the exception of Manstein, who was far superior to him.

The largest organised retreat of the Russo-German war, operation *Büffel*, was a withdrawal to better positions after the battles for Rshev. It was conducted by Kluge with two of his armies, 9th Army under Model and 4th Army under Heinrici.

When the staff of his Army Group became the centre of the military 'resistance', Kluge was the only *Feldmarschall* of 1940 who had retained an active troop command. Leeb and Bock had been relieved. Rundstedt was *OB* West, at that time an insignificant command. Reichenau had died of a stroke. List had been dismissed. Witzleben was on a lengthy sick leave.

The military 'resistance' felt that it needed an active *Feldmarschall* at its head, and Kluge was the only available choice. Kluge was unable to cope with such a role. Historians have labelled him a 'flailing reed', a 'watch', which Tresckow had to wind up every evening, but which stopped before daybreak. Kluge always hesitated. However, he went further than other high-ranking officers, in talking repeatedly with high-ranking members of the civilian *resistance*. He exchanged letters with Dr Goerdeler. Kluge never hid the fact that Hitler's death was a prerequisite of his active participation in a plot. When Beck phoned him on 20 July, and told him that Germany's destiny was at stake, Kluge replied that, quite simply, a failed attempt at assassination had occurred. On that day, Kluge was *OB* West. Paris was the only place where operation *Walküre* was successful, until late at night on 20 July. Lieutenant Colonel Caesar von Hofacker, Stauffenberg's liaison man in Paris,

---

32 P. Steinbach, *Hans-Günther von Kluge-Ein Zauderer im Zwielicht*, in R.Smelser/ E.Syring (ed.), *Die militärische Elite des Dritten Reiches, 27 biographische Skizzen*, Berlin 1998, p. 288 (henceforth: Steinbach)

pressed Kluge to continue with *Walküre*, in spite of the failed attempt on Hitler' life. Kluge replied: "If the swine were at least dead."[33]

Kluge also came under attack for having been the only General who denounced a comrade. After the plot had failed, he had indeed reported General von Stülpnagel's actions to *OKW*. However, Kluge knew that both he and Stülpnagel were already doomed and, prior to writing his report, he had taken Stülpnagel aside. He had proposed to him that he should at least try and save himself, by donning civilian clothes and disappearing 'somewhere'. Stülpnagel refused. Kluge was also attacked for his obsequious last letter to Hitler, before he took poison. It has never been established if the letter reached Hitler. Steinbach questioned why Kluge found it necessary to write in that vein, at the moment when he had nothing to lose. But Kluge had to think of his family.

After the 20 July, *Sippenhaft* had been introduced, to cover the arrest of family members of participants in the plot who had escaped trial by committing suicide. Later, it was extended to next of kin of commanders who had surrendered a city and become prisoners-of-war. Kluge found the appropriate words about himself in his last talk with Gersdorff on 28 July 1944. Gersdorff implored him to order his Army Group back into Germany and to make a new attempt to kill Hitler. He added that Kluge then had to decide between being condemned by history, or being remembered as the saviour of last resort. All great men had faced the choice between such decisions. Kluge put his arm around Gersdorff's shoulder and replied: "Gersdorff, *Feldmarschall* von Kluge is simply not a great man."[34] Steinbach concluded his essay about Kluge: "A negative figure among the German military, whose name will never adorn a *Bundeswehr* barracks."[35] A Kluge barracks has never been considered. Germany has also been spared a barracks named after Manstein.

History may well come to judge Kluge in a more positive light than do his present critics. Kluge committed suicide, and all his personal papers disappeared. Therefore, there is no reply to the accusations levelled against him. There is no doubt that Kluge had recognised the criminal nature of the regime and that he was convinced that it had to be removed. Thun-Hohenstein quotes an entry in the diary of Captain Hermann Kaiser: " In his understanding, Kluge is 'horse-lengths' ahead of Manstein." [36]

Manstein was no less aware of the crimes of the Third Reich than Kluge. In the Crimea he had taken an active part in them. His repeated and close to endless statements after the war, that he knew nothing, are a blatant lie. "We knew nothing" was an easy excuse for many Germans after the war. Every German knew at least something. Many knew more and the *Feldmarschalls* knew most. Manstein also had knowledge of the extermination camps after Stahlberg had informed him. A relative of Stahlberg, Mareille Schweitzer, had been deported to Auschwitz. Stahlberg heard of it while on leave in Berlin 1943 and told Manstein after his return:

---

33 Recalled by General von Falkenhausen after the war who was present at the talk between Kluge and Hofacker. Also in E. Zeller, *Geist der Freiheit. Der zwanzigste Juli*, Munich 1965, p. 411

34 Gersdorff, p. 151

35 Steinbach, p. 321

36 Thun, p. 222

I did not spare him the name of Auschwitz. It was a place from which no one returns. His face began to twitch. I tried to speak without emotion, but I got the impression that he found it increasingly difficult to listen. He remained silent. I asked him if I should continue. He replied, "Yes, by all means.[37]

In May 1944, at Dresden, Stahlberg met Achim Oster, General Oster's son. He told him that Manstein considered all accounts about Auschwitz, and other extermination camps, to be unbelievable, and that he refused to listen to them.[38] Recent research has established that knowledge of the extermination camps was quite widespread amongst the German public.

Superficially *Generaloberst* Fromm, commander in chief of the *Ersatzheer*, may well be judged in a manner similar to Kluge. The position of *Ersatzheer OB* was more important than the command of an Army Group. Fromm had more troops under his command than did any other Army Group commander. He was in regular contact with the heads of war production industry, a number of whom belonged to or at least sympathised with the civilian resistance. Fromm had previously let his officers understand that he supported the idea of a *coup d'état*. On one occasion he had said to them that it would be best for Germany if Hitler took his own life.

On 20 July he had his close subordinates arrested, after he had spoken with Keitel, but before Stauffenberg returned to Berlin. He had heard from Keitel that Hitler had survived. At his headquarters, Fromm had four of the main actors shot in the evening hours of 20 July. They were General Olbricht, Colonel Mertz von Quirnheim, Stauffenberg, and Stauffenberg's adc Lieutenant von Haeften. Fromm granted Beck's request to be permitted to shoot himself. It turned out that he had done them a favour. They were spared a show trial before the unspeakable Freisler, and an execution by slow strangulation. An hour later, Fromm found himself under arrest. He was indicted for cowardice on 20 July, sentenced to death, spared the gallows, and shot on 12 March 1945.

Accusations made by Joachim Fest in his Video, that Fromm acted in order to save himself at the expense of his subordinates, do not stand up to scrutiny. Fromm knew that he himself was lost, but made efforts to permit his associates such an exit as was possible under the circumstances. (For details, see the recent biography of Fromm by Professor Kroener, Paderborn 2005).

The staff of Army Group Centre became the largest cell of the military 'resistance' during the whole war. Through Tresckow and Gersdorff, the path finally led to Manstein. Tresckow had a close personal relationship with Manstein. Kluge was one of the Army Group commanders with whom Manstein talked most frequently. When Manstein took over his command of Army Group Don, Kluge had warned him of the dangers arising from a direct subordination to Hitler. In his talk with Gersdorff, Manstein had explicitly referred to Kluge's authority.

Tresckow was Ia of Army Group Centre. He had begun to build up his cell while the Army Group was still under the command of his uncle, *Feldmarschall* von Bock. In an essay on von Bock, in the same anthology as Peter Steinbach's chapter

---

37   Stahlberg, p.354
38   Kosthorst, p.199

about Kluge, Horst Mühleisen labels von Bock 'Soldier without *Fortune*'.[39] Tresckow's talent had been recognised at an early stage, one of his first regimental commanders told him: "You will either end your career as Chief of the *Generalstab* or you will perish as a rebel on the scaffold."[40]

Tresckow had long departed from his early National-Socialist views. In the 1920s he had written an article in which he described "Anglo-American demo-cratic capitalism, also called Jewish capitalism, as an idea that would lead to an enslavement of humanity by merchants."[41] At a speech at the Potsdam officers' club in 1929, he had urged the officers of his regiment to educate their soldiers in National-Socialist spirit and break the monopoly of international finance.[42] All that was long buried. After Stalingrad, Tresckow said to Stahlberg:

> Our *Generalstab* no longer deserves its name. Only the collar patches and the crimson stripes remain. Clausewitz and Moltke the elder no longer exist. Hitler only wants subaltern aides in the *Generalstab*, aides in the service of a major criminal.[43]

Tresckow made continuous requests for transfer to his staff of officers whom he knew to share his opinions. His friend and regimental comrade Schmundt agreed with every demand. Obviously, Tresckow had never confided in Schmundt, but, as head of the army's personnel department, Schmundt knew many *Generalstab* officers. A number of the officers demanded by Tresckow belonged to the highest Prussian aristocracy. Their negative attitude to the party was no secret. Schmundt must have suspected that there was more behind Tresckow's request than simply a demand for qualified officers. Sebastian Haffner wrote that a list of the conspirators executed after 20 July reads like a page extracted from the Gotha almanac.[44] Gersdorff recalls that Schmundt once said to him that he had the impression that Tresckow disapproved of the *Führer*. However, he himself had known him over so many years that he trusted him entirely.[45]

When Tresckow received the *Barbarossa* and Commissar Orders, he implored his uncle von Bock to fly to Hitler and strongly protest, even resign his command if the orders were not withdrawn. On his way to Bock, he said to Gersdorff:

> If we cannot convince the *Feldmarschall* to do everything, even at his personal risk, to obtain a repeal of this order, Germany's honour will be lost for ever. This will remain for centuries. Not only the leaders of National-Socialism will be found guilty, also you and I, my wife and your

39   H. Mühleisen, *Fedor von Bock-Soldat ohne Fortune*, in R. Smelser/E. Syring (ed.) *Die Militärelite des Dritten Reiches. 27 biographische Skizzen*, Berlin 1998, p. 60
40   Scheurig, p. 77
41   T. Hamerow, *Die Attentäter.Der 20. Juli-von derKollaboration zum Widerstand*, Munich 1999, p. 20 (henceforth: Hamerow)
42   Ibid
43   Stahlberg, p.223
44   Haffner, p. 70 ff
45   Gersdorff, p. 118

wife, our children, the woman who just walks down the street and the child who plays ball across the street.[46]

Bock said to Tresckow: "He will simply throw me out." Tresckow replied: 'At least, history will credit you with having chosen an honourable exit.' Bock could not be convinced he should fly by himself. He sent Gersdorff, who obviously could not approach Hitler, and could only report that he had been unable to accomplish anything. When Bock received Gersdorff's report, he said to his staff: "I put on record that *Feldmarschall* von Bock has protested."[47]

In August 1941, Bock's adc, Major von Hardenberg, witnessed a major *Judenaktion*, the euphemism for mass shooting of Jews, which became part of the *Wehrmacht* jargon. It was the massacre of close to 10,000 Jews by *Einsatzgruppe* B at Borissow. Hardenberg had observed it while flying at low altitude over the town. He immediately reported what he had seen to Tresckow and also to a friend of his, who served on the staff of 16th Army commanded by *Generaloberst* Busch. Tresckow again implored his uncle to fly to Hitler and protest. Bock again refused.

Busch said to his staff officer: "This is a political matter that does not interest us. Perhaps it should interest us, but we are not allowed to meddle. What can we do?"[48] With a similar remark, Busch had already been severely reprimanded by Beck in 1938. Busch had expressed doubt that a soldier could be allowed to concern himself with matters that were the responsibility of politicians. Beck replied angrily that every officer of the *Generalstab* had a duty to concern himself with questions of military politics and had to clearly express his opinion.[49]

Schlabrendorff recalled a conversation with Busch. Busch told him that he had once served as assistant judge at the *Volksgerichtshof.* Since he knew nothing about legal matters, he had decided to vote for a death sentence in every instance, even if the 'learned' judges held another opinion.[50] During a war-game in March 1940, Guderian explained how he intended to proceed, after having crossed the Meuse. Busch, who commanded 16th Army, suddenly broke in: "I don't believe that you will be able to cross." Guderian replied: "Certainly, no one will ask you to try."[51]

During the first weeks of the Russian campaign, Manstein was compelled to halt his advance and come to the rescue of Busch's 16th Army, which due to Busch's faulty leadership, was suddenly in danger of becoming encircled. One may well ask how an officer, who was simply stupid, and bereft of moral standards, who had failed in every command entrusted to him, could be promoted to *Feldmarschall.*

Gersdorff decided to make an entry in the war diary of Army Group Centre under his own signature: "In all my talks with comrades, I am questioned about mass shootings of Jews. I feel that shootings of Jews, prisoners-of-war and commis-

---

46   Gersdorff, p. 87, henceforth: Gersdorff. Also Scheurig, p. 101.
47   Gersdorff, p.89. Scheurig, p. 98 ff
48   Krausnick, p. 206
49   K-J. Müller, *Das Heer und Hitler. Armee und nationalsozialistisches Regime 1933– 1940*, Stuttgart 1969, p.335 (henceforth: Müller)
50   Schlabrendorff, p. 51
51   Guderian, p. 82

sars are considered to be a violation of the honour of the German Army and its Officer Corps."[52]

Kluge took over command of Army Group Centre, when Bock was dismissed after the failure of the offensive against Moscow. In him, Tresckow had a more amenable candidate. Kluge had provided Tresckow with a moral weapon. Kluge was among the first commanders to receive a monetary gift from Hitler. On his 60th birthday, Schmundt had brought him a check for 250,000 marks and a particularly cordial letter from Hitler: "For your birthday, my dear *Feldmarschall*. 125,000 marks can be used for an expansion of your estate, *Reichsminister* Speer has been informed."

Later such gifts became a matter of routine. 250,000 marks remained the basic amount, but a number of recipients begged for increases of up to one million marks, in order to purchase a desirable estate. Gersdorff describes how Tresckow, himself, and Kluge's adc, Captain Philipp von Boeselager, had strongly urged Kluge not to touch the money.[53] Surprisingly, Hitler attached particular importance to that gift. In a situation meeting, after Kluge had committed suicide, he complained:

> I have personally promoted him twice. [Every *OB*, who was not already a *Generaloberst* in 1939, was promoted at least twice. The only exception was Blaskowitz, who was denied further promotions after his strong protest against the excesses in Poland in 1939]. I have awarded him the highest decorations, I have made him a gift of a large sum of money, to permit him to buy an estate. I have granted him a sizeable monthly increase to his *Feldmarschall* salary. [The monthly tax-free amounts paid to a *Generaloberst* (2,000 marks) and a *Feldmarschall* (4,000 marks) were simply increased salaries]. Never before have I suffered such a personal disappointment.[54]

During the years of Kluge's command, three attempts on Hitler's life occurred at his Army Group. In every instance, Hitler escaped by pure chance. In January 1943, Lieutenant Colonel Georg von Boeselager had planned to have Hitler shot by ten officers of his cavalry regiment in the officers' mess. It was on the occasion of one of Hitler's visits to Army Group. Kluge had to be informed since he had to be kept out of bullet range. Kluge hesitated again. He indicated at first that he approved of the idea. Then he made a turn-around and said that it would not be honourable to shoot a man at the dinner-able, and that other high officers would likewise be endangered.[55] The plan was abandoned. Georg von Boeselager was later killed in action. His brother Philipp survived the war. In 2004, he attended the D-Day anniversary celebrations as an official guest of the French government and was awarded the *légion d'honneur*.

On 13 March 1943, Hitler visited Army Group's Centre headquarters at Smolensk. Fabian von Schlabrendorff, Tresckow's cousin, placed two British 'clam' grenades in Hitler's plane. The 'clams' had been provided by Oster, as they

---

52   War diary Army Group Centre, vol. 1, entry by Gersdorff, December 9, 1941
53   Gersdorff, p. 124
54   Lagebsrpechungen, p. 279
55   Gersdorff, p. 124 ff

were more efficient than German explosives. The grenades had been put into a parcel and were given the shape of two bottles of Cointreau liquor. During luncheon, Tresckow asked Colonel Brandt from *OKH* to take the parcel as gift to Colonel Stieff. Schlabrendorff timed the ignition at thirty minutes after the plane's departure and set it off before Hitler boarded the plane. For unknown reasons, the grenades failed to detonate and Hitler landed safely at his headquarters at Rastenburg.[56]

On 31 March 1943, Hitler visited an exhibition of captured Russian armament at the arsenal building in Berlin. Gersdorff had succeeded in being invited by Model to accompany him. Tresckow had been able to replace Kluge with Model, since Kluge was needed in the event Hitler was killed. Model was looked upon as totally subservient to Hitler and Tresckow felt that the two might as well be blown up together. Gersdorff carried two 'clam' hand grenades in the pockets of his overcoat and had ignited them for explosion ten minutes after entering the exhibition hall. Hitler literally ran through the building, refused to look at the arms displayed and left after two minutes. Gersdorff succeeded in flushing the grenades down a toilet. After his return to Army Group, he told Kluge what had happened. Kluge was aghast: "Gersdorff, for heaven's sake, what have you done?" Gersdorff replied: "I did the only thing that the circumstances dictated."[57]

In August 1943, Kluge was severely injured in a car accident and remained incapacitated until July 1944, when he was appointed *OB* West. His staff was dispersed. Army Group Centre then came under the command of Busch. Fate had it that Busch, of all people, was indirectly involved in a later attempt to kill Hitler. On 11 March 1944, Busch attended a situation meeting at Hitler's residence at Berchtesgaden. He was accompanied by his adc, Captain Eberhard von Breitenbuch, an active member of the 'resistance', who had promised Tresckow to attempt to kill Hitler on the first occasion that presented itself. Breitenbuch carried a loaded gun in his pocket. When he wanted to enter the room together with Busch, they were stopped by an *SS* officer on guard, who told them that no adc were permitted to attend. Busch protested and said that he needed Breitenbuch's help in presenting his account. The *SS* officer remained adamant and said that Busch had to manage with his own papers, without help from Breitenbuch. Tresckow encouraged Breitenbuch to make other attempts. Breitenbuch refused and said that his nervous system could not permit a repeat performance. "One can do this only once." Breitenbuch accompanied Busch on his last meeting with Hitler, on 20 March 1945, in Hitler's Berlin bunker. He recalls that Busch was elated after his talk with Hitler, and that Hitler had told him that the great turnaround would now occur and the war would be won.[58]

A 'desperate' wooing of Manstein?

Manstein's critics charged him with having turned down increasingly desperate entreaties by the 'resistance' and thus having compromised its success. That charge must be contradicted. One can certainly criticize every high commander who

---

56   Schlabrendorff, p. 78 ff
57   Gersdorff, p.133. Also Scheurig, p.151, Hoffmann, p.335 ff
58   Hoffmann, p. 389 ff

refused to join the 'resistance'. With few exceptions, all acted in the same manner as Manstein. A desperate wooing of Manstein never took place. Undoubtedly, there was a major interest in gaining Manstein's adherence. Manstein was not popular with his fellow generals, but all recognised his military supremacy and had indicated that they were prepared to subordinate themselves to him. No *Feldmarschall* would have agreed to be placed under Kluge's orders.

Manstein could only be reached through his staff, but Manstein's staff was not Kluge's staff. The dominant personality in Manstein's staff was General Busse. Busse was feared and suspected by many of his fellow officers. He was a tough disciplinarian and a good commander. Later he asserted himself as Commander of 9th Army during the final battle for Berlin. However, he was intolerant, viewed as unprincipled, and known to be strongly attached to the regime. He was the brother-in-law of General Wilhelm Burgdorf. After Schmundt died of wounds sustained on 20 July, Burgdorf had succeeded Schmundt as Hitler's *Wehrmacht* adc and head of the Army's personnel department. Burgdorf had never seen active troop command during the war. He was an alcoholic and totally devoted to the regime. History would label him the 'grave-digger of the German Officer Corps.' He was one of the two Generals who carried the poison to Rommel after 20 July, and told him that he had either to commit suicide or face trial at the *Volksgerichtshof.* Burgdorf remained at Hitler's side until the end and shot himself after Hitler committed suicide.

Whether Busse was influenced by Burgdorf remains an open question The family relationship with Burgdorf was however sufficient to prevent visitors to Manstein from talking candidly in Busse's presence. The only active member of the 'resistance' on Manstein's staff was the Ia, Colonel Schulze-Büttger, who was hanged in the aftermath of 20 July. Stahlberg does not count. Schulze-Büttger had been an adjutant of Beck before the war. Stahlberg wrote that Tresckow had brought Schulze-Büttger into Manstein's staff.[59] Long before Stahlbergs book was written, Manstein could show that he himself had requested Schulze-Büttger, after Busse had been promoted from Ia to chief-of-staff. [60]Manstein was always eager to obtain the best talent available.

Manstein talked with Tresckow, Stauffenberg and Gersdorff. His relations with Tresckow were close, the difference in rank and age not withstanding. Tresckow had been instrumental in bringing about the first meeting between Hitler and Manstein that had given Manstein the possibility of presenting his *Sichelschnitt* plan to Hitler. On three occasions, Manstein had requested Tresckow as chief-of-staff, first for his Motorized Corps in 1941, then for 11th Army and finally for Army Group Don. He was always turned down and told that he did not need such a 'bright brain' and that Tresckow would be more useful with less capable commanders. All three tried to obtain Manstein's adherence to the 'resistance', but gave up after realising that it was hopeless. That was the end of the 'desperate wooing'.

During all three meetings, only Stahlberg was present in his outer office, adjoining Manstein's workroom. Manstein's talks with Tresckow and Gersdorff took place behind closed doors. In later years Stahlberg had to limit his account to

59   Stahlberg, p. 284
60   Letter from Manstein to Schlabrendorff, 1947, in Manstein/Fuchs, p. 204

what was told to him by third parties. During Manstein's meeting with Stauffenberg, the door was open and Stahlberg never left his room during their talk. His book gave the most detailed account available of the conversation. However, his chapter about the events leading up to July 20 has to be read with care. It contains much fiction, since Stahlberg grossly exaggerated his own part in the 'resistance'.

Manstein's talks with Stauffenberg, Gersdorff and Tresckow

Stauffenberg

Stauffenberg came to Manstein's headquarters at Taganrog, on 26 January 1943. Fighting at Stalingrad had not yet come to an end. Zeitzler had asked Manstein to receive him. On 25 January, he phoned Manstein:

> I have a request. I have asked my Ia, Major Count von Stauffenberg, to fly to Army Group Don to morrow, and report about new line-ups of Russian volunteer units, particularly those from the Caucasian provinces. I would highly appreciate if you could see him personally. Please tell me if the date is convenient.

After Manstein agreed, Zeitzler added:

> May I add a personal request? I view Stauffenberg as one of the most talented younger officers of the *Generalstab*, perhaps the most talented. Since I intend to promote him, I would attach great value to your personal impression of him. I would greatly appreciate it if you could find the time to talk to him at some length.[61]

Stauffenberg arrived, together with Generals Fellgiebel and Schmundt. General Fellgiebel was head of communications at *OKW*. He was hanged after 20 July. Stahlberg wrote that Stauffenberg extended his hand and said: "I am Stauffenberg, you must be Stahlberg."[62] This is obviously one of Stahlberg's inventions. Stahlberg was not a known figure who had to be recognised immediately. Stahlberg then continued to exaggerate: "Stauffenberg had greeted me with my name, before I had the time to introduce myself. Someone, certainly Tresckow, must have told him that he had to make sure that Stahlberg was in the adjoining room when he talked with Manstein."[63] Whatever Stauffenberg had in mind, he was not in need of assistance by Stahlberg. When Zeitzler sent Stauffenberg to Manstein, Tresckow was not at *OKH*, he was still Ia at Army Group Centre, and had no advance knowledge of Stauffenberg's visit.

Manstein talked with Schmundt for more than two hours behind closed doors. Stahlberg wrote that he was surprised at the length of that discussion.[64]

---

61   Ibid, p. 264
62   Ibid., p.265
63   Ibid, p. 265
64   Ibid, p. 263

However, there was no reason for such surprise, Manstein gave an account of his meeting in *Verlorene Siege*[65] and in letters to his wife. The reason for a lengthy meeting with Schmundt was obvious. *Spitzengliederung* and unified command, at least in the East, were Manstein's pet themes. Since he could make no headway in his direct approach to Hitler, he took advantage of every meeting with Schmundt to present his view, as he knew that Schmundt had Hitler's ear.

After Schmundt left, Manstein talked for a few minutes with Fellgiebel. Then Stauffenberg went into Manstein's room. Stahlberg's account of their conversation is given in its relevant parts:

> ... Stauffenberg was very precise in his presentation. I soon felt that Manstein was impressed, I heard him say repeatedly: "Very good, my friend" ... Suddenly, there was no more talk about Cossacks and Turkmenians ... The discussion now centred around Stalingrad and the situation of Army Groups Don and A ... I had the impression that Manstein now wanted to end the meeting ... Stauffenberg got up and said: "I respectfully ask for permission to continue." Manstein replied: "Very well, my friend, what more is on your mind?"

Stauffenberg said that he could not accept that the loss of 6th Army at Stalingrad was due only to operative errors. Stalingrad was not the first error in the East. The war against Russia was nothing but a chain of errors. Manstein immediately agreed. The war had been badly planned. Had he been asked to draft the plan, it would have been totally different ... "However, you have to accept facts and also the fact that 6th Army is lost at Stalingrad".

Stauffenberg replied that he was not prepared to simply write off Stalingrad. The sacrifice of hundreds of thousands of soldiers had no relation to what may have been the sense of that battle ... Manstein said that it was part of an officer's duty in wartime to recognise that a battle could be lost ... "Give me one example in military history, where a war was won without losing at least one battle?"

Stauffenberg replied:

> I am not convinced. We have already agreed that the whole campaign in the East, even if assumed that it was necessary, was marred by a chain of errors. Who can tell that this will not continue? Since the failure of our offensives during the autumn and winter 1941, our armies in Russia have repeatedly come close to collapse. In the South, only the brilliant leadership of *Feldmarschall* von Manstein has prevented the front from breaking down ...

Stauffenberg saw *Spitzengliederung* and the structure of command on the Eastern front as the root of all evils. Those bold words received a surprising reply. Manstein agreed.

There was no reason for Stahlberg's surprise. Manstein had often complained to Hitler directly about the *Spitzengliederung*. He was however not prepared to take part in illegal activities, either directly or indirectly ... Stauffenberg reverted. If no one took initiatives, things would remain the same and finally end in total catastrophe. Manstein disagreed violently. His own ideas would never lead to a catas-

---

65   *Verlorene Siege*, p.437

trophe. A catastrophe would occur as a result of the initiatives suggested by Stauffenberg ... Suddenly Stauffenberg said 'Tauroggen.'

Tauroggen was a small village in Lithuania, where the Prussian General Yorck, who served in Napoleon's army, had switched sides after the French retreat from Russia and concluded an armistice with the Russian unit, commanded by another Prussian officer, General Diebisch. Yorck had thus disobeyed an order by his King who charged him with disloyalty. However, the King had become a vassal of Napoleon. Yorck's action was the signal for a revolt against Napoleon all over Prussia and the King regained his liberty.

Manstein reacted violently. The present situation was not comparable to Tauroggen and Stauffenberg had better watch his tongue. Stauffenberg countered skilfully. Manstein had misunderstood him. He had not mentioned Tauroggen with the intention of suggesting that they reached out to the Russians. That was out of the question. He had mentioned Tauroggen as an example of creating a *fait accompli*. There were conditions when a *fait accompli* was called for. Tauroggen was a symbol of highest loyalty. Manstein then said: A war is only lost when one admits that it is lost. One has to wait for Hitler to show understanding, that would certainly happen."[66]

Many years after the war, Stahlberg talked with Stauffenberg's biographer, Wolfgang Venohr, who questioned him about Stauffenberg's talk with Manstein:

> I can still see Stauffenberg ... He was very blunt in his questions, he literally went on the offensive. I had the impression that he had come thoroughly prepared. He obviously tried to convince Manstein. Manstein was not prepared to face the consequences of Stauffenberg's ideas. He was totally loyal to Hitler. The supreme commander, to whom he had sworn his oath of allegiance, was simply taboo. He could never consider using force for any intervention at the highest level.[67]

Venohr was strongly critical of Manstein. Stahlberg had told him that he had asked Manstein about his impression of Stauffenberg. Manstein had replied that Stauffenberg was a very intelligent man. The talk with him had been interesting, at times brilliant. But Stauffenberg had tried to convince him that the war was lost and he did not agree. Venohr commented: "Manstein's replies to Stauffenberg tend to reduce the talk between them to simple military shop-talk. They are a dismaying testimony of voluntary intellectual suppression, and of political ignorance."[68]

The meeting ended on a very friendly note. Manstein said to Stauffenberg that he had enjoyed the opportunity: "What do we need a *Generalstab* for, if two of its officers cannot speak uninhibitedly with each other." He added: "Criticism is the salt of obedience." Stauffenberg looked surprised. Manstein asked him if he knew who was the author of that sentence. Stauffenberg said: "I don't recall, maybe Clausewitz or Moltke?" Manstein smiled and said: "I admit, I don't recall it myself." One can assume that Manstein wanted to have Stauffenberg understand

---

66   Stahlberg, p.265
67   Venohr, p.174
68   Ibid.

that he need not fear that he would report this conversation. Manstein then invited Stauffenberg to stay for dinner.

Without doubt, Manstein could have terminated his exchange, with a much junior officer, at any moment of his choice. He did not know that Stauffenberg was a talkative man who would repeat this conversation to a number of his friends. After 20 July, Manstein's name was mentioned in several records of Gestapo interrogations.

Stahlberg wrote about a phone call from Zeitzler to Manstein, on the day following Stauffenberg's visit. When Zeitzler questioned Manstein about his impression of Stauffenberg, Manstein is reported by Stahlberg to have said: "An outstanding personality. But Stauffenberg has remained too long at *OKH* and he now tends to involve himself in matters that are none of his business. I feel that the time has come to send him to the front for a short period."[69]

Stauffenberg's biographer, Peter Hoffmann, contradicts Stahlberg and shows that Zeitzler had already recommended Stauffenberg's promotion to lieutenant-colonel and his transfer to North-Africa in October 1942. Manstein had said directly to Stauffenberg: "Get some fresh air at the front and get out *OKH*, this 'shithole'." [sic]. Manstein had repeated those words in his talk with Zeitzler.[70] Stahlberg added another fantasy: "I had the feeling that Zeitzler knew more about Stauffenberg than he let appear."[71] That was obviously impossible. In January 1973, Zeitzler was still the National-Socialist chief of the *Generalstab*, Stauffenberg was not yet a leading figure in the 'resistance'.

Given Breithaupt's strong dislike of Stahlberg, his criticism of Stahlberg's account is not surprising. He wrote:

> Stahlberg's recollections were written fourteen years after the death of his former commander, and forty-four years after the end of the battle for Stalingrad. It is an astonishing account. That the witness felt capable, after such a lapse of time, of giving a *verbatim* account of a long verbal duel is remarkable. Stahlberg's account conveyed the impression of a passionate exchange about strategy, in which the young officer intended to show his desire for a *coup d'état*, by talking about creating a *fait accompli*. He even referred to Tauroggen, as a request directed at the *Feldmarschall* to remain true to his honour as an officer.[72]

Stahlberg's 'inconceivable' memory is easy to explain. When Stahlberg entered his service with Manstein, Manstein ordered him to make immediate detailed notes of every conversation that he attended or overheard.[73] Given the importance of this talk, it can safely be assumed that Stahlberg made close to *verbatim* stenographic notes. Breithaupt then makes great case of a talk of his with Brigadier General *Bundeswehr* Raban von Canstein. Canstein was a close friend of Stauffenberg and the two met a day after Stauffenberg's talk with Manstein. Breithaupt wrote that Canstein's comments put Stahlberg's account to rest. If one reads the three pages

---

69   Ibid.
70   Hoffmann, Stauffenberg, p. 270
71   Stahlberg, p. 271
72   Breithaupt, p.61
73   Stahlberg, p. 230

that Breithaupt devoted to Canstein, one is surprised to see that they hardly differ from Stahlberg's account. Canstein also mentions 'Tauroggen' and confirmed it in his appearance on Knopp's video. (Canstein was the *Fähnrichsvater* of Lieutenant von Schmeling-Diringshoven, for whom Manstein intervened in his protest against the introduction of racial laws in the army.)

On 27 January 1943, Manstein wrote to his wife:

Yesterday, Schmundt, Fellgiebel and a Count Stauffenberg were here. I had a very long talk with Schmundt and I hope that it served at least some purpose. The others came with their concerns as if I were able to help them. I am always moved by the trust shown in me. But how can I change things which are not in my power?[74]

However, Stauffenberg's talk with Manstein shows that he did not limit himself to mere 'concerns'. Stauffenberg left, bitterly disappointed. He wrote to his wife that Manstein's replies were not the language of a *Feldmarschall*. In Knopp's video, Canstein quotes a sentence by Stauffenberg, which is reported in many works about the 'resistance': "Every *Feldmarschall* knows, none is willing to act."[75] At a later conversation with *Generalleutnant* von Thüngen, one more officer who was hanged after 20 July, Stauffenberg exclaimed: "The blockheads have their pants full with 'shit and straw' in their brains, they simply don't want."[76] In Tunisia, he told his divisional commander, *Generalleutnant* von Broich: "Manstein said to me, if you don't stop immediately with your utterances, I will have you arrested."[77] In a post-war statement, Manstein took strong exception:

It is totally untrue that I threatened Stauffenberg with arrest. I have tried to do my best in assisting a most worthy younger comrade, by listening to his justified concerns. I may have cautioned him to be more careful in his own interest, since not every *OB* might be as tolerant as myself when hearing his criticism of Hitler.[78]

In a letter of 30 October 1972, Manstein wrote to one of his foreign correspondents:

I did not recognise any intention on Stauffenberg's part to attempt to convince the high commanders to take steps against Hitler by means of a *coup d'état*. I am unable to judge if he had such intentions, or if caution led him to disguise them.[79]

In the same letter, Manstein refers to Busse, who could confirm his statement. When Busse was questioned, he said that he could only guess. He added that Manstein would not have failed to inform him of a talk with Stauffenberg about a

---

74 Quoted in Breithaupt, p.64
75 Hoffmann, Stauffenberg, p. 267
76 Hoffmann, p. 267
77 Ibid
78 Statement by Manstein, November 15, 1962, reproduced in Hoffmann, Stauffenberg, p. 267
79 Letter from Manstein to Williams, in Hoffmann, Stauffenberg, p. 267

possible removal of Hitler.[80] Obviously, Stauffenberg would not have talked in such a manner with Manstein, had Busse been present. In February 1943, Stauffenberg said to Broich that he did not intend to convince high commanders to take joint steps against Hitler. He was convinced that it would serve no purpose. Hitler could only be removed by force. Stauffenberg wanted a *coup d'état* and was searching for a commander who was ready to take the lead. He found it personally difficult to reach his final decision, since he was a devout Christian, but the fatherland and the German people required the supreme sacrifice. All high commanders approached by him shared his views, but none was willing to act.[81]

The contradictions in the literature on the talk between Manstein and Stauffenberg will never be put to rest. Stauffenberg was shot on 20 July, Manstein confined himself to defending his reactions. Manstein and Stauffenberg never met again after their talk on 26 January 1943.

Gersdorff

On 8 August 1943, Gersdorff visited Manstein at his headquarters at Zaporoshe. Gersdorff was then a colonel and Ic of Army Group Centre. Immediately after the meeting, Gersdorff wrote a long account. In the foreword to his recollections he pledged his word of honour, as an officer, that he had faithfully mentioned every detail, even if he could not vouch for every single word.[82] In the Prussian Officers' code of ethics, the 'word of honour' had a mythical value, higher than an oath. An officer was permitted to pledge his 'word of honour' only under exceptional circumstances. If it turned out that he had not spoken the truth, he was cashiered. Gersdorff's report is contained, without deletions, in every serious work on the 'resistance'. Manstein made a detailed entry in his diary immediately after the meeting, in which he summed up the topics that were discussed, without reproducing the verbal exchange of opinions.[83] One can therefore follow Gersdorff's chapter in his recollections.

The meeting was held behind closed doors. Stahlberg only claims to have heard loud voices.[84] Gersdorff wrote:

> Before I left for the headquarters of Army Group South at Zaporoshe, Kluge said to me: Inform *Feldmarschall* von Manstein that after a successful *coup d'état* I will ask him to assume the post of Chief of *Generalstab* of the *Wehrmacht*, a *Generalstab* with authority over Army, Navy and *Luftwaffe*. He insisted that I tell Manstein that he, Kluge, although senior in date of promotion, was ready to place himself under his orders. Tresckow had given me letters from Goerdeler and Popitz, who was a former Prussian minister of finance. Both of them implored the generals to take action. Tresckow had cautioned me to show these documents to Manstein only if I was convinced that he would respect their

---

80 Statement by Busse, in Hoffmann, Stauffenberg, p. 545, footnote 142
81 Ibid, p. 267
82 Gersdorff, p.10
83 Manstein/Fuchs, p. 184 ff
84 Stahlberg, p. 319

confidentiality. He further ordered me not to say a word in the presence of General Busse, chief-of-staff of Army Group South.

After arrival at Zaporoshe, I spoke with Schulze-Büttger and another *confidant* of Tresckow, Manstein's adc, Lieutenant Alexander Stahlberg. Both expressed scant hope that Manstein could be influenced in our direction. They arranged a meeting with him 'under four eyes'. We then had the following conversation:

M: You have come from Army Group Centre. I will ask my chief-of-staff to join us.

G: If General Busse is present, I will only be able to report about the military situation at Army Group Centre. I will not say a single word about the real purpose of my visit to you.

Manstein gave me a surprised look and said: Then 'just shoot'. (*Schiessen Sie los*)

I then began with a topic that I knew would find an open door with Manstein, the *Spitzengliederung*, which was widely discussed at all staffs. I said: *Feldmarschall* von Kluge has increasingly grave concerns about the continuation of the war. The confusion about the authorities of *OKW* and *OKH*, and the increasingly *dilettante* interventions of Hitler in operations, are bound to lead soon to a breakdown of the front in the East. One has to make clear to Hitler that he is on his way to a catastrophe.

M: I could not agree more. But I am the wrong man to convey such a message to Hitler. Enemy propaganda is now describing me, without any doing of mine, as the man who is purported to attempt to challenge Hitler's authority. He now distrusts me. Only Rundstedt or Kluge can approach him on this subject.

G: Perhaps all *Feldmarschalls* should jointly go to Hitler and put a pistol to his chest.

M: Prussian *Feldmarschalls* don't mutiny.

In the video of the German public television channel ARD about Manstein, Philipp von Boeselager makes an angry comment: "They have to mutiny if it is necessary, that's why they have been made *Feldmarschalls*. If they don't have the guts, they could have remained battalion commanders, then they need not mutiny."

G: There are enough examples in Prussian history where high commanders have acted against the will and the orders of their King. It is sufficient to recall Seydlitz and Yorck. Apart from those, Prussian *Feldmarschalls* never faced a situation like the present. Such a unique situation requires unprecedented means. We are likewise of the opinion that a joint action by the *Feldmarschalls* is doomed to failure. At Army Group Centre we have long been convinced that every possible step has to be taken to save Germany from a catastrophe.

M: In other words, you intend to kill him.

G: Yes, like a mad dog.

Manstein leapt up, ran agitatedly across the room and shouted: 'I will have no part in this. It would result in the destruction of the army.'

G: You have already admitted that Germany will be destroyed if nothing happens. The foremost concern is Germany and the German people, and not the army.

M: I am first and above all a soldier. You don't know the Front as I do. I speak daily with soldiers of all ages and with young officers. I can see the enthusiasm in their eyes when they speak about the *Führer*. They will never understand an action against him. This will certainly lead to a civil war within the Army.

G: I also often visit the Front and I speak with young officers. I admit that a majority remain enthusiastic about Hitler. But I know many who feel differently. Above all, I am convinced that officers and soldiers will remain totally obedient to their commanders, and execute any order given by them. If Hitler disappears, soon no one will even talk about him.

I had become very excited when I made this outburst and I immediately understood that I had gone too far. Manstein contradicted me energetically. He remained strongly with his conviction and repeated over and over again that he would never take part in an action that would lead to a destruction of the Army. Manstein could certainly have arrested me earlier. I had been too outspoken about the necessity to kill Hitler. I preferred to leave Goerdeler's and Popitz' letters in my pocket. In view of Manstein's unbending attitude, I could not risk putting the lives of these men in his hands.

Since our continued discussions made me recognise that I could not convince Manstein, I remembered the selfless message which *Feldmarschall* von Kluge had asked me to convey: "*Feldmarschall* von Kluge has requested me to ask you if you will be prepared to become Chief of the *Generalstab* of the entire *Wehrmacht*, should a successful *coup d'état* occur."

Manstein made a slight bow and said: "Please convey to *Feldmarschall* von Kluge my gratitude for his trust in me. *Feldmarschall* von Manstein will always be loyally at the service of every legitimate government." That was the end of our conversation.[85]

Manstein's reactions call for comment. Manstein has to be given credit for letting Gersdorff present his views without inhibition. Gersdorff had gone much farther than Stauffenberg. Stauffenberg had only intimated a *coup d'état*, but Gersdorff had clearly demanded to have Hitler killed.

Without doubt, Kluge was well ahead of Manstein his understanding.

Manstein was not the 'wrong man' to raise the problem of *Spitzengliedung* in a talk with Hitler, he did so repeatedly, even after his talk with Gersdorff. One has to assume that he did not want to approach Hitler in this particular context.

"I am first and above all a soldier", cannot be taken seriously, a *Feldmarschall* is more than just a soldier. Kosthorst qualifies this statement as a "hypostasis, or the

---

85   Gersdorff, p. 134 ff

settled notion of a soldier's conception, a windowless monad, or indestructable closed unit of a belief, totally divorced from morality and political understanding."[86]

Manstein's reply, to Kluge's agreement to subordinate himself to him, recalls old German officers' jargon: *'Hannemann, geh Du voran'* (*Hannemann*, you be the one to take the first step.) "It would result in the destruction of the army" could confirm my view of Manstein's personality. The Army may be destroyed, but, if Manstein became its chief of *Generalstab*, it would continue to prosper. In his biography of Stauffenberg, Peter Hoffmann wrote that Manstein's reply only made sense if Manstein, at that time, had already recognised the legitimacy of a government formed by the 'resistance'.

"You don't know the front as I do. I speak daily with soldiers of all age and with young officers" is a defensive statement. Manstein was never close to frontline soldiers. "Manstein could certainly have arrested me earlier". Manstein certainly could have done so, but he did not have Gersdorff arrested, nor did he report the meeting. One can assume that Manstein would not have betrayed the confidence of Goerdeler and Popitz, had Gersdorff given him their letters.

Gersdorff added to his account:

> I was in fear of arrest until my plane took off. Manstein had every right to send me up before a summary court-martial and immediately have me shot. But he kept his silence, even after 20 July. In spite of my disappointment, I will always be grateful to him.[87]

In the last chapter of his memoirs, Gersdorff wrote:

> I owe my survival to *Feldmarschalls* von Manstein and von Kluge. Both were aware of my views and both knew of my attempt to blow myself up with Hitler. Both had full knowledge of all my activities in the 'resistance'. One word by either would have been sufficient to deliver me into the hands of the Gestapo.[88]

Since Breithaupt only searched for reasons to discredit any critic of Manstein, he omitted both those statements. Instead, he wrote that "Gersdorff conveys the astonishing impression of having been in danger of an arrest by Manstein."[89] The impression was far from astonishing. It was Gersdorff's first ever meeting with Manstein, and he had no advance knowledge of Manstein's attitude.

Tresckow

Without any question, the only thing known about Manstein's last meeting with Tresckow on 25 and 26 November 1943, is that it took place. After the war when Manstein was accused by Schlabrendorff of having denounced Tresckow, he wrote a number of statements about their last encounter. While he was able to establish that Schlabrendorff's charges were unsustainable, his account of his last talk with Tresckow lacks conviction.

---

86   Kosthorst, p. 194
87   Gersdorff, p. 136 f
88   Ibid. p. 207
89   Breithaupt, p. 81

Tresckow was always careful, to extremes. His discretion saved many conspirators from being discovered. He never uttered a negative word to third parties about comrades who had not followed his entreaties. Even after his disappointment with Manstein, he was eager not to compromise him and sent him a letter of sympathy through official channels, when Manstein was dismissed in March of the following year.

After Tresckow's suicide, the *Wehrmacht communiqué* of 24 July 1944 said: "During the battle, *Generalleutnant* Scheller, and the chief-of-staff of an army, *Generalmajor* von Tresckow, found a heroic death in the foremost line of the front." The commander in chief of 2nd Army, *Generaloberst* Weiss, eulogised him in an order of the day:

> On 21 July, the chief-of-staff of 2nd Army, *Generalmajor* von Tresckow, was killed in action during a reconnaissance mission. We bow our heads in deep awe and sorrow. This outstanding officer was a truly chivalrous man and embodied a brilliant mind, spiritual grandeur and genuine German virtues. With our deepest gratitude we take farewell of this model man, whose loss is a heavy blow for all of us in difficult times. His memory will remain with us as a shining example and encourage us to fulfil our soldierly duty to the very utmost.[90]

On 20 July, the Gestapo had yet no inkling of Tresckow's part in the 'resistance'. His name appeared for the first time in the Gestapo reports on 27 July, and then with a question mark:

> Police: Police was to become part of the Ministry for Interior Affairs under a commander with the title Chief of the German Police. (*Chef der deutschen Polizei*). *Generalmajor* von Tresckow, recently killed in action. (Probably committed suicide).[91]

Tresckow's role in the 'resistance' only became known when Stieff and von der Schulenburg confessed under torture. Tresckow was at first buried in his family grave plot. Thereafter, his body was brought to the Sachsenhausen concentration camp, where it was identified by his cousin Schlabrendorff. After the identification, it was cremated.

Tresckow's biographer, Bodo Scheurig, made an indirect reference to the last talk between Manstein and Tresckow:

> Manstein cannot be converted. Contrary to all his experience, he still thinks that he can convince Hitler. He opposes use of force; it would lead to a collapse of the front. The idea that the Russians would invade Germany precludes any action by force, as does the request for unconditional surrender.

> Tresckow made a massive attempt.

> The *Feldmarschall* remains uncompromising and requests a second meeting, late evening. His partner feels that there is 'at least slight prog-

---

90   BA-MA, RH 20-2/938
91   Kaltenbrunner reports, p. 61

ress', but 'still it is enough to drive you up the wall.' Tresckow gave up. He would not bother anymore with Manstein.[92]

Breithaupt immediately attacked Scheurig. He quoted a letter from Tresckow to his wife and concluded that Scheurig had lumped two different occurrences into one and the same paragraph. In his view, the sentence with 'slight progress' referred to Tresckow's last talk with Manstein, the one with 'enough to drive you up the wall' to a later conversation between Tresckow and friends of his at *OKH*. Breithaupt continued: "Given Scheurig's standing as a historian, it is difficult to believe that he only made an unconscious confusion between two different quotes."[93] It would have been easy for Breithaupt to put the question directly to Scheurig. However, Breithaupt felt that 'slight progress' indicated some withdrawal by Manstein from his 'draw theory'.[94] No such indication can be found, neither in *Verlorene Siege* nor in any post-war statement by Manstein.

Manstein's only mention, during the war years, of his last meeting with Tresckow was a letter to his wife of 27 November 1943:

Tresckow could not fly back yesterday, he stayed over the evening. We played bridge. It is always interesting to talk with him. I had once thought to request him as my chief-of-staff. But at this time, I feel that this is no longer advisable. Much as I like him and appreciate his pleasant personality and his intelligence, he is simply too clever for the present difficult situation. He pays too much attention to the dangers, the difficulties, and all other negative aspects. I am obviously aware of them, but I am able to overcome my feelings. If there is someone on one's side, who has a clear view but closes his eyes to positive aspects, he will become a burden.[95]

When Manstein went into his room with Tresckow, he told Stahlberg that he only wanted to be disturbed if matters of utmost urgency required his immediate attention. Stahlberg wrote:

The talk between the two must have taken a dramatic turn. I had to go twice into the room. Both were standing at the fireplace in a state of utmost agitation. Manstein was trembling over his whole body in a manner I had never seen before. Tresckow had tears of despair in his eyes. I got the impression that it was a continuation of Manstein's talk with Stauffenberg. Tresckow being more candid, was becoming increasingly passionate.[96]

The words "Manstein's body was trembling" were simply copied by Stahlberg from the first edition of Schlabrendorff's book:

Tresckow refused to give up. Manstein was so impressed by Tresckow's review of the situation and by his appeals to his own responsibility that he trembled over his whole body. But he could not convince himself to reply

---

92   Scheurig, p. 175
93   Breithaupt, p. 85
94   Ibid
95   Letter in possession of the Manstein family, quoted by Breithaupt, p.86
96   Stahlberg, p. 282

with a simple "Yes". Tresckow had preached to a deaf man. Finally, Manstein became afraid of Tresckow's influence. At the end of 1943, the army's personnel department had proposed Tresckow as new chief-of-staff of Manstein's Army Group. Manstein's refusal was sharply worded. Schmundt was surprised and asked Manstein why he had declined Tresckow. Manstein replied that "Tresckow was a most capable *Generalstab* officer but that he had a negative attitude toward National-Socialism." As a consequence of that statement, which Schmundt reported to Tresckow, Tresckow's military career came to an end. Manstein had prevented Tresckow from reaching a position of considerable military authority, which would have permitted him to mobilize military strength against Hitler at the decisive moment.[97]

After Schlabrendorff's book went on sale, Manstein wrote to him from his prison cell:

> My relationship with Tresckow can be described as one of mutual high esteem, compounded by personal friendship, in spite of the age difference. I would have been a total fool if I had tried to damage my most faithful supporter who, thanks to his friendship with Schmundt, was not without influence.[98]

Whether Tresckow still remained Manstein's most faithful supporter can be doubted. On April 6, 1943, Tresckow had made an entry into his diary:

> Manstein has military and operational capability, but he understands nothing about politics and lacks erudition. He does not see political requirements and he shows complete indifference and opposition to remedying the urgent problems of the German people.[99]

At that time, Tresckow knew that the war was lost and he was not interested in a further career. He was promoted to *Generalmajor* and became chief-of-staff of 2nd Army, and remained in high staff positions until his suicide. The position of chief-of-staff of an Army is important, but it carries no power, since the chief-of-staff cannot order under his own name and he has no authority over troop mobilization and movement.

Although Schlabrendorff retracted his charges against Manstein 1959, Joachim Fest took them up again his book that appeared in 1998. He gave Schlabrendorff's first edition as his source, without mentioning Schlabrendorff's corrected second edition:

> Tresckow's hopes of reaching a key position from where he could support a *putsch* by military means at the front, were not fulfilled. The army's personnel department had proposed him for chief-of-staff of Manstein's Army Group South. Manstein had refused. When questioned by Schmundt, Manstein

---

97   Schlabrendorff, p. 114
98   Text of the letter in Breithaupt, p. 84, without indication of the exact date.
99   Hoffmann, Stauffenberg, p.555

made the highly dangerous statement: Tresckow is an outstanding officer, but he has a negative attitude towards National-Socialism.[100]

In *Verlorene Siege*, Manstein referred to Schlabrendorff's charge:

A man, close to Tresckow, has written that I had refused Tresckow as my chief-of-staff because he was not a reliable National-Socialist. Every one who knows me, will confirm that I never paid attention to the political views of my associates.[101]

Schlabrendorff was a man of total integrity who later became a senior judge at the constitutional court of the Federal German Republic. The first edition of his book appeared in 1946. His Swiss editor, Gero von Gaevernitz, wrote that he had already begun to write it in the second half of 1945. When he met Schlabrendorff for the first time, Schlabrendorff still wore the dress of a concentration camp inmate. On 3 February 1945, he had stood before Freisler's court and waited for the death sentence that his lawyer had told him was unavoidable. During a recess there was an air-raid. Freisler was killed by a falling beam in the air-raid shelter. He had taken the Schlabrendorff file into the shelter and it was burned. When his trial was resumed, Schlabrendorff was able to convince Freisler's successor, Dr Krohne, that he had confessed under torture. He was acquitted and sent to the Sachsenhausen concentration camp for identifying Tresckow's body. He was obviously still in shock and inclined to believe accounts from third parties.

Manstein's own account of his meeting with Tresckow, reproduced here in excerpts, is not convincing:

My last talk with Tresckow occurred in late autumn or the winter of 1943. We were in agreement that our supreme command was not up to its task. Tresckow said that things could not continue as at present. I told Tresckow that the only way out was to convince Hitler to give up Supreme Command in the East and to appoint a responsible Chief of the *Generalstab*. I added that he would hardly choose me for any of these positions and that we would soon clash. ... We only talked about military leadership. He advanced neither moral nor political arguments. I had no reason to bring them up, since all my time was taken by military considerations. Furthermore, I had as little knowledge of the crimes committed in the East as had other soldiers, whose time was fully taken up by their duties at the front. Peter Hoffmann commented: if Manstein says 'as little', at least he does not say 'nothing'. 'As little' can likewise mean 'much' since many knew much.[102]

Tresckow knew about the massacre at Borisov, but made no mention of it during our meeting. We only talked about the insufficiencies of our high command and here he brought no new ideas. I had thus really no reason 'to tremble over my whole body'. That was never my style. Tresckow gave me no indications of his plans. My own position was never in doubt. I thus had no reason to arrive at an unequivocal 'Yes!' Whether

100   Fest, p. 226
101   *Verlorene Siege*, p. 226
102   Hoffmann, Stauffenberg, p. 559, footnote

my position was correct or erroneous is beside the point. One can only ask if I refrained from reaching a decision through cowardice or weakness of character, or if I tried to escape responsibility with veiled expressions. Neither was the case. I still don't know why Tresckow was not totally candid with me.[103]

That statement rings hollow. Tresckow would hardly have travelled to Manstein to enjoy a game of bridge and to discuss *Spitzengliederung* with him. They had discussed the topic in many of their previous meetings. Tresckow had sent Gersdorff to Manstein. When Gersdorff's entreaties led nowhere, Tresckow made a last attempt to win Manstein over. Tresckow may not have mentioned Borisov, but that is hardly relevant. Borrisov was one of the first mass murderers of Jews. Since then many more had occurred and both Tresckow and Manstein knew about them, Manstein's denials not withstanding. It cannot be ascertained if Tresckow had knowledge of Manstein's order of the day of 20 November 1941, or of his crimes in the Crimea. But he knew the 'Reichenau-order' that had served as model for Manstein's order of the day. It had been distributed to all units in the East. If Tresckow wanted to convince Manstein, war crimes in the East would have been his main topic.

Did Manstein break faith with Beck?

The *Bundeswehr* celebrated Manstein's eightieth birthday with a *Grosser Zapfenstreich*. Brigadier General *Bundeswehr* Achim Oster published an outraged letter in the influential weekly *Die Zeit*, under the heading: *Ein falscher Zapfenstreich – Manstein und die Bundeswehr* (a wrong *Zapfenstreich* - Manstein and the *Bundeswehr*):

Every year, officers and soldiers of the former *Panzer* troops assemble at the *Panzer* academy at Munsterlager. In the honour grove, with monuments for fallen *Panzer* soldiers, they remember their fallen comrades. This year, on the eve of Memorial Day, they witnessed a *Grosser Zapfenstreich*, the most solemn military testimonial to a living man, *Feldmarschall* von Manstein, who will shortly turn eighty.

If the purpose was to have old soldiers show their appreciation of a highly talented and often successful former comrade – fine. However, we cannot recall that similar honours were rendered to *Generaloberst* Halder on his eightieth birthday. He was a man, who by 1938, planned to rise against the destroyer and the desecrator of our fatherland. He spent the last months of the war, together with his courageous spouse, in a concentration camp.

The Manstein celebration took place in the grounds of the *Bundeswehr* with its active support. If the purpose was to create a new role model for the present German army, care for its 'good' name compels us to issue a stern warning.

Erwin Rommel was not a convinced National-Socialist, but had been converted into an enthusiastic follower. In North Africa, dire distress forced him to think anew. As a man and a soldier of high character,

103 Manstein/Fuchs, p. 206 f

consumed by love for his fatherland, he drew the consequences that led him to reach for the hemlock cup.

Erich von Manstein was never a National-Socialist. His sharp brain, and the arrogance of the old guard officer, always saw through the *Pinkelstratege*, as he used to call Hitler. In the end, Manstein finally regarded Hitler with utter contempt. Brought up in the best traditions of the Prussian *Generalstab*, he was not only the most outstanding of all *Quartiermeister*, but also, in his thoughts and his plans, he was particularly close to his chief, General Ludwig Beck. Everyone knows how patient and how imploring Beck could be. He tried to gain the close support of his 'disciple' after their joint work in the past, but he must have felt a tragic breach of faith had taken place.

Becks's struggle to gain Manstein's support was made harder by the uncontested standing that the *Feldmarschall* continued to enjoy in the whole army, and also with the younger *Generalstab* officers and with the front line troops. A courageous initiative by Manstein, supported by the army's power, could perhaps have led to an overthrow of the regime, even without an attempt to kill Hitler.

But in his talks with those who, without consideration for their personal danger, had decided to put an end to the misery, Manstein remained true to the old guard jargon: *Hannemann, geh Du voran*! A successful *coup d'état* would have seen Manstein immediately side with his former mentor. And therein lies his breach of faith.

Here was not a supporter of the regime, consumed with loyalty to the *Führer* to the very end. No, the most brilliant mind among the military commanders had long recognised where all that would lead. His way was shown to him by a man whose memory he still purports to cherish. He had gained his authority on the battle-field, bore a distinguished soldier's name and carried the baton of a *Feldmarschall*. All this may well have tipped the balance and led to salvation.

He had his reasons for abstaining. Seen against the background of history, there can only be one conclusion: he was 'weighed in the balance and found wanting.' Failure in decisive hours is not a personal but an historic guilt. No one will blame Manstein for not having been a hero. But a *Grosser Zapfenstreich*, a role model for the *Bundeswehr* – NO![104]

One has to agree with many of Oster's statements. A *Zapfenstreich* was not due to Manstein, whether it was due to Halder may be questionable. Manstein was certainly not a role model for the *Bundeswehr*, neither was he a hero. The only *Feldmarschall* who deserves to be called a hero was Erwin von Witzleben. Had a *coup* against Hitler succeeded, Manstein would certainly have been among the first to side with the new rulers. Oster's contention, that a participation by Manstein the 'resistance' could have succeeded, without a physical removal of Hitler, is more than doubtful.

But Beck never wooed Manstein and Manstein never broke faith with Beck. Faith can only be broken if there was a previous commitment, and Manstein never

---

committed himself to Beck's opinions. Relations between Beck and Manstein suffered an increasing alienation. However, it was one-sided. Beck made increasingly negative remarks about Manstein. Later he spoke of him in open contempt, but Manstein never said a negative word about Beck. Like most German generals, Manstein had welcomed Hitler's rise to power. Beck had gone much further and written to Ms Gossler that 30 January 1933 was the first beam of light in his life, after the defeat of 1918. Manstein would have known of Beck's first doubts. When Manstein was replaced as *Oberquartiermeister* I, there were only doubts about Beck. Beck could have confided in him, but that did not happen.

Beck was not the resistant 'from the very first moment', as he is described in a number of books. At first he had only doubts. Then he hesitated, and finally he turned to open opposition and paid with his life. When Halder replaced Manstein as *Oberquartiermeister* I, he tried to convince Beck that Hitler never could be swayed, once he had made up his mind. Beck only found the lame reply: "But I have sent him a lengthy memorandum". Halder told him that Hitler was not the kind of man who could be impressed by memoranda.[105]

On 18 January 1940, Beck told Halder that an attack in the West would lead to a catastrophe. He drew up a plan for an action against Hitler in Berlin. Halder said that it was too early. Beck replied that, after all, Halder was an 'old rider' and should know that a strong heart was required to jump over an obstacle. Halder replied testily, that he was known to have been an opponent of Hitler and his regime from the very beginning, and that he was not in need of such reproaches.[106] Klaus-Jürgen Müller related the incident. He added that it must have been personally embarrassing for Beck, to be reminded by Halder, that Halder had recognised the dangers of the regime at an earlier time than himself.[107]

Manstein was unaware of all that, but, suppose he had known. Manstein was no recruit, he was already a *Generalleutnant* and, already at that time, viewed as the future commander in chief of the army. He was master of his own decisions. They were shown to have been erroneous and history has already rendered its verdict. In his talk with Röhricht, Tresckow quoted a sentence from Nietzsche: "The future of Germany's culture rests with the sons of Prussian officers". Kosthorst added:

> The future can also be gambled away. And it has been gambled away! The military elite, the product of the *Generalstab*, was the only body in Germany that had the means to remove the NS-regime. Its duty was not confined to military achievement, it was also duty bound to assure the welfare of the nation. It failed in that duty, although it had been long aware that the war was irretrievably lost. History proved that failure.[108]

The exact time that Beck began to dissociate himself from Manstein has not been determined. Perhaps it was already prior to Beck's decision to have Halder replace Manstein as *Oberquartiermeister* I. Beck may well have been irritated by Manstein's letter to him of 21 July 1938, in which Manstein implored him not to resign as head of the *Generalstab*. It contained the sentence: "After all, the *Führer*

---

105   Müller, p. 325
106   Ibid, p. 556
107   Ibid, footnote 502
108   Kosthorst, p. 87

has always shown a totally correct grasp of the political situation." Beck made a hand-written comment: "and what about now?" Beck may have felt additional anger at another sentence by Manstein. Manstein wrote that, " I know that no one longs with greater fervour than you for the final destruction of Czechoslovakia". However, Manstein could have had in mind a memorandum by Beck of 29 May 1938. Beck had written: "Czechoslovakia is a creation of the Versailles dictate. It would be unbearable for Germany and ways must be found to eliminate Czechoslovakia, if necessary, even by means of war."[109] In the 1920s, Seeckt had expressed himself in a similar manner about Poland.

In conclusion to his memorandum, Beck stated that present international constellations did not permit the use of military force. Some of Manstein's sentences may appear cynical. But they can also be interpreted as a suggestion for a way to overcome the difficulties indicated by Beck. Manstein wrote:

> Taken together, all our present steps, the build-up of fortifications, mobilization of additional units, assembly of motorized units close to our western border, may well be considered as an open preparation for war by us, or a threat of war, which is undoubtedly justified by present political circumstances. Since the western powers do not want war, our political-military leadership should take advantage of this attitude and induce the West to put pressure on Prague. At first, it would be by granting further autonomy to national minorities. Once that was achieved, Czechoslovakia would become undermined to an extent that would permit her final disappearance by military action on our part.[110]

Conceivably those sentences led Beck to content himself with his short and non-committal reply. He did not even mail it, but kept it for possible communication to Manstein a forthcoming visit to Berlin.

After Manstein's dismissal as *Oberquartiermeister* I contacts between Beck and himself were only sporadic. Therefore there was never a "patient and imploring" struggle, by Beck, to gain Manstein's adherence to his views. Manstein wrote:

> During the war, I met Beck only once. It was after the campaign against, and even perhaps after our victory over France. I don't recall the exact date. I paid a call on him at his home at Berlin-Lichterfelde. At that meeting, he did not say a word about a possible *coup d'état*, or a removal of Hitler by force. Probably he abstained because my wife was present. During the war, I received a letter from Beck, around Christmas 1942. He gave a classic review of the general situation and wrote that the war could not be won ... I replied that I could not dispute his conclusions. However, I was so preoccupied with the situation of my Army Group that I simply could not find the time to reply in detail. Beck concluded his letter with an exhortation to make every effort to avoid loss of life. That had always been my preoccupation. I added that a war was only lost when one admits that it is lost, but, in my view, this was still far from being the case. On the contrary, I was convinced that, after our successes at

---

109   BA-MA, RH-N 28/3
110   BA-MA, RH 09-28/4

Charkov and on the Dnepr in March 1943, that it was still possible to achieve a draw, provided supreme command was up to its task.[111]

History has proved Beck right and Manstein wrong. History will record Manstein as a failure, but not as a disloyal man.

Not surprisingly,Manstein and his followers were outraged by Oster's letter. The old tale of Oster's father, the 'traitor' Oster who had 'betrayed' Germany's attack in the West, was again brought up. Furthermore it was 'scandalous', that Brigadier General Oster had publicly objected to a ceremony which had been ordered and commanded by his superior, General Ulrich de Maizière, the *Bundeswehr* inspector general. Manstein's faithful shield-bearer Busse wrote: "The *Feldmarschall* is heads above such pamphlets. I will not lower myself to the level of the Oster letter. After all, who is *Herr* Oster?"[112]

Did Manstein have advance information of the date of July 20?

Stahlberg produced a fairy-tale. He wrote about a conversation with Manstein, some time in mid-July, but does not mention the date:

"*Herr Feldmarschall,* I feel duty bound to inform you that the *Führer* will be killed today or on one of the next few days." Pause. A long pause. No reply. After some time, which I felt was an eternity, he said, "Repeat what you have just said." I repeated my words.

After another eternity, came the question that I had expected and to which I had prepared my answer all through the previous night. "Who told you that?" I replied immediately, "General Fellgiebel." After another long silence, over many kilometres, I felt that I had to ask him, "Should I have abstained from informing you?" He replied immediately, "No, you had to inform me." I drew a long sigh of relief. [113]

That is simply laughable. Manstein may have harboured paternal feelings for Stahlberg, yet such a familiar conversation between the *Feldmarschall* and a young reserve lieutenant, on a topic of such importance, is simply unthinkable. Sentences like, "the two us now know quite a lot", were more appropriate for a beer hall *Stammtisch.*

Stahlberg then continued to 'spin his yarn'. He wrote that Fellgiebel often referred to him as 'a saviour in distress'. He purports that he had visited the *Führerhauptquartier* on 11 July, and that General Fellgiebel had told him, "You have arrived at the right moment. Stauffenberg is at Berchtesgaden and has the bomb in his briefcase. Now the time has come when Manstein is no longer bound by his oath. Now he has to know. When will you see him?"[114]

Stahlberg as 'saviour in distress' requires no comment. If a senior general such as Fellgiebel really wanted to convey such a message to Manstein, he would have turned to a senior officer, perhaps Colonel Brandt at *OKH*. Brandt was a member

---

111   Manstein/Fuchs, p.208
112   Wrochem, p. 343
113   Stahlberg, p. 391
114   Ibid, p.368

of the plot and was wounded by splinters from Stauffenberg's bomb. His involve-
ment was not known. On the following day, the daily press published a lengthy
eulogy. However, Brandt talked in his delirium and his part was uncovered. He
died after some hours. All the newspapers were immediately withdrawn from
circulation. General Fellgiebel was not sufficiently naive to believe that Stahlberg
could influence Manstein regarding his oath of allegiance.

Tresckow's legacy

In the last days before 20 July, Tresckow and other leading members of the 'resistance' were convinced that the attempt was doomed to failure. On the eve of the
Allied landing in France, Tresckow said to Stahlberg:

> It is almost certain that we will fail. But how will future history judge the
> German people, if not even a handful of men had the courage to put an
> end to that criminal? As yet, only a few Germans know of the many atro-
> cious crimes committed by the *Nazis*. Only at the highest military level is
> everything known. But one day, everybody will know. And they will then
> fall upon those who knew and who did nothing to prevent them. There-
> fore Hitler has to be killed, at all costs, *coûte que coûte*.[115]

Before blowing himself up, Tresckow said to Schlabrendorff:

> Now everyone will attack us and besmirch us. I continue to be convinced
> of the justice of our cause. Hitler is not only Germany's arch-enemy, he is
> the arch-enemy of the whole world. In a few hours, I will stand face to face
> with the Almighty. I can defend what I did with the cleanest conscience. If
> God had promised Abraham that he would not destroy Sodom if only ten
> just men were found there, I hope that God will show mercy to Germany
> for our sake. None of us may complain about our end. Everyone who
> joined us has agreed to 'wear the Nessus shirt'. A man's ethical value
> begins at the moment when he is ready to sacrifice his life for his convic-
> tion.[116]

Having put on the 'poisoned shirt' of Nessus, and failed in their attempt to
assassinate Hitler, they knew that they would lose their lives.

Recognition in post-war Germany and the rest of the world took much longer
than Tresckow had hoped for. German opinion polls during the 1970s showed
that the attitude of the German people towards the 'resistance' ranged from ambivalent to downright negative. In Britain and the USA, 20 July was at first discarded
as a failed attempt by some mutinous generals. Gersdorff recalls that in his prisoner-of-war camp, he was shown a memorandum written by an American Captain
Franz-Joseph von Trautmannsdorff, a scion of an Austrian aristocratic dynasty,
who had emigrated to the US. According to Trautmannsdorff, most of the
conspirators were Prussian *Junker*. Motivated by personal ambition, they wanted

---

115   Ibid, p.380
116   Schlabrendorff, p. 153

to seize power at the last moment, to replace the present dictatorship with an even worse one of their own.[117]

Professor Theodore Hamerow shows the results of opinion polls conducted in Germany in 1951/52. Only 41% of those questioned felt that the 'resistance' was justified. 36% gave 'another answer', and 23% had no opinion. 20% said that 'resistance' during the war was legitimate. 34% felt that it would have been preferable to wait until after the war. 31% refused to answer. Hamerow quotes the British author, Anton Gill, who wrote in 1994 that relatives of the conspirators, bearers of illustrious names, had told him that their names were a distinct disadvantage in post-war Germany.[118] In his video, *Operation Walküre*, Joachim Fest gave the results of opinion polls conducted in 1970. 60% of the German population knew nothing about 20 July. Of those who recalled it, 40% viewed it a positive. 7% thought it a negative. The remainder had no opinion. 52% could not recall a single name of the conspirators.

A memorial service for Witzleben's adc, Count von Schwerin-Schwanenfeld, on the first anniversary of his execution, was permitted by the Allies only if no mention was made of his activities in the 'resistance'. He had to be described as an officer killed in action. At his trial, Schwerin-Schwanenfeld had faced Freisler's gutter language with exceptional courage. *Generaloberst* Hoepner's farewell letter to his wife, written in haste before he was dragged to the gallows, was kept under lock and key by the Allies for ten years. It was then handed to his wife, but only as a photostat.

Schlabrendorff's book gave a detailed description of Gersdorff's attempt to blow himself up with Hitler. When the book became available in the prisoner-of-war camps, Gersdorff was surprised to see that his fellow officers suddenly ignored him and did not return his salute. He requested a meeting with the senior German general, *Generaloberst* Hollidt, and requested a meeting with all officers, to read a statement, in which he confirmed what Schlabrendorff had written. Hollidt refused and told him: "You are apparently not aware of your position. A few days ago, I received a visit by a delegation of generals. They requested your immediate transfer, or they would see to it that the SS officers in the camp would kill you." Gersdorff wrote that he simply laughed. He was on friendly terms with the SS inmates. He had told them of this attempt and found sympathetic understanding. It was the old story again. Generals, who had remained incorrigible, wanted once more to hide behind the SS.[119]

When the totally insignificant *Generalleutnant* Engel, who, as a captain, had served as Army liaison officer to Hitler in 1933, was granted an early release from captivity, Gersdorff went to the American camp commander and asked him why he was not accorded a similar favour. He was told: "Engel had always obeyed orders, therefore he was not dangerous. You have given preference to your conscience and shown that you were prepared to disobey. We have to consider you

---

117   Gersdorff, p.193 f
118   Hamerow, p. 410, with reference to A.Gill, *A Honourable Defeat. A History of German Resistance to Hitler 1933–1945*, New York 1994
119   Gersdorff, p. 201

as being dangerous and have to keep you in custody."[120] Later, Gersdorff applied for entry in the *Bundeswehr*, but met with a refusal.

Major Remer, who had quelled the uprising in Berlin on 20 July, was immediately promoted to colonel. Before the end of the war he rose to *Generalmajor*. He joined a party of the extreme right. At a meeting, he made a speech in which he described the conspirators as a bunch of traitors, paid by the Allies. He received an insignificant prison sentence of a few months.

In East German schoolbooks, the 'resistance' movement was described as having been led by the German Communist party, *KPD*.

> From the first day of the Hitler regime, the *KPD* led the struggle against the regime. The anti-fascist 'resistance' was part of the class struggle of the working-class against the bourgeois monopoly. Communists, Social-Democrats, members of the middle-class, pacifists and youths of all opinion joined the 'resistance'. But all recognised the leadership of the *KPD*. Admittedly, Stauffenberg had "some contact with Beck and Dr Goerdeler", but he wanted above all to make peace on all fronts, establish a democratic regime in Germany, and create good neighbourly relations with the USSR. Therefore he searched for a co-operation with the 'resistance' led by the *KPD*. Unfortunately, the *KPD* could not prevail against the reactionary majority among the conspirators.[121]

This calls for some comment. In 1933, the *KPD* had already become insignificant. In the last years before Hitler's appointment as Chancellor, an increasing number of its members had switched sides. Jokingly, they were described as 'beefsteaks', outside 'brown', inside 'red'. The *KPD* had to act in secret, and took to the 'underground'. After the signing of the Hitler-Stalin pact, and until Germany's attack against Russia, the Communist parties in Germany, and in occupied Europe, were openly supportive of the German war effort. The day after German troops entered Paris, the publishers of the Communist daily, *L'Humanité*, went to the German military commander and asked for permission to continue publication.

In 1953, a monument was erected in the courtyard of the *Bendlerblock* building, where Stauffenberg and his comrades were shot on the evening of 20 July. The building was declared an official memorial. However, *Bundeswehr* barracks were named after generals of the *Reichswehr* and the *Wehrmacht*, before similar recognition was granted to the men of 20 July.

On 19 July 1954, Theodor Heuss, the first President of the German Federal Republic, finally made a speech in which he acknowledged the merits of the 'resistance': "In this hour, we acknowledge our gratitude for the idealism and the longing for a rule of law, shown by the men whose heroic death was an inspiration

---

120   Ibid, p. 204

121   H. Markmann, *Der 20. Juli 1944 und der deutsche Widerstand gegen den Nationalsozialismus in den Schulbüchern beider deutschen Staaten*, in G. Ueberschär (ed.) *Der 20. Juli. Das andere Deutschland in der Vergangenheitspolitik nach 1945*, Berlin 1998, p. 188 f

for freedom. Their blood removed the shame with which Hitler had sullied the German name."[122]

122   H. Bott (ed.) *T.Heuss, Würdigungen, Rede, Aufsätze und Briefe aus den Jahren 1949–1955*, p.424

Chapter 6

Manstein and the 'Commissar Order'

At his trial, Manstein was found guilty of compliance with the 'Commissar Order', the infamous order of 6 June 1941, that called for the immediate execution of every Red Army Commissar after capture. The tribunal found evidence that fourteen commissars were shot at 11th Army, and a further five handed over to the *SD*. However, it could not conclusively determine if commissars were executed at Manstein's LVI Motorized Corps, during the initial weeks of the war in the East. Manstein did not contest the figures. In *Verlorene Siege*, Manstein wrote that the shootings of commissars at 11th Army was in conformity with martial law. "The few Commissars who were shot were not taken prisoner on the battlefield. They were arrested in the rear, and shown to have been partisans or party functionaries. They were thus treated in accordance with martial law."[1] Manstein, of all people, ought not to have used terms such as 'international law' or 'martial law' in connection with 11th Army on the Crimea.

Searching for exact numbers of executed commissars is somewhat meaningless, since it has never been possible to determine how many commissars were shot in compliance with the 'Commissar Order'. Between July and December 1941, the Red Army lost close to 4 million prisoners-of-war. Since every Russian unit, down to company level, included a commissar, more than 30,000 commissars would have had to be shot, if the order were carried out to the extent desired by Hitler. The commissars who were executed did not even come close to that number.

The 'numbers game' continues to be played in German revisionist history. Its purpose is to set off German suffering against the sufferings that the Germans brought upon other nations. It tries to reduce the responsibility of the *Wehrmacht* for its crimes during the war of extermination in the East. Obviously, the execution of one single commissar, shot in compliance with the 'Commissar Order', is just as criminal as the shooting of thousands, or tens of thousands. The 'numbers game' is not confined to commissars.

In his book *Keine Kameraden* (No Comrades), Christian Streit arrives at a total of 3 million Russian prisoners-of-war, who perished in their camps.[2] For years, German revisionist historians disputed Streit's figures, claiming that they were exaggerated. When Soviet intelligence became available, it showed that the data given by Streit was on the low side. Alfred Streim wrote of 'at least' 2,530,000.[3]

---

1 *Verlorene Siege*, p. 177
2 C.Streit, *Keine Kameraden. Die Wehrmacht und die sowjetischen Kriegsgefangenen 1941–1945*, Bonn 1997 (henceforth: Streit)
3 A. Streim, *Sowjetische Gefangene in Hitlers Vernichtungskrieg, Berichte und Dokumente 1941–1945*. Heidelberg, 1982

Joachim Hoffmann, who saw the German attack on Russia as a preventive war, arrived at 2 million victims.[4]

Whether 2 or 3 million Russian prisoners-of-war perished, as a result of ill-treatment in their camps, the guilt of the *Wehrmacht* remains the same. 6 million dead have become a symbol for the victims of the Holocaust. The analysis by the foremost Holocaust historian, Raul Hilberg, arrives at a total of 5.1 million.[5] There is no dispute about the number of Jews murdered by the *Einsatzgruppen* in Russia, since their commanders were always eager to boast, with exact figures of their victims after every execution.

Manstein was one of the top commanders who lodged a strong protest against the 'Commissar Order'. It is established that he did his utmost to prevent it from being carried out. The main criticism that can be levelled against him, in this particular context, lies in the strategy adopted by his lawyer Paget, and his own rambling defence at his trial. Paget wrote that Manstein had 'forbidden' the execution of the order.[6] This is obvious nonsense. Although Paget would increasingly show himself an admirer of the *Nazi* regime, and an apologist of the racial extermination in Poland and in Russia, that sentence of his is evidence of his ignorance of the chain of authority in the Third Reich. No general could ever forbid the carrying out of an order by Hitler. The best he could do was to express a wish to his subordinates that an order not be executed. There is evidence that Manstein did so in connection with the 'Commissar Order'.

Manstein's attitude toward the 'Commissar Order' deserves to be emphasised, since opposition to the 'Commissar Order' was not as frequent as the memoirs of German commanders want to imply. Manstein's predecessor at 11th Army, *Generaloberst* Eugen Ritter von Schobert showed himself a ruthless executioner of commissars. Manstein described Schobert as a 'Bavarian noble mind', a 'commander whom his soldiers cherished in their hearts.'[7] 'His heart was with his soldiers' or 'his soldiers cherished him' are typical stereotypes in the memoirs of German generals. One might just as well say that a commander, whose heart is not with his troops, can never be a good commander. A typical order, issued by the 'Bavarian noble mind', contained the sentence, "Better to take charge of too many than too few."[8]

At his trial before the IMT, (Case 12, also called the *OKW* trial) *Generaloberst* von Salmuth described Schobert as having been a man totally devoted to Hitler, who would blindly follow any order issued by him." A few days later, Salmuth retracted his statement and said, that "Schobert could not be included among the National-Socialist believers. He was a decent and honourable man, a pure idealist. If he followed Hitler's ideas, it was only because he believed in them as in the 'amen' at the end of a prayer."[9] General Wöhler, chief-of-staff of 11th Army, saw Schobert as "a man who believed in Hitler and who was totally convinced that

---

4   J. Hoffmann, *Stalins Vernichtungskrieg 1941–1945*, Munich 1995

5   R.Hilberg, *Die Vernichtung der europäischen Juden*, Frankfurt 1990, vol.3, p.1.299 (henceforth: Hilberg)

6   Paget, p. 161

7   *Verlorene Siege*, p. 208

8   Krausnick, p.216.

9   IMT, Case 12, p.3.889 and p. 3.913 (henceforth: IMT, Case 12)

Hitler had a historic mission. However, I do not feel that Schobert can be viewed as an enthusiastic follower of the National-Socialist party line."[10]

When *Generalleutnant* Karl Hollidt, a deeply religious man, who commanded 5th Infantry Division in 11th Army, received the 'Commissar Order', he sank into depression. He turned to his Corps Commander, General Erik Hansen, and told him that his faith forbade him to persecute people who had fallen into his power, but only on the grounds of different political views. Hansen replied that the order was valid for the whole Front in the East and that he could do nothing. Hansen then made an appeal to Schobert, who told him that "Hollidt was a soldier who had to carry out orders. Orders received from highest authority may not be discussed."[11]

Wöhler had already received a dressing-down from Schobert. He had proposed to him to limit executions to the commissars who had committed crimes, who under general law were subject to the death penalty. Schobert told him sternly: "One cannot throw an order, sent *ex cathedra*, into the waste paper basket or simply put it into the files."[12] At Nuremberg, Wöhler stated that he had a guilty conscience, adding that he could not request his 'relief' on ground of disagreement with his commander about a *Führer* order. Later, in the Crimea, Wöhler had no such qualms about the execution of Jews by the *Einsatzgruppen* and repeatedly put troops of 11th Army at their disposal. When Manstein succeeded Schobert at the head of 11th Army, Wöhler immediately questioned him about his attitude, and felt relieved when Manstein told him that he opposed the 'Commissar Order'. [13]

At Nuremberg, in his plea for *OKW* and the *Generalstab*, Dr Laternser stated,

When Hitler mentioned this plan, which had been prepared solely by him, in his address to the Generals in March 1941, he immediately encountered the strongest rejection from all commanders present. They had been raised in a spirit of humanity and soldierly ethos. All attempts of the Generals at *OKW* and *OKH* had failed to put a halt to formalising Hitler's views in a written order. The 'Commissar Order' was issued, the commanders of Army Groups and Armies either abstained from forwarding it to the units under their command, or they gave instructions to disobey it. They acted in full knowledge of their risk of being severely punished for open disobedience of an order, by their Supreme Commander, in war-time. An additional order by the Commander in Chief of the Army, Brauchitsch, to preserve discipline, accomplished the desired effect. It gave the commanders at the front the tool they needed to act according to their conviction. The military leadership thus knew that the 'Commissar Order' was not complied with at all Army Groups and Armies.[14]

Those are indeed elevated words, but they are simply not true. There never were "all efforts by *OKW* and *OKH*". Obviously, no commander could refuse to communicate the order to his subordinates. Statements made by some Generals in

---

10   Ibid, p. 5.562
11   Friedrich, p. 595
12   IMT, Case 12, p. 5.580 also Friedrich, p. 597
13   Ibid, p.5.582
14   Also quoted in Streit, p. 45

their memoirs, that they had never received the order, have been exposed as lies. Guderian wrote that he had never seen the *Barbarossa* Order nor the 'Commissar Order'. Perhaps Army Group Centre had refrained from communicating them to him.[15] The *Barbarossa* Order was even more horrible than the 'Commissar Order'. It gave German soldiers, and persons in *Wehrmacht* employment, a free hand to commit crimes against the Russian civilian population, without having to face prosecution.

Guderian's statement is shown to be untrue, by an order from General Joachim Lemelsen, commander of XLVII *Panzer* Corps in Guderian's *Panzergruppe* 2. General Lemelsen had protested against the shooting of prisoners-of-war in a general manner, but added that "prisoners, who could be shown to have been commissars, had to be immediately taken aside and shot, in each instance upon an order given by an officer to the firing-squad."[16]

Lemelsen's order is a typical example of the divisions in the mentality of the German officers. On one side, a continued adherence to military tradition, that prisoners-of-war may not be molested, on the other, an abandoning of the same tradition, as soon as the victim is a representative of the *Bolshevist* system. The Ia of 17th *Panzer* Division in Lemelsen's Corps, confirmed that the 'Commissar Order' had been transmitted to him through normal channels, ie XLVII Corps, by direct instruction from Guderian.[17] Furthermore, Guderian reported directly to *OKW* that his *Panzergruppe* 2 had taken only few prisoners-of-war during the first days of the campaign, but that by the beginning of August, 170 commissars had been 'shunt off' ie *abgeschoben*.[18]

Undoubtedly, a refusal by a high commander to communicate the 'Commissar Order' would have been immediately communicated to Hitler, and the general responsible would have been severely punished. However, there is no record of any General punished for that reason. German archive documents show that the 'Commissar Order' was carried out in all units of the army, the only exception being *Generalmajor* Hans-Heinrich Sixt von Armin's 17th *Panzer* Division.[19] Brauchitsch's 'additional order', mentioned by Dr Laternser, did not concern the 'Commissar Order', but part II of the *Barbarossa* Order. It read:

II. 1. Acts committed by soldiers of the *Wehrmacht* or persons in its employment against enemy civilians, even if they are crimes under military law, need not be prosecuted. Military courts may order prosecution only if such acts endanger discipline or the safety of the troops. This includes, *inter alia*, severe acts of sexual molestation, deeds resulting from a criminal disposition of the perpetrator, or deeds that show a danger that troops may become dissolute.

2. Such deeds should be seen against the background that the military collapse of 1918, the sufferings of the German people, and the internal

---

15 Guderian, p. 138
16 Streit, p.104
17 Ibid, also in minutes of the Nuremberg trial, vol. 35, p. 156 ff
18 BA-MA, RH 21-3/v. 423
19 Förster, p.1.063, with reference to diary Halder, vol. 3, p. 243

struggle against National-Socialism with its many victims, were decisively due to *Bolshevist* influence. No German is allowed to forget this.[20]

Brauchitsch's additional order, of 24 May 1941, had the wording:

… All Commanders have to keep in mind that individual acts of violence committed by solders cannot be permitted, and they have to prevent a development of unruliness in their units. The individual soldier must never get the feeling that 'he can simply do what he wants' in Russia. In every case he has to obey orders by his officers. I request that this be made totally clear down to the smallest unit. Immediate steps by officers, in particular Company Commanders, must strive to maintain strict discipline, (*Manneszucht*), the foundation of our previous successes.[21]

Brauchitsch stated at Nuremberg that he had issued an additional order of his own to soften the impact of the 'Commissar Order'.[22] This statement is likewise not true. On 8 June 1941, Brauchitsch issued a directive that civilian political commissars, who are treated separately in the 'Commissar Order', who can be shown to have acted in a hostile manner against the *Wehrmacht*, or who can be suspected of such intentions, have to be taken aside after capture, and shot in an 'inconspicuous (*unauffällig*) manner.'[23] The reader will have to judge, if 'inconspicuous shooting' of civilian commissars is a softening of an order, which was mainly concerned with military commissars.

Literature

British and American books on the Second World War make only scant reference to the 'Commissar Order'. Neither Pierre Masson nor Matthew Cooper mention it in their books on the *Wehrmacht*. In his book on the Russo-German war, Albert Seaton makes a few statements about the part played by commissars in the Red Army. The 'Commissar Order' is only mentioned in a footnote, which bears no relation to reality:

It was originally intended, that the German Army should shoot the commissars on capture, and it appears that the *OKH* framed a draft on the *Führer's* order. Halder, according to his diary on 6 May, seems to have been briefed on the drafting of such orders by the Judge Advocate's Department. A draft order was sent from *OKH* to *OKW* for concurrence. Later, an attempt was made to withdraw the order, it being understood that the *SD* (*Sicherheitsdienst*) would carry out the executions.[24]

Seaton expressed himself in a similar vein his work on the German Army:

---

20 *NOKW* 3357
21 M. Messerschmidt, *Die Wehrmacht im NS-Staat. Zeit der Indoktrination*, Hamburg 1969, p. 25 (henceforth: Messerschmidt)
22 Ibid, p.p. 257. Also minutes of the Nuremberg trial, vol. 22, p. 622
23 Minutes of the Nuremberg trial, vol. 22, p. 624 f
24 Seaton, War, p.54, footnote 8

Then followed the notorious order by which the Red Army commissars were to be denied the treatment normally accorded to prisoners-of-war. The draft orders for those, following the *Führer*'s order, appear to have been actually initiated in the *OKH* and sent to the *OKW* for concurrence.[25]

In Liddell Hart's anthology on the history of the Russian Army, the 'Commissar Order' is not mentioned. Only one essay deals with the commissars during the Russian civil war.[26] John Eriksson likewise failed to mention the 'Commissar Order' in his book on the Soviet high command.[27] Authors of works on purely military history can hardly be blamed for practically ignoring the 'Commissar Order', since it had no effect upon military operations. It only resulted in a fanatical will by the commissars to fight until the very last, since they knew the fate they had to expect.

However, for different reasons, most Russian works of military history ignore the 'Commissar Order'. *IVOVS* limits itself to one short sentence in its first volume: "Tens of thousands of Russian prisoners-of-war died in the fascist camps."[28] The background for this silence is obvious. In the official Soviet version, Russian prisoners-of-war were simply not allowed to have existed. The Germans captured Stalin's son from his first marriage, Captain Yakov Djugashvili. They then approached Stalin through diplomatic channels for an exchange of important prisoners. Stalin is known to have replied: "We have no prisoners-of-war, only traitors." Most of the Red Army's prisoners-of-war, who returned home after the victory of Germany, were immediately arrested, under the provisions of article 58 b of the penal code of the RSFSR, and sentenced to several years in the *Gulag*.

Stalin's personal order Nr. 270 contained a paragraph to the effect that next-of-kin of commanders and political officers who had surrendered, were to be arrested. No assistance was to be granted to families of ordinary soldiers. When Stalin was informed about his son's capture, he immediately ordered that his daughter-in-law be arrested and kept in isolation. After Yakov Djugashvili was shot in his camp, under circumstances which have never been clarified, Stalin ordered her release.

In 1943, I, as a refugee in Switzerland, spent a few months as an interpreter in a camp for escaped Russian prisoners-of-war. Even at that time, the Russians expressed fear for their fate after their return to their homeland. One of their spokesmen, Lieutenant Ivan Klimenko, succeeded in escaping from the Soviet repatriation commission, headed by General Dragun. Klimenko obtained Swiss asylum after the war. He is mentioned in Nicolay Tolstoy's *Victims of Yalta*.[29] The Russian internees received parcels of groceries and medical supplies from home, at regular intervals, only because the Soviet authorities feared that inspections of the Swiss camps by the Red Cross, and by foreign diplomats, could reveal their lack of

25   Seaton, Army, p. 168
26   L. Shapiro, *The Birth of the Red Army*, in B. Liddell-Hart (ed.), *The Soviet Army*, London 1956, p. 24 ff
27   J. Ericksson, *The Soviet High Command. A Military-Political History*, London 1962
28   *IVOVS*, vol. 1, p. 551
29   N. Tolstoy, *Victims of Yalta*, London 1977, p. 381

interest in their countrymen. The gifts were also intended to create the illusion among the internees of a hearty welcome upon returning home.

Discrimination against former prisoners-of-war continued during the *Glasnost* period. Streit's book on the mistreatment of Russian prisoners-of-war was translated into Russian immediately after its publication in 1978. However, it was kept under 'lock-and-key' as a 'top secret' document.[30] In 1992/94, the *Voyenno-Istoritcheskyi Zhurnal* printed excerpts in fourteen consecutive issues. During his famous speech at the 20th Congress of the Russian Communist party, Krushchev proclaimed an amnesty for former prisoners-of-war. However, no formal rehabilitation occurred. In 1987, the official daily newspaper of the Soviet government, *Isvestia,* demanded that the honourable reputation of former prisoners-of-war be officially recognised. The Red Army immediately objected. Its official publication, *Krasnaya Sviezda,* wrote in a lead story, that capture in war was "only shame, corruption and dishonour." In December 1994, President Yelzin signed a decree that restored the rights of former prisoners-of-war. However, they were not permitted to take part in the parade on Red Square, held in celebration of the fiftieth anniversary of victory.

Even today, Russian authors remain reluctant to write about the commissars and are less than eager to give details of their activities during the war. The book by Nekrich and Heller, *History of the Soviet Union,* was permitted to appear in 1980, after having circulated in typed clandestine shape. Even in it, there is only one short sentence: "One month before the beginning of their attack on the USSR, the High Command of the German ground forces had ordered that all captured political functionaries had to be immediately liquidated."[31]

A Russian historian, Michael Morozov, wrote a book on the general history of the Red Army.[32] Morozov defected to the West. His book appeared in 1982 and is written in German. It gives a detailed account of the changes in the status of the commissars, while avoiding writing about their activities. The Commissars were certainly no innocent angels. The Stalin 'terror' was largely based on denunciation. Many commissars did denounce their commanders as 'enemies of the people'. That had no bearing on the criminal character of the 'Commissar Order'. Whatever deeds the Commissars may have been guilty of against their own people, they were not under the jurisdiction of German law and courts.

A German history of the *Wehrmacht,* with appeal to a wider public, still remains to be written, in spite of the availability of exceptionally comprehensive documentation at various German archives. For the German readership that is regrettable. They are restricted to foreign writings that, in recent years, have become the subject of increasingly heated dispute. It was ignited by an exhibition, *Vernichtungskrieg. Verbrechen der Wehrmacht 1941 bis 1944* (War of extermination. Crimes of the *Wehrmacht* 1941–1944). The exhibition was shown in a number of German and Austrian cities in the 1990s. It attracted hundreds of thousands of visitors, and led to violent debates in the *Bundestag.*

---

30 Streit, p. 23
31 M. Heller/A. Nekrich, *Ot zhimnego dvorca do kremlyovskoy steni. Ocherkyi sovietskoy istoryi ot 1917 do nashich dneyi,* Moscow 1980, vol. 2, p.80
32 M. Morozov, *Die Falken des Kremls. Die sowjetische Militärmacht von 1917 bis heute,* Munich 1982

The exhibition was closed down, after two historians, one Polish and one Hungarian, showed that a number of photographs, purported to show mass shootings by the Germans, were in fact pictures of executions by the NKVD, before the Germans penetrated Russia. The mix-up was gross negligence by the organisers, the Hamburg Institute for Social Research. Genuine photos were available in more than sufficient quantity. Disputes between German historians, about the part played by the *Wehrmacht* in crimes committed in the East, are beginning to abate. Among serious German historians there is a consensus that many commanders and units of the *Wehrmacht* were guilty of 'unspeakable crimes'. That has to be welcomed, for the Germans must finally come to terms with their past, and view their Army of the Second World War as it really was.

When discussions about the *Wehrmacht* exhibition became increasingly violent, a group of prominent German personalities published an anthology, *Die Soldaten der Wehrmacht*,[33] (Soldiers of the *Wehrmacht*), with the purpose of contradicting the more radical elements of the exhibition. It was produced under pressure of time and is therefore of doubtful quality. Whilst a few chapters are written by eminent historians, most are typical examples of revisionist literature.

Sources for that chapter are the works of:

* Manfred Messerschmidt, *Die Wehrmacht im NS-Staat, Zeit der Indoktrination* (The *Wehrmacht* in the NS-State. Years of indoctrination.)
* Christian Streit, *Keine Kameraden.* (No comrades.)
* Jörg Friedrich, *Das Gesetz des Krieges. Das deutsche Heer in Russland 1941 bis 1945. Der Prozess gegen das Oberkommando der Wehrmacht.* (Laws of war. The German Army in Russia 1941–1945. The trial of the *OKW*.)[34]
* Jürgen Förster, *Die Sicherung des Lebensraumes* (securing the '*Lebensraum*'.) in volume 4 of the *MGFA* anthology on the Second World War.[35]
* Horst Rohde's chapter *Politische Indoktrination in höheren Stäben und in der Truppe untersucht am Beispiel des Kommissarbefehls* (Political indoctrination at staff and troop level – seen against the example of the 'Commisar Order'), in *Die Soldaten der Wehrmacht.*[36]
* Krausnick/Wilhelm's standard work about the *Einsatzgruppen*, includes the minutes of the Nuremberg trial and of IMT, case 12 and the minutes of Manstein's trial.[37]

Only Rohde's chapter deals exclusively with the 'Commissar Order'. It is an example of revisionist attempts to reduce the level of *Wehrmacht* responsibility for crimes committed in the East. It also coupled personal attacks on authors who

---

33 *Die Soldaten der Wehrmacht,* H.Poeppel, W.-K., Prince of Prussia, K.-G.von Hase (ed.), Munich 1998 (henceforth: *Soldaten Wehrmacht*).

34 J. Friedrich, *Das Gesetz des Krieges. Das deutsche Heer in Russland 1941–1945. Der Prozess gegen das Oberkommando der Wehrmacht,* Munich 1993 (hencforth:Friedrich)

35 J. Förster, *Die Sicherung des Lebensaums,* in *Das deutsche Reich und der Zweite Weltkrieg,* vol. 4 of the *MGFA* anthology, Stuttgart 1983, p.1.030-1.978 (henceforth: Förster)

36 Ibid, p.124–159

37 Minutes of the Manstein trial, English version, Holocaust Memorial Museum Yad Vashem, Jerusalem, some pages without number (henceforth: Trial)

disagreed. Rohde criticized Streit for only showing documents that were part of the evidence presented at trials for war crimes.[38] However, that is not true. Streit shows reports from 17 major units, with reports on the execution of commissars.[39] Meanwhile, Rohde limits himself to documents from ten units, mostly Divisions, and some transit camps. Rohde views the laconic style of reports about commissar executions, such as 'one commissar shot according to orders', 'enemy dead 3,053, among them three commissars', 'one commissar executed' etc, as evidence of no political tendencies in the execution reports. One could certainly question if there were more to report about the executions. The reports prescribed by *OKH* only requested numbers and not additional descriptions. Rohde furthermore argued that terms like 'shunt-off', 'treated in accordance of regulations', need not necessarily mean executions.[40] He overlooks the fact that such euphemisms were common practice in German reports, in efforts to replace too many direct mentions of executions. Rohde's repeated efforts to show that the 'Commissar Order' was not carried out to the extent foreseen by Hitler, are somewhat superfluous, since there is no disagreement on that point, regardless of the political views of historians.

During his years as head of *MGFA* history department, Professor Messerschmidt came in for strong criticism, often accompanied by unnecessary personal attacks by revisionist authors. While Messerschmidt at times presented one-sided views, an objective historian has to recognise that his standard work, with its wealth of material, has laid the foundations for the present debate about the *Wehrmacht*.

Friedrich's book, of more than one thousand pages, remains the only comprehensive account of the IMT Case 12 trial. Friedrich does not write in the usual dry, close-to-boring style, which is the trademark of many German historians. He often adds sarcastic comments of his own, but every statement of his is supported by incontrovertible documentary evidence.

The 'Commissar-Order' – the planning stage and the final wording.

Hitler's speech to his generals on 30 March 1941 and the planning

On 30 March 1941, in a speech to his commanders, Hitler issued general outlines of the methods with which the war was to be conducted in the East. The meeting was attended by some 250 Generals who were expected to command Army Groups, Armies, Corps and Divisions in the East, and their chiefs-of-staff. Manstein was present as one of the Corps Commanders. Halder jotted down stenographic notes in his diary. Italics are in the original:

> Colonial duties! *War between two philosophies of life.* Devastating judgement of Communism, which is antisocial crime. Communism is an enor-

---

38 Ibid, p. 148
39 Streit, p.88 ff
40 Ibid, p. 137

mous danger for the future. We must retreat from traditional military comradeship. The Communist was never a 'comrade', and will never be a 'comrade'. It is a war of extermination. Even if we do not understand this, we will still vanquish the enemy. But in thirty years from now we will face the same communist enemy again. We are not making war to preserve the life of the enemy.

War against Russia:

Elimination of the Commissars and communist 'intelligentsia'. The new states to be created must be socialist states, without any 'intelligentsia' of their own. On no account can a new intelligentsia be permitted to develop. A primitive socialist 'intelligentsia' is sufficient. War must be waged against the poison of subversion. This is no matter for courts-martial. The commanders have to know their duties. They have to lead. Troops will defend themselves with the same means with which they are attacked. Commissars and GPU-men are criminals and will be treated as criminals.

Soldiers may not become detached from the officers. Officers have to take their decisions in accordance with the feelings of their soldiers. (Halder added his own note: War will be different from the war in the West. In the East, hardship looks mild, when viewed against the future.) Officers have to overcome any apprehension for themselves. (Note by Halder: order by Commander in Chief of the Army.)[41]

That speech was the first indication of the methods with which the war against Russia was to be conducted. 'War of extermination' is clearly mentioned and the emergence of the 'Jewish-*Bolshevist* subhuman' is not far away. Already, back in 1933, Reichenau had voiced similar views:

All that is rotten in the state has to disappear, this can only be achieved by terror. The party will be ruthless against Marxism. Duty for the army: guns ready for battle. No assistance, if people turn to the Army for help from persecution.[42]

Even before the attack on Russia, the slogan of the subhuman had penetrated the orders of the day issued by the German Commanders. Later, it became commonplace.

During the autumn months of 1941, *Generaloberst* Strauss, *OB* of 9th Army, requested, in contravention to all international conventions, the use of Russian prisoners-of-war for work of a military purpose. He added that the Russians should consider themselves lucky if they were given two thirds of the rations available to German soldiers. Naturally 'Asiatic subhumanity' had to remain confined to camps. But their employment by the *Wehrmacht* would provide them for the rest of their lives with the advantage of having obtained knowledge of German discipline.[43]

---

41   Halder personal diary, vol. II, p. 336 f.
42   Streit, p. 57
43   Förster, p. 1.056, with reference to BA-MA, RH 23/219, *AOK*9, Ia, Nr. 4346

One may add that the Soviet government had turned to Germany in June 1941, through diplomatic channels, with a request that both sides observe the Geneva Convention. No German reply was received. Hitler's repeated order to the Commanders, to adapt themselves to the feelings of their soldiers, could be a sign that he was somewhat uncertain of their approval. No General, who had listened to that speech, could claim after the war that he had no knowledge of the criminal methods foreseen in the East.

Halder declared that he wrote down his notes to show his disapproval after the war. That was a usual post-war argument of German Generals – in the case of Halder it is simply a lie. Pursuant to the address of 30 March, Halder issued an order, under his own signature, stipulating harsh measures against the civilian population in occupied territories in the East:

Any attempt of active or passive resistance by the civilian population has to be nipped in the bud with sharp measures. A self-assured and drastic attitude towards the hostile population is the best means for prevention. At an early stage, clear knowledge must be obtained as to whom the Army can rely on in occupied territories. Such parts of the Russian population who are hostile to the Soviet state and system, must be made useful to German interests, if necessary, by means of some material advantages and the granting of modest liberties.[44]

At Nuremberg, Brauchitsch stated that strong protests were voiced by all Generals after Hitler had left the room, and that he had told them that he would not comply with Hitler's requests, but with orders under his own signature. Why did such protests only occur after Hitler had left the room? Why not in his presence? Had Hitler then relieved 'all the generals' and had them arrested? With whom could he conduct his war against Russia, if all commanders of Army Groups, Armies, Corps, Divisions and their Chiefs-of-staff had been dismissed on one day? Reality is often at odds with German Generals' post-war statements. Brauchitsch later issued a number of orders, in the spirit of Hitler's address, under his own name. Little is known about the objections of German Commanders to the methods with which the war in the East was conducted.

Manstein was present when Hitler made his speech on 30 March 1941, although he significantly omitted to mention it in *Verlorene Siege*. Had he done so, he would not have been able to keep to his many post-war statements that he knew nothing about the criminal methods used in the East. During his years as Commander in Chief of the Army, Brauchitsch was never able to lodge a protest with Hitler, since Hitler immediately cut him off and showered him with insults.

On 7 December 1941, Halder noted in his diary: "The last days are again shattering and disgraceful. The Commander in Chief of the Army has become a 'mailman'." Hitler talked directly to Army Group Commanders without bothering to inform him.[45]

---

44   *OKH*/GenStdH. Gen.Qu/Abt. Kriegsverwaltung, Nr.II/0315/41, gKdos. Chefs. 3.4.41, BA-MA. RH 22/v.11
45   Messerschmidt, p. 259

On 6 May 1941, *Generalleutnant* Eugen Müller, in charge of structural matters at *OKH*, sent a first draft to *Generalmajor* Walter Warlimont, Jodl's deputy at *OKW*:

Political functionaries and commanders ie commissars, represent an increased danger for the security of our troops and the pacification of occupied territories. If such persons are captured in combat, or arrested in another manner, they have to be brought immediately to an officer, at least a Company Commander. The officer will call two more military, either Officers or Non-Commissioned Officers, in order to determine if the prisoner in question is a commissar. If this can be established in a manner deemed sufficient, the Company Commander will immediately order the execution of the prisoner and supervise the carrying out of the execution.

The Commissars at Red Army units are political functionaries. Their speedy discovery and their isolation is of overriding importance, since they will continue their propaganda activities among other prisoners-of-war. If possible, they should be shot at collection points for prisoners-of-war, at the very latest when in transit-camps. Functionaries with the party administration, as well as other political personalities captured by the troops, will be treated in the same manner as commissars. Political functionaries at industrial plants, or other economical entities, will only be arrested if it can be shown that they have acted against the interests of the *Wehrmacht*. On no account may captured political functionaries and commissars be 'shunted-off' to the rear.[46]

Warlimont wrote in his memoirs that he was 'most painfully surprised', that the Commander in Chief of the Army had found it necessary to put Hitler's guidelines into a written order, to be communicated to the troops. Until then, they had only been known to a small group of officers and probably already forgotten. Warlimont refers further to a hand-written comment of his on Müller's draft: "Please examine if a written order is at all required."[47] Warlimont's "painful surprise' can be doubted, particularly since he received a life sentence at the IMT. It may be assumed that Warlimont simply wanted to 'pass the buck' to Keitel, Jodl, Brauchitsch and Halder. It will be difficult to find logic in his statement. If supreme command wanted to have the 'Commissar Order' carried out throughout the Eastern front, a written order was obviously required.

A number of drafts went back and forth from *OKW* to *OKH*. Their text offers no particular interest, except for an impatient hand-written note from Jodl on one of the drafts which read: "Finally, the paper has to be shown to the *Führer*. Since we can expect reprisals against captured German airmen, we had better word the 'Commissar Order' as a reprisal measure of our own." Reprisals against whom? The commissars or other functionaries who had no previous contact with the Germans? Streit feels that Jodl's comments are evidence of Jodl's understanding that the 'Commissar Order' violated international law,

---

46   W. Warlimont, *Im Hauptquartier der deutschen Wehrmacht 1939–1945. Grundlagen-Formen-Gestalten*, Bonn 1964, p. 178 (henceforth: Warlimont)

47   Ibid, p. 179 f

and of his personal approval only provided some mysterious wording could be added.[48]

The final wording

The 'Commissar Order' was given its final wording at *OKH* on 6 June 1941 and distributed in 340 copies to the commanders, down to division level:

> In the fight against *Bolshevism*, the enemy is not expected to act in accordance with conventions of humanity and international law.
>
> The troops must remain conscious:
>
> 1. In this struggle, forbearance and observation of international law towards these elements is out of place. They are a danger for our security and the peaceful administration of conquered territory.
>
> 2. The Commissars are the creators of barbaric and Asiatic combat methods. They must be dispensed with immediately and with utmost severity. The troops must be given to understand that any mercy shown to commissars endangers their security and the peaceful administration of conquered territory. Therefore, when captured during battle or when resisting capture, commissars must be executed immediately. Commissars are not recognised as soldiers. International law concerning prisoners-of-war is not applicable to them. They will be separated from other prisoners and liquidated.[49]

The remainder of the document contained detailed instructions of the procedures under which the order was to be executed. It required regular reports, about the number of Commissars shot, to be sent to *OKW*. Some corps and divisions sent daily reports, others lumped them together in communications at intervals of two weeks.

The order was signed by *Generalleutnant* Eugen Müller and counter-signed by his adc Major Bernhard Bechler. Bechler told Rees that he was "very proud to have his name appearing on an order. At that time, victory was obvious. And had we won, everything would have been fine."[50] In a later part of the movie 'War of the Century', Bechler boasted of his heroic hand-to-hand fighting at Stalingrad, before being taken prisoner. Bechler was careful not to tell Rees anything about his later life. In captivity, Bechler joined the *BDO* and immediately spied on his comrades. After his liberation, he became the first minister of the interior of the Eastern German province of Brandenburg. He was then taken into the *NVA* as a *Generalmajor*, registered as an informer (*IM*) with the East German secret police, the *Stasi*, and denounced his superiors. When his wife was arrested, he repudiated her in a public statement, obtained a quick divorce and married a communist functionary. After the re-unification of Germany, his first wife published her story.

---

48   Streit, p. 47
49   N *OKW* 1076
50   Rees, p. 33.

The mention of 'barbaric Asiatic' methods of war, which would be repeated in countless appeals by German commander, can cause some surprise, since Germany's only strong ally was Japan. No German General ever attempted to explain what Asiatic methods consisted of. Furthermore, only 25% of the Soviet population were of Asiatic origin

The IMT described the 'Commissar Order' as "one of the most heinous, despicable orders ever issued by any army."[51] The IMT insisted upon the word 'army.' More atrocious orders had been issued by the *Nazi*-Regime, such as the *Barbarossa* Order and the *Euthanasia* Order of 1 September 1939, which was the forerunner of the Holocaust. However, the drafting of the 'Commissar Order' was the work of *OKH* and it was issued under its responsibility.

The 'Commissar Order' in practical terms

Shootings of captured commissars began on the first day of the Russian campaign. Although, until the repeal of the order, the total number of executions has never been established, many commanders were careful to remove execution reports from the diaries of their units. It became increasingly evident that the expected *Blitzkrieg* victory was not to be. Such figures, as can be gathered from archive documents that were not destroyed, show that they were greatly in excess of what German generals wanted to imply. Förster shows that *Panzergruppe* 4, under Hoepner, reported 172 executions up to 19 July 1941, 2nd Army, under von Weichs, 172 shootings up to 24 July 1941. *Panzergruppe* 3, under Hoth, showed 130 executions by the end of July 1941, and 44th Infantry Division, 122 by the end of September 1941.[52]

A table presented by Streit, based upon archive documents of reports chosen at random, shows 1,008 Commissars executed at all three Army Groups during the months of June to December 1941.[53] Streit emphasised that his table was far from complete and that he only intended to show the style in which the report documents were worded. [54]Rohde arrived at 700 executions at most. However, he confined himself to the statement without attempting to go into details of the many reports which, taken together, showed much higher figures.[55] A flat statement, without any attempt at substantiation, is of little value.

A number of Generals had already protested against the order at an early stage of the fighting. Their objections were solely motivated by military considerations, due to the unexpected course taken by the operations. Only Manstein advanced moral arguments and stated that the 'Commissar Order' was contrary to all military traditions and ethics ie *unsoldatisch*. In his rambling defence at his own trial, Manstein buried the ethical value of his objections in a thicket of utter confusion.

On 23 September 1941, General Müller wrote to *OKW* and requested to have the order reviewed, against the background of the military situation that had developed:

---

51   IMT, Case 12 (*OKW* Trial), p. 90
52   Förster, p. 1.064, with reference to the archives of the units mentioned by him
53   Streit, p. 88 f
54   Streit, p. 88 f
55   *Soldaten Wehrmacht*, p. 142

The commissar is aware that 'death waits for him' if he is captured. There-fore many continue to resist until the very end and order their troops to do likewise. In the present situation there are signs of relaxation of the will to fight on, by the Russian soldier. Should the 'Commissar Order' be suspended, further desperate resistance may become increasingly para-lysed. This will spare us many casualties. Perhaps we should strive instead for greater efforts of propaganda. The Commander in Chief of the Army shares these views, which have been presented to him. He feels that they deserve careful attention and that a review of the treatment of captured commissars must now be considered.[56]

Jodl gave a hand-written reply on the back page of Müller's note: "The *Führer* has taken note of the proposals and declines any change in the treatment of captured commissars."[57]

The increasing strength of Soviet resistance was obviously not as a result of orders issued by the commissars. The expected *Blitzkrieg* had never materialised. Many Russian commanders felt increasingly that the Germans had finally found their masters. Doubts about the value of the 'Commissar Order' had set in at an early date. Even by 2 July 1941, when the *Wehrmacht* still felt confident of its success, *Generalleutnant* Kurt Brennecke, chief-of-staff of Army Group North, instructed the chief-of-staff of *Panzergruppe* 4: "I deem it necessary to destroy the *OKH* order, to avoid it falling into enemy hands and being used as propaganda against us."[58]

On 14 August 1941, *Panzergruppe* 3 raised objections:

The treatment of captured commissars has become known to the Russians and led to increased resistance. It would have been preferable to have commissars executed far back in the rear area. Most captured Red Army offi-cers and soldiers say that they are aware of the special treatment of captured commissars. They had obtained extensive knowledge from captured docu-ments, and from commissars who had succeeded in escaping after capture.[59]

On 17 September 1941, *General der Panzertruppe* Rudolf Schmidt, commander of XXXIX Corps lodged a particularly strong protest with 16h Army, under Busch:

The campaign in the East has shown that the *Bolshevist* resistance by far exceeds all our expectations. The Red Army has a corps of younger offi-cers and non-commissioned officers who have shown ample evidence that they can keep its troops together, both in attack and in defence.

The pre-Revolutionary leadership has emigrated, but the younger intelligentsia and the working class are committed communists. Every attempt of an overthrow of the regime has always been 'nipped in the bud' with brutal force. It was nonsensical on our part to imagine that the war could lead to a revolution against the Soviet system. We can daily see that

---

56 *NOKW* 200
57 Messerschmidt, p. 406, footnote 1.348, with correction of a statement by Warlimont
58 *NOKW* 3136
59 *NOKW* 1904

that the commissars continue to fight because they know that we will shoot them on capture. Such feelings will increase as the war progresses. The Russian people are not given any idea about our future intentions for them.

As a first step, the 'Commissar Order' must be cancelled forthwith. As long as the commissars defend themselves against certain death, they will stick together. Even our threats are sufficient to weld them together. If a commissar knows that he can save his life by deserting, the general 'will-to-resist' may become more relaxed. In a broader perspective, it is of paramount importance to show the Russian people a positive future.[60]

Only General Schmidt showed some political vision. The other protests were motivated solely by the strong resistance of the Red Army and fears that the Russians would obtain knowledge of the 'Commissar Order'. Yet, in spite of his protest, General Schmidt complied with the order. In his list, Streit shows that 20th *Panzer* Division reported to Schmidt's XXXIX Corps that it had executed twenty, up to 5 July. He quotes reports from other Divisions of the Corps about the execution of commissars during the first two days of the campaign.

By the end of winter 1941, the number of Russian prisoners-of-war decreased drastically and few more commissars were captured. Hitler could now be convinced that the 'Commissar Order' had missed its purpose. On 6 May 1942, he decided to suspend it, "in order to strengthen the wish of the Russian soldiers to surrender or to defect. For this purpose, an attempt should be made to show to the commissars that they can perhaps save their lives."[61] The 'suspension', in fact the repeal of the 'Commissar Order', remained in force until Germany's defeat.

Excursus: The Commissars in the Red Army – German ignorance and reality

German ignorance

During the Second World War, the Germans were undisputed masters at issuing orders in total ignorance of their background. No German General, regardless of his attitude to the 'Commissar Order', had the slightest inkling of what a Commissar was, what his functions were, or what he represented. No one had ever attempted to acquaint himself with the many facets of the Soviet system. It was easier to rely on Hitler's speech of 30 March 1941 and the description of the commissar in the 'Commissar Order'. Manstein shared that ignorance, his stuttering defence at his trial gave ample evidence.

A general never sees a commissar. He is not present at his capture and the 'Commissar Order' calls for execution immediately after identification. Commissars were identified by a star, surrounded by a hammer and sickle on their right sleeves. As soon as they heard about the 'Commissar Order', many commissars removed them. Therefore General Müller was in a rush to write to *OKH* on 14 July

---

60   *NOKW* 2413
61   *NOKW* 1807

1941: "With the rapid progress of our advance, there is an increasing danger that commissars will slip unidentified into prisoner-of-war camps. The Ic have to be ordered never to relax in their search for commissars."[62]

Streit wrote:

> Knowledge of the Commissars was restricted to articles in the NS press and the recollection of some former *Freikorps* soldiers. Significantly, not a single document in the files of the authorities that participated in the drawing up of the 'Commissar Order', mentioned any effort to obtain a reliable view of the Commissar institution. Neither the military nor the political leadership had any interest in such research.[63]

The 'knowledge' that was imparted to the soldiers is shown in circular Nr. 116 to the troops (*Mitteilung an die Truppe*) of June 1941:

> Everybody knows what a *Bolshevist* is if he has looked at the face of a Red Commissar. No theoretical explanations are necessary. It would be an insult to animals if the facial traits of these slave-drivers of men, many of whom are of Jewish origin, were to be described as animal. They embody the inferno and the personified hatred of noble humanity. The Commissars personify the mad hatred of the sub-human against noble blood. The masses whom they drive to death with all their means of ice-cold terror and stupid indoctrination could have led to the end of all meaningful life, if they had not been halted at the last moment.[64]

Friedrich gave the text of leaflets that German planes dropped behind the Russian lines, with appeals to murder Commissars:

> Kill the executioners and the Commissars, don't believe your swindlers and your political leaders. Cross the lines and come over to us. Kill all Commissars and all Jews. They are your misfortune.

> Turn your bayonets around and join us in our fight against the cursed Jewish Commissars. Transform the Red Army into a genuine Russian Army. Then you will have peace, liberty, bread and your own country.

> Beat the Jewish Commissar. His mug (*Fresse*) longs for a brick. Beat the Jews! Beat the executioners, the Commissars. Don't believe your fraudulent leaders. Kill all Commissars and Jews. They are your misfortune and your destruction. Come over to us.

Friedrich added the ironic comment: "The *Wehrmacht* was apparently looking for accomplices. The main purpose for killing Commissars and Jews is to liberate the Russian people from their slave-drivers."[65]

Messerschmidt quoted the text of another circular to the German troops, *Mitteilung an die Truppe* Nr. 115

---

62 *AOK* 18, Ic, Nr. 2.034/41
63 Streit, p. 58 f
64 Circular to the troops Nr. 116 in vol. 116 'Rescue in highest danger', June, 1941, Messerschmidt, p. 327 f
65 Friedrich, p. 403

"This is the face of *Bolshevism*". "We all know what *Bolshevism* looks like. It has joined hands with nihilism, which has always been part of the Russian soul. Nihilism includes the Latin word 'nihil', that is 'nothing'. It means that the nihilist believes in nothing, that he feels no bond to anything and that he is not committed to any value. Nihilism is a state of total moral exhaustion. It shows a brittle character, rotten to the very core. Russian-Jewish *Bolshevism* is built upon the destruction of all moral values."[66]

Messerschmidt added a comment:

Just as National-Socialism was never able to engage in a serious and scientific confrontation with Marxism, *Wehrmacht* propaganda was satisfied with presenting the soldiers with a bogey-man against whom any means of destruction had to be used.[67]

The historian Hans-Alfred Jacobsen emphasised that

the 'Commissar Order' cannot be treated in an isolated manner. It is part of the total context of the political intentions of the NS-leadership and its orders of political, economical and military content, in particular the ones concerning the annihilation of parts of the Russian population.[68]

Reality

Military commissars have existed in a number of armies over the centuries, in civil wars or in territories recently conquered where the situation lacked security. The French Army of the Revolution had introduced commissars by a decree of the Convenant of 15 December 1792. On 14 December 1900, 1,900 commissars were appointed in the Russian Imperial Army in Manchuria, after that territory was incorporated in the Tsarist Empire. They were temporary institutions, and were removed as soon as the situation became stabilised. In the Red Army, a totally politicised body, they remained a permanent feature until 1942.

The word 'commissar' was surrounded by an aura of mystique in Soviet vocabulary. The first government Ministers were called 'People's Commissars' and political commissars were found at all levels of society. The creation of the Red Army in 1917, was accompanied by the setting up of a 'Department for Organisation and Agitation' within the 'All-Russian Committee for Organisation and Formation of the Red Army.' The Committee was soon renamed 'Department for Agitation and Instruction.' The members of the Committee, both men and women, were first named 'political commissars.' In April 1918 that was changed to 'war commissars.'

The first war commissars were appointed during the Civil War. Trotsky was the first Commander in Chief of the Red Army and understood quickly that he could not do without officers recruited from the former Tsarist forces. Since he

---

66   Messerschmidt, p. 326
67   Ibid
68   H-A. Jacobsen, in M.Broszat, H-A. Jacobsen and H. Krausnich (ed.), *Anatomie des Staates. Konzentrationslager, Kommissarbefehl, Judenverfolgung,* Olten 1965, p. 170

could not feel sure of their loyalty towards the new regime, commissars were appointed as their watchdogs.

The status and the authority of the commissars were subject to regular changes. In 1929, Stalin had gained total political power after the elimination of Bukharin's 'right' opposition. However, the self-conscious leadership of the Red Army had retained some independence until it was hit by the Great Terror in 1937.

Up to 1924, the fundamental element of many controversies was the authority of officers to issue orders. In 1924, a difference was made between officers who were members of the Communist party, and those who decided not to join the party, or who had applied for membership but had not yet been admitted. If an officer was a party member, he had sole command authority. He had an assistant for political matters, the 'Sampolit', but military orders only required his signature. If an officer was not a party member, even military orders required the counter-signature of the Sampolit.

After the murder of the Leningrad party head, Sergei Kirov, on 1 December 1934, Stalin made two attempts to bring the Army commanders under his sole authority. Both attempts were only partially successful. On 22 September 1935 Stalin agreed to the requests by the commanders to re-establish the former Tsarist officers ranks, with the exception of the generals, who remained *Kombrig, Komdiv, Komkor* and *Komandarm*. In 1935 the new rank of Marshal of the Soviet Union was created and conferred upon the *Komandarm* Voroshilov, Budennyi, Tukhatchevsky, Bliukher and Egorov.

The most senior commissars received the ranks of Army Commissars of the first, second and third rank, which were the equivalent of Army, Corps and Division Commanders. 26 November 1935 witnessed one of the typical farces of the Stalin era. A new function "General Commissar of the Soviet Union" was established and conferred upon the head of the secret police, Genrikh Yagoda. All military and civilian institutions were subordinated to him and Yagoda thus ranked as the most powerful man in the Soviet Union after Stalin.

Three days later, on 29 November 1935, after an outcry from the leadership of the Red Army, a 'correction' was officially published: "The decree of 26 November 1935, contained an 'inaccuracy' requiring additional precision. Yagoda was no longer 'General Commissar of the Soviet Union, he now became 'General Commissar of State Security.' During the Bukharin show trial in 1938, Yagoda was sentenced to death. At the end of 1935, the institution of war commissars was suspended.

When the Great Terror hit the Army in 1937, the highest commissar, Yan Gamarnik, shot himself when he was about to be arrested. On 11 May 1937, War Commissars were re-established in a manner more than strange even for official Soviet legislation. There was no formal decision by the Central Committee of the Party or the government, such decisions always appeared on the front page of the press. Instead, a short paragraph on the last page of the daily party newspaper *Pravda*, mentioned: "The government has found it necessary to create an institution of military commissars in every military district and every Red Army unit." Gamarnik's successor, Smirnov was arrested and shot a year later. Lev Mechlis, one of the most vile figures of the Stalin era, was appointed his successor as Army

Commissar of the first rank and immediately instituted a regime of total terror in a terror regime.

After the war against Finland, during the winter of 1940/41, the authority of the commissars was partly curtailed and their counter-signature on orders of commanders no longer required. The commissar was now the deputy of commanders at all levels, without having the right to intervene in military decisions of the commanders. Commissars were now attached to every Red Army unit, down to and including company level. The company commissar was called *politruk*, commissars, above company level and up to divisions, were simply named 'commissars.' At Army and 'front' levels, several commissars were grouped into 'war directorates'. The head of a directorate was often a high ranking political personality. During the war, Krushchev, Zhdanov and Bulganin headed directorates and were given temporary military ranks. Krushchev was made a Lieutenant-General.

Since the *politruks* had not been mentioned in the 'Commissar Order', an Army Group commander asked *OKH* if *politruks* were to be considered as being commissars. General Müller did not know what a *politruk* was. On 18 August 1941, he asked *OKW* for clarification. *OKW* replied on August 18, "Political assistants at company level, *politruks*, are political commissars and have to be treated in conformity with the 'Commissar Order.'[69]

After the Russian victory at Moscow, the prestige of the Russian Generals increased rapidly. On 9 October 1942, the War Commissar Institution was abolished, only the directorates at Army and Front level were maintained. The former war commissars were integrated as regular officers into the Army and acted as aides of the commanders in matters of ideology and politics. At times, they were given minor assignments, such as the distribution of party literature or procurement of suitable clothing.

The commissar can be defined as a Red Army officer who had gone through the normal military training, and who was given both command authority and entrusted with propaganda and political supervision. They were certainly soldiers. One of Manstein's arguments in his defence was that commissars were not soldiers. Marshal Konev had begun his military career as a commissar. Marshal Meretskov had also served as commissar.

The 'Commissar Order' at Army Group North

Manstein's commanders

At the beginning of the war against Russia, Army Group North was commanded by *Feldmarschall* Ritter von Leeb. It consisted of 16th Army, under *Generaloberst* Busch, 18th Army, under *Generaloberst* von Küchler, and *Panzergruppe* 4, under *Generaloberst* Hoepner. *Panzergruppe* 4 consisted of Manstein's LVI motorized Corps and Reinhardt's XLI motorized Corps. Busch's bungled leadership soon endangered 16th Army and Manstein had to come to his rescue. He had to halt the

---

69   *OKW*-WFst/Abt.L. (IV /Qu), Nr.001797/41, g Kdos.

advance of his Corps and was transferred to 16th Army, under which he remained until he took over 11th Army in the South.

Feldmarschall Wilhelm, Ritter von Leeb

Leeb was number five on the army's seniority list. He had been retired from active service during the *Revirement* with simultaneous promotion to *Generaloberst*. During the Sudeten crisis, he was reactivated and given command of 12th Army, with Manstein as his chief-of-staff. After the Munich agreement, he was once more retired. When the war broke out, he was reactivated and given command of Army Group C in the West. After the victory over France he was promoted to *Feldmarschall*. On 16 January 1942, he requested to be relieved from his command of Army Group North and was succeeded by Küchler. He saw no more active service during the remainder of the war.

When Leeb received communication of the 'Commissar Order' he is reported to have requested his chief-of-staff, *Generalleutnant* Kurt Brennecke, to inform the Commanders of all units of his Army Group, that he opposed the order and that he was not going to control its execution.[70] The officer, who kept the war diary of Army Group North, added that he had listened in on a conversation over the phone between Leeb and Küchler. During it, Leeb said that he could not stop the order, but that he recommended simply boycotting its execution.[71]

As in many German post-war statements, some elements of ambiguity remain. Already on 18 June 1941, four days before the outbreak of hostilities in the East, Army Group's Ic/AO, the staff officer under the Ic, responsible for enemy intelligence, Major Walter Heinemeyer, issued an order: "The Russian commissars are known, and have to be quickly disposed of. Police have a liaison officer at Ic, political commissars are to be handed over to him."[72] To whom were the commissars known? Certainly not to the German Generals, who knew nothing about them, apart from the wording of the 'Commissar Order'. The police liaison officer was no less ignorant, since no German institution had ever attempted to gain knowledge or understanding of any Soviet institution.

In a letter to *Panzergruppe* 4 of 1 July 1941, Brennecke wrote: " Give instructions to your troops, that prisoners already incorporated into working units, may not be shot at a later date."[73] If executions at a later date are prohibited, prior executions had obviously occurred. Furthermore, if the 'Commissar Order' was to be boycotted, why was it necessary to forbid the later shooting of men who, according to the general's statements, were never intended to be shot? When Brennecke was questioned by the IMT about this order, he found only a lame reply: "Perhaps there was a special case that I can't remember."[74] 'Special case' and 'absence of recollection' were standard arguments in defence statements by German generals.

Ritter von Leeb was certainly not a contemptible man. He had knowledge of crimes committed in the areas under his command, but he was also known to have

---

70 IMT, Case 12, p. 2.535, testimony by Brennecke.
71 IMT, Case 12, p.2.534 ff, testimony by Dr. Heinemeyer
72 BA-MA, RH 22/v.221, page 66
73 *NOKW* 3136
74 IMT, Case 12, p. 2547

done his best to prevent them. He never made it easy for himself, in the end he requested to be relieved from his post.

Generaloberst Erich Hoepner

History will record Hoepner as a somewhat puzzling personality. In 1938, he was part of Halder's plans for a *coup d'état* attempt. In the war against France, he showed himself a rousing and successful *Panzer* Commander and was called 'daredevil' Hoepner. At the onset of the war against Russia, he was the commander who issued the most inflammatory hate appeals against *Bolshevists* and Jews. The commander of *Einsatzgruppe* A, Dr Walther Stahlecker, emphasised "his very close, even heartfelt co-operation with Hoepner's army".[75] Krausnick felt that it need not signify Hoepner's approval of the murders committed by the *Einsatzgruppe*.[76] However, one may ask what else 'heartfelt co-operation' could mean, since every *Einsatzgruppe* was only concerned with mass murders of innocent people. During the winter of 1941/42, Hoepner was cashiered from the Army for contravention of Hitler's stay-put order. He was forbidden to wear uniform.

On 20 July 1944, Hoepner was made Commander of the *Ersatzheer*, after Fromm had been put under arrest by the conspirators. Then he simply wasted time. When urgency was needed, he requested a written order, in due military form, to confirm the appointment to his new command. Thereafter, Hoepner engaged in meaningless phone calls with the commanders of the *Wehrkreise*. When they told him that Keitel had informed them that Hitler had remained unscathed by the bomb, he told them to obey orders from Keitel. After the failure of the *putsch*, he assumed responsibility for his actions. Fromm, who had been a close friend of his over many years, offered him the possibility of committing suicide. Hoepner declined. At his trial, Freisler showered him with insults and he was hanged, two hours after the death sentence was passed on him.

Hoepner's Ic, Captain Robert Bruns, recalled that Hoepner, after receiving the 'Commissar Order', made a disgusted gesture with his hand, left the room, and left it to Bruns to read out the text of the order.[77] Hoepner's adc, Lieutenant Werner Bothe, had a somewhat different account. He wrote that Hoepner received the order a few days ahead of the German attack at Allenstein, in East Prussia, and that he had ordered Bothe to read out the text to his officers. According to Bothe, Hoepner then said: "You have listened to this, but mark my words, where I command, no prisoner-of-war will be executed."[78] Such words notwithstanding, Hoepner showed himself again a dare-devil in the execution of the 'Commissar Order'. On 17 July 1941, Bothe reported to General Müller, through the channel of Army Group North: "Up to 101 commissars shot."[79] On 22 July, Bothe cabled Reinhardt: "Political commissars. Report immediately about the execution of he

---

75 Krausnick, p. 236
76 Ibid.
77 IMT, Case 12, p. 3.625
78 *Hoepner Symposium*, professor Dr.Oswald Hahn (ed.), Nuremberg 1982, p.1982
79 *NOKW* 1674

'Commissar Order' during the period 22 June–19 July. Exact figures have to be added. Next report to be sent on 3 August, again with exact figures."[80]

Streit's table shows that the 'Commissar Order' was executed with particular diligence at Hoepner's *Panzergruppe*. Between 2 July and 8 July 1941, it reported 101 executions. However, only four took place at Manstein's Corps, the remainder occurred with Reinhardt.[81] Regardless of how unreliable the figures may have been, such a discrepancy does not arise fortuitously. Obviously, Manstein had been able to convey to his subordinates his opposition to the 'Commissar Order', in a particularly strong manner, and had obtained their adherence to his views.

Army Group North and the 'Commissar Order' before the IMT, case 12

Case 12 was not confined to Army Group North, and the 'Commissar-Order' was only one point of the indictment. Ritter von Leeb was the senior indicted officer and became the unofficial spokesman for all the accused. Dr Laternser and his team of defence lawyers had agreed upon a common strategy on all charges. With regard to the 'Commissar order', it was rendered ineffective by a conspiracy of all generals. All figures about the executions of commissars were fictitious, and had the sole purpose of deceiving Hitler. This strategy was soon shown to be untenable. Had all generals been willing or able to form a joint conspiracy against Hitler, there would not have been a world war. The IMT rejected the contention out of hand and stated in its verdict:

> The order has been carried out throughout the army. Some contend that, on occasions, inflated or totally fictitious statistics about the number of assassinated political officials were reported. The hard and undeniable fact remains that many were executed in cold blood, in violation of rules of war and humanity.[82]

At times, the questioning of Leeb turned close to grotesque. The judges were clearly impressed by his personality. Leeb was a Bavarian, but in his appearance and his bearing he was close to the prototype of a Prussian *Feldmarschall* of times gone by. All the judges knew of his career. As a young lieutenant of 24, he was part of the German contingent that in 1900 repressed the Boxer uprising in China. In 1938, he published his classic book about defence (*Die Abwehr*) which was part of the curriculum of military academies in a number of countries. Professor Yehuda Wallach told Georg Meyer that Leeb's book was part of his teaching of Israeli infantry officers in military history and tactics.[83]

The judges had already received copies of many of Leeb's memoranda, in which he warned against a war of aggression. They also had a written record of Leeb's last talk over the phone with Hitler, when he requested his relief from duty.

---

80   Ibid
81   Streit, p. 80
82   IMT, Case 12, p. 95
83   Meyer, Leeb, p. 35, footnote 66

Leeb had said to Hitler: "There is a responsibility which I have to bear alone. Above all, I am responsible to the Lord and to my conscience."[84]

On the other side, some statements by Leeb sounded disconcerting, to the extent that the judges treated them with scorn. In some instances, this was unfair. Leeb had pleaded his ignorance of a number of actions charged to him in the indictment. He had said that he was not informed of the death by malnutrition and bad treatment of prisoners-of-war, since such information rested with the quartermasters of the armies in his Army Group. The tribunal commented: "It was an incredible and shameful attempt to pass on responsibility to his subordinates."[85] However, it had overlooked that the relatively small staff of a German Army Group had no quartermaster of its own, and was therefore dependent on information obtained from the much larger staffs of its armies.

In accordance with the agreement reached between the accused and their team of lawyers, faked reports became the core of Leeb's defence against the charge of compliance with the 'Commissar Order.' Leeb stated that, given the number of Russian prisoners, the reports had shown figures of commissars shot were far too low. That was hardly logical. If reports were faked, in order to make it appear that the generals had complied with the order, the figures would have had to be increased, not reduced. That point led to the following exchange between Leeb and the prosecution.

Q: Your statement results in the hypothesis that the Commissars were first identified and then purposely spared. Is this your contention?

A: Yes. Anyway, they were not executed, neither those who were identified and of course also those who were not identified.

Q: In other terms, the order was never carried out?

A: I hope so."[86]

"I hope so" shows that Leeb already had doubts about the strategy of faked numbers. Leeb then stated that all reports from his Army Group were sent to *OKH*. This led to ironical questions by the prosecution in its cross-examination.

Q: Since you state that your Army Group sabotaged the order, *OKW* and *OKH* must have been aware of this.

A: I have no idea what *OKW* and *OKH* thought.

Q: This was obviously a poor attempt of sabotage, would you not agree? If you transmitted reports, with the intention of deceiving you superiors, and on purpose reported a low number of Commissars, do you expect the court to believe that you engaged in sabotage?[87]

---

84   IMT, Case 12, p. 2.648
85   Friedrich, p. 399, with reference to the brief of the prosecution, p. 43
86   IMT, Case 12, p. 2,471
87   Ibid.

With his mention of *OKH*, Leeb made it necessary for the court to call Halder. As chief of the *Generalstab*, Halder was one step closer to the 'throne' than Leeb. Halder stood in special 'good grace' with the Americans, who, already in 1946, had appointed him as head of a research group of 150 German officers, who were employed by the History Division of the US Army. Halder's work continued until 1961 and he was awarded the American 'Meritorious Civilian Service Award.' Since he now had to be called, he appeared officially as witness for the prosecution.

In his testimony, Halder referred to Brauchitsch's directive about the 'inconspicuous' shooting of commissars. He stated that commissars were not to be shot immediately upon capture, but only after a thorough questioning. Thus, the commissars could never have known about their future fate. Halder failed to realise that his statement placed the responsibility of the executions straight on the higher commanders, who had conducted the 'thorough examination'. If commissars were not shot immediately upon capture, their execution did not take place in compliance with the 'Commissar Order', but after order by the high commander in every instance. Friedrich comments ironically: "Thus the commissars had the privilege of meeting a lawful death in their prison camps."[88] The tribunal found it difficult to follow Halder's reasoning:

Q: Do you really intend to imply that this was a weakening of the 'Commissar Order'?

A: The Commander in Chief of the Army had ordered that the execution of commissars had to take place outside the combat zone, after quiet reflection, and no longer influenced by the anger of the preceding fighting. It meant that we had been able to assemble deserters in an orderly fashion.

Q: I fail to understand you. At first, you want to convince us that the 'Commissar Order' was never carried out. Now, you suddenly state that you wanted to obtain a repeal of the order, because it prevented Russian soldiers from surrendering or from deserting into the German lines. How could Russian soldiers be aware of an order that was never carried out?[89]

The questionings became increasingly confused. Leeb's Ic, Major Karl-Friedrich Jessel, stated that he himself had inserted the faked numbers in Army Group's reports, after agreeing upon them with the staff officers of the armies and the *Panzergruppe.*

Q: What sense did it make to bother the armies with such nonsense? Why did you not simply invent the numbers?

A: This could have spelled great trouble for the armies, since there were *OKH* liaison officers at their staffs. If the numbers reported were contradictory, it would be reported to Hitler and the commanders could have found themselves in a most uncomfortable position.

Q: You imply that *OKH* spied upon the commanders?

---

88   Friedrich, p. 400
89   IMT, case 12, p. 2150

A: No, certainly not, this is not what I intended to express. There was never any spying by *OKH*. But contradictions could arise, if Army Group reported one number and an Army another. Therefore prior agreement was required.[90]

Gersdorff likewise appeared for the defence. When the 'Commissar Order' was distributed, he was Ic/AO at Army Group Centre and had made a formal entry of protest into Army Group's war diary under his personal signature. In 1945, he had been promoted to *Generalmajor*. He testified:

Hitler was never able to control the execution of the order. Apart from our moral objections, we feared that it would increase the Russian will of resistance. Around 5,000 Russians deserted monthly to Army Group Centre. The Russians tried to prevent this by drastic means and propaganda slogans that all prisoners-of-war would be executed. Recall that a Commissar asked me during his questioning when he would be shot.

Q: Was this not their usual destiny?

A: No, this was just a propaganda slogan.[91]

To define the 'Commissar Order' as a propaganda slogan was more than a bit thick.

Gersdorff wrote in his memoirs in 1977, the 'Commissar Order' was no longer a propaganda slogan, but new contradictions appeared:

The 'Commissar Order' was seldom carried out. I have been able to save the lives of a number of high-ranking commissars, who had to be brought to Army Group's staff for questioning. We asked them to remove their insignia, in order to be able to treat them as ordinary prisoners-of-war. Unfortunately, many were denounced by their own comrades in prison camps. Executions at the front occurred mainly in instances when German soldiers had come across mutilated bodies of their fallen comrades. The commissars were highly popular with their fellow soldiers and were looked upon as being the 'mother' of the company. They had every reason to fight desperately, since they preferred to die in combat, rather than being shot after capture.[92]

If the 'Commissar Order' was only seldom carried out, why did all commissars choose to fight desperately? And if they were highly popular with their fellow soldiers, why were they denounced by them?

At the end, respect for Ritter von Leeb prevailed. He was acquitted of the charge of compliance with the 'Commissar Order', the court agreed to his contention that he had objected to it in every possible manner.[93] He was only sentenced for having communicated the *Barbarossa* Order. That communication to his Armies was recorded in Army Group's war diary.

---

90   IMT, Case 12, p. 2,206 ff
91   Ibid. p. 2,150 ff
92   Gersdorff, p.100 f
93   IMT, Case 12, p.136

However, the tribunal found that this point had to be seen against Leeb's many positive actions. There was no doubt that Ritter von Leeb had never been a National-Socialist. When Hitler was appointed Chancellor, Leeb is on record for having said: "A salesman, who has good merchandise, does not have to praise it with the shouts of a vendor at a street market."[94] The IMT stated in its conclusions:

> Ritter von Leeb was not a supporter of National-Socialism nor of its doctrines. He was the commander of hundreds of thousands of men in a campaign of gigantic proportions and responsible for the well being of the civilian population in the very large areas under his control. It is significant that the prosecution could not produce a single criminal order under his signature or with any sign of approval by him.[95]

Leeb was sentenced to three years, the most lenient sentence of imprisonment ever handed down by the IMT. His years as a prisoner-of-war were set off against the verdict and Leeb left the courthouse as a free man. His successor as commander in chief of Army Group North, von Küchler, was sentenced to twenty years.

Manstein – the 'inverted chain of command' and his defence at his trial

The 'inverted chain of command'

"I was compelled to tell my superiors that the 'Commissar Order' would not be complied with in my corps."[96] Thus Manstein wrote in *Verlorene Siege* about his reaction to the 'Commissar Order'. Manstein said he had communicated his disapproval of the 'Commissar Order' up the chain of command to his two superior commanders, Leeb and Hoepner. This was not required, since both had already communicated their opinion to him. Friedrich, who seldom missed an opportunity to make sarcastic comments about Manstein's vanity, wrote: "They did not inform him, he informed them. This is how he liked to see himself."[97]

Manstein wrote further that 'it was obvious that all my superiors shared my views'.[98] This was however far from obvious. While Ritter von Leeb and Hoepner had similar opinions, the latter at least until the beginning of the campaign, it cannot be assumed as a foregone conclusion with Busch. But, regardless of the absence of intellectual and moral level with Busch, he must have had enough understanding that there was some danger in engaging in an open dispute with Manstein. Therefore he was probably well advised to take note of Manstein's communication without replying.

It would have been more interesting to know exactly what Manstein told his subordinates, however he does not mention it. There is no reason to doubt that he was firm in his opposition to the order, when communicating it to them. Paget

94   Müller, p. 40
95   IMT, Case 12, p. 144.
96   *Verlorene Siege*, p. 277
97   Friedrich, p. 596
98   Ibid

contributes yet another piece of nonsense. He wrote that Manstein had, at first, decided to conceal the 'Commissar Order' from his division commanders. But his Ia, Major Dethleffsen, had warned him that the divisions cold obtain knowledge from other sources.[99] There was however no need to obtain knowledge that was already available at all divisions, since Manstein's predecessor, Ritter von Schobert, had communicated the order to them, and he ordered ruthless compliance. Furthermore, if one wants to tell commanders that one does not wish for their compliance with an order, the order in question must obviously be known to them. Manstein told Paget, that his Division Commanders unanimously shared his views.[100] Such unanimity may be seriously doubted. One of his Divisions was the *Waffen-SS Totenkopf* Division, which was commanded by the infamous *SS-Gruppenführer* Theodor Eicke.

After the First World War, Eicke could never find stable employment. He tried several times to join the police but was always sacked after stints of a few months. After the *Nazis* came to power, Eicke was the first commander of the Dachau concentration camp. Later he became head of the central organisation of all concentration camps. During the war in France, the *Totenkopf* Divisions had committed many war crimes. One of its companies, commanded by *SS-Obersturmführer* Fritz Knöchlein, had ordered the summary shooting of 100 British prisoners-of-war. Knöchlein was sentenced to death by the British after the war and hanged.[101] It is somewhat hard to imagine Eicke agreeing to arguments based on ethics, however he would certainly not have dared to contradict Manstein to his face. Had he done so, it is easy to imagine Manstein's reaction. In France, Hoepner had already shouted at Eicke that he was not a soldier but a 'simple butcher'.

The 'inverted' chain of command is probably the key to the unreliable numbers. The conspiracy theory can be left aside. A General 'orders', he does not 'express' wishes. The authority of his orders goes unchallenged, compliance with his wishes remains a decision by his subordinates. Since no General, not even the 'flamboyant Manstein'[102] could order disobedience, he could only express his wish. An Army Commander can rely upon his corps commanders, a Corps Commander upon the commanders of his divisions. If he does not trust them, he has them relieved of duty. The Division Commander communicates the wish from above to his regiments, every regiment to its battalions, and the Battalion Commander to his companies. With every step downwards, readiness to comply with the wish becomes increasingly difficult, since at low levels, convinced National-Socialists may report on their commanders.

---

99 Paget, p. 160

100 Ibid

101 Details about Eicke in a chapter by C. Snydor, *Theodor Eicke, Organisator der Konzentrationslager*, in R.Smelser/E. Syring (ed.), *Die SS Elite unter dem Totenkopf. 30 Lebensläufe*, Paderborn 2000, p. 147 ff and in *Theodor Eicke, SS-Obergruppenführer und General der Waffen-SS*, in A. Schulz/G. Wegmann (ed.), *Die Generale der Waffen-SS und der Polizei. Die militärischen Werdegänge der Generale, sowie der Ärzte, Veterinäre, Intendanten, Richter und Ministerialbeamten im Generalsrang*, Bissendorf 2003, vol. 1, p. 280 ff

102 Friedrich, p. 598

General Hollidt made a convincing statement at his trial before the IMT. Manstein described Hollidt as "a man with a firm and serious mind, but at times bereft of drive. As a former infantry man, he could at times become depressed when hearing about the sufferings endured by the infantry."[103] Hollidt had succeeded in convincing the IMT of his opposition to the 'Commissar Order'. When he was asked why he transmitted it, accompanied by a wish, he replied: "Had I ordered disobedience to the order, I would have put myself at the mercy of all my subordinates."[104]

Streit emphasised that non-compliance with the order was only assured at a level where all officers involved knew each other so well that they need not fear reporting by the fanatics among their comrades. Probably the regiment staff was the lowest level where such conviction could be found.[105] The wishes of the Commanders could take strange formulations. General von Salmuth commanded XXXIII Corps in 11th Army. In a performance evaluation, Manstein had rated him suitable for command of an Army, but added that he was not a rousing personality.[106] Salmuth testified at his trial:

> I have discussed the 'Commissar Order' with my division commanders. I told them that I did not wish to see it carried out. I added, it is written somewhere in the Bible: 'Seek and ye shall find.' If this is true, the opposite is likewise true. If you will not seek, you will not find.[107]

The numbers that are finally communicated to *OKH* start at the lowest level. The lieutenant is in command of the execution squad, or the soldier, who takes the captured commissar aside and puts a bullet in his head. Friedrich calls him the "sly Ulysses, the unknown *Wehrmacht* soldier."[108] Some number had to be given, no report could write "order not executed in compliance with wishes." But was the first number always reliable? In some instances, yes. But in others the lieutenant or the soldier may have been too lazy to write an immediate report, but first preferred to get drunk. He could easily choose a number at random, since he knew that no later control took place. The first individual reports were then added up at the next level, and transmitted further, until they reached the division.

The Division Commander thus received a number of additions from individual reports that he cannot control. The numbers passed on by him to his superiors depended upon his attitude to the 'Commissar Order'. If his view was positive, he may increase the number, to show at highest level how eager he was to comply with a *Führer* order. If he was opposed to the order, he may decrease the numbers and point out that it only resulted in increased strength of resistance by the Russians. Since that was indeed the case, the order was repealed, and a conspiracy of the generals was never required.

---

103   *Verlorene Siege,* p. 532
104   IMT, Case 12, p. 4.335
105   Streit, p. 19
106   *NOKW* 141
107   IMT, Case 12, p. 3.888
108   Friedrich, p. 600

Manstein's defence at his trial

During the 'case 12' trial at the IMT, Manstein was in jail in Britain. The tribunal had considered calling him as a witness, but changed its mind and Manstein spent only a few days at Nuremberg. Dr Laternser obviously communicated all the records to him and told him about the failed strategy of the faked numbers. The 'formidably intelligent Manstein' (Beevor) had undoubtedly recognised this by himself. In his own trial, he never reverted to that argument. Neither did Manstein repeat Paget's statement that he had forbidden the execution of the order. Manstein was no lawyer, but he was far more intelligent than Paget, and he obviously knew that no tribunal would believe such a statement.

Manstein's indictment of 'compliance with the Commissar Order' was rather weak. Manstein had only to thank Paget and himself for having been found guilty. A good defence strategy would have been easy. Manstein could state that he had immediately recognised that the 'Commissar Order' contravened international conventions about the conduct of war. He could have added, that it was not in his power to forbid its execution, since it was a direct order from Hitler. But he had communicated his opposition in unmistakable words to his subordinates. He had also done everything in his power to prevent it from being carried out. Manstein could likewise have pointed out the small number of commissars shot at LVI Corps and 11th Army. He could have emphasised that he could not control every single action in the rear areas of his command. Any good lawyer would have advised him accordingly, but Manstein did not have a good lawyer. Paget was the head of his defence team.

Manstein held a strong hand, but he did not play his trump cards. Instead, he engaged in totally confused and often incoherent declarations. On one occasion it led the tribunal to interrupt him and admonish him, and tell him to stop making long speeches.

It cannot be ascertained whether Manstein simply followed Paget's advice, or whether he intended to show his own convictions. He had indeed said to Paget on their first meeting:

> I am not concerned about what is going to happen to me. My life already belongs to the past. My own concern is my personal honour, and the honour of the German soldiers, who fought under my command. Your soldiers should know well that we fought as gentlemen throughout the war. You British have been convinced by *Bolshevist* propaganda that we acted like savages in the East. This is not true. In an unprecedentedly cruel war, we have always observed strict discipline and fought like honourable soldiers. I shall spare no effort to defend the honour of the German Army.[109]

Perhaps Manstein was guided by those thoughts when he formulated his statements. On the other hand, many of the absurdities advanced by him clearly show Paget's language. Paget repeated them in his book, at times in an even more emphatic manner. But he could also have made things easy for himself and simply copied the minutes of the Manstein trial.

---

109   Paget, p.96

At the beginning of the proceedings, Manstein saw fit to lecture the court.

Since the judges have no personal experience of the Soviet system, and are unable to understand the Soviet leadership, the system of Commissars and the Asiatic Russians in general, they have to be first informed and then convinced, that the Soviet methods rendered the brutal German reprisals unavoidable. The tribunal has to be convinced that the war in the East had an Asiatic aspect throughout. We could not escape such a framework if we did not want to be at a disadvantage. Therefore we had no other resort, but to apply ourselves the methods of the enemy, scorched earth, execution of prisoners-of-war, reprisals against partisans, although that was never wanted by me.[110]

"Never wanted by me?" Suddenly Manstein personifies not only the Army but all German measures in the East. He did not realise that, with those words, he assumed responsibility for the *Barbarossa* Order, which was the root of the subsequent cruelties in the East. Neither the *Barbarossa* Order, nor the 'Commissar Order' were reprisals, both were issued before hostilities began.

After his introductory statement, Manstein's cross-examination began:

Q: When you were a student at the *Generalstab*, was the Hague Convention Nr.4 not part of the curriculum?

A: I was certainly aware of the basics of the Hague convention. But I also feel that every decent soldier knows how to conduct himself in war, and the various Hague conventions leave many questions unanswered. The people who drafted them obviously knew nothing about the Commissar institution, that was a novelty. Likewise they could not foresee the bombing of civilian towns, nor the war in the air. In such cases, the conscience of the decent soldier remains the guideline.

Q: Did you not know that the Soviet Union proclaimed on 1 July 1941, only a few days after you invaded Russia, that she would treat prisoners-of-war in a manner strictly in accordance with the Hague conventions?

A: On 1 July my *Panzer* Corps was 100 kilometres ahead of the front line and I obviously did not receive a copy of the Soviet proclamation. But in those days I could certainly see that the Russians acted differently, since we recovered the bodies of soldiers of my Corps who had been assassinated after capture. Both my adc and myself had decided to never allow ourselves to be captured alive.

Q: Don't you feel that executions, as they possibly occurred at some Soviet units, were a reaction to the execution of the 'Commissar Order'?

A: I don't think so. I have no evidence that the 'Commissar Order' led to them, but it can't be excluded. But I want to state clearly that the Commissar system was not limited to a political control of the troops, their main duty was without doubt, as fanatical Communists, to instil a ferocity into combat which is unusual in normal combat between soldiers.

---

110 Trial, page without number

Q: Does your statement imply that combat was ferocious because it was a war between two ideologies?

A: Yes, this was part of it.

Q: What created a war between ideologies?

A: The politicians.

Q: In other terms, the 'Commissar Order' created a war between ideologies?

A: No! The war between ideologies had totally different causes than the 'Commissar Order'.

Q: But you obviously knew that the 'Commissar Order' was a gross violation of the Hague conventions.

A: I have already said that I disapproved of it and did not carry it out, because I considered it to be unsoldierly and that was sufficient for me. My attitude was due to my conviction that it would not serve the discipline of my troops and the esteem in which they were held, if people, regardless of their functions, were shot after being captured in open fight. I had no need for further consideration. I was certainly not qualified to judge if my government acted legally or illegally. If it comes to this, that every soldier has to examine this, then the soldier decides what his government is allowed.

At this point, the prosecution lost patience: Will you please answer my question instead of making long speeches. I am putting questions to you and it is in your own interest if you would reply to them instead of engaging in long speeches."

Then the cross examination continued:

Q: Are you really serious in your contention that the commissars were not soldiers?

A: In my opinion this is at least doubtful.

Q: But they fought and they wore a regular uniform.

A: Yes, but they were not soldiers, they were politicians.

Q: Is it impossible for a politician to be a soldier?

A: No certainly not, but these people were attached to the troops in a political function and not as soldiers.

Q: In other terms you imply that international law and justice are only matters which a soldier regards as being part of his honour. Is this really what you mean?

A: No, this is not what I wanted to convey. In my opinion international law and justice are the result of a soldier's personal experience in war.

Q: And what is your definition of soldiers' honour? What is the exact meaning of your expression 'things which are in opposition to our concept of military honour?

A: A soldier's honour is a virtue in itself. It is independent from any general context. It does not rely on individual talent, nor upon international conventions. I am convinced that every soldier knows what a soldier's honour is. It is an ethical concept, not a paragraph in some legal book.[111]

Manstein/Fuchs contend that the defence team was convinced that their defence would lead to an acquittal.[112] One could reply that Manstein should perhaps have been acquitted of the charge relating to the 'Commissar-Order'. However, the line of defence chosen by Paget and himself rendered his sentencing unavoidable.

Manstein's comments in *Verlorene Siege* were no less muddled than his testimony:

> The status of the political Commissars in international law is certainly open to doubt. They were certainly not soldiers. Had a *Gauleiter* been attached to me as a political watchdog, I would not have considered him as having been a soldier.[113]

Some of Manstein's confused arguments require comment.

- The commissar institution was not a novelty when the Hague conventions were signed. However, prior to the creation of commissars in the Red Army they were only temporary *ad hoc* institutions and there was no reason for the authors of the Hague convention to include them in their text. In defence of Manstein, it must however be said, that he could not be expected to search the Hague conventions for institutions about which he knew nothing. At his trial, it was more difficult for him to plead ignorance, but this would have required an effort by Paget to enlighten him about the status and the background of the commissar institution.
- 'Soldierly' is a vague notion, which can be used by anyone according to his own concept. However, it must be said again defence of Manstein, that he could find no better argument in stating his rejection of the order towards his subordinates.
- "The commissars were no soldiers." How else can officers, who bear military uniform and participate in combat, be defined? Paget adds: "What were these commissars? The prosecution said that they were part of the Russian armed forces. The prosecution never defined them as having been soldiers and, without doubt they were never soldiers at all."[114] The contradiction between "part of the Russian armed forces" and "they were never soldiers at at all" obviously escaped Paget's logic. Likewise, Paget was unaware that the question, whether the commissars were soldiers, was a central argument of the prosecution. "Are you really serious in your contention that the commissars were not soldiers?"
- "I was certainly not qualified to judge if my government acted legally or illegally." In other terms, Manstein views the soldier as being above the law.

---

111 Trial, page without number. The text of Manstein's interrogation is likewise reproduced in Manstein/Fuchs, p. 299 ff

112 Manstein/Fuchs, p. 289.

113 *Verlorene Siege*, p. 176 f

114 Paget, p. 116

Not unexpectedly, Paget adds a personal comment and states that Manstein was never concerned with legality. This is yet another of Paget's inventions, since Manstein had paid attention to legality on more than one occasion. When questioned about the *Barbarossa* Order he had stated that the paragraphs, which rendered German soldiers immune from prosecution for crimes committed against civilians, were not illegal, because the speed of the German advance would not permit the setting up of military tribunals in time.[115] Manstein was likewise aware of article 147 in the German Military Penal Code that renders any subordinate responsible, for compliance with an order from his superior, if he knew that the order covered a deed punishable under criminal law. Manstein could only have argued that an order by Hitler outranked an article in the penal code. However, he could certainly not say that he was not required to pay attention to the law.

- In *Verlorene Siege*, Manstein wrote that there could certainly be some doubt about the status of the commissars in international law. If anyone had doubts about a status in international law, one would have to concern oneself with legality. Manstein reached the summit of absurdity when he was questioned about the handing over of prisoners to the *SD*: "There was an order issued by *OKW* to hand over prisoners and this is certainly not illegal. After all, I was myself informed by the British, while being a prisoner-of-war, that I was to be handed over to the Home Office."[116]

- "An 'unusual' ferocity in combat, which is not normal in combat between soldiers". Manstein does not say what 'normal' ferocity in combat between soldiers means. The ferocious fight in the East resulted from the strength of the Red Army. Combats did not become less ferocious after the repeal of the 'Commissar Order'. Manstein does not explain what he meant by 'normal ferocity in combat between soldiers'.

- Manstein's comparison between the 43 *Gauleiters* and the tens of thousands of commissars is simply laughable. Manstein would have been more logical, had he compared the commissars to the *NSFO*, the *Nationalsozialitischer Führungsoffizier*-who were the officers in charge of political indoctrination, and who were attached to all *Wehrmacht* units from battalion upwards in December 1943. A German draft order, prepared when the *NSFO* were introduced, stated explicitly that the *NSFO* were the *politruks* of the *Wehrmacht*.[117] One can easily imagine Manstein's reaction if the Soviets had issued an order to shoot every *NSFO* upon capture.

- "Every soldier knows what a soldier's honour is." At first, Manstein talks about the 'decent soldier' This is acceptable, but 'every soldier?' Were all of the 18 million German soldiers paragons of virtue? Does a pimp, who dons a military uniform, suddenly turn into a man who is permeated by ethics? Pimps and other trash exist in every army.

- Finally, Manstein fails to realise that by denying the Commissars soldier's status, he aligns himself with the proponents of the 'Commissar Order.'

---

115 Manstein/Fuchs, p. 289
116 Trial, p. 2,138
117 Messerschmidt, p. 450

Conclusion: Was Manstein's sentence for compliance with the 'Commissar Order' justified?

The reply had already been intimated. If it were decided that every general had to be sentenced in whose area of command commissars had been executed, no exception could be made for Manstein. If individual responsibility is the issue, Manstein could have been acquitted. His muddled defence at his trial is not relevant. Manstein had not neglected the duties that devolved upon him as Corps and Army Commander. The Army commander is vested with territorial authority, responsibility for prisoners-of-war, and civilians in his area of command. However, he can only be held responsible, if illegal intentions are brought to his knowledge in sufficient time to permit him to prevent them, and he still lets matters take their course. There is no evidence that Manstein had advance information of the fate of the commissars in the rear of 11th Army.

After being sentenced, Manstein wrote to Paget: "No one could have defended me better than you. My gratitude and my admiration are due to the man who had the courage to show past events as they really occurred, and who took a firm position against enemy propaganda, which will soon disappear."[118]

For once, Paget was able to find a truthful reply: "As things turned out, nothing of what I had done, had been of the slightest use to Manstein."[119]

---

118   Paget, p. 234 ff
119   Ibid

Chapter 7

Manstein and the Holocaust

Manstein was one of the major perpetrators of genocide among German high commanders. During the months of his command of 11th Army, 33,000 Jews were murdered by Ohlendorf's *Einsatzgruppe* D, in the southern Ukraine and in the Crimea. On 16 April 1942, *Einsatzgruppe* D reported to the Ic/AO of 11th Army:

> The Crimea is free of Jews. (*Von Juden ist die Krim freigemacht.*) Occasionally some small groups are still discovered in the North. Wherever Jews have been able to hide with forged identity papers, experience has shown that they are soon discovered.[1]

Although the number of victims is confirmed by every work dealing with the Holocaust, Paget finds it appropriate to write: "I 'personally' do not believe that more than 2,000 or 3,000 Jews have been murdered in the Crimea. Naturally this is also a heinous crime."[2] Paget does not indicate how he arrives at his 'belief'.

Many other German generals co-operated actively with the *Einsatzgruppen*. In some instances the number of victims was larger. At the massacre at Babi Yar, in which troops of 6th Army participated, more Jews were murdered in a single day than during the whole period of Manstein's command. Given the monstrousness of the extermination of Jews, comparisons between figures can be dispensed with.

However, Manstein was in a unique situation. Other generals, who worked hand-in-glove with the *Einsatzgruppen* were constantly on the move and already away from future *Judenaktionen*, after the ones in which they had ordered their troops to participate had come to an end. Many Army commanders were replaced at regular intervals. With Manstein, matters were different. After some initial progress, his 11th Army had become stuck in the Crimea until July 1942. Manstein remained its Commander during an unusually long time. Manstein himself wrote that the Crimea was one of the few theatres of operations during the war in the East, where an Army could operate independently.[3]

Distances between cities in the Crimea were short. What happened in one location became immediately known in the whole peninsula. At the *Einsatzgruppen* A, B and C, their commanders were frequently replaced. Ohlendorf remained commander of *Einsatzgruppe* D during the whole time of Manstein's command of 11th Army. Ohlendorf could never approach Manstein. It is doubtful if Manstein ever saw him, let alone spoke with him. Ohlendorf complained at Nuremberg that neither on service matters, nor for a social encounter, Manstein had never invited him personally.[4]

---

1   BA-MA, RH 20-11/488
2   Paget, p. 242
3   *Verlorene Siege*, p. 277
4   Friedrich, p. 609

The reports of *Einsatzgruppe* D were sent to 11th Army's Ic/AO, Major Hans-Wolf Riesen and the Army's chief-of-staff, Colonel, later *Generalmajor*, Otto Wöhler. More documents about 11th Army's co-operation with the *Einsatzgruppen* are available in the German military archives than for any other German Army. In many units, the staff officers took care in destroying them. At 11th Army, all were preserved.

In the mid-1930s, Wöhler, at that time a colonel, had said to his subordinates in Breslau: "We have sufficient experts. What we need are men of strong character."[5] At 11th Army, Wöhler showed himself an expert, but there was little evidence of character. Manstein described Wöhler as 'faithful' Wöhler,[6] the 'upright and straightforward Lower Saxon, who did not hesitate to talk in unmistakably plain German with a protégé of Himmler.' Manstein refers to Ohlendorf.[7] During his own trial after the war, 'faithful' Wöhler became increasingly faithless and never hesitated to put the blame on Manstein. When questioned about the 'Commissar Order', Wöhler testified:

Q. What measures did Manstein take, or did you yourself take, to prevent your subordinates from carrying out the order?

A. I don't know of any measures taken by Manstein. I personally was not empowered to take any measures, since the 'Commissar Order' fell into the responsibility of the *OB* and not of his chief-of-staff. Perhaps I may have taken some measures, I can't recall it. But if it happened, only the Army Commander was responsible. But I simply can't remember any instance.[8]

Paget makes one of his many strange comments about Wöhler: "If Manstein were to be acquitted, what could be done with Wöhler, whose only crime was to have served under Manstein?"[9] Paget could have easily found the answer to his rhetorical question. Wöhler was sentenced to eight years, long before Manstein's trial took place.

The background for the mild verdict against Manstein, in connection with the genocide, was the hesitation of the Russian and Allied tribunals to prosecute the Holocaust. After Germany's surrender, a number of the most cruel perpetrators were immediately recruited by the CIC, which felt that their 'expert knowledge' of communism could be put to use. In the four-hour movie by Marcel Ophuls, about Klaus Barbie, the 'butcher of Lyon', a number of former CIC officers appear and tell of their close co-operation with Barbie. They later helped Barbie to escape to Latin America, with forged identity papers, when the French government demanded his extradition. It took more than forty years before Barbie was finally handed over to the French. He was sentenced to life imprisonment.

Eichmann, and also Dr Mengele, who supervised the 'selections' of the victims on the ramp of the Auschwitz extermination camp, were provided with forged

---

5   Meyer, Heusinger, p. 618
6   *Verlorene Siege,* p. 259
7   Ibid, p. 533
8   IMT, Case 12, p.5.761 and Friedrich, p. 597
9   Paget, p. 224

papers by the International Red Cross and the Vatican. Generally that was done by Bishop Hudal, rector of the Santa Maria del Anima in Rome and confessor of the German Catholic community in Rome, after requests by the Americans. Eichmann managed to escape to Latin America. In 1960, he was kidnapped by the Israelis in Argentina, brought to Jerusalem for trial, condemned to death and hanged. Dr Mengele fled from one Latin American country to the next. He was never arrested, although his identity was widely known. He died in Brazil.

At the *Einsatzgruppen* trial (case 9) before the IMT, thirteen death sentences were handed down, only four were executed. The remaining sentences were reduced to periods of between fifteen years and life, but all were released after a few years. The British were engaged in civil war with the Jews in Palestine and were less than eager to judge people who had participated in the extermination of Jews. The French prosecution did not want to have the Vichy government's complicity for the fate of the French Jews become an issue at the Nuremberg trial.

In the Soviet Union, the 'doctors' plot' was already under preparation and Stalin had developed plans to deport the whole Jewish population to Siberia. After Stalin's death in 1953, the 'doctors' plot' was officially exposed as a fraud and the physicians were set free and rehabilitated. Even in the 1960s, Holocaust was a taboo word in the Soviet Union. A monument erected at Babi Yar did not mention that the victims were Jews, the memorial stone mentioned only Soviet citizens. Energetic prosecution of the Holocaust took place only in Poland, Hungary and Czechoslovakia. There, all the death sentences were carried out. The Holocaust literature deals mainly with the ghettos and the extermination camps.

Relatively little attention is paid to the murders committed by the *Einsatzgruppen*. Approximately 4 million Jews were murdered in the extermination camps, but a number of inmates survived. Their extermination was expected, but that was prevented by the rapid advance of the Red Army. Thus they were able to tell their stories, and write books about their experiences. Close to 1 million victims of the *Einsatzgruppen* were exterminated, save for a few individual survivors. They were not killed by a last 'bullet in the head' that should have been fired by the commander of the death squad. Only one major German work of 700 pages, written in co-operation by Helmut Krausnick and Hans-Heinrich Wilhelm, is entirely devoted to all the *Einsatzgruppen*.[10] In 2003, Andrej Angrick published his doctoral thesis of some 800 pages about *Einsatzgruppe* D. *Besatzungspolitik und Massenmord. Die Einsatzgruppe D in der südlichen Sowjetunion 1941–1943.* (Occupation policy and mass murder. *Einsatzgruppe D* in the southern Soviet Union 1941–1943).

The main sources for this chapter are the reports of *Einsatzgruppe D* and 11th Army. This chapter is the first publication in Holocaust literature to give a complete account in a separate section for every city in the area controlled by 11th Army where *Judenaktionen* took place. (*Judenaktion* was the expression used by the Germans in the East about executions of Jews). Many of the reports are also mentioned in works by Krausnick and Wilhelm. However, they are interspersed with reports of massacres in other areas, and sometimes only reproduced in part. Krausnick does not concentrate only on a single Army. Heinz Höhne's *Der Orden*

---

10   H.Krausnick/H.Wilhelm, *Die Truppe des WeltanschauungskriEinsatzgruppees. Die Einsatzgruppen der Sicherheitspolizei und des SD 1938–1942*, Stuttgart 1981 (henceforth:Krausnick)

unter dem Totenkopf, die Geschichte der SS continues to be the standard work about the *SS*.[11]

All reports in this chapter are taken from the German military archives, other German archive sources, and the Nuremberg *NOKW* documents. Post-war historic impact was not a consideration in mind when *Einsatzgruppen* reports were written. They were daily routine reports, and their historic importance only became clear after the war. Their reliability was not contested by any of the defence attorneys at the trial of the *Einsatzgruppen, IMT* Case 9. Other sources are the works by Jörg Friedrich, Christian Streit, Raul Hilberg's standard work about the extermination of the European Jews, the minutes of the IMT trials, case 9 and case 12, and the minutes of the Manstein trial.

Manstein's testimony as a witness at the Nuremberg trial of the major Nazi war criminals

Manstein was questioned, under oath, about the *Einsatzgruppen* and about the murder of Jews. In both instances he committed outright perjury. He stated that the only thing he knew about the *Einsatzgruppen* was that they had been given the task of preparing the political administration of the occupied territories, and of supervising the political behaviour of the civilian population. Höhne comments that

> Manstein's statement was a typical example of the schizophrenia of the German commanders, which facilitated the murders committed by the *Einsatzgruppen*. The Generals purported to see in Heydrich's commandos, normal units of defence of the rear area. But they also knew that they had been given special tasks. Those were special tasks that the Commanders were more than happy to leave to them, without making further enquiries.[12]

When questioned about the shooting of Jews, Manstein stated that he had never heard of them.[13]

At his own trial, Manstein repeated his mendacious statement about the *Einsatzgruppen*. As to the shootings of Jews, his memory had to be refreshed. When Manstein took over the command of 11th Army, he immediately issued an order from his headquarters at Nikolayev, which made specific reference to murders of Jews. A number of works quote the order as stipulating that no executions were to take place at a distance of less than 200 kilometres from his residence.[14] Although that order is preserved in the archives of 11th Army and mentioned in the minutes of the Nuremberg trial, Krausnick feels that Manstein's authorship is not estab-

---

11   H.Höhne, *Der Orden unter dem Totenkopf, Geschichte der SS*, Hamburh 1966 (henceforth Höhne)

12   Ibid, p. 326

13   Both statements are recorded live on a movie produced by the public German television station ARD.

14   BA-MA, RH 20 – 11/488 and minutes of the trial against the major Nazi war criminals, vol. IV, p. 354 ff

lished beyond doubt.[15] No doubt is left about another text, which Wöhler confirmed at his own trial. Wöhler testified:

> I remember without any doubt that *Feldmarschall* von Manstein, during the first days after his assumption of command of 11th Army, was informed that shootings of Jews had taken place in the rear. He issued an immediate order forbidding such actions. Because those actions had occurred somewhere in the rear, I believe that it was in Kichinev, but I am not entirely sure of the location, *Feldmarschall* von Manstein immediately sent his adc to his chief quartermaster. He was held responsible that such *Schweinereien* would not happen in the areas under his command. This was certainly not an order given with 'a twinkle in the eyes', it was issued in total severity and with the strongest emphasis.

That order is reproduced by Alfred de Zayas in his chapter about the Nuremberg trials in *Die Soldaten der Wehrmacht.*[16] De Zayas adds the next sentence of Wöhler's testimony. "Since that day, 11th Army has never received further information about the execution of Jews."[17] Given the large number of reports by the *Einsatzgruppen* that were initialled by Wöhler, or signed by him with his full name, and similar orders that he issued on behalf of 11th Army, his statement was an outrageous lie. A general who fights for his life at his trial, may be forgiven for not speaking the truth. A historian like de Zayas cannot be permitted to use such a statement in his effort to absolve the *Wehrmacht* from crimes committed in the East.

Furthermore, on the very day Manstein assumed his command of 11th Army, a *Judenaktion* took place at Nikolayev. Nikolaus Pauly, who belonged to Company 2 of *Feldgendarmerie* (military police) 683 which was responsible for Manstein's personal safety, stated in 1962:

> Shots were heard and Manstein ordered me to find out what was happening. I went into the birch forest. There I told a man from the SD about the order which I had received from Manstein. He replied that this was neither Manstein's nor my business and I was asked to leave immediately. Later I heard from an old woman that Jews had been driven into the forest and shot.

Pauly adds that he had spoken with Manstein's driver, *Feldwebel* Nagel, about the incident.[18] Relations between Manstein and his driver were very close. In *Verlorene Siege* Manstein mentions Nagel repeatedly. When Nagel was killed in action, Manstein devotes two pages to his eulogy. Nagel would hardly have avoided to inform Manstein about his 'sacking'.

Manstein was now forced to correct his testimony.

Q: "Did your chief quartermaster, amongst others, really know of your objection, if you had one, as you said you had, to the *SD* shooting Jews, or anyone else?"

---

15 Krausnick, p.226
16 *Soldaten, Wehrmacht,* p. 468
17 Ibid.
18 Wrochem, p. 61

A: "I did not talk to him about the shootings of Jews because at that time I never knew of that matter. *With the exception of the order which I had passed on, by my adc, in Nikolayev.* (author's italics) I do not remember that I ever discussed the matter with him because I knew nothing about it."[19] Manstein fails to explain how one can issue an order about an action of which one knows nothing.

In *Verlorene Siege*, Manstein wrote: "Rumours which circulated in the homeland, never reached the front and least of all us."[20] "Least of all, us?" Again, Manstein set himself apart. His unit was not less 'the front' than other units. However, if a rumour reaches the front and, by chance, does not get through to Manstein, it may just as well have not existed.

Manstein's statement is contradicted by a 'V.I.' (*Vertrauliche Information,* secret information memorandum) of the Party chancellery, Nr. 66/881 of 9 October 1941:

In the framework of 'the final solution' of the Jewish question, rumours are being spread among the population, in several parts of the *Reich,* concerning very severe measures against the Jews, particularly in the East. Investigations have established that such rumours, most of them exaggerated or distorted in their content, can be traced to soldiers on leave from the East who have witnessed such occurrences.[21]

Rumours from the homeland had not reached Manstein particular, nor the front. In fact they took the opposite route.

Krausnick comments that,

German literature and segments of public opinion over the years stuck to a *cliché.* Apart from the *SS,* no one in German had any knowledge of *Nazi* atrocities, least of all the murder of Jews. In spite of total secrecy and the unchallenged power of the *SS,* whoever were able to gain some insight were horrified, and immediately opposed it actively, at danger to their own life.[22]

At Nuremberg, *SS-Obergruppenführer* von dem Bach-Zelewski appeared for the prosecution. When the prosecution asked him if the *Wehrmacht* was aware of the methods used in the fight against partisans, and the murder of Jews, he replied that such methods were known everywhere, and certainly by the military leadership.[23] A testimony by von dem Bach-Zelewski need not be accepted at face value. He had himself taken an active part in the murder of Jews, and had commanded the crushing of the Warsaw uprising in 1944. Von dem Bach-Zelewski added that he was disgusted by the sudden denial of actions, which only a short time previously had been accepted by everyone, by some even considered as having been

---

19 Trial, p.2.138
20 *Verlorene Siege,* p. 603
21 Reproduced in J. Wallach, *Feldmarschall Erich von Manstein und die deutsche Judenausrottung in Rußland* article in the annual of the Institute for German history, University Tel Aviv, 4/1957, p. 457-472, henceforth: Wallach
22 Krausnick, p. 598
23 Minutes of the Nuremberg trial against the major Nazi war criminals, Vol.32, p. 470 ff

'holy'.[24] Still, one cannot exclude that von dem Bach-Zelewski was eager to save himself, by his readiness to testify against his former accomplices. However, his statements were confirmed by General Roettiger, who later was to become the first inspector of *Bundeswehr* ground forces. General Roettiger testified: "The fight that we conducted against the partisans, had the real purpose of serving as a model for the ruthless extermination of Jews, and other undesirable elements."[25]

In reality, such testimonials are hardly required, since officers and soldiers of every large unit of the *Wehrmacht* took an active part in the crimes committed by the *Einsatzgruppen*. They had acted on direct orders from their commanders. So it is obvious that not a single German general can plead ignorance.

Direct reports to Manstein

Manstein received at least three direct reports from eyewitnesses, ie the officers of his Army, who had watched mass executions of Jews.

Report by Captain Ulrich Gunzert

Captain Gunzert attended a course for *Generalstab* candidates in 1942. He was sent for a short period to 11th Army's staff and witnessed a mass execution that he described in Knopp's video:

> Many layers of corpses were in the ditch. After every volley, an *SD* man descended into the ditch. If there were survivors, he fired a bullet into their heads. It was a mass murder. I will never forget the faces of the men and women who waited for their end. When I tried to intervene, an *SS* man told me: 'Disappear, this is no business of yours.' I then reported what I saw to Manstein and asked him to do something. Manstein refused. He was not concerned with what happened in the rear. He had more important things to attend to. He simply retreated to his military duties, and expressly forbade me to mention to others what I had witnessed. His behaviour was a flight from responsibility and a moral failure.[26]

Report by Colonel Eberhard Finckh

Colonel Finckh was the quartermaster of Army Group South. In 1944, he was transferred to Carl-Heinrich von Stülpnagel's staff in Paris. He participated in the 20 July actions in Paris and was hanged on 30 July 1944. In October 1943, Army Group's headquarters were in a suburb of Vinnitsa in the Ukraine. Stahlberg received a phone call from Finckh, requesting an urgent meeting. Stahlberg does not mention the exact date:

---

24   Krausnick, p.598 with reference to the New York Jewish magazine *Der Aufbau, Leben eines SS-Generals*, 12/35, 1946, p.40 (The magazine is published in German).
25   Ibid, p. 478 ff
26   Gunzert's account also in Knopp, p. 191

He had to speak to me immediately about a horrible matter. Two *Generalstab* officers had called upon him. They had witnessed a mass execution of Jews in a forest area that was part of Army Group's territory. The executions had been carefully planned and were well organised. The killers wore *SD* uniforms. I asked Finckh if he knew how many Jews were shot. He replied that his two witnesses had asked one of the *SD* men, and received the reply, 100,000. Finckh added that he had wanted to inform me before reporting to Manstein. Were Manstein to call him, he could be at his headquarters in less than one hour.

I returned and had tea with Manstein. As soon as the orderlies had left the room, he asked me why Finckh had wanted to see me. I replied: 'A horrible thing, the executions of Jews are taking place in our area.' Manstein became testy and asked why Finckh had chosen to talk to me instead of directly reporting to him. I replied that Finckh had wanted me to prepare him for his account, and that he would come immediately if Manstein wanted to get his direct report. Manstein asked me if Finckh had mentioned any figures and I replied, 100,000.

Manstein exploded! '100,000 is totally unbelievable. Even if we accept the story that 100,000 were shot at one single location, can someone tell me how such a number of bodies can be disposed of? Such rubbish is evidence that you and your friend have become victims of a filthy propaganda intrigue. As a young lieutenant during the First World War, I have already had my fill of enemy propaganda lies. This is certainly not the time to become victims of such tricks. We have recently exchanged recollections about the opening ceremony of the Berlin Olympic games that both of us had attended. There were some 100,000 spectators in the stadium. If one has this view in mind, let somebody try and explain to me how one can carry away such a number of corpses in order to conceal an execution. Tell your friend Finkh that I will not stand for such fairy-tales. If he wants to talk to me, I will agree to see him. I asked him if I should call Finckh. He told me to wait, he first wanted to think this over.[27]

In a conversation with the historian Bodo Scheurig, Stahlberg said that Manstein added: "Is it really negative if Jewry with its danger for Germany will be decimated?"[28] Stahlberg added that Manstein did receive Finckh on the following day. He purposely closed his door to Manstein's office during their talk. He knew what would be said and he did not want to experience a second shock.

Manstein's outburst calls for some comments. An execution of 100,000 Jews never took place on a single day. Perhaps the *SS* officers were simply bragging, but they could also have referred to the total number of victims of the *Einsatzgruppen*. In that case the number was realistic. But major actions did regularly occur. One need only be reminded of the massacre at Babi Yar, in which 33,788 Jews were slaughtered in 48 hours, on 29 and 30 September 1941. The massacre of 14,500 Jews at Simferopol required three days. When the massacre at Borisov took place in October 1941, Sergeant Soennecken, employed as interpreter at Army Group

27   Stahlberg, p.344 f
28   Wrochem, p.71

Centre, met with a Russian police officer, David Ehof, who had volunteered for service with the Germans. Ehof told him that he was going to shoot 8,000 Jews during the night. When Soennecken expressed doubts that an execution of this order of magnitude could be carried out within a few hours, Ehof told him that this was not the first time he succeeded in such a matter. He was no amateur. He and his men were quite capable of carrying out the killings within the time prescribed.[29]

The removal of such a number of corpses was not as difficult as Manstein wanted to imagine. It could not be accomplished in one single day, but not many days were needed. Such matters were taken care of by *SS-Standartenführer* Paul Blobel. His *Sonderkommando* had supervised the massacre at Babi Yar, and became expert in the removal of corpses. In June 1942, Blobel was ordered by the head of the Gestapo, *SS-Gruppenführer* Heinrich Müller, to remove all traces of mass executions. Blobel was sentenced to death in the *Einsatzgruppen* trial (IMT, Case 9) and hanged. He had testified:

> During a visit to Kiev, in August 1943, I supervised the burning of corpses that had been buried in a mass grave. The ditch was approximately 55 metres long, 3 metres wide, and had a depth of 2½ metres. After the cover of the ditch was removed, gasoline was poured over the corpses. It took approximately two days before the corpses were entirely consumed by the flames. They were then covered with earth and no traces remained. As the Red Army approached, it was unfortunately no longer possible to remove all traces from other burial sites.[30]

Previously, Blobel had conducted some unsuccessful experiments with dynamite. The commandant of the Auschwitz concentration camp, Rudolf Höss, testified before the IMT:

> Blobel had erected some furnaces and filled them with wood and gasoline. He then tried to blow up the bodies with dynamite but this did not succeed. Therefore I had to assist him in finding other methods. The ashes were simply strewn into the forest and the bones were ground to dust in a mill. The work was done by commandos of Jews brought from Auschwitz. They were shot after completion of their work. I was able to constantly supply such commandos.[31]

Blobel felt that all his murders had been carried out in strict accordance with international law: "Shootings of men and women who were suspected of espionage and sabotage, and who could cause damage to German soldiers and property, would entirely conform with the Hague conventions."[32]

Report by Captain Philipp von Boeselager

Boeselager called upon Manstein a few days after Finckh. He had talked to the same two officers, who had mentioned a figure of 250,000. Manstein responded in

---

29 Krausnick, p. 576 ff
30 IMT, Case 9, p. 108
31 Ibid, p. 109 f
32 Ibid, p. 166

the same manner as he did to Finkh. Instead of the Olympic stadium he mentioned the *Deutschlandhalle*, a huge indoor sports arena in Berlin, that could accommodate up to a quarter of a million spectators.[33]

The hidden page in 11th Army's war diary

Manstein's knowledge of mass executions was further established by a passage in 11th Army's war diary that had been covered with a white tape. Firstly, Manstein's own account, which, true to habit, he turned into an anecdote, just as he did whenever unpleasant facts concerning him were uncovered:

> While this act of a 'costly vengeance' [Manstein borrows the title of Freda Utley's book about the war crime tribunals] was in process, one of the prosecutors suddenly discovered that a page in 11th Army's war diary was covered by a tape. What a discovery! Surely this would show something which could be used against me. With great care the tape which covered the secret was removed. What kind of a shameful act by me would now appear? I had no idea of the tape, since I was forced to sign the diary but never had sufficient time to read it. This was the duty of my chief-of-staff. Once the tape was removed, the prosecutor read the uncovered text and became increasingly taken aback and embarrassed. The text read: 'We expect a new Army commander. He is a *Herr* and somewhat difficult. But one can speak frankly with him.' Finally the judges smiled at each other.[34]

Manstein described the event as a 'comical interlude'. It may well have been reduced to that, had not the following page also been covered by a tape. The chief prosecutor Elwyn-Jones ordered Manstein to read the text to the court: "The Army commander does not wish that officers become onlookers of executions of Jews. This is unworthy of a German officer."[35] Beevor comments that German military logic, in another of its distortions of cause and effect, does not appear to have acknowledged the possibility that officers had already shamed themselves by furthering the aims of a regime capable of such crimes.[36]

The first excesses in Poland

Wanton massacres of Jews had already occurred during the campaign in Poland and continued after it had ended. Railway coaches bringing soldiers to the front were painted with: '*Wir fahren nach Polen, Um Juden zu versohlen*' (We are on our way to Poland to beat up Jews). Some killings were committed by individuals, police, *SS*, and soldiers, others by *Wehrmacht* units of up to regimental strength. At that time, a few German generals protested, most remained silent bystanders. The groundwork for the later horrors in the East was already laid in 1939. It only required future consent by the generals for them to be put into practice.

---

33 Testimony Philipp von Boeselager on the ARD video.
34 *Verlorene Siege*, p.209
35 Paget, p. 173
36 Beevor, p. 55

Manstein could not write about those excesses in *Verlorene Siege*. Such a mention would have shown him to be already a liar, when he stated that he had never heard of mass murders of Jews.

A selection of protests voiced by higher commanders.

Generaloberst List, commander of 14th Army: "Looting, ... wanton executions, mistreatment of people without defence, rape, burning of synagogues."[37]

General von Cochenhausen, town commander of Warsaw:

> Illegal requisitioning – in other terms, simple plunder, has grown in Warsaw to such an extent that it can only be called a disgrace of the whole German Army. Excesses committed by drunken officers have turned into a daily routine. The police are unreliable. The civilian population suffers total misery. In spite of its needs, massive purchases of goods needed by the population take place and the officers are the ones who set the bad example. I am acting against such excesses with the most rigorous means. I want a court-martial to put an end to them within 24 hours. We have to succeed in putting an end to this undignified situation.[38]

A court-martial of a unit within 3rd Army sentenced a sergeant of the field-police to a nine-year term. An *SS Sturmbannführer* was sentenced to three years for shooting 50 Jews in a synagogue at Narev, after they had completed repair work at a bridge. On hearing the sentences, General von Küchler, commander of 3rd Army, quashed the verdict as being too lenient and ordered a new trial. However, the guilty men were pardoned before new proceedings began, after Hitler had declared a general amnesty on 4 October 1939, for crimes committed by Germans in Poland.[39] Küchler became the target of Himmler's strong anger, because he had called the *SS*-unit a blot on the honour of the Army.[40] Küchler was the only Army commander in Poland who was not promoted to *Generaloberst* after the campaign. List already held that rank before the war.

General Petzel, commander of I Corps, wrote that the conduct of the soldiers was totally undignified.[41] *Generaloberst* Ritter von Leeb, whose Army Group C had remained in the West during the Polish campaign, heard of events in Poland, and wrote to Brauchitsch on 19 December 1939, that the behaviour of the German soldiers in Poland was unworthy of a nation of culture.[42] Knowledge of German behaviour in Poland had quickly spread to other theatres of war.

On 25 October 1939, *Generaloberst* von Brauchitsch addressed the following message to the whole Officer Corps:

> The performance and the success of operations in Poland cannot hide that some of our officers simply lack firm control. An alarming number of instances are evidence of illegal actions, such as illegal confiscation of prop-

37 *NOKW* 1621
38 Krausnick, p. 598 with reference to BA-MA, RH 20-8, O.Qu.P. 1032, L.2
39 Krausnick, p. 81
40 Ibid, p.81
41 IMT, Vol.35, p. 89
42 Ibid. p. 98

erty, theft committed by officers, threats or mistreatment of subordinates while totally drunk, disobedience in the sight of their soldiers. All of this has had dire consequences on the conduct of subordinates. Rape of a married woman, etc, show the manners of mercenaries that have to be condemned with the utmost severity. Those officers, regardless if they have acted carelessly or on purpose, are 'destructive weeds' who have no place in our Officer Corps. I will refrain from giving individual names or mentioning the punishments that have been meted out. I want to emphasise that the manner in which an officer conducts himself in war will be decisive in his peacetime evaluation.[43]

Generaloberst Johannes Blaskowitz, who had commanded 9th Army during the campaign and who was made supreme commander East after the Polish surrender, wrote two strong memoranda of protest against the German behaviour in Poland.

It is totally inept to slaughter some 10,000 Jews or Poles as happens now. It will neither cause the Polish population nor the Jews to disappear. On the contrary, the size and the manner of the massacres lead to serious damage. It complicates whatever problems there are and increases their danger.

1. Enemy propaganda is provided with the best imaginable tool. What foreign broadcasts have reported until now is only a small fraction of what has been going on. World wide, protests will increase and cause us great damage, particularly since the hideous deeds have taken place and cannot be contradicted by any evidence.

2. Behaviour of commanders, who witness such crimes without reacting, deserves no further mention. Their reputation is irremediably damaged, not only in the eyes of the Polish population. The greatest danger for the soul of the German people will be its boundless coarsening and moral depravity. It will soon spread like an epidemic across the whole German nation. There is no doubt that the Polish people, who have to witness such deeds without being able to defend themselves, will be driven to despair and will fanatically support every movement of resistance and vengeance. Segments of society, which would never have considered an uprising, will now seize every opportunity and become resolute fighters. The many small peasants, who would have worked peacefully for us, had we treated them with decency, will be compelled by our behaviour to join every rebellion.

3. The feeling of the troops towards the *SS* and the police is disgust and hatred. Every decent soldier is repulsed by crimes committed in Poland by officials of the *Reich*, which furthermore have the appearance that they are committed under my authority. They cannot understand that such deeds remain unpunished.[44]

---

43   BA-MA –N 104/3
44   *NOKW* 3011

Blaskowitz appended a letter from General Wilhelm Ulex, commander of the southern border area:

> There is only way out from this undignified situation that casts an indelible blot upon the honour of the whole German people. It is to immediately dismiss all members of the police, including their highest commanders, who have been content to watch such events without taking action and to replace them with units that have kept their honour.[45]

Hitler immediately replaced the Military Government with a Civilian Administration under Hans Frank, after saying that war was not conducted with Salvation Army methods. "Soldiers have to remain with their military assignment, they are not allowed to govern or to administrate."[46] Blaskowitz remained the only *Generaloberst* of 1939 who was never promoted to *Feldmarschall.*

On 4 February 1940, *Feldmarschall* August von Mackensen, the only surviving German *Feldmarschall* of the First World War, wrote to Brauchitsch:

> As a man becomes older, he has to watch carefully that age has not reduced his creativity. After reaching the age of 90, I have decided not to involve myself any longer with matters that are not concerned with my private life. However, I am still the most senior German officer. Many turn to me, sometimes with wishes, but more often with their concerns.
>
> During these weeks our concern is with the spirit of our unique and successful Army. The concern results from the crimes committed in Poland, looting and murder that take place before the eyes of our troops, who appear unable to put an end to them. An apparent indifference has serious consequences for the morale of our soldiers and it is damaging to the esteem of our Army and our whole nation.
>
> I am sure that you are aware of these events and that you certainly condemn them. These lines intend to convey my daily growing concern at the reports that constantly reach me, and I have to ask you to take up this matter with the highest authority. The messages I receive are so numerous, many come from high ranking persons and from witnesses. As the most senior officer I cannot keep them to myself. In transmitting them to you, I fulfil my duty to the Army. The honour of the Army and the esteem in which it is held must not be jeopardised by the actions of hired subhumans and criminals.[47]

For the first time, the term 'subhuman' appears in a German document, however, not in relation to Jews, but to German soldiers.

Paget purports to know better: "The German soldiers behaved well in Poland. Maybe some synagogues were set ablaze, and some Jews were occasionally subjected to humiliation."[48] (At that point, the tribunal lost patience and asked Paget if he was trying to make jokes.)

---

45   Krausnick, p. 102 f. The complete documents are in BA-MA, RH 53 – 22/23
46   Minutes of the trial against the major Nazi war criminals, vol.XXIX, p. 435
47   BA-MA, H 08-39/314, Estate Mackensen.
48   Paget, p. 157

Manstein was chief-of-staff of Rundstedt's Army Group South and thus had knowledge of every event reported to it. In one of these reports about three soldiers who had mistreated a Jew, raped his daughter and had looted Jewish shops, a note from Manstein is appended: "How long will it finally take before this matter is dealt with by a court-martial?"[49] But other reports were not passed on by him to his Army Group Commander, such as a draft order submitted to him on 8 September 1939: "Concerning discipline: Present excesses are incompatible with the honour of the *Wehrmacht* and every German soldier. I request that the strongest possible steps are immediately taken to put a stop to them." The following comment is appended:

> The draft has been shown to *Generalleutnant* von Manstein, Chief-of-staff of Army Group South, for communication to the Army Group Commander, *Generaloberst* von Rundstedt. Communication refused by *Generalleutnant* von Manstein. Signed: Langhaeuser, Ic of Army Group South.[50]

Langhaeuser's draft was prompted by the beatings of Polish prisoners of war and violence against Polish civilians. The 'Langhaeuser incident' came up at the trial of the *OKW* and the *Generalstab* at Nuremberg. Langhaeuser explained that he wanted Rundstedt to issue a general order against such excesses, to be communicated to all units in Poland. Manstein refused to communicate the draft to Rundstedt, because it did not contain evidence referring to specific actions, as if such 'evidence' was required.[51] By refusing to pass on the draft, Manstein prevented an order by Rundstedt which was sorely needed.

Many Jews had attempted to flee to German occupied territory after the Red Army had marched into Poland. Manstein added a note to an order by Rundstedt to Reichenau: "Use all means to prohibit the influx of Upper Silesia by Jewish refugees."[52] Reichenau added: "If required, by armed force."

Paget adds one of his unintelligent comments: "Had Manstein known that the Jews would be exterminated in Poland, I feel that the Jews should have praised him for having taken all measures preventing them from returning."[53]

The Massacre at Konskie.
Reality and Manstein's attempt
at a tasteless humoresque

The events at Konskie were brought up at Manstein's trial. The massacre followed the death of the police general Roettig. Roettig had been killed in action during a regular combat, but his death was reported as a murder by *Einsatzgruppe* II. It had been set up during the Polish campaign. The *Einsatzgruppe* set up a 'murder investigation commission', which was ordered to find out if inhabitants of the neigh-

---

49   Krausnick, p. 76
50   Ibid, p. 77
51   Paget, p.154 f
52   Trial, p. 396
53   Paget, p. 157

bouring township of Konskie could be found among the 'perpetrators'. As a first step, *Einsatzgruppe* II shot twenty hostages, without making any reference to the death of General Roettig. Then General von Reichenau, commander of 10th Army, ordered the arrest of all male civilians, aged 18 and over, at Konskie and its neighbourhood – in all some 5,000 people. They were brought into a camp at Konskie and carefully searched. Some 120 Jews, Poles and Polish soldiers, who had donned civilian clothes, were found to wear underwear with bloodstains, although they had not taken part in combat. This rendered them suspect of having gained possession of German money and they were thus convinced to have "ordered the massacre of German soldiers." They were shot. The famous film producer Leni Riefenstahl happened to be present. She was horrified by what she saw, and made an immediate report to Army Group South.

Manstein chose to write about the Konskie massacre as follows:

> One day, a well known film producer and actress appeared at our head-quarters, accompanied by a team of cameramen. She said that she was following in the footsteps of the *Führer* and had been ordered by Hitler to make a movie at the front. Such an activity, in particular by a woman, was most displeasing to us soldiers. But there was Hitler's order that could not be cast aside. She looked quite nice and bold, like an elegant partisan woman, who had bought her dress at a *Rue du Rivoli* luxury store. Her beautiful hair, like a flaming lion's mane, surrounded her interesting face, with its eyes close together. She wore a kind of ancient Roman tunic, breeches and soft leather boots. She carried a pistol at her belt. Her arma-ment was completed by a long knife inserted in the shaft of her boot, in Bavarian fashion. This appearance caused us to be somewhat perplexed. I had to accompany her to *Generaloberst* von Rundstedt, to permit her to present her mission to him. The old gentleman received her in his usual charming manner but soon brought her back to me.
>
> I had no choice but to organise her visit. With her team she drove to Konskie, headquarters of 10th Army. [Leni Riefenstahl had been acquainted with General von Reichenau since before the war. Manstein does not mention her name in his account.] She soon returned. Some shootings had already previously occurred at Konskie and the civilian population had taken part in them. A crowd had gathered on the market-square and one anti-aircraft lieutenant had become nervous. This created an unnecessary panic. It led to senseless shooting, which resulted in some victims. The movie team happened to witness this regrettable scene and our lady returned completely shaken by what she had seen. The officer was convicted of manslaughter, sentenced to loss of rank, and to some years in jail.[54]

In other words, a story of the kind that "regrettable things happen in wartime."

---

54 *Verlorene Siege*, p. 43 ff

Barbarossa – the Generals' hate appeals

In the weeks preceding the attack against Russia, the German Commanders had already issued strong anti-Semitic orders to their troops. The protest in Poland had been replaced by Hitler's speech of 30 March 1941. The Generals now attempted to outbid themselves with appeals to violence that were tantamount to murder. No great mental effort was required. The notion of the Jewish-*Bolshevist* subhuman had already entered the officers' language during the years of the Weimar Republic. Streit wrote that the appeals had put a final end to the 'classification' of generals. The 'totally conservative' Rundstedt, the purported 'expert only' Manstein, the *Nazi* Reichenau, and the conservative military resistance man Stülpnagel, in their relation to the death squads all followed the same compulsion.[55]

Generaloberst Hoepner, Commander of *Panzergruppe 4.* 2 May 1941:

> The war against Russia is the consequence of the fight that we are compelled to wage, in order to preserve our existence, to guarantee the economic independence of Greater Germany, and all of Europe that has come under her domination. It is the old struggle of the Germans against the Slavs, the defence of European culture against the Muscovite-Asiatic flood, the throwing back of Jewish *Bolshevism.*
>
> This struggle must lead to the annihilation of today's Russia and requires methods of unprecedented brutality. Every military action has to be inspired by an iron will of a merciless destruction of the enemy. No mercy will be shown to the leaders of the Russian-*Bolshevist* system.[56]

On 6 July 1941, Hoepner issued an additional order, asking "for good and fair treatment of the loyal population". He added that "individual acts of sabotage should simply be charged to communists and Jews."[57]

Generalfeldmarschall von Reichenau, commander of 6th Army, 10 August 1941, some weeks before he issued his infamous order of the day: "Executions of criminals, *Bolshevists*, and mostly Jewish elements are carried out by units of the *SD* of the *Reichsführer SS* and chief of the German Police."[58]

General der Infanterie Karl von Roques, *Korück*, the Military Commander of the rear area of Army Group South: "If acts of sabotage occur without the perpetrators having been discovered, search should not be made among Ukrainians, but confined to Russians and Jews. All measures of reprisals to be taken against them."[59]

General der Infanterie Carl-Heinrich von Stülpnagel, Commander of 17th Army, 30 July 1941:

> If an act of sabotage cannot be shown to have been committed by an Ukrainian, the village elders have to be ordered to name Jewish and communist inhabitants. This will encourage the population to engage in

55   Streit, p. 113
56   *NOKW* 2510
57   Krausnick, p. 219
58   *NOKW* 1654 and 2176
59   *NOKW* 1691

denunciation ... Many members of the Russian youth organisation *Komsomol* have remained behind. If urgency is required, they are easy to get hold of. In particular, Jewish members of the *Komsomol* have to be considered as the standard bearers of sabotage and the formation of juvenile criminal bands.[60]

In a letter of 21 August 1941 to the department of propaganda at *OKW*, Stülpnagel had written: "Request to German propaganda: increased fight against Jewry. Total enlightenment about Jewry is a must."[61]

Back in 1935, Stülpnagel had already written in a memorandum: "The 'snitching' attitude of the commissars, who are mostly Jewish, reminds one of the worst years of the beginning of the Soviet system. Since Jews are averse to military duties even in the Soviet Union, most Russian officers view them with distrust."[62]

General der Infanterie von Salmuth, Commander of XXX Corps, 2 August 1941:

> The fanatical will of the communist party and the Jews to halt the progress of the German *Wehrmacht*, must be broken at all costs. Special units are here in charge. At one location, *Wehrmacht* troops have unfortunately taken part in such an action. Soldiers are only permitted to do this, if expressly ordered by their commanders.[63]

Salmuth refers to the massacre at Kodyma in which troops of his corps had participated. The massacre will be described, in detail, in the part of this chapter dealing with *Judenaktionen* in all cities under control of 11th Army. If soldiers may participate in massacre on direct orders by their commanders, such orders were obviously given, in spite of the post-war denials of the generals.

General der Panzertruppe Reinhardt, Commander of XLI Corps, May 1941: "It is the old struggle of the Germans against the Slavs, the struggle of European culture against the Muscovite-Asiatic flood, and the defence against Jewish *Bolshevism*"[64]

This order is identical with Hoepner's order. Reinhardt's Corps was part of Hoepner's *Panzergruppe* 4. Perhaps Reinhardt's staff officer was too lazy to write an order of his own, and simply copied Hoepner's paper with Reinhardt's signature added.

Finally an order by Manstein, 12 June 1941: "This war demands acts, without mercy, against Soviet trouble-makers, snipers, partisans and Jews."[65]

Did the generals really believe all their nonsense? It cannot be excluded. Since none had ever made an effort to acquaint himself with the Soviet Union, it was obviously easier to remain with *Nazi* propaganda slogans. Still the question remains, why they found it necessary to issue such orders, especially as after the war, they were relentlessly eager to distance themselves from such edicts.

---

60   Krausnick, p. 219
61   BA-MA, RW 4
62   BA-MA, H 1/661
63   BA-MA, RH 20 –11/488
64   *NOKW* 2012
65   *NOKW* 2018

Krausnick stated that the generals may well have believed in what they wrote, since the belief that the Russian-*Bolshevists* were subhuman was part of their credo. Their orders were a justification of their own actions.[66] Friedrich advances the opinion that the generals consciously invented a fairy tale:

> The Generals explained to their soldiers, in great detail, the murders committed in the East. The Jews were the standard-bearers of *Bolshevism* and the war was started because they had to be exterminated. The Jews held the threads between the Red Army and the regions that the Germans had already liberated. There, the former holders of sovereignty had to be totally eliminated. Other former subjects of the Soviet power had to be treated harshly, but fairness had to be shown to them, provided they accepted their new masters.
>
> Those slogans, which were spread across the whole Eastern Front, have been exposed at Nuremberg as ideological nonsense. The Jews were never the main agents of the central authority of the Soviet Union. They were the weakest element in the Soviet population. No other population group was more adaptable, and none encountered more hostility. The Generals had simply created a legend. This is not unusual. No war can be conducted without legends. With the stab-in-the back legend, the Generals had branded the Jews and the Socialists as the culprits of their defeat in the First World War. Did they believe it? It was unimportant. They believed that it was useful. Generals are not interested in truth, their only interest is in success.[67]

Streit is of the opinion that the Generals, who had opposed the war against France, had learned their lesson. They were now convinced that the future was with the National-Socialist leadership and wanted to publicly show their loyalty to the party line.[68]

Perhaps an easier formulation can be found. Hitler had little interest in the extent to which the Generals adhered to the party line. It was sufficient for him that they obeyed his orders. He did not need the Generals to convince the German people of his propaganda, the Generals were only too happy that Hitler confirmed their traditional prejudice against Eastern European Jews. The Generals had opposed Hitler's war in France because they feared defeat. The German victory in France had proved Hitler right. The Generals now expected a new victorious *Blitzkrieg* against the Soviet Union and wanted to be part of every effort, including official propaganda, and to share in the glory of victory.

Generals are not only interested in success, their main ambition is glory. When Dr Popitz was interrogated by the Gestapo, after 20 July 1944, he was asked how he felt that he could succeed in his attempt. Since he knew that he had forfeited his life, he could permit himself a joke, and said:

> My proposal would have been, on the first day of the war, to cover the whole chest of every general with decorations. Then, every day, as long as

---

66 Krausnick, p. 220
67 Friedrich, p. 252
68 Streit, p. 55

there were decorations left on his uniform, one decoration was to be removed. This would have brought the war to a rapid conclusion.[69]

Without doubt, the *Einsatzgruppen* were elated by these orders, since they immediately saw that the Generals did not intend to place any obstacles in their way. Manstein's testimony at his trial is a good example of German ignorance:

> I was of the opinion that there was a direct link between the *Bolshevik* system and Jewry. Jews could be found in many high positions, both in politics and in the Red Army. During a visit to the Soviet Union, I met a number of commanders of the highest ranks who were Jews. Jews could also be found in sizeable numbers among saboteurs and partisans. Therefore I was not surprised that *OKH* had warned us against them. I don't deny that the *Nazi* policy had embittered the Jews against us, so we had no choice but to take preventive measures, to keep them from bringing their hatred into action.[70]

If 'prevention' is replaced by 'extermination', then Manstein and his comrades certainly showed themselves efficient.

Manstein's 'watch' had come to a halt in 1917. History was a subject that had always remained alien to him. Since Manstein was not allowed to see anything during his visits to the Soviet Union, except what the Russians showed him, he knew nothing, except what he had been permitted to see. The Jews, who had remained in the territories occupied by the Germans, never represented any danger to the *Wehrmacht*. The only danger the Germans could never overcome was the increasing strength of the Red Army. The Jews in leading positions in the Russian communist party, in the immediate aftermath of the revolution, had never had Jewish interests on their mind.

On the contrary, in a number of his writings, Trotsky was openly anti-Semitic.[71] In 1907, Stalin had published a series of openly anti-Semitic articles in a local newspaper in Baku, in which he suggested that the party should organise *pogroms*. After the revolution, Zionism and all other Jewish political movements were immediately forbidden. When Manstein visited the Soviet Union, the only Jewish member of the *Politburo* was Kaganovich, who will not be recorded by history as a 'philo-Semite'. The only high ranking Jewish Red Army commanders whom Manstein met were Generals Yakir and Feldman, both of whom were shot in 1937. The highest ranking Jewish Red Army General during the Second World War was Lieutenant General Yakov Kreiser, who was only promoted further after Stalin's death.

The Jews were the only official nationality of the Soviet Union that had neither a territory of their own, nor an official language. Every citizen in the Soviet Union held Soviet citizenship. In addition, every recognised population group had its own nationality. The small region of Birobidjan, in the Far East, which had been offered to the Jews as a replacement for Palestine, was a simple farce. Very few

69 R. Hildebrandt, *...die besten Köpfe, die man henkt. Ein tragischer Auftakt zur deutschen Teilung und der Mauer,* Berlin 2003, p. 141 f – A. Hildebrandt (ed). (henceforth:Hildebrandt)

70 Trial, p.1.937

71 J. Nedava, *Trotsky and the Jews,* The Jewish Publication Society of Philadelphia, 1971

Jews agreed to settle there. In 1937 further settlement of Jews was forbidden, under the pretext that the Jews in Birobidjan could be turned into Japanese spies. There were only a few Jewish partisan units. A number of them were destroyed by larger anti-Semitic partisan units. In provinces occupied by the Germans, where active anti-Semitism had existed over many years, Jews who had been able to escape were often caught by the local population, and handed over to the Germans. "The partisan movement, which always emphasised the cruelty of the German occupiers, seldom mentioned the massacre of the Jews by the *Einsatzgruppen*. It feared that the murders could find sympathy among local anti-Semites."[72]

Not unexpectedly, Paget felt bound to add his wisdom:

> The Germans regarded the Jews as the rulers of *Bolshevism*. With regard to the Ukraine, this was to some extent the case. The Jews were the only people in the Ukraine who stood firmly behind the communist regime. They had good reasons, since the communist government was the first of its kind in Russia which protected them against *pogroms*.[73]

Paget's statement is no less beside the point than Manstein's testimony. During the civil war, many *pogroms* occurred in the Ukraine. Some were organised by the Reds, some by the Whites, depending upon who had temporary control of a given area. After the civil war, Jews were practically excluded from public functions in the Ukraine. At the beginning of the war not a single Jew belonged to the leadership of the Ukrainian party or held any functions in the Ukrainian government. The Jewish Kaganovich had taken good care of their removal during his period as first secretary of the Ukrainian communist party. There was not a single Jewish partisan unit in the Ukraine. There were units that fought against the Germans, others fought both against the *Wehrmacht* and against the Red Army. After the Red Army recaptured Kiev, Army General Vatutin was murdered by one of those units. A Ukrainian underground movement remained active until the mid-1950s.[74]

The summit of absurdity was reached by the search list of the 'advance command Moscow', a sub-command unit of *Einsatzgruppe* B, under *SS-Oberführer*, Professor Dr Franz Six. The command had the assignment to arrest 'important personalities' after the German capture of Moscow. The names contained on its list were classified as being 'particularly dangerous' or 'less dangerous'. The *Politburo* members, Krushchev and Berya, and the *Politburo* candidate Kossygin, were not even mentioned. Breithaupt, who even to-day knows no more about the Soviet Union than Franz Six knew in 1941, described the Georgian Berya as having been a Jewish intellectual. He was neither.

The famous pianist David Gilels was listed as 'particularly dangerous'. The not less renowned violinist, David Oistrakh, was not mentioned. The totally harmless former chess world champion, Dr Emanuel Lasker, who had briefly emigrated to the Soviet Union in 1935, was classified as 'less dangerous'. In 1939 he had already left for the USA. The former chief of the *Gulag* administration, Boris Berman, was included among the 'particularly dangerous'. However, by 1938 he

---

72   J. Armstrong (ed.), *Soviet Partisans in World War II*, Madison 194, p. 279, also quoted in Friedrich, p. 414

73   Paget, p. 194

74   H. Kostiuk, *Stalinist Rule in the Ukraine*, Institute for the Study of the USSR, Munich 1966 and B. Levitskyi, *Die Sowjet-Ukraine 1944–1963*, Cologne 1964.

had already been shot. The 'advance command' from Moscow did not proceed beyond Smolensk. Six assisted *Einsatzgruppe* B in its murders, since it had fallen somewhat behind in the prescribed number of victims.[75] Six was sentenced to twenty years by the IMT, Case 9 (The *Einsatzgruppen* trial). He was set free after a few years and spent the remainder of his life in lucrative business ventures, as a publisher, executive consultant and marketing expert.

The three 'Murder' orders of the day. *Feldmarschall* von Reichenau, *Generaloberst* Hoth and General von Manstein

The Reichenau order of the day

On 10 October 1941 *Feldmarschall* von Reichenau, Commander of 6th Army, released the following order of the day:

Subject: Behaviour of the troops in the East:
There is insufficient clarity about the behaviour required by troops toward the *Bolshevist* system. The main purpose of the war against the Jewish-*Bolshevist* system is the annihilation of all its means of power, and the extermination of Asiatic influence upon European culture.

This confronts the troops with duties that go beyond one-sided traditional soldierly norms. The soldier in the East is not only a fighter in accordance with the art of war, he is likewise the bearer of a relentless popular ideology, and the avenger of all the bestialities committed against the German people and nations related to her by common blood.

Therefore the soldier has to have full understanding of the necessity of the just punishment inflicted upon subhuman Jewry. It is likewise necessary to put down any attempts of uprising in the rear, which are usually instigated by Jews.

The battle against the enemy behind the front is not taken seriously enough. Malicious and cruel partisans and degenerate women are still treated as prisoners-of-war. Snipers in civilian clothes or wearing parts of uniforms, and tramps are treated like decent soldiers and sent to prisoner-of-war camps. Russian officers, who have been captured, tell with a sneer of contempt that Soviet agents are roaming peacefully in the streets of captured cities and are often fed by German field kitchens. Such an attitude by the troops is simply thoughtless. Time has now come for their superiors to awake them to the requirements of the present struggle.

Giving food at field kitchens to the civilian population and to prisoners-of-war who are not performing work for the *Wehrmacht*, is just as much a misunderstood humanity as the giving away of cigarettes and

---

75   L. Hachmeister, *Der Gegenforscher. Die Karriere des SS-Führers Franz Alfred Six,* Munich 1998

bread. The soldier is not allowed to give away to the enemy what the homeland lacks under great privations, and what has been carried to the front with the greatest difficulty. This prohibition also extends to goods captured from the enemy. They are a necessary part of our catering.

During their retreat the Soviets had set many buildings ablaze. The troops are only interested in extinguishing the fires, if the buildings can be preserved as their quarters. In all other eventualities, the destruction of symbols of the former *Bolshevist* system, even buildings, is part of the framework of the war of destruction. Historic or artistic considerations cannot be given consideration in the East. Command will issue the necessary orders for preserving raw material resources and production entities that are necessary to our war effort.

Disarmament of the population, in the rear of the fighting troops, has total precedence, given the difficult transportation conditions to the front. Whenever possible, captured arms and equipment have to be carefully preserved and put under guard. If combats do not permit this, all captured arms and equipment have to be immediately destroyed. If armed partisans are discovered in the rear, draconian measures must be implemented. Such measures must also extend to male civilians who could have had the possibility to avoid armed attempts or to stay away from them. The indifference, shown by many who pretend to be hostile to *Bolshevism*, has to give way to a clear decision to actively participate in the fight against it. If this does not happen, no one has the right to complain if he is considered to be an adherent to the Soviet system and treated as such. Fear of German measures must be stronger than apprehension of the loose remainder of Red Army units.

While remaining remote from future political considerations, the soldiers have to comply with two overriding duties:

1. Total destruction of *Bolshevist* heresy, the Soviet State and its Army.

2. Merciless annihilation of alien maliciousness and cruelty, thus preserving the security and life of the German *Wehrmacht* in Russia.

Only in this manner will we be true to our historic mission, to liberate the German people for all time to come from the Asiatic-Jewish peril.

From the Commander in Chief. Signed: von Reichenau, *Generalfeldmarschall.*"[76]

On 28 October 1941, *OKH* communicated the *Reich*enau order to the three Army Group Commanders in the East with an accompanying letter:

By order of the Commander in chief of the Army, an order of the day by the Commander of 6th Army about the conduct of the troops in the East is attached, which the *Führer* considers to be excellent. The Commanders are requested to issue orders of a similar content, if this has not already been done. Signed: Wagner, by order[77]

---

76 IMT, vol.XXXV, p. 84 ff. also *NOKW* D-411
77 Oberkommando des Heeres, Gen.St.d.H./Gen. Qu.Abt.K. Verw.(Qu. 4/B) 11 74
    98/41 g.H.Qu. OKH, 28.20.41

Feldmarschall von Rundstedt, Commander of Army Group South, wrote to three of his Army Commanders, von Manstein–11th Army, Hoth–17th Army, von Kleist- 1st *Panzer* Army, and his *Korück*, that he was 'in full agreement' with Reichenau's order of the day. He asked them to 'consider' issuing similar orders, provided they had not already done so under their own initiative, after adapting them to local considerations.[78]

Einsatzgruppe C, which operated in the area of Reichenau's 6th Army was particularly elated:

> As far as the future is concerned, we can certainly expect active support by 6th Army. *Feldmarschall* von Reichenau has clearly indicated in his order of 10 October 1941 that a Red Army soldier has to be considered as being a representative of *Bolshevism* and treated as such.[79]

The wording of the Reichenau order shows the same anomaly as the communication of the 'Commissar order' by the high commanders to their subordinates. A General gives orders to his troops, he does not ask for their understanding. He assumes that his soldiers understand him, if they do not, they have to obey without understanding. Krausnick voices the opinion that some younger officers were outraged at the actions of the *Einsatzgruppen* and that Reichenau wanted to call them to order.[80] In other terms, it was not the generals, who swore after the war that they had known nothing, but younger officers and soldiers, who had opposed the murders of the *Einsatzgruppen* and who had to be corrected by the generals in their 'erroneous' views.

Reichenau was not a client of Paget, so there was no need for Paget to concern himself with his order of the day. But since Reichenau's order served as model for Manstein's order of the day, Paget could not refrain from commenting on it in a particularly distasteful manner:

> Just let us replace German hatred with our own. We could have easily issued the following document. In their attitude toward the *Nazi*-system, our soldiers are less than mindful of their duties. They have always to be aware that the main purpose of our war against the Prussian *Nazi*-system is the total elimination of its diabolical influence upon Europe's cultural life. The soldiers are therefore faced with duties that reach far beyond normal military concepts. The soldier is no longer a simple combatant, he likewise embodies the democratic ideal. He is the avenger of all the cruelties committed by the Germans. The soldiers must be conscious of their duty to exercise a strong but at the same time just retribution upon the German Huns.

Paget asks: "Does that sound much different from the stuff we distributed in 1944 and 1945"?[81]

---

78 *NOKW* 309
79 *Einsatzgruppe* C, EM 128, November 3, 1941, also quoted in Krausnick, p. 261
80 Krausnick, p. 256
81 Paget, p. 194

The Hoth order of the day

On 17 November 1941 *Generaloberst* Hoth issued an order of the day that was not an adaptation of the Reichenau order but was formulated by himself. The wording can cast doubt upon Hoth's sanity. The document is so full of repetitive venom and hatred, that it is sufficient to reproduce the relevant parts.

Hoth begins with a lengthy introduction, in which he turns himself into a historian:

> It has become increasingly clear to us during the summer that irreconcilable views fight each other in the East. On the one side are German feelings of mastery and race, and century long soldierly values. On the other are Asiatic doctrines, inflamed by the primitive instincts of a small number of intellectuals, mostly of Jewish origin. There is fear of the whip of oppression, disregard of ethical virtues, descent into moral abyss, readiness to throw away their own valueless life.
>
> Every day our conviction becomes stronger that the future has intended the German people to reign supreme over Europe, thanks to the superiority of its race and the accomplishments of its leadership. We clearly recognise that our mission is to save European culture from Asiatic barbarism ... Five months of uninterrupted successes have brought this campaign to a victorious conclusion. The once powerful Red Army is no longer capable of organised operations and cohesive resistance ... During the winter, operations will not come to a complete stand-still. The *Führer* will not demand the impossible from the German soldier. No German troops will be exposed to the rigours of the Russian Winter. We know that we are fighting a strong and bitter enemy. Such a fight can only end with the annihilation of one. There is no room for compromise.
>
> Russia is an Asiatic state, it is not European. Every step into this enslaved and joyless country shows the difference. We have the duty to liberate Europe, and in particular Germany, for a future free from the destructive strength and pressure of *Bolshevism*.

Then follows the order of the day:

> The soldiers have to be the first to understand the necessity of hard measures against elements void of popular and racial honour. They are the pallbearers of *Bolshevism*, the messengers of murder and the agents of the partisans. The Jewish subhuman had already caused great damage to our fatherland, now he is the agent of currents hostile to Germany world-wide and wants to be the bearer of vengeance. His extermination is an imperative of self-preservation. A soldier who is critical of our measures, does not remember the former destructive and treasonable poisoning of our own people by Jewish-*Bolshevist* elements.[82]

Every sentence of Hoth shows his feeble-mindedness. The German is a master by right of birth, and the superiority of his race makes it incumbent upon him to assume the leadership of Europe. If the Russian is already prepared to throw his valueless life away, why does he need the assistance of the German soldier? Hoth was soon to experience for himself the extent to which the Red Army was still capable of strong defence and major operations, since his Army was one of the victims of the Russian counter-offensive at Moscow. Later, in 1942 at Stalingrad, and in 1943 at Kursk, the armies under his command were practically destroyed. The German soldier soon paid the price for the scant attention given to the Russian winter.

The Manstein order of the day

On 20 November 1941, Manstein issued the following order of the day to his 11th Army:

> Since 22 June, the German people have engaged in a struggle for life or death against the *Bolshevist* system. This war is not conducted in traditional manner, solely against the Russian Army, and it does not follow European rules of war. Fighting continues behind the front. Partisans, and snipers in civilian clothes, attack individual soldiers. Small units attempt to destroy our supply lines with mines and other infernal tools. *Bolshevists*, who have remained behind, continue to impose terror and disquiet on a population liberated from *Bolshevism*, and thus attempt sabotage of the political and economic pacification of the country. Industrial plants and harvests are destroyed and the urban population is exposed to famine.
>
> Jewry is the centre, between the enemy in the rear, and the remaining units of the Red Army that are still capable of fighting. More than anywhere else in Europe, Jewry holds all keys of political leadership and administration, trade and handcraft, and it is the cell of all disturbance and potential uprisings.
>
> The Jewish-*Bolshevist* system has to be exterminated for all times. It must never be permitted again to penetrate our European *Lebensraum*.
>
> The German soldier not only has the sole duty to destroy the military means of this system, he is also the standard bearer of a popular idea, and an avenger of the cruelty against himself and the whole German people.
>
> Combat in the rear is not paid sufficient attention. The soldier has to participate actively in disarming the population, in controlling it, and arresting all loafing soldiers and civilians. He has to see to the removal of all *Bolshevist* symbols. Every sabotage has to be punished immediately and with the most radical means, every symptom has to be reported without delay.
>
> The food situation in Germany makes it necessary for the troops to live with what is available in occupied areas, and to see that a maximum quantity of available foodstuff is sent to the homeland.
>
> In enemy cities, much of the population will have to remain hungry. Humanity arising from a lack of understanding cannot be permitted to divert food from the homeland by distributing it to the civilian population and to prisoners-of-war, unless they perform work for the *Wehrmacht*.

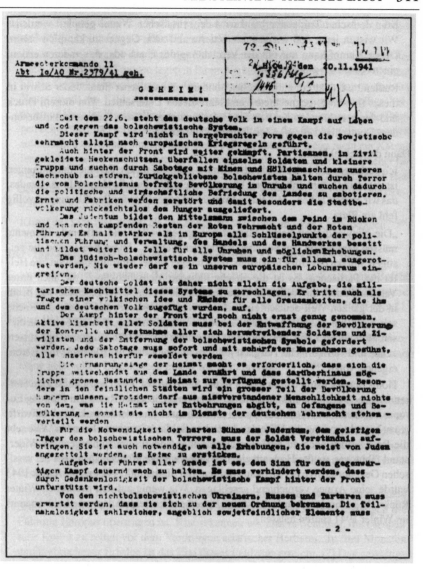

Manstein's order of the day of November 20, 1941.

The soldier has to show understanding for the harsh punishment meted out to Jewry, the spiritual flag bearer of *Bolshevist* terror. This punishment is necessary, to nip in the bud all attempts of uprisings that are mostly inspired by Jews. Commanders of all ranks have to keep their soldiers constantly aware of the spirit of the present struggle. Lack of reflection must not be permitted to aid the *Bolshevist* struggle in the rear of the front line.

- 2 -

einer klaren Entscheidung zur aktiven Mitarbeit gegen den Bolschewismus weichen. Wo sie nicht besteht, muss sie durch entsprechende Mass-
nahmen erzwungen werden.
Die freiwillige Mitarbeit am Aufbau des besetzten Landes be-
deutet für die Erreichung unserer wirtschaftlichen und politischen
Ziele eine absolute Notwendigkeit.
Sie hat eine gerechte Behandlung aller nichtbolschewistischen
Teile der Bevölkerung, die z.T. jahrelang gegen den Bolschewismus
heldenhaft gekämpft haben, zur Voraussetzung.
Die Herrschaft in diesem Lande verpflichtet uns zur Leistung,
zur Härte gegen sich selbst und zur Zurückstellung der Person. Die
Haltung jedes Soldaten wird dauernd beobachtet. Sie macht eine feind-
liche Propaganda zur Unmöglichkeit oder gibt Ansatzpunkte für sie.
Nimmt der Soldat auf dem Lande dem Bauern die letzte Kuh, die Zuchtsau,
das letzte Huhn oder das Saatgut, so kann eine Belebung der Wirt-
schaft nicht erreicht werden.
Bei allen Massnahmen ist nicht der augenblickliche Erfolg ent-
scheidend. Alle Massnahmen müssen deshalb auf ihre Dauerwirkung ge-
prüft werden.
Achtung vor den religiösen Gebräuchen, besonders der der moha-
medanischen Tartaren, muss verlangt werden
Im Verfolg dieser Gedanken kommt neben anderen durch die spätere
Verwaltung durchzuführenden Massnahmen der propagandistischen Aufklärung der Bevölkerung, der Förderung der persönlichen Initiative
z.B. durch Prämien, der weitgehenden Heranziehung der Bevölkerung zur
Partisanenbekämpfung und dem Ausbau der einheimischen Hilfspolizei er-
höhte Bedeutung zu.
Zur Erreichung dieses Zieles muss gefordert werden:

Aktive Mitarbeit der Soldaten beim Kampf gegen den Feind im Rücken
Bei Nacht keine einzelnen Soldaten,
Alle Fahrzeuge mit ausreichender Bewaffnung,
Selbstbewusste, nicht überhebliche Haltung aller Soldaten,
Zurückhaltung gegenüber Gefangenen und dem anderen Geschlecht,
Kein Verschwenden von Lebensmitteln.

Mit aller Schärfe ist einzuschreiten:

Gegen Willkür und Eigennutz,
Gegen Verwilderung und Undiszipline,
Gegen jede Verletzung der soldatischen Ehre.

Verteiler:
bis Rgt. und
selbst. Btl.   Der Oberbefehlshaber:

Manstein's order of the day of November 20, 1941.

Ukrainians who are not *Bolshevist*, Russians and Tartars must be expected to accept the new order. The indifference of many purported anti-*Bolshevist* elements has to be replaced by an unequivocal readiness, to work actively with us in the struggle against *Bolshevism*. If this is not done, under their own volition, it has to be enforced by us.

A voluntary participation in the reconstruction of the country by the population is an absolute prerequisite for attaining our desired political and economic objectives. It makes it incumbent upon us to show justice to such parts of the population that have been fighting heroically against *Bolshevism* over many years.

Our domination of this country makes it incumbent upon us to show performance and hardness towards ourselves, and to refrain from consideration of individuals. The behaviour of our soldiers is under constant observation. It has to render enemy propaganda invalid and prevent any such attempts. If a soldier takes the last cow, the last chicken, the last breeding sow, or the last seeds from the farmer, the economy cannot be revitalised.

Immediate results of our measures are not a cornerstone of our success. Future and lasting effects have to be taken into account.

Religious customs, especially those of the Muslim Tartars, have to be respected.

Future measures of the administration have to be assisted by explanations of propaganda to the population, and by the encouragement of local initiatives, such as premiums, increasing participation in the fight against partisans, and the development of a local police force.

Our aim requires: Active co-operation by the soldier against the enemy in the rear. Every vehicle has to be provided with sufficient arms. Attitude towards the population must be self-conscious, restraint has to be shown towards prisoners-of-war and women, waste of foodstuff must be prohibited. No arbitrariness, no selfishness, no unruliness and lack of discipline, and no violation of soldierly honour."

To be distributed down to Battalion level.

Signed: The Commander in chief v. Manstein[83]

Manstein was less aggressive than some of Reichenau's statements about the civilian population, but he was more violent than Reichenau in his appeals for measures against the Jews. Manstein demanded respect for religious customs, especially those of the Muslim Tartars. That sentence gave Paget the opportunity to charge Manstein with the responsibility of the later fate of the Tartars: "The best proof Manstein's humane policy is that the *Bolshevists* found it necessary to deport most of the Crimea's population to Siberia after the war. Poor guys (sic)"[84] Of course, Manstein had no responsibility for the future tragedy of the Tartars. They were one of the nations, like the Balkars, the Chechens, the Ingushi, the Kalmycks, the Karachai, who were collectively deported to Siberia in 1944, after the Red Army had re-occupied their territories.

Did Manstein believe his own nonsense that the *Wehrmacht* defended itself against the Jews and not against the "remaining units of the Red Army still capable of fighting"? That was obviously unthinkable. He happened to be Commander of the 11th Army that had to defend itself against the "remaining units of the Red Army still capable of fighting". He could hardly convince his troops, who had to fight the remnants of Red Army in the rear of the former front, after Manstein's first offensive on the Crimea had turned into failure. Had the Jews possessed the strength that Manstein attributes to them, they had not become the victims of the

---

83   BA-MA, RH 20-11/519
84   Paget, p. 57

smallish *Einsatzgruppen*, but would have destroyed them with ease. Apparently Manstein succeeded in convincing Wöhler.

Wöhler testified at his trial:

> If this attempt on our Army or some other step occurred – I assume that such a thing had indeed taken place – one has to assume that the 'intelligentsia' must have had prior knowledge of such plans and participated in their execution.[85]

Apparently Wöhler ignored the fact that the Russian 'intelligentsia' was almost totally concentrated in Moscow and Leningrad and could not be found in the small Crimean townships. Wöhler was looked on as a capable chief-of-staff. He should have known something about the distribution of the Crimean population that was under control of his Army. Wöhler added in his testimony: "In Germany, we have had the misfortune to experience the Jewish-*Bolshevist* system at close range in the years following the end of the First World War."[86] It seemed that Wöhler had not sufficient intelligence of his own to know that the German Jewish intelligentsia had made an essential contribution to the 'golden years' of the Weimar Republic, before the Third *Reich* put an end to all creative German culture. Like many German officers, he had apparently concentrated his mental efforts exclusively on military details.

When Manstein was confronted with his 'order of the day' at his trial, the 'New York Herald' wrote: "Erich von Manstein shifted uneasily when the prosecutor showed him a copy of the document."[87] Manstein's first reply was that he could not remember it. "I have to state that I have no recollection whatsoever of this document."[88]

Given the far-reaching importance of that order, this is more than surprising, especially if Manstein's exceptional memory of unimportant details is taken into account. In *Soldatenleben*, he devoted pages to his visits to Russia, gives a detailed description of the apartment of General Uborevitch in a house 'exceptionally' equipped with a lift and who employed a home servant. He also wrote at length about a gala dinner, during which Marshal Budennyi constantly drank his health, after having removed the bottles of mineral water and exclaimed: "Nix Narsan, only Schampanski".[89] In *Verlorene Siege*, he wrote in detail about every castle in which he spent his nights during the battle for France. He mentions one castle owned by the liquor manufacturer Cointreau, that contained a painting showing Cointreau surrounded by leading statesmen of the world. He found it so tasteless that he had it removed.[90] When his memory was refreshed by the tribunal, Manstein engaged in increasingly muddled accounts:

> I now recall that I received the Reichenau order with an accompanying letter from Rundstedt. When I received the order, I took no steps at all. I did not like it, and, on account of the relations of close confidence that I

---

85   *NOKW* 3237, also Friedrich, p. 632
86   IMT, Case 12, p.5.861
87   *New York Herald,* September 6, 1949
88   Trial, p.1.930
89   *Soldatenleben,* p. 134 ff.
90   *Verlorene Siege,* p. 149

had with *Feldmarschall* von Rundstedt, I believed that I could wait, since *Feldmarschall* von Rundstedt would probably come to see me in the near future. On that occasion, I intended to discuss the matter with him and to tell him that I did not like the order, and that I would not pass it on. I was always opposed to orders of propaganda. They are harmful to discipline, and, as a soldier, I oppose any kind of propaganda.

I received the same order again from *OKH* at a later date. At that time I was involved in a very heavy battle around Izyum and I had no time for such matters. When tension decreased, I ordered my Ic to draft an order somewhat similar to the one by General von Reichenau. At that time, partisan danger had increased on the Crimea and I had to warn the troops. Later, I heard that Reichenau had issued his order after one of his divisional headquarters in Kiev had been blown up by partisans. [Manstein confused the dates. The headquarters in question had been blown up more than a month before Reichenau issued his order, the massacre at Babi Yar took place as a reprisal.] Before I issued my own order, a Romanian headquarters was blown up. My Ic then submitted a draft order to me that had followed the general lines of the Reichenau order. I still did not like it and requested that the last sentences were removed. But I have to point out that the sentence "has to be exterminated" refers to the system and not to human beings.[91]

It can be doubted if such subtleties were understood by the soldiers. In any case, they were certainly not grasped by the soldiers of 11th Army, who actively participated in the elimination of human beings. In a conversation with fellow Generals in the prisoner of war camp Trent Park, which was monitored by the British, General von Choltitz, in 1941 a Lieutenant Colonel and commander of Infantry Regiment 16 in 11th Army said: "The most difficult task of my career, which I fulfilled with the greatest possible consequence, was the liquidation of the Jews" [92]

Streit wrote:

> With regard to Manstein, one is entitled to ask what an Army commander, who had listened to Hitler's speech of 30 March 1941, and who had not remained isolated from what had happened during the war in the East, could have had concretely in mind, when he wrote about the harsh punishment meted out to Jewry for which the soldier had to show understanding.[93]

In a letter to his wife, Manstein wrote:

> "Then they showed me an order of the day, issued by 11th Army. It was obviously intended to show my untrustworthiness. It was a kind of propaganda order that I had never liked, but which apparently had been written by my Ic and then signed by me. I simply could not remember it at all. But in the last part, I had explicitly insisted against any arbitrariness or

---

91 Trial, p. 1.932 ff
92 S. Neitzel, "Abgehört. Deutsche Generale in britischer Gefangenschaft 1942–1945", Berlin 2005, p.258
93 Streit, p. 118

violation of soldiers' honour, therefore the order of the day certainly must be seen in a positive light.[94]

Manstein claims that he had not written the first part of his order concerning the Jews but at his trial he identified himself with its content: "The part concerning the Jews is entirely correct. Undoubtedly it is not exaggerated."[95]

As to the second part of his order about which Manstein expresses pride, Martin Oldenburg writes:

> Manstein only opposed wanton confiscations by his troops while combats were still proceeding and he was interested in a quiet rear area. When Sevastopol was about to fall in June 1942, Manstein gave the order to confiscate the 'last cows' in order to provide meat for his soldiers. Obviously at this point Manstein had no more interest in the well-being of the civilian population. Manstein's successor as territorial commander of the Crimea, General Franz Mattenklott, had to face the new situation. In a letter to *Heeresgruppe* South of September 6, 1942, Mattenklott warned against making promises which could not be kept.[96]

When Manstein was asked if he knew that Jews had been shot as a consequence of his order of the day, he replied:

> Soldiers, who had happened to be eyewitnesses to such occurrences, did not report them to me at that time. Had I received such a report, I would have intervened immediately. Perhaps there was such fear of the SS, that soldiers, instead of immediately reporting the *Schweinerei* to me, have kept it to themselves and waited until now to come out with the truth.[97]

Since *Wehrmacht* soldiers were subject to Army jurisdiction only and could not be deferred before an SS tribunal, they had no cause for 'such fear'.

Captain Gunzert was an eyewitness who did not wait 'until now'. He made an immediate report to Manstein, who did not immediately intervene. Better said that Manstein did indeed intervene, by telling Captain Gunzert that he refused to intervene. Friedrich is of the opinion that a soldier who had read Manstein's order of the day, could well look at the *Schweinerei* as a compliance with his commander's order.[98]

For obvious reasons, post-war literature paid more attention to Manstein's order of the day than to those issued by Reichenau and Hoth. During the 1930s, Reichenau was an important personality in the *Reichswehr* ministry, during the Second World War his command of armies and Army Groups was not outstanding and he died a few months after having issued his order.

Hoth was an outstanding *Panzer* commander. But in the larger historic context of the war, he was a nobody. His troops named him the 'poisoned dwarf'. One can therefore doubt if he was popular with his soldiers, although Manstein described him as man, who took pleasure in cheerfulness when surrounded by

---

94 Manstein/Fuchs, p. 242 f
95 BA-MA, N 507/v.8. Bl. 214
96 Oldenburg, p. 95 f
97 Trial, p. 1.397
98 Friedrich, p. 639

younger officers. Manstein wrote further that Hoth's soldierly rectitude even impressed his judges at the IMT.[99] How little Hoth impressed his judges can be gathered from the minutes of his trial. Apart from Wöhler, no other general was subject to more mockery. Hoth had given himself the merit of the postponement of a *Judenaktion* at Artemovsk. His chief-of-staff should have recognised that postponement was the equivalent of an order forbidding him to proceed, but he did not understand that.

In its verdict against Hoth, the IMT wrote:

> His testimony tends to show that his subordinates should have cathode-ray-tubes in their brains, enabling them to grasp the ideas that resulted from his honourable character. He thought that they should have the courage to disobey an order, while he himself lacked such courage. Either the rays which resulted from his character were too weak or the brains of his subordinated were not sophisticated enough to comprehend them.[100]

Hoth was sentenced to 15 years.

Manstein was a 'somebody'. Many who gained knowledge of his 'order of the day' after the war, are at a loss to understand, because they feel that Manstein simply could not have uttered such words. Lieutenant General *Bundeswehr* Freytag von Loringhoven states on Knopp's video: "This is simply incomprehensible. I could never imagine that this was written by Manstein:" Since the existence of the order could not be denied, explanations were searched for as Manstein's defenders found it difficult to come to terms with. General Winfrid Martini criticizes the fact that Manstein repeated some of Reichenau's indecent expressions but added that he was left with no choice.[101] This was not so, since Rundstedt's request (*Bitte*) was not worded in the manner in which high-ranking officers gave orders to each other. In such cases, 'I order' was always replaced by '*Ich bitte*'. Rundstedt's *Bitte* suggested merely to his Army commanders that they consider issuing an order resembling the Reichenau order.

Manstein had a simple choice. He was not compelled to issue an order, he should never have allowed himself to issue it. Only Manstein and Hoth had followed Reichenau's example in issuing similar orders of the day of their own. All the other Army commanders either ignored the Reichenau order, or some transmitted it as an appendix with no comments of their own. General von Mackensen, commander of III Motorized Corps, wrote an order of his own, which was the opposite of the vulgarity of the orders by Reichenau, Manstein and Hoth. Mackensen strongly blamed the conduct of the troops and other German institutions in the East. They had put an end to the attitude of parts of the local population that, at first, had taken a positive view of the German invaders. Not every Russian, who looked like a *Bolshevik*, could be looked on as an enemy. Officers should exercise care when receiving denunciations.[102]

In 1969, Manstein's past again caught up with him. The prosecutor's office in Bonn asked the Central Office for War Crimes at Ludwigsburg if there was mate-

---

99   *Verlorene Siege*, p. 533
100 IMT, Case 12, p. 185, also Friedrich, p.931
101 W. Martini, *Das Achim Oster Ei* in *Soldat im Volk*, Mai 1968, p.2
102 BA-MA, RH 24-3/136

rial available concerning Manstein. The Ludwigsburg office transmitted a copy of Manstein's order of the day and the minutes of his testimony at his trial. The Bonn prosecutor initiated an investigation against Manstein on grounds of "suspicion of murder' and trasmitted the file to the prosecutor's office at Munich. The Munich prosecutor suspended the investigation in a *preliminary* manner (underlined in the original), because the treaty between the Allied occupation authorities and the German Federal public forbade prosecution by German courts of actions already tried by Allied courts. The word 'preliminary' referred to the possibility that this treaty might be changed in the future.[103]

Halder stated at Nuremberg that all Army commanders should simply have thrown the Reichenau order into the fire. After the war, the German generals suddenly knew what they should have done. When Reichenau issued his order of the day, Halder transmitted it to the armies with his warm recommendations, and added that Hitler had found it to be excellent. Klaus Hammel wrote in *Soldaten der Wehrmacht*, that

> Manstein's order was certainly not a page of glory in the annals of German military history. The argument was advanced by some, that such incredible sentences were simply a preamble, and that they were intended to encourage the troops to act in a correct manner, by employing a National-Socialist style. But that argument can be dismissed as a glossing over of facts. But an appreciation of Manstein's personality must also take into account the leaflet that he had written himself and ordered to be inserted in the service book of every soldier of his Army.[104]

Hammel refers to Manstein's 'Ten Commandments' to his troops in Russia in which he admonishes them to behave in a chivalrous manner towards the population.[105] Hammel's chapter is yet one more example of the many shortcomings in *Die Soldaten der Wehrmacht*, where inessential is opposed to essential. Manstein's 'Ten Commandments' are lofty, but no one is compelled to observe them. The 'Ten Commandments of the Bible' are likewise not universally observed. A man, who does not follow them, turns into a sinner. Little if any chivalrous conduct by the Germans in Russia remains on record.

On 29 August 1942, the Ukrainian Archbishop, Count Andreas Scheptycky, wrote to the Pope:

> When the German Army appeared to liberate us from the *Bolshevist* yoke, we experienced at first a feeling of some relief. But that lasted no more than one or two months. Step by step, the Germans introduced their regime of incredible terror and corruption. Today, the people feel that the German regime is even worse, worse in a diabolical manner than *Bolshevism*. It simply appears that a band of madmen or of rabid dogs have descended upon the poor population.[106]

---

103 Wrochem, p. 379

104 K. Hammel, *Kompetenzen und Verhalten der Truppe im rückwärtigen Heeresgebiet*, in *Soldaten, Wehrmacht*, p. 218 ff

105 Complete text in Breithaupt, p. 129 f

106 F. Seidler, *Die Kollaboration 11939–1945. Zeitgeschichtliche Dokumentation in Biographien*. Munich 1999, p.484 ff

Pius XII replied with one his 'meaningless' letters.

Hammel's chapter is not limited to Manstein and his convictions, it concerns the competence and the attitude of all German troops in the occupied territories in the East. Hammel should therefore not have limited himself to Manstein's 'Ten Commandments', but likewise have included Keitel's 'guidelines for the conduct of the troops in Russia'. The future 'resistance' movement member, Carl-Heinrich von Stülpnagel, had ordered it to be inserted into the service books of the soldiers of his 17th Army. It was an adaptation of Hitler's speech of 30 March 1941.[107]

It is totally irrelevant to determine if Manstein's order responded to his personal conviction. The only essential thing is that he chose to issue it. Even Paget, who seldom has difficulties in finding arguments in favour of Manstein, could only write: "This is the only order signed by Manstein and even this is held against him."[108]

In an essay about Manstein, Enrico Syring writes:

> ... one could perhaps believe that Manstein, in his attempt to toady to National-Socialism, intended to strongly recommend himself for higher positions. Curiously, his order was issued at a time when Brauchitsch's dismissal as Commander in Chief of the Army, in the near future, was already imminent. Manstein was looked upon as one of his successors.[109]

Such speculations have little value. The only essential point is that the order was issued, that it was obeyed, and that Manstein became one of the active 'perpetrators' of the genocide.

The *Einsatzgruppen* – General Organisation. *Einsatzgruppe* D and Otto Ohlendorf

The first *Einsatzgruppen* were established in 1938 and operated in Austria, Czechoslovakia and Poland. Their duties were different from their followers in Russia. In a book dealing mainly with Manstein and their activities in Russia, they are not relevant.

When the war against Russia began, four *Einsatzgruppen* were set up. *Einsatzgruppe* A was under Dr Stahlecker. *Einsatzgruppe* B was commanded by the chief criminologist of the *Reich, Reichskriminaldirektor* Nebe. He was already recognised as Germany's leading crime expert before the Nazis took power. *Einsatzgruppe* C was under Dr. Rasch and *Einsatzgruppe* D was commanded by Ohlendorf. The commanders of *Einsatzgruppen* A, B and C were exchanged at regular intervals. Dr Stahlecker was killed in action on 23 March 1943, Nebe and Dr Rasch requested to be relieved in October 1941. Ohlendorf remained as head of *Einsatzgruppe* D until the end of the fighting on the Crimea.[110] *Einsatzgruppen* A, B

---

107   *AOK* 17, Ia/Ic/AO, 298/41 gKdos.Chefs. May 4, 1941
108   Paget, p. 196
109   E. Syring, *Erich von Manstein – das operative Genie,* R.Smelser/E.Syring (ed.), *Die Militärelite des Dritten Reiches, 27 biographische Skizzen,* Berlin 1998, p. 337 (henceforth: Syring, Manstein)
110   Complete table in Krausnick, p. 644 ff

and C consisted of approximately 1,000 men each. The smaller *Einsatzgruppe* D numbered 600.

Every *Einsatzgruppe* worked through sub-units, the *Sonderkommandos* (Sk) and the *Einsatzkommandos* (Ek). The 'advance command Moscow' was renamed Sk 70, after it was halted at Smolensk. The Sk followed the front line troops closely. The Ek operated in the rear. On the Crimean peninsula, front and rear were seldom separated and the Ek of *Einsatzgruppe* D were employed alongside, with its Sk. *Einsatzgruppe* D consisted of Sk 10 a, commanded by Seetzen, later by Christmann. Sk 10 b, was commanded successively by Persterer and Jedamcyk. Sk 11a, commanders were Zapp, Nach and Herrmann. Sk 11b, commanders were Müller, Dr Braune and Schulz. Ek 12, was Nosske followed by Herrmann and Schulz. When massacres took place in small townships or villages, with relatively few Jewish inhabitants, the Sk and Ek were in turn divided into sub-units of 10–15 men, who rejoined their centres after completing their murders.

The commanders of the *Einsatzgruppen*, the Sk, and the Ek were intellectuals with an academic level above most *Wehrmacht* commanders. Franz Six was a university professor, Dr Rasch held two doctorates. Dr Braune, who conducted the murders at Simferopol and Eupatoria was already, at age 32, a high ranking official at the German ministry of the interior. Woldemar Klingelhöfer, who succeeded Six as commander of Sk 70, was a well known opera singer. Ernst Biberstein, who commanded Ek 6 at *Einsatzgruppe* C, was a Protestant priest. Paul Blobel, who had commanded the Babi Yar massacre, and was responsible for the disposal of the victims' bodies, was an architect of repute. That men of such calibre joined the *Einsatzgruppen* is not too surprising. Many intellectuals are known to have become eager followers of any regime.

The ordinary soldiers in the Sk and the Ek were partially recruited from police battalions. A number had been declared unfit for military service, others were simply 'trash'. Few were professional criminals, most were 'simply ordinary men' (Christopher Browning), who had turned into 'willing executioners' (Daniel Goldhagen).

After the war, the 'Milgram Test' was conducted with the help of electrical equipment at the University of Yale. 'Teachers' pressed electrical buttons in a closed room, and transmitted the shocks to 'students' in another room. The 'test' has shown that men totally void of criminal instincts, could become ready to obey orders, including murder, if the experiment was repeated often enough. At the end of the experiment, 60% of the 'students' were ready to obey every order.

Höhne comments:

> The real horror, in the total bestiality of the murder of the Jews, was that thousands of otherwise honest family men, eagerly engaged in organised murder. They felt satisfied at the day's end to have acted as law-abiding, ordinary citizens, who would never consider straying away from the virtues of their private lives. The sadism was only one of the elements of the massacres. It was not even desired by the SS leadership. On the contrary, Himmler was fascinated by the idea that the murders had to be accomplished in a clean, factual manner. The SS man had to commit murder, ordered from above, in a personally decent fashion.[111]

---

111 Höhne, p.351

Paget views the men of the *Einsatzgruppen* as representatives of the remains of Christian tradition (!): "These men were simply not bad enough to persist in their deeds. The criminal *Nazi*-system had tried to eradicate every trace of Christianity, but it had not entirely succeeded."[112]

The duties of the *Einsatzgruppen*, and the general principles of their co-operation with the *Wehrmacht*, were first laid out in the 'Wagner-Heydrich agreement'. It was signed on 28 April 1941, between *Generalmajor* Eduard Wagner, Chief Quartermaster at *OKH* and *SS-Obergruppenführer* Reinhardt Heydrich, head of the *SD*.[113] Wagner participated in the 20 July plot and committed suicide on 21 July 1944. Heydrich, who had been appointed *Reichsprotektor* in the Czechoslovak Protectorate in 1942, was killed in Prague by Czech partisans in that same year. The agreement did not contain details about the tasks of the *Einsatzgruppen*. They can be summed up as the organised killing of all communist functionaries, 'Asiatic inferiors', gypsies, and Jews.

The first orders to the *Einsatzgruppen* were given verbally. Curiously, the word 'order' is totally absent from the Wagner-Heydrich agreement. This enabled Ohlendorf to construct a line of defence at the *Einsatzgruppen* trial. A detailed description is given by Angrick.[114] Ohlendorf claimed that the order to murder all Jews was given orally at Pretsch, where the *Einsatzgruppen* received their training. Ohlendorf added that the order was given orally by SS-*Gruppenführer* Bruno Streckenbach, head of the personnel department at *RSHA*. Streckenbach was considered a useful alibi since he was a prisoner of war in Russia and Ohlendorf was apparently convinced that the Russians would execute him. Ohlendorf felt that he could claim that he and his comrades had acted upon higher order. "They can't hang all of us". However Streckenbach returned from captivity and immediately denied the statements attributed to him.

A letter, signed by Heydrich on 2 July 1941, contained the first details in writing:

> The following must be executed:
>
> All functionaries of the *Komintern* and all professional politicians in the ranks of the Communist party.
>
> Senior, medium rank and radical functionaries of the Party Central Committee and of the regional and provincial committees.
>
> Peoples Commissars.
>
> Jews in state and party employment.
>
> Other radical elements, saboteurs, propagandists, snipers, assassins, agitators, etc.[115]

In their own reports, the *Einsatzgruppen* left no doubt as to what was expected of them. A report from *Einsatzgruppe* C from October 1941 listed all persons

---

112 Paget, p.200

113 *NOKW* 2080

114 Angrick, from page 70 onwards

115 Reproduced in Krausnick, p. 157

subject to execution. It explained the extent to which they were considered as having been guilty, and simply adds, "Jews in general."[116]

For functionaries, their former duties were briefly described.

For Jews a mention of 'belonging to the Jewish race' was sufficient.[117]

Some of the reports would mention additional justification, such as 'impertinent and provocative behaviour,' 'distribution of pamphlets,' or 'unwillingness to work.' But in most cases, no such details were provided, since all Jews were by definition subject to execution.

In a report by *Einsatzgruppe* C the following persons were listed as subject to immediate execution:

- Political functionaries, looters and saboteurs, active Communists and bearers of political ideology, Jews who have escaped under false pretence from a prisoner-of-war camp, agents and informants of the NKVD.
- Persons who have been guilty of lies and attempts to influence witnesses in trials against ethnic Germans.
- Persons guilty of Jewish sadism and lust for vengeance, undesirable elements, members of Russian gangs, partisans.
- Persons who supplied gangs with food, rebels and agitators, neglected juveniles and Jews in general.[118] Given this 'definition', it is doubtful that there was a single citizen of the Soviet Union who was not liable for execution.

Co-operation between the *Wehrmacht* and the *Einsatzgruppen* were laid out in the Wagner-Heydrich agreement and an *OKH* order, signed by Brauchitsch on 28 April 1941. Executions by the Sk were to be performed outside the area in which the troops were stationed. This soon became more theory than practice, since commanders increasingly requested the presence of *Einsatzgruppen* units in their front line areas. Streit described the separation between *Wehrmacht* and *Einsatzgruppe* as being a simple *cliché*.[119] *Einsatzgruppen* commandos were instructed to follow the troops at a short distance and to report to the commander of the rear area, the *Korück*. The nearer the Sk came to the front line, reports were no longer sent as routine to the *Korücks,* but communicated directly to the Ic/AO of the front line units involved.

A representative of the security police and the *SD* was attached to the staff of every Army to organise 'centralised steering' ie *zentrale Steuerung* of the *Einsatzgruppe* commandos activities. The representative was usually the chief of the *Einsatzgruppe* commandos attached to the Army. The commander of the *Einsatzgruppe* was its representative with the *Korück*. Duties of the representative were to bring the instructions of the *SS* main office (*RSHA*) to the knowledge of the Army commander without delay, and to remain close contact with the Army's Ic/AO. The Ic/AO was required to co-ordinate the activities of the *Einsatzgruppe* with his Army's military requirements.

---

116   Krausnick, p. 150 f
117   Report about an action in the vicinity of Leningrad, Feburary 25, 1942, Krausnich, p. 158
118   EM 111, October 12, 1941, reproduced in Krausnick, p. 158
119   Streit, p. 51

The first direct co-operation between *Wehrmacht* and *Einsatzgruppen* had thus been formalised. By February 1941, Brauchitsch had admonished the generals who had opposed the excesses in Poland, to try and likewise understand Himmler's point of view.[120] Whatever separation still persisted, soon turned into fiction, since the commanders continuously demanded that the commandos of the *Einsatzgruppen* be brought into their immediate neighbourhood. Streit gives some examples:

On 21 June 1941 an Sk had joined the front units of 291st Division within 18th Army and conducted a 'punitive action' against Jews.[121] *Einsatzgruppe* A was commanded by Dr Stahlecker. He recalled his very close and friendly relationship with *Generaloberst* Hoepner. They had reached an agreement with the staff of Hoepner's Army, on the latter's strong request, that Sk were to be attached to every unit taking part, in the advance of the attack against Leningrad. Co-operation was also very close with Army Group Centre. All *Wehrmacht* units constantly requested close *SD* presence. Our help was highly appreciated. On a number of occasions, *Wehrmacht* units were put at our disposal. Our wishes were always complied with.[122]

Co-operation between Army Group South and *Einsatzgruppen* C and D was particularly close. *Einsatzgruppe* C reported that Army Group South had requested keeping all Sk as close as possible to the front lines.[123] From the very first day of the campaign, units of *Einsatzgruppe* C never remained in the rear and the *Wehrmacht* never stopped urging the Sk not to slow down their progress to the front.[124] The Ek, which operated in the area of Stülpnagel's 17th Army, reported that it was encouraged by a particularly heartening feeling against the Jews.[125] Ohlendorf reported that relations with *AOK* 11, at that time still under Schobert's command, were particularly warm.[126] Streit emphasised that neither Himmler nor Heydrich had a particular interest in praise from the *Wehrmacht*. The active co-operation by the *Wehrmacht* was certainly not the result of pressure by them on the military commanders.[127]

In December 1941, 17th Army requested Ek 4b to shoot all the Jewish inhabitants of the city of Kremenchug, after unknown saboteurs had destroyed the Army's communication cables on three different occasions.[128] In December 1941, Halder called all the Army Commanders in the East to a meeting at Orsha. All erupted in a hymn of praise about the *Einsatzgruppen*. "They are worth their weight in gold, they secure our communications and thus make it possible for us to

120   Streit, p. 51
121   BA-MA, RH 58/219
122   BA-MA, RH 58/217
123   Streit, p. 110 f
124   BA-MA, RH 58/218 and Streit, p. 110 f
125   Ibid
126   Ibid
127   Streit, p.112
128   Hilberg, vol. 2, p. 266

use our troops for other purposes."[129] The urging of the commanders reached such an extent that *Sturmbannführer* Lindow at the *SS* Main office (*RSHA*) exclaimed angrily: "The secret state police does not have to play the part of the executioner of the *Wehrmacht*.[130]

The methods used in the murders

Krausnick described one of the standard actions:

> We are in 1941. At one township in the occupied Soviet Union, a number of men, women and children, unarmed citizens of the occupied areas, are informed by special bodies of the National-Socialist system of power, that they will be resettled. They had already been registered. Now they are ordered to assemble in the market square and to deposit their valuables as a 'precautionary measure'. They are then put on lorries and made to believe that they will be transported to their resettlement destination. However, the lorry suddenly halts at a place in open fields. Until that moment, the commanders are eager to let the victims believe in the resettlement. As long as this lasts, they have an easy game. If they succeeded in maintaining their deception until the last moment, they would proudly report their 'skilful organisation.'
>
> But now, the camouflage disappears. Close to the place where the lorries come to a halt, a deep anti-tank ditch or a mass grave has already been dug. The victims are ordered to undress until they are naked. They are then led to the edge of the ditch, told to remain standing or to kneel down and are shot. Bodies that do not fall into the ditch, after being shot, are pushed or thrown into it. If this procedure appears too complicated, the victims are ordered to jump into the ditch, drop to their knees and are then shot. At the end, the head of the command or his deputy tries to make sure that all are dead, if he has doubts, he fires a bullet into their head.[131]

When the Germans attacked Russia, the Russian Jews were unaware of what lay in store for them. During the years of appeasement, the Soviet press did not report the anti-Semitic policies of the Third *Reich*. Foreign newspapers and magazines were not available to the Russian people. 95% of the Russian Jews, approximately 5 million people, still lived in the former area of settlement. During the Czarist years, Jews were not allowed to live in the major cities, unless they had obtained an academic degree with distinction, or were able to pay the taxes imposed on merchants of the first guild. After the revolution, limitations on the right of residence were lifted, and intellectual Jews moved to the large cities. The majority, mostly farmers and small craftsmen, remained in 'the pale'.

Recollections of the First World War had persisted. Then, the Germans had pursued a friendly policy towards the Jews in Russia,. The Jews were regarded by the Imperial German government and Army as allies, against the Czarist regime

---

129   Höhne, p. 338 f, with reference to P. Bor, *Gespräche mit Halder*, Wiesbaden 1950
130   Höhne, p. 338
131   Krausnick, p. 13 f

and its *pogroms*. Moreover the Germans were eager to retain the support of American Jewry who had opposed American entry into the war as an ally of *Czarist* Russia.

When the Imperial German Army penetrated a Russian township, posters were immediately displayed in Yiddish and were signed by Ludendorff, 'To my dear Jews.' When the Red Army entered Poland in 1939, thousands of Jews fled into the provinces occupied by the Germans. The first German troops that entered the Soviet Union were looked on by the Jews as liberators from the Soviet yoke. Last minute warnings by the Soviet authorities were ignored.

When the Prince Friedrich Theodor zu Sayn und Wittgenstein appeared at Kamenka on a government mission, he was greeted by a Jewish delegation with a proclamation:

> We, the citizens of Kamenka, which was formerly part of the estate of your ancestors under whose protection the Jews prospered, welcome your arrival. We wish you long life and fortune. We hope that the Jewish population will continue to live in safety under your protection, and enjoy the same sympathy bestowed on it by your blessed ancestors. We hope that you will likewise take the sympathy and the gratitude into account, which the Jewish population has always shown your illustrious family.[132]

The Prince was not impressed. He told the Jews that they were an evil, and he requested the town commander to make them wear the Jewish star and do hard labour without payment.[133]

On 12 July 1941, Schröter, a *Sonderführer*, (a functionary, who was conferred an *ad hoc* military rank for a determined period), reported to the *Reichskommissariat Ostland*:

> The Jews are ignorant of our attitude. They know nothing about how they are treated in Germany or in Warsaw, although quite close. They ask us if we would make a difference between them and other Russian citizens. While they do not expect that they will enjoy the same rights as other Russians, they trust that they will be left in peace, if they diligently pursue their work.[134]

As soon as news of the killings by *Einsatzgruppe*an began to spread, a massive flight started. The commanders of the *Einsatzgruppe* had to increasingly report, 'with regret', that not sufficient Jewish victims were left in the cities. *Einsatzgruppe* B reported on 15 August 1941:

> The intellectual Jews in the cities have been able to flee as our armies advanced. It will therefore be hardly possible to proceed with the elimina-

---

132 Hilberg, p. 330 based on a report of the Prince of his visit to Russia, August 28–September 1, 1941
133 Ibid.
134 Ibid.

tion in the same numbers as at present. The Jewish element has been very much reduced.[135]

'Hardly possible', perhaps, but still, sufficient Jews were left to kill close on 1 million.

Otto Ohlendorf

The most detailed biography of Ohlendorf is given by Höhne, in his book about the *SS*. A recent German-American anthology about leading *SS*-figures contains a chapter about Ohlendorf by the American historian David Kiterman. Kiterman had several talks with Ohlendorf's widow. He was allowed to see Ohlendorf's correspondence with his wife before and during the war, and also in the last months of his life, while he awaited his execution.[136]

Ohlendorf was born in 1907, the fourth son of a farmer. Even at school, he developed an active interest in politics and became a member of the right-wing *Deutschnationale Volkspartei*. In 1925, while still at high school, he joined the *NSDAP* with the low membership number of 6,531, which entitled him to wear the golden party badge.

Ohlendorf studied law, economics and constitutional science at three German universities. At Kiel he was a student of Professor Jens Jessen who, at that time, was close to the party. Later Jessen became a prominent member of the civilian 'resistance' and was hanged after 20 July. His widow told Kiterman that she was very bitter when Ohlendorf refused to come to the help of her husband in spite of her many entreaties.[137] After Ohlendorf graduated as a junior lawyer, Jessen arranged a one year scholarship for him at the university of Pavia. Ohlendorf had intended to write a doctoral thesis about the political and corporate aspects of Fascism, and then embark on an academic career. For unknown reasons he did not proceed with his plans, and he never obtained a doctorate.

However, he was certainly the most advanced intellectual among the heads of the *Einsatzgruppen*. Speer described him as one of the most brilliant brains of National-Socialism.[138] Kiterman does not share this elevated opinion and views Ohlendorf as a man of exaggerated ambition but, at best, of average intelligence.[139] Ohlendorf soon made a name for himself as a 'grouch'. He developed a philosophy of his own about the party that was distant from the official party line. On 6 February 1934, he wrote to his wife: "Something has been shattered within me. The easy and secure feeling with which I fought for National-Socialism in the past

135 P. Klein (ed.) *Die Einsatzgruppen in der besetzten Sowjetunion 1941. Tätgkeits-und Lageberichte des Chefs der Sicherheitspolizei und des SD,* Berlin 1997, p. 30
136 D. Kiterman, *Otto Ohlendorf, 'Gralshüter des Nationalsozialismus',* in R.Smelser/E. Syring (ed.), *Die SS, Elite unter dem Totenkopf, 30 Lebensläufe,* Paderborn 2000, p. 378-393 (henceforth: Kiterman)
137 Kiterman, p. 386 f
138 A. Speer, *Der Sklavenstaat. Meine Auseinandersetzung mit der SS,* Stuttgart 1981, p. 123
139 Kiterman, p. 382

has gone."[140] Some of his remarks were reported to the Gestapo. He was forbidden from making public speeches and was arrested for a short time. After his release he fell into depression. Jessen recommended him to his friend, Professor Reinhard Höhn, who was the head of a central department at the *RSHA*.

Höhn took a liking to Ohlendorf and convinced him that the *SD* was a suitable place of work for him. Ohlendorf joined the *SD*. Höhn was one of the National-Socialists who dreamt of a reform of the party according to their image. Ohlendorf was happy to have found a superior who shared his critical mind. Ohlendorf started to be endlessly critical, often simply for the sake of criticism. He disapproved of the 'blood and earth' romanticism of Dr Walter Darré. The Minister of Agriculture's ideas led to a law that a country estate could only be inherited by the eldest son, and never divided between all the heirs. The party had degenerated from a *Führerstaat* into a pluralistic anarchy and had become degenerate.

In one of his many memoranda, Ohlendorf wrote:

> The National-Socialist economy and the impact of rearmament are sources of unbearable tensions. On the one side, major conglomerates are continuously strengthened, while private trade and industry are increasingly pushed into the background. Wage and price control turn into havoc. We have the duty to set limits to such tensions if we do not want to witness a breakdown. The *SD* must play an important part in continuously reporting about the public mood.[141]

As long as Höhn's position remained undisputed, Ohlendorf had nothing to fear. Höhn felt that the *SD* needed intellectuals, like Ohlendorf, to put a halt to excesses in brutality. Ohlendorf became head of a newly established central *SD* Economics Department, which employed a number of business administration graduates. He wrote a thesis titled, '*Economics in the NS-State*,' in which he criticized rearmament as a source of uninterrupted tension in the economy. Höhn was satisfied with the performance of his pupil and, in 1937, had him appointed as head of the staff of a new central Department II. It was charged with analysis of all economic activities of the state.

His opinions did not render Ohlendorf popular with the *SS* leadership. Manstein had described him as a *protégé* of Himmler, without mentioning him by name. This was certainly not the case. Himmler criticized Ohlendorf's reports as being defeatist and far too pessimistic. He either tore them up, or returned them to Ohlendorf without having read them. In his eyes, Ohlendorf was an 'unbearable Prussian, devoid of any sense of humour, certainly not a soldier figure, but simply a 'damned intellectual'. Himmler told his Finnish masseur, Felix Kersten, that Ohlendorf, with his mediaeval views, saw himself as National-Socialism's knight of the holy grail.[142] Kersten's massage was able to relieve Himmler's increasingly unbearable stomach pains. Kersten made good use of his influence and succeeded in saving many lives during the last year of the war.

Himmler's dislike of Ohlendorf did not stand in the way of Ohlendorf's promotions. However, after the war, Ohlendorf maintained that Himmler always

---

140 Ibid, p. 381
141 Ibid, p. 385
142 Ibid, p. 385

rejected him, both as a person and as a proponent of his views. Because of his 'outstanding merits in Russia', Ohlendorf was made an *SS-Oberführer* on 9 November 1941. In October 1944 he was proposed for promotion to *Gruppenführer*, as a reward for his exemplary attitude and outstanding performance. There was no contradiction in Himmler's attitude. Himmler disliked Ohlendorf as a person, and considered his economic theories as being close to infantile. However, the mass murders that Ohlendorf conducted with special intensity, as head of *Einsatzgruppe* D, totally complied with Himmler's wishes.

Höhn was satisfied with his pupil and promoted Ohlendorf as chief-of-staff of the central IIa department of the *SD*. He was given the assignment of analysing all segments of the German economy in continuous reports. He also had to give accounts of the popular reaction to every new step taken by the authorities. (*Meldungen aus dem Reich*.) As long as Höhn's authority remained unchallenged, Ohlendorf was safe, since his reports reflected the views of Jessen and Höhn. But Höhn was not *persona grata*, ie a welcome guest, in party circles outside the *SD*. As a result of a personal quarrel with the party historian, Professor Walter Frank, who was supported by Streicher, Höhn was dismissed from the *SD*. He escaped to Sweden for a short time.

Suddenly, Ohlendorf found himself without a mentor in the party's inner circle. Himmler gave him a dressing-down and Heydrich dismissed him from his position as chief-of-staff. Ohlendorf first returned to his former 'Trade' department and then intended to leave the *SD* entirely. Himmler and Heydrich refused his resignation and wanted to keep his economic knowledge at their direct service. Ohlendorf found an intermediary solution. He became head of a Department for Trade in the Ministry of Economics, while at the same time remaining head of the 'Trade' department of the *SD*.

When the *Einsatzgruppen* were formed in 1941, Ohlendorf applied for membership. He contended to have done so with distaste. His widow told Kiterman that he was afraid of being labelled a coward.[143] He had already succeeded twice in avoiding military service. However, nothing in his life up to that moment, could foresee that he would turn into one of the most appalling mass murderers in Holocaust history. Some of his intellectual comrades, among them Professor Six and Heinz Jost, succeeded in obtaining other assignments after a short period. Walter Schellenberg was able to completely avoid service with the *Einsatzgruppe*. Ohlendorf became commander of *Einsatzgruppe* D attached to Army Group South, and operated in Bessarabia and the Crimea. When Manstein took over command of 11th Army, their paths crossed.

Ohlendorf developed his own execution techniques. Shootings were only to be carried out by collective action. No single man of his *Einsatzgruppe* was ever permitted to act as a sole executioner. He experimented with killing by gas in lorries, but soon discarded it, because he wanted to spare his men 'mental strain.' "After the killing, the bodies which were covered with blood and excrement had to be removed from the lorry and the executioner was thus confronted with his own action, the moment of truth. Ohlendorf wanted to spare him"[144]

---

143 Ibid. p. 385
144 Höhne, p. 336

Kiterman quotes from a number of letters by Ohlendorf to his wife. He took pride in stating that his reports never contained exaggerations such as the ones written by the other *Einsatzgruppen*. He had always made a careful count of the victims before reporting their numbers. He was happy that his transfer to Russia had put an end to the constant quarrels in his offices in Berlin. As he was totally fed up with them, he stayed with his *Einsatzgruppe* longer than his colleagues. Furthermore, he was convinced that his work in Russia brought a greater contribution to National-Socialism than his writings at the *SD*. He could have returned to Berlin several times during his years in Russia, but he preferred to "hold out on the spot".[145]

Co-operation between 11th Army and *Einsatzgruppe* D was closer than in other armies. Krausnick emphasised that 11th Army made the most frequent use of its authority to direct the progress of the *Einsatzgruppe*. They constantly requested the presence of its commandos in the front area.[146]

Hilberg estimates the total number of victims of *Einsatzgruppe* D to be as high as 100,000, possibly even more in southern Ukraine, the Crimea, and the Caucasus.[147] The reports from *Einsatzgruppe* D and its Sk show a figure of 91,678 killed by 8 April 1942.[148] During the period from 11 November 1941 to 11 December 1941, *Einsatzgruppe* D reported the execution of 17,645 Jews, 2,054 Krimchaks, 824 gypsies and 212 Communists and Partisans. Up to 11 December 1941, the total number of victims reached 75,881 executions.[149] The Krimchaks were a small sect with some thousands of members in the Crimea. They practised the Jewish faith but their racial origin was not established. They did not register themselves as Jews, so Berlin decided after a query by *Einsatzgruppe* D, that the Krimchaks were racial Jews, but that their execution had to be reported separately. Another Jewish sect in the Crimea, the Karaites, were considered to be racially 'Aryan' and were not executed.[150]

After the German surrender, Ohlendorf was appointed for a few days as head of an economic department in Speer's ministry for economics and production, in the government of Hitler's appointed successor, *Grossadmiral* Karl Dönitz. He was then arrested and sentenced to death by the IMT – Case 9. Since his testimony was required in later trials, his execution was postponed over a number of years. All observers at the trials where Ohlendorf appeared, either as accused, or as witness, are unanimous in their statements that he cut a most impressive figure.

The American Justice Michael Musmanno, who sentenced Ohlendorf to death by hanging, described him as:

> good-looking, a man of balanced temperament, forthcoming and polite. He conducted himself like a man who possessed born dignity and intelligence. He was able to tell his story with the gift of a professional author. He was slim, with elegant facial traits. He had carefully combed brown hair and looked at the audience with a penetrating expression in his

---

145 Kiterman, p. 386 f
146 Krausnick, p. 212
147 Hilberg, p. 1,294
148 *NOKW* 6281
149 *NOKW* 2834
150 Queries by the town commanders of Simferopol and Feodosia, both November 16, 1942 and reply from *Einsatzgruppe* D in BA-MA, RH 23/72

greyish blue eyes. He had a pleasant voice, his hands were particularly well groomed and he moved around in an elegant and self-assured manner. Next to Hermann Göring, he was undoubtedly the most impressive personality among the accused at all the trials.[151]

Ohlendorf was hanged in 1951. Among his direct subordinates only Dr Braune suffered the same fate. [152]

The IMT trials, Case 9 and Case 12 – who told the truth?

Ohlendorf

In his plea at Case 12, Dr Laternser stated:

> It remains for the tribunal to decide if it has more belief in the statements of *SS*-commanders, such as Schellenberg, Ohlendorf, and Rohde, who, driven by hatred, attempt for a last time to draw the military commanders into their own downfall, or in the words of these officers, whose personalities have certainly impressed the court.[153]

Dr Laternser's clients were less than impressive when they testified in their defence. Küchler can be given as one of many examples. In Poland, Küchler was one of the generals who raised his voice against the behaviour of his troops. After 1940, he made an immediate turn around. His 18th Army was the first major German unit sent to the East during the preparation of operation *Barbarossa*. His first order to his Corps Commanders in Poland stated: "I request that every soldier, in particular every officer, immediately abstain from criticism of any measures inspired by popular feeling and directed against the Jews, Polish minorities, and representatives of the Catholic church."[154] When questioned about an order, signed by him, that compelled the Jews to wear the Jewish star, Küchler replied: "Look, I am testifying under oath and I really can't. I can only answer according to my recollection. If I tell you that I did not sign such an order, you will immediately produce a paper bearing my signature."[155]

That was also Kuchler's reply to the charge of the murder of 240 women. On 25 December 1941, troops of his XXVIII Corps murdered the women, who were inmates in an asylum for the mentally deranged at Markeyevka. It was recorded in the war diary of the Corps, and ended, "The *Herr Oberbefehlshaber* has given his agreement to the execution". Then, at his trial, Küchler said,

> I am unable to explain this entry. Perhaps there has been confusion between *Oberbefehlshaber* and *AOK*. War diaries were kept by younger

---

151   Kiterman, p. 389
152   Kiterman, p. 389
153   H. Laternser, Verteidigung deutscher Soldaten, Plädoyers vor Alliierten Gerichten, Bonn 1950, p. 34
154   *NOKW* 1531
155   Friedrich, p. 619

officers, some of them belonged to the reserves. As I have said, there were daily heavy combats, many men were overextended. I continue to be terribly plagued by this recollection, since it reflects upon my humanity.[156]

With that last sentence Küchler became a living image of self-pity.

Or perhaps Hoth, whose 'soldierly rectitude' was described by Manstein as having impressed his judges. Hoth quoted the already mentioned order by his chief-of-staff, to postpone a massacre of Jews at Artemovsk until the situation at the front was clarified.

Q: "How could your chief-of-staff order the postponement of a massacre of which the Army, according to you, knew nothing?

A: "Well, this is the point. He could not order anything. One had to try and reason and even lower oneself to begging. This was a most displeasing situation. Men were roaming around in the areas under our control who paid no attention to our orders.

Q: "From the point of view of the enemy, where was the difference between a policeman and an irregular combatant?

A: "He wore a uniform, he did not hide his weapon, he was under the authority of a commander, but he did not follow the orders ... well, may be, this can't be said in this manner ... "[157]

Furthermore, Dr Laternser made things too easy for himself. A General can certainly lie, and a mass murderer, who has no doubt of his final fate, can speak the truth. A statement by Ohlendorf against a general like Wöhler, let alone Manstein, can certainly give cause for doubt. But only if both can build their contradictory statements upon unimpeachable evidence. If the statements by the generals mainly consist of 'I can't recall', or 'I was never informed', they become worthless. Ohlendorf was able to produce copies of the reports by his *Einsatzgruppe*, requests by the *Wehrmacht* town commanders, and orders issued by 11th Army in support of every statement made by him. Not one of the defence attorneys in the *Einsatzgruppen* trial attempted to contest the contents of the reports and orders. None were issued for the purpose of post-war justification, all were daily routine accounts, the importance of which came to light only after the war.[158]

In its verdict in Case 9, the IMT stated:

> The history of the *Einsatzgruppen* and their bloodthirsty murders has not been compiled in the years since the war. The reports were written on a daily basis, as these crimes occurred and by the men who committed them. They reflect a particular eagerness not to leave out the slightest detail.[159]

In his testimony at Case 9, Ohlendorf confirmed that 33,000 Jews were killed during the time of Manstein's command. He added:

---

156 Ibid, p. 436
157 Ibid, 450
158 Krausnick, p. 337
159 IMT, Case 9, p. 147

All our actions took place under the responsibility of the Army commander. He alone had territorial sovereignty and total executive power. He was master of life and death. His responsibility was never curtailed.[160]

Manstein's knowledge is also confirmed by an entry in 11th Army's war diary under the heading: 'Results of the resettlement'. One of the euphemisms used by the *Wehrmacht*. That was followed by a table showing all the executions committed in 11th Army's area.[161] In its verdict in Case 9, the IMT stated that no doubt remained about the complicity of 11th Army.[162]

Ohlendorf never denied what he did, on the contrary, he took pride in his actions. In the death sentence imposed upon him, the IMT stated:

Regardless of the crimes with which he is charged, he was certainly not guilty of evasive behaviour as a witness. This cannot be said of the other accused. With a candour, which one must wish to have been devoted to a better cause, Otto Ohlendorf gave his account of how he received the *Führer*'s orders and how he carried them out. He never denied that he had ordered murder, he only stated that he had acted on orders. After having been himself indicted and sentenced, he appeared voluntarily as a witness at four other trials before the IMT and confirmed his testimony before us without limitation or hesitation. He never denied that he had committed murders, and gave a detailed description of the divisions of his Sk and Ek into smaller sub-units, and a full account of his collection of the victims' property and their despatch to Berlin. In his view, Germany had been compelled to attack Russia in self-defence. The security of the troops to which his unit was attached had made the measures taken by him necessary, and he had carried them out without hesitating.[163]

Ohlendorf reserved his contempt for the Generals who denied their participation in his actions. In a letter, smuggled out from his prison to his wife, he wrote that he was "utterly disgusted with the commanders who simply denied their past, and who covered their oath of loyalty to the *Führer* with a web of treason and lies."[164] In 1947, he managed to send another letter to his wife, in which he explained what had moved him and thousands more to engage in the wholesale slaughter of Jews: "Even after the war, Jewry has continued to sow hate; and it reaps hate again. What else could we have done when confronted with demons at work, engaged in a struggle against us?"[165]

Friedrich concludes:

In all matters subject to dispute, only the mass murderer has spoken the truth, and the generals lied. They were accomplices and denied it. Only

160   Case 9, p. 137
161   BA-MA, RH 19 VI/457, OAU/Qu.2, *AOK* 11
162   IMT, Case 9, p. 137
163   Case 9, p. 147
164   Höhne, p. 476
165   Ibid. p. 393 f

because the accusation levelled at Manstein is so incredible that many simply refused to believe it, his reputation has escaped total blemish. [166]

Wöhler

Ohlendorf did not testify at Manstein's trial. However, he was one of the main witnesses against Wöhler at the procedures of IMT, Case 12. The individual *Judenaktionen* in which 11th Army played an active part will be treated in detail in the section of this chapter dealing with the massacres in every township under 11th Army's control.

Wöhler was first questioned as to how it was possible that he had no knowledge of the reports from 11th Army *Korück* 553, *Generalleutnant* Heinrich Doehla, nor of the reports sent to him by his Ic/AO, Major Riesen. At first, Wöhler replied that 11th Army's headquarters and the staff of the *Korück* were stationed at different locations.[167] He immediately recognised that this was unsustainable.[168] Then a cross-examination ensued:

Wöhler: "The *Korück* reports never reached me since they were part of territorial authority and responsibility. I was adviser to the Army Commander in all matters related to operations and tactics. The chief quartermaster reports directly to the Army Commander, apparently he failed to submit his reports to Manstein. The deputy quartermaster never reported to me."

Q: "Was the deputy quartermaster not under obligation to keep you informed of events which had occurred in the rear?"

A: "No."

Q: "Why did the quartermaster department conspire against you?"

A: "I find it difficult to give a satisfactory reply."

Q: "Why did Major Riesen not find it necessary to communicate his reports to you?"

A: "I have long searched for a reply to this question, but I was never able to find one, at least none that was convincing."[169]

Since Wöhler had initialled many of the reports which he claimed never to have seen, also issued orders in his own name or on behalf of *AOK* 11[170], those statements of his require no further comment.

Wöhler's defence attorney Rauschenbach then asked Ohlendorf how he could charge Wöhler with complicity in Ohlendorf's massacres. He was faced with a barrage of Ohlendorf's answers to which he was unable to find a reply:

A: "When such things occurred, over a whole year, in locations under direct Army control. The local Sk and their sub-units had to co-ordinate every action of theirs with the Ic officers of every division, or the military town commanders. So I simply can't imagine that the staff officers of the Army had remained ignorant. Especially, after they had to be asked for their consent and then provided the assistance required. This is simply common sense."

---

166 Friedrich, p. 641
167 IMT, Case 12, Minutes, p. 5,914 ff
168 Ibid.
169 Ibid
170 Details in the section about *Judenaktionen* in locations under 11th Army's authority

Q: "After you had selected the undesirable elements, how did their liquidation take place?"

A: "They were shot in accordance with military procedures."

Q: "Where they shot at the place where they were arrested or transported to another location?"

A: "No, they were shot outside the township, in a manner which prevented the inhabitants from witnessing it."

Q: "How did they reach their place of execution? Did they walk or were they transported?

A: "In a general manner, they were transported in lorries."

Q: "How did you obtain the lorries?"

A: "In the case of large-scale shootings, lorries were provided by the Army. In other instances, we had to take them where we could find them, either from our own stocks or whatever vehicles the quartermasters could give us."

Q: "Have you received direct assistance from 11th Army's staff?"

A: "Yes."

Q: "Did the staff officers of 11th Army, who assisted you, have knowledge of the ultimate fate of the victims?"

A: "Since we had to tell them why we needed their assistance, and also the size of the assistance which they were asked to provide, we had obviously to inform them what this was needed for."

Q: "When you gave your explanations, did you tell the staff officer that you needed his help to complete your massacres?"

A: "The commander of the Sk, or of the sub-unit, went to the town commander and discussed all the details with him."

Q: "When you went into an area where Jews or other undesirables could be found, did you go there on your own initiative or did you receive orders?"

A: "I think that I have already made it clear that orders concerning a given area, where a Sk or a Ek had to penetrate, were given by the Army. The Army gave precise orders as to which areas, which command had to be directed there, what equipment was to be supplied and how long we had to remain there."

Q: "And did those officers know that you had to go there to catch and kill Jews and other undesirables?

A: "This was not the original purpose of sending us into a given area. Our orders were to ensure the security of the area and commands have also gone into places where there were no Jews. Such locations did exist. The purpose of the orders given by the Army was to ensure general security. The commands then also killed other undesirable elements, in accordance with the *Führer* orders."

Q: "Was the elimination of all Jews part of your security considerations?"

A: "Yes, this was the essential element of the *Führer* order."

Q: "In other terms, whenever you were sent somewhere to liquidate people who were considered to be a security risk for the *Wehrmacht*, Jews were part of them?"

A: "Yes, of course, this was part of our assignment."

Q: "Were the *Wehrmacht* officers with whom you discussed your orders aware of this?"

A: "The Ic and the Ic/AO, who had to take care of the details, obviously knew."

Q: "When you received orders to go into a certain area and to get hold of undesirable elements who were considered to be security risks, from whom did you receive your orders? From the Division, the Corps or the Army?"

A: "The orders were obviously given by the Army, since the Divisions received their orders from the Army. The Army decided upon the Commands that were given to every Division. The movements of the Division were ordered by the Army. The Divisions could thus not issue orders of their own to the Commands, such orders were always issued by the Army."

Q: "You imply that the order came directly from the Army?"

A: "Yes, they were always issued by the *AOK*."

Q: "Did you receive such orders while the accused, Wöhler, was chief-of-staff of 11th Army?"

A: "Yes."

Q: "Who signed the orders, the Army commander of the chief-of-staff?"

A: "They were signed by the chief-of-staff, on behalf of the *AOK*." [171]

The incessant flows of Ohlendorf's detailed reports that descended upon 11th Army should have quickly aroused Manstein's suspicions. The transmission of Ic/AO reports to the Army commander is subject to decision by the Army's chief-of-staff. However, the reports contravened an order that Manstein had issued 'with utmost emphasis' and 'without a twinkle in his eyes.' Wöhler would hardly have failed to inform him of such disobedience.

At the end, the tribunal lost patience with Wöhler's 'lack of awareness'. Wöhler had declared: "We did not know that the National-Socialists wanted to kill Jews only because they were Jews." [172]

Friedrich comments:

> Since Wöhler had previously admitted that he had provided the *Einsatzgruppen* with ammunition and kept careful copies of all reports about the massacres, his 'lack of awareness' must be described as a 'qualified lack.' [173]

Wöhler invented a new term, 'official lack of awareness': "I deny that the *SD* has informed the Army commander or any staff officer of the 'other' element of its assignment trough official channels. I know now that it was not allowed to do so." [174]

Another comment by Friedrich:

> Still, *Einsatzgruppe* D could report to 11th Army through Ic/AO that the Crimea was 'free of Jews'. It was a sentence which Wöhler could only understand if he was aware of Ohlendorf's 'official' mission. Although Ohlendorf never refrained from putting blame on 11th Army, he did not claim that he had informed it of his mission 'through official channels'. He only said that he had had to assume that his 'official mission' was

---

171   IMT, Case 12, p. 9.268 and 5.742. Also Friedrich, p. 633 f and 641 ff
172   IMT, Case 12, p.5.738
173   Friedrich, p. 667
174   IMT, Case 12, p.5.565

known. This was simply common sense and his many reports about executions could hardly have left a doubt.[175]

The IMT referred to Wöhler's 'lack of awareness' in its sentence:

Without the shadow of a doubt, the slaughter of 90,000 civilians by those police units could not have taken place without the knowledge of 11th Army's chief-of-staff, unless he was totally incompetent. The accused certainly did not convey an impression of incompetence, and no mention of his incompetence can be detected in his many positive evaluations by his superiors.[176]

Some revisionist books describe Wöhler as an opponent of National-Socialism. During the Second World War no trace of opposition ever appeared. During the German retreats in Summer 1944, Wöhler was commander of Army Group South and had withdrawn into Romania. He was furious when he saw that Jews were still living unmolested in all Romanian towns. At the beginning of the war in the East, many Romanian troops had taken part in massacres. However, since the summer of 1942, Antonescu increasingly doubted a favourable outcome of the war and had forbidden further deportations of Jews. After most of the Romanian Army was destroyed at Stalingrad, Jews were no longer molested in areas under Romanian control. Wöhler could no longer order executions and was reduced to issuing outraged orders:

Jews are returning to Jassy by the day. The town should be evacuated. This is hardly possible, since the Jews have obviously bribed the city officials. At Barlad, Jews have even bought clothing and canned food from German soldiers. I have ordered the arrest of these creatures. Conclusions: Jews have to disappear.[177]

Instead of killing Jews, the German soldiers now found it more attractive to engage in trade in second-hand clothing. When Wöhler heard that German officers and soldiers were regular guests at Jewish homes, he was outraged and issued an order:

Undignified and shameless behaviour by German soldiers makes a mockery of our National-Socialist education. Such behaviour must immediately be stamped out with utmost severity. Whoever has relations with Jews, the greatest enemies of the German people, is not worthy to be a German soldier.[178]

Social contacts between Jews and German soldiers had inevitably resulted in *Rassenschande,* sexual relations between Jews and non-Jews, which were prohibited by the German racial laws. "Such things have occurred in Jassy, as a consequence of social contacts."[179] Wöhler could now only limit himself to orders requiring

---

175   Friedrich, p. 667
176   IMT, Case 12, p. 279
177   *NOKW* 3422
178   *NOKW* 3439
179   IMT, Case 12, p. 5.865

protection against venereal disease.[180] When the court asked him why he had inserted racial concepts in this order, Wöhler replied: "I had to use racial wordings to explain my order. This was something everyone understood at that time."[181]

Only a few months later, with final defeat and retaliation approaching, Wöhler himself understood it no longer. A new understanding caught up with him and he 'discovered' humanity. As commander of Army Group South, he had visited a concentration camp in January 1945 and provided medical help to Jewish inmates, who had contracted epidemic typhus. He testified that, "I remember halting with my car at the fence of the camp. Many Jews saw me and removed their hats to show their gratitude."[182]

Judenaktionen in townships controlled by 11th Army

This section contains the relevant extracts from all archive documents related to the murders committed by *Einsatzgruppe* D, in the areas under the territorial authority of 11th Army. Only such parts as relate directly to the massacres are given. Some reports contained more than one hundred pages, in which the *Einsatzgruppe* endeavoured to show its ignorance of the political conditions in their areas of operation, and to show the even greater ignorance of the Army commanders. Large-scale massacres required the Sk or Ek to be divided into several local sub-units. In such instances, only one description is given, since the others are identical, except for the names of the commanders involved. The language of the reports is purposely not embellished in the translation, in order to preserve the vulgarity of the original.

The section covers both the command periods of Schobert and Manstein, in order to show that co-operation between *Einsatzgruppe* D and 11th Army had already become a daily routine in Schobert's time, and that Manstein inherited a ready made instrument, with no changes in the Army's staff.

Some reports are unsigned, they were apparently transmitted as an annex to other documents. At times, euphemisms were used. The words 'execution' and 'shooting' are then replaced by 'resettled,' 'cleansed,' 'treated according to orders.' Jews are at times replaced by 'partisans' and 'Commissars.' Those terms were often chosen at random, for the sake of bringing variation in the definition of the victims. Apparently the *Einsatzgruppen* feared that remaining with the term 'Jew only', might have a negative effect, since pictures of executions were often shown on German newsreels. One such newsreel, reproduced on the ARD Video, shows a group of civilians being led to execution and described as partisans. "Their hiding place has been uncovered. The bandits who have remained alive have been captured. This rabble can expect no mercy." A manual prepared for a *Wehrmacht* officers' training course contains the sentence: "The partisan is the Jew and the Jew is the partisan." Many orders issued by Army commanders contained the equation

180 Ibid
181 Ibid, p. 5.866
182 Case 12, p. 5,682 f

'*Bolshevist* = partisan = Jew'. [183]The *Einsatzgruppen* had thus latitude in their choice of terminology.

Personal relations between Wöhler and Ohlendorf were tense. When Wöhler turned to Ohlendorf, Ohlendorf created difficulties, and Wöhler repaid him in kind. Wöhler saw himself as a colonel, decorated with both Iron Crosses. He was soon to become a general and an Army commander in his own right, while Ohlendorf was an *SS-Standartenführer*. He did not even belong to the *Waffen-SS* and had only 600 men under his command. In other words, at best a battalion commander. At Nuremberg, Ohlendorf complained: "This is the way I was treated."[184] Wöhler felt that he was entitled to order Ohlendorf around, and that Ohlendorf had to remain total respect of his military rank. Ohlendorf saw in Wöhler one of many thousands of colonels who could be replaced at any moment, while he represented the real power. Wöhler never objected to Ohlendorf's massacres. The main area of contention between the two was the *OKH* order of 28 April 1941, which gave the *AOK* the authority to decide where and when the *Einsatzgruppen* should be put into action. Ohlendorf had little respect for *OKH*, which had no authority over the *SD*. His only interest was the accomplishment of his "historic" mission that had kept him from returning to Berlin. He felt that his success would be assured if he was allowed to plan, independently, where and when to bring his Sk and Ek into action, without any interference by 11th Army. A first clash between Wöhler and Ohlendorf occurred in August 1941. Ohlendorf testified:

> During the first six weeks of the campaign, 11th Army intended to entirely integrate my Sk and Ek. I gave them their first marching orders. Then the Army began ordering them around and deciding what they had to do. I had already clashed with the Ic of 11th Army, Major Ranck. Since I was not prepared to comply with his instructions, he complained to the Army's chief-of-staff, colonel Wöhler. He told me that things could not continue in that way and that agreement had to be reached on all points under contention. In particular, it remained the right of the Army to give me orders where to go, how to determine the size and the compositions of my Sk and my Ek, and where to send them.[185]

By July, Wöhler had threatened Ohlendorf with having him recalled to Berlin if co-operation with *AOK* 11 was not quickly improved. This was the instance that Manstein alluded to, when he wrote that "Wöhler did not hesitate to talk in unmistakably plain German with a *protégé* of Himmler." Tensions between *Einsatzgruppe D* and *AOK* 11 quickly subsided, when the staff of the Army saw that Ohlendorf's independent actions facilitated its work. Ohlendorf showed himself to have a better view as to where his presence was urgently required.

---

183   Krausnick, p. 248
184   IMT, Case 12, p.623 f and Friedrich, p. 644
185   IMT, Case 12, p. 9.079 and Friedrich, p. 637

Judenaktionen during the time
of Schobert's command

The first three orders by 11th Army

11th Army's first order to *Einsatzgruppe* D was issued on 3 July 1941, and signed by Wöhler:

> A *Sonderkommando* is attached to DVK 2 (*Deutsches Verbindungskommando*, German liaison command unit with the Romanian armies). Every step taken by it will be reported to *AOK* 11, department Ic/AO by transmission through DVK 2. All captured military equipment is to be immediately handed over to DVK 2 which will in turn send it to *AOK* 11, Ic/AO.[186]

On 12 July 1941, 11th Army sent a request to Army Group South: "*Sonderkommando* of *Einsatzgruppe D* to be sent into the area of 11th Army. Acknowledge receipt of communication."[187]

Order by *AOK* 11 to *Einsatzgruppe D*, Sk 11b:

> ... Sk 11b will immediately seize all unreliable elements (partisans, saboteurs, remaining groups of enemy soldiers not yet captured, parachutists in civilian clothes, Jews, leading communist personalities etc). Sk 11b will report all steps taken by it to the Ic/AO ... After completion of its mission, Sk 11b reports to *AOK* 11 and receives further orders for its new assignments.[188]

Already these first orders are sufficient evidence that 11th Army was informed about the activities of *Einsatzgruppe* D from the very first days of the war and that it immediately initiated an active co-operation.

Wöhler's order of 22 July 1941, prohibiting taking photographs of mass shootings

On 22 July 1941, Wöhler issued an order related to pictures, taken by German soldiers, of an execution of Jews by Romanian troops:

> A recent incident makes it incumbent on me to issue the following order. Given the lack of importance attached to the value of human life in the East, German soldiers may become witnesses of actions such as mass executions, murders of civilian prisoners and Jews that they are unable to prevent but which are contrary to the German sense of honour.
>
> It should be obvious to every sane person that such contemptible actions may not be photographed nor mentioned in letters sent home. Photos which are made and passed on, and reports, are a violation of discipline and decency in the *Wehrmacht* and will be severely punished. All

---

186   BA-MA, RH 20-11/488
187   BA-MA, RH 20 –11/488 with copy to Army Group South
188   Krausnick, p.212

pictures, together with the negatives and reports, are to be immediately turned over to the Army's Ic/AO with a mention of the name of the photographers and the writers. An inquisitive watching of such events is below the dignity of the German soldier.

Signed: Wöhler, chief-of-staff, on behalf of *AOK* 11[189]

The Ic of 46th and 27th divisions ordered the communication of the order to every soldier of their units on 27 and 29 July 1941.

This document calls for the following comments:

1. Wöhler already had knowledge of the mass execution of Jews by 22 July 1941.

2. Since pictures were being taken by German soldiers, they likewise had knowledge. Pictures must have been taken in large quantities, otherwise Wöhler's order would not have had to be communicated to every soldier of the divisions involved.

3. Wöhler's order was not obeyed, the taking of pictures continued. The many photographs and amateur films, unearthed after the war, are sufficient evidence.

4. Accounts in letters from soldiers to their relatives and friends at home continued to be written, as shown in the already mentioned report of the party chancellery.

5. What was known to the troops, was likewise known to the Division Commanders who also received a copy of Wöhler's order.

The Romanenko incident

On 7 September 1941, Schobert issued a personal order to execute Vladimir Romanenko by hanging. Schobert had already ordered *Einsatzgruppe* D to search all bunkers for any fugitives who were considered to represent a danger for German troops. If they could not prove their identity, they were to be shot without further investigation.[190] Schobert repeated his previous order: "Better take care of too many than too few."

After Romanenko had been hanged, it turned out that he was neither a Jew nor a partisan. He was simply a mentally ill man. Ohlendorf was irritated. His mission consisted of killing Jews. He knew that the mentally ill were 'taken care of' by another department of the *SD*. He wrote an angry letter to *AOK* 11: "The verbal communication by the Army commander was based upon totally false premises. Romanenko had never threatened any units of 11th Army, nor had he asked to refrain from working as he had been ordered. Since Romanenko was mentally retarded, and had admitted that he had been sent to an asylum for mentally retarded on three previous occasions, his execution took place on 9 September 1941, on grounds of inherited mental illness.

When Wöhler was first shown the Romanenko file, he expressed disbelief: "The man has been handed over by *Generaloberst* von Schobert to the *SD*. There must have been something against him, he must have agitated and demanded stoppage of work."

---

189 *NOKW* 2523
190 Krausnick, p. 199

Q: "The documentation shows clearly that the man was acquitted of the charges brought against him."

A: "Yes, I can no longer contest that he was simply mentally ill and that he was executed on biological grounds."[191]

Czernovits

Report by Ek 10 b of *Einsatzgruppe* D to Army Group South with copy to 11th Army, 9 July 1941:

Ek 10 b arrived at Czernovits on Sunday, 6 July 1941, at 6.15 pm. An advance unit had already arrived on the previous day, established communication with Romanian troops, and arranged for living quarters.

... Based on our search list and new lists prepared by us, the arrest of Communists and Jews began on 7 July. On 8 July, a major action was carried through. Practically the whole Jewish leadership was arrested. On the following day, around 100 Jewish Communists were shot by the Ek. Together with executions carried out by Romanian troops and police units, 500 Jews were shot between 8 and 9 July. ... Signed: Persterer, SS-*Sturmbannführer* and commander of Ek 10 b, and certified by Major Riesen in the name of 11th Army.[192]

At his trial, Wöhler blamed Major Riesen: "I was never informed that shootings of Jews had taken place. Obviously Major Riesen knew, since he had signed the document, but I did not know."[193]

Delzy

Report by Sk 10 a, 12 July 1941: "First indications show that 50% to 80% of the inhabitants are Jews. This number is probably inflated ... Many wealthy Jews have escaped. A patrol entered a house in which 15 Jews had been shot by the Romanians. Some were still alive and were finished off with a bullet in the head. Synagogues which have remained undamaged have been brought into the same state as the remainder." Signed: "Seetzen, *SS-Obersturmbannführer*."[194]

Nikolayev (first report)

Report by Sk 11a for the period of 18 August to 31 August 1941:

After entering Nikolayev, a sub-unit of three men searched all civilians who had been brought into transit camps for prisoners of war. 4,000 men and women were questioned.

---

191 IMT, Case 12, p. 5.912 and Friedrich, p. 617
192 BA-MA, RH 23/72
193 *NOKW* 2948, Friedrich, p. 617
194 BA-MA, RH-20-11/488

The examination made it necessary to arrest 227 suspect Jews, political functionaries and former prison inmates. Signed: Zapp, *SS-Sturmbannführer.*[195]

Kichinew

Report by Ek 12, *Einsatzgruppe* D, July 1941 (no day indicated):

Until now, 551 Jews executed, 151 for having participated in acts of sabotage and 400 as a reprisal for shooting by unknown persons at German ambulances and giving torch signals to enemy aircraft. The remaining Jews have been enclosed in a ghetto.[196]

Report by Sk 11a, *Einsatzgruppe* D, August 1941 (no day indicated): "After search of a transit camp, 68 Jews were executed after they had been convicted of communist agitation."

Wöhler made a comment which Krausnick qualifies as being particularly 'revealing': " I am sure that an enquiry must have taken place. I can't imagine that the reports were simply written in order to soothe Army's conscience."[197] Wöhler added that he had no recollection of the *Judenaktion.*

The events in Kichinew led to Manstein's order which was issued 'without a twinkle in his eyes.'

Kodyma

The circumstances of the massacre at Kodyma were unique among all the *Judenaktionen* in the area of 11th Army. Not on the grounds of the number of victims – 'only' 96 Jews were shot – but because of the flurry of reports that described the circumstances under which the massacre had taken place. Had they not concerned an action of mass murder, one may be tempted to feel that they were part of a 'comedy'. No less than three reports were devoted to the event, one by the field police, a second by *Einsatzgruppe* D and finally one by *AOK* 11. Only a final analysis by Friedrich makes it possible to obtain a coherent picture of what had occurred.

11th Army's XXX Corps, commanded by general von Salmuth, whom Manstein had criticized for not being a rousing personality, had been held up at Uman by the 'remnants of the Red Army which were still capable of offering some resistance.' Since Salmuth feared that the tough disciplinarian Schobert would administer him a stern rebuke, he was in a hurry to rejoin the bulk of the Army and instructed his troops to actively assist the *Einsatzgruppe* in its removal of any obstacles in his way.

Report by the field police to *AOK* 11, 7 August 1941:

On 1 August 1941, a Ukrainian peasant woman presented herself at our headquarters. She told us that some fifty Jews had assembled on the previous day at the Kodyma school. The woman could neither read nor

---

195   BA-MA, RH 23/27
196   *NOKW* 2948, Friedrich, p. 617
197   Krausnick, p. 223, with referece to IMT, Case 12, p. 5.833

write, but she had been employed by Jews as a domestic servant over many years, and was therefore able to understand the Jewish jargon.

She reported that the Jews had planned to launch an attack on German staff headquarters, and the German troops who camped in the open. The Jews had heard from young guys that the German staff headquarters were insufficiently guarded and that their planned action stood a good chance of success. At the same time, they intended to set the harvest on fire. They had already called for reinforcements by other Jewish and communist elements from neighbouring townships.

As a result of this information, the Jewish quarter of the city was surrounded on 1 August, at 3 pm ....The Jews were brought from their homes ... Some Jews attempted to escape and had to be prevented by firearms. After a short while, 500 Jews were assembled in the market place. All Jews were carefully searched and it was shown that almost every Jew carried large sums of money ... Many Jews had packages of cash, watches and jewellery pieces. The valuables were immediately confiscated by the SS-Sk.

98 Jews were shot on the same day by the Sk. A further 300 have been retained as hostages, 60 Ukrainians have been set free ... We intend to strongly object to the assertions of the Jews that the German staff headquarters were not sufficiently guarded by us. Day and night, the troops and all their equipment were under constant protection by armed guards and the attack which the Jews had planned would have been easily nipped in the bud ...

Signed: Scholz, commander of the field police unit.[198]

Report by Sk 10b to XXX Corps, with copy to *AOK* 11, 12 August 1941:

After a Ukrainian woman made a report which was transmitted to XXX Corps, the corps command requested us to make an investigation. The Ukrainian woman had stated that a secret meeting had taken place at Kodyma. Some 50 Jews had planned to attack German military installations. Already on previous occasions, the Jews had behaved in a refractory manner towards German soldiers. The Jewish manager of a mineral water plant had forbidden the distribution of water to the German soldiers and had threatened them when they tried to enter his plant. Other Jews had assembled, in groups of ten to twelve, and behaved in an aggressive manner.

After the Ic of XXX Corps had put 400 soldiers at our disposal, the centre of the town, which is almost entirely inhabited by Jews, could be searched thoroughly ... Since the Jews persisted in their bad behaviour, with some even trying to escape or barricading themselves in their homes, fire-arms had to be repeatedly used. Warning shots had to be fired at the city's population, since many tried to free the Jews who had been arrested, or who had otherwise disturbed our work. After our search was completed, around 400 Jews had been arrested. Most of them had fled their homes when our troops advanced and had found refuge in Kodyma.

After questioning, it was established that 98 had participated at meetings hostile to the Germans or that they belonged to the Jewish intelligentsia ... A further 175, all of them Jews, could not be shown to have offered active resistance to the Germans. For the time being, they were put into a *Wehrmacht* transit camp as hostages, while the 98 were liquidated after completion of their identification. The execution took place with the assistance of the *Wehrmacht*, which put a firing-squad of 24 men at our disposal. Our own sub-command numbered 12 men. An attempt to escape during the execution could be easily prevented by using fire-arms. Signed: Prast, *SS-Hauptsturmführer*.[199]

The sub-unit of Sk 10 b numbered 16 men. Under normal conditions this was sufficient to shoot 98 Jews, even 400, without outside assistance. But the Jews at Kodyma apparently belonged to the Jewish intelligentsia which, according to Manstein and Wöhler, provided the strongest assistance to such units of the Red Army 'still capable of fighting'. Since they had also behaved in a 'most refractory manner', the 'generous' assistance of Salmuth's soldiers was required.

Report by the Ic of XXX Corps to Ic/AO *AOK* 11: In its introductions, the report repeats the statements made by the Ukrainian woman. It continued:

After having received the report by the Ukrainian peasant woman, we immediately contacted Ek 10a at Olchanka and requested it to come quickly to Kodyma, in order to prevent the execution of hostile plans by the Jews and the *Bolshevists* against German installations and troops. The search of the Jewish quarter was conducted by *SS-Hauptsturmführer* Prast with the assistance of 300 *Wehrmacht* soldiers whom we had put at his disposal.

Result: 400 Jews were arrested and questioned in the market square of Kodyma. We were surprised to see that many of them had come from Balty, Soroky and Yampol, which had already been occupied by us. The field-police units immediately informed our Ic about the indications given by the Ukrainian woman ... The SS-Sk conducted the search ... It was found out that, besides the Jewish residents of Kodyma, many had come from Bessarabia and other neighbouring townships and had found refuge with local Jews ... Thus, the indications by the Ukrainian woman were shown to have been true ... 98 Jews were shot on the same day by the Sk ... On 1 August 1941, the Jewish quarter was surrounded at 3 pm ... The Jews were taken from their homes ... Some attempted to flee and had to be shot. No signs remain of further actions by Jews and *Bolshevist* against the *Wehrmacht*. Signed: The chief-of-staff of XXX Corps, *Oberst* Botsch.[200]

An entry in the war diary of 11th Army reads: "Preparation of an attack by Jews and members of the *Komsomol* in Kodyma. All the leaders and other suspects have been shot."[201]

---

199 BA-MA, RH 20-11/488
200 BA-MA, RH 20-11/488
201 BA-MA, RH 20-11/488

This time even Wöhler's patience was exhausted. He prepared a draft order: "The report about the executions of 96 people at Kodyma requires an order to take the severest steps if such incidents are repeated."[202] The Ic/AO of 11th Army simply put Wöhler's draft into a file, with the hand-written notice that nothing remained to be done in this case, nor ordered for the future.[203]

Friedrich succeeds in bringing some order into this confusion:

When the Ukrainian informer threw herself into the arms of the inter-preters at 198th division, her babbling immediately fell on open ears. She denounced the troublesome Bessarabian Jews and the *Bolshevists* who wanted to sabotage the sale of grain. The *Wehrmacht* officers had carefully studied the orders from the highest commands and knew that they were in the middle of the cradle of Jewish-*Bolshevism*. Therefore the report of the Ukrainian woman was plausible. Subversive elements had torn down posters with official *Wehrmacht* communications to the civilian popula-tion. Armed NKVD battalions continued to roam through the neigh-bouring countryside, this could not be doubted.

The woman pretended to have overheard 50 Jews and Communists during a secret conspiracy meeting. Surprisingly she was unable to provide the field police with any relevant detail. Who belonged to the conspiracy group? Where did it hide? But according to highest instruc-tions, 'the group simply had to exist'. The reports indicated Kodyma, therefore the group must have been at Kodyma.

400 persons were questioned in the market square. According to the reports, the whole questioning took place between 3:25 pm and 7 pm. That amounts to 225 minutes. Interpreters were needed, thus every indi-vidual questioning took 45 seconds at the most. Some Ukrainian resi-dents of Kodyma had confirmed the statements by the woman and identified Jews. Curiously, those were Jews whom they did not know. They were refugees from Bessarabia. There were practically no Jewish residents in Kodyma before their arrival. Hence the surrounded Jewish quarter, which 400 soldiers had carefully searched, could, at best, have consisted of only one or two houses. But where did those Jews live who had only recently arrived? Apparently, in houses that were inhabited by Russians and Ukrainians who had to be arrested first, then threatened with arms, and thereafter set free.

To sum up: The Germans had indeed conducted a round-up in the centre of the city, mainly inhabited by Romanians and Ukrainians. The Jews had apparently found refuge there. Perhaps it was a sudden gesture of hospitality? The indication by the field-police, that the Jews were "care-fully searched for money, watches and jewels" points to the real back-ground. Three weeks after the completion of the massacre, the staff of 11th Army continued to request further written reports from all partici-pants. The soldiers were particularly enraged at the Jewish manager of a mineral water plant, who had refused water to a *Wehrmacht* unit under

---

202   BA-MA, RH 20-11/488
203   Krausnick, p. 240 f

the burning heat of an August day. Therefore the *Wehrmacht* had to retreat, thirsty, to its barracks.[204]

At his trial, Salmuth hardly showed himself as 'rousing'. A Corps Commander knows all the units under his command, but Salmuth did not know where his 400 men at Kodyma belonged. "They were just a lot of individual soldiers who roamed around the countryside. Today they happened to be at Kodyma, they left after a few hours, tomorrow, they were somewhere else."[205] Thus, they were a crowd without a commander. However, the field- police had taken pains to report that they had camped in good order, both during the day and at night, and that they were carefully guarded. Therefore, they had hardly left 'after a few hours."

Salmuth complained at his trial:

I have to say that things have taken a strange turn. What happened here? An uprising had to be suppressed. The soldiers had to assume that the culprits were chased according to rules. All soldiers of the corps were under orders to act without consideration against the Jews. But, understand, not against the Jews as such, only if they could be shown to have committed an offence.[206]

Salmuth was sentenced to twenty years.

After completing the massacre at Kodyma, Sk 10a proceeded to Pechanka where it discovered new victims. In his report to *AOK* 11 of 5 August 1941, *Korück* 553 stated: "Just as I arrived, 10 Jews were shot by the *SS*-commando, because they had attempted to sabotage harvest work."[207]

Ananyev

A report by town commander Ananyev to *Korück* 553, 3 September 1941, stated:

The Jews at Ananyev had threatened a blood-bath among the ethnic German residents as soon as the Germans troops would be forced to retreat from the city. Therefore, the field-police made a round up and shot some 300 Jewish men and women on 28 August 1941. Signed: Town commander, (name illegible).[208]

General order by AOK 11 to all Corps concerning attitude towards enemy espionage and sabotage, 5 September 1941:

In all areas which require strong security, the Corps have to create a no-man's-land … Simple supervision of the front lines is insufficient. Both Corps and *Korücks* have to conduct swoops at regular intervals, arrest all suspicious civilians and check their residence permits. Civilians who can be suspected of sabotage, espionage, or partisan activities have to be immediately shot by the field-police. Residents who have arrived from

---

204   Friedrich, p. 619 f
205   IMT, Case 12, p. 4.026
206   Case 12, p. 4,035
207   *NOKW* 2925, Friedrich, p. 626
208   *NOKW* 1712, Krausnick, p. 271

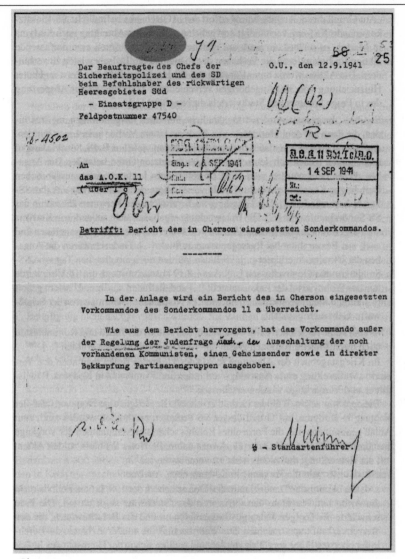

Cherson

other townships, who have no identity papers showing their town of origin, and all Jews have to be handed over to the *SD*. If such people are discovered in transit camps, the camp commanders have to hand them over immediately to the *SD*. No exception is to be made for young boys and girls whom the enemy often prefers to put in as spies and saboteurs.

Signed: Wöhler, signature confirmed by Major Riesen, Ic/AO[209]

---

209   BA-MA, RH 20-11/488

Judenaktionen during the time of Manstein's command

Cherson

Report by *Einsatzgruppe* D to *AOK* 11, 12 September 1941. The report reached 11th Army three days before Manstein assumed command. On 26 September, it was transmitted to the Army's quartermaster department, shown to Manstein and initialled by him. This report was part of the prosecution's evidence at Manstein's trial:

> The report shows that an advance unit has already taken care of the "Jewish problem'(these words are underlined four times by 11th Army's quartermaster department) and has also succeeded in discovering a secret transmitter and in eliminating communists and partisans who had remained in the city.[210]

That short statement is followed by a lengthy addendum:

> On 20 August 1941, a small advance command had entered the city to assume the duties of Sk 11a. The small command immediately began to take the first steps in solving the *Judenfrage*, to protect German ethnic minorities and to destroy the bearers of *Bolshevism*. Then the situation in this city, with 100,000 inhabitants, suddenly changed. On 24 August 1941, the Red Army opened a heavy artillery barrage ... Several German unit headquarters were forced to withdraw from the town.
>
> Since Sk 11a had already begun its duties, it decided to face the danger and remain. The task was not easy, because enemy action proved to be a strong obstacle. Feelings were depressed ... Many expected a return of the Reds and feared their retaliation. The mission of Sk 11a was completed between 22 August 1941 and 10 September 1941. Already by 23 August 1941, Jews were ordered to register and to wear the Jewish star ....The Jews were then ordered to suffer hard-labour and were concentrated in a few streets. There is no intention to establish a permanent Jewish quarter ...
>
> The *Judenfrage* was thus initially solved in a first step ... Sk 11a then carried out the following executions: 400 Jewish men and 10 Jewish women were shot in reprisal for acts of sabotage and destruction of communication equipment. 11 political criminals were arrested, their leader was hanged, and the remainder were shot ... Sk 11a numbered 15 men, no losses occurred. On 5 September 1941, 72nd division left for Bereslav. The commander of Sk 11a reported to him about the actions of his command. The General had already been informed by his Ic and he expressed his gratitude and appreciation. The town commander, Lieutenant Colonel von Rochow, also conveyed his thanks.

---

210   BA-MA, RH 20-11/488

At his trial, Wöhler testified that he had initialled the report because he could not imagine that it referred to a large-scale massacre of Jews.[211]

Genichesk

In October 1941, a massacre took place on the outskirts of Genichesk. The killing was carried out by men of Sk 10a, in the presence of officers and soldiers of 11th Army's 22nd Division. A report to *AOK* 11 mentioned 'horrifying details'.[212] The circumstances of this massacre were strange, to the extent that, once again, only an analysis by Friedrich succeeded in clarifying what had occurred. Friedrich likewise shows the strange aspects of the co-operation between 11th Army and the *Einsatzgruppe*. The 11th Army showed approval of the massacres, provided they were conducted in accordance with regulations.

After the massacre was completed, Major Riesen sent a reprimand to Ohlendorf, who outranked him. As a *Standartenführer*, Ohlendorf held a rank equivalent to colonel:

> The Ek attached to 22nd Division is stationed in the Division's combat zone. I expect that any measures, in particular executions in public in the city centre, the recruiting of Ukrainian auxiliary units etc, be only taken after previous agreement with the Ic of the Division. An officer of the division witnessed the execution and complained that it had taken place in the city centre.

Ohlendorf was not prepared to accept a rebuke that said he was not able to conduct executions in a prescribed manner, without the assistance of an Army intelligence officer. Even at Nuremberg, he was still very proud of his methods. He immediately questioned *Obersturmbannführer* Seetzen, the commander of Sk 10a. Seetzen replied that obviously no executions had taken place in the centre of the city. Orders of this kind were only issued by him if he felt it necessary to instil fear of reprisals among the population. He requested an immediate investigation to clarify how such incorrect reports had reached 11th Army.[213]

Seetzen attached a report by *Untersturmführer* Spiekermann. It described the events in detail. Spiekermann and three of his men had commanded the execution of the Jews in Genichesk on 2 and 4 October 1941. Genichesk was located on the shores of the sea of Azov and had 17,000 inhabitants. Spiekermann wrote that the killings took place outside the city's limit, at a distance of 500 to 800 metres from the last houses. No civilian had been able to watch. However, a number of soldiers of the 3rd Infantry Battalion had suddenly appeared, and remained at a distance of 100 metres. They were repeatedly ordered to disappear but refused. Spiekermann and his three aides were unable to put an end to this lack of discipline. They would have had to erect barriers and detach guards. 'But I want to emphasise that the executions were carried out exactly in the prescribed manner.'

Spiekerman's report was sent to the Ic/AO of 11th Army, who requested a reply from the Ic of 22nd Division. The division phoned the 65th Regiment, the

---

211 IMT, Case 12, p. 5920
212 Krausnick, p. 242
213 *NOKW* 641

Regiment then phoned 3rd Battalion. On 12 October, 3rd Battalion sent a report in writing:[214]

> The execution did not take place in the centre of Genichesk, 3rd Battalion had never made such a report. The shootings were conducted on a square on the outskirts of the city, as shown on the attached map. The houses close by are inhabited both by soldiers and by civilians, who had become involuntary witnesses. An artillery battery is stationed in the immediate neighbourhood. The road is used both for transportation of military equipment and the evacuation of the civilian population. The execution could be watched from the offices of the battalion and the whimpering of the victims was clearly audible. On the next morning, a heap of abandoned clothing had remained at the place of execution and large crowds had gathered. The clothes were to be destroyed. The mass grave in which the victims were buried can be seen. It is the best evidence of the place where the shootings took place.

The report leaves an oppressive feeling. Four policemen were apparently sufficient to kill all the Jews of a medium size township. If this took two days, the victims must have numbered several hundreds. Obviously, the policemen recruited a Ukrainian auxiliary unit, provided it with arms and carefully searched all the houses. The policemen felt capable of carrying out the shootings, but were apparently unable to force a few soldiers to leave. The battalion heard the whimpering of the victims, but did not intervene and preferred to complain about the disturbance in written reports to the regiment. "The clothes left over by the victims caused irritation. There is always need. But the battalion wants to keep its men from sensation-seeking and from plunder."[215]

Nikolayev (second report)

Manstein's first headquarters as Commander of 11th Army were at Nikolayev.

Report from Ohlendorf to *AOK* 11, 9 October 1941: Concerns: Report about the activities of the *Einsatzgruppe* and further plans. The Jewish question has already been taken care of. Further attention is required for the uncovering of partisans. During the past weeks, *Einsatzgruppe* was mainly concerned with political pacification and protection of ethnic German settlements.[216]

General order by AOK 11 to all units of 11th Army, Ic/AO, 'Partisan activity,' 10 October 1941:

> Partisan groups are continuously joined by Jews. Army troops and all police and security of the Army, secret field-police units, police stations, and commandos of the *SD* have to act jointly.
> Signed: Wöhler[217]

---

214 *NOKW* 3453
215 Friedrich, p. 644 ff
216 BA-MA, RH 20-11/488
217 BA-MA, RH 20-11/341

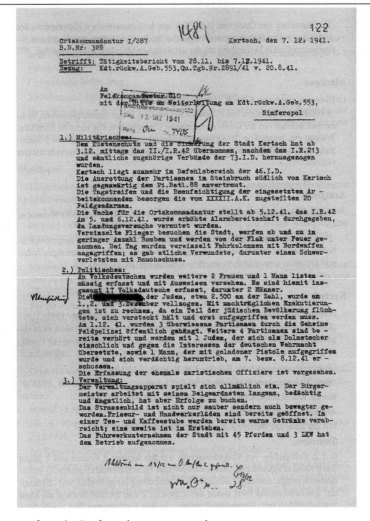

Documents from the Simferopol town commander.

Melitopol

Activity report by the town commander, 13 October 1941:

Town command has arrived in the city on 8 October 1941. Contact was immediately established with the *SD* (*Obersturmbannführer* Seetzen). In the evening hours of 10 October 1941 the town was visited by General Doehla [*Korück 553*] and the chief-of-staff of 11th Army. Reports about their visits have already been sent to *AOK* 11.

Political matters: The city and its suburbs had 85,000 inhabitants, of which 45% Russians, 40% Ukrainians, 13% Jews and 2% ethnic Germans. When we occupied the city, some 40,000 inhabitants had remained. All

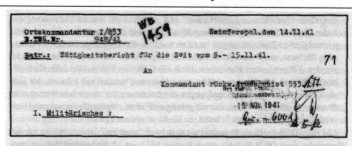

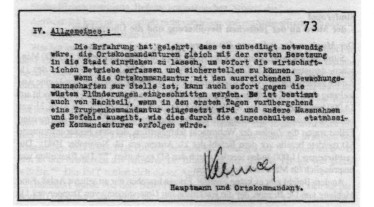

Documents from the Simferopol town commander.

Jews, 2,000, have been executed by the *SD*. The population has shown confidence in the German soldiers, in particular the Ukrainians are grateful for their liberation." Signed: "Kleiner, Captain and town commander.[218]

Kachovka

Report by the town commander to *Korück* 553, 20 October 1941:

… Originally 13,000 inhabitants, 48% Ukrainians, 30% Jews, 6% ethnic Germans and others. Only 8,200 are left. The 'cleansing' of Jewish and

---

218   BA-MA, RH 23/72

Communist elements have already been carried out by the *SD* with the assistance of Ukrainian militia. Before the war, some 800 communists are believed to have lived here. ...

Signed "Johannes, Major and town commander."[219]

Mariupol

Report by the town commander to *Korück* 553, 29 October 1941:

8,000 Jews have been executed by the *SD*. The vacated Jewish apartments have been taken over by town command. Clothing and underwear removed from the Jews will be collected, cleaned and then distributed to hospital, prisoner-of-war camps and ethnic Germans.[220]

Armyansk

Report by the town commander to *Korück* 553. 30 November 1941:

As protection against partisan activity and to ensure the safety of the troops stationed in the town, it became unavoidable to render the 14 Jewish inhabitants, men and women, harmless. The execution has been carried out on 26 November 1941.[221]

Kerch

There were two reports. First, the report by the town commander to *Korück* 553, 22 November 1941: "The registration of the Jewish population has not yet been completed. Given the difficult situation of food supply in the city, the liquidation of the Jews will be accelerated."[222]

Second, the report by the town commander to *Korück* 553, 7 December 1941: "Political situation: Three more ethnic Germans, two women and one man, were found, registered and provided with identity papers. Altogether 17 ethnic Germans, among them two men, have now been registered."

Report about the executions: The word 'execution' is in the typewritten original, it was obliterated with thick black colour and replaced in handwriting by: 'resettled.' The 'correction' was omitted in the remainder of the document, which referred to plain 'executions'.

The execution of 2,500 Jewish men, women and children has taken place on 1, 2 and 3 December. Further executions must be expected, because part of the Jewish population has fled, gone into hiding and has to be found. On 1 December 1941, three partisans were hanged in public by the field-police. Four more partisans have already been interrogated and were shot on 7 December together with a Jew, who had managed to sneak in as an

219   BA-MA, RH 23/72
220   *NOKW* 1529
221   *NOKW* 1532
222   BA-MA, RH 23/72

interpreter and who translated in a manner damaging to the interests of the *Wehrmacht.* Medical service is assured by 27 physicians, among them 9 Jews who have been provisionally exempt from actions by Sk 10 a.[223]

The expression " a Jew, who had managed to sneak in as an interpreter' has to be seen against the background of an order by *OKH* of 10 November 1941, forbidding the employment of Jews as interpreters.

Yalta

Activity report by the town commander, 12 December 1941: "A ghetto has been put in place. The resettlement of the Jews has already been completed."[224] The town commander obviously overlooked the contradiction. 'Ghetto' means concentration of Jews in a closed quarter of a city. 'Resettlement' means completed execution.

Simferopol – the massacre of all the city's Jewish inhabitants and the 'watch action.'

The massacre

Simferopol was the capital of the Crimea. It numbered 120,000 habitants, 15,000 were Jews. 11th Army took the city on 1 November 1941. On 20 November 1941, *Einsatzgruppe* D received a written request from 11th Army to have all the Jews of Simferopol shot before Christmas. 11th Army was ready to provide all troops and equipment that were needed.[225] 11th Army had estimated that 14,000 Jews had remained in the city. As often, the *Wehrmacht* got its numbers wrong. Already by 14 November 1941, the *SD* had instructed the town commander to inform 11th Army: "The remaining 11,000 Jews will be executed by the *SD*"[226]

The order is not in doubt. Questions remain unanswered to this day, as to why it was issued. A detailed report by Dr Braune, who commanded the massacre, contains exact indication on the dates on which it occurred, the designation of the units that 11th Army put at the disposal of the *Einsatzgruppe,* and the description of every part of the city where the massacre was carried out.[227]

Why the sudden decision about the advanced date for the execution? Friedrich asks the rhetorical question: "Was the *Generalstab* really concerned about the date? Did Manstein's racial hatred not permit him a postponement of three months of an execution, while his campaign in the Crimea had entered into a critical phase?" Friedrich answers: "No, this has to be excluded." Indeed, there was no racial hatred with Manstein, only indifference. Perhaps indifference is even worse than hatred. Hatred has a motive, indifference has none.

---

223   BA-MA, RH 23/72
224   *NOKW* 1591
225   IMT, Case 9, p. 607 f.
226   BA-MA, RH 23/72
227   BA-MA, RH 23/86

Obviously, there was no order signed by Manstein, such matters were left by him to his chief-of-staff and to his quartermaster. However, it is difficult to contradict Ohlendorf's testimony at his trial:

Q: "In other terms, *Feldmarschall* von Manstein had issued direct orders to you about the executions at Simferopol without any prior request by you?"

A: "No, I can't express myself in that manner. But given the organisation of the Army, it is obvious that the chief quartermaster cannot give instructions of this kind without the prior consent of the Army commander. I can't state, without the shadow of a doubt, that Manstein has issued a specific order about the date. I can only say that logic dictates that this must have occurred."

Q: "In other terms, it is logical, even probable that Manstein knew, and that he instructed his officers to issue corresponding orders?"

A: "I find it impossible to believe that a staff officer can issue such an order on his own authority."[228]

Why the sudden hurry? Since all Simferopol Jews had to be shot anyway, no precise indication of a given date was required, but the order expressly insisted upon it. Did Manstein really believe that the early removal of the defenceless Jewish community would permit him to keep his original promise to Hitler to conquer the whole of the Crimea before Christmas? This is likewise unthinkable, one cannot imagine that the best brain among the German generals could conceive of such a stupidity. Probably, an answer will never be found. All Holocaust historians are unanimous in putting the responsibility straight at the doorstep of 11th Army.

Raul Hilberg, who is always more than careful in determining individual guilt, considers the affidavits presented by Dr Braune as being entirely trustworthy.[229] The IMT was likewise convinced:

> Since the Simferopol Jews were to be executed anyway, there was no need to specify a date in advance. The fact that the execution was formally ordered to take place at a specified date, and had to be completed before Christmas, is an obvious evidence that 11th Army had issued a corresponding order.[230]

Ohlendorf was surprised by Manstein's order and was irritated. He saw himself as a meticulous planner and all his schedules had suddenly been thrown overboard. Friedrich wrote: "He had acted on the Crimea, covered by highest authority and certainly not upon the orders of an Army Commander. He was not prepared to share his murders with anyone."[231] He had already sent his Sk and Ek to other locations, and Dr Braune's Sk was not able to conduct a massacre of such dimensions on its own. Therefore assistance by 11th Army was needed, something which Ohlendorf always preferred to avoid, because he knew that his usual quarrels with Wöhler and 11th Army's staff could not be avoided. Furthermore, the date requested by Manstein cast a shadow over his Christmas mood, and spoiled a Christmas party which he intended to celebrate with his men. In his testimony before the IMT, Ohlendorf stated:

228   IMT, Case 9, p. 692
229   Hilberg, vol. 2, p.318
230   Case 9, p. 137
231   Friedrich, p. 660

The command of 11th Army requested to have the Simferopol Jews executed before Christmas. We received the order from 11th Army's liaison officer and Braune had to enter into talks with 11th Army, since we were unable to carry out this liquidation with our own means. The Army agreed to put the troops and material required at our disposal and we were thus able to begin the execution before Christmas.

Q: "Did 11th Army keep its promise and assist you during the execution?"

A: "The Army provided us with lorries, drivers, gasoline and units of field-police. But I have to add the following. The staff officer of 11th Army knew that the liquidation would have to take place, meaning at some other time. Thus no special order was required in this instance. He expected that the massacre would take place under similar circumstances, but at a date three to four months later than now suddenly ordered."[232]

Dr Braune added:

> The Army suddenly said, we want this done before Christmas. I have never been able to understand the reasons for this order. Perhaps the Army was guided by operative considerations, or there was lack of living space. Perhaps there was food shortage. We had heard that the Army had feared that hundreds of thousands could die during the winter from malnutrition, since there was a general shortage of food.[233]

The bulk of the Simferopol Jews, 13,000 men, women and children were executed over three days, from 11 December to 13 December 1941. The 1.500 Krimchaks had already been murdered on 9 December. The executions were only completed on 11 January 1942, when Dr Braune's Sk, assisted by sizeable forces of 11th Army, hunted down remaining Jews who had succeeded in hiding.

On 8 January 1942, *Einsatzgruppe* D reported:

> Sub-commandos succeeded particularly in smaller townships to make them 'free of Jews'. Over the last few weeks, 3,126 Jews, 85 partisans, 12 looters and 120 Communist functionaries were shot. In Simferopol, Krimchaks and gypsies were also liquidated.[234]

On 29 November 1941, the Simferopol town commander reported to *Korück* 553:

> On 29 November 1941, 50 male inhabitants of Simferopol were shot, as measures of retaliation:
> A German soldier had been killed by walking into a mine-field which had not been reported as being dangerous.
> A German *Feldwebel* had been assassinated.[235]

---

232   IMT, Case 9, p. 607 f and 9.280. Also Friedrich, p.660
233   IMT, Case 9, death sentence against Dr. Braune, p. 188
234   *NOKW* 3258
235   *NOKW* 1590

A number of smaller scale executions were reported in a series of messages sent by the particularly sanguine town commander, Major Kupferschläger.[236]

At Nuremberg, Dr Braune was still unable to free himself from the sad memory of the spoiled Christmas party. Höhne comments:

The Germanic noblemen always remained true to themselves. Doped philistines, who conducted their bestial work with typical German self-pity and then thought with sentimental tears about their women and children at home.[237]

Dr Braune testified: "All our thoughts were with our wives and children at home. Had the decision been left to us, we would have postponed the date."
Q: "You knew that women and children were also going to be shot?"
A: "Yes, this was the heaviest burden which we had to carry."[238]
During his testimony, Dr Braune referred time and again to the Christmas party:

After the execution had been completed, Ohlendorf organised a Christmas celebration which was attended by the whole staff of 11th Army. Everybody, who has had the occasion to listen to an address by *Herr* Ohlendorf about religious matter, knows that he was most capable of appealing to religious feelings.

Q: "Did he dwell upon religion?"
A: "I can't recall any words of his. I don't know if he mentioned the Christ, but I know how Ohlendorf feels about such matters."
Q: "But he did make a speech? Did he say anything of religious significance?"
A: "I really can't remember details."
Q: "Did anyone present pray on Christmas day?"
A: "I don't recall"
Q: "Did anyone pray for the Jews whom you had murdered a few days before?"
A: "I really don't recall if anyone prayed for the thousands of Jews."[239]
In his account of the Simferopol massacre, Paget became shameless:

All that happened, was the removal of some 300 elements from a building, where they had hidden. Not all of them were Jews, they were simply elements, who were suspected of belonging to the 'resistance' movement. A number of our witnesses recall that they had continued to live in Jewish homes at Simferopol and that they had attended services in the local synagogues. There was also a Jewish flea market, where Jews sold icons and other goods during all the months Manstein stayed in the Crimea and after he left.[240]

---

236   BA-MA, RH 23/72, BA-MA, RH 23/80, BA-MA, RH 23/86
237   Höhne, p. 334
238   IMT, Case 9, p.3.256 f
239   Case 9, verdict, p.186 and minutes of Case 9, p. 3.256 f
240   Paget, p. 199

Witnesses? Not a single survivor from Simferopol testified at Manstein's trial. An old man, Michal Mervinets, appears on the ARD Video 'Hitler's soldiers'. He leans on the shoulder of his grandson and tells how the last bullet of the executioner failed to kill him.

Paget then adds:

> I am of the opinion that at the time, when the Germans arrived in the Crimea, extermination policy had given way to security policy. Jews were no longer killed because they were Jews. Some Jews were selected and killed because they belonged to sabotage groups. Jews who were not under suspicion continued to live in full security in the townships.[241]

This sentence would have given pleasure to David Irving. It is hardly necessary to add that wholesale extermination of the Jews had not yet begun when the Germans reached the Crimea and that the extermination camps only began to function in 1942.

Rumours about the shootings had spread and *Einsatzgruppe* D found it necessary to file a complaint on 7 January 1942:

> Rumours of execution in other areas cause great difficulties to the execution of our plans in Simferopol. Accounts by Jews and loose talk by German soldiers spread knowledge of our actions against the Jews. Total executions by *Einsatzgruppe* D up to this date: 75,881.[242]

Paget became suddenly worried:

> Even if it could not be proved that Manstein had any part in the Simferopol massacre, this point was difficult for us. If mass executions of such magnitude took place, [it was no longer 300 elements], how is it possible that Manstein knew nothing about them?[243]

But Paget soon found comfort: "Since Manstein was such an honest man, I am sure that the tribunal believed him."[244]

Manstein felt it necessary to turn to God as a witness: He told Paget:

> I had a somewhat strange feeling that I had the Lord's protection. It would have been impossible for me to continue with my military duties, had I known about the atrocities committed by the *SD*, since the Lord would no longer have protected me.[245]

Wöhler was likewise questioned about the Simferopol massacre at his trial:

Q: "Have the 50 men of Dr Braune's Sk arrested the 11,000 victims and shot them or did they have assistance from the *Wehrmacht*?"

A: "I don't know how they were able to do to this. I can't find an explanation."

Q: "Would it have been possible for you to take 50 of your men, arrest 11,000 victims and execute them?"

---

241   Paget, p. 199
242   *NOKW* 2834
243   Paget, p. 198
244   Ibid
245   Ibid, p. 26

A: "I am unable to answer, because I have never given this matter a thought, nor have I ever made such an attempt."[246]

Very true indeed and logical. The chief-of-staff of an Army does not himself assemble 11,000 victims. He gives his orders to have them assembled, and, if necessary, he assists with units of his Army. He leaves the shootings to the commander of the Sk.

In 1970 Hauck admitted that AOK 11 had indeed placed troops, weaponry and lorries at the massacre at Simferopol. Hauck's line of defence can be summarized: AOK 11 had to expedite the execution of the Jews because any delay would have jeopardized the security of 11th Army. The *Einsatzgruppe* would have massacred the Jews without the assistance of 11th Army but this would have taken longer and carried the risk of an uprising of the Simferopol Jews and the other inhabitants of Simferopol against 11th Army. The absurd idea that the defenceless Jews of Simferopol, together with the anti-semitic Tatars and Ukrainians would join in an uprising was accepted by the Munich prosecutor and the investigations against Hauck were terminated because he had 'erroneously' acted under constraint. The prosecutor's office wrote: … "the decision to have 11th Army assist the *Einsatzgruppe* must obviously have been taken by the *OB* of 11th army, *General der Infanterie*, later *Generalfeldmarschall* Erich von Lewinski, named von Manstein." [247]

The 'watch action'

After completion of the *Judenaktion* at Simferopol, 11th Army suddenly discovered that it was in need of watches. Manstein ordered Wöhler to find out from Ohlendorf if there were left-overs from the victims of the Simferopol massacre and to request them for his troops.

Had the documents concerning this action not been preserved in the original, with Manstein's and Wöhler's hand-written "Yes," and their initials on the top, the obvious conclusion would be that this tale is a slander by their enemies. Since when does a general, who commands an Army of close to 300,000 men, take a personal interest in a few watches and instructs his chief-of-staff, a *Generalmajor*, to make a formal request for them? Such matters are dealt with by a junior officer at Army's quartermaster department.

The 'watch action' had already come up at previous war crime trials, but it had evinced only passing interest. It was not a crime, article 250 of the Hague convention allows for the confiscation of captured enemy property. It was simply Hannah Arendt's 'banality of evil'.

Ohlendorf knew that his time had finally arrived. Since he had always been treated as a battalion commander, he refused to take Wöhler's call and connected him to the *SS-Haupsturmführer* Seynstahl, whose rank was the equivalent of company commander. He then wrote to Wöhler:

> The representative of the Chief of the Security Police and the *SD* with the commander of rear area South.
> *Einsatzgruppe* D

---

246   IMT, Case 12, p. 5.915. Friedrich, p. 628
247   Wrochem, p.381 with reference to Staatsarchiv Munich, 22 Js 201/61

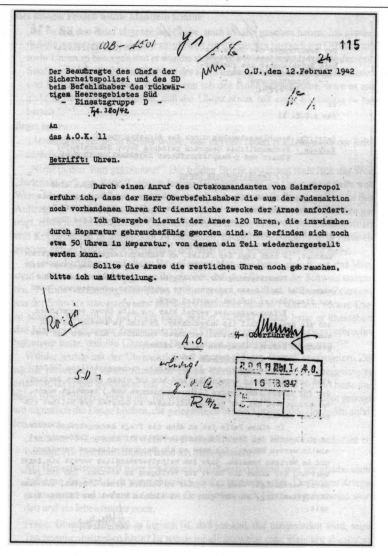

The two letters from Ohlendorf about the 'watch action'.

Diary number 381/42

To *AOK* 11

The town commander of Simferopol has informed me that the *Herr Oberbefehlshaber* requires the watches that still remain from the *Judenaktion*. I herewith transmit to the Army 120 watches that have been repaired. Some 50 additional watches remain the repair shops and part of them may be usable after adjustments. If the Army requests these remaining watches, I expect corresponding information.

The two letters from Ohlendorf about the 'watch action'.

Signed: Ohlendorf, *SS-Oberführer*[248]

On top of this letter a hand-written '*Ja*' followed by 'W' [Wöhler] and 'vm' [von Manstein].[249]

AOK 11 persisted and Ohlendorf wrote a second letter to Wöhler. Every line breathes his satisfaction to teach Wöhler a lesson on how booty goods had to be

248 BA-MA, RH 20-11/488
249 BA-MA, RH 20-11/488

disposed of in strict accordance with official regulations, even if they were of little value:

> The representative of the chief of security police and the *SD* with the commander of rear area South
> *Einsatzgruppe* D
> Diary number: 381/42
> To *AOK* 11
> 12 February 1942
> Subject: Confiscation by *Einsatzgruppe* D
> Background: Telephone conversation between *Generalmajor* Wöhler and *SS-Hauptsturmführer* Seynstahl, 12 February 1942
> 1. Confiscated watches:
> The watches confiscated during the *Judenaktion* have been collected according to official regulations. Watches which have value (gold or silver) have been sent to the *Reich* treasury in accordance with official rules for valuables. Other watches, which are of so low value that they cannot be put at the public's disposal, have been handed over against payment, on some occasions free, depending upon circumstances, to members of the *Wehrmacht* (officers and soldiers) or to the personnel of *Einsatzgruppe* D.
> A condition for the handing over of these watches was proof that the owner's watch had been lost or damaged in combat, or that an additional watch was required for service purpose.
> Experience shows that only old watches are found and that most of them are no longer fit for use. A number have been repaired in the meantime and can be disposed of in the manner indicated above.
> 2. Confiscated rubles:
> Rubles that had been secured during the *Judenaktion* have been collected according to official regulations. Except for small amounts required for official purpose, (payment of wages etc) all have been transferred to the credit of the account of the *Reich* at the *Reichskreditkasse*, in accordance with official regulations. In one instance, I have been asked if ruble amounts can be put at the disposal of the city of Simferopol. I have indicated that the *Reichskreditkasse* is the only official recipient. I have added that I am obviously prepared to put the monies at the disposal of 11th Army, provided I obtain a written receipt in due order. I am not authorised to put any sum at the disposal of a third party, such as the city administration of Simferopol, since the funds are the property of the *Reich*.
> Signed: Ohlendorf, SS-*Oberführer*[250]

On top of the letter: "Yes' W. [Wöhler]

When this matter was brought up at Manstein's trial, Manstein became confused and claimed:

---

250   BA-MA, RH 20-11/488

Yes, since I have initialled the letter, I must have 'seen' it. I think that this matter is easy to explain. I asked the officer in charge to procure more watches. He contacted the mayor of Simferopol. Simferopol was the largest city in the Crimea, obviously there were watch shops and repair shops in the city. Even if I had 'read' the letter, I would never have imagined that the watches came from an execution.[251]

Paget added: "To someone who did not know what had happened to the Jews, the letter obviously meant nothing."[252]

"Easy to explain?" "Never have imagined?" The document explicitly mentions the word *Judenaktion*, an expression that had become part of the standard *Wehrmacht* vocabulary in the East. If Manstein was in need of watches, why did he send Wöhler to Ohlendorf, who was hardly a wholesale dealer? It would have been sufficient to send a low ranking officer of his quartermaster department to the few co-operatives and state owned department stores at Simferopol. After the termination of the NEP, no privately owned retail stores remained anywhere in the Soviet Union.

In his introductory plea for Manstein, Paget had said that the watches were a consignment from Switzerland and therefore legitimately confiscated enemy goods.[253] Paget was not perturbed by the absurdity of an idea that Switzerland would send watches on consignment to retailers in Simferopol in war-time, he also overlooked that Manstein had stated at Nuremberg that he believed that the watches had come from Germany.[254]

Wöhler was grilled at his own trial. At first, he tried his luck at flimsy arguments. He could not avoid recalling the incident, since he had talked to *SS-Hauptsturmführer* Seynstahl and initialled both letters. He said that Manstein had asked him, sometime during the winter of 1941/42, what had become of the valuables that must have been left over after the 'resettlement " of the Jews:

> I therefore turned to Ohlendorf and put the question to him. It never occurred to me that we were talking about plunder. I had no reason to believe that we were talking about left-overs from people who had been killed. In such case, the number of watches must have been much more important. German prisoners-of-war in America have also had their watches confiscated and they are still alive.

Q: "Do you really think that it is logical that someone, who is being "resettled", parts with his pocket watch? Perhaps he would have left a large clock in his living room behind, but hardly a pocket watch."

A: "Yes, it was easy for him to carry a pocket watch, but perhaps he needed a cart and exchanged his watch against a cart, if I may give this as a possible example."

---

251 Trial, p. 1,945 f
252 Paget, p. 197
253 Trial, page unnumbered, also quoted in P. Leverkuehn, *Verteidigung Mansteins*, Hamburg 1950, p. 37. Leverkuehn mentions the Swiss origin but omits the consignment.
254 O. v. Wrochem, *Die Auseinandersetzung mit Wehrmachtsverbrechen im Prozeß gegen den Generalfeldmarschall Erich von Manstein*, monthly magazine of *Institut für Zeitgeschichte* 3/1997, p. 345 wth reference to collected volumes IMT, vol. 20, p. 675

Q: "I think that, after you have read the documentation, you can't have any doubt that the watches were simply confiscated. They were obviously not purchased by the *Einsatzgruppe*. Now, you suddenly say that they were taken from people who were arrested or who may have been shot for any reason. Why does your document explicitly refer to *Judenaktionen*? The Jews were not the sole saboteurs, other saboteurs certainly also had watches, which were not less useful to 11th Army than the ones taken from Jewish victims. Don't you finally want to admit that you had to know that the owners of the watches had been murdered by the *SD*? This is the only question which I am putting to you and I request a simple 'Yes' or a 'No' as an answer."

A: "My answer is 'No'. If I kill someone, I don't need to confiscate his valuables, they automatically belong to me. I already have them. But if I arrest him for some reason or if I want to have part of his belongings, even gold is mentioned here, then I confiscate it."[255]

When he saw that he was making no progress, 'faithful' Wöhler became faithless. "I deny that I have reached any decision on my own. Everything was decided by the Army Commander. The request for watches was a direct order by him. Of course, *Judenaktionen* are not testimonials of friendship. Everybody knows that. I really don't know why *Feldmarschall* von Manstein got involved in this, why he wanted to know details."

Q: "I want to know if you have heard that the watches were handed over to 11th Army?"

A: "This is possible."[256]

Wöhler defended himself as an officer of the *Generalstab* and wanted to point out the limits set to his authority. Friedrich quoted a statement by Halder at Nuremberg, that the nimbus, ie the cloud over the German *Generalstab* was due to the secrecy that surrounded its activities. No one could look into it, but the world knew that the machine functioned. Friedrich added: "Thus the motives that lay behind the extermination of the Jews remained hidden in secret. But the extermination functioned."[257]

Order by AOK 11 about the conduct of partisan warfare – 15 December 1941

> The partisans on the Crimea are under the leadership of the Russian intelligentsia (heads of hospitals, managers of industrial plants, scientists etc) It is not surprising that only 100% convinced communists are put into positions of leadership. This, in turns, guarantees a partisan leadership of high quality. Whenever the slightest suspicion arises that the local population does not actively oppose the partisans, the strongest means of retaliation have to be employed, burning down of villages, shootings … All Jews have to be handed over to the *SD*. Captured partisans have to be hanged. A table on the gallows has to state: 'This is a partisan who has refused to surrender.'

---

255   IMT, Case 12, p. 5.905. Friedrich, p. 670
256   IMT, Case 12, p. 5.905. Friedrich, p. 671
257   Friedrich, p. 671

Signed: Major Stephanus, head of the staff for the fight against partisans, Ic/Ia.[258]

Dr Georg Meyer comments:

The results of the combat against the partisans were sobering. It was never possible to overcome the danger resulting from guerrilla warfare. This particular war, part of the general war, resulted from the cruelty of the brutal German measures in occupied territories that defied imagination. Once again, the military leadership had to face its inferiority, and not only on the battlefield.[259]

The refusal of the Russian population to co-operate with the Germans against the partisans is logical. The partisans may have behaved in a cruel manner towards their own people, but when the choice lies between domestic and foreign terror, the local population will always turn against the occupiers.

Order by AOK 11 to all Corps of the Army, 8 January 1942.

AOK emphasises that general orders by the *Führer* must become known to every soldier. This concerns in particular the orders in which the *Führer* develops in detail the methods to be used in the East. Only if this becomes known to every soldier, can he be expected to act in full compliance with them. But it has to be avoided that copies of such orders can fall into the hands of the enemy. The Corps have to report:
 1. That the orders have been communicated.
 2. That they have been destroyed after communication to the troops.
 Signed: The chief quartermaster on behalf of *AOK 11* (name illegible).[260]

This order is typical for the mentality of the German armies in the East. Criminal orders may be communicated, and commanders may also issue similar orders of their own, since Manstein wrote to Beck, in his letter of 21 July 1938, that the *Führer* has always shown a totally correct grasp of the political situation. Hitler's speech of 30 March 1941 confirmed the old prejudices of the German Generals against Eastern European Jews, so the generals felt that the first successes in the war against Russia were their confirmation. Perhaps the common soldiers had not yet grasped this, therefore all efforts must be made to hand him copies of the orders by the *Führer*. Only then can one be sure that he will comply with their spirit. But on no account must the documents be permitted to fall into the hands of the enemy, because he can then resort to retaliation.

---

258   BA-MA, RH 20 – 11/341
259   Meyer, Heusinger, p. 242
260   BA-MA, RH 23/88

Eupatoria

The massacres at Eupatoria were not a *Judenaktion*, they were a combined action of *Wehrmacht* and *Einsatzgruppe*. Units of the Red Army had made a surprise landing at Eupatoria and other Crimean cities on 4 January 1942. Manstein's plans for finishing the conquest of the Crimea before Christmas were to grind to a halt. In the cities retaken by the Russians, strong demonstrations of hostility against the Germans erupted. After Eupatoria was retaken by the Germans on 9 January 1942, *AOK* 11 issued an angry communiqué:

> On 4 January, enemy forces, supported by the local population, succeeded in landing at Eupatoria and occupying part of the city. Immediate counter-attacks by the German Army repulsed and then annihilated the units of the Red Army that had succeeded in landing.
>
> During its advance into the Crimea the *Wehrmacht* acted in accordance with international law and soldierly tradition and fought only the armed forces of the enemy. It trusted the population, tried to alleviate its conditions, and did its best to quickly remove the destruction caused by the retreating Soviets.
>
> Most of the population had shown its appreciation of the German efforts. But some have engaged in a shameful abuse of the trust shown to it by the Germans. They had hidden arms and taken part in combats against the Germans after units of the Red Army had succeeded in landing. After first showing appreciation, the inhabitants of Eupatoria shamefully abused the trust the *Wehrmacht* had shown them. They had pretended to be friendly to the Germans, but at the same time they had secretly stored weapons and engaged in open combat against our troops after the Russian landing.
>
> By this criminal action, the inhabitants of Eupatoria have placed themselves outside of international law. The guilty have been ruthlessly executed and their houses destroyed. The German High Command gives this last warning to the population of the Crimea and to all who hope that they can secretly act for a return of the Soviets.[261]

After the Germans recaptured Eupatoria, reprisals began and 1,200 civilians were shot. Many Jews were among them, their exact number has never been ascertained. The actions were commanded by Major Riesen. By an order of *AOK* 11, signed by Wöhler, Riesen had already been appointed as the Army's plenipotentiary for fighting partisans in the area under 11th Army's authority. All reports about partisan activity had to be channelled to him. He was authorised to put Army troops at the disposal of *Einsatzgruppe* D.[262] A second order issued by Wöhler had appointed the commander of the field-police, Dr Hermann, as chief-of-staff for units of 11th Army engaged in fighting of partisans. The Ia of all corps commands had to report to him.[263]

---

261 BA-MA, RH 20 23/80
262 BA-MA, RH 20 – 11/341
263 BA-MA, RH 20 –11/341

After the fighting in Eupatoria had come to an end, Major Riesen arrived in the city. He intended to leave the reprisals to the Sk commanded by Dr Braune, but Ohlendorf refused. His mission was the organised killing of Jews and not to engage in reprisals in retaliation of a set-back suffered by 11th Army, due to faulty military leadership. Once more, the Army wanted his men to do things which its officers considered to be below their dignity. Ohlendorf only agreed that Dr Braune was attached to Major Riesen's units as an 'expert'.

Dr Braune was an invalid, who had been declared unfit for war service, but he knew more about the careful organisation of mass executions than the officers of 11th Army. The soldiers were no less brutal than Dr Braune's men, but they lacked the latter's organisational talent, and executions were conducted at random. Ohlendorf testified that the 'expert' Dr Braune was 'outraged' at the amateurish handling of the reprisals by 11th Army's officers and soldiers.

> The Army had failed in its preparations. Many unpleasant incidents had occurred and Braune had to intervene, in order to re-establish order and avoid even worse mishaps. The Army commander had issued an order to shoot the whole adult male population of Eupatoria.

Then Ohlendorf became sentimental: "There is no greater damage to the human soul than to be forced to execute defenceless victims."[264]

The town commander complained that "a more careful investigation before the shootings should have been called for."[265]

Major Riesen testified at the *Einsatzgruppen* trial: "I commanded the reprisals upon express order by the Army commander. The commander of *Einsatzgruppe* D delegated three SS-officers, among them SS-*Sturmbannführer* Dr Braune. We selected 1,184 men, who had already been assembled. I led them in a closed group, accompanied by 90 soldiers from an anti-aircraft unit and by the SS-officers, in a march of one hour, to the site of the execution, where they were shot. During the walk, some shots were fired at us from houses. The snipers were killed by hand-grenades or sub-machine-gun fire. 20 to 30 tried to escape during the march, they were immediately shot. Dr Braune gave instructions for the conduct of the execution. He had not taken part in hand-to-hand fighting with the partisans."[266]

Manstein was confused when Eupatoria came up at his trial. He often repeated himself, therefore only the relevant parts of his testimonial are given:

> I never gave an order for reprisals at Eupatoria nor anywhere else. Had I issued such orders, reprisals at Feodosia would have been called for, where German soldiers were murdered in a bestial manner with the help of civilians after the Red Army's landing. But even in this case I did not order any reprisals ... I ordered an investigation at Eupatoria, because I had the impression that the town commander had failed in his duty ... I had him informed that he would be shot if he did not immediately retake his positions ... This is the only time when I mentioned the word 'shooting' at Eupatoria ... I remember this distinctly ... No, I had no knowledge what-

---

264   IMT, Case 9, p. 264. Friedrich, p. 663
265   BA-MA, RH 23/79
266   *NOKW* 584

soever of the reprisal action conducted by Major Riesen at Eupatoria … I had only received information that 1,300 partisans had been killed during the fighting. If 1,000–1,300 partisans were shot one by one or after capture, or if they were shot while still bearing arms, is uninteresting. But if a total of 1,300 partisans were shot at Eupatoria, it is hardly possible that 1,184 of them were killed after the fighting had come to an end.

Q: "Did you give your intelligence officer an order to conduct an action of reprisal?"

A: "I never gave him any order for a reprisal. I did not even see him, since he was at Simferopol, while my headquarters were at Sarabus." The distance between Simferopol and Sarabus was less than 15 kilometres.

Q: "Whom did you call to your headquarters?"

A: "I called the Ic of the Army, who was Riesen's immediate superior. I may have told him that Riesen, who was apparently asleep when the combats occurred, should go to Eupatoria and find out what had happened. But I would never have given a staff officer, who is glued behind his desk, to conduct an action of reprisal. Had I ordered such an action, I would obviously have turned to the commander of 105th Infantry Regiment on the spot, the 'valiant'[267]Colonel Müller and not to a man who spends his time behind a desk."[268]

Thus Wöhler's most trusted aide, Major Riesen, suddenly becomes a desk officer and a 'dope'. His position as 11th Army's Ic/AO was far more important than the command of the regiment by Colonel Müller. At Eupatoria, Colonel Müller must have gained *prima facie* knowledge of the valour required in the administration of an occupied area. In 1944, he was to be promoted to *General der Infanterie* and made commander of the fortress of Crete. In 1944, the Greeks sentenced him to death for war crimes committed on Crete, and he was shot.

General Müller showed the depth of his military knowledge when he relieved General Hossbach as commander of 4th Army. He reported to General von Natzmer, chief-of-staff of his Army Group commander, *Generaloberst* Rendulic and told him: "I am a good non-com and I know how to execute an order. But I understand nothing about strategy or tactics. Please tell me what I have to do."[269]

Not surprisingly, Paget feels it necessary to add his comment about Eupatoria: "I tend personally to believe that the Germans simply sent all the Russians captured during the street fights into prisoner-of-war camps, regardless if they had taken part in the combats or not."[270]

Here Paget contradicts the testimony of his client since Manstein had admitted that executions had taken place.

Manstein's statement about the Eupatoria massacre is a lie. Not because of Riesen's report – here Manstein's defender could argue that it was a matter of contradictory evidence. However Manstein's staff officers testified after the war that the order had been given by Manstein. Angrick writes:

267   *Verlorene Siege,* p. 230
268   Trial, p. 1.956
269   J. Thorwald, *Es begann an der Weichsel,* Stuttgart 1953, p. 129
270   Paget, p. 177

While fighting was still going on at Eupatoria, Colonel Müller received a direct query from Manstein if civilians had taken part in the uprising. Only five hours later – Angrick describes this short time as evidence that Müller's investigation has been most superficial – Colonel Müller reported that a number of Red Army soldiers had landed in civilian clothes and that the civilian population had indeed taken part in the uprising. On June 10, 1964, Riesen testified at the Munich prosecutor's office that the Ic of 11th Army, Major Werner Ranck, had informed him that Manstein had ordered reprisals to be taken. In his own statement at the Munich prosecution on October 10, 1965 Ranck denied having transmitted Manstein's order and said that it had been communicated to Riesen by Wöhler. "When Riesen returned, he told me that he had acted upon an order by either Wöhler or Manstein." Wöhler testified on October 10, 1965 and denied having transmitted the order to Riesen. Riesen had received the order directly from Manstein. (Wöhler had already been tried by the IMT and could not be charged again by a German court).[271]

After the mass reprisals were completed, the usual murders of Jews by *Einsatzgruppe* D took place in neighbouring townships. Already during the combats after the Russian landing, *Einsatzgruppe* D mentioned an order of 7 January 1942, by the commander of Army Group South, at that time Reichenau, that all male Jewish inhabitants of Eupatoria were to be 'resettled.'[272] The town commander of Eupatoria reported on 21 January 1942: "The apartments of the Jews who had been 'resettled' have been taken over by the *SD*. As in the documents relating to the massacre at Kerch, 'executions' is replaced in handwriting by 'resettled'. Clothes, table-ware and furniture have been 'taken care of.'[273] Field command unit (*Feldkommandantur*) 810 reported on 5 December 1941 that "a Russian civilian who apparently belonged to the Jewish race was arrested."[274] Three days later, the same command "handed over eight apparently Jewish civilians for further treatment by the *SD*."[275] Motorized Gendarmerie Unit 683 reported had already reported on 29 November 1941: '*Jews without stars:* The Jew Musil Tujal was discovered at Simferopol in November 1941 not wearing the star. He was handed over to *Sonderkommando* 11b."[276] A handwritten note from Corporal Flugler at the staff of Major Kupferschläger of 17 January 1942, for transmission to *Korück 553*: '23 Partisans and Jews had hidden 15 kilometres north-west of Eupatoria. They were discovered and shot. Major Kupferschläger will submit the report.[277]

On 9 January 1942, Major Kupferschläger wrote to the commander of the secret field-police at Simferopol:

---

271   Angrick, p. 488 f
272   BA-MA, RH 23/180
273   *NOKW* 1727
274   *NOKW* 1594
275   *NOKW* 1596
276   *NOKW* 1594
277   BA-MA, RH 23/80

I want to insist upon the following. In my opinion, which is shared by all other commanders, none of the arrested who had possession of fire-arms, or just one single bullet, or one item of equipment to be used for the manufacturing of ammunition, or a radio transmitter etc, should have remained alive for one more night. I refer to the order of 10 November 1941, which makes the death sentence mandatory for possession of arms.

If the *Wehrmacht* does not act with utmost vigour, incidents like those that occurred at Eupatoria or Feodosia will take place at other locations. Arguments like 'I did not know that there was a transmitter in my cellar' have to be discarded. Every culprit always claims that he was innocent.

The life of one single German soldier has more value that the lives of hundreds of Russians. If we limit ourselves to shoot people who have been proven guilty, our actions serve no purpose. Better shoot a number of innocents. Since my time is taken up with meetings, you will phone me, at 6 pm at the latest, that people who have been released from arrest, are again under arrest. I order you to refrain from any further releases.[278]

A report by Field Command unit 810, of 15 February 1942 introduced a new euphemism for executions:

"In the village of Ikor, a Jewess was found to have a hostile attitude towards the Germans. Together with a three year old child and a new-born child she was treated in accordance with regulations."[279]

Some further reports from the same *Feldkommandantur* mention:

"Arrest of a civilian who is suspected to belong to the Jewish race."[280]

"Eight persons, suspected to be Jews have been handed over to the *SD* at Eupatoria for further investigation of their identity."[281]

Such 'imprecisions' could only occur in reports by *Wehrmacht* units, Ohlendorf would have taken care to determine the exact racial affiliation before writing his reports.

Sarabus

Manstein's headquarters were at Sarabus, some 15 kilometres distant from Simferopol. Sarabus is a tiny hamlet that does not even appear on the map of the Crimea in the Soviet World Atlas containing 250 maps.[282]

On 30 January 1942, *Einsatzgruppe* D reported that units of Sk 12 had arrived at Sarabus.[283] In its report for the period 1 January to 13 January, a staff officer at the Gendarmerie reported to 11th Army's quartermaster: "Arrest of Jews, partisans

---

278 BA-MA, RH 23/80
279 BA-MA, RH 23/79
280 Ibid
281 Ibid
282 World Atlas, Moscow 1967, Crimea, Map # 27
283 *Einsatzgruppe* D, EM 162, January 30, 1942

and other suspicious elements. Their resettlement will be taken care of in co-operation with the *SD*."[284]

Dchanskoy

Report by *Korück* 553, Ic, 1 January 1942, covering the period 16–31 December 1942, sent to *AOK* 11, Ic/AO on special request:

> A special incident, the setting up of a Jewish concentration camp at Dchanskoy led to several meetings between *Korück*, *AOK* 11, the gendarmerie and the *SD*. The *SD* had refused to proceed with this matter, the shooting of the inmates, since it did not have sufficient men at its disposal. After *Korück* had agreed to provide men from the gendarmerie, the *SD* agreed to issue an order for this action.
>
> Signed: Teichmann, Major.[285]

Report by town commander II/939 pursuant to order by *Korück* 553, January 1942:

> "The local *Judenaktion* was carried out by the Simferopol *SD* on 23 December 1941."[286]

Karasubasar

Report from town commander to *Korück* 553, 14 February 1942:
"Karasubasar had 8,789 inhabitants, only one Jew. However, we succeeded in discovering two Jews who had gone into hiding and delivered them to the *SD*."[287]
Poster in Russian displayed in the town square:

> To all inhabitants of Karasubasar and neighbouring townships: The town is put on notice that anyone who will provide assistance of any kind to partisans, enemy parachutists or other hostile elements, receive them or hide them, know about their residence and refrain from reporting it to the German authorities will be shot.[288]

A report from *Einsatzgruppe* D, 2 January 1942, stated that by the end of the year Karasubasar was *judenfrei*.[289]

Feodosia

Feodosia was one of the Crimean cities where the Red Army had made its surprise landings at the end of 1941 and beginning of 1942. It was retaken by the Germans after a few days. Only the Kerch peninsula remained in Russian hands until late spring 1942. Manstein was thus reduced to fighting a two-front war, the Kerch

---

284 *NOKW* 1283
285 BA-MA, RH 23/91
286 BA-MA, RH 23/79
287 BA-MA, RH 23/75
288 BA-MA, RH 23/75
289 BA-MA, RH 23/75

peninsula in the East and Sevastopol in the West. His attack on Sevastopol had to be postponed until the recapture of the Kerch peninsula.

Since before the Russian landing at Feodosia, *Einsatzgruppe* D had reported on 2 January 1942 that its Sk 10b, 11a and 11b had succeeded in rendering Feodosia *judenfrei*. This was premature, a sizeable number of future victims were left who had to be murdered after the Germans recaptured the city.

On 28 February 1942, the military town commander, Major Teichmann, sent a long report to *Korück 553*. Major Teichmann seems to have been particularly proud of his accomplishments, since his paper is the longest of all the accounts of the deeds of the *Einsatzgruppe* on the Crimean peninsula. It contains many repetitions. Only the relevant parts are reproduced here:

> ... Political matters:
> ... Up to 15 February 1942, Sk 10 b shot 36 Jews, 19 members of the NKVD, 12 partisans and 12 youths. The 36 Jews, both men and women, had succeeded in hiding in the city and were uncovered by the Sk. Six Jews were in possession of forged passports, five had taken part in the mutilation of wounded German soldiers, and some had acted as guides for the Red Army marine soldiers, who had succeeded in landing.
> ... The following arrests were immediately conducted.
> 1. Michael Goldstein, Jew, guilty of mistreatment of German wounded and prisoners taken during the Russian landing.
> 2. Feodor Jasnitzky, Jew ...[290]

Report by Sk 10b, 27 March 1942, to *AOK* 11, describing the 'combing' of the city: The report begins with a long, self-congratulatory description of all the obstacles that the Sk had been able to overcome:

> 1. Background of the 'combing': Observations made by Sk 10b during its cleansing operations showed that many unsecured parts remained in the city and were inhabited by unreliable elements. Since the front line was close by, a rapid 'combing' was required, in order to arrest all suspects and then execute them.

> 2. In peacetime, Feodosia was one of the main ports of the Soviet Navy and had always been a main pillar of *Bolshevism*.

> 3. The work of the police and the Sk was interrupted by the landings. 'Combing' had to be resumed at the earliest possible moment, since many inhabitants of Fedosia, who were fit for work, simply refused to appear, engaged in sabotage, and rendered reconstruction work difficult. Also, we had cause to fear new landings by the Red Army and therefore could not delay our action, in spite of the unexpected difficulties that had arisen.

> 4. Sk 10b was too weak to conduct the whole operation in one sweep. The city had to be divided into four districts that were searched separately. [This is followed by a number of pages of self-praise, describing the efforts of the Sk in overcoming the unexpected difficulties that had been placed in its way.]

---

290   BA-MA, RH 23/79

... The first rounding-up began on 5 March 1942 ... 351 persons were arrested and brought to the Sk. 64 men, who were capable of outdoor work, and who lingered lazily around, were sent to prisoner-of-war camps. 13 persons, among them 4 women, were brought into the city jail, the remainder were set free. The 13 arrested were guilty of the following offences:

Four were Jews and two had forged passports, probably forged by themselves ...

Three Jewesses likewise carried forged passports, probably forged by their husbands ...

All thirteen were shot ...

The second round-up took place on 5 March 1942. The *Wehrmacht* had put 360 soldiers at the Sk's disposal. 447 were arrested and delivered to the Sk for further examination. 15 were sent to jail for 'special treatment'. Six of them were Jews, three held passports forged by the NKVD, three were Jewesses ... After questioning, all 15 were shot. The *Wehrmacht* succeeded in seizing goods which had been hoarded. The 'combing' of the city could now be considered as having been successfully completed.

Conclusions: For safety purposes, every house in the city was searched and every inhabitant carefully questioned. Unreliable elements were withdrawn from the city and liquidated. Security has therefore been improved and if a new Soviet attack should occur, the *Wehrmacht* has been brought into better positions of resistance. Our action has also contributed to a positive education of the population.[291]

This long report is a typical display of the mentality of the men of the *Einsatzgruppe* and of the soldiers of 11th Army, who took an active part in the massacre. A landing by the Red Army is sufficient to cause 'gratitude' from the population for its 'generous' treatment by the Germans in helping them to disappear. Therefore, a re-education is required, in particular for 'creating joy' in working for the occupier, which has remained somewhat absent until now. The small Sk is unable to complete its assignment with its own staff. Although the Jews will be executed without further ado, many suspicious elements remain the city and they have to be carefully screened, before a decision is reached about their fate.

But the *Wehrmacht* generously puts 300–400 soldiers at the Sk's disposal and the re-education only requires a few additional days. Forgery of passports and other identity papers by the Jews, is particularly revolting since it delays their punishment. Property seized must be carefully put under lock and key since the men of the Sk and the soldiers are always eager to engage in plunder. Some elements of uncertainty remain, since it cannot be excluded that the "remainders of the Red Army, who are still capable of fighting", will attempt a new landing. Therefore better defence positions have to be set up.

A report by the town commander of Feodosia to *Korück* 553 for the period 16–30 April 1942, included: "Two persons, who were suspected of hostile actions, one Red Army soldier and one Jewess handed over to the *SD* for further

---

disposal."[292] An attached addendum included: "During the second half of April 1942, 43 persons were executed, among them 22 Jews."[293]

In 1965 Manstein was forced to admit that *Wehrmacht* units had participated at the Feodossia massacre. He wrote: "There is no excuse for the participation of the *Feldgendarmerie* at the mass execution of Jews at Feodosia." One of Manstein's arguments was that the officers and soldiers of the *Feldgendarmerie* had not served in the *Reichswehr* and that they were ignorant of the *Reichswehr's* 'code of honour'.[294] It is always the same story. 'The others' are always guilty, only Manstein is innocent.

Bakhtiassaray

Report by the town commander to *Korück* 553, 28 February 1942: "In Backtiassaray, 90 Jews. They are not wealthy and live in modest homes. The *SD* has completed their shooting on 31 December 1942."[295] 'Shooting' is crossed out in handwriting in the original, and replaced by 'resettling".

The final report

A report by *Einsatzgruppe* D covering the period 1 February to 15 February 1942, stated: "1,451 people have been shot, among them 920 Jews, 45 partisans, 12 plunderers, saboteurs and asocial elements. Total number of our executions up to this date, 86,642.[296]

On 16 April 1942, *Einsatzgruppe* D issued the report already mentioned at the beginning of the chapter, 'The Crimea is free of Jews'.[297]

The Crimea was indeed free of Jews, however there remained other regions in Southern Russia that were under Ohlendorf's control and he continued with his murders.

Mein Führer, what will be the fate of the Jews?

Manstein put this question to Hitler in 1942. Hitler was always annoyed when this matter was brought to his attention. During a visit to the *Berghof*, Henriette von Schirach, the American born wife of Baldur von Schirach, former head of the *Hitlerjugend* and later *Gauleiter* of Vienna, mentioned to him:

> *Mein Führer*, I happened to have seen a train carrying Jews to deportation at the Amsterdam railway station. It was terrible to look at those poor

---

292 *NOKW* 1717
293 *NOKW* 1717
294 Wrochem, p.370
295 BA-MA, RH 20-11/488
296 IMT, Case 12, p. 3.359
297 BA-MA, RH 20-11/488

people and they were brutally handled. Do you know about this and do you permit those things to happen?"[298]

Hitler immediately left the room and Henriette von Schirach was barred from further visits to the *Berghof*.

Although Hitler had mentioned, for the first time on 30 January 1939, before the beginning of the war, the elimination of the Jewish race in Europe in a number of public speeches, he never signed a document ordering its implementation. This gave David Irving the opportunity of writing that the destruction of Jews was the sole work of Himmler, without any participation by Hitler. This is obviously absurd and a further example of the stories spread by David Irving. Such a unique and far-reaching measure could never have taken place without a sanction by Hitler.

In his recollections, written in a Polish prison before his execution by hanging, the commander of the Auschwitz extermination camp, Rudolf Höss, confirmed that he was called to Himmler's headquarters. He was told by Himmler that Hitler had decided upon the final elimination of all Jews who had remained in territories under his power. Höss was then named by Himmler as the man in charge of the mass exterminations in the death camps.

Manstein testified about his talk with Hitler:

> I remember having talked about this matter with Hitler during a luncheon. I can't recall the exact date. Perhaps it took place during one of my visits to the *Führerhauptquatier* in 1942, or after the fall of Sevastopol, maybe also in autumn 1942, when my Army was sent to the North. I asked Hitler whether he had any future plans for the Jews. He gave me an evasive reply. The Jews had to be given an autonomous territory, naturally under our control, that meant somewhere in the East. I had already heard rumours that a kind of Jewish territory had been set up at Lublin.[299]

Manstein's question may appear naive since he knew what had happened to the Jews in the East. However, Manstein was never naive. In 1942, he knew that Germany stood no more chance of winning the war. Even if he still pretended to believe in his 'draw theory', it was clear to him that an understanding by the Allies with Hitler was out of the question. Therefore, post-war history had to be considered and he knew that he would be called to account for his deeds. His question to Hitler was intended to prepare an alibi.

Manstein had signed only one document with his full name, his order of the day of 20 November 1941, which he considered so unimportant, that he later declared that he could not even remember it. He had initialled a number of documents, but he could pretend that initialling was simply a routine when a document was shown to him, and that he did not waste his time in reading it. He had never met Ohlendorf face-to-face, and felt that he could deny any of his statements. His question to Hitler served his purpose, to show his ' official ignorance.'

---

298   T. Junge, *Bis zur letzten Stunde. Hitlers Sekeretärin erzählt ihr Leben*, Munich 2002, p. 101
299   Trial, p. 1.946 f

Manstein's responsibilty – who is a 'perpetrator' of the genocide?

Every active participant in the genocide was a 'perpetrator'. The least important ones were the guards in the extermination camps, who pushed the victims into the gas-chambers, or the commanders of the *SD*, who put the final bullet in the head of his victims. The higher the rank of the 'perpetrator', the heavier his responsibility. No general shoots a Jew with his own hands. It is done by his low-ranking subordinates who comply with his orders. Eichmann laid his hand upon a Jew on only one occasion, when he slapped the Vienna Chief Rabbi Löwenherz in the face, a few days after the *Anschluss*. He immediately apologised and saw to it that Löwenherz remained unharmed in Vienna until the end of the war.

Eichmann 'only' organised the transportation of millions of Jews from occupied Europe to the extermination camps. The executives of the German state railways 'only' prepared the timetables for the trains to the camps with typical German diligence and saw to it that transportation of the victims was paid with the monies which had previously been stolen from them. Rudolf Höss was an ideal husband and a caring father. He never touched a Jew at Auschwitz. He 'only' made exact calculations of the gas chambers and the crematoria required for the daily disposal of the victims, supervised their construction and saw to it that they functioned without interruption. When questioned by the Polish tribunal after the war, if he had any feeling about his deeds, he replied that he simply found them 'boring'.[300]

Manstein was commander in chief of an Army. The Army commander is the supreme territorial authority. He holds executive command over the area under control of his Army and is the guarantor of law and order, responsible for the fate of the civilian population. The IMT does provide for certain limits of his responsibility. A government could limit the authority of the military commander in specific instances, but as long as there were no official orders from above that prevented him from opposing illegal activities, he had a duty to prevent them.[301] The responsibility of Manstein for the fate of the Russians was never officially curtailed. The IMT granted the commander further restrictions of his responsibility.

> The commander cannot talk his way out, by stating that his government had dispatched people into his area who had committed crimes against the civilian population and engaged in murders. However, the court must be convinced that he neglected his personal duties. It has to be shown that the crimes were either committed on his personal orders or that he showed negligence in the supervision of his subordinates. A commander

---

300 The execucion of Höss on a special gallow erected at Auschwitz was delayed for months, to give him the opportunity of writing his memoirs, R. Höss, *Kommandant in Auschwitz*, Munich 1985. All Holocaust historians agrree that his book is a singularly revealing document.

301 *NOKW* 1978

can thus only be held responsible for the murder of Jews if, firstly, he was aware of such events and, secondly, if he was at the time, aware of them.[302]

In his compliance with the 'Commissar Order', Manstein could indeed justify himself with the exemptions provided by the IMT. However, this was not the case with his responsibility for the genocide. His order of the day of 20 November 1941, on its own, is sufficient to label him as a 'perpetrator'. The consequences that followed that order are clearly established. Manstein had received direct reports of murders from eyewitnesses. He could certainly not put an end to the deeds of the *Einsatzgruppe*, but he was duty bound to carefully investigate what was reported to him.

He took the easy way out and chose to ignore reports that reached him. He had received regular reports about the murder of Jews from his staff, and initialled them. He had ordered the execution of the Simferopol Jews months in advance of the date that had been originally decided. In no single instance can he claim lack of awareness. A strange sentence by Manstein's admirer Brett-Smith has to be quoted: "Undoubtedly the *Einsatzgruppen* were responsible for bestialities in both Poland and Russia. But Manstein was not the sort of man to countenance them."[303]

For the determination of Manstein's responsibility, an analysis of his personality lacks relevance. There was not one Manstein who protested against the introduction of racial laws in the Army, and who protected the Jewish physician at Kolberg, and another Manstein who became an active participant in the genocide. Dr Jekyll and Mr Hyde were fiction. Manstein always remained the same Manstein. His motives are likewise without importance. Manstein shared the prejudices of the German officers against the Jews. Manstein's knowledge and understanding of the Soviet Union did not exceed the low level of the remainder of the German generals. The Crimea, with its mixed population, always remained a total mystery to him.

If the Manstein of the 1930s was the same Manstein of the 1940s, an explanation for his changed behaviour must be found elsewhere. Manstein remained Manstein. But Lieutenant von Schmeling-Diringshofen, his *protégé* in his protest against the racial laws, and the half-Jewish physician in Kolberg, were not the same Jews as those in Russia. Like most of his fellow German generals, Manstein had swallowed the notion of the Jewish-Bolshevist *Untermensch*. The *Untermensch* has no God-given right to life. If he is not a disturbance, he may be permitted to exist, but if he is looked upon as a trouble-maker, he can be killed without hesitation.

Surprisingly, the first loud protest against the notion of the *Untermensch* was voiced not by a *Wehrmacht* general, but by a very high ranking *SS*-official. In September 1942, Gunther d'Alquen, the editor-in-chief of the official *SS*-periodical *Das Schwarze Korps* said to Himmler:

Our men in the field don't know where they have to put their arse[sic]. And believe me, if they read this booklet put out by you, they will react in a loud voice and in unmistakable words: 'The guys on the other side who are fighting us and who are beating us up, who have better tanks than ourselves, and who know as much about tactics and strategy as our

302   IMT, Case 12, p. 122, lengthy analysis in Friedrich p. 918 f
303   Brett-Smith, p. 235

commanders, they are *Untermenschen*? What kind of *Obermenschen* are we then?'[304]

Sebastian Haffner emphasises that the genocide was not a war crime, but a real crime, something 'entirely different'. He writes:

> The understanding of the special aspect of Hitler's mass murders is blunted if they are classified as war crimes. Hitler's mass murders can only be understood if one is aware that they were not war crimes but something 'entirely different'. The shooting of prisoners-of-war in the heat of combat, the executions of hostages in partisan warfare, the aerial bombing of civilian populations, the sinking of passenger vessels during the U-Boat war; those are all war crimes, certainly horrible, but better forgotten by both sides after the end of hostilities. Mass murder, planned extermination of entire population groups, killing of human beings like vermin, all these are things 'entirely different'.[305]

In Haffner's eyes, things 'entirely different' are

- the genocide of the Jews,
- the euthanasia-order,
- the mass murder of the Polish leadership and the Polish intelligentsia, which cost more than a million Poles their lives, and
- the lives of the three million Russian prisoners-of-war, who perished in the camps run by the *Wehrmacht*.

Whether Manstein's refusal to consider the reports sent to him, or his own deeds, are deemed as having been war crimes or real crimes is hardly important. Regardless of the definition, Manstein must be included among the major 'perpetrators.'

304　Höhne, p. 470
305　Haffner, p. 181

Chapter 8

Manstein, the Man

Conclusion

Nikita Krushchev is buried in the graveyard of the Moscow Novodevitchi Monastery, not far from the grave of Stalin's second wife, Nadeshda Alleluyeva. He is the only former leader of the Soviet Union who has not been granted a resting-place in Red Square. Lenin's body still rests in his mausoleum. Stalin and Breshnev have their graves, with their statues, in the space behind the mausoleum. Andropov and Chernenko are buried in the walls surrounding Red Square.

The monument to Krushchev was sculpted by the famous artist Ernest Neizvestny. It consists of two vertical halves, one white and one black. The white half symbolises the de-Stalinisation introduced by Krushchev, and the gradual liberalisation introduced during his years in power. The black is intended to show his earlier participation in Stalin's Great Terror. Perhaps a 'grey' coloured layer should have been introduced in the centre of the stone, between the black and white halves. It would have hurt the aesthetics of the monument but would have come closer to the truth. Only a few men are totally black or totally white, there is always a 'grey' area.

A tombstone for Manstein could well have been sculpted in a similar manner, using both black and white. Manstein was a towering personality. Without doubt he was the *Wehrmacht*'s best commander. Compared with him, other *Feldmarschalls* were average at best. His operating methods continue to be part of the curriculum of military academies world wide, including the Israeli army. I have already quoted a statement by Seaton in the introduction to this book: "Among Manstein's successes were his contributions to the French campaign, the overrunning of the Crimea, and the containing of part of the spring 1943 offensive in the Ukraine. He achieved little else." Had that been the limit of Manstein's performance, it would have been sufficient to place him among the most eminent captains of modern times, but Manstein achieved much more.

Seaton does not mention Manstein's performance as a *Panzer* Corps commander during the first weeks of the Russo-German war. There he showed himself the equal of the very best German *Panzer* commanders, despite Halder denying him sufficient equipment. Nor does Seaton mention Manstein's operations during the last months of his command. At that time he repeatedly succeeded, if only temporarily, in re-establishing lost positions with only meagre means at his disposal. Likewise, Seaton ignores his last brilliant stroke, just a few weeks prior to his dismissal, when he succeeded in extricating the 1st *Panzer* Army from a major Kessel. The Army commander, *Generaloberst* Hube, had developed a different plan that had been approved by Hitler. Manstein succeeded in convincing both of them to adopt his solution, but only after threatening Hitler that he would resign his command if it were not.

Manstein's *Sichelschnitt* plan was more than just a contribution. Had it been his only achievement, it would have been sufficient to include him among the greatest military minds of military history. His plan was far superior to the Schlieffen plan of the First World War. The Schlieffen plan contained no alternatives if its original version did not succeed. Manstein did consider alternatives, and proposed solutions to deal with them. Manstein was not the only commander whose successes were considered to be a 'mere' contribution. The victor of the battle of El-Alamein was Montgomery. In Churchill's memoirs it was Alexander, a general about whom his fellow officers used to say that it was never difficult to search for his ideas because he had none.

There is little doubt that Manstein, had his career taken place in the Imperial German Army, would have risen to the very top position to which he aspired in the *Wehrmacht*. But he could not achieve it under Hitler's dictatorship. The historian Andreas Hillgruber writes:

> Bismarck was a statesman who subordinated war to politics, but left operations to his military experts, as in the spirit of the teachings of Clausewitz. Under the conditions of the Bismarck era, a commander such as Manstein would have been recorded in history as one of the most brilliant minds that the Prussian-German *Generalstab* had produced in its 130 year history.[1]

Liddell Hart describes Manstein as the 'most dangerous opponent' of the Allies. This is one of Liddell Hart's exaggerations, due to his boundless admiration for Manstein. No German general could every present a danger to the Allies. The *Wehrmacht* was far too weak. Germany had already lost the war, from the day the first German soldier crossed the Polish border. *Generaloberst* Friessner wrote:

> We know now that it had been a major mistake to start the war, and later to attack the Soviet Union. The leaders of the *Generalstab*, with *Generaloberst* Beck at their head, had opposed Hitler's plans for war since before 1939. They knew that the *Wehrmacht*, in its structure and equipment at that time, was not up to the requirements of a modern world war. As responsible men, imbued with morality, they were not prepared to gamble the nation's fate.[2]

However, there is little doubt that had he been born in one of the countries with which Germany was at war, Manstein would have risen there to the very top military. Neither Eisenhower, Montgomery nor Zhukov came close to his military prowess.

Manstein's staff officers revered him. When he was dismissed, all of them requested their immediate transfer. Obviously, none was eager to serve under his successor Model, since they knew what kind of behaviour awaited them. Whenever Model was given a new command, senior staff officers of his new unit requested their transfer. But that was not the main reason, officers had to serve even under the most unpleasant commanders. Manstein's staff officers felt that his dismissal occurred under particularly shameful conditions, that it was only due to Hitler's personal dislike of Manstein, and that his performance could not be faulted.

---

1 Manstein/Fuchs, p. 139 (henceforth Hillgruber)
2 H. Friessner, *Verratene Schlachten*, Hamburg 1963, p. 223 (henceforth Friessner)

Manstein's orders, which he issued in his curiously high-pitched voice, often gave the impression that he simply followed suggestions by his subordinates. Stahlberg wrote:

> He never used words like 'I order you'. When he gave me an order, he would say: "Please take care that … " or " I would be grateful if you would arrange the following." "Please put me in touch with … " Real authority is always linked to trust. Manstein was a *Herr.*[3]

At the *Truppenamt* it was considered a privilege to be among Manstein's pupils. All the officers taught by him later rose to high command positions. Seaton wrote that Manstein could be very unpleasant towards subordinates.[4] But it depended towards whom. Manstein had little patience with officers whom he considered to be *Kommisskopf* and they quickly felt his lack of patience. One of his adc, Rudolf Graf, told Knopp:

> Manstein was in many ways a warm-hearted and sensitive man, qualities which he endeavoured to hide behind an abrasive appearance. He liked straightforward answers and hated false subordination. Whoever was slow to see the point, would quickly feel his impatience.[5]

His military superiority was acknowledged by all generals, even by the many who strongly disliked him as a person. *Feldmarschalls* senior to him, in date of promotion, declared themselves ready to subordinate themselves to his command, should a situation arise where a single supreme commander was required.

In *Soldatenleben*, Manstein had written that he was born with a military inheritance. He could have added that he was born with an inherent military superiority. Wherever he served, he showed himself to be the number one. At cadet school he was already the *primus* among the 'Selecta' pupils. During the First World War, General von Schutzendorff said that Manstein was the best adc he ever had. He had not completed the training of a *Generalstabs* officer. Prior to the First World War he had spent only one year at the military academy. During the war, he had gone through the few short weeks of the 'Sedan' course. Yet, as soon as Manstein joined the *Truppenamt,* he emerged as the most brilliant brain of the institution.

Like other large scale institutions, world wide, the *Generalstab* was permeated by bureaucracy. Guderian endlessly pleaded for his independent *Panzer* arm. His commanding officer, Colonel von Natzmer, replied, "To hell with your *Panzer,* your vehicles have to transport flour." With his, "leave the church in the centre of the village, you can't do everything by yourself", Manstein had immediately found the right reply to Guderian.

Manstein was arrogant and very ambitious. Every talented officer is ambitious. Francis Bacon had written that depriving a soldier of ambition was like removing the spurs from a horse-rider. One of the few high commanders devoid of personal ambition was Moltke the elder. He said that to look at a growing tree gave him more pleasure than a victorious battle. He never criticized his fellow-officers, or officers whom he had defeated in battle. His criticism was only directed at himself.

---

3   Stahlberg, p. 239
4   Seaton, Army, p. 216
5   Knopp, p. 159

After his victory over France in 1871, he wrote: "Now I have risen to the top, mainly through luck. And many better men have disappeared into oblivion."[6]

As the war progressed, Manstein's unbridled ambition and his overbearing manner caused many of his fellow officers to view him with unease. When he was promoted to *Feldmarschall*, General Heusinger wrote to his wife: "Has he now reached the limit of his ambition? I don't believe it." The more the fortunes of war deserted Manstein, the more his arrogance increased. At the end, he became the victim of a hubris that led him to look down on his opponents. He even favoured absurd plans, provided they were carried out under his command. Hélie de Saint Marc wrote: "As men rise higher and their prestige becomes a dominant factor, their complacency clouds their better judgement."[7]

Manstein's contempt for the Red Army remained unaltered after his dismissal. When the Russians launched their major offensive against Army Group Centre in June 1944, Manstein had already been dismissed, but he followed operations on the map. When Stahlberg showed him the direction taken by the Russian armies and asked for his opinion, Manstein replied: "Fortunately for us, the Russians know how to fight, but they know nothing of the art of leadership. They will soon halt and await new reserves."[8] The Russian generals who commanded the *Bagration* offensive and who, according to Manstein, knew nothing about the art of leadership, were their best commanders. They did not halt, but defeated the *Wehrmacht* in what might be called 'the major Cannae' of the Russo-German war. The German art of leadership was represented by the least capable of the *Wehrmacht* commanders, Ernst Busch, who was quickly removed and replaced by Model. Manstein's fellow generals saw the Red Army command in a different light.

Generaloberst Friessner:

> The leadership of the Red Army rose increasingly to the highest standards. Their generals had repeatedly visited us before Hitler came to power. They had taken part in our exercises. I have learned to respect them as very attentive and intelligent pupils. Undoubtedly, after Stalingrad, their performance was way beyond our expectations. They had an unsurpassed mastery in quick movements, in the displacement of *Schwerpunkte* and in

---

6 Uhle-Wettler, p. 128 f
7 Colonel de Saint-Marc was one of the officers who took part in the *putsch* against de Gaulle. He had fought valiantly in the war, was taken prisoner and escaped. After his arrival in France he was betrayed to the Gestapo and spent two years in the Dachau concentration camp, where he suffered daily torture. After the war, he fought in Indochina and then in Algeria. Like a number of officers of his rank, he felt betrayed by de Gaulle's politics – when assuming power, de Gaulle had proclaimed that Algeria would remain for ever French. Saint Marc commanded the elite unit of the French army, the 1st regiment of the foreign legion. After the *putsch*, he was sentenced to ten years in prison and loss of rank. De Gaulle, who was never tender with his enemies, recognised that Saint-Marc was an exception, solely motivated by honour and without any personal ambition. Saint Marc was released from prison after a few years, was made a commander of the Legion of Honour and became a prolific writer whose books are published world wide.
8 Stahlberg, p. 385

the establishment of bridgeheads which became the basis for later major offensives.[9]

Generaloberst Halder:

In 1941, the Red Army commanders had failed with their tactics of defending every inch of their soil. So it was interesting to see how they were able to turn to a flexible art of command. Their command operations were the equal of the best German performances. Opposed to this, Hitler more and more deviated from flexible command, and became confined to the purely defensive, without any operational ideas.[10]

Generaloberst Guderian:

During the war, the Red Army had an increasing number of the most capable commanders. Their inexhaustible reserves made it possible to find the best candidates for high commands.[11]

General der Panzertruppe Balck:

You have to give it to the Russians! Their highest commanders are simply great … All respect for their understanding, their tenacity and their talent of organisation."[12]

Manstein often contradicted Hitler, to his face, after he had become an army group commander and thus directly subordinate to Hitler. He did not hesitate to use strong expressions like 'nonsense' in his disagreements with the *Führer*. However, the value of such contradictions should not be exaggerated. The worst fate that could befall a general who contradicted the *Führer*, to his face, was dismissal from his command. Contrary to what German generals asserted after the war, objecting to Hitler face-to-face was not more dangerous than for a British general to protest an order by Churchill, or for an American general to voice his objections to Roosevelt. Contradicting Stalin was a different matter. If that occurred, the life of the Red Army General was in danger.

When he felt that a danger to his career had arisen, Manstein lacked courage. At this point, I go into the imaginary 'grey' area of the tombstone that was never erected. 150 years earlier, the French *Maréchal* MacMahon had already said that generals are 'the last people from whom courage can be expected'. Albrecht Haushofer wrote, 'self-assurance is a personal freedom of action that can only rarely be found among people who appear to have freedom of action.'[13] Manstein had shown courage when he protested against the introduction of part of 'the racial' into the army. Later, when he felt some danger to his position, he sacrificed his subordinates, as in the case of General Sponeck. At Stalingrad he refused to issue an order that could have saved the lives of thousands of soldiers. He preferred to follow the orders of the *Pinkelstratege* Hitler.

---

9   Friessner, p. 222

10 Halder, *Hitler als Feldherr*, Munich 1949, p. 56

11 H. Guderian, *Russian Strategy at War*, in B. Liddell Hart (ed.) *The Soviet Army*, London 1956, p. 129

12 H. Balck, *Ordnung im Chaos, Erinnerungen 1893–1945,* Osnabrück 1981, p. 398

13 Hildebrandt, p. 47

Gerd Schmueckle, later to become a four-star general of the *Bundeswehr*, was at that time a young front-line officer. He is on record as saying that "Manstein did not feel it incumbent upon himself to issue an order that could have saved the lives of many soldiers at Stalingrad. It did not diminish our respect for his military capacity, but we no longer believed in his courage."

Manstein was never close to his soldiers. Colonel Reichhelm was Model's Ia and was present when Manstein turned his command over to Model. Reichhelm told me that he had spent a few days at Manstein's headquarters, and that he admired the quiet manner in which Manstein issued his orders. Since Reichhelm was accustomed to Model's outbursts, his admiration is not surprising. But he also said that he was astonished that there was no bond between Manstein and the front-line troops. Some people have reproached Manstein for not returning the salute of his subordinates. This was however unfair. Manstein's cataracts had rapidly become worse and he was often unable to see others, except through a blur. *Verlorene Siege* conveyed the impression that Manstein looked at his soldiers as statistics. Survivors of the battle for Sevastopol appeared on Knopp's video. They complained that Manstein looked at them merely as chess pieces that he moved around at will. They added that Manstein's promise to Hitler, to take Sevastopol at all costs, before Christmas 1941, was a crime against his soldiers.

Another part of the 'grey' area is Manstein's attitude towards the 'resistance' movement. Does Manstein deserve particular praise for not having reported Stauffenberg and Gersdorff? None whatsoever. Had he acted as he did, while other generals had reported members of the 'resistance' movement who approached them, all honour would have been due to him. But no other general reported anyone, although many were approached. Manstein simply remained true to the old tradition of the German Officer Corps, that one did not report officer comrades.

But Manstein's replies to Stauffenberg and Gersdorff were simply shameless. He was approached by the two young officers, both of whom had decided to do what had to be done at the risk of their lives, namely, to kill Hitler. Stauffenberg detonated the bomb on 20 July 1944. When it failed to kill Hitler, Stauffenberg paid with his life on the same day. Gersdorff escaped, only by a miracle, when Hitler unexpectedly cut short his visit to the armoury. When both asked for Manstein's support, he hid behind meaningless phrases, like "Prussian *Feldmarschalls* don't mutiny", or " I am first, and above all, a soldier." In other words:

> You do what you feel has to be done. If you succeed, you have created a new situation where I may be able to be useful. If you fail, you will lose your lives, but I will not be compromised. If things go your way and Kluge wants me to serve as chief of a new and genuine *Generalstab*, I will always be at the disposal of a legal government.

In Manstein's mind, 'legal' was obviously intended to mean 'effective.'

During the first months of 1943, General Beck wrote a long letter to Manstein which he emphasised that the war could not come to a 'favourable' end. Manstein described this letter as a 'classic review'. But he replied, in an impertinent manner, that a war was only lost when one admitted that it was lost. Then he reverted to his 'draw theory', which was beginning to be viewed as absurd by a number of his fellow generals. He then added that his military duties did not leave sufficient time to reply in detail to Beck's letter. Manstein was known to spend most of his evenings playing bridge. Surely he could have sacrificed one or two sessions, as a gesture of elementary politeness. Beck was, after all, the man to whom he owed his early career and his subsequent rise in the military hierarchy.

In a number of fields, such as literature and classical music, Manstein was an extremely well read man, in particular if one takes into account that he never received a higher education beyond the *Abitur*. After the war, in his letters to his wife from prison, he quoted Tolstoy and showed that he had not only read him but that he understood his philosophy. His conversations with Stahlberg, about Mozart and Bruckner, gave evidence of a knowledge and understanding of classical music far beyond the average amateur.

Colonel Reichhelm told me that he met Manstein and his daughter during the yearly Bach-festival at Ansbach in the 1960s. During an intermission, they walked through the gardens and had an intensive talk about Bach's music and various forms of its interpretation. Reichhelm was himself a gifted musician. He played second violin an amateur string quartet at the age of 90. He said that it was obvious to him that Manstein was well acquainted with the works of Bach, and that he had a clear opinion as to how they should be played.

However, in other no less important fields, particularly world politics and history, Manstein understood practically nothing. Some of his statements are simply childish. When he encountered Alsatian soldiers in French uniforms, he wrote that, "it was tragic to meet these wonderful German boys as enemies."[14] The tragic fate of the Alsatians, condemned to live at regular intervals under German or French domination, entirely escaped him.

King Michael I of Romania, of the Hohenzollern dynasty, became the 'treacherous Hohenzollern offspring.' "Who could guess that a member of the Hohenzollern dynasty would betray Germany?"[15] Manstein could well have expressed himself in similar manner about the British royal family that changed its German name Battenberg to Windsor only during the First World War.

Manstein then attacked Churchill: "In his hatred of Hitler and his regime, and of Prussian Germany, Churchill simply overlooked the greater danger that threatened Europe, i.e. the Soviet Union and Stalin."[16] A greater danger than Hitler? Churchill had written: "No one for the last twenty-five years, has been a more consistent opponent of Communism than I. I will unsay no word that I have spoken about it."[17] Any ally in the struggle against Hitler was obviously welcome to him. But it was Hitler who increasingly admired Stalin. Hitler often expressed his regret that he had not proceeded against his own generals, as Stalin did with the leadership of the Red Army, during the years of the Great Terror.

In his unpublished memoirs, *Generaloberst* Adam wrote that Rundstedt and his fellow generals who sat on the *Ehrenhof* (the court of honour) which expelled officers involved in the plot of July 20 from the army and delivered them into the hands of the monstrous Freisler at the people's court, had forever forfeited their

---

14 *Verlorene Siege*, p. 134.
15 Ibid, p. 289
16 Ibid, p. 155 f
17 W. Churchill, *The Grand Alliance*, Boston 1950, p. 371

military honour.[18] How would General Adam have judged the deeds of his former protégé at the *Truppenamt*, had he obtained knowledge of the events in the Crimea?

It is unimportant that the Holocaust was ordered by Hitler and not by Manstein. Manstein did not initiate it he simply remained indifferent to it. Manstein could not prevent the actions of the *Einsatzgruppen*. The physical elimination of all Jews was Hitler's foremost aim. However, Manstein could have prohibited any participation by his soldiers in those murders.

But Manstein issued 'orders of the day', in particular his order of 20 November 1941, that were a direct appeal to murder. He actively supported the actions of the *Einsatzgruppen* whenever it was in his interest. He put his troops at their disposal when their own forces were insufficient. He requested the execution of 14,500 Jews in Simferopol, months ahead of the date foreseen for their execution. Manstein received regular reports of the murder of Jews in areas under his territorial authority. It was his duty to immediately investigate and go directly to Hitler with the knowledge he had obtained. Instead, he ignored the reports. In fact, he wrote in his memoirs, that he had obtained knowledge of such horrors only after the war. He would not have had any success in making such reports. No one could influence Hitler in that area, but it would have then been his duty to resign his command, and leave the responsibility to his successor. Had Manstein acted in that manner history would have recorded him a hero, and his successor would have had to bear the responsibility for the subsequent events.

In *Soldat im 20. Jahrhundert*, one finds the rhetorical question: "How much did Manstein know?" It was easy for Stahlberg to appear on the ARD Station and say: "He knew everything, I had always kept him informed." Perhaps that statement was superfluous. The many reports initialled by Manstein are sufficient evidence of his knowledge.

Even worse, was a statement by Breithaupt: "Information must be kept away from Manstein. The *Feldmarschall* must be permitted to concentrate exclusively upon his military duties. He is already in permanent dispute with Hitler. If information is brought to his knowledge, about political events and crimes committed in his area, it may lead to his dismissal. The *Feldmarschall* is indispensable. He would be especially so after a successful *coup d'état*.[19] Every word in that statement defies reason!

Manstein could not be allowed to ignore what happened in his areas, since it was not his military duties that were paramount, but his reputation in history. In 1941, there was not yet any dispute between Hitler and Manstein. On the contrary, Manstein stood high in Hitler's favour. A *coup d'état* was not even under consideration at that date. And was Manstein to be indispensable after a successful *coup d'état*? Can anyone imagine, that after a successful assassination of Hitler, the new leadership who took over would have turned to Manstein? He had turned a deaf ear to all their entreaties. Beck was foreseen as the first provisional Head of State, in the event of a successful *coup*. Can anyone imagine that he would have wasted a minute on Manstein, whom he totally despised?

---

18   W. Adam, *Erinnerungen*, handwritten manuscript at the BA-MA, p. 649
19   Breithaupt, p. 90

That Manstein, even after the war, refused to acknowledge any guilt, cast an irremovable stain on his reputation. A poem by Franz Grillparzer contains the verse:

> *Und die Grösse ist gefährlich,*
> *und der Ruhm ein leeres Spiel;*
> *was er gibt, sind nichtige Schatten*
> *was er nimmt, es ist so viel.*

Manstein's memoirs were among the first to appear after the war, and became the bench-mark for those who followed suit. Were Manstein and his fellow generals naive in their belief that subsequent generations would accept their arguments?

Friedrich writes:

> If one takes the statements of all the accused, it means that in the territories under Soviet authority, in 1940, total secrecy permitted 3,000 policemen, under the watchful eyes of more than 3 million German soldiers, in full view of 60 million Soviet citizens under German rule, to murder more than 2 million people, without anyone saying a word about the events to any *Wehrmacht* General. That was the argument of an entire, German, post-war, generation. Obviously, it is unbelievable.

Albrecht Haushofer was under no compulsion to make any public confession of any guilt. He paid with his life for his part in the 'resistance' movement. Yet he felt that he had a responsibility which he had to transmit to future generations. In his 39th "Moabiter Sonnet" he wrote:

> *Ich trage leicht an dem, was das Gericht,*
> *mir Schuld benennen wird; an Plan und Sorgen;*
> *Verbrecher wär ich, hätte ich für das Morgen*
> *des Volkes nicht geplant, aus eigener Pflicht.*
> *Doch schuldig bin ich anders als Ihr denkt,*
> *Ich musste früher meine Pflicht erkennen,*
> *Ich musste schärfer Unheil Unheil nennen,*
> *mein Urteil hab ich viel zu lang gelenkt …*
> *Ich klage mich in meinem Herzen an,*
> *Ich habe mein Gewissen jahrelang betrogen,*
> *ich hab mich selbst und andere belogen,*
> *ich kannte früh des Jammers ganze Bahn,*
> *ich hab gewarnt – nicht hart genug und klar!*
> *und heute weiss ich, was ich schuldig war:* "[20]

Haushofers 36th sonnet could well have been written for Manstein:

> *Den ersten reut vielleicht, was er getan,*
> *den zweiten höchstens was er unterliess.*

---

20   Kosthorst p. 183. The 'Moabiter Sonette' are a collection of poetry which Haushofer wrote in Moabit prison while awaiting his execution. He was shot by an SS-command during the last days of the war.

Den dritten reut, dass er nicht schärfer stiess,
dem Abgrund näher, seiner Kugel Bahn
Ein vierter jammert noch um Amt und Rang
Der nächste fühlt von allem sich entlastet.

Even Keitel, Hitler's most obedient servant among the *Feldmarschälle*, finally recognised his guilt and walked 'like a man' to the gallows. Manstein kept his silence to the very end.

Manstein compounded his crimes in the Crimea by introducing a deliberate policy of famine. It caused many among the civilian population, not only Jews, to die of hunger.[21] For another part of the 'black' half of the imaginary tombstone, Manstein must share the blame with his fellow commanders. They continued to pursue a senseless war, for close on three years, when it was apparent that defeat was already inevitable. Millions of soldiers and civilians lost their lives for nothing.

In 1996, Father Lothar Groppe, SJ, published a devastating criticism of Manstein a Berlin newspaper. Father Groppe, born in 1929, is the son of General Theodor Groppe. In September 1939, General Groppe had ordered the soldiers of his division to shoot at a mob who intended to start a *pogrom* against the Jews who had remained in the Sarre area. After castigating Manstein's infamous order of the day of 20 November 1941, which he calls 'one of the most shameful documents ever issued by a German officer', Lothar Groppe wrote: "It must have been clear to Manstein's brilliant mind that, after Stalingrad, the war was lost. How could his conscience permit him to sacrifice millions of additional military casualties and civilian dead, only to satisfy the *Pinkelstratege*, as he often contemptuously referred to Hitler?

When Manstein wrote that 'the soldier has no right to refuse obedience', he shows that for an officer of his high rank he is surprisingly ill-informed. At the cadet school in Lichterfelde, where he began his schooling, he could not have failed to see the plate with the words: "Prussian obedience is the consequence of a free decision and not of obsequiousness." In the offices of the Bendlerstrasse, where he worked for years at the *Truppenamt* and at the *Generalstab*, the walls are adorned with the words of Moltke the elder: "Obedience is a principle, but man stands above principle."

One cannot demand of anyone that they kill a criminal tyrant if their conscience forbids such an act. But one must expect that every high-placed commander should show an equal respect for the fate of his subordinates. Manstein is dead. He now has to answer to 'another judge'. But his subservience, which cost millions of soldiers and civilians their lives, can never be forgotten. Compared with this guilt, all his achievements descend to total insignificance.

Father Groppe concluded his article with a reference to his father. He wrote:

A German general, who did not demand that 'harsh punishment' be meted out to the Jews, but who protected Jews against the actions of an enraged mob, had written: "A commander is responsible for the well-

---

21 For details, the recent doctoral thesis of Dr. Manfred Oldenburg, *Ideologie und militärisches Kalkül – die Besatzungspolitik der Wehrmacht in der* Sowjetunion, Cologne 2004. Dr. Oldenburg is able to substantiate every statement of his with incontrovertible documentary evidence.

being of his subordinates and, if circumstances require it, he has to sacrifice his life for their well-being. This was the spirit in which officers of the Imperial German Army were brought up." Never can Manstein be considered to have been a role model.[22]

The late Clemens *Graf* von Kageneck, a highly decorated *Panzer* officer, holder of the Knight's Cross with Oak Leaves, told me that he happened to encounter Manstein by chance, during the last weeks of the war. He had implored Manstein to support his active fellow generals, with his moral authority, in their refusal to carry out Hitler's 'Nero' order, calling for the destruction of all German infrastructure. Manstein refused and replied: "The principle of obedience to highest authority has to prevail."[23]

After the war, the German commanders tried to justify themselves by claiming that the Allied demands for unconditional surrender, and the rules laid down at Yalta and Potsdam, left them no choice but to continue fighting to the bitter end. This cannot be taken seriously. The demand for unconditional surrender took place in 1943, when Stalingrad was already 'past history'. Yalta was almost at the end of the war. The Potsdam conference took place after the German surrender.

Another argument of the commanders was equally spurious. It was expressed in the hope that the alliance between Russia and the Western allies would break apart to Germany's benefit. Indeed, there was often tension in the alliance. At first, when Stalin complained about the Allied delays in opening a second front, and later, towards the end of the war, when it became evident that Stalin would create what Churchill called the 'iron curtain'. But once Hitler's crimes had become common knowledge, any understanding with Hitler was unthinkable for Franklin D. Roosevelt and Winston Churchill. Until his death, Roosevelt had some illusions about Stalin. But Churchill never wavered in his mistrust of Stalin's intentions. However, Hitler was never an alternative for Churchill.

Scruples were a minor concern with Stalin, who was always guided by his own interests, and the alliance with the Western Allies served him well. On the ground, his troops were beating the Germans in every encounter after 1942. The fact that the Red Army continued to bear the brunt of the fighting on the ground, convinced him that Western opposition to his plans for Eastern Europe would remain within boundaries acceptable to him.

Stalin was never above cheating others, but he did not suffer being cheated himself. On 22 June 1941, Hitler succeeded in cheating Stalin into the belief that he, Hitler, would faithfully abide by the Hitler-Stalin pact, as indeed Stalin himself had done. This belief in Hitler cost Stalin millions in casualties and prisoners-of-war. It brought the German Army close to Moscow, Leningrad and then deep into the Ukraine, before Stalin was able to assemble his greater strength, and deal the Germans their first decisive defeat at Moscow. Surely, he would never expose himself to a second deceit by Hitler.

So, who benefited from the senseless continuation of the war? Some generals got additional decorations, others were promoted, until they in turn were sent home.

22　*Feldmarschall im Zwiespalt*, in Märkische Zeitung, December 10, 1996
23　Letter from Kageneck to the author, September 6, 2004

On 23 September 1918, Ludendorff had gone to the Emperor and declared that Germany could no longer win the war. He said that an armistice had to be sought, with power transferred to the parliamentarians, as they were in a better position to negotiate. True, Ludendorff spoiled part of his patriotic action by adding the sentence: "Let them (the parliamentarians) now eat the soup they've cooked." It was a statement that gave birth to the 'stab-in-the-back' legend. But two months earlier, the German Army had stood for the second time at the gates of Paris. A number of French ministers seriously favoured leaving Paris and retiring to the South. In September 1918, the Imperial Army was still much stronger than was the *Wehrmacht* after Stalingrad. Was no *Wehrmacht* commander capable of matching Ludendorff's patriotism?

To this very day, German historians continue to search for an explanation of Manstein's 'split personality'. None of their explanations is successful. Probably there is no such thing as the absolute truth. At his only meeting with Manstein, Rommel had called him an 'illusionist'. But this was caused by Manstein's statement to him that Hitler would relinquish supreme command and turn it over to him, if the situation turned to despair. Rommel had never served in the East. At the time of his meeting he was certainly unaware of Manstein's crimes.

Guido Knopp ended his chapter on Manstein with the words: " He was a soldier – not less, but certainly not more."[24] Obviously, a *Feldmarschall* is more than just a soldier. But with his endless repetitions of 'I am a soldier', 'we soldiers', Manstein has certainly contributed to Knopp's statement. Professor Yehuda Wallach wrote: "Manstein was perhaps a good expert commander, but he was a small man." Manstein was more then 'perhaps a good expert commander", and he was certainly not 'a small man."[25]

In his account of a meeting between Manstein and the last German ambassador to Britain, Herbert Dirksen, Stahlberg came closer to the truth. He wrote:

In a way, the paths taken by both men, Ludendorf and Manstein, were similar. Both had served their country in high-level positions, both had become the victims of dictators who followed old established rules, but only as long as they were of use to them. I got the impression that they simply lived in a wrong generation. Neither was apparently able to grasp that what was the rule in the 19th century was no longer valid in the 20th.[26]

Professor Kosthorst, who is highly critical of Manstein, added:

The *Feldmarschall* believed in an illusionary transposition of the principles of the Imperial State into Hitler's *Führerstaat*. He apparently felt compelled to serve it in total obedience. In this faulty logic he was unable to believe in the crimes that were reported to him, since he considered it unthinkable to serve a criminal.[27]

---

24 Knopp, p.226.
25 Y. Wallach, '*Feldmarschall von Manstein und die deutsche Judenausrottung in Russland*, in the annual of the institute for German history, Tel Aviv university, 4/1975, p. 472
26 Stahlberg, p. 383.
27 Kosthorst, p. 204

In *Verlorene Siege*, Manstein turned into a censor of all his fellow commanders. It was an attitude which had led *Der Spiegel* to describe him as 'the most self-satisfied' of German military memoir writers. What Manstein did was not only contrary to German officers' tradition, it was also unnecessary since, with the exception of Halder, he had no personal accounts to settle. Manstein used a perfidious method. At first, he is highly complimentary about the victims of his pen, then a poisoned arrow is introduced, and at the end the compliments again emerge.

One of his main targets was Brauchitsch, an easy victim, since he died before *Verlorene Siege* and thus could not defend himself. A conflict between Manstein and Brauchitsch had arisen even before the war. In 1936, Brauchitsch commanded the East Prussian *Wehrkreis*. Beck had given him specific instructions for a war-game and ordered Manstein to be present when the conclusions were presented. Brauchitsch's conclusions did not meet with approval by Beck or Manstein. General Heusinger wrote that the incident led to a latent hostility between Manstein and Brauchitsch that never abated.[28]

Manstein wrote about Brauchitsch with an opening compliment:

> He was a very capable commander. But he did not belong to the very top class of high commanders, like von Fritsch, Beck, von Rundstedt, von Bock and Ritter von Leeb. Nevertheless, he has to be considered as one of the top generals, and he had certainly shown the capacity to act as commander in chief of the army. (Then follow the poisoned arrows.) I will not deny him a strong will-power, although this was mainly negative. He let decisions be proposed to him rather than reaching them himself. Perhaps he avoided this because he felt that he was not up to a personal decision. He was not a fighter by nature … He could never win the complete trust of his subordinates and of his soldiers … His unquestionable charm never conveyed the impression of personal warmth … (At last, the usual final compliment.) Regarding Brauchitsch's relationship with Hitler, I am convinced that this basically noble man was simply destroyed by that ruthless dictator.[29]

Manstein's description of Brauchitsch calls for some comment. Before the war, Beck, Fritsch, Rundstedt, Bock and Leeb belonged to the very top league of commanders. During the war, neither Fritsch nor Beck held any command, and the performances of Bock, Rundstedt and Leeb hardly deserve the compliments that Manstein showers on them. They certainly did not show themselves superior to Brauchitsch.

During his lifetime Manstein would never know what his fellow generals really thought of him. His reputation had remained at such a height that no one dared to go public with their opinions. General Heusinger wrote almost daily to his wife. In a number of his letters he did not hide his contempt of Manstein, but in public, he was always full of praise. After Manstein died, the constraints disappeared. The opinions of Paulus and of Heusinger have already been mentioned, and other voices joined the chorus. *Generaloberst* Beck, who took his own life on 20 July

---

28   Heusinger, Kopf, p. 40
29   *Verlorene Siege*, p. 71 ff

1944, had already voiced his contempt of Manstein, in particular in his talks with the ambassador, Ulrich von Hassell, who was hanged after 20 July 1944.

On one occasion, von Hassell had described all the *Feldmarschalls* as a 'bunch of hopeless sergeants'.

Beck: "Although I have appreciated him for years, I felt no regret at his dismissal."[30]

Beck described the disappointing attitude of his former *Wunderkind* protégé as 'the result of his weakness of character.'[31]

> Manstein's attitude is better understood by his weak character than by his statements that 'one has to do everything to prevent the Russians from entering Germany'. Such an event would not result from a successful *putsch*, but rather from a failed *coup d'état* that prolonged a senseless war and unavoidably brought the Russians into Germany.[32]

"Beck intended to defer Manstein and Paulus to a court-martial if he was invested with the necessary authority."[33]

Generaloberst Halder: "Manstein was always the prototype of the *Junker* and the militarist, to whom the brutality of Ludendorff, and his indifference to the means employed, was his model and his personal law."[34]

"Manstein searched for a direct relation with Hitler behind my back. He succeeded."[35]

Albert Speer: "Loyalty! A word constantly used, not only by Keitel and Kesselring, but also by Blomberg, Manstein and Kluge, to put an end to their doubts."[36]

The historian Andreas Hillgruber quotes: "Manstein's failure and guilt is due to his incapacity to realise that the exceptional situation of the years 1933–1945 could not be compared to previous Prussian 'moral' commands."[37]

Probably the best portrait of Manstein has been recently painted by Philipp von Boeselager, on the ARD video, 'Hitler's soldiers':

> Manstein was the outstanding strategic head of the *Wehrmacht*. He possessed an artistic brain, he was certainly no *Kommisskopf*. His understanding was razor-sharp. He was well read and had an extraordinary memory. He knew how to command, he did not run along the front but he prepared his every step carefully. He never reported a comrade, as that was 'not done' by a German officer. But he never dared to contradict Hitler in questions of real importance. When he received reports of the murder of thousands of Jews and gypsies in the area of his command, he simply refused to listen. As *Feldmarschall* he had to take responsibility for deeds committed in the rear of his command area. If he was not prepared

30   Knopp, p. 211
31   Ibid
32   Hoffmann, p. 343
33   A. Kluge, *Schlachtenbeschreibung*, Olten 1974, p. 274
34   Knopp, p. 159
35   Ibid, p. 177
36   A.Speer, *Spandauer Tagebücher*, Frankfurt 1975, p.283
37   Manstein/Fuchs, p. 379

to do this, he should have remained a battalion commander. He should have taken a political step against Hitler, but he was never able to do this. He would probably have been dismissed, but his life was not at stake. The soldier risks his life daily, a *Feldmarschall* has a greater duty to risk his head. The German Generals of the Second World War were no military failures, they were superior to the commanders of the First World War. But they were political failures. They alone had the power to put a stop to the continuation of a war already lost.[38]

Four-star General of the *Bundeswehr*, Dr Günther Kiessling:

My feelings about Manstein have always been ambivalent. I recognised the value of his military leadership and felt that his burial with military honours was justified. But, with him, not all that glittered was gold. In his biography of Stauffenberg, Wolfgang Venohr shows the shady side of his character, and the memoirs of Alexander Stahlberg have greatly increased my reservations.[39]

When Manstein died in 1973, the *Frankfurter Allgemeine Zeitung* wrote in its obituary:

The perfection of military art turns into a farce, if criminal mentality pervades a country's leadership to the point where an officer can use his military knowledge to prolong senseless butchery. The most typical example of this dilemma, in Germany in this century, is presented by the personality and the actions of *Generalfeldmarschall* von Lewinski, named von Manstein. Victories that Manstein describes in his memoirs as 'lost' victories, increased the disaster, instead of putting an end to it. Military knowledge was thus perverted into a contribution to inhumanity.[40]

As the years have gone by, criticism of individual commanders such as Manstein has given way to attacks against the *Wehrmacht*. This is logical, a general does not shape world history unless he takes one step further and, like Bonaparte, Eisenhower and de Gaulle, he becomes his country's ruler. But when writing about the *Wehrmacht*, authors stand on the brink of an abyss.

On the tactical and operational levels, the *Wehrmacht* was without doubt the best of all armies of the Second World War. Even in the battles it lost, and in the disasters of the last year of the war, it inflicted more casualties on its enemies than it suffered on its own side. It had the best generals and, in particular, the best corps and divisional commanders. However, strategically it was a failure, and wars are won by strategy.

In moral values, the German generals of the Second World War showed themselves to be dismal failures. Gersdorff wrote:

In my opinion, during the First World War, the commanders of German Army Groups were not up to the military standards of Generals such as von Manstein, von Bock and von Rundstedt. But they showed more character

---

38   ARD Video 'Hitler's soldiers' and the accompanying book, Berlin 1998, p. 161 f.
39   G. Kiessling, *Versäumter Widerspruch*, Mainz 1993, p. 300 (henceforth Kiessling)
40   *Frankfurter Allgemeine Zeitung*, July 15, 1973

than the German commanders of the Second World War. I know that it was easier for Generals in the Imperial Army to keep their old established values, because they could be certain that the leadership of the country would not issue orders to them which were incompatible with their military honour. Certainly my late father, and many of his comrades, would have reacted more forcefully, had they been issued the orders given to the Generals of the *Wehrmacht*. Contrary to many opinions advanced after the end of the Second World War, I am convinced that the idea of 'resistance' had stronger roots in the German Empire than in the Third *Reich*. By 'resistance,' I mean that more attention was paid to conscience than to obedience. Prussian history can show many examples where such 'resistance' led to action. Perhaps the many oaths which the soldiers had to swear, first to the Emperor-King, than to Ebert, Hindenburg, and finally to Hitler, have had a nefarious, even wicked, influence.[41]

In Goethe's *Faust*, part one, Faust exclaims: "*Was Du ererbt von Deinen Vätern hast, erwirb es um es zu besitzen*" (What have you inherited from your ancestors? take good care to continue to abide with it). The *Wehrmacht* commanders had inherited many virtues from their ancestors, but they chose to cast them aside. Personalities like General Groppe, did not belong to the mainstream, they were exceptions. In 1933, *Generaloberst* von Hammerstein-Equord said to Secretary of State Ernst von Weizsäcker: "Hitler happens to be our destiny. We have to bear with him for ten years."[42] His timetable was wrong by only two years. The remainder of his statement must be ignored, since in 1933 the Generals could have prevented that destiny.

The *Bundeswehr* has made great efforts to distance itself from the traditions of the *Wehrmacht*. but as frequently happens in Germany, it jumped from one extreme to the other. Goethe had already complained that Germans have a tendency of 'searching for extremes'. (*dass der Deutsche alles bis zu einem Äussersten treibet!*). No army can be built up without traditions from its predecessor, however it is difficult to discover *Wehrmacht* traditions which should be perpetuated in the *Bundeswehr*. Military parades, such as those in France on 14 July and 11 November, and in Britain on the Queen's birthday, do not take place in Germany. A unit of the *Bundeswehr* took part in the farewell ceremony for Alexander Haig at SHAPE. Adelbert Weinstein wrote in the *Frankfurter Allgemeine Zeitung:*

> The intimidated young soldiers who represented the *Bundeswehr* at Cateau looked like a military caricature. Many stumbled when they attempted to keep pace in marching. Their uniforms did not fit. The inspector-general must have felt his stomach turning upside down.[43]

Conceivably, the main inheritance of the *Wehrmacht* has been to turn a nation that had always been proud of its soldiers, into the most anti-militaristic nation in Europe.

---

41 Gersdorff, p. 137
42 Müller, p. 60. His timetable
43 A. Weinstein, *Der Leutnant stolperte unbeholfen* (the hopelessly stumbling lieutenant), in *Frankfurter Allgemeine Zeitung,* July 2, 1979

In the concluding chapter of his book, *Höhe-und Wendepunkte deutscher Militärgeschichte*, Uhle-Wettler wrote: "Perhaps German military history has reached its end."[44] Given the misery that the German military brought upon the world, during the Second World War, one has to render thanks to destiny.

In 1834, Heinrich Heine had already foreseen what was liable to happen one day. "If you hear it crash, like you never have heard it crash before, then know, 'the German thunder' has finally broken loose. A drama will be played in Germany that will make the French Revolution appear to have been a harmless idyll."

Uhle-Wettler added: "One thing is certain. If German military history has come to an end, something disappears which many nations would view with respect. Were it their own history, they would look at it with the highest esteem."[45] There has never been a lack of respect for German military prowess. But after the Second World War, no esteem can remain for the *Wehrmacht* and its commanders, who succeeded in perverting their traditions of many generations.

Martin van Creveld emphasizes:

Nothing in my study of the fighting power of the *Wehrmacht* should be construed as an acquittal of the *Wehrmacht* from its responsibility for the events of 1939–1945. On the contrary, the outstanding organisation of the *Wehrmacht*, particularly at the lower level, and the totally professional Officer Corps, made it possible for them to be used as an instrument of a ruthless policy of aggression, accompanied by many crimes against humanity. A great majority of its officers and its soldiers were ready to obey the most criminal orders, and to participate in their execution. Although the *Wehrmacht* did not start the war, did not create the concentration camps, and did not decide upon the extermination of the Jews, those crimes could not have been committed without its active assistance. What remains is a heavy guilt from which there can be no acquittal. I can only hope that the Germans will never endeavour to acquit themselves.

Martin van Creveld is a favourite of German revisionist historians because he extols the fighting qualities of the *Wehrmacht*. All their books are full of quotations from his works. This paragraph could be found only after a lengthy search in an 'irritated' chapter by Andreas Broicher in *Soldaten der Wehrmacht*. [46]

Kunrat von Hammerstein, son of the *Generaloberst*:

The commanders of the *Wehrmacht*, most of whom were no National-Socialists, bear a heavy responsibility that they cannot pass on to Hitler. Therefore one should not create a new commander 'myth', to further the setting up of a new *Wehrmacht*.[47]

General of the *Bundeswehr* Dr Kiessling:

Obedience is a duty for every soldier, but it is not identical for all ranks. The higher the rank, the more 'contradiction' to orders is not only

---

44 Uhle-Wettler, p. 279
45 Uhle-Wettler, p. 279
46 *Soldaten Wehrmacht*, p. 446
47 Frankfurter Hefte, 11, 1986, p. 454

possible, but becomes a duty. The fate of the *Wehrmacht* leadership was determined by its weak and late 'contradictions' that therefore remained unnoticed. The 'contradictions' were necessary when it became evident that the war was lost. In spite of that knowledge, the commanders of the *Wehrmacht* chose to obey the dictator and continue a useless war. No one can absolve them from that guilt.[48]

Conceivably all traditional military history has come to an end. Every era has its termination. In the fifth act of Shakespeare's 'Troilus and Cressida', Hector says:

> The end crowns all,
> And that old common arbitrator, Time,
> Will one day end it.

Great powers, that wage war against others, have disappeared. All that remains is one military superpower. When it takes to arms we no longer see a traditional war, but an execution, in which computers and other technological elements, play a more important part than the commanders. Saint-Marc wrote: "Modern wars are conducted with aims that remain unclear. The demands of the media exceed the requirements of the battlefield. The real 'aims' of war become more and more obscure".

This German book was completed six months after the end of the Iraq war. It is doubtful if many remember that the coalition troops were commanded by a General Franks. But most know about the Cruise missiles and Stealth bombers.

A second form of modern war, the guerrilla war, is beyond the capacity of traditionally schooled commanders. The victors are men like Tito, or the Vietnamese General Giap, who have never undergone any traditional military training. After the end of the Vietnam War, an American Colonel said to a Vietnamese Colonel: "You know that you have never vanquished us on the battlefield." The Vietnamese Colonel pondered his reply for a brief moment and said: "This may indeed be true, but it is of no importance."[49]

---

48   *Warum sie trotz allem nicht aufgegeben haben* in *Das Parlament*, 28. April/5 Mai 1995, p. 4
49   F. Uhle-Wettler, *Der Krieg. Gestern – Heute – Morgen*, Hamburg 2001, p. 178

Photographs

Generaloberst Ludwig Beck (Ullstein Bild)

Generalfeldmarschall Walther von Brauchitsch (Biblio Verlag)

Generaloberst Heinz Guderian (Biblio Verlag)

Generaloberst Franz Halder (Biblio Verlag)

Generaloberst Hermann Hoth (Biblio Verlag)

Marshal of the Soviet Union Andrei Yeremenko (Biblio Verlag)

Generaloberst Alfred Jodl (Ullstein Bild)

Generalfeldmarschall Wilhelm Keitel (Biblio Verlag)

Generalfeldmarschall Erich von Manstein, 1943 (Ullstein Bild)

A post-war photograph of von Manstein, taken in the early 1950s (Ullstein Bild)

Generalfeldmarschall Walter von Reichenau (Ullstein Bild)

Marshal of the Soviet Union Konstantin Rokossovski (Biblio Verlag)

Marshal of the Soviet Union Georgi Zhukov (Biblio Verlag)

Oberst Claus Schenk *Graf* von Stauffenberg, seen here whilst on leave in 1940 with two of his children, Franz Ludwig and Heimeran (Ullstein Bild)

Generalmajor Henning von Tresckow (Ullstein Bild)

Marshal of the Soviet Union Vasili Chuikov (Biblio Verlag)

Generaloberst Kurt Zeitzler (Biblio Verlag)

Memorial headstone of Khrushchev at Novodevichy Cemetary (Biblio Verlag)

TIME from 14.1.1944 (Biblio Verlag)

Bibliography

Abenheim, D. *Bundeswehr und Tradition. Die Suche nach dem gültigen Erbe des deutschen Soldaten*, Munich 1989

Abetz, O. *Das offene Problem. Ein Rückblick auf drei Jahrzehnte deutscher Frankreichpolitik*, Cologne 1951

Adam U. *Judenpolitik im Dritten Reich*, Düsseldorf 1972

Adam W. (*Generaloberst*) *Erinnerungen*, unpublished manuscript, BA-MA

Adam, W. *Der schwere Entschluß*, East Berlin 1965

Addington, L. *The Blitzkrieg Era and the German General Staff 1865–1941*, New Brunswick 1971

Alexander, M. *The Republic in Danger. General Maurice Gamelin and the Politics of French Defence 1933–1945*, Cambridge 1992

Aly, G. *Hitlers Volksstaat. Raub, Rassenkrieg und nationaler Sozialismus*, Frankfurt 2005

Aly, G. *Endlösung – Völkerverschiebung und der Mord an den europäischen Juden*, Frankfurt 2005

Amouroux H. *Le peuple du désastre, 1930–1940*, Paris 1976

Andronikow, I. & W. Mostowenko *Die roten Panzer, Geschichte der sowjetischen Panzertruppen 1920–1960*, Munich 1963

Angrick, A. *Besatzungspolitik und Masaendmord. Die Einsatzgruppe D in der südlichen Sowjetunion 1941–1943*, Hamburg 2003

Anon. *Die Wehrmachtberichte 1939–1945*, Munich 1985, 3 Bände

Anon. *Encyclopedia Judaica*, Jerusalem 1973, 15 volumes

Anon. *IMT, Fall 9, Das Urteil im Einsatzgruppen-Prozeß*, East Berlin 1963

Anon. *Krushchev Remembers*, Toronto 1970

Anon. *Krushchev Remembers, The Last Testament*, London 1974

Anon. *International Military and Defense Encyclopedia*, Volume 5, Washington 1991

Anon. Istoria *Vielikoi Otetschesvennoy Voijnu Sovietskojo Sojuza – 1941–1945*, Moscow 1963, 6 volumes,

Archiv, Peter (Hrsg.) *Spiegelbild einer Verschwörung. Die Kaltenbrunner-Berichte an Bormann und Hitler über das Attentat vom 20.Juli 1944. Geheime Dokumente aus dem ehemaligen Reichssicherheitshauptamt*, Stuttgart 1961

Bagramyan, I. *So schritten wir zum Sieg*, East Berlin 1984

Balck, H. *General der Panzertrupe. Ordnung im Chaos. Erinnerungen 1893–1948*, Osnabrück 1981

Barnett, C. *Hitler's Generals*, New York 1989

Beaufre A. *Mémoires*, Paris 1961

Beck, L. *Studien*, Stuttgart 1955

Beevor, A. *Stalingrad*, London 1998

Beevor, A. *The Battle of Berlin*, London 2002

Below, N. von Als *Hitlers Adjutant 1937–1945*, Mainz 1945

Benoist-Méchin, J. *Der Himmel stürzt ein. Frankreichs Tragödie 1940*, Düsseldorf 1958

Benoist-Méchin, J. *Soixante jours qui ébranlèrent l'occident,* Paris 1956
Benz, B. & H. Graml,H. (eds.) *Biographisches Lexikon zur Weimarer Republik,* Munich 1988
Berben P. & B. Iselin *Les Panzers passent la Meuse, 13.5.1940,* Paris 1967
Bialer, S. *Stalin and his Generals, Soviet Military Command, Memoirs of World War II,* London 1984
Bloch, M. *L'étrange défaite. Témoignage écrit en 1940,* Paris 1990
Blumentritt, G. von *Rundstedt, The Soldier and the Man,* London 1952
Boeddecker, G. *Der Untergang des Dritten Reiches,* Berlin 1985
Böhler, J. *Auftakt zum Vernichtungskrieg. Die Wehrmacht in Polen 1929,* Frankfurt 2006
Bracher, K. *Zeitgeschichtliche Kontroversen – um Faschismus, Totalitarismus, Demokratie,* Munich 1984
Bradley, D. & R. Schulze-Kossens (Hrsg.) *Tätigkeitsbericht des Chefs des Personalamtes, General der Infanterie Rudolf Schmundt, fortgeführt von General der Infanterie Wilhelm Burgdorf,* Osnabrück 1984
Breithaupt, H. *Zwischen Front und Widerstand – Ein Beitrag zur Diskussion um den Feldmarschall Erich von Manstein,* Bonn 1994
Brett-Smith, R. *Hitler's Generals,* London 1976
Brochhagen, U. *Nach Nürnberg – Vergangenheitsbewältigung und Westintegration in der Ära Adenauer,* Berlin 1999
Browning, C. *Die Entfesselung der Endlösung. Nationalsozialistische Judenpolitik 1939–1945,* Munich 2003
Bryant, A. *The Turn of the Tide – Based on the Diaries and Autobiographical Notes of Fieldmarshal, the Viscount Alanbrooke.,* London 1959
Bücheler, H. *C-H von Stülpnagel, Soldat, Philosoph und Verschwörer,* Frankfurt 1989
Bücheler, H. *Hoepner, ein deutsches Soldatenschicksal des XX. Jahrhunderts,* Herford 1980
Bussche, A. *von dem Eid und Schuld,* Göttingen 1947
Calic, R. *Reinhard Heydrich – Schlüsselfigur des Dritten Reiches,* Düsseldorf 1982
Carell, P. *Unternehmen Barbarossa,* Frankfurt 1966
Carell, P. *Verbrannte Erde,* Frankfurt 1972
Chamberlain P. & C. Ellis *Britische und amerikanische Panzer des Zweiten Weltkrieges,* Munich 1972
Chamberlain, P. & H. Doyle *Encyclopedia of German Tanks of World War Two,* London 1993
Chandler, D. *The Campaigns of Napoleon,* New York 1966
Chauvineau, N. *Une invasion est-elle encore possible?,* Paris 1938
Chuikov, V. *Garde auf dem Weg nach Berlin,* Bonn 1959
Chuikov, V. *The Beginning of the End – The Battle for Stalingrad,* London 1963
Churchill, W. *The Grand Alliance,* Boston 1950
Churchill, W. *Their Finest Hour,* London 1959
Clausewitz, C.von *Vom Kriege, Bonn 1980* (19. Taschenbuchausgabe)
Clemenceau, G. *Grandeurs et Misères d'une Victoire,* Paris 1930
Cooper, M. *The German army 1933–1945, its political and military failure,* London 1978

Cross, R. *Citadel, The Battle of Kursk,* London 1993

Dansette, A. *Les Présidents des la République – de Louis Napoleon Bonaparte à Vincent Auriol,* Paris 1953

d'Astier de la Vigerie, F. *Le ciel n'était pas vide 1940,* Paris 1952

Davidson, E. *The Trial of the Germans, An Account of the Twenty-Two Defendants before the International Military Tribunal at Nuremberg,* New York 1966

Doerr, H. *Der Feldzug nach Stalingrad,* Darmstadt 1955

Domarus, R. *Hitlers Reden und Proklamationen 1932–1945,* Munich 1983

Donelly, T. & S. Taylor *Clash of Chariots, The Great Tank Battles,* New York 1996

Doumenc, A. *Histoire de la Neuvième Armée,* Paris 1945

Dunn, W. *Kursk – Hitler's Gamble,* London 1997

Dupuy, T. *A Genius for War. The German army and General Staff, 1807–1945,* Fairfax 1984

Einbeck, E. *Das Exempel Sponeck,* Bremen 1970

Eisenhower, D. *Crusade in Europe,* NewYork 1948

Enfer, J. *10 Mai-25 Juin 1940. La Campagne de France,* Paris 1990

Engelmann, J. Manstein, *Stratege und Truppenführer. Ein Lebensbericht in Bildern,* Friedberg 1981

Engert, J. (ed.) *Soldaten für Hitler – Begleitbuch zur gleichnamigen ARD Serie,* Göttingen 1957

Epifanow, A. & H. Mayer (eds.) *Die Tragödie deutscher Kriegsgefangener in Stalingrad von 1942 bis 1956, nach russischen Archivunterlagen,* Osnabrück 1996

Erfurth, W. *Die Geschichte des deutschen Generalstabes 1918–1945,* Göttingen 1975

Erickson, J. *The Road to Berlin,* London 1983

Erickson, J. *The Road to Stalingrad,* London 1973

Erickson, J. *The Soviet High Command. A Political and Military History 1918–1941,* London 1962

Eschenburg, T. *Die Republik von Weimar – Beiträge zur Geschichte eines improvisierten Demokratie,* Munich 1984

Faber du Faur, M. von *Macht und Ohnmacht – Erinnerung eines alten Offiziers,* Berlin 1944

Fest, J Das Gesicht des Dritten Reiches, Munich 1963

Fest, J. Staatsstreich, *der lange Weg zum 20.Juli,* Berlin 1994

Foerster, W. *Ein Soldat kämpft gegen den Krieg – aus nachgelassenen Papieren des Generalstabschef Ludwig Beck,* Munich 1949

Foerster, W. *Generaloberst Ludwig Beck – Sein Kampf gegen den Krieg,* Munich 1952

Foertsch, H. *Schuld und Verhängnis. Die Fritsch-Krise im Frühjahr 1938 als Wendepunkt in der Geschichte der nationalsozialistischen Zeit,* Stuttgart 1961

Fonvielle-Alquier, F. *Les Français dans la Drôle de Guerre 1939–1940,* Paris 1971

Förster, J. *Die Sicherung des Lebensraums in Das Deutsche Reich und der Zweite Weltkrieg, Band 4,* edited by the Militärgeschichtlichen Forschungsamt, Stuttgart 1983

Friedrich, J. *Das Gesetz des Krieges,* Munich 1997

Friedrich, J. *Der Brand, Deutschland im Bombenkrieg 1940–1945,* Munich 2002

Frieser, K-H *Blitzkriegs-Legende, Der Westfeldzug 1940,* Munich 1996

Frieser, K-H. *Krieg hinter Stacheldraht. Die deutschen Kriegsgefangenen in der Sowjetunion und das Nationalkomitee Freies Deutschland,* Mainz 1981

Frieser, K-H. *Schlagen aus der Nachhand – Schlagen aus der Vorhand, Die Schlachten von Charkow und Kursk, in Förster, W.(Hrsg.), Gezeitenwechsel im Zweiten Weltkrieg? Die Schlachten von Charkow und Kursk im Frühjahr und Sommer 1943 in operativer Anlage, Verlauf und politischer Bedeutung,* Hamburg 1996

Frießner, J. *Verratene Schlachten,* Hamburg 1956

Gamelin, M. *Servir, Paris 1955,* 3 volumes

Ganzenmüller, J *Das belagerte Leningrad. Die Stadt in den Strategien von Angreifern und Verteidigern,* Paderborn 2005

Gaulle, C. de. *Mémoires de Guerre,* Paris 1955

Gaulle, C.de *Vers l'Armée de Métier,* Paris 1944 (2nd ed.)

Gehlen, R. *Der Dienst – Erinnerungen 1942–1971,* Mainz 1971

Gerlach, H. *Die verratene Armee – Ein Stalingrad Roman,* Munich 1957

Gerlach, H. *Odyssee in Rot – Bericht einer Irrfahrt,* Munich 1966

Gersdorff, R.Frhr.von *Soldat im Untergang – Lebensbilder,* Frankfurt 1979

Gibson, H. (ed.) *The Ciano Diaries 1939–1943,* New York 1946

Gilbert, G. *Nürnberger Tagebuch. Gespräche der Angeklagten mit dem Gerichtspsychologen,* Frankfurt 2001

Gilbert, M. *Endlösung – ein Atlas,* Reinbeck 1982

Gilbert, M. *The Holcaust. The Jewish Tragedy,* London 1986

Giordano, R. *Die Traditionslüge – Vom Kriegerkult in der Bundeswehr,* Cologne 2000

Gisevius, H. *Bis zum bitteren Ende,* Zürich 1946

Giziowski, R. *The Enigma of General Blaskowitz,* London 1997

Glantz, D 'Prelude to Kursk. Soviet Strategic Operations, February – March 1943' in Förster, W. (Hrsg.) *Gezeitenwechsel im Zweiten Weltkrieg? Die Schlachten von Charkow und Kursk im Frühjahr und Sommer 1943 in operativer Anlage, Verlauf und politischer Bedeutung.* Hamburg 1996

Glantz, D. *From the Don to the Dnepr Soviet Offensive Operations, December 1942–August 1943,* London 1991

Glantz, D. & J. House *The Battle of Kursk,* Lawrence 1999

Goldhagen, D. *Hitler's Willing Executioners – Ordinary Germans and the Holocaust,* London 1997

Gorbatov, A. *Years off my life,* London 1964

Gorce, P. de la *La République et son Armée,* Paris 1963

Görlitz, W (ed.). *Generalfeldmarschall Wilhelm Keitel - Verbrecher oder Offizier?,* Göttingen 1961

Görlitz, W. *Der deutsche Generalstab,* Frankfurt 1969

Görlitz, W. *Der Zweite Weltkrieg 1939–1945,* Stuttgart 1952

Görlitz, W. (ed.). *Paulus – Stalingrad, Lebensweg und Nachlaß des Generalfeldmarschalls.* Bonn 1964

Gosztony, P. *Hitlers Fremde Heere,* Düsseldorf 1976

Goutard, A. *La Guerre des Occasions Perdues,* Paris 1956

Grandmaison, L. de *Deux Conférences,* Paris 1912

Greiner, H. *Die oberste Wehrmachtsführung 1939–1943,* Wiesbaden 1952

Grigorenko, Pjotr. *Erinnerungen,* Munich 1981

Grossmann, V. *Life and Fate,* London 1958

Grossmann, V. *Stalingrad,* Moskau 1946

Guderian, H. *Achtung – Panzer. Die Entwicklung der Panzerwaffe, ihre Kampftaktik und ihre operativen Möglichkeiten,* Stuttgart 1938

Guderian, H. *Erinnerungen eines Soldaten,* Wels 1951

Gunsburg, J. *Divided and Conquered. The French High Command and the Defeat of the West 1940,* London 1979

Hachmeister, L. *Der Gegenforscher – die Karriere des SS-Führers Franz Alfred Six,* Munich 1949

Hackl, O. Generalstab. *Generalstabsdienst und Generalstabsausbildung in der Reichswehr und der Wehrmacht 1919–1945. Studien deutscher Generale und Generalstabsoffiziere in der Historical Division der US Army in Europe, 1946–1961,* Osnabrück 1999

Haffner, S. *Anmerkungen zu Hitler,* Frankfurt 1981

Haffner, S. *Geschichte eines Deutschen. Die Erinnerungen 1914–1933,* Stuttgart 2000

Hahn, O. (ed.) *Hoepner Symposium,* Nürnberg 1982

Halder F. *Kriegstagebuch 1939–1942,* Stuttgart 1964

Halder, F. *Hitler als Feldherr,* Munich 1949

Hamerow, T. *Die Attentäter – Der 20 Juli, von der Kollaboration zum Widerstand,* Munich 1999

Hammerstein, K. *Frhr.von Spähtrupp,* Stuttgart 1963

Hartmann, C. Halder, *Generalstabschef Hitlers,* Paderborn 1951

Hausser, P. *Waffen-SS im Einsatz,* Göttingen 1953

Heer, H. & K. Naumann (eds.) *Vernichtungskrieg, Verbrechen der Wehrmacht 1941–1944,* Hamburg 1995

Heiber, H. (ed.) *Lagebesprechungen im Führerhauptquartier – Protokollfragmente aus Hitlers militärischen Konferenzen 1942–1945,* Stuttgart 1962

Heuer, G. *Die deutschen Generalfeldmarschälle und Großadmirale,* Baden 1979

Heusinger, A. *Der 'unbequeme' operative Kopf, in Nie außer Dienst, zum achtzigsten Geburtstag von Generalfeldmarschall Erich von Manstein, 24 November 1967, mit Beiträgen von Ulrich de Maizière, Walther von Schultzendorff, Adolf Heusinger, Theodor Busse, Andreas Hillgruber, Walter Wenck,* Cologne 1967

Heusinger, A. *Befehl im Widerstreit- Schicksalsstunden der deutschen Armee 1923–1945,* Stuttgart 1952

Heydecker, J. & J. Leeb *Der Nürnberger Prozeß – Bilanz der tausend Jahre,* Cologne 1979

Hilberg, Raul *Die Vernichtung der europäischen Juden,* Frankfurt 1990

Hildebrandt, R & A. Hildebrandt (eds.)...*die besten Köpfe, die man henkt. Ein tragischer Auftakt zur deutschen Teilung und Mauer*, Berlin 2003

Hilger G. & A. Meyer *The incompatible Allies – A memoir history of German-Soviet relations*, New York 1953

Hillgruber, A. *Die ideologisch-dogmatische Grundlage der nationalsozialistischen Politik der Ausrottung der Juden in den besetzten Gebieten der Sowjetunion und ihre Durchführung 1941–1944* in German Studies Review, vol. II, Nr.3, October 1979, New York

Hoffmann, P. Claus Schenck, *Graf von Stauffenberg und seine Brüder*, Stuttgart 1992

Hoffmann, P. *Widerstand, Staatsstreich, Attentat – De Kampf der Opposition gegen Hitler*, Munich 1979

Höhne, H. *Der Orden unter dem Totenkopf – die Geschichte der SS*, Munich 1978

Höhne, H. *Die Machtergreifung. Deutschlands Weg in die Hitler Diktatur*, Hamburg 1983

Höhne, H. *Gebt mir vier Jahre Zeit – Hitler und die Anfänge des Dritten Reiches*, Wien 1996

Höhne, H. *Mordsache Röhm. Hitlers Durchbruch zur Alleinherrschaft 1933–1945*, Hamburg 1984

Höhne, H. *Canaris – Patriot im Zwielicht*, Munich 1976

Horne, A. *To loose a battle – France 1940*, Boston 1969

Höß, R. *Kommandant in Auschwitz*, Munich 1985

Hoßbach, F. *Zwischen Wehrmacht und Hitler – 1934–1938*, Göttingen 1965

Hubatsch, W. *Hitlers Weisungen für die Kriegsführung 1939–1945*, Frankfurt 1962

Hürter, J. *Hitlers Heerführer. Die deutschen Oberbefehlshaber im Krieg gegen die Sowjetunion 1941/42*, Munich 2006

Jäckel, E. *Frankreich in Hitlers Europa. Die deutsche Frankreichpolitik im Zweiten Weltkrieg*, Stuttgart 1966

Jäckel, E. *Frankreich in Hitlers Europa. Die deutsche Frankreichpolitik im Zweiten Weltkrieg*, Stuttgart 1966

Jacobsen, H.A. *Der Fall Gelb*, Wiesbaden 1957

Jacobsen, H.A./Rohner, L. (Hrsg.) *Entscheidungsschlachten des zweiten Weltkrieges*, Frankfurt 1960

Jacobsen, H-A. *Der zweite Weltkrieg in Chroniken und Dokumenten*, Darmstadt 1961

Jacobsen,H & H. Krausnick *Die Anatomie des SS Staates- Konzentrationslager, Kommissarbefehl, Judenverfolgung*, Olten 1965

Janssen, K. & F. Tobias *Der Sturz der Generäle – Hitler und die Blomberg-Fritsch-Krise 1938*, Munich 1994

Jentz, T. *Die deutsche Panzertruppe 1933–1945*, Wölfersheim-Berstadt 1998–1999

Jeremenko, A. *False Witnesses*, Moscow, n.d.

Jeremenko, A. *Tage der Entscheidung – Als Frontenbefehlshaber an der Wolga*, East Berlin 1964

John, A. *Kursk '43 – Szenen einer Entscheidungsschlacht*, Bonn 1993

John, O. *Falsch und zu spät – der 20. Juli 1944*, Munich 1984

Jong, L. de *Die deutsche fünfte Kolonne im Zweiten Weltkrieg*, Stuttgart 1959

Junge, T. with the assistance of Melissa Müller *Bis zur letzten Stunde. Hitlers Sekretärin erzählt ihr Leben*, Munich 2002

Keegan, J. *The Second World War*, New York 1989

Kehrig, M. Stalingrad, *Analyse ud Dokumentation einer Schlacht*, Stuttgart 1974

Keilig, W. *Die Generale des Heeres*, Friedberg 1983

Keilig, W. *Rangliste des deutschen Heeres 1944/45*, Friedberg, n.d.

Kern, E. *Der große Rausch – Rußlandfeldzug 1941–1945*, Zürich 1948

Kershaw, I. *Hitler, 1889–1936 – Hubris*, London 1998

Kershaw, I. *Hitler, 1936–1945 – Nemesis*, London 2000

Kersten, F. *The Kersten Memoirs – Totenkopf und Treue*, London 1956

Kießling, G. *Versäumter Widerspruch*, Mainz 1993

Klein, P. (Hrsg.) *Die Einsatzgruppen in der besetzten Sowjetunion 1941. Tätigkeits-und Lageberichte des Chefs der Sicherheitspolizei und des SD*, Berlin 1997

Kleist, P. *Zwischen Stalin und Hitler*, Bonn 1950

Klink, E. *Das Gesetz des Handelns – Die Operation Zitadelle 1943*, Stuttgart 1966

Kluge, A. *Schlachtenbeschreibung*, Frankfurt 1983

Knopp, G. *Hitlers Krieger* (book to accompany the ZDF TV series), Munich 1988

Kogon, E. *Der SS-Staat*, Frankfurt 1946

Kolomyec M. & M. *Swirin Kursk 1943*, Warsaw 1999, 2 volumes

Koltunow,G. & B. Solowiev *Kurskaya Bitva*, Moscow 1970

Koniew, I. *Aufzeichnungen eines Frontenbefehlshabers 1943/44*, East Berlin 1978

Korfes, O. *Der Zweite Weltkrieg 1939, Wirklichkeit und Fälschung*, East Berlin 1959

Kosthorst, E. *Die Geburt der Tragödie aus dem Geist des Gehorsams. Deutschlands Generale und Hitler – Erfahrungen und Reflexionen eines Frontoffiziers*, Bonn 1998

Kostiuk, H. *Stalinist rule in the Ukaine – A study of the Decade of Mass Terror 1929–1939*, Munich 1960

Kotze, H. Von & H. Krausnick (eds.) *Es spricht der Führer – 7 exemplarische Hitler-Reden*, Gütersloh 1966

Krausnick H. & H. Wilhelm *Die Truppe des Weltanschauungskrieges – Die Einsatzgruppen der Sicherheitspolizei und des SD 1938–1942*, Stuttgart 1981

Krausnick, H., H. Deutsch & H. von Kotzen (eds.) *Helmuth Groscurth, Tagebuch eines Abwehroffiziers 1938–1940*, Stuttgart 1970

Krivosyew, G. (ed.) *No more secrets! Losses of the Soviet Armed Forces in war, military operations and conflicts. A statistical research*, Moscow 1993

Kroener, B. *Der starke Mann im Heimatkriegsgebiet. Generaloberst Friedrich Fromm. Eine Biographie*, Paderborn 2005

Krushchev, S. *Krushchev on Krushchev. An Inside Account of the Man and his Era, by his son, Sergei Krushchev*, Boston 1990

Kunz, N. *Die Krim unter deutscher Herrschaft 1941–1944*, Darmstadt 2005

Langer, W. *Our Vichy Gamble,* New York 1947

Le Goyet, P. *Le mystère Gamelin,* Paris 1975

Leber, A., W. Brandt, K.Bracher (eds.) *Das Gewissen steht auf – Lebensbilder aus dem deutschen Widerstand 1933–1945,* Mainz 1984

Leppa K. *Generalfeldmarschall* Walter Model. *Von Genthin bis vor Moskaus Tore.* Nürnberg 1982

Leverkuehn, P. *Verteidigung Mansteins,* Hamburg 1950

Lewytski, B. *Die Sowjet-Ukraine 1944–1963,* Cologne 1964

Liddell Hart, B. *Geschichte des Zweiten Weltkrieges,* Wiesbaden 1970

Liddell Hart, B. *The Other Side of the Hill,* London 1978

Liddell Hart, B. (ed.) *The Soviet Army,* London 1956

Lill, R. & H.Oberreuter (eds.) *20. Juli – Porträt des Widerstands,* Düsseldorf 1984

Lochner, L. (ed.) *Goebbels Tagebücher aus den Jahren 1942–43 mit anderen Dokumenten,* Zürich 1948

Longerich, P. *Davon haben wir nichts gewusst. Die Deutschen und die Judenverfolgung 1933–1945,* Munich 2006

Lottman, H. *Pétain, Hero or Traitor,* London 1958

Luther, M. *Die Krim unter deutscher Besatzung im zweiten Weltkrieg.,* Berlin 1956

Macksey, K. *Guderian – Panzer General,* London 1975

Malinowski, S. *Vom König zum Führer. Sozialer Niedergang und politische Radikalisierung im deutschen Adel zwischen Kaiserreich und NS-Staat.,* Berlin 2003

Manstein, E. von *Aus einem Soldatenleben,* Bonn 1958

Manstein, E.von *Verlorene Siege,* Bonn 1955

Manstein, R.von & T. Fuchs *Soldat im 20. Jahrhundert,* Munich 1981

Marx, K. & F. Engels. *Werke,* East Berlin 1956

Maser, W. *Adolf Hitler,* Munich 1971

Maser, W. *Nürnberg-Tribunal der Sieger,* Wien 1977

Masson, P. *Die deutsche Armee – Geschichte der Wehrmacht 1935–1945,* Kirchheim 1996

Mayenburg, R.v. *Blaues Blut und Rote Fahnen. Revolutionäres Frauenleben zwischen Wien, Berlin und Moskau,* Munich 1969

Mehner, K. (ed.) *Die geheimen Tagesberichte der deutschen Wehrmachtsführung im Zweiten Weltkrieg Osnabrück 1988,* 13 Bände

Meier-Welcker, H. *Aufzeichnungen eines Generalstabsoffiziers 1939–1942,* Feiburg 1992

Meissner, H. & H. Wilde *Die Machtergreifung – Ein Bericht über die Technik des nationalsozialistischen Staatsstreichs,* Stuttgart 1958

Mellenthin, F. von *Panzerschlachten,* Neckargmünd 1963

Mellenthin, F. von *Schach dem Schicksal,* Osnabrück 1989

Messenger, C. *The Last Prussian, a biography of Field Marshal Gerd von Rundstedt,* London 1991

Messerschmidt, M. *Die Wehrmacht im NS Staat,* Hamburg 1989

Messerschmidt, M. *Die Wehrmacht in der Endphase, Realität und Perzeption in Stuttgart im zweiten Weltkrieg,* Gerlingen 1989

Messerschmidt, M. *Was damals Recht war...NS-Militär-und-Strafjustiz im Vernichtungskrieg,* Essen 1996

Meyer, G. *Adolf Heusinger, Dienst eines deutschen Soldaten 1915 bis 1964,* Hamburg 2001

Meyer, G. *Personalfragen beim Aufbau der Bundeswehr in Adenauer und die Wiederbewaffnung, Bd. 18,* Rhöndorfer Gespräche, Bonn 2000

Meyer, G. (ed.) *Wilhelm Ritter von Leeb, Tagebuchaufzeichnungen und Lagebeurteilungen aus zwei Weltkriegen,* Stuttgart 1976

Michalka, W. (ed.) *Der Zweite Weltkrieg, Analysen, Grundzüge, Forschungsbilanz,* Munich 1989

Militärgeschichtliches Forschungsamt (eds.) *Anfänge westdeutscher Sicherheitspolitik 1945–1956,* Munich 2001, 4 Bände, Sonderausgabe

Minart, J. Vincennes, *Secteur 4,* Paris 1945

Model, H. & D. Bradley (eds.) *Generalfeldmarschall Walter Model (1891–1945). Dokumentation eines Soldatenlebens,* Osnabrück 1951

Morozow, M *Die Falken des Kremls – die sowjetische Militärmacht von 1917 bis heute,* Munich 1982

Müller, K. *Das Heer und Hitler – Armee und nationalsozialistisches Regime 1933–1940,* Stuttgart 1969

Müller, M. *Das Mädchen Anne Frank. Eine Biographie.,* Munich 1998

Müller, R. & H. Volkmann (eds.) *Die Wehrmacht – Mythos und Realität,* Oldenburg 1999

Müller, V. (K.Mammach, ed.) *Ich fand das wahre Vaterland,* East Berlin 1963

Müller-Hildebrand, B. *Das Heer 1933–1945. Entwicklung des organisatorischen Aufbaus.* Darmstadt 1969

Murray, W. *Strategy for Defeat. The Luftwaffe 1933–1945,* Washington 1983

Nedava, J. *Trotzky and the Jews,* Philadelphia 1971

Nehring, W. *Die Geschichte der deutschen Panzerwaffe 1916–1945,* Berlin 1969

Neitzel, S. *Abgehört. Deutsche Generale in britischer Gefangenschaft 1942–1945,* Berlin 2005

Nekrich, A. & M. Heller *Die Geschichte der Sowjetunion 1940–1980,* Königstein 1982

Nekrich, A. & P. Grigorenko. *Genickschuß – Die Rote Armee am 22.6.1941,* Frankfurt 1969

Oldenburg, M. *Ideologie und militärisches Kalkül. Die Besatzungspolitik der Wehrmacht in der Sowjetunion 1942,* Cologne 2004

Overmans, R. *Deutsche militärische Verluste im Zweiten Weltkrieg,* Munich 1999

Paget, R., Earl of Northampton *Manstein – seine Feldzüge, sein Prozeß,* Wiesbaden 1952

Philippi, A. & F. Heim *Der Feldzug gegen Sowjetrußland 1941–1945,* Stuttgart 1962

Piekalkiewicz, J. *Krieg der Panzer 1939–1945,* Gütersloh, n.d.

Piekalkiewicz, J. *Stalingrad – Anatomie einer Schlacht,* Munich 1970

Piekalkiewicz, J. *Unternehmen Zitadelle, Kursk und Orel Die größte Panzerschlacht des 2.Weltkrieges,* Hersching 1989

Piekalkiewicz, J. *Ziel Paris, Der Westfeldzug 1940,* Munich 1986

Plettenberg, M. Guderian. *Hintergründe eines deutschen Soldatenschicksals 1948–1945*, Düsseldorf 1950

Plivier, T. *Stalingrad*, Berlin 1946

Prételat, L. *Le destin tragique de la Ligne Maginot*, Paris 1950

Prioux, R. *Souvenirs de Guerre 1939–1943*, Paris 1947

Proske, R. *Wider den Mißbrauch der Geschichte deutscher Soldaten zu politischen Zwecken. Eine Streitschrift.*, Mainz 1996

Prozeßprotokolle IMT, Prozeß gegen die Hauptkriegsverbrecher, IMT, Fall 12 – OKW Prozeß, Prozeß gegen Manstein, stenographisches Protokoll (engl. version)

Rees, L. *Hitlers Krieg im Osten*, Munich 2000

Richardson,W. & S. Frei (eds.), *The Fatal Decisions*, London 1956

Rigg, B.M. *Hitlers jüdische Soldaten*, Paderborn 2003

Ritter, G. *Carl Goerdeler und die deutsche Widerstandsbewegung*, Stuttgart 1954

Röhricht, E. *Pflicht und Gewissen, Erinnerungen eines deutschen Generals 1932–1944*, Stuttgart 1965

Rokossovsky, K. *Soldatski Dolg*, Moscow 1970

Rotmistrow, P. *Stalnaya Gvardya*, Moscow 1984

Rotmistrow, P. *Tankovoye srazhenie pod Prochorovkoy*, Moscow 1960

Roton, G. *Années Cruciales*, Paris 1947

Rousset, L. *Histoire Générale de la Guerre Franco-Allemande*, Paris 1886

Ruby, E. *Sedan – Terre d'épreuve. Avec la deuxième armée mai-juin 1940*, Paris 1948

Saint Marc, H. de. *Die Wächter des Abends*, Friedberg 2000

Schall-Riaucourt, H.von. *Aufstand und Gehorsam. Offizierstum und Generalstab im Umbruch, Leben und Wirken von Generaloberst Halder, Generalstabschef 1938–1942*, Wiesbaden 1972

Schellenberg, W. *The Schellenberg Memoirs*, London 1956

Scheurig, B. Freies Deutschland. *Das Nationalkomitee und der Bund deutscher Offiziere in der Sowjetunion 1943–45*, Frankfurt 1984

Scheurig, B. *Henning von Tresckow*, Hamburg 1973

Scheurig, B. (ed.) *Verrat hinter Stacheldraht? – Das Nationalkomitee Freies Deutschland und der Bund deutscher Offiziere in der Sowjetunion 1943–1945*, Munich 1965

Schlabrendorff, *Fabian von Offiziere gegen Hitler*, Zürich 1959

Schmädeke, J. & J. Steinbach. (eds.) *Der Widerstand gegen den Nationalsozialismus – Die deutsche Gesellschaft und der Widerstand gegen Hitler.*, Munich 1984

Schmidt, P. *Statist auf diplomatischer Bühne 1923–1945. Erlebnisse des Chefdolmetschers im Auswärtigen Amt mit den Staatsmännern Europas*, Bonn 1953

Schmiedecke, H. & P. Steinbach (eds.) *Der Widerstand gegen den Nationalsozialismus – die deutsche Gesellschaft und der Widerstand gegen Hitler*, Munich 1985

Schmückle, G. *Ohne Pauken und Trompeten. Erinnerungen an Krieg und Frieden*, Stuttgart 1982

Schramm, P. *Kriegstagebuch des Oberkommandos der Wehrmacht 1940–1945*

Schramm, W.von *Verrat im Zweiten Weltkrieg – vom Kampf der Geheimdienste in Europa, Berichte und Dokumentation,* Düsseldorf 1967

Schröter, H. *Stalingrad...bis zur letzten Patrone,* Klagenfurt 1968

Schukow, G. *Vospominiania i Ramyshlenia,* Moscow 1965

Schumann, W. (ed.) *Deutschland im Zweiten Weltkrieg. Der grundlegende Umschwung im Kriegsverlauf (November 1942 bis September 1943,* East Berlin 1973

Seaton, A. *Stalin as Warlord,* London 1976

Seaton, A. *The German Army 1933–1945,* New York 1982

Seaton, A. *The Russo-German War 1941–1945,* London 1971

Seidler, F *Die Militärgerichtsbarkeit der deutschen Wehrmacht – Rechtssprechung und Strafvollzug,* Munich 1991

Seidler, F. *Die Kollaboration 1939–1945. Zeitgeschichtliche Dokumentation in Biographien,* Munich 1995

Senger und Etterlin, F. von *Krieg in Europa,* Frankfurt 1960

Sereny, G. *Albert Speer, Das Ringen mit der Wahrheit und das deutsche Trauma,* Munich 1995

Seydlitz-Kurzbach, W. v. *Konflikt und Konsequenzen, Erinnerungen,* Hamburg 1977

Shtemenko, S. *The Soviet General Staff at War,* Moscow 1970

Siegler, F. *Frhr.* von (comp.) *Die höheren Dienststellen der Wehrmacht 1933–1945, Im Auftrage des Instituts für Zeitgeschichte Munich,* Stuttgart 1963

Simonow, K. *Days and Nights,* New York 1945

Smelser, R. & E. Syring *Die Militärelite des Dritten Reiches – 27 biographische Skizzen,* Berlin 1998

Smelser, R. & E. Syring *Die SS, Elite unter dem Totenkopf – 30 Lebensläufe,* Paderborn 2000

Smith, B. & A. Peterson (eds.) *Heinrich Himmler- Geheimreden 1933 bis 1945 und andere Ansprachen,* Frankfurt 1974

Sokolovsky, V. *Military Strategy – Soviet Doctrine and Concepts,* New York 1963

Solowiev B. *Kutuzi i Rumyancev protiv Citadel in Voyenno-Istorichesky Zhurnal,* Moscow 1998, Band 4

Solowiew, B. *Wendepunkt des Zweiten Weltkrieges. Die Schlacht bei Kursk,* Cologne 1984

Spears, E. *Assignment to Catastrophe,* London 1954

Speer, A. *Der Sklavenstaat, Meine Auseinandersetzung mit der SS,* Stuttgar 1981

Speer, A. *Erinnerungen,* Berlin 1969

Speer, A. *Spandauer Tagebücher,* Frankfurt 1973

Stahlberg, A. *Die Verdammte Pflicht – Erinnerungen 1942–1945,* Frankfurt 1994

Stein, M. *Generalfeldmarschall Erich von Manstein – Kritische Betrachtung des Soldaten und Menschen,* Mainz 2000

Stein, M. *Generalfeldmarschall Walter Model – Legende und Wirklichkeit,* Bissendorf 2001

Stein, M. *Österreichs Generale im deutschen Heer – Schwarz/Gelb, Rot/Weiss/Rot, Hakenkreuz,* Bissendorf 2002

Steinberg, J. *Deutsche, Juden und Italiener – der italienische Widerstand gegen den Holocaust,* Göttingen 1992

Streit, C. *Keine Kameraden – Die Wehrmacht und die sowjetischen Kriegsgefangenen*, Stuttgart, 1978

Taylor, T. *Die Nürnberger Prozesse – Kriegsverbrechen und Völkerrecht*, Zürich 1951

Taylor, T. *Sword and Swastika*, New York 1952

Taylor, T. *The March of Conquest – The German Victory in the West 1940*, London 1959

Thorwald, J. *Das Ende an der Elbe*, Stuttgart 1950

Thorwald, J. *Es begann an der Weichsel*, Stuttgart 1953

Thun-Hohenstein, R., *Galeazzo Graf von Der Verschwörer – General Oster und die Militäropposition*, Berlin 1982

Tippelskirch, K.von *Geschichte des Zweiten Weltkrieges*, Bonn 1959

Tolstoy, A. *Victims of Yalta*, London 1977

Töppel, R. *Die Offensive gegen Kursk 1943 – Legenden, Mythen und Propaganda*, Dresden 2001 (dissertation)

Trevor-Roper, H. (ed.) *Hitler's Table Talks 1941–1944*, London 1953

Ueberschär G. & W. Vogel *Dienen und Verdienen. Hitlers Geschenke an seine Eliten*, Frankfurt 1999

Ueberschär, G. *Generaloberst Franz Halder. Generalstabschef, Gegner und Gefangener Hitlers*, Göttingen 1991

Ueberschär, G. & W. Wette *Stalingrad, Mythos und Wirklichkeit einer Schlacht*, Frankfurt 1993

Ueberschär, G. (ed.) *Der 20. Juli. Das andere Deutschland in der Vergangenheitspolitik nach 1945*, Berlin 1998

Ueberschär, G. (ed.) *Hitlers Militärische Elite - Vom Kriegsbeginn bis zum Weltkriegsende*, Darmstadt 1998

Ueberschär, G. (ed.) *Hitlers Militärische Elite – Von dem Anfang des Regimes bis Kriegsbeginn*, Darmstadt 1996

Ueberschär, G. (ed.) *NS-Verbrechen und der militärische Widerstand gegen Hitler.*, Darmstadt 2000

Uhle-Wettler, F. *Der Krieg, Gestern – Heute – Morgen?*, Hamburg 2001

Uhle-Wettler, F. *Erich Ludendorff in seiner Zeit – Soldat, Stratege, Revolutionär – Eine Neubewertung*, Berg 1995

Uhle-Wettler, F. *Höhe – und Wendepunkte Deutscher Militärgeschichte*, Mainz 1984

Uhlig, H. *Der verbrecherische Befehl in Vollmacht des Gewissens*, Frankfurt 1965

van Creveld, M. *Die deutsche Wehrmacht, eine militärische Beurteilung in Die Wehrmacht, Mythos und Realität*, ed. R.Müller & H.Volkmann, im Auftrag des Militärgeschichtlichen Forschungsamts, Oldenburg 1999

van Creveld, M. *Fighting Power – German Military Performance 1914–1945*, Potomac, Md. 1981

Varillon, P. *Joffre*, Paris 1956

Venkow, I. 'Archivbestände in Rußland zu den Operationen im Frühjahr und Sommer 1943' in Förster, R. (Hrsg.) *Gezeitenwechsel im Zweiten Weltkrieg? Die Schlachte von Charkow und Kursk im Frühjahr und Sommer 1943 in operativer Anlage, Verlauf und politischer Bedeutung*, Hamburg 1996

Venohr, W. *Stauffenberg – Symbol der deutschen Einheit – eine politische Biographie*, Berlin 1968

Volkogonow, D. *Stalin, Triumph and Tragedy*, London 1991

Volkogonow, D. *Trotzki, Das Janusgesicht der Revolution*, Düsseldorf 1992

Wallach, Y. 'Feldmarschall Erich von Manstein und die deutsche Judenausrottung in Rußland' in *Jahrbuch des Instituts für Deutsche Geschichte*, University of Tel Aviv 4/1975

Warlimont, W. *Im Hauptquartier der deutschen Wehrmacht 1939–1945*, Bonn 1962

Wassiliewski, A. *Delo Vsei Zhisny*, Moscow 1974

Wegner, B. *Hitlers politische Soldaten Die Waffen-SS 1933–1945*, Paderborn 1997

Weinberg, G. (commentary) *Hitlers Zweites Buch*, Stuttgart 1961

Werth, A. *Russia at War*. New York 1964

Weygand, M. *Mémoires, Paris 1957*, 3 volumes

Wheeler Benett, J. *The Nemesis of Power – The German army in Politics 1918–1945*, London 1956

Wieder, J. *Stalingrad und die Verantwortung des Soldaten*, Munich 1962

Williams, J. *The Ides of May – The Defeat of France May–June 1940*, London 1968

Wrochem, O. von 'Rehabilitation oder Strafverfolgung. Kriegsverbrecherprozeß gegen *Generalfeldmarschall* Erich von Manstein im Widerspruch britischer Interessen', in *Mittelweg 36*, Heft 3/1997

Wrochem, O. von *Erich von Manstein. Vernichtungskrieg und Geschichtspolitik*, Paderborn 2006

Wrochem, O.von 'Die Auseinandersetzung mit Wehrmachtsverbrechen im Prozeß gegen den *Generalfeldmarschall* Erich von Manstein' in *ZfG 46* (1998).

Yeremenko, A. *False witnesses*, Moscow, n.d.

Zeidler, M. 'Reichswehr und Rote Armee 1920–1933. Wege einer ungewöhnlichen Zusammenarbeit. Beiträge zur Militärgeschichte' in *Militärgeschichtliches Forschungsamt, Bd.36*, Munich 1993

Zitzewitz, C. v. *Am Wendepunkt des Zweiten Weltkrieges. Ein Erlebnisbericht. Als Verbindungsoffizier beim AOK 6 in Stalingrad vom 25. November 1942 bis 20. Januar 1943*, unpublished manuscript in BA-MA

Index

The following names are not mentioned separately in the index: Adolf Hitler, Erich von Manstein, most of the commanders and members of the *Sonderkommandos* and *Einsatzkommandos* of the *Einsatzgruppen*, the town commanders on the Crimea and the officers and soldiers of the secret field police, authors not mentioned in the text and quoted in the endnotes only.